The Politicization of Islam

The Turban for the Crown
The Islamic Revolution in Iran
 Said Amir Arjomand

The Arab Press in the Middle East
A History
 Ami Ayalon

Iran's First Revolution
Shi'ism and the Constitutional
 Revolution of 1905–1909
 Mangol Bayat

Saddam's World
Political Discourse in Iraq
 Ofra Bengio

Islamic Reform
Politics and Social Change in Late
 Ottoman Syria
 David Dean Commins

King Hussein and the Challenge of
 Arab Radicalism
 Jordan, 1955–1967
 Uriel Dann

Nasser's "Blessed Movement"
Egypt's Free Officers and the July
 Revolution
 Joel Gordon

The Young Turks in Opposition
 M. Şükrü Hanioğlu

Preparation for a Revolution
The Young Turks, 1902–1908
 M. Şükrü Hanioğlu

Cross-Cultural Encounters and Conflicts
 Charles Issawi

The Fertile Crescent, 1800–1914
A Documentary Economic History
 Edited by Charles Issawi

The Politicization of Islam
Reconstructing Identity, State, Faith,
 and Community in the Late Ottoman
 State
 Kemal H. Karpat

The Making of Saudi Arabia, 1916–1936
From Chieftaincy to Monarchical State
 Joseph Kostiner

Eunuchs and Sacred Boundaries
 in Islamic Society
 Shaun Marmon

The Imperial Harem
Women and Sovereignty in the Ottoman
 Empire
 Leslie Peirce

From Abdullah to Hussein
Jordan in Transition
 Robert B. Satloff

THE POLITICIZATION OF ISLAM

Reconstructing Identity, State, Faith, and Community in the Late Ottoman State

Kemal H. Karpat

UNIVERSITY PRESS

2001

OXFORD
UNIVERSITY PRESS

Oxford   New York
Athens   Auckland   Bangkok   Bogotá   Buenos Aires   Calcutta
Cape Town   Chennai   Dar es Salaam   Delhi   Florence   Hong Kong   Istanbul
Karachi   Kuala Lumpur   Madrid   Melbourne   Mexico City   Mumbai
Nairobi   Paris   São Paulo   Shanghai   Singapore   Taipei   Tokyo   Toronto   Warsaw

and associated companies in
Berlin   Ibadan

Copyright © 2001 by Kemal H. Karpat

Published by Oxford University Press, Inc.
198 Madison Avenue, New York, New York 10016

Oxford is a registered trademark of Oxford University Press.

Library of Congress Cataloging-in-Publication Data
Karpat, Kemal H.
The politicization of Islam : reconstructing identity, state, faith, and
community in the late Ottoman state / Kemal H. Karpat.
p.   cm. — (Studies in Middle Eastern history)
Includes bibliographical references and index.
ISBN 0-19-513618-7
1. Turkey—History—1878–1909.   2. Turkey—History—Mehmed V, 1909–1918.   3. Islam
and state—Turkey.   4. Panislamism.   I. Title.   II. Studies in Middle Eastern history
(New York, N.Y.)
DR572.K28   2000
320.54'09561'09034—dc21   99-053429

1 3 5 7 9 8 6 4 2
Printed in the United States of America
on acid-free paper

Preface

The idea of this book has been in my mind since the start of my academic career. I would have written it sooner if I had accumulated all the necessary information and devised the proper approach and methodology. I felt that much of what has been written and said about the transformation of the Ottoman state and the rise of modern Turkey (and other Muslim nation-states) ignores some key factors of change or relates them to each other in an incomplete and erroneous fashion. In particular, I thought it faulty to regard modernity and Islam as engaged in a deadly struggle. To do so ignores the impact of the economic, social, cultural, and international factors that created modernity and changed the social political environment in which Islam operated. In other words, Islam and Islamic society need to be considered separately, and the change in society should not be seen as equivalent to the transformation of the faith. Consequently, I have viewed the Ottoman transformation as caused by concrete, tangible factors, both internal and external, and have regarded Islam as an instrument of legitimacy, mediation, balance, psychological support, mobilization, defense, and so on, during the transformation of the community into a new unit of organization, the territory-based nation and state. Islam became the instrument of change and adaptation as much as it was politicized as the ideology of cultural self-preservation and opposition to colonial rule.

The approach and methodology of this work were devised to take into account every major domestic and international factor that affected the transformation of the Ottoman society and state as well as to reconsider the true role of Islam and of the sultan-caliph in this process. The involvement, via Islam, of the lower classes in the transformation of the social structure; the changes in the traditional concepts of state, community, faith, and authority; and a series of other topics have been given proper consideration. The book deals with Islamic revivalism as part of the general process of socioeconomic and cultural transformation; it is not meant as a calculated effort to join the current heated discussion about Muslim fundamentalism. The work is also an effort to present as complete as possible a holistic picture of the Ottoman state—with all its political, economic, social, and cultural dimensions so that the course of Ottoman-Turkish Islamic modernization may be properly understood.

A substantial part of the work deals with Sultan Abdulhamid II (r. 1876–1909), who is seen as an absolutist ruler and the main force behind the Ottoman modernization and, also as caliph, its legitimizer and the architect of its Islamization. He also successfully maintained the territorial integrity of the Ottoman state during a thirty-year period that was crucial to the modernization process, and he prepared the ground for the rise of modern Turkey. The modern identities that emerged during this transformation were nurtured by grassroots folk religion and culture as much as by the ethnonational models imposed from above by the ruling elites.

I commenced work on this book some twenty years ago, when access to Ottoman archives was exceptionally difficult. Since 1989 the use of the archives has been greatly liberalized, and consequently a dozen or more scholars, mostly Turks, have published dissertations and books on the Hamidian period, based in part on the materials used in this work. To the extent possible all these works are indicated in the references. The length of the manuscript forced me to leave out much factual information and elaborating on the meanings behind the facts (although such meaning and implications may be self-evident to the reader).

I would like to thank a few people for their help in preparing this work. The late Hayri Mutluçağ's knowledge of the archives, sources, and documents, as well as his insights into the Young Turks and early Republican eras proved to be of vital importance. Deniz Balgamiş provided dedicated research assistance and typed various drafts and revisions as did Steve Hahn, whose help was enhanced by his computer expertise. Barbara Husseini provided editorial assistance and advice. I would like to thank the Graduate School at the University of Wisconsin–Madison for its financial help, which made possible several research trips and stays in Turkey. Last but not least, as a person who has paid dearly in his life for his critical and inquisitive mind, I take special pleasure to thank the United States of America for providing me the opportunity, security, and the environment to work, think, and express myself in full freedom. I have used the Turkish spelling of titles and names except for some well-established English usages. A key to Turkish pronunciation has been provided. All translations are mine unless otherwise indicated.

Madison, Wisconsin   K.H.K.
April 2000

Contents

Note on Pronunciation

The following Turkish letters are pronounced approximately as follows:

ş   *sh* as in "sharp"
ç   *ch* as in "cherry"
c   *g* as in "George"
ö   *e* as in "erring"
ü   *ew* as in "few"
ğ   silent *g* as in "higher"
â   *a* as in "palm"

All capital and lowercase *i*'s are set roman.

The Politicization of Islam

Introduction

General Theme

This work deals with the social, cultural, and political modernization and ethnic transformation of the Ottoman state, and the role of Islam and Sultan Abdulhamid II (r. 1876–1909)—referred to here simply as Abdulhamid—in conditioning and directing that transformation and modernization.

The Ottoman state, like the rest of the Muslim world, was exposed to capitalism and the threat of violent European occupation in the nineteenth century. Capitalism undermined, among other things, the economic-social foundation of the *vakif, imaret*, and above all the state-controlled land system, which maintained and assured the society's unique Islamic cultural features. And the European occupation put an end to the Islamic *devlet*, or state, which had guaranteed the survival of the Muslim institutions and ways of life and perpetuated the rule of a variety of rulers and dynasties, who often used Islam to legitimize their authority. Capitalism also stimulated the development of private property and the market forces that existed in various embryonic forms in all Muslim societies and increased trade and profits and the production of local agricultural commodities. All these structural developments, aided by increased literacy, a modern (European) school system, the press, and so on, created new Muslim middle classes with rationalist modes of thinking that appraised their own social position and Islamic culture in a critical and worldly manner.

The collapse of the traditional Islamic state in turn freed the community from the rule of its political elites and opened the way for the community to seek for means based on its own intellectual and spiritual resources to assure its cultural and religious survival The popular revivalist movements of the nineteenth century, for example, were the reaction of Muslim grassroots communities to the economic, cultural, and political transformation of classical Muslim society, as well as a local-regional effort at adapting Islam to changed circumstances within an orthodox-Islamic frame of reference. Where the state had disappeared, Muslims tried to reform society, or community; where the state survived, elites sought to reform the state. These efforts to reform the state or the society-community were endeavors that produced vastly different results. The state appeared as the means for preserving the community's

3

Islamic culture and its identity, but also as the instrument used by the social and bureaucratic elites to perpetuate their domination. The rise of the individual would provide a new vantage point to evaluate the role of the state and the function of the faith; modernism in a way was rational individualism.

The Ottoman state, the only major independent Muslim state, found itself besieged by demands from the states and rulers at the periphery of the Muslim world to help them retain their independence and Islamic way of life. It was under growing pressure from England, France, Russia, and Italy, first to accept a series of "reforms" designed primarily to facilitate the reception of the capitalist system and then to initiate its own dismemberment by according autonomy and independence to its Christian subjects, whose middle class had developed substantially. The struggle of the Ottoman Muslim middle class (which controlled most of the state lands and converted them into private property) and the non-Muslims (who were masters of the foreign and, to a somewhat lesser extent, domestic trade) was eventually resolved in favor of the Muslims, thanks to their control of the state, the educational system, and the army. In the second half of the nineteenth century, the Ottoman state became the religious center of the Islamic world, not only because it had vital control of the Hicaz (province harboring the main Muslim holy places) and the *hac* (Arabic: *hajj*—pilgrimage to Mecca) and because the modern reforms promised to revive it (its victory over Greece in 1897 was celebrated throughout the Muslim world) but also and especially because of a growing demand for a Muslim political center. It is in the context of these developments that Sultan Abdulhamid appeared as the *religious* leader of the Muslim world in its would-be unity. The West stigmatized Abdulhamid as the enemy of civilization and enlightenment, although in fact he admired the West and praised Christianity for freeing itself from dogmatism. He introduced a series of widespread reforms, including modern education, that laid the foundation of the modern Middle East in general and Turkey in particular. Abdulhamid and his advisors were as much advocates of change and renewal as they were apologists for the faith, for tradition, and believers in Islam's compatibility with science and progress.

In more concrete terms, the basic theme of this work is the study of a variety of economic, cultural, and social forces, both domestic and international, which forced the traditional Ottoman corporatist state, first, to create a common Ottoman political identity for all its citizens, regardless of faith and language and, then, to realign itself religiously, culturally, and politically with the most numerous of those citizens: the Muslims. This process of "Ottomanization" sought to remold all existing ancient identities, well preserved under the old system, into something new, which could be referred to as "re-Islamization," "Turkification," "Arabization," or the like, and which involved a cultural and political transformation and identity change without parallel in earlier Islamic history. This radical transformation was a consequence of change, class differentiation, education, the discovery of ethnoregional history, and so on, and of geographic factors that produced a certain homogenization at one level and promoted diversity and differentiation at another.

The Ottoman state was established at the periphery of Muslim world, on the lands of the Eastern Roman Empire, known as Byzantium—not by fanatical *gazis* seeking to spread Islam through holy war but by a group of tribal chiefs, mystical fraternities of craftsmen, and other Anatolian elements, including some Christian lords of west

Anatolia and the Balkans, many seeking to escape the Mongol onslaught of the thirteenth century. Until its expansion into the Muslim Middle East in the sixteenth century, it remained geographically a predominantly East European state. Primarily interested in power, economic rewards, and group survival, and with no dominant tribal or social group emerging as leader, the early Ottoman leaders, who eventually became the state elite, created a state above tribal, ethnic, and social ties and, through it, consolidated their position as a status group. By virtue of circumstances rather than by following any plan, the state developed as an entity that was sui generis. Its own institutions, laws, and culture appeared in Islamic guise but were also in harmony with the political-cultural and unique ethnoreligious environment of Southeast Europe and the Turks' own folk culture and faith.

The need for accommodation between the sociopolitical environment and their own faith shaped, in part, the philosophy and governing attitudes of the Ottoman bureaucrats. While reserving all government power to themselves as a status group, they developed a sophisticated sense of pragmatism, flexibility, and relativism, which usually enabled them to shape their ruling institutions to the requirements of the time while preserving cultural and institutional continuity in appearance and in essence.

The state, or, in practice, the bureaucracy, was simultaneously the guardian of the Islamic faith, the agent of change, and the mediator between ethnoreligious and cultural groups in the old order. The initial period of rapid growth in the fourteenth to sixteenth centuries was followed by two centuries of relative stagnation and challenge from within and without. Finally, pressures stemming from structural changes caused by the slowly expanding capitalist system and the state's inability to understand fully the nature of the economic challenge and its cultural, political, and military effects caused the state to initiate changes designed to perpetuate its own existence. The government expanded its centralized authority and introduced into the countryside changes that would allow it to control resources and monitor relations between various social groups and ethnoreligious communities—and willy-nilly involve them ultimately in the exploitation by and defense of the "fatherland" (the territorial state), which the centralized authority controlled. From the start there were both an official state view and a private image of the fatherland: the first stemmed from calculated practical considerations; the second, from historical experience and cultural attachment. The challenge of a developing civil order forced the state to engage in a series of "reforms" that engendered new social groups, with their own interests and orientations, and ultimately created extraordinary confusion about the state's own essence, mission, role, and legitimacy. Thus, the new civil order turned out to be the partner or the antagonist of the state that created it, depending on the internal or international circumstance prevailing. However, the resulting conflicts and their periodic resolutions did not stem the march of the "new" toward final victory but were mere facets of the synthesis resulting from the interaction of the traditional factors and values, the creation of individual and group identity was also one of the results of the interaction. Consequently, in this study I have attached special importance to ethnicity as source of identity, but I have not viewed faith and linguistic, political, and ethnic identities as exclusive. On the contrary, I have emphasized the fact that in the classical Ottoman state ethnic identity coexisted with religious identity among both Muslims and Christians; and in the age of modernity, the blend of faith and ethnicity and the change in their order of priority gave each major ethnic group in the Ottoman state its specific "national" characteristics. The emergence of the Turks as an ethnic community (and eventually as a nation) was the consequence both of the blend of faith and ethnicity and also of the drive toward modernity, the latter becoming a pervasive ideological force akin to a new faith that accompanied the emergence of the modern-day Turks.

The late Ernest Gellner found that the "deep" Turkish commitment to modernity is not "rigidly tied to any elaborate and constraining doctrine" but gives the "impression that the Turkish commitment to modernization of the polity and society has, or initially had, both an Ottoman and a Koranic quality."[1] After stressing the role played by the state, Gellner theorized that the Turks are headed for "an unselfconscious blend of Kemalist republicanism and urban Islam, fusing Turkish and Muslim identity in an apparently seamless web of symbol and sentiment, as Ottoman and Islamic identity had once been fused. Being a good citizen and a Muslim may blend once again."[2] In more than one way this study focuses on that original historic fusion, in order to show how the state sought to reshape the old Ottoman-Muslim identity, first by integrating it with ethnicity and later by redefining it to accord with the state's perception of a modern national identity while formally rejecting the Ottoman-Muslim content.

In sum, this work attempts to study the transformation of the Ottoman state in the nineteenth century by emphasizing identity changes in the major ethnic groups, especially the Muslim groups of Anatolia and Rumili (the Balkans), who developed new ethnonational identities in interaction with their previous universalist Ottoman and Islamic ones. It provides also some information on the "national" question among Arabs.

Capitalism, Social Change, and Religious Revivalism

The impact of the capitalist system on the Ottoman statist socioeconomic structure began to be felt as early as the eighteenth century and led, after 1830, to the speedy commercialization of agriculture, the privatization of state lands (which initially accounted for 60 to 80 percent of the arable land in the Balkans), and, in time, to changes in the economic foundations of such characteristic Muslim cultural institutions as the *vakifs* and *imarets*. When those vital supports of the old Islamic political-cultural system were eliminated or forced to adapt to the capitalist system, the sociocultural and political transformation took on a unprecedented worldly quality, depth, and scope in the Muslim societies of Asia and the Ottoman Empire, which had evolved and changed continuously and dialectically for centuries around their own cultural axes but explained such change as God-ordained.

Historically, Muslim societies have always changed, but the intellectual assessment of such change—that is, the rational search for its causes—seldom, if ever, properly linked cause and effect. Everything was attributed to divine will, thus avoiding the internalization and understanding of change and the search for corresponding means to cope with its effects. Simply put, the concept of a divine and immutable social order was invoked by practically all ruling Muslim elites in order to perpetuate their own economic and political supremacy, using Islam to legitimize it. But then, foreign occupation, however undesirable, freed the Muslim masses from the "tutelage" (actually domination) of their own state elites and helped the rise of a new, modern sense of community. This was a self-defense reaction that unintentionally generated new modes of thought that induced Muslims to look to their past and seek rationally the causes of their plight and then to look for remedies that might be found in their own spiritual and mental resources. Foreign occupation thus unwittingly helped revive the Muslim community's memory of the past golden age—*devr-i saadet* (happy age)—at the same time as it revealed the state's political and military inability to protect the faith, and undermined its legitimacy as the unquestionable authority over the community. Consequently, in the occupied Muslim lands, the eclipse of the Islamic state led gradually to the revival of the community as a basic unit of social organization and stimulated the educated modern and traditional elites to search for some means to reassert and maintain its Islamic identity and culture.

Knowingly or not, some Muslim elites in the occupied lands collaborated with the European powers, in many instances as a subordinate social group, but in others as an economic partner and cultural intermediary. The subservience of both traditional and new leaders to the new order and their emergence as a semicolonial, although modernist, middle class having a rationalist outlook alienated the masses and allowed the rise of new types of populist leaders to confront the challenges created by the capitalist system and European occupation and to chart an "Islamist" course of action for their society. Thus the greatest revolution in the entire history of Islam materialized as a series of popular Sufi revivalist movements, which surged up from among the lower classes under the guise of reviving the faith, but actually sought to find an "Islamic" accommodation to the new order of things. (This accommodation with the new order in the Ottoman Empire, as indicated later, was carried out by an independent "Islamic" state and its "Muslim" ruler, and the political effect of mass action including political fundamentalism as distinct from religion, was felt less there.)

Twenty-five or so revivalist movements arose during the nineteenth century, often led by self-appointed, popular religious leaders. They took the Prophet himself as a model of action and thought, believing that he had used faith as well as practical skill to create an ethical, law-abiding Muslim society out of the debauched and hedonistic pagan society of Arabia. The vision of the Prophet Muhammad as a model human in the service of God, coping with the myriad problems in the society he governed, played a crucial role in all these Sufi—and neo-Sufi—revivalist movements by humanizing the dogma. The *hadis* (tradition or saying attributed to the Prophet) was the key and legitimizing vehicle in the modern, humanist *ihya* or renaissance-reformation of Islam. The forms and terminology of the revivalist movements were traditional, though their essence as mechanisms for accommodating the Muslim societies to changed social and political realities was new.

The popular revivalist movements found themselves more often than not opposed to their own new middle classes, especially the intelligentsia. Regardless of whether it called itself "modernist," "Islamic," or "Westernist," the intelligentsia adapted itself to the new circumstances and claimed elite status by virtue of its education under the new system. The modern (Western) educational system, with its rationalist modes of thought, proved to be the most revolutionary force in helping or, rather, compelling the Muslim intelligentsia—both modernist and traditionalist—to reassess its own history and define its identity according to Western standards and methods of reasoning—although few admit this orientation—or, more properly, the universal rational standards that were the mark of early Islam. The modernists—both those in the service of Europe and those in opposition to it—occupied the new political, economic, and educational centers of power and wrote their own history as a lament on underdevelopment and the search for culprits. The availability of print technology facilitated the rise of a modern press and brought about a revolution of knowledge, giving the upper hand to the modern intelligentsia over the traditionalist conservatives, who eventually used the same printed word to disseminate their own views.

Revivalism, Reforms, Ottomanism, and Sultan Abdulhamid II

The Ottoman state, almost alone in the Muslim world, possessed sovereignty and an independent Muslim ruler, the sultan-caliph, who had a sophisticated political organization at his disposal and could claim legitimately to be the defender of Islam. The caliphate that gave the Ottoman sultan the credentials to defend the faith also provided legitimacy for carrying out reforms, although few people acknowledged the profoundly reformist policy of Abdulhamid. Moreover, as caliph—that is, as the head of the Muslim community—the sultan had enough moral authority to oppose the revivalist popular movements when they threatened the social-political status or, when it suited him, to accommodate them and incorporate their views into the prevailing system. This was, in a nutshell, Sultan Abdulhamid II's policy vis-à-vis the revivalist movements. Yet a degree of conflict was inevitable. Headed by traditionalist, lower- or middle-class leaders, revivalist movements outside the Ottoman Empire began mainly at the grassroots level and appealed to the community of believers to defend both the faith and the community against European occupiers. In contrast, in the independent Ottoman state, the modernist reform movements were initiated at the top by political elites, headed by the sultan-caliph, and aimed chiefly at saving the state. They were willing to use the faith to achieve their end, even though the old relation between the state and faith had already lost much of its sustaining religious philosophical basis. This development, paradoxically, brought to an end the de facto separation of faith and state that prevailed in the government practices of the classical Ottoman era—the supposed *din-u devlet* (fusion of state and faith), notwithstanding. Instead, modernization eventually provided the state with a new argument for abolishing the faith's relatively autonomous sphere and monopolizing all sectors of power, even, when necessary, using the faith for its own benefit in the name of "secularism." The problem that Turks would eventually face, therefore, was how to free the faith from the autocracy of the state rather than vice versa, as usually claimed by some so-called secularists. (In self-defense, the community reacted by maximizing its Islamic features to the extent that a large section of Turkey's population is more "Islamic" than many Muslim countries that unlike Turkey do not consider themselves "secular." Even in the nineteenth century, many foreign observers found Egypt and India more modern and reformist than Turkey.)

Although the policy pursued by the first of the reformist sultans, Selim III (r. 1789–1807), maintained the de facto traditional separation of faith and state, Mahmud II (r. 1808–39) undermined this separation by abolishing the popular religious orders, Janissaries, and provincial notables and their role in limiting de facto the state (sultan's) authority—a role that had heretofore assured a relatively autonomous sphere for the faith. Subsequently, the reforms in the Tanzimat era (1839–76) initiated by Abdulmecid (r. 1839–61) made a basic departure from the idea of the state as a status group standing on its own traditional foundations and having its own legitimacy and sought to base the state on a concept of "nation," which consisted of individuals residing within a well-defined territory and sharing a common citizenship and political culture. This was the essence of Ottomanism, which would force a redefinition of state, faith, community, and freedom as it inadvertently moved toward giving political expression to the individual's primordial identities within the nation-state. This individualistic orientation, however, arose within the organizational and institutional framework of the "Turks'" political culture, which was premised partly on the supremacy of state authority. Inevitably, the clash between individualism and authoritarianism, as well as between irreligiosity or worldliness and piety and communalism, became an essential feature of Turkish modernism and as much its driving force as the "challenge" and "response" that the late Arnold Toynbee regarded as key feature of the Western world.

Indeed, social mobility, occupational diversification, and the appeal of the revivalist and other popular religious movements were propelling into the public arena members of the lower urban groups, variously referred to as "the people," or "the nation," "public opinion," and so on. The sultan and his constitutionalist adversaries, who had arisen in the 1860s, both sought to harness the political potential of the masses; Abdulhamid appealed to their religious traditions and loyalty toward the ruler, and the constitutionalists promised them the totally new concept of political freedom and material betterment. In short, the sultan, the revivalists, and the constitutionalists all preached versions of populism that were in line with their own philosophies and expectations. The revivalists practiced a community-based religious populism at the grass roots; the sultan promoted religious populism, managed, orchestrated, and contained by the state—in other words, himself—from the top; and the constitutionalists preached an institutional populism that took concrete form first in the Constitution and Parliament of 1876–78, then reappeared in the period 1908–18. Thus, "populism" became a convenient support for both traditional absolutism and modernist authoritarianism, including the Republic.

Because the new populist upsurge promoted by the revivalists represented at once a return to the faith and a challenge to the elitist political and social order, Sultan Abdulhamid, although sympathetic to the revivalists' pietist aims, feared the political and cultural consequences of their populism. Certainly, the ferment created by the revivalist movements seemed likely to result in far-reaching change. As action-oriented populist movements, they unintentionally served as channels through which the lay folk culture, ethnic and regional identities, and the economic aspirations of the lower classes percolated upward and challenged, in the name of the faith, the "deviationist" culture of the elites, which was actually a protest against the unjust social and economic order and its political bases. When Abdulhamid resorted to absolutism in order to control the masses and the elites alike, he was using a strategy that itself became a major source of conflict and that engendered, in reaction, seminal political developments, including liberalism. Sultan Abdulhamid and the revivalists sought to restore the vitality of the faith, society, and state, but, in doing so, ended up turning Islam into an ideology.

Islam as an Ideology of Mass Mobilization and the Concept of Civilization

Antonio Gramsci has pointed out that, contrary to Marx and Engels's view that ideology is the instrument of class rule only for the bourgeoisie or the proletariat, it can also be used by the traditional classes of craftsmen, peasants, and common people. Gramsci further argued that, historically, organic ideologies, which are specific to given structures, possess the psychological capacity to organize the masses that arbitrary, rationalistic, or "willed" ideologies lack.[3] Using this distinction, we can say that the revivalist orders used Islam as an historically organic ideology to mobilize the masses in defense of the society and its faith, and Sultan Abdulhamid used the same Islam as a "willed" ideology to try to mobilize the masses in defense of the Ottoman state. The revivalists and the sultan were Muslims sharing the same faith, but, in the name of that faith, the sultan sought to preserve the statist elite order while the masses sought liberation from its rule.

In a more Marxian sense, the rise of ideology in the Muslim world in general and the Ottoman Empire in particular resulted from the rise of a new bourgeoisie that initially served as an intermediary between the state and the community but later made the latter its cultural, economic, and social power base, at times opposing the ruling government elites. The introduction of a primitive capitalism and the privatization of state lands, coupled with modern education and its rationalist modes of thought, produced a middle class whose individualism, interest orientation, and dynamic awareness of its sociocultural roots made it substantially different from its traditional counterpart. With its commercial and intellectual, as well as agrarian connections, this middle class played an especially decisive role in the transformation of the countryside throughout the Muslim world.

In the end, substantial numbers of Muslims, including the Ottomans, adopted new patterns of political and social organization, such as territorial nationhood, and either developed new identities or gave new meaning to existing ones while outwardly preserving their Islamic identities. The late Ernest Gellner, discussing relations between state and nation, attached primary importance to the existence of the state, claiming that nationalism emerges only in a milieu where the existence of the state is taken for granted and where there is the necessary moral-political climate: "So the problem of nationalism does not arise where there is no state."[4] Although Gellner devoted his main attention to modern nationalism in the industrializing society, his observations also apply to such preindustrial societies as the Ottoman one, where the state still played a crucial role in social engineering and the rise of nationalism.

It should be repeated that, in the Ottoman case, the existence of a state with a legitimate ruler and a bureaucracy that served and defended it helped to contain this transformation within manageable bounds and direct it toward predetermined ideals of society, nation, and state. There is no question that Europe stimulated the change in Muslim society by serving both as a challenge to its cultural and political autonomy and as a model to be followed. But it is erroneous to think that, even in their most Westernist phase, Ottoman reformists accepted Europe without qualification as a model of change. Rather, they tried to create new mediating concepts that allowed them to acquire the science and the arts of the West that were supposedly in harmony with their own culture and emerging ethnocultural identity.[5]

The concept of *medeniyet* (civilization) devised by the Ottoman intelligentsia-bureaucracy opened a neutral avenue for change by separating civilization from its cultural-religious content—that is, culture as they saw it—and legitimizing civilization as a universal, superior form of life—a distinction not too different from that drawn by the Germans between civilization and culture. The term *medeniyet* does not exist in classical Islamic literature, for the Turks coined it from the Arabic *madina* (city) as their counterpart to the newly devised French concept of *civilisation*.[6] It meant, therefore, a higher level of social order, morality, refinement, grace, good manners, development (*umran*), and secure, comfortable living; and it was the opposite of ignorance, stagnation, passivity, unproductive existence, and primitiveness. In the eyes of such early users of the word as Sadik paşa in 1838 and Ibrahim Şinasi, "civilization" was both a lofty principle and pragmatic necessity that could be acquired through individual effort as well as through state-sponsored training and education and would be beneficial to the society as a whole. By the end of the nineteenth century most elites, both conservative and liberal, deemed civilization a highly desirable value (and commodity) and the yardstick of national achievement. Even the most conservative Muslim thinkers began to view Islam not only as a community of believers but also as a civilization with material components, in some ways openly defying Islam's emphasis on spirituality. Civilization and economic development were eventually seen as being closely related; the idea was spelled out by Mehmed Cavid bey (1875–1926), the finance minister of the Young Turks (1908–1918) and author of a four-volume study of economics based almost entirely on Leroy Beaulieu's work.

The Turks' own cultural predisposition toward *medeniyet* had various historical roots. The ancient Turks of Central Asia, who lived on the fringe of the fertile lands where the great Chinese, east Roman, and Islamic civilizations flourished, became heirs to all of these civilizations, in varying degrees. Although the Turks subsequently produced their own Selçuki and Ottoman civilizations, neither had an aristocracy to identify with it and make it the cultural characteristic of their class or ethnic group. By contrast, the Persians and Arabs not only left their own ethnolinguistic mark on their Islamic civilization but, in the age of nationalism, eventually claimed that it was the product of their national genius. (Discussion of the civilization of Uigurs and other Turkic groups falls outside of the scope this work.)

In the nineteenth century, however, the idea of *medeniyet* created overnight a new way for the Ottoman bureaucracy-intelligentsia to measure their society's achievements and devise an identity accordingly. Because no other institution or group yet aspired to achieve its own civilization, the state appeared to be the only instrument capable of such achievement. Consequently, assuring the survival and supremacy of *devlet baba* (the father or mother state) acquired undisputed priority and legitimacy as the instrument of civilization (that is, modernization) and the bureaucracy-intelligentsia—included the military—became its supreme and exclusive agent and used it to legitimize their political supremacy and absolutism. They could thus label their opponents "reactionary" and neutralize them on behalf of their new religion, civilization, or modernization.

Conflicting Christian and Muslim Concepts of Civilization and Islamism

Ottomanism came into existence as a key reformist concept and policy mainly after 1856. Aiming to produce "equality" between Muslims and non-Muslims and to center political unity on common Ottoman citizenship, it transformed the subjects of the sultan into citizens of the state and opened the way to turn religious faith into a personal matter. In theory, Ottomanism was intended to depersonalize authority and shift it to institutions, but it also spurred a variety of administrative reforms. These facilitated the political ascendancy of the local notables and literati, who gave new strength to the sense of regional and ethnic identity and economic interest.

From the very start the ideas of civilization became entangled with religious perceptions that gave it different meanings among Christians and Muslims and determined the ultimate shape of Ottomanism. As new Christian elites rose from the ranks of the lower classes and were educated in modern schools they came to regard their own faith as their main link to Europe. They believed that being a Christian made them a partner in the European civilization and conferred automatically upon them a status "superior" to that of their "underdeveloped" Muslim rulers. A humble, only half-schooled Balkan Christian peasant considered himself superior to the most learned and refined Muslim. In any event, Balkan Christians conveniently blamed Islam and the Ottoman Turks, its supposed promoters, for preventing them from reaching the level of European civilization to which their faith entitled them. Most Ottoman Christians viewed Ottomanism as an ideology designed to perpetuate the Muslim character of the state and to promote the Muslims' cause; and, indeed, Ottomanism ended by identifying itself with the largest religious and ethnic group— that is, the Muslims—and, ultimately, in the last years of the Young Turks, with the Turks. Because most Ottoman Christians were Orthodox, however, they differed significantly in spirit, mentality, and political outlook from Western Christians, whether Catholic or Protestant. This is a fact seldom mentioned.

To achieve unity among Ottoman Muslims, Sultan Abdulhamid adopted the ideology of Islamism after 1878. Regarding all the Muslims of the Empire as an *ümmet* (from *ummah* or the universal religious community), the sultan tried to make them the political foundation of his state. Islamism thus supplied, perhaps inadvertently, an ideological content to Ottomanism, and the two became facets of a single ideology that bound the Muslims together for a while. Because Ottomanism, accompanied by modern education and class differentiation, stimulated the growth of regionalism and local culture, it also imparted a powerful ethnolinguistic bias to the Christians' religious view of civilization. Simultaneously, it provided Ottoman political and intellectual elites with a window through which to look at the historical origins of their state; thus they came to define it as the patrimony, not of the sultan, but of a new, rather vague ethnic type of *millet* (nation), which they claimed to represent, challenging therefore the sultan's authority.

Turks, Communities, and Ethnicity

A major theme of this work is the transformation of ethnic groups into ethnonational communities; it focuses specifically on the different stages of development among the Turkic groups in the world and, finally, on the emergence of Turkishness (ethnic identity) and Turkism (nationalism) in the Ottoman Empire. Although the founders of the Ottoman Empire had consisted of tribal groups, merchant-craftsmen, and Sufis, mostly Turkish in origin, the state did not, despite abundant evidence to the contrary, display conscious awareness of its ethnicity. Instead, as Anthony D. Smith has described them, the ethnic Turks in the Ottoman Empire, living as they did in villages and as tribes, represented mainly *ethnic categories*: they were more aware of their Islamic identity and more strongly attached to their kin, village, and region than to their ethnicity.[7] Eventually, the Empire also included several major *ethnic communities*, among them Greeks, Serbians, Bulgarians, and Arabs, each of which possessed a collective proper name, a myth of common ancestry, historical memories of statehood, elements of common culture, an idea of a specific homeland, and a sense of group solidarity. The Turkic groups of Kazan, Crimea, and Azerbaijan likewise constituted ethnic communities not very different from those of the non-Turks in the Ottoman Empire. The Muslims of Russia, consequently, played an important role in defining—or misdefining—the developing ethnonational identity and nationalist ideology of the Ottoman Turks, just as they, in return, were themselves profoundly influenced by the modernization movement and the educational system of the Ottoman Empire. This study therefore, takes into account the impact of the pan-Islamism-pan-Turkism of Russia's Turkic peoples on the Muslim Ottomans, and vice versa.

National Identity and Turkish Nationalism: A Synthesis

The genesis of Turkish nationalism was a multifaceted process occurring in several stages of identity accretion proceeding from universal Ottomanism and Islamism to specific ethnic Turkishness and Turkism. It was the unplanned result of structural transformation, special differentiation, and migration, as much as the product of the state's efforts to direct the identity-forming process toward a predetermined end. In the process, the state often ignored the new identities, sometimes emerging in traditional garb, that social change created. Ultimately Anatolia and, to some extent, Rumili, the heartland of the Ottoman state, witnessed the creation of a new nation with, first, an Ottoman and, later a Turkish label. This new nation consisted of the old Turkic stock of Anatolia and Rumili and the numerous other ethnic or converted Muslim groups that were indigenous to those lands or had migrated and settled there. Similarly, the Arabs underwent the same process of "nationalization" under old "Arabic" labels, although the resulting Arab nations were new. As a consequence, on either side of a Turko-Arabic zone, running through Syria and Iraq, arose a Turkish and several Arab nations. This study will attempt to review and revise in light of more realistic social, historical, and ideological perspectives the "nationalist" ideas of Ziya Gökalp and Yusuf Akçura and, very briefly, Arab "nationalism" in the Ottoman context.

The Turkish "national" awakening, to use a stereotype just for the sake of clarity, followed a unique course of evolution. It started among the upper echelons of the bureaucracy, as an interest in the ethnic origins of the holders of *hükümet* (the executive power) and in the language of the state. History textbooks used in the modern schools of the nineteenth century used the *hicra*, the migration of the Prophet from Mecca to Medina in A.D. 1622, as the start of "national" history, whereas textbooks in the military schools traced the beginning of the "national" history to its ethnic roots in Central Asia. In truth, the language of the Ottoman state always was Turkish, and the Enderun, the famous palace school that trained top-level administrators, used Turkish as the language of instruction throughout its existence. It is not surprising, therefore, that these facts supplied the arguments to claim that political leadership in the Ottoman state had always been "Turkish." This "newly discovered" Turkishness of the Ottoman state, however, was really a more recent by-product of Ottomanism and Islamism, which had imbued ethnicity with a unique cultural substance. In other words, Ottoman and Islamic historical identities and experiences had been brought into the realm of consciousness and internalized under the label of Turkishness, a sense of cultural-historical ethnicity that separated the Ottoman Turks from Russia's Turkists, whose ethnicity derived from lineage (*soy*) and race (as will be discussed in due course).

Ottoman Relations with Europe

In the seventeenth century, there was a degree of chaos and uncertainty as to the nature of change in the Ottoman classical order. Their inability to devise a remedy for this unsettled state resulted in Ottoman weakness, while Western Europe emerged as a powerful economic and military entity and Russian military power increased. Thus was born the "Eastern Question."

It is incorrect to claim that Ottoman weakness stemmed from ignorance about achievements and events taking place in the West. Sultan Mehmed II (r. 1451–81) exchanged letters with the pope and sent Turks to Italy to study painting. The oldest surviving map of America, drawn in 1513, was in Ottoman hands. The writings of Katip Çelebi (1600–57) on geography, history, and even on nationality show that Ottomans were aware of some of the major issues of their time and eventually of the French Revolution. What they did not understand, at least for a while, was the nature of the changes that were transforming the Western world and steadily affecting their own society.

In any case, the Eastern Question and the need of England, France, Russia, and the Hapsburgs to find moral and political justification for partitioning the Ottoman lands were the most important, although not the first, factors that drastically altered the Ottomans' internal and international policies. While the Ottoman state adopted a series of reforms intended to strengthen the state and to prevent its partition, Russia, England and France were calling for reforms in the name of modernity, freedom, justice, and a variety of other ideals: reforms not always implemented in their own countries. They were hardly interested in a true Ottoman revival, at least not in its old imperial form.

Its alliance with Europe during the Crimean War and the Paris Treaty of 1853–56 rapidly and unexpectedly moved the Ottoman state into the European political, cultural, and economic orbit; but the war with Russia in 1877–78 and the partisan European attitude toward Balkan events in 1875–76 shattered the illusion of Europe's friendship. During the ensuing long and painful reappraisal of Ottoman relations with Europe, the Ottomans were placed in the difficult position of wishing to acquire the civilization of Europe while fending off its imperialist ambitions and decrying its anti-Muslim attitudes.

The nature of the Ottoman relations with Europe and Russia is, thus, a major theme running throughout this book. Those relations cannot be viewed only from a strategic perspective, for religious differences were often magnified into conflicts of civilization and culture and used to justify military-political actions. Such differences often exerted a powerful influence on Ottoman-European relations at the same time that developments in Ottoman society were pointing toward cultural understanding, rather than cultural confrontation, with the West. Sultan Abdulhamid, hard pressed to maintain the territorial integrity of the Ottoman state, used the caliphate as an instrument of internal unity, conveying to posterity a false image of himself as a pan-Islamist intent on mobilizing the Muslim world against the West. In fact, Abdulhamid used the caliphate not only to unify the Ottoman Muslims but also as an instrument to legitimize his reforms, which produced profound changes in practically all fields of activity. At the same time, he sought to maintain friendly relations with England and France, which were effectively seeking to partition the Ottoman territories. Nonetheless, supposedly in order to restore the Muslims' true "Islamic" identity, the sultan gave the caliphate and the faith a hitherto nonexistent ideological force. Such a profoundly revolutionary act, in turn, altered forever the nature of relations between the state and the ruler, between the ruler and the ruled, and between the individual and religion. Ottoman foreign relations, then, are rightly regarded as having played a seminal role in the political, economic, and ideological transformation of the Ottoman state.

The Caliphate, Islamism (Pan-Islamism), and Abdulhamid II

No other Muslim ruler in history faced such momentous decisions as Abdulhamid. A practicing Muslim and an absolutist, but also a firm believer in modernization, he admired Europe and its civilization, but not its "culture." He hoped that Muslim societies would somehow emulate the reforms that had revitalized Christianity and their societies, which, despite change, remained faithful to their own identity and faith. Abdulhamid preserved all the reforms introduced by his predecessors and opened new avenues of change, including the letters and sciences, that greatly widened the intellectual horizons of Ottoman modernization and, paradoxically, brought the elites closer to European culture. In other words, while claiming due recognition and re-spect for Islamic civilization, Abdulhamid opened it to the West. It was during his reign that private enterprise gained momentum, the privatization of state lands ac-celerated, and that the first modern Muslim bourgeoisie began to rise, first in the agrarian and then in the commercial sector. His association with and manipulation or adroit suppression of the popular Sufi movements not only minimized their ill effects but also allowed the sultan to bring these movements and some of their ideas into the mainstream of Islam and state policies.

Abdulhamid was handicapped by a number of personal shortcomings, such as a tendency toward suspicion and secrecy, fear of delegating authority, distrust of oth-ers, and his belief in the efficiency of absolutism, which he attempted to turn into a formal theory of government. Because he believed firmly in the indivisibility of au-thority, in the divine origin of his royal prerogatives, and in his historical mission to assure the survival of the state as the patrimony of the House of Osman, he made absolutism the mark of his reign and used the caliphate to legitimize it. Thus Abdulhamid's understanding of his faith and of his position and authority as sultan and caliph was markedly different from that of his predecessors. A substantial part of this work, therefore, revolves around the person of Sultan Abdulhamid, the office of the caliphate, and the ideology of Islamism.

Although Islamism was a new and modern ideology wrapped in traditional reli-gious garb, only its conservative aspect received much attention, being given the name "pan-Islamism" and condemned as a doctrine of anti-European Islamic unity. "Pan-Islamism" has been used in Western political and academic circles for a century or more to indicate merely a dark-age ideology, without any definite agreement on its content, scope, and goals. Dwight E. Lee was absolutely correct when he wrote, more than half a century ago, that there is "no study of Pan-Islamism that reveals satisfac-torily the exact details of its rise and development during the latter half of the nine-teenth century."[8] The most typical definition of the concept was that given by the German orientalist and colonial adviser to his government, C. H. Becker, early in the twentieth century, after interest in it had passed its zenith. Becker called pan-Islamism a movement toward "realization of an Islamic ideal, the unity of the Muslims in the world under the direction of a leader [imam] commanding the world community."[9]

Despite the imprecise and varied applications of the term, there has been general agreement that Sultan Abdulhamid, in his capacity as the caliph for all Sunni Mus-lims in the world, was the principal proponent and practitioner of pan-Islamism for his own political purposes.[10] The theory that the sultan was the driving force behind the rise of this ill-understood ideology is bolstered by the fact that the term came into frequent use among European scholars only after Abdulhamid's ascension to the throne in 1876 and chiefly after 1878, when the final partition of the badly battered Ottoman state appeared to be imminent. Accusations that Abdulhamid was foment-ing the pan-Islamic movement as an anti-European bigotry arose mainly following the Ottoman rift with France and England during the years 1878–82. That was after England had occupied Cyprus and then Egypt, and France had been encouraged by England and Germany to take Tunisia in order to compensate it for the loss of Alsace-Lorraine. These land grabs caused a profound anti-European revulsion throughout in the Muslim world. However, the author of one article in an English magazine stated that "history will some day recognize in Abdul Hamid II, Sultan and Khalif, one of the most striking figures . . . even one of the master-minds, of our times," and described the sultan as inspired by a central idea "throughout his reign,—namely, the revival of the spiritual authority to which he lays claim as heir to the Khalifate, in order to compensate for the curtailment of his temporal dominions as Sultan."[11] The writer then defined pan-Islamism as a confrontation of Islam against Christendom and the civilization of Europe, rather than as a struggle against colonialism or an effort to preserve and revive the Islamic societies.

Almost from the start, there were challenges to the notion that pan-Islamism was an ideology that Abdulhamid had created for strictly political reasons, but few people paid attention to those contrary views. In 1906, for example, Arminius Vambery, who was well acquainted with the Muslim world and knew Abdulhamid personally, wrote of the sultan's "pan-Islamic missions" to Bukhara, Afghanistan, and India: "It would be idle to attribute to this exchange of mission some far-going political importance, for the predominant feature was of a religious character."[12] Decades later Dwight E. Lee and Anthony Reid criticized the prevailing emphasis on the very sort of political interpretation Vambery had warned against. Specifically, Lee charged that most studies either viewed pan-Islamism as a simple ideology for mobilizing the Muslim East against the Christian West or attributed its rise to a single source or individual.[13] Likewise, Reid, who studied pan-Islamism in Indonesia, disputed the idea that "every outburst of pan-Islamic enthusiasm formed part of a centrally directed international movement," and he doubted that Turkey had an exclusive or overwhelming role in leading any such movement.[14]

The Muslims' own views about the nature, scope, and goals of pan-Islamism also differed sharply from the standard European notions. The insightful Behdjet Wahby bey, whose writings found acceptance among a few well-informed scholars such as Vambery, claimed that the Europeans saw a "Muslim peril" following the pattern of the "yellow peril" and coined the term pan-Islamism to express this view. He emphasized that pan-Islamism was not the grouping of "Moslem communities under the flag of some despotism which would urge them on to carnage; nor is it the political union of peoples professing the same religion. It is neither an occult religious sect nor a secret political association; it is merely a free and complete expression of progress in Moslem societies."[15] Wahby bey's important article is worthy of extensive quotation, for it relates to many other points stressed in this study. In the author's view, pan-Islamism was

> a compact tacitly entered into by the most enlightened classes of the Mussulman nations, with an object which is purely moral and intellectual . . . [and a search for] a common ideal, that of Progress, and in a common aspiration, that of Liberty. . . . The aim of Pan-Islamism then is to liberate these three hundred millions of human beings from *any yoke whatsoever that would maintain them in a state of ignorance* and degradation, and that would constitute an obstacle to the free development of their moral and intellectual faculties. It is the awakening of the Islamic conscience, struggling against the aggressor, be he Pope or Khalifa.[16]

Although the Europeans and some Muslim intellectuals differed sharply about its meaning and goals, the nineteenth and early twentieth centuries witnessed the rise of a unique Islamic ideology, whether looked at in its international dimension and called "pan-Islamism" or regarded only in its internal transformational aspect and called "Islamism."

Islamism/pan-Islamism had no parallel in Islamic history. It was a European-type movement of liberation and change, clad in Islamic garments and apparently led by the traditional head of the Muslim community, the caliph. In other words, it was a modern, progressive Islamic movement, the outward traditional aspects of which obscured its modern character and led it to be condemned as anti-European and regressive. Even the term *pan-Islamism* was non-Islamic. E. G. Browne, D. S. Margoliouth, and several Muslim scholars have ascertained that it did not exist in Arabic, Turkish, or Persian until it was borrowed from Europe.[17] Probably coined by Franz von Werner and Arminius Vambery around the period 1873–78, it was popularized by Gabriel Charmes in works written in 1881 or 1882.[18] Frequent use of the term began after those dates, as England and especially France became suspicious that Istanbul was planning to incite revolutions in Tunisia, Egypt, and other occupied Islamic lands—suspicions encouraged by Russia.

The Islamic term for the unity of the Muslims, *ittihad-i Islam* (Muslim union), apparently was popularized by the Ottoman poet Namik Kemal in a defense of Islam in an article written in 1872, when the Muslims were incensed by Russia's occupation in the 1860s of the Central Asian Muslim hanates (khanates), with which the Ottoman state had long-standing relations. It was again in 1872 that Esat efendi, the secretary of the trade court, issued a pamphlet entitled *Ittihad-i Islam*, urging Muslims to unite against foreign occupation, mainly Russia. The pamphlet was given wide circulation in Mecca and Medina during Abdulhamid's reign and was used as the evidence of his "pan-Islamist" propaganda. Anyway, it is clear that the concept of some sort of Muslim union existed among the intellectuals long before Abdulhamid's enthronement and that it was mainly a reaction stirred by Russia's occupation of Central Asia. There is no indication, however, that Namik Kemal or anyone else developed this idea of a Muslim union as a concrete ideology at that time or thereafter or that the idea was ever put in practice. (These matters are dealt with at length in the body of this work.)

Clearly, "pan-Islamism" and "Islamism" are exceptionally complex movements. They cannot be described in one or two general statements or dismissed as "primarily a sentiment of cohesion" manipulated by Sultan Abdulhamid, as W. C. Smith put it.[19] From the European standpoint, pan-Islamism appeared to be a militant international Muslim political movement of opposition to the West, antagonistic primarily to its Christian faith and its civilization, which some thought derived directly from Christianity. By contrast, the Muslim masses and middle classes, in particular the intellectuals, regarded Islamism as a movement of regeneration and modernization and as an effort to mobilize Muslims, not merely for political and cultural self-defense against Western colonialism, but also for self-renewal and progress. By the last quarter of the nineteenth century, many Muslim modernists and conservatives came to share common aspirations, despite sharp differences in the ways they proposed to achieve their goals. Both talked about "restoring" a glamorized version of the society's old vigor and purity to assure its moral and physical survival, along with the survival of its Islamic identity and traditions. This was, in fact, a form of nationalism in Islamic garb and a transformational process of widespread scope.[20]

A proper study of Islamism/pan-Islamism as the central instrument of transformation must encompass the delineation of its origin and evolution, as well as the impact upon it of shifting political and social circumstances and foreign relations. In addition, Islamism must be related to other movements and historical developments. As Dwight E. Lee concluded:

> [A] satisfactory and fundamentally sound historical treatment [of Panislamism] can be made only if Islamic sources can be studied. Furthermore, in such a study of Pan-Islamism not only must the intellectual and political development in all the various Moslem countries be clearly understood, but also the international relations of the great powers toward one another and toward the Islamic countries must be taken into account.[21]

Consequently, I have viewed Islamism in the context of the social and political changes and religious movements found in various Muslim countries, even though my emphasis is on the Ottoman state. I have attempted to relate Islamic doctrinal issues to empirical facts, foreign relations, and the cultural religious attitudes of policy makers in the Ottoman Empire and Europe. Such a broad empirical-theoretical approach may occasionally result in ambiguity, but it can also provide, I hope, a better understanding of events in the Ottoman Empire during its last five decades.

In sum, this work aspires to examine all the background forces that, by conditioning the transformation (and ultimate disintegration) of the Ottoman Empire, opened the way for the emergence of nation-states in the Middle East and the Balkans, especially modern Turkey. International events as well as domestic political, economic, structural, cultural-religious, and educational factors are considered to the extent they contributed to the transformation. This multifaceted historical-conceptual study is the culmination of many years of observation and research into a mass of original and published sources. It is both "post"-modernist and postorientalist, though it owes an intellectual debt to all these studies and in particular Karl Deutsche's theory about identity changes that occur when smaller traditional social units disintegrate and then restructure themselves into larger ones under the impact of mass communication. This approach also draws on the work of E. P. Thompson and Clifford Geertz, who emphasized the importance of popular Islam, the role of religion in politics and the *local* cultural roots of nationalism. Also taken into account are Max Weber's insights into how belief systems shape group behavior and notions of legitimate authority, Karl Marx's ideas on the dynamics of class formation, Joseph Shumpeter's theory about the genesis of the bourgeoisie, and Durkheim's concept of anomie. In addition, the concluding chapters on nationalism have benefited from the classical writings on nationalism, for example, Hans Kohn, and the more recent works of E. J. Hobsbawm, Ernest Gellner, Benedict R. O'G. Anderson and Anthony D. Smith, although I have departed from their mostly Eurocentric models or sought to add "native" dimensions, that is, the crucial role of the community, religion, and the input of the local and regional elites.[22] Finally, I am indebted as well to the works of Bernard Lewis and Niyazi Berkes, who have dealt with many of the issues studied here, as well as numerous other recent works by younger scholars in Turkey and the West who have opened new intellectual perspectives on the transformation of the Muslim world and relations with the West.

1

Islamic Revivalism

Popular Roots of Islamism (Pan-Islamism)

General Characteristics of the Revivalist Movements

The last decades of Ottoman history cannot be understood properly without taking into account the revolution from below caused by the revivalist movements. The most important event in the history of Islamic societies was the disintegration of the old social order and the resultant restructuring of almost all the traditional social and political institutions and the emergence of new modes of thought all deemed to be "contemporary" or modern. That vast structural transformation was caused, first, by the market forces of capitalism and the often ensuing European occupation of the Muslim lands and, second, by the reforms that the Ottoman state, and other Muslim governments that had preserved their political independence, instituted to assure their survival.

The upswelling from below made the Muslim masses gradually conscious of their social situation and identity, which then were politicized and redefined. The emergence of new Muslim middle classes was another development largely attributable to an interaction between the capitalist market forces and the native society's structure, traditions, and values. Although the transformation of Islamic societies has been viewed as being almost solely of the work of the "transforming elites"—usually bureaucrats and intellectuals who openly espoused Western ideas—the majority of both the traditionalist, conservative masses and the middle classes also became advocates of change in harmony with their Islamic ethos. Islamism, as it emerged during the reign Abdulhamid II, therefore sought to combine change with Islamic values in a way that satisfied all the people, not merely the newly rising elites.

The revivalist movements mobilized and politicized the Muslim masses by bringing the *nâs* (people) into the political arena, and turned them into a force not only opposed to the European powers but also to their own governments, elites, and ulema. In turn, most of the revivalist populist movements found themselves opposed by the occupying European powers, the native religious and cultural establishment—often including reform-minded leaders—and their own ulema, who had perfunctorily managed the people's lives without regard for the essence of their faith or their worldly aspirations. Revivalist groups, representing folk Islam and using the Sufi *tarikat*

20

(paths) inadvertently upheld local, ethnic, and cultural ties while still considering themselves to be part of the universal *ümmet*. (Even today, for example, Muslim immigrants in the United Kingdom—who are mainly from Pakistan—are divided into two groups: the numerous Barelwi, who tend to be new arrivals led by a Sufi *pir* from the home country and who use the mosques to support their ethnic and regional identity, and a smaller group led by Deobandi ulema, who claim to represent true Islam.)

A third way, or compromise, between "low" and "high" Islam occurred in areas such as the Ottoman state, where the state-government formally maintained its Islamic credentials and could direct revivalist ideas into the mainstream of Islam. The result was a new sense of Islamic religious identity that seemed to be separate from and supersede the local community identity by giving Muslims a political sense of belonging to the universal *ümmet*, while nurturing their sense of ethnic and linguistic identity. That the two seemingly contradictory developments—that is, the fragmentation of the traditional *ümmet* into ethnolinguistic units and the broadening and politicization of the religious identity—occurred at the same time and, rather than obstructing, actually supplemented each other will be illustrated in the chapters on nationalism and other issues. Suffice it to say here that the Nakşbandia Sufi order in its modern reincarnation played a significant role in the Ottoman state, notably in its Turkish-speaking part, in merging the revivalist fundamentalism of the lower classes into the established orthodoxy, even as the movement itself became more populist, "national" (Turkish), and modern Islamic. Thus, while the established local customs and ways of life gained visibility and acceptance, the faith also inched toward becoming a more global, abstract, and unifying ideology. In the Ottoman state, Sultan Abdulhamid gave this drive toward globalization and political Islamization new momentum by making the caliphate a central institution for all Muslims without challenging local customs, traditions, and ethnic and linguistic identities. By the end of his rule, the sultan identified himself as both a Turk and a Muslim.

European occupation and influences not only destroyed the traditional Muslim political system and the economic and social institutions that had sustained it but also produced a new social stratum. Now, a new type of middle class arose to communal prominence, through personal initiative and the manipulation of market forces and government power, and challenged the old elites, who had owed their position and wealth mainly to the state. The new middle class, especially its agrarian wing, accepted the ethical standards and cultural values of the traditional order but also adopted the rational business rules and the profit motive of the capitalist market system. Consequently, the revivalist movements tended to regard the members of this new class, especially the intelligentsia, as somehow part of their own faith, culture, and community but also as deviating from the "true path" by accepting the "enemy's" practices and values.

The twenty-four or twenty-six revivalist movements of the nineteenth century started as local or regional movements seeking a return to the basic foundations of Islam—the Koran and the Sunna—and gradually, or in some cases simultaneously, became militant movements of resistance against Russian, Dutch, French, English, and Italian occupation of Central Asia and the Caucasus, the East Indies, North Africa, and Egypt. Their leadership came from the lower urban, upper agrarian, and tribal segments of the middle classes as well as from some of the old religious elites—usually those associated with reformist ideas. In pursuing their aim to renew the society and oppose foreign occupation, the revivalist-fundamentalist movements of the nineteenth century, unlike most of today's fundamentalist movements, may be seen as vehicles for adapting to the changed socioeconomic and political environment. Most contemporary fundamentalist movements are critical of the modernism of the early Islamic "reformers," whose wholesale "modernization" they regard as having been harmful to the integrity and purity of Islam. Actually, the roots of many of the contemporary fundamentalist movements are found in internal political causes, rather than revivalism.[1] They have arisen as a reaction to the disorientation caused by rapid economic development and to the fear that the materialistic modern world has corrupted the ethical system.[2] It is also to be argued that modern fundamentalism is a reaction both to European mercantilism, which limited local, internal, and external trade, and to land reform, industrialization, and the imposition of state controls over religious institutions.[3] The early revivalists, on the other hand, as John O. Voll explains, emphasized the idea of *tajdid* (renewal), which describes a "longstanding and continuing dimension of Islamic history," the idea of renewal being attributed to a saying of the Prophet that "God will send to this umma (the Muslim community) at the head of each century those who will renew its faith for it."[4] What was subject to change and renewal was the social "environment" in which the faith operated, not the faith itself. As Voll put it, the *islah* (reform) was "an effort of socio-moral construction or re-construction making use of a normative standard found in the Quran and the Sunna of the Prophet";[5] and as the social environment underwent change, it enhanced the staying power of the Koran and Sunna.

Sayyid Abul 'Ala al-Mawdudi (1903–79) claimed that the sole criterion of *ihya*—revival—in the religious field was whether "one interiorized or not the action of revival" and, implicitly, also of the social revival deriving eventually from it.[6] In contemporary Turkey there is widespread interest in the notion of *ihya*, the title under which Ibn Taymiyya's and Mawdudi's works, as well as one book in English have been translated and reprinted.[7] It should be noted that Mawdudi criticized Sirhindi, Shah Valilullah Dehlevi, Sayyid Ahmad Barlevi, and other early revivalists for borrowing popular mystical elements from Sufism and for failing to understand that the Muslims among whom they were active had only superficially observed the faith. According to Mawdudi, *tajdid* did not consist of renewed knowledge of Muslim writings only but also all contemporary writings on science and technology. The problems of the century, and their solution, called both for a knowledge of the Koran and Sunna and for a correct diagnosis of those problems. Mawdudi, who founded the Jamaat-i Islami in 1941, opposed nationalism as conflicting with Muslim universalism, but he soon faced the unavoidable fact that the survival of the Muslim community of India depended on the creation of its own territorial state and the development of its own "national" language and identity, as eventually actually happened with the establishment of Pakistan. In effect, Mawdudi seemed to have misunderstood the Indian revivalists' dual acceptance of faith and society, each one with its own characteristics.[8]

On another level of analysis, the revivalist movements relied on the community, not the state, to make their political-religious stand. The English, French, Dutch, and Russian occupation and capitalism had eliminated the old Muslim political and social elites, or limited greatly their field of activity and material possessions; but above all they deprived the Muslim societies of the support, custodial role, and guidance of the state, so these societies had to confront the challenge of occupation and the resulting change on their own. The community replaced the state, except within the borders of the Ottoman Empire, as the chief Muslim social, cultural, and political unit. Because it faced the creative challenge of devising by itself the means to maintain its Islamic identity and faith and, as well, to find an explanation for its plight, the Muslim community was forced to examine its own culture, creed, and inner self.[9] The revivalists relied on the existing tribal, ethnic, and linguistic bonds among the believers to achieve an "Islamic solidarity" but did not deliberately promote narrow tribalism or ethnic segregation to the detriment of the universality of *ümmet*. Nevertheless, by speaking a particular language and abiding by the social customs and culture of a given region and group, they did in fact promoted a certain local culture, which later turned into a "national" culture in cases where the movement succeeded in laying the foundation of a future state (as in Saudi Arabia and Libya). The struggle against central authority and taxation obviously strengthened the appeal of localism and its religious expression—that is, of revivalism.

All the revivalist movements were Sufi in origin, except for that of the Wahhabis of Arabia, whose formal revivalism was confined to the faith and did not seek the renewal of society. The Sufis' Islamic credentials, despite occasional accusations of heresy and hedonism, were impeccable. In the nineteenth century, Sufism (or neo-Sufism) departed from its early esoteric and pacifist views and adopted a social, communal, and populist understanding of the faith. It may be asserted that the revivalist movements represented a form of grassroots Islamic democracy, the first known expression of which appeared in the War of Liberation in Turkey in 1919–22 and, later in some political parties after the 1960s. The issue of the meaning and significance of the dynastic component of Islam was destined to cause deep rifts among the future intelligentsia.

The revivalists devised methods of mass communication and mobilization and often used the *hac* to disseminate their views and methods. Ultimately, their ideas and the strategy of mass mobilization were adopted by the intelligentsia, who amplified them through the use of new media, such as the newspaper.

Sultan Abdulhamid adopted, reshaped, and augmented many of the basic methods and ideas of the revivalists to create a modern state ideology. The sultan's relatively successful use of Islamism, with all its often conflicting progressive and conservative nuances, would not have been possible had the ground not been prepared by these movements. Because the revivalists' powerful populist bases enabled them to appeal to centuries-old cultural and religious values as well as to worldly aspirations shared by the Muslim masses, they forced many crowned heads, including Abdulhamid—who supported all Islamic movements, provided that they did not challenge his power—to acknowledge the power of the masses. The belief in the power of the masses produced new types of leaders ready to challenge the political establishment. Abdelkader of Algeria and Şeyh Şamil carried on a brief correspondence as the new popular leaders of Islam because the Ottoman caliph was passive toward French and Russian expansion, but their own limited resources undermined their anticolonial initiative.

The revivalist movements embodied two basic trends found in one way or another in practically all the past discourses concerning the affairs of Islamic society. The first trend, represented by the orthodox *asharite* (rigid) thought, as reformulated and embodied in the Islamic dogma by Muhammed al-Ghazzali (d. 1111), called for the restoration of the pristine faith as in the days of the Prophet. The second trend was introduced by periodic revivalist movements of short duration and scope, whose call for the return of Islam to its original essence included an accommodation with the worldly order. These were not successful, for they lacked mass support, organization, and ideological political leadership. Both trends, the first represented by Wahhabis and the second by the Sanusis and Nakşbandis (both of which had subbranches), were evident in the Ottoman state. As mentioned, Sultan Abdulhamid's Islamism was, among other things, an effort to mediate between these two trends through a variety of practical measures. On one hand, he appeared formally to adhere to the *asharite* dogma in order to preempt the appeal of the Wahhabis; on the other, he adopted and implemented a variety of changes that would coopt and satisfy the aspiration of the revivalists and of the awakening masses, but without identifying the sultan with any of them. In effect, the sultan became a practical mediator who reconciled the two Islamic trends of thought but alienated the modernist liberals (Westernists) as reformism in the Ottoman state turned into a struggle for power.

The rest of this chapter is a general survey of four revivalist movements, because they were the prototypes that affected the ideological, cultural, social, and political transformation of the Ottoman state during its last decades, notably during Abdulhamid's time. The Wahhabis are analyzed because their movement had great political repercussions and differed in significant ways from the rest of the revivalist movements; the movement of Sayyid Ahmad Barelvi and his followers, known mistakenly as the Wahhabis of India, is studied both because it best embodies the local and cultural features of the revivalist movements in general and because it probably had some indirect impact on Şeyh Khalid, whose Nakşbandia—rather neo-Nakşbandia—order acquired great power in the Ottoman Empire. The muridists of the Caucasus and the Sanusiyya of Libya are dealt with because of their profound impact upon the political destiny of their lands and, as well, upon the ideological transformation of the Ottoman state. It is essential to note here that not a single revivalist movement arose as a result of the sultan's direct or indirect effort. In fact, although he was in close contact with the Rifaiyya, Mevleviyya, and other Sufi orders that supported him, he arrested, persecuted, and reportedly liquidated some Kadiri and even Nakşbandi popular *şeyh*s or religious leaders.

The Wahhabis: Their Stormy Relations with the Ottomans

The *muwahiddun* (believers in unity), unitarian monotheists, or Ikhwan, have been idealized as the first modern movement for Islamic renewal and one that influenced subsequent revival movements. This is a view that, to this author, seems incorrect (although it is one still held by some scholars).[10] Articulated by Muhammad Abd al-Wahhab (1703–92), the founder, and termed by its opponents "Wahhabism," the basic tenets of the doctrine seem similar to those of other revivalist movements, but the similarity is at a superficial level only. Under the banner of Islamic purity, the Wahhabis actually stood in opposition to the transition of the Muslim society to a higher level of political organization and certainly caused the Ottomans serious internal and international difficulties.

Abd al-Wahhab was born in Nejd but traveled extensively in the east and became upset by what be considered the corruption of Islam. He was a follower of the Hanbelite school of Islamic thought, as expressed in the fourteenth century by Ibn Taymiyya (1263–1328). The Hanbelites were the least tolerant of the four main schools of Orthodox Islam, being strongly against the elements of popular Islam that the other schools tolerated, or even embraced. Particularly, the veneration of various religious leaders as saints, whose tombs then became places of pilgrimage, was inveighed against by Ahmad Ibn Hanbal (d. 855). This was even more case with Ibn Taymiyya, who had personal reasons for despising the Mongols (his parents had been forced to flee the Mongol invasions) and who held that their subsequent conversion to Islam was false, as they still retained many of their old practices. It was Ibn Taymiyya's view that *cihad* (Arabic: *jihad*—holy war) could properly be called against even Orthodox Muslims if their practice of Islam was not suitably pure.

The austere doctrine preached by Abd al-Wahhab did not find acceptance among Muslims until he returned to Nejd and settled in al-Dariyeh. There he found a princely ally, Muhammad Ibn Saud, who became a follower and brought his family and his tribe with him. They rose up to combat *shirk* (the veneration of saints and tombs), to oppose tribalism, blood warfare, *taqlid* (imitation), and *icma* (Arabic: *ijma*—consensus) beyond that reached by the original Companions of the Prophet. They wanted to return the religion and the society to the state of authentic purity that prevailed at the time of the Prophet, rejecting the scholarly embellishments of the medieval period and relying only on the Koran and the Sunna for direction. *Ictihad* (Arabic: *ijtihad*—interpretation) of these original principles was to be permitted, if properly done. In following these ideals, Wahhabis were fanatical and fiercely intolerant.

That this austere version of Islam should arise in the Central Arabian peninsula is perhaps not surprising: climate, terrain, and the scarcity of resources in the area made for a harsh life, and geographical isolation protected the sparse population from the impact of market forces until the discovery of oil in the twentieth century; in contrast, by the middle of the nineteenth century, Iraq, the coastal areas of Syria, Anatolia, and Egypt had all been drawn into the market sphere, and their societies had experienced change accordingly. The Wahhabis had little use for the Ottomans, considering them as the source of the despised *shirk*, and they were indifferent to the sultan's position as caliph, at least until Abdulhamid's reign.[11]

The Wahhabis at first mainly extorted tribute from the pilgrimage caravans, at times causing a complete cessation of this economically important (to the şerifs of Mecca and the Hicaz administration) activity. Just after the turn of the century they began attacking the settled, relatively prosperous areas of southern Iraq, pillaging and destroying not only tombs and monuments of saints but also the evidences of material progress, which they termed *bida* (innovation), that undermined the purity of the faith.

Finally, the Wahhabis turned on the holy cities, occupying Mecca in 1806 and destroying the ornamental embellishments of the tombs of all the great Muslim leaders, including that of the Prophet himself. The news of this destruction profoundly disturbed many Muslims, particularly those from Asia, where the cult of the dead was an important part of the local culture and had survived bitter opposition from the religious establishment. I encountered in 1990 in Medina a middle-class citizen, a shop owner, from eastern Turkey. We met in the Cennet-ul Bakiye, the cemetery across from the Haram mosque of Medina, where I was searching for the grave of Şeyh Şamil and he was trying to locate the tomb of Osman, the third caliph. Our searches were unsuccessful, for the Wahhabis had reduced all the tombs to uniform piles of earth. The man was exceptionally angry because the guards did not allow him to pray facing the Prophet's tomb but forced him to turn to Kibla, that is, toward the Kaaba in Mecca. "I came here to be close to the Prophet and to his human remains," he said. "They are more meaningful to me than a black, lifeless stone." Similar views were put forth by other Muslims, including Omar al Kattab.

The conquest of Mecca brought home to the Ottoman administration the true political nature and significance of the Wahhabi movements and the House of Saudi. The sultan condemned the Wahhabis, and the *kazasker* (chief judge) of Rumili, Abdullah Tatarcik efendi, issued a *fetva* (religious opinion) declaring that the obligation to perform the *hac* to Mecca was "gayri vacip" (not necessary or binding) as long as Mecca was under Wahhabi occupation. In 1811, at the behest of the Porte (the prime minister's office), Mehmet Ali of Egypt launched a campaign to conquer the Wahhabis and break their power. This campaign lasted until 1818. Finally, Ibrahim paşa, the son of Mehmet Ali of Egypt, captured and razed al-Dariyeh and freed Mecca. The news that he had captured Abdullah ibn Saud and his four sons was celebrated with three days of festivities in Istanbul. Cevdet paşa, the official Ottoman historian for the period, stated that Abdullah ibn Saud and his companions were interrogated for three days and asked to identify the goods taken from the Prophet's tomb; some items were identified and returned, but not the precious stones (apparently pocketed by Ibrahim paşa's own people). Eventually Abdullah was executed in the public square.[12] The relief felt by society at large was similar to the deep satisfaction that followed the liquidation by the state of the anti-Sufi puritanism and vigilantism of the fundamentalist order of the Kadizadelis in 1683. This movement, started by Kadizade Mehmet (b. 1582 in Balikesir), was a reaction both to the state's domination of religion and, especially, to drastic changes in Ottoman society's living habits after the institutions of the classical age disintegrated and the new world order began to emerge.[13] Fanaticism and intolerance never appealed much to the Muslim public; even in the early days of Islam, the Kharijites, with their unwillingness to accept that circumstances should temper the rigors of the ritual, were not popular.

Ottoman-Saudi relations became increasingly unsteady as the nineteenth century wore on. Faisal ibn Turki (the Great; d. 1866), who ruled from 1834 to 1838, was returned to power again in 1843 until 1865, after the Egyptian hold on the Hicaz was broken and he was released from captivity in Cairo. Although Faisal regained his *kaymakamlik* (governorship) of Nejd, he immediately sought the support of the British (and of Muhammad Ibn Awn, the *şerif* of Mecca), in order to expand his authority over Bahrain and the Trucial Coast. When the British turned him down, Faisal sought Ottoman help against the British. Faisal's son Abdullah (r. 1865–71), however, reached an agreement giving the British a foothold in Arabia, which London exploited adroitly.

The Saudi flirtation with territorial ambitions in the Gulf induced the Ottoman administration in Baghdad under Mithat paşa (governor of Baghdad from 1868 to 1872) to capture the important province of Hasa (Hassa) in 1871 and then to help the Rashidi dynasty of Jabal Shamar, ruling north of Nejd, to take power in Hasa. These measures neutralized temporarily the Saudi princes, while the Ottoman throne underwent great turmoil in 1876 and during the war of 1877–78. The Rashidis, who relied heavily on the Shammar tribe aimed at making Hail, their capital, rival Mecca and Medina, however unrealistic it may sound. It seems that worldly ambitions took precedence over religious beliefs.

Under Sultan Abdulhamid, relations with the Saudis improved, as the sultan did his best to remain on friendly terms with them. He did not try to punish Abdul Rahman ibn Saud (son of Amir Faisal), who briefly ousted the Rashidis from Riyadh in the years 1889–1891. Instead, when the Saudi prince was forced to take refuge in Kuwait, the sultan did not pursue him but actually provided Abdul Rahman and his son Abdulaziz with a pension. Winning over the Saudis was part of Sultan Abdulhamid's plan to coopt the Saudis-Wahabbis and to solidify his control and influence over the Muslims under Ottoman sovereignty while neutralizing British moves. The Saudis were not much interested; they had their own plan to lead the Islamic world. As it turned out in the end, this plan was financed by Western money.

In 1902 Abdul Rahman's son, Abdulaziz ibn Saud, conquered Riyadh. Then, as early as 1903, he reverted to the policy of his grandfather Faisal, seeking British help to oust the Ottomans from the strategic province of Hasa. Sultan Abdulhamid tried to pacify Abdulaziz by appointing him *kaymakam* of Nejd (still under Ottoman rule), but Abdulaziz promptly moved to conquer Qatar and Abu Dhabi, only to be stopped by the British. However, the political resident in Bushire, Sir Percy Cox, was aware of the help the Saudis could render the British and tried to come to terms with them, an approach that gained further momentum after Abdulaziz defeated and killed Abdulaziz Ibn Mutaib Ibn Rashid in 1906.

The Ottoman-Saudi rift intensified after the Porte imposed the levy of customs fees at Hasa and widened the use of Turkish. This resulted in new tribal support for the Saudis, but the British refrained from giving their full support to the Saudis in order not to aggravate their already delicate relations with Istanbul and the emir of Mecca, whom they were grooming as a potential Arab caliph. However, the British defended Kuwait against Istanbul and thus helped consolidate its de facto autonomy. The uncertain and precarious situation of Nejd, in turn, compelled Istanbul to consolidate further its authority in the Hicaz, by far the most important Arab province, by coming to terms with the emir of Mecca. The collapse and disintegration of the Ottoman state in 1918 left Arabia prey to local contenders. In 1924 Abdulaziz succeeded in conquering Mecca and Medina once more, defeating Şerif Hüseyin and consolidating the Saudi rule over the Hicaz.

Up to this point, the *cihad* had been used exclusively against Muslims; however, when the Ikhwan demanded to continue the *cihad* in Iraq, Transjordan, and Kuwait in order to oust the British, Abdulaziz enlisted the support of the ulema and liquidated the Ikhwan at the battle of Sibillah in 1930. Two years later Nejd and the Hicaz were formally united and Ibn Saud was declared king of Arabia. In short, the Saudi house had relied on Wahhabism when convenient, challenging Abdulhamid's control of the Hicaz and the holy places that legitimized de facto his claims to the caliphate; but ultimately the Saudis asserted political rule over the Arabian peninsula and assumed the kingship. Only in 1987, feeling the pressure of a truly religious challenge to his rule, did King Fahd adopt the title "Custodian of the Two Holy Places," which the Ottoman sultan had used since the sixteenth century.

As for the Wahhabi movement, its interest lay in total devotion to the rituals of the faith. The Wahhabis did not share the curiosity of the revivalist movements outside Arabia about the source of Europe's material strength; nor did they pursue the inner spiritual and personal experience sought by the Sufis. Instead, the Wahhabis condemned (and still condemn) Sufism and its means, such as mysticism and chanted prayers, as deviations from Islam. The Sufis revered not only the Message (Koran) but also the Messenger (Prophet) and saw the two as reinforcing each other. The Wahhabis accepted the Message and the Messenger's mission of being God's voice but ignored the Messenger as a person. In the end, the apparent absolute formal devotion to ritual religion that endeared the Wahhabis to many pious Muslims and stirred the admiration of some European scholars left the majority of Muslims unsatisfied.

The Indian Revivalist Movement: Sayyid Ahmad Barelvi

The movement of Sayyid (Syed) Ahmad Barelvi established a broad popular foundation for revivalist Islam in India, had some role in shaping Şeyh Khalid's new Nakşbandi teachings, indirectly contributed to the Indian Muslims' extraordinary support for the Ottoman state, and prepared the ground for the panislamist Khilafat movement. Finally, it engendered in the British a paranoid fear of Indian Muslim revolt, which probably prevented London from attacking, first, the Ottomans and, later, the nationalists of Mustafa Kemal. (This movement should not be confused with the Hizb al-Ahnaf of the Barelwis of Ahmed Riza Han [1856–1921], although both movements were Sufi and originated in the same area—but not the same town—in Uttar Pradesh.)

Indian "Wahhabism" probably was the most authentic prototype of a modern, revivalist, populist militant movement, and hence will be explained in some detail. Indian revivalism was a Sufi movement with long historical roots in the Nakşbandia-Mucaddidiyya teachings of Ahmat Sirhindi. The literature on these Indian revivalists is very scanty, Sir William Hunter's work, published in 1871, being one of the earliest and best-known sources.[14] Hunter strongly condemned the "Wahhabis," as he called them, for their struggle against the British, but he undertook an honest inquiry into the root cause of the movement. He concluded that changes in the status of two basic Muslim institutions, the *vakif* and the *imaret* (which he referred to as public endowments created by Muslim dignitaries), were paramount in fueling the rise of the revivalists in India. In this assessment Hunter was correct, and it is appropriate here—though redundant to the specialist—to discuss these institutions, the *vakif* and the *imaret*, in some detail. The *vakif* is a foundation established by an individual through the dedication of personal property or its revenue to sustain social, educational, and/or cultural activities. The *vakfiye* is the constitutive act of the *vakif* and represents the donor's free decision. The *vakif* is governed by the Şeriat, which, being above state-issued regulations, makes *vakif* property theoretically immune to expropriation and to the intrusion of *kanunname*, the "secular" law. The state role is confined to ensuring that the property is used according to the donor's wish. Thus, through the *vakif*, a person could sponsor a series of social, educational, and cultural activities to fulfill a religious obligation and help maintain the Islamic character of society and also to give it a specific direction according to the donor's ideas. The *vakif* was a mechanism of social adaptation and subtle engineering but it took out of the market substantial amounts of property, including land; in the last quarter of the eighteenth century about 30 percent of the land in the Ottoman state was in the hands of the *vakif*s. The situation of the *imaret* was somewhat different. It consisted of large tracts of conquered state, or *miri*, lands given to high state dignitaries, officials, and other special people. In the Ottoman Empire such holdings, known as *hass*, were returned to the state upon the dignitary's death, except in the case of the imperial family, while in other Muslim areas, such as in India, they passed to heirs. The recipients of such property used the income to build palaces for themselves but also marketplaces, mosques, schools, bridges, and variety of other public edifices. In fact, most of the historical monuments in the Muslim countries, consisting of works usually named after the sponsor (sultans, viziers, or other dignitaries or their children), were financed with income from such lands. The *vakif*s and the *imaret*s, both exempt from taxes, were the material support bases of Muslim culture and identity, for they often represented a blend of the local and universal features of Islam; a mosque in Malaysia or Istanbul, for instance, has features common to all mosques as well as unique local architectural characteristics. However, late in the eighteenth and throughout the nineteenth century some of the *vakif*s and almost all of the state or domains land gradually lost their earlier tax-free status.

The European powers appropriated wholesale the *miri* and *imaret* lands, which they regarded as public domain that should become their property, since the conquest made them the successors of the Muslim states. In the Ottoman Empire, where the centralized government was in need of revenue, it either confiscated the *vakif* lands under various pretexts or brought them under direct state administration, partly in order to siphon their income to the state institutions that had taken over many of the functions, notably in education and social service (health), carried out by the *vakif*s in the past.[15] In addition, as the pressure for commercialized agriculture increased, much *vakif* and then *miri* land was privatized to become part of the commodities production system. (see chapter 4). The process varied from country to country: for example, in Crimea, the Russian generals and their associates acquired the land of the *han* and the *mirza*s (mid-level nobility), while in North Africa the communal property was transformed into private holdings. In any case, the result was the same: namely, the destruction of the basic economic foundation that provided for a Muslim way of life, often at the grassroots level. The bureaucrats and the old imperial elites often adapted themselves to the new situation by associating themselves with the new regime, whether European or a new Muslim central administration, but such adaptation at the grassroots level was difficult if not impossible. The Muslims in India viewed this situation as a direct threat to their faith, and although the English accorded them full freedom of religion, that "freedom" was deprived of its economic and social basis. Thus, in a major way, the "Wahhabis" in India represented a grassroots reaction to the havoc created by the land policies of the British.

Hunter stated that the British had toyed with the idea of acquiring some rights over the *vakif* and the princely (domain, or *miri*) lands in India as early as 1772 but did not do so until 1819. Then, in 1828, the British adopted the Land Resumption Act, taxing *vakif* and *miri* lands and dealing a crushing blow to Muslim traditions. James Grant, the revenue officer in Bengal, claimed that one-fourth of the province lands transferred by the earlier Muslim rulers to individuals were domain lands.[16] The consequences are best described by Hunter himself, when he speaks about the 1.1 million pounds in taxes collected in Bengal from formerly tax-exempt *vakif* and *miri* lands.

> A large part of this sum was derived from lands held rent free by Musulmans or by Muhammadan foundations. The panic and hatred which ensued have stamped themselves for ever on the rural records. Hundreds of ancient families were ruined, and the educational system of the Musulmans, which was almost entirely maintained by rent-free grants, received its death-blow. The scholastic classes of the Muhammadans [which] emerged from the eighteen years of harrying [the period when the Land Resumption Proceedings asserting the title of the British to the Muslim state lands were drastically enforced] absolutely ruined: . . . The Muhammadan Foundations suffered most. . . . We demanded an amount of proof in support of rent-free tenures, which, in the then uncertain state of real property law, they could not have produced in support of their acknowledged private estate.[17]

The true significance of the much maligned movement of Sayyid Ahmad Barelvi becomes clear in light of the conditions described above. Qeyamuddin Ahmad claims that the movement, apart from its political aspects, represented an important attempt at a socioreligious reformation of the Indo-Musulman society.[18] Information on Ahmad's work is based on a series of fundamentalist writings, including *Waqa-i Ahmadi* or *Tarikh-i Kabir* and the *Sirat-i Mustaqim* (which comprise the sayings of Sayyid Ahmad and are regarded as the manifesto of the movement), as well as on the records of the police and the published sources.

Sayyid Ahmad Barelvi (Brelwi) (1786–1831) was born in Bareilly (Barelui). After his learned father's death in 1800, he went to Lucknow and then to Delhi in search of employment. In Delhi he became a disciple of Shah Abdulaziz, the son and the spiritual heir to Shah Waliullah, who himself was a disciple of Sirhindi.[19] Shah Waliullah was a Sufi and a Nakşbandi, as was Shah Abdulaziz. Waliullah had claimed that monarchy was contrary to the early republican tradition of Islam and that it had undermined the freedom of *ictihad* as well as free thinking and initiative in Islam. According to Waliullah, Islam was built on its followers' character, which in turn was shaped by certain moral and spiritual principles rooted in the Koran and *hadis*. The individuals formed the cells of the community, and if the cells degenerated, then the community itself would degenerate. Waliullah did not believe that the reforming of a few individuals at the top could lead to the regeneration of the Muslim society. Instead, he advocated the reform of the community as a whole, to be achieved through a widespread mass movement.[20] Islam, according to Waliullah, was a revolutionary movement for the emancipation of mankind based on the moral and spiritual principles in the Koran and Sunna. Waliullah held that the believer should have direct personal access to and develop his/her own understanding of the Koran, rather than rely on a few interpreters or ulema; eventually he translated the Koran into Persian.

Sayyid Ahmad Barelvi followed the basic teaching of Waliullah, although with considerable modification. In matters of faith, he objected to the innovations brought by the Sufis, including their concept of *tawhidi wujud* (unity with God, which presumed an insight into divine truth and masked sensual pleasure), their interpretation of fate (*kadir*, which ran contrary to the orthodox view of predestination), and their excessive dependence on the *pir* (the leader). He also criticized the offering of *nazr-u-niaz*, food and prayers to please the soul of the dead, and the expensive ceremonies related to marriage, circumcision, and mourning. As a Sufi, Sayyid Ahmad stressed observance of an ethical code and the unity of Islam; he took the *biat* (allegiance) in all four major Sufi orders of India: Chishti, Sohrawardi, Kadri, and Nakşbandi.

Sayyid Ahmad went on the *hac* in 1821, well after he had begun preaching his own views and after the Wahhabis of Arabia had been ousted from Mecca. There is no evidence that in Mecca he was in contact with the Arabian Wahhabis, but having already been called Wahhabi, Sayyid Ahmad and his followers were probably highly suspect in the eyes of the Ottoman authorities in Mecca.

Sayyid Ahmad Barelvi's movement was a new type of genuine Islamic populist, communal movement, geared to the needs and ways of the Indian Muslims. Wilayat Ali, who took over the leadership of the movement after Sayyid Ahmad's death in 1831, held meetings at his home where the Koran and the *hadis* were taught in the simple local language, so that people could understand their meaning. Indeed, the Koran was translated into Urdu and "copies distributed in large numbers among the members of the gathering [which] included women, children and uneducated laymen."[21] In time, Sayyid Ahmad's brotherhood became a mass political movement, aimed not only at regenerating the faith but also at mobilizing the society against the British. Sayyid Ahmad traveled throughout north India recruiting followers; in 1826 he moved to the northwest provinces, where he established a base of operation for his fight against the British. There he also fought—unsuccessfully and unnecessarily—the Sikhs, who were obstructing his access to Kashmir. After inflicting severe defeats on the British army, Sayyid Ahmad was eventually defeated and killed in the battle for Balakote in 1831. His *halifas* (disciples) then continued their struggle under the leadership of the Sadiqpur family of Putna, whose wealth, influence, and learning gave a new vitality to the movement.

The Faraizi movement paralleled that of Barelvi. This fundamentalist social movement originated in the Faridpur district under the leadership of Haci Şeriatullah (b. 1764), who had spent twenty years in Mecca. When Mir Nisar Ali (or Titu Mir), the next leader, offered his *biat* to Sayyid Ahmad during their meeting in Mecca, their movements merged. The Faraizi was essentially a social movement directed against the *zamindar* (landlords) and the British, but in matters of doctrine its views coincided with those of Sayyid Ahmad, making the merger easy and logical.[22]

Sayyid Ahmad placed the utmost importance on monotheism and *ictihad*, while he redefined *cihad* as a defensive struggle providing a means of mass mobilization to protect and preserve one's own religion and the society's Islamic identity. The upper echelons of Muslim society and the religious establishment in India regarded Sayyid Ahmad as preaching ideas alien to Islam and as not being a true Muslim; they criticized him for, among other things, taking the title of imam and *amir-ul mu'min* in the northwest provinces in 1826. Actually, Sayyid Ahmad rejected the government position and advised religious leaders not to become involved in public administration, and he implemented this principle in the areas under his control; his followers even sought the support of the Hindus against the British.

It is incorrectly assumed that Barelvi activity faded away after its peak period, from about 1815 to 1831. That it still existed in 1864 is indicated by the arrest and trial at Ambala of several leaders, who were sentenced to life terms (although most of them were released after 1882). Meanwhile, the ulema of northern India and the Calcutta Muhammadan Society formally declared that *cihad* against the British was unlawful because the ruler did "in no way interfere with his Muhammadan subjects in the Rites prescribed by their Religion, such as Praying, Fasting, Pilgrimage, Zakat, Friday Prayer, and Zama'at, and gives them fullest protection and liberty in the above respects in the same way as a Muhammadan ruler would do"; also, the upper classes believed that the "Muhammadan subjects had no strength and means to fight with their rulers."[23] The Barelvis, on the other hand, regarded the British "freedom of religion" as meaningless, for the faith had been deprived of its supporting Islamic economic and social foundations that gave vitality and meaning to the five principles of the faith; they seem to have realized that faith alone was unable to defeat the superior technology of the British.

Sayyid Ahmad Barelvi's movement also dramatized emerging Indian class differences in the understanding of Islam, the British, society, and justice, differences that were duplicated throughout the Muslim world. Qeyamuddin Ahmad stressed that Sayyid Ahmad's movement pursued, along with the moral rejuvenation of society, concrete sociopolitical goals, such as social justice and progress in all its forms.[24] In addition, Sayyid Ahmad's movement is credited with lessening the hold of the *maulavis* (religious men) on the laity, with helping better the status of widows by facilitating remarriages, and with introducing a variety of other social improvements. Hunter's writings made the movement's more worldly goals apparent to the British, as did the writings of Sayyid Ahmad han, a close friend of the British.[25]

It is the contention of this writer that the revivalist movements, though legitimizing themselves in the name of moral-religious regeneration, also espoused social, economic, and cultural goals; and, in fact, while upholding the society's Islamic identity and culture, they implicitly advocated a variety of changes that would be reflected in the Muslims' patterns of living, identity, and culture. The Indian revivalists elevated the local language to a higher level, not for ethnic or nationalist reasons but for emancipation and religious enlightenment. "An important, but neglected side-result of the Movement," states Qeyamuddin Ahmad, "was the impetus it gave to the growth of the Urdu language, particularly Urdu prose writing. Like all missionary movements, it laid great emphasis on the use of the vernaculars in its attempt to carry its message to the masses."[26] Urdu thus became the Indian Muslims' "national" language, thanks in part to the revivalism of Sayyid Ahmad Barelvi, who also was among the first in the Muslim world to initiate the use of the printed word to transmit knowledge—in this case revivalist, revolutionary knowledge. His books, *Taqwiyat al-Iman* (Reinforcing faith) and *Sirat al-Mustaqim* (True path), were the first works with religious content to be published in relatively great quantities in the 1820s and 1830s and to be made available to large numbers of Muslims in India and beyond. In terms of tactics and organization, the Barelvis turned religion into an ideology that was used to achieve popular mobilization, social justice, and to establish mass organization; for this reason, the British and the Muslim establishment labeled their movement and methods "subversive," "un-Islamic," and "antigovernment."

After the 1870s some Indian Muslim intellectuals began to adopt views similar to those promoted by the Barelvis. Sayyid Ahmad's view that Muslims shared a common faith and needed common institutions and practices helped increase Indian interest in the Ottoman caliphate and its Islamist ideology. The Sepoy Revolt of 1857 was in part nourished by Barelvi's teachings, and the British even asked the ruling Ottoman sultan, Abdulmecid, to intercede as caliph to calm the rebels. Later, Sultan Abdulhamid knew that the Sepoy Revolt had imbued the British with a fear of Islamic unrest and would use that fear in promoting his realm's interest. However, Abdulhamid himself feared popular religious movements and Sayyid Ahmad Barelvi's antimonarchist views, which threatened the established Muslim sociopolitical order that Abdulhamid represented, defended, and promoted.

Nakşbandia-Muridiyya

The Nakşbandia-Muridiyya played a crucial role in encouraging a worldwide rise in Islamic political consciousness and in linking the political and ideological developments in the Caucasus and the Ottoman state. Muridism, so named for the Russian term for a Sufi Nakşbandi brotherhood, was a grassroots populist social movement and a political and military organization led by a *şeyh* (or imam) who enjoyed the total devotion of his followers (*murid*s).[27] The imam was simultaneously *murşid* (spiritual guide, teacher), chief administrator, and army commander, and the bonds between the imam and the *murid*s stemmed directly from the imam's *irşat* (teachings), which were regarded as the expression of love for God. The doctrine of *gazavat* (holy war) was an expression of the faith, a means to fight the Russian occupation, to spread the faith, and to achieve social reform. The imam followed the Prophet and Sunna in every possible way, striving to make himself a living model.

Muridism was basically a Nakşbandi popular resistance movement, and, like all other revivalist movements, it had unique local and regional characteristics, while sharing the universal ideas of Islam.[28] The Nakşbandia-Muridiyya (as it is properly called) did not start out as a pan-Islamic movement, although political and military factors soon forced it to transcend the Caucasus and become a universal Muslim model for attachment to and defense of the native land, an attachment that became part of true faith. The transformation of muridism into a militant resistance movement had deep historical roots that drew sustenance from the accumulated resentment of the Caucasian Muslims against Russian expansionism and its threat to their faith.

The Russian offensive into the east Caucasus that began under Peter the Great remained stalled for over half a century after reaching the Terek River, which was then described by Russia as the frontier between Islam and Orthodox Christianity, represented by the sultan and the czar respectively. Catherine II finally resumed the drive, defeating the Ottoman army in the war of 1768–74 and forcing the sultan to sign the

Küçük Kaynarca Treaty of 1774, which left to Russia practically all the Ottoman lands north of the Black Sea and east of the Dnieper and isolated the Caucasus. The Kuban River now became the new Caucasian frontier, separating the mountains and their tribal population in the south from the conquered areas in the north. Cossacks and Russians gradually settled the northern areas and established a string of towns and forts from the Black Sea to the Caspian. The Ottomans, meanwhile, rebuilt the port of Anapa on the Black Sea and turned it into a major fortress, commanding the communication line between south and west. Both Russia and the Ottoman state tried to gain influence among the Caucasian tribes by courting their leaders, who enjoyed great power and prestige and the almost absolute loyalty of their kin. Then Russia began again to move southward. It subdued various tribes and, in 1783, by the Treaty of Georgiefs, gained the right to settle Russians in Georgia, Imretia, and Mingrelia. Finally, in 1801, Russia annexed Georgia, thus effectively cutting off the Muslim areas in the north from the Ottoman-held lands in the south. The final conquest of the Caucasus seemed imminent when General Alexander I. Ermalov became governor in 1816.

The Nakşbandia-Muridiyya movement arose in the circumstances of the Russian offensive; its beginnings can be traced to Şeyh Mansur Ushurma. Born in 1732 in the village of Aldi near Grozny, Mansur was a member of one of the Chechen non-Turkish but orthodox Muslim tribes. The assertion by Muratoff—and the Italian press—that Mansur was a renegade Italian in the service of the Turks is absolutely false.[29] He studied with the ulema in Grozny, mastering Arabic, and upon his return home he started his missionary work among the Muslim tribes of the northeast. Mansur's initial objectives appeared to be mainly religious and moral, inspired by his belief that the deteriorating social and moral standards of the Caucasian tribes and the widening social differences were undermining Islam.[30] The *aul*, or village, headed by a chieftain was each tribe's basic social unit. Federations or confederations of *aul*s obeyed the orders of a tribal aristocracy divided into numerous tribes speaking different languages. The mountaineers often fought with each other, but the leading families of the Circassian tribes (Abaza, Beşiler, Shebsbuz, Natachkack, Kanartov, Besleney, Mohos, Kemguy, Notukay, Njeduh, Zan, etc.) in the west apparently established a hierarchical order of representation topped by the Beşiler beys, through whom the Ottoman government communicated with the rest of the tribes.[31] The political systems of the tribes in the central and east Caucasus ranged from democracy to feudalism and autocracy. Some tribes practiced slavery; others engaged in continuous warfare stemming from family feuds, vendetta, disputes over territory and booty, and matters of honor; still other tribes engaged in agriculture, trade, and crafts and produced many learned men.

Şeyh Mansur Ushurma was a Nakşbandi Sufi who claimed that all believers were equal before God, thus obliquely criticizing the feudal order, slavery, and the lavish living of the beys (or *beǧs*) and *han*s, some of whom had converted to Christianity in order to benefit from incentives offered by the Russians. The oppressed peasantry and the tribes responded enthusiastically to Şeyh Mansur's call to *gazavat* (holy war), to fight against the surviving elements of paganism and animism, against social inequality, and against the Russians and, especially, their local followers, who were regarded as the source of evil.[32] Driven by sheer necessity, Mansur associated himself with Istanbul, although he always considered himself independent of the Porte.

Alarmed by the extraordinary success of Şeyh Mansur among the Kabardians and Chechens, the Russians attacked and destroyed his stronghold at Aldi, only to have their own entire army liquidated by Mansur's men. Finally, Mansur was captured by the Russians in 1790 and executed in St. Petersburg on 13 April 1794.

Mansur's relations with the Ottomans set a precedent and laid the foundation for future relations between the muridists and Istanbul that the Russians called "pan-Islamism." The later Russo-Turkish wars of 1806–12 and 1829–30, gained Bucak (southern Basarabia) and the ports of Anapa and Poti, through which Turkey had supplied arms and aid to the Circassians, the Chechens, and the Dagestanis, for the Russians. The Caucasus, especially the muridists, was almost totally isolated from the Ottomans and left to its own resources in the fight against the Russians.

Subsequently, the Nakşbandia-Muridiyya movement entered the second phase of its history. The movement's literature from this period indicates that the initial muridist teachings about Islamic unity, equality, and purity of faith were accompanied by a distinct ideological and "national" call. Now the tribes as a whole acted as if they considered themselves as belonging to a special entity—that is, a nation that was Islamic in name but Dagestani in practice. Once more, the universal was used to promote the local and regional. The new Muslim Dagestani-Caucasian entity (pro-tonation) consisted of Circassians, Avars, Lezgis, and so on, but the terms *Dagestan* and *Dagestani* (*Dagistan, Dagistani,* or *Dagistanli*), which in the past had connoted a geographic area, began to acquire national-cultural meaning, defining a political identity shared by most of the northeastern Caucasian Muslims. The muridists used the struggle with Russia to turn the original tribal version of Islam into a new belief system that transcended the tribe and became the source of a new broader identity. Even today, after seventy years of communist rule, the territory still is known as Dagestan, and the people of the area often refer to themselves as Dagestanis, although linguistically, ethnically, and historically they are different from one another.

This second phase of the Nakşbandia-Muridiyya movement began at the end of the 1820s, under the leadership of Gazi Muhammad ibn Ismail al-Gimrawi, or Gazi Molla (b. 1793). In a few spectacularly successful years, Gazi Molla sought to neutralize and/or liquidate the tribal leaders who had "deviated from the true path" and cooperated with the Russians. Recognized as imam in 1829, Gazi Molla used the *gazavat* to convert to Islam several pagan tribes, such as the Galgan and Kists and, especially, the Ingush, although a number of tribes and their leaders remained loyal to the Russians. Gazi Molla defeated the Russians several times but was killed at the battle of Gimri (Ghimree) in 1832. After a short period under the leadership of Hamza (d. 1834), who also took the title of imam, the movement's leadership was assumed by Şeyh Şamil, who had been severely wounded at Gimri.

The Nakşbandia-Muridiyya movement is normally associated with the name of Şeyh Şamil, who, in turn, is usually portrayed as a Muslim patriot fighting a long guerilla war against the Russians, rather than as a Nakşbandi upholding the principles of his faith.[33] Indeed, the glorification of Şamil as a military leader obscures both his extraordinary popular appeal and his role as a revivalist leader and social reformer.

Şamil belonged to one of the Avar tribes and was related by marriage to Gazi Molla. It appears from a recently discovered manuscript, "Diwan al-Mamnun" by Hasan al-Algadari, that both Gazi Molla and Şeyh Şamil were initiated into the şeriat and *tarikat*—that is, the Nakşbandia—by al-Algadari, whose grandfather, Şeyh Muhammad al-Yaraghi, had introduced Şeyh Khalidi's teachings into Dagestan. The Khalidi teachings thus signaled a basic transformation in the Islam of the Caucasus as it did in the Ottoman state.

Şamil introduced a centralized administration and a Muslim judiciary. The *adat* courts, which had perpetuated the feudal rule of the *han*s and beys, were replaced by religious courts that enforced the Şeriat. Şamil created a *beyt-ul mal* (treasury) to support his army and to finance the regular training of his soldiers, while establishing steady communications with the villages and their militias. His was, in effect, a centralized, modern type of government founded on the Koran and Sunna; the *naib*s (deputies) directly responsible to the center administered the provinces, levied taxes, recruited *murid*s, and trained an army in the strict discipline and warlike traditions rooted in past tribal warfare.[34] The fight had become an all-out national war for survival and liberation, the "nation" being founded on Islam. Thus, Muratoff, in the usual mode of anti-Muslim sensationalism, wrongly sees Şamil's war as an end in itself and as a vehicle for self-purification and self-sacrifice.[35] The hostilities between Şamil's forces and the Russians escalated further after Şamil refused to appear before Czar Nicholas I to pledge personal submission and allegiance. General Golovine finally attacked Şamil in 1839. The campaign culminated in the famous battle for the Akhoulgu (Akhulgah or Ahulgo), which fell to the Russians only after Şamil had inflicted heavy losses on the czar's army. Although his ninety-day resistance made him hero throughout the Caucasus and the Muslim world, Şamil learned at Akhoulgu that a rebel force, however dedicated, had little chance of success against a regular army. Consequently, he adopted guerilla tactics and was victorious everywhere, reconquering all of Dagestan. When the Crimean War broke out in 1853, Şeyh Şamil, after an initial drive southward, remained passive during the war to the surprise of the Russians (and of some Turks unaware of the real situation). Nevertheless, Russia was forced to keep a large force in the Caucasus in order to secure its lines of communication.

The Paris Treaty of 1856, although putting the seal on the Russian defeat, brought no relief to Russia's Muslims or Şamil. Instead, the new czar, Alexander II, decided to put an end to Şamil's revolution. General Baryatinski began his offensive with a large army divided into three corps, not unlike the Russian attack on Chechnya in 1999–2000, which besieged the *murid* forces from three sides. Şamil fought for three more years, but after his attempts to negotiate a peaceful settlement with the Russians failed, he was forced to make a last stand in the village of Gunib. Although Şamil had only five hundred followers with him, Prince Baryatinski concentrated forty thousand men with forty-eight guns to ensure the capture of a man who had proved himself to be the greatest guerilla leader in the history of war.[36] Şamil agreed to surrender in the village mosque only after the Russians "promised his safe conduct to the Khalife (Sultan) in Constantinople. This last [the third] offer fell on willing ears among Shamil's remaining followers. . . . Shamil finally accepted their will and gave himself up."[37]

Şamil was taken to St. Petersburg, where Alexander II received him with honors and gave him a large house near Kaluga. Eventually the czar permitted Şamil to go on the *hac* to Mecca. On the way the şeyh stopped in Istanbul, and the population gave him an extraordinarily enthusiastic welcome that lasted for days, until the Porte, afraid that the popular demonstrations were escalating into antigovernment shows, hastened Şamil's departure. He passed away on 4 February 1871 in Medina and reportedly was buried near the tomb of Abbas, the Prophet's uncle. Meanwhile, the Russians engaged in brutal expeditions against the Circassian tribes, killing tens of thousands of them in pogroms, some of which were organized as spectacles for the officers. In what was one of the first forced emigrations in modern history, over a million Caucasians were forced to migrate to Ottoman lands in the years 1862–65.[38] Many more migrated there from 1865 to 1920 and played a seminal role in the social and cultural transformation of the Ottoman state.

Some Russian writers believed that muridism originated in Istanbul and that Şamil and his predecessors followed the caliph's instructions both in disseminating their creed and in fighting the czar's armies. During the Turko-Russian war of 1828–29, for example, General Yemanovil (Emanuel) in a letter told the beys, chiefs, *kethudas*, and other Muslim leaders in the Kuban, "[Y]ou were deceived by [Istanbul's] exhortations on behalf of religion, but thanks to the Almighty's mercy and goodwill our soldiers have defeated" the enemy. He scolded the leaders: "We know by experience that you ignored the promises you offered us up till now and never carried them out" but still promised them help and understanding and urged them to remain faithful to the czar.[39] The Russians, as did the British and French, regarded the Caucasian Muslims as driven solely by religious fanaticism rather than by need and aspirations for human dignity; but for all practical purposes the Caucasus became a model of resistance and bravery.

Articles in newspapers and books, the growing number of Caucasian pilgrims to Mecca who stopped or stayed for years in Istanbul, the presence of Caucasian women in the sultan's harem and of Caucasian men at the sultan's court all helped increase communication between Istanbul and the Muslim Caucasus. So too did the many immigrants whose tribal and religious leaders became part of the Ottoman establishment and the thousands of Caucasians enrolled in the special units of the regular army and irregular militias active in the Balkans and Anatolia. Because many Caucasian leaders and immigrants already were members of the Sufi *tarikats* in their countries of origin, their coming greatly increased the size and influence in the Ottoman state of the popular Sufi orders, especially the Nakşbandia. In fact, since the flow of Muslims from Dagestan, south Caucasus, and Central Asia to Istanbul had started in the early 1830s, the Ottoman government had been worried that the Russians would consider the unauthorized migration a violation of the Treaty of Adrianople (art. 13). Consequently, the Porte ordered its governor in Trabzon to legalize the emigration by signing an agreement with the Russians;[40] after 1859 that agreement was used as a pretext by Russia to force out the Caucasian Muslims. Once assured of their safety in the Ottoman state, Caucasian religious leaders sought to aid their brethren left behind. For instance, several living in Istanbul volunteered in 1853 to go to Dagestan and Georgia to mobilize the Muslims against Russia; and Dagestani Hasan efendi, a member of the ulema and of the aristocracy of Dagestan who had immigrated twenty years earlier to the Ottoman state, offered his propaganda services to the government.[41] (The same sort of thing happened in the Chechen-Russian war of 1994–95, as the children and grandchildren of immigrants went to fight along with the Chechens and the Abkhazians.)

Şeyh Şamil's relations with Istanbul need to be placed in the proper perspective: Was he an agent of the caliph or a free patriot fighting for his country's independence? Some Ottoman documents can shed light on this issue. Soon after the war with Russia started in 1853, the governor of Erzurum was instructed to honor Şeyh Şamil and other Caucasian leaders with special decorations and gifts. Eventually Sultan Abdulmecid issued an imperial *hüküm* (order, proclamation), dated 9 October 1853, informing Şeyh Şamil that because the Russians threatened Ottoman independence, military preparations were being undertaken in the Trabzon and Erzurum areas and that it was time for the "entire Muslim nation to ally in unity" ("umum millet-i islamiye ittifak u ittihad") without regard for life and property and be ready for battle. The sultan suggested that Şamil establish communication with the *han*s of the east Caucasus so that the Russian army could be attached from all sides. Finally, the Ottoman ruler informed Şamil that he was sending several of his own officers to serve under Şamil's orders and asked him to establish communications with Abdi paşa, the commander of the Caucasus army.[42] Şeyh Şamil, in a letter sent to the Ottoman commander of the Anatolian forces, answered that he had invited the *han*s and dignitaries of the Caucasus and Circassia and that all "have agreed to become a subject-servant of the sultan, who is the imam of the Muslims" ("imamu-l muslimin olan padişahimizin bir bendesi olduk").[43] It may be deducible from the tone of this correspondence that Şamil served at the discretion of the sultan. The content and essence of the letter, however, showed a clear difference from the usual deferential etiquette of the address to sultan. True, Şeyh Şamil expressed readiness to help the Ottoman army, but he also asked that the sultan move his troops to Guru first, to complete the strategic preparations and reassure the Caucasian Muslim commanders that they had Istanbul's actual support. After the expected link-up between Imam Şamil and the Ottomans failed to materialize (for the Russians defeated Abdi paşa's large army), Şamil retreated back to his own lands.[44]

For the rest of the Crimean War, Şeyh Şamil remained rather passive, despite exhortations from Istanbul to engage in further hostilities against the Russians. Mahmud Celaleddin paşa, who served the Ottoman government most of his adult life, stated in his memoirs that "after the [Crimean] war started the Dagestani tribes, who had long fought the Russians under the command of Şeyh Şamil, instead of intensifying their struggle in order to aid the Ottoman state, signed a peace treaty with the enemy and remained neutral, and consequently they could not be trusted."[45] The truth is that by 1855 Şamil was militarily exhausted and the Ottomans were unable to provide him with much help. In the ultimate analysis, the actual relations between Istanbul and Şeyh Şamil seem to have been conditioned by mutual military interests rather than by religious considerations. Indeed, the correspondence between Istanbul and Şamil deals primarily with such military matters and conspicuously lacks evidence of the "religious fanaticism" or subservience to Istanbul of which Şamil has sometimes been accused, only to be rehabilitated and then condemned again. Some Russian intellectuals in the czarist regime gave Şamil positive coverage, among them Chernyshevski, Lermantov, and Tolstoy, who immortalized him in his novel *Haji Murat*, about an ally who turned against Şamil. Early Soviet literature also adopted a positive view of Şamil, as seen in the textbooks of A. V. Shestakov and A. M. Pankratova. He was hailed as an able administrator, reformer, military leader, and a patriot interested mainly in the independence of his nation. During World War II the Soviets even contemplated forming a tank column called Shamil and having the religious leaders proclaim a *cihad* against Germany. This positive view changed after 1947–50. The assault on Şamil started with the attack on muridism by K. G. Adzhemian, an obscure member of the Union of Soviet Writers. Despite nearly unanimous criticism of Adzhemian's thesis that Şamil was an aristocratic, feudal reactionary, supported by Turkey and England, who opposed the "civilization" brought by the czarist regime, the Communist Party eventually upheld his views, as did M. D. Bagirov, the first secretary of Soviet Socialist Republic of Azerbaijan. The rehabilitation of Şamil began after Bagirov's dismissal and Stalin's death. Many writers who had denounced him, including A. V. Fadeev, began to recant, especially after the conference on history held late in January 1956, and the twentieth party congress.[46]

Şamil played a basic symbolic role; he was the catalyst that speeded up the renewal process and the transformation of the community's religious consciousness into a political one. He became a model for many Muslims by the force of his personality, the strength of his convictions, and, especially, because of his military achievements. His successful resistance to the Russians occurred at a point in history when many people regarded Islam as doomed to perish and the Muslims as destined to fall under foreign rule. The community was reviving and renewing itself while the only truly independent Muslim state, that is, the Ottoman Empire, sought for ways to use the community to assure its own survival. To the Muslims from Asia and Africa who convened as pilgrims in Mecca, Şamil's bravery and ability to disseminate the faith among the pagan and nominally Muslim tribes of the Caucasus symbolized Islam's vitality and will to live. He was "a hero," as the noted Azeri scholar Mirza bey (1802–1870) put it, "and a maker of modern heroes," who superseded ethnic, national, and geographic boundaries.[47] Today Şamil is still venerated throughout the Muslim world as a hero and symbol of patriotism and of something else more difficult to define: of a faith willing to break shackles of the traditional version of the "faith" in order to achieve real faith. Books and plays are written about him, a film is being made about him in Turkey, several songs are dedicated to him, and his name is given to streets and villages.[48] He inadvertently helped popular Islam, including the Nakşbandia Sufi order, to gain power and a following, and he gave religious populism a degree of respectability among the new Ottoman intelligentsia, some of whom were of Caucasian origin. The hundreds of thousands of Caucasian immigrants in the Ottoman state, some of whom had fought with him, played a significant role in mythologizing Şamil's memory, and also in popularizing the Nakşbendi teachings.

It is my contention that the early revivalist movements had populist, egalitarian, and potentially democratic aspects that inspired fear and suspicion among the Muslim crowned heads, whose legitimacy and authority stemmed not from the will of the community but from stereotyped "Islamic" principles, reinterpreted to suit their purposes. These governments accused the revivalists of undermining the "true" Islam in much the same fashion as today's Muslim authoritarian regimes condemn the defenders' democracy as "fundamentalist" in the name of "secularism" and "modernism." The Ottoman government feared that the popular appeal of Şamil and his followers would be likely to turn into political opposition. Şamil was quickly spirited away from Istanbul. Dagistanli Gazi Mehmet paşa, a relative of Şeyh Şamil who had reached the rank of *ferik* (marshal), was exiled in 1883 to Tayif in Arabia because he made remarks questioning the sultan's high-handed actions (see chapter 4).[49]

In conclusion, Şamil's religious-military movement became a powerful nationalism with defense of the homeland—fatherland—as its main goal, even though the idea of a territorial fatherland and allegiance to the territory was alien to classical Islam. Şamil's deep attachment to his ancestral lands probably derived from his traditional tribal background, but through Islam (and in direct conflict with classical Islamic practice) he was able to convert this feeling of territorial attachment into a respected practical political principle. While the Nakşbandia-Muridiyya respected the caliph and obeyed him to some extent because of his symbolic Islamic position, at the same time it was critical, as were most other revivalist movements, of the ruling Muslim political and social establishment. The revivalists saw the decadence of the Islamic society as originating not in the faith but in its outdated political organization and leadership and, ultimately, in its leaders' separation from society.[50] Thus the Nakşbandia-Muridiyya movement appears to have been a national one, its strength and durability stemming from an emerging new type of identity, that was both local (Caucasian) and universal (Islamic).

The Nakşbandia-Muridiyya movement retained its political vigor, but its religious form changed soon after Şamil's demise in 1859. The Chechens in the Kadiriyya movement took over and continued the struggle under different leadership and under changed circumstances. They pursued the same national goals, always expressing them in Islamic terminology, for Islam and national identity had come to be synonymous. After the defeat of Şamil, the Kadiri (Qadiri) order had arisen rapidly in Dagestan and Chechnya, partly in order to assert the Chechen identity that had been blurred during Şamil's life. The leader was Kunta Hajji Kishiev, a Kumyk—a Turkic group—shepherd who turned missionary after a visit to Mecca and a stop in Baghdad at the tomb of Şeyh Kadir Gilani (who supposedly had initiated Kunta into the order). At the beginning, Kunta adopted a pacifist attitude in line with his mystic and ascetic orientation, but by 1863 he began to fight the Russians. The latter had not interfered in Kadiri religious practices until the czar became afraid of their strength. The Kadiris also adopted the classical view that Muslims could not live under infidel authority. Eventually, the Kadiris attracted a large segment of Şamil's former Nakşbandi fighters. By the time the Russian authorities arrested Kunta Hajji in the mid-1860s (he was declared insane and placed in a hospital-prison, where he was poisoned in 1867), the order had spread into all of north Caucasus. It was the Kadiri Chechens who converted the remaining pagan Ingush to Islam in the years 1863–70. After Kunta's deportation, his mother acted for a while as the head of the order, and her tomb is today one of the most sacred places in the Caucasus. Soon, however, the order split into four groups (*wirds*), each headed by a *halifa* or *vekil*, a successor to the original leader. Each group, although collaborating closely with the others, had its own organization and leaders, which made suppression of the movement very difficult.[51] The Nakşbandia made a comeback and fought both the czarist and Bolshevik troops from 1918 to the mid-1920s, the leader of the anti-Bolshevik fighters being the grandson of Şeyh Şamil, namely Said bey. The Bolsheviks defeated the Nakşbandi, but their place soon was taken by the Kadiris. Some Chechen cooperated with the Bolsheviks (many Chechen communists were secret members of the order), but the friendship proved to be short-lived. In 1928 the Bolsheviks attacked the Caucasian *tarikat*, only to be dragged into a lengthy and costly civil war that lasted until 1936.

A new Sufi-led revolt in north Caucasus started in 1941 and lasted until 1947. After 1944 most of the Chechen-Ingush and the smaller groups of Balkars and Karachais were deported to Central Asia and Siberia. Thanks to the deportees, the most radical branch, of the Kadiris, the Vis (Uweys), rapidly gained followers among the Kazakhs, Uzbeks, and Kirgiz. The deportees were rehabilitated in 1956 and allowed to return to their native lands, where their influence on practically all Muslim activities and places of worship has been steadily increasing. The Chechens established their own independent muftiate; the first mufti, himself a Chechen, came from Alma Ata—where I interviewed him—where he had been deputy to the Kazakh mufti, the latter having declared independence from Tashkent. The Chechen mufti had studied in the Middle East and spoke Arabic. Boris Yeltsin accused the Chechens of being fanatic "Muslim fundamentalists": apparently three hundred years of history had taught Russians nothing. (The Soviet literature refers to the Kadiris as *Zikirist* or *jumpers* and to Nakşbandia as *murid* and *şeriatists*.) Chechnia declared its independence in November 1991 and eventually confronted Yeltsin with a delicate situation. (The war in Chechnya in 1994–95, followed by renewed fighting in 1999–2000 is just one more, perhaps the last, episode in the Chechen resistance to Russian occupation.)

The Russians habitually viewed every Muslim reaction to their rule as a consequence of "religious fanaticism" and blamed Istanbul as the instigator. Such was the case, for instance, in the Andijan Revolt of 1898. Madali Ishan Muhaddam Ali Khalifa (b. 1856 in Kashgar) started his uprising in the village of Ming Tube near Andijan-Uzbekistan: its immediate purpose was to restore the Kokand hanate and to stop the deterioration of Muslim morals after the Russians confiscated *vakif* and *amlak* (state) lands. A spindle maker, the leader joined the Nakşbandia and became a *murid* and then successor to Sultan Khan Tore, a famous *ishan* (*şeyh* and saint). In 1887, Madali, as he is popularly called, went on the pilgrimage to Mecca; then, in Medina, at the tomb of the Prophet, he swore to rid the Fergana of Russian rule. His "revolt" consisted of a short-lived attack on the Russian barracks that lasted only fifteen minutes. At the court, where about 417 people were tried, Madali complained not so much against the Russians as against the moral decay of his own society. He had written to Abdulhamid, asking him as the caliph to intercede with the Russian czar to restore the Şeriat but apparently received no answer;[52] a letter purporting to be accompaniment of a *halat* (overcoat) allegedly sent by Abdulhamid to Madali was a forgery. Political national revolts in Caucasia continued to take a religious form until contemporary times.

African Revivalism: Sanusia and the Ottomans

The Ottoman caliphate's Islamic (pan-Islamic) relations with Africa evolved in a manner markedly different from those with Asia. Central Asia and the Caucasus had ancient political, cultural, religious, ethnic, and linguistic ties with the Ottoman Turks, but North Africa, prior to the sixteenth century, had none. The early Ottoman presence in North Africa west of Egypt in the sixteenth century resulted not from conquest but from a sort of informal coalition between Turks and the native population against Spanish expansion. During this early association with the Ottomans, North Africa enjoyed considerable local autonomy, self rule, and tax exemptions. In the eighteenth century, however, the Ottoman bureaucracy increased taxes and infringed upon the autonomy of the districts and the local notables, who tried to oppose the Ottoman power by courting tribal support; those living in western Algeria aligned themselves with the Moroccan *şerif*s. After the French occupied Algeria in 1830, North Africa drifted back to closer relations with the Porte and the Ottoman sultan-caliph out of sheer political necessity rather than out of any special love for the caliph; but difference between these two motivations subsequently became meaningless.

At first, the French invasion of Algeria in 1830 had compelled Amir Muehiddin and his son Amir Abdelkader (1807–1883; known as al-Jazairi in the Arab world) of the powerful Banu Hashim tribe to seek, like the notables of west Algeria, Moroccan help. When they discovered that the *şerif*'s rule was worse than that of the French, Abdelkader sought to mend his relations with the Porte. (On his way back from *hac* he had stopped in Damascus to visit the famous Nakşbandi-Mucaddidi, Şeyh Ziauddin Khalid (Shahrazuri), whose teachings also affected Gazi Molla and Şeyh Şamil and gave the Ottoman Nakşbandia its contemporary features. Apparently, Abdelkader and his father were initiated into the order's teachings by Şeyh Khalid himself.) Abduljelil Temimi has pointed out that Abdelkader wrote to Sultan Abdulmecid as early as 1840, addressing him as the caliph of the believers and the Muslims' last hope for survival and asking for his help.[53] The Ottomans did not support Abdelkader, because of his earlier anti-Ottoman stand and his initial reluctance to support the pro-Ottoman tribes that had joined the anti-French resistance. Meanwhile, the major anti-Ottoman and antimonarchist religious group, the Tijaniyya order (est. 1781), became discredited in the eyes of the nationalists when it sided with the French; they opposed war as long as their freedom of worship was granted.

After fiercely fighting the French, Abdelkader was defeated in 1847 and taken to France. In 1852 he was allowed to migrate to the Ottoman state; he settled first in Bursa in western Anatolia and then in Damascus, where he received generous pensions from the sultan. A number of Algerians and other Muslims followed Abdelkader and established several colonies in Syria, stirring French fears that the Ottoman state could use the Algerian refugees to create trouble for them in North Africa.[54] The Algerian refugees in Istanbul did in fact become a center of resistance to the French and helped to further mobilize the population against Europe. The Crimean War of 1853–56, which made the Ottoman state a temporary partner in the European coalition against Russia, soothed the French fears, but the Algerian Revolt of 1871 convinced the French that Istanbul had become the nest of anti-French "pan-Islamist" plots. Consequently, the French began to look upon the conquest of Tunisia and southern Sahara as necessary to consolidate their rule in Algeria. The escalation of French imperial ambitions turned the initial local anti-imperialist struggle of the Algerians into a large resistance movement spread over all of North Africa. Eventually this French expansion threatened south Libya and the existence of the emerging Sanusiyya order, which rapidly transformed itself from a peaceful, pietiest order into a militant resistance movement associated with the Ottoman caliph.[55]

The Sanusiyya transformation can easily be chronicled. Muhammad Ali bin al-Sanusi (1787–1859), founder of the Sanusiyya brotherhood, was born in Algeria and followed the teachings of Mevlay Arabi al-Darkawi (who was instrumental in the creation of the anti-Ottoman Tijaniyya) and later went to study in Fez in Morocco.[56] When he returned to Algeria, he met with the Tijani opposition and then went first to Tripoli, which was under Ottoman rule, and then, in 1824, to al-Azhar in Cairo. Soon becoming disillusioned with the conservative atmosphere of the institution, he went to Mecca, where he met Ahmad Idris al-Farsi, who shared his reservations about the conservative radicalism of the Wahhabis. Although accepting many of the views of Ibn-Taymiyyahah and the Hanbali concerning the importance of orthodoxy and of the traditional Muslim institutions, the two remained attached to neo-Sufism and the belief that the *ictihad* was still in force.[57]

Sanusi established his own *zaviye* (lodge and center of prayer and teaching) at Cebel Alim-Kubay in Arabia until, faced with the opposition of the Meccan religious establishment and of some Ottoman administrators, who feared he was a crypto Wahhabi, he returned to Tripoli about 1840. The governor of Tripoli, Ali Ashkar paşa (rumored to have joined the brotherhood), welcomed Sanusi and his followers. Because the French were prepared to arrest him, Sanusi established his lodge in al-Beyda in Cyrenaica, which became the main center of the order until 1857. Returning to Mecca in 1846, Sanusi stayed there for seven years to write numerous works and gain further influence among the ulema of Mecca, who finally came to accept him, although his success in urban areas was still less than among the tribes, whose culture and customs he knew how to cultivate. Mainly in response to pressure from his followers, Sanusi returned to North Africa and moved his headquarters further south to Jaghbug, which commanded the trade routes to Egypt and Cyrenaica and was strategically better suited to help the order spread Islam to Central Africa. In 1900 there were 143 Sanusi *zaviye*s: 45 in Cyrenaica, 25 in Fezzan, 15 in Waday, and the others in Kanem.[58]

A detailed analysis of the Sanusiyya's relations with Istanbul indicates that, at the beginning, each regarded the other with considerable mistrust. According to a recent Turkish study, the Sanusiyya leader believed the Ottoman political order was doomed to disintegrate and did not want to condemn his own brotherhood to death by harnessing it to the service of Istanbul.[59] Şehbenderzâde Filibeli Ahmed Hilmi (1865–1914), a little-known anti-Hamidian intellectual who spent many years in exile in Fezzan, was a great admirer of Muhammed al-Sanusi but considered his distrust of the Turks and his dislike of modern ways to be his major shortcomings. It was Hilmi's belief that Abdulhamid did not help Islam or the cause of Muslim unity;[60] but in the end, al-Sanusi realized that the Ottoman state could be a deterrent to the French advance into the Sahara and North Africa, and Istanbul. In turn the sultan, overcoming his early mistrust, decided to help the order and benefit from its influence among the tribes of the Sahara. Already the Ottoman government had officially accepted the Sanusiyya as the representative of the local people (that is, of the tribes), exempted their lodges from taxation, and accorded them the right of sanctuary while the Sanusiyya helped Istanbul collect taxes.[61] When Muhammad al-Sanusi died in

1859, his place was taken by his minor son, Muhammad al-Mehdi al-Sanusi (1844–1902), although for a while a council of *khalifa*s exercised authority in his stead.

The French occupation of Tunisia in 1881 profoundly changed Ottoman-Sanusiyya relations and forced both sides into active collaboration, making Cyrenaica a Turco-Sanusiyya condominium. The order became a militant anti-French, then anti-Italian, resistance organization. Despite its alliance with Istanbul, the Sanusiyya managed to retain their independence, doctrine, and local character and eventually transformed themselves into a national movement, which, helped by international circumstances, in the 1950s created its own national state under the name of Libya. (Ottoman-Sanusiyya relations will be studied again in chapter 12.)

Conclusion

Except for the Wahhabis of Arabia, the revivalist movements analyzed in this chapter were all orthodox, neo-Sufi movements and were influenced by the Nakşbandia, the orthodox preachers of revivalism. All were popular, egalitarian movements, driven from below, and sought to regenerate and revive Islamic society morally from the inside, unwittingly taking account of the changed social order but claiming to return to the religious fountainhead. This made them, in the ultimate analysis, truly revolutionary and potentially democratic political movements. Their strict orthodoxy was matched by their worldly, activist outlook and by their wish for solutions to the concrete problems of their societies. For them, these solutions lay in changing the social and political environment through a correct and realistic interpretation and application of the Koran and Sunna. They were the champions of *ictihad*, or freedom of interpretation, expressing this in a variety of informal ways, and they sought to involve the community in political action. The revivalists appealed simultaneously to their local and regional audiences and to a worldwide Muslim community without any apparent contradiction: the single unit found expression in the universal. They were, in fact, upholding local culture, and customs, and language as firmly as they were defending the absolute supremacy of the faith.

Most of the revivalist movements were led by a new brand of Sufis, whose militancy contrasted sharply with the peaceful, pious, and socially reclusive attitude of classical Sufism. The transformation of the Sufis into guerilla fighters, army commanders, and even state leaders resulted from their belief that *cihad* was not only an effort at personal spiritual enhancement but also a struggle against *fitna*, the lapse and degradation of the faith and, ultimately, against those who caused it, be they foreign occupiers or Muslim rulers. The Sufis believed that in order to achieve self-transcendence the soul must be eternally free and independent of any oppression, limitation, and encroachment—all likely burdens under foreign rule and emulation of Europe. Because any individual Muslim is free to call the *cihad*, the Sufis did exactly that in order to achieve the "re-Islamization of society."[62]

If analyzed from a socioeconomic perspective, the revivalist movements must be seen as grassroots reactions both to the disintegration of the classical Muslim social order and to the rise of a primitive capitalism and its social by-product, the interest-oriented middle classes, who cooperated with the establishment and Europe. Much of the traditional religious establishment, unable to absorb intellectually the idea of social change, even while adopting it in daily life, insisted on a rigorous and formal adherence to the rituals of Islam and often viewed this as sufficient to fulfill their religious duty. The revivalists were personally pious and practiced the "works"—the five principles—but attached equal importance to inner faith (*iman*) and to a healthy social environment, which was considered essential for achieving purity of the faith. In this context, the revivalist movements provided individuals from the lower classes with an Islamic vehicle to express their criticism of the traditional Muslim political establishment and the established Islamic hierarchy that was ready to serve the state uncritically. The revivalists generated, without defining them in concrete terms, concepts of social and civic responsibility that remained faithful to the essence of the faith.

The revivalist populist movements also expressed criticism of the Muslim governments' absolutism. They saw despotism and absolutism as forms of tyranny, regardless of their traditional Islamic legitimacy; this issue later was taken up by liberal intellectuals and reformulated in terms of European liberalism. Meanwhile, in an indirect fashion, the revivalists supported the endeavors of some classical Muslim thinkers, including Ibn Taymiyya, to "open the gates of *ictihad*," blaming the political order for closing them when it prohibited free interpretation of the Koran and Sunna. The "closing" had coincided with the emergence in the eleventh century of absolutist Muslim rulers, who used the state to control economic resources and assure themselves enormous power and wealth, while using Islam to legitimize their acts. Opening the gates of *ictihad*, therefore, would lead to the questioning of the sacred immutability of the sociopolitical order that had perpetuated the rule of both the wise and the unfit sultans and *han*s. The revivalists' relativist view of the social and political order was, in the Islamic context, truly revolutionary.

The revivalists' methods of organization and of securing the involvement of the community in action were as important as their ideology and left a permanent imprint on Islamic societies. They were able to mobilize people at the grassroots level and stimulate them to mass action and guerilla warfare. For the first time ceasing to be merely perfunctory terms, the "people" (*nas*) and the "community" (*ümmet*) acquired concrete form and demonstrated a will of their own. The revivalists restored to the community its old prerogative—as seen by the Kharijites at least—as a major regulatory social and political institution whose will (*ijma*) was exercised not by a handful of self-appointed leaders and learned men (ulema), but by the community as a whole. This was the first step toward a form of democracy, still waiting for some implementation in most of the Muslim world: in the end the elites, "modern" or traditionalist, have shown themselves to be lacking a sense of moral and social responsibility and have generally refused to share power with their followers.

The revivalists also served as channels for upward communication, allowing the cultures, worldviews, aspirations, and expectations of the Muslim lower classes to penetrate to the decision-making level. Thus a series of natural human attachments, such as the love of one's birthplace or *vatan* (fatherland) and ethnic and linguistic loyalties, gained a degree of respectability and social and political validity. Obviously, the traditional Islamic governments never promoted or recognized attachment to one's birthplace (*hubb ul-vatan*), language, and ethnicity as principles of organization, although some *hadis*es recognized their existence. Attachment to territory and ethnicity itself were not outside the faith: "A revival of ethnic consciousness . . . thus involves a revival of religion rather than its negation."[63]

Although the fundamentalist movements have often been seen as strictly a reaction to the dislocations caused by European occupation, the reaction was not directed against Europe as a civilization but against its brazen belittling of Islam and calculated violations of Islamic traditions and customs. Europe takes up relatively little space in the revivalist literature, most of which is dedicated to the internal situation of Muslim society. European and Russian expansionism was only the catalyst that brought the Muslim society's problems into the open and transformed them into causes for the revivalists, helping convert the believers' religious consciousness into a political one. Revivalism was mainly a Muslim political ideology of regeneration and adaptation to a changed social environment and the expressions of yearnings and hopeful expectations, that oscillated between utopianism and realism; it was not yet cast in the form of Muslim nationalism.

None of the revivalist movements aimed at creating a pan-Islamic unity or a Muslim union centered on the Ottoman caliphate: they had began outside the Ottoman religious and political establishment and were often in conflict with it. The Nakşbandia and the Sanusiyya cooperated with the caliph, but mainly because of military and political necessity and also for a variety of administrative, fiscal, and economic incentives. Sultan Abdulhamid, a social and political archconservative, feared the populist militant movements and sought to use the state apparatus and his caliphal position to deflect and neutralize the radicalism of the revivalist masses by satisfying some of their worldly aspirations and to coopt, whenever possible, the leading cadres of the orders into the system. His strategy was successful on both counts, damping down the radical populist fires and creating a new urban, middle-class, religious-national leadership group. The inherent intellectual inability of the popular revivalist orders to create a theoretical framework that could both satisfy their worldly aspirations and revive Islamic orthodoxy within the context of a "modern" state left the field open to middle-class intellectuals, led mainly by the new Nakşbandia, a group that arose as the result of the combined effect of socioeconomic changes in the Ottoman state, revivalist activity, and the pervasive government presence, and that changed the Ottoman religious outlook, as shall be discussed in chapter 4, on middle classes.

However, after helping spell out some of the key issues facing the Muslims in the nineteenth century and psychologically conditioning society for change, while at the same time teaching it to preserve its Islamic identity and culture, the revivalist movements faded away. It is a gross historical error to regard the twentieth-century fundamentalist orders as their continuation. The old revivalists were active in coping with change, while many contemporary fundamentalists are reacting against the effects of change as well as against the oppressive political regimes responsible for the economic poverty and moral deprivation of the Muslim lower classes—often brought about in the name of "science" and "modernity." Much of the essence of the revivalist thought of the nineteenth century has entered into the fabric of popular Islam in the form of heightened self-consciousness, a desire to enjoy material well-being, and even a longing for some sort of democracy, combined with the wish to retain the faith. Abdulhamid obviously did not have a blueprint for the change needed to assure the state's survival and cope at the same time with the populist Islam. He only reacted to the threat of internal events, and to international pressures, and his reactions then developed into policies, as shall be seen. The revivalist movements promoted or upheld, unwittingly, the local and regional idioms, which became their means of communication, and generated a sense of local and regional consciousness alongside heightened awareness of their ties to an ideal universal community. The "national" states, such as Saudi Arabia, bear witness to the marriage of the universal and particular embodied in the revivalist movements. The Saudis deny that their regime is "national," although the Wahhabist features of their state make it just a dynastic Arab "national" state, despite its claims to represent the "true" Islam, a claim that in fact expresses nationalist ideology of the regime.

2

The Precursors of Pan-Islamism
Peripheral Islam and the Caliphal Center

The idea of Islamic unity remained an alien concept to Muslim rulers until the nine-teenth century, despite the pervasive feeling of religious communality and brother-hood among the mass of believers. Prior to the nineteenth century, in spite of a few vague and isolated calls for unity, the Islamic states failed to develop a concept of unity or to achieve a military alliance against the West or Christendom, or even against the Crusaders who occupied the heartland of the Middle East from the eleventh to the thirteenth centuries. The Muslim rulers used the call to *cihad*, or holy war, to fight each other instead of the perceived enemies of Islam. They were far more concerned with their personal economic, political, and military power than with the fate of Islam or of their Muslim subjects, although the faith gave them their legitimacy and the subjects furnished them with taxes and manpower. The famous Timur (Tamerlane, Timurlenk), who claimed to be a good Muslim, crushed the Golden Horde in 1395 and thus indirectly helped the Muscovy principality to annihilate and annex the Kazan hanate in 1552; and he also nearly put an end to the Ottoman state by defeating and incarcerating Beyazit I in 1402.

The Ottoman sultans probably came closest to living up to the image of an ideal Islamic ruler, but ultimately they, too, placed their state interests above Islam. At the peak of their power they ignored both the desperate calls for help coming from the last Muslims of Spain, decimated by the Spanish Reconquista, and the cries of the Kazan Muslims, whose hanate was destroyed by the Orthodox crusade of Russia. Like their counterparts in the West, the Ottoman sultans remembered religion only when they needed the faith to enhance their image or enlist popular support. The Mogul and Ottoman sultans tried unsuccessfully for over one hundred years to achieve an alliance, not in order to unite the Muslims but to destroy Shiite Iran. The Muslim rulers thus ignored the *tawhid* (unity) that is central to Islam, both as a koranic com-mandment and as a political principle that permeates its entire spirit. Only the Mus-lim masses appear to have maintained an idealized yearning for *tawhid*, along with a sense of shared values, universal Islamic identity, and solidarity with each other.

The relentless European advance and subjugation of the Islamic lands in the nine-teenth century forced the peripheral Muslim leaders to call for some sort of alliance with the Ottoman state, looking to the sultan-caliph in Istanbul as a potential source of military and economic help that could thwart European plans to occupy their lands. To support their demands, they referred to pacts of allegiance with the Ottomans enacted by their predecessors and proposed to renew and reinforce the old pledges by adopting the Ottoman flag and by minting coins with the caliph's name on them. The universality of the Ottoman caliphate became a fait accompli in the nineteenth century, thanks to the widespread need of the Muslim leaders to unite around one central institution in order to oppose the Europeans.

The Muslim rulers' appeals to the caliph were justified in Islamic terms, but the caliph's actual power derived from his position as sultan, for the caliphate had no formal military, economic, or political power and no recognized international status of its own. It possessed, however, a supreme symbolic position that could be used for practical political purposes, as the British first demonstrated when they tried to use the caliphate for their own ends in India and Central Asia and thus helped enhance its international stature and visibility. The Muslim rulers who sought to secure and maintain authority with the caliph's aid represented a new breed of leaders. The fact that these new leaders sought the legitimacy of their power in the good of the people and the faith rather than in the ascriptive rulers of kinship was a major departure from the past.

Nevertheless, it should be emphasized that the effort of the Muslim leaders at the periphery of the Islamic lands to achieve some sort of Islamic unity around the Ottoman caliph was a strictly self-interested political initiative confined to a small group of elites rather than a move representing the consensus of the community. Actually, the caliph's help could enable the Muslim *havas* (elites) to preserve not only the society's Islamic character but also the obsolete social and economic structures and their own monopoly of power. Yet, at some point both the *avam*—that is, the commoners involved in the fundamentalist movements—and the *havas* looked upon the Ottoman sultan-caliph as their potential savior, thus giving Istanbul an extraordinary prestige and potential influence.

Sultan Tipu of Mysore

The case that may be regarded as the starting point of the new relations between Istanbul and the Muslim periphery was that of Feth Ali, known as Tipu (1750–99), the sultan of Mysore.[1] His father, Haidar Ali, had fought the British successfully and allied himself with the French, establishing contact with France at Porto Novo in February 1782; upon his death in that same year, Tipu succeeded him. Sultan Tipu thus inherited from his father the legacy of a French alliance that exacerbated his already strained relations with the British. One year after England and France signed a peace treaty in 1783 at Versailles, Tipu also signed a treaty with the British at Mangalore; but Tipu and the British remained mutually suspicious, largely because Tipu invaded the British protectorate of Travancore and because the nizam of Hyderabad and the Hindu Marathas, both London's friends, wanted back the territory lost to Haidar Ali and Tipu. These circumstances impelled Sultan Tipu to send a large embassy to Istanbul with several letters addressed to the sultan and the grand vizier.[2] The embassy left Seringapatam, the capital of Mysore, on 17 November 1785 and reached Istanbul on 25 September 1787; it returned to Tipu's camp in January 1790.[3]

Tipu's letter to the sultan, written in Farsi, paid him the highest compliments as the caliph of the Muslims (in a section amounting to a third of the letter), then proposed the exchange of a port on the Malabar coast for Basra. Tipu also offered to build a canal to bring water to Necef (the Shiite holy place) in Iraq and asked Istanbul to provide some artisans to help Mysore manufacture weapons, glass, paper, and so on.

I. H. Qureshi, the noted Indian Muslim historian, claims that Tipu's main purpose for sending the embassy to Istanbul was to confirm and legitimize his title as the sultan.[4] The Mogul sultan in Delhi had refused to confirm Tipu's title, his father having "usurped" Mysore from the titular rajah. Tipu proposed to Istanbul "co-operation in political and economic spheres" through "trade relations, factory establishments, new arms and naval power."[5] Tipu also described how the *nasrani* (Christians) attacked Muslims, forced conversions and transformed mosques into churches. He eulogized his own actions in defending the faith and the believers and asked the caliph to help him mobilize the Indian Muslims against the British.

Abdulhamid I, in his answer to Tipu,[6] expressed his own woes, accusing the Russians of having deceived the Muslims (Russia induced the *han* of Crimea to declare independence in 1774 and in 1783 had annexed that country) and vowed to retake Crimea by *gaza* (holy war).[7] As for Tipu's requests, such as the exchange of ports and other matters, however, the sultan stated that the governor of Basra would deal with them—an old and tried way to procrastinate. Abdulhamid I appears to have viewed Tipu's call for help as a request from a lesser Muslim ruler and as an acknowledgment of Istanbul's primacy, thanks to the sultan's caliphal title.

In 1795 Tipu and the French engaged in an exchange of letters revolving partly around the French-Ottoman friendship and the Mysore-French alliance. The French described the Ottoman sultan as one of the few rulers in Europe who had remained at peace with France (during the revolutionary wars), implying that the highest Muslim figure was their friend. In sum, the French sought to enlist Tipu's help against the English, while the Mysore sultan hoped to use the French to defend his domain against the British and their local allies.

Apparently the exchange of letters, some of which have come to light recently, alarmed the British.[8] The governor general of Calcutta, the earl of Mornington, better known as the marquess of Wellesley (1760–1842), saw in Sultan Tipu's alliance with the French—and in Tipu's entente with the ruler of Afghanistan—a potentially grave threat to the British position in India. Consequently, he mobilized the Marathas and the nizam of Hyderabad against Tipu; he also began exerting diplomatic pressure on him though the Ottoman sultan-caliph, who had become overnight an ally of Britain, thanks to the French invasion of Egypt in 1798. The new Ottoman sultan, Selim III (r. 1789–1807), wrote—or was persuaded by the British to write—a letter to Tipu that was conveyed to him in the record time of two months by the British representative in Madras, just before the final British attack on Seringapatam started. A little while later, an Ottoman emissary was sent to Tipu with Sultan Selim's second letter, which is more or less identical to the first, except for some up-to-date information on events in Egypt. The Ottoman emissary, however, reached Mysore well after Tipu's death on 4 May 1799.[9]

In his first letter, Selim III spoke about French ingratitude and about their perfidious attack on Egypt under "one of their generals, named Bonaparte." According to

Selim, the French invasion of Egypt endangered Mecca and Medina because the French planned to divide Arabia into various republics and then attack and "extirpate all Musulmans from the face of the earth."[10] The French, Selim III charged, intended to liquidate all sects and religions under their doctrine of liberty. After heaping further accusations and insults on the French, the Ottoman sultan advised Tipu to "refrain from entering into any measure against the English, or lending any compliant ear to the French," who were the enemy of the sublime Porte.[11] Selim's letter, courteous and respectful of Tipu, did not mention his caliphal position or Tipu's obligation to obey him as such.

Wellesley immediately sent the Ottoman sultan's letter to Tipu adding to it his own rather revealing message. He told Tipu to pay close attention to the Ottoman declaration of war against France and to the sultan's alliance with the "British nation" and stressed the lofty position of the caliph. He urged Tipu to manifest his "zeal for the Mussulman faith by renouncing all intercourse with the common enemy of every religion, and the aggressor of the head of the Mahomedan church."[12] Furthermore, Wellesley emphasized that "the French have insulted and assaulted the acknowledged head of the Mahomedan Church" and concluded with the exhortation "May the admonition of the head of your Faith dispose your mind to the pacific propositions" advanced by him, Wellesley. Specifically, Tipu was to cut off his relations with the French and receive the British ambassador to discuss relations (surrender).[13] Soon after, on 4 May 1799, the British and their allies, including the Muslims, stormed Seringapatam, killing Tipu in the battle, and put an end to the Mysore sultanate.

Tipu had answered Sultan Selim III's first letter. In his reply, dated 10 February 1799, Tipu paid respect to the sultan and described at length the British efforts to take over southern India. He made special reference to his first embassy sent to Istanbul, about which "the English receiving information . . . with hearts inflamed, immediately conceived that all the tribes of Islam were about to league together for their destruction." Tipu wrote further that the English were determined to "subdue the whole of Hindustan and to subvert the Muslim religion" and went on to describe the anti-Muslim deeds of the Marathas as well as his own plans to provide help to the custodian of Mecca to fight the Wahhabis.[14]

The correspondence between the Ottoman sultans and Tipu provides some clues to the genesis of the idea of "pan-Islamism" and the caliph's role in it. Apparently the British were the first to see the caliphate as the potential center that could not only mobilize and unite Muslims—and induce them to fight for England but also soothe some Indian Muslims, who perceived London to be the enemy of Islam. The Ottoman ruler appeared at this stage rather unaware of the potential of the caliphate—or unwilling to use it—for political purposes; the English, however, seemed to have a clear and concise opinion about the caliphate's potential influence over other Muslims. Indeed, by the end of the eighteenth century, London seemed sure that the caliphate could be used to tame the Muslims under its rule and to establish an Islamic front directed against its enemies, Russia in particular. On the other hand, Tipu, his personal motives notwithstanding, proposed something truly revolutionary: namely, to turn the caliphate into the real political center of Islam and use it to oppose European encroachment. These two basic ideas determined the direction taken by the caliphate in the nineteenth century.

A petty Muslim ruler he may have been, but Tipu nevertheless had a vision that transcended his immediate personal and imperial interests. He had relatively modest origins, being close to the ordinary Muslims, and was genuinely interested both in the welfare of his subjects and the maintenance of an integral Muslim existence in India. He has been described, perhaps with exaggeration, as a democratic-minded populist ruler who believed that "power resides with the people" and viewed the pyramids of Egypt and the wall of China as "monuments not so much to the memory of men who ordered them to be built but to the agony and toil, blood and tears of those unfortunates who . . . built [them]."[15] In sum, Tipu was the first Muslim ruler in modern times to reach beyond the borders of his realm, actively seeking broader Muslim political alliances against the "enemies of Islam"—that is, England and France —only to realize that other Muslims regarded these "enemies" as friends, at various times and under certain circumstances and differing views of the interests of Islam.

The Achehnese Case

The people of Atjeh (Atchin, Achin, Acheh, or Ashi) occupy a special place in the history of Muslim resistance to European colonialism. Their contribution to the rise of international Islamic consciousness and to the stature of the Ottoman caliphate was overwhelming and pacesetting. Atjeh, originally a petty Muslim state located in the northwestern part of Sumatra, eventually became a flourishing empire. In 1563, when threatened by the Portuguese, the Achehnese ruler, Ala'addin Riyat Shah al-Kahhar (r. 1537–71), asked for help from Istanbul.[16] Out of nineteen ships sent from Istanbul, only two vessels seem to have reached Atjeh, but their armed crews apparently remained there—which may explain why in the twentieth century there were some "Turks" living in Bandar Atjeh—formerly Kotaradja. In any case, there is enough evidence to support the view that in the sixteenth century the Achehnese sultan accepted the Ottoman sultan's suzerainty, although with little practical consequence. After this short political intercourse, Ottoman relations with Atjeh remained dormant until the nineteenth century, when the Achehnese faced the Dutch.

In 1824 the Dutch pledged to England that they would not extend their rule to the north of Sumatra and, consequently, abstained from occupying Atjeh, in effect recognizing its independence. In a new treaty signed in 1871 and aimed primarily at controlling the piracy that originated in reaction to economic hardship in Atjeh, the Dutch succeeded in removing this restriction. In 1873 the Dutch landed troops on Achehnese territory and began a long and costly war that lasted until 1910 and was never actually won.[17] After the death of Sultan Muhammad Shah (r. 1815–38), during whose reign the first Dutch-English agreement was signed, Ali Ala'addin Mansur Shah, known as Sultan Ibrahim (r. 1838–70), took over. Mansur acted as ruler until 1857 and maintained close relations with the ulema, by that time the leading resistance group against the Dutch.

Two important factors influenced both the Achehnese response to the Dutch threat and the renewal of Achehnese-Ottoman relations. First was the existence of a sort of democracy in Atjeh, whereby the sultan was elected and exercised many of his ruling prerogatives in consultation with the uleebalangs (the local landlords), the ulema, and, to a somewhat lesser extent, the traders (the lords also controlled trade). Atjeh thus seems to have possessed some organizational structure capable of reaching the masses and mobilizing them. The second factor was the country's geographical position, open to the sea, which permitted a relatively large number of Achehnese to make the annual pilgrimage to Mecca and easily reach Istanbul, the orthodox center and seat of the caliphate.

In Atjeh the political-military resistance to the Dutch became inseparable from the revivalist-modernist drive, which spread in many parts of Indonesia and Malaysia. Unitarist in essence, Atjeh's special type of Islamism chose Mecca as its symbolic center and eventually looked upon the caliph in Istanbul as its potential political ally, leader, and legitimizer. As Anthony Reid has indicated, many South Asians, including Achehnese pilgrims in Mecca, became members of the orthodox Sufi orders, especially of the Nakşbandia and Kadiriyya brotherhoods, although these orders apparently were not found earlier in Atjeh proper.[18]

By the middle of the nineteenth century a şeyh from Menangkaban became the head of the local Nakşbandia order, which was regarded as the "main source of a permanent Mecca-orthodox influence in Sumatra." Because this şeyh "brought a Turkish flag from Mecca when he returned a few years before 1850," his teachings were "originally associated with Turkey."[19] Indeed, the Sumatran colony at Mecca appeared to be one of the strongest supporters of orthodoxy. C. Snouck Hurgronje thus reported in 1885 that the members of this "colony [possibly Java] were distinguished by their scorn for their own half pagan country, and their naive respect for the idealized land where all institutions were presumed to be in accordance with the law of the Prophet."[20]

The Achehnese embassies to Istanbul must be viewed in the light of the historical, political, and social factors and circumstances discussed above. Mansur Shah apparently realized that the Dutch would not abide forever by the agreement with the British signed in 1824, and he decided to take advantage of the truce to consolidate his position through a union with Istanbul. Mansur made his first contact with the Ottomans between 1848 and 1850, when his envoy met the Ottoman governor Hasip paşa in Jedda.[21] According to the governor's communication, the Achehnese envoy wished to convey to the Ottoman sultan Mansur Shah's desire to confirm the old "ties of allegiance" (*rabita-i tabiiyet*), and he asked that an Ottoman flag and a boat be dispatched to "Ache in the country called Java [*sic*]." Another person (whose name is not given) went from Atjeh to Istanbul and declared that, although his country had established a "special relationship" with England, the Porte was the real master of the land, for Atjeh had accepted the Ottoman suzerainty as early as the sixteenth century, and the Achehnese "could read the Friday *hutbe* (*khutba*) in the name of the sultan."[22]

After the grand vizier and his advisers debated the request at some length, they asked the sultan to reconcile the apparent contradiction between Atjeh's "special relationship" to England and its desire to accept Ottoman sovereignty in such a way as to retain the Ottoman rights without infringing upon those of the European powers. The grand vizier also recommended that information on the situation be obtained from the Achehnese pilgrims in Mecca and that a special Ottoman official be sent "in secret and disguised" (*hafiyen ve tebdilen*) to study the situation on the spot.[23] It may be noted that the sultan's reply approving the recommendations came on 11 August 1850 (2 Şevval 1266)—that is, four days after the grand vizier's memo was drafted. Many researchers have been impressed by the speed with which the Ottoman bureaucracy worked when it wanted to.

The initial contacts were followed by a more formal embassy to Istanbul, consisting of Molla Muhammad Gavs and şeyh Ismail, who delivered Mansur Shah's letter to the sultan. Mansur, claiming that his country had been part of the Ottoman state since the sixteenth century, asked the caliph to protect it against Dutch incursions and interference. In exchange, he pledged on his own and his people's behalf total *tabiyyet* (submission) to Istanbul through the reading of the Friday *hutbe* in the caliph's name and the paying of taxes. He provided extensive information about his country's material wealth and military power and promised not to be a financial burden on the Ottoman state. Mansur Shah asked the Ottoman sultan to send him instructors who, in addition to Arabic, knew "the languages of France and the English" and could "provide modern military instruction" ("asakir-i nizamiyenin üsül-ü talimini öğretmek") and an expert to mint new coins in the caliph's name.[24]

The Ottoman officials, after receiving the information about Atjeh's location and economic resources (it produced sugar, coffee, black pepper, cloves, rice, wheat, etc.), debated the issue in the Ottoman Meclis-i Valâ (High Supreme Council).[25] The members of the council were very impressed by the great importance attached by Atjeh to the Ottoman sultan's position as caliph and by how it cherished the Ottoman memory (several cannons that had been sent in the sixteenth century were preserved). In the end the Ottoman officials decided that their government was economically and strategically ill placed to provide any help, but they did not reject outright Mansur Shah's request outright because of the applicant's royal stature and because some "twenty to twenty five thousand pilgrims went annually to *hac*" from Sumatra, as well as for other reasons.[26] In the formal answer to Mansur, the Porte glorified the Ottoman sultan's position as the imam of the Muslims and the caliph to the Prophet ("imam-i Muslimin ve halife-i hazreti Seyyidul-Murselin") and said that the matter was referred to Mustafa paşa, the governor of Yemen, for consideration and action.[27] Mustafa paşa did indeed contact Mansur, and eventually the sultan issued a *ferman* (decree) accepting the shah as a subordinate and his realm as part of the caliph's domains. Nothing further came out of this mission, nor from an Ottoman request to the Dutch for permission to establish a consulate in the Dutch colonies, although a consulate was later established in Batavia.

In 1869 when the Dutch intention to subdue Atjeh by force became more evident, Mansur, working through the *amir* of Mecca, and the *vali* of the Hicaz, Muammer paşa, appealed once more for help and offered again to place his country entirely under Ottoman rule.[28] In view of the "large number of Muslims in those areas who need protection and [offer] allegiance to the Sublime Sultanate," the Porte decided to send Pertev efendi, the former *kaymakam* of Musawa' (Masua), who spoke Arabic and "was aware of the politics of the time and knew the area," to contact Mansur and determine the exact situation in Atjeh.[29] He was instructed to camouflage his mission as an inspection tour of Yemen and use the occasion to strengthen the population's attachment to the sultanate and to study the reasons for the fighting between the tribes of Meşaleha and Hakem.[30]

After the Dutch attacked Atjeh in 1873, the next sultan Mahmud Shah (r. 1870–74), referring again to the pact of submission in the sixteenth century, renewed his predecessor's request through his vizier, Abdurrahman az-Zahir, a *sayyid* (descendant of Hassan, the Prophet's grandson) related to the *şerif* of Mecca. He wrote that although the Achehnese had repulsed the Dutch, the latter were preparing a massive new attack on his country.[31] Whereas the earlier Achehnese embassies to Istanbul were hardly noticed, az-Zahir's mission met with great public enthusiasm, thanks to reports in the newly emerging Ottoman popular press. *Basiret*, the populist newspaper, urged the government to acquiesce to Atjeh's demand, as did Mithat paşa—the populist constitutionalist leader—who was opposed to the sultan and was building a popular constituency for himself. (Mithat urged the Porte to mediate the Dutch-Atjeh conflict.)

Mithat's efforts were undermined by the Russian ambassador, Ignatiev, who (always mindful of Russia's own restless Muslims) got his friend Grand Vizier Mahmud Nedim (Nedimov) paşa to persuade Sultan Abdulaziz to withdraw the mediation offer. Fearful of popular reaction, Abdulaziz replaced Saffet paşa, the minister of foreign affairs, with Reşit paşa only a few hours after he had informed the Dutch of the withdrawal of the offer. Public support for Atjeh's cause in Istanbul apparently encouraged Abdurrahman az-Zahir to reiterate his position—he even had the letters of the late Mansur Shah read in a cabinet meeting—but the final result was still negative.[32] The envoy soon was sent home empty-handed, though honored with a medal and gifts, while the Porte sent an abject memorandum to the Dutch seeking understanding for the delicate position in which the Achehnese requests had placed the caliph and begged for compassion for the Muslims of Sumatra.[33]

Sultan Abdulaziz eventually paid for his failure to live up to his popularly expected caliphal duties. His abandonment of Atjeh plus his cold treatment of Şeyh Şamil alienated the population and the *softa*, the students in the religious schools, and encouraged Mithat's group to oust him in 1876. Abdulaziz's successor, Sultan Abdulhamid II, aware of the power of the "people" and, especially, of the manipulators behind it, did his best to repair the damage to the Islamic cause by opening a *şehbenderlik* (consulate) in Batavia in 1883 and keeping himself informed about the situation of the Muslims in India and Dutch colonies in East Asia.[34]

The Dutch military triumph in 1873 and the subservience of the gentry and the commercial interests to the Dutch colonial administration left the ulema as the only credible group speaking on behalf of the community and its values.[35] Hurgronje had seen the tensions in Sumatran society as a conflict between *hüküm* (Islamic law) and *adat* (indigenous customs) and urged the Dutch government to uphold the *adat* and its representatives—that is, the *uleebalang*. In that way he hoped to restore the harmony between the peasants and the lords that supposedly had been disrupted by Islam and its representatives, the ulema. As James T. Siegel has pointed out, however, Hurgronje had overlooked the central, multifaceted representative functions assumed by the ulema, who stressed on behalf of Islam the equality of men and not their social roles.[36] These were preparatory steps for the Sarekat Islam (Muslim Union), founded in 1912 in Indonesia and incorporating at least three currents of thought: a strong anticolonialism, a new national identity rooted in Islam and in Atjeh's own experience, and a desire for change in order to strengthen the society morally and materially.[37] National revival and a revived Islam, as usual, were indistinguishable from each other and were a challenge to the old order, including the old Muslim establishment.

The Achehnese correspondence with the sultan-caliph demonstrates that the Ottoman ruler seemed more interested in upholding the principles of international law and not interfering in the affairs of other nations than in expanding his authority over other Muslims. Consequently, the Achehnese had to base their struggle for independence and cultural self-preservation on their own resources; the Achehnese sultan became the leader of the popular resistance to the Dutch occupation, while the ulema allied with and mobilized the masses. Local resistance to the Dutch seemed to have bolstered the local and regional character of Achehnese Islam as much as it strengthened its attachment to Muslim universality and preserved the ulema's credibility and respect. Atjeh played a seminal role in shaping the culture, identity, and even the language of modern Indonesia while retaining its own regional and historical identity. The centralizing policies and the exploitation of its economic resources by the Jakarta government and a variety of other causes produced tensions that resulted, in 1953, in an open Achehnese uprising followed by unrest and then, in 1988–99, by a full-fledged movement for autonomy and self-government. The local and regional culture and history failed to melt, mesh, or harmonize with the central drive to create a modern Indonesian culture and identity, in which Islam became a subculture of the national one promoted by the central government.

The Muslims of the Comoro Islands

Some modernists, including some members of the new middle classes, to be discussed later, visualized the caliphate in a dynamic manner, as a modern force capable of mobilizing their society and even providing leadership to independence movements, while the traditionalists still regarded it as a repository of Islamic traditions and values and defender of the social status quo. For the most part, the attitudes of the old and new Muslim elites toward the caliphate reflected their own social origin, philosophical outlook, political attitudes, and expectations. The new middle classes acquired power and position, largely to the detriment of the traditional elites, as a result of the European occupation and the social change that went with it. The old elites tried to stem the rise of new groups by asking for the caliph's help. The case of Henzevan Island in the Indian Ocean illustrates well how this process took place.

Henzevan (Hinzuan, Anjouan, Johanna), Mayotte, Grand Comoro (Ngazija), and Moheli (Mohella) are the four major islands in the Comoro group. The French occupied Mayotte and made it a colony over the period 1841–43, but there was an interval of over forty years before the French occupied the other three islands in 1886.[38] The British were allowed to open a consulate on Henzevan in 1848, and Josiah Napier, the first consul and, especially, his successor, William Sunley (d. 1877), introduced plantation agriculture and obtained special concessions to engage in a variety of enterprises, such as sugar refining. Sultan Abdullah, who took the throne in 1855, became a great friend and admirer of Sunley and also engaged himself in plantation agriculture.

The sultan brought a workforce from Mozambique, armed his slaves to form a private army, and chose to reside in a special mansion outside the capital, thus facilitating the emergence of a new social order in Henzevan, one based on capital and hired labor. Initially the sultan ruled the island with the help of the Grand Council (Council of Henzevan), composed of the notables, mostly ulema, who had the right to correspond with foreign powers. After acquiring wealth and forming his own private army, however, Sultan Abdullah apparently began to ignore the council and to implement arbitrarily a variety of reforms that upset the status quo. Eventually the British ousted Sunley, who had used his influence over the sultan to his own advantage, but he continued to reside in Henzevan and expanded his businesses.

Upset by the growing impact of the new economic order on traditional society and the continuing association of Sultan Abdullah with Sunley, the Council of Henzevan petitioned the caliph in Istanbul to intervene to restore the old order.[39] That the petitioners were "spokesmen of Islam," as self-described, and community leaders is indicated by their titles: Seyyid Abdurrahman Bin-i Sultan Ulvi, Seyyid Meku Bin-i Sultan Ahmet, Muhammed bin-i Kadi-ul Muslimin, Ali bin-i Şeyh Ahmet, Seyyid bin-i Şeyh Ali, Seyyid Ebubekir Bin Abd-i Rab, Fazil bin-i Ali Kadi-ul Muslimin, and Imam Ebubekir bin-i Ali. They belonged to the dominant aristocratic class of chiefs, mostly of Arabic origin, some claiming descent from the Prophet, from among whom came the sultans and viziers.[40] Addressing the caliph as *halife-i seyyidus sakaleyn, hamidul-harameyn* (the successor of the Prophet and protector of the holy cities) and as "the holder of the seat of the great caliphate and the head [*reis*] and leader [*pisua*] of the Muslim nation," they informed him that the "Christians are pressuring us and are preventing us from following the laws of the *Şeriat* as decreed by God and his Prophet. They want to inflict upon us the same treatment imposed on the country of Mayota and its inhabitants by the French who occupied unjustly the above mentioned country and destroyed the mosques and forced the population to abandon Islam."[41] The council members informed the caliph that they had delegated Seyyid Muhammad Ibn-i Sultan and Seyyid Abdullah ibn-i Sultan (the two were brothers related to the ruler of Henzevan) to present their case to the caliph in Istanbul "*as the holder* of the seal [*uzma*] of caliphate and ask him *since they had no other office to address*" (emphasis added) to come to the aid of his Muslim subjects and followers and to save their Islamic way of life.[42]

The ruling Ottoman sultan-caliph, Abdulaziz, finally decided to send an emissary with a message advising the ruler of Henzevan in the Comoro Islands to provide relief and security to the Muslims on the island.[43]

Yakub bey's Relations with the Ottoman Sultans: A Reinterpretation

Yakub bey (1820–77) has received considerable scholarly attention since the days when he established in east Turkistan (Sinkiang) an independent state centered in Kaşgar (Kashgar) and Yarkand, and ruled it under the titles *beg* (bey), *atalik gazi, badevlet,* and, finally, *amir* (*ul-Muminin*) given to him by the Ottoman caliph-sultan. Some scholars have regarded Yakub bey as an adventurer who exploited the political turmoil in Central Asia to gain power for himself and then tried to establish a dynasty by seeking support and legitimacy—like Tipu of India—from higher Muslim forums. But lately there has been a steady positive reappraisal of this ruler. He has been compared to Nadir Shah and credited with the establishment of a sovereign state and a modern administration.[44] This section is an addition to the efforts to reassess Yakub bey as a new type of Muslim ruler, giving a social and ideological consideration to his activities in the context of local dynastic conflicts, international politics, and Islam.

Yakub bey had a modest background and relied on local civilian groups, such as the merchants of Andijan, and the general population to gain power. He was, in fact, a new type of Muslim ruler, who sensed that the sultan-caliph in Istanbul, as the head of the Muslim community, was potentially a more powerful and reliable source of strength than were whimsical local dynasties—despite their illustrious past—concerned primarily with their own interests. Known as Khojas, those dynasties started with Khoja Ahrar in the fifteenth century, who was essentially an adviser to the lay ruler. His descendants, however, became rulers themselves. Like many other Muslim potentates in Asia and Africa, Yakub bey came to believe that an alliance with the caliph in Istanbul would neutralize the influence of the Khojas and assure his throne.

East Turkistan acquired its Muslim Turkic identity as early as the eighth century and, through the subsequent centuries became a sort of literary, linguistic, and religious cradle of Turkishness. The Chinese, who had always regarded east Turkistan mainly as a defensive outpost rather than as an integral part of their domain, lost much of their control of the area during the rule of the Monguls—the descendants of Cengiz han (Genghis Khan). Eventually, in the fifteenth and sixteenth centuries, the Cengizids split into several opposing groups, and then the religiously oriented Khojas, claiming descent from the Prophet, gradually gained influence and power over the rulers in both east and west Turkistan. The two main factions contending for power, the Black and the White Mountaineers (Karataulu and Aktaulu) fought each other, occasionally seeking Kalmuk, Chinese, or even Russian support, as the situation dictated.

The Chinese consolidated their hold on Kaşgar in 1760 and, favoring trade with west Turkistan, they permitted the establishment in Kaşgar of various Kokand merchant communities headed by elders, or *aksakal,* nominated by the *han* of Kokand.[45] They also allowed the han of Kokand to tax the merchandise sold by the Muslim merchants in Kaşgar. The rising economic power of the Kokand (Andijani) merchants and the desire of their leaders, the *aksakal,* for autonomy, coupled with the ambition of the Khoja families, generated a series of anti-Chinese revolts, those of Vali Han Töre (1855) and Muhammed Emin Khoja (1864) being the better known ones.

In reaction to the uprisings the Chinese dismissed the *aksakal,* cut off relations with Kokand, and curtailed the privileges under which the Andijani merchants had prospered. The Muslim merchants and the segments of the local population of Kaşgar were opposed to the Chinese, but also to the heavy taxes and mistreatment by the Khojas, who were involved in every anti-Chinese revolt. The times seemed ripe for the rise of a different type of ruler, one who drew his legitimacy from his effort to benefit the population, not merely from his inherited rights.

Born in 1820 in Pişkent, a prosperous town near Taşkent (Tashkent), Yakub bey was the son of Pir Mohammed Mirza (Mehmet Latif), a *kadi* (judge). (His claim to descent from Timur was unfounded.) Yakub married a Tatar woman and had three sons: Kuda Kul bey, Kuli bey, and Haj Kuli bey. He soon entered the service of the Kokand ruler, Khudayar han. Ousted several times, the *han* managed to regain his throne and keep it until the Russians conquered his state in 1876. Yakub bey, despite participating in several of the internal revolts, kept his position and distinguished himself in the effort to hold off the Russians, initially in the lengthy defense of the fort of Ak Mescit. (Renamed Perovskii after the Russian general who took the fort, it became known as Kizil Orda, or Red Army, in Kazakhstan. It has now reverted to its old name.)

Meanwhile, in Kaşgar the disintegrating power of the Manchu rulers encouraged local revolts, which brought into picture the Kokand rulers, always eager to regain their influence in eastern Turkistan. Buzurg han, the only surviving son of Jihangir bey of the Khoja dynasty, was sent to Kaşgar to reconcile the various contending factions striving to fill the power vacuum left by the departure of the Chinese. Yakub bey was charged to assist Buzurg in gaining control of Kaşgar; but their relations deteriorated, and eventually Yakub imprisoned and then exiled the rather inept Buzurg. Once in full command of operations, Yakub bey took Kuça (1867), Korla (1869), and Turfan (1871), but not Ili (Kulca), which was occupied by the Russians in July 1871 as a precaution.

The Russians feared that Yakub bey's successes would jeopardize the security of their newly conquered territories in western Turkistan, notably Kokand, and open the area to British penetration. Indeed, William Henry Johnson's two visits to Yarkand in 1864 and 1865, the journey of Robert Shaw, a tea planter from Kangra in the Himalayas, and the visit of George Hayward to the area under the auspices of the Royal Geographical Society, raised the Russian fears of British expansionism. Actually, Yakub bey mistrusted the British and began to seek diligently to contact them in India only after he clashed with the Russians. A British mission to Kaşgar headed by Douglas Forsyth in 1870–71 could achieve little, however, because Yakub bey was away campaigning.[46]

Yakub bey's relations with the Porte began as early as 1868–69, when his nephew and ambassador, Yakub Töre han, made his second trip to Istanbul. The Russian occupation of Kokand (1875) and their establishment of a protectorate over Buhara (Bukhara) (1868) and Khiva (1873) increased the apprehension of both Istanbul and London and therefore led them to support Yakub bey.[47] Yakub bey, in turn, welcomed the opportunity to legitimize his ruling position, wrested from the Khojas, by receiving the caliph's blessing and to strengthen that position with British military support if possible.

Yakub bey's foreign policy must be in part credited to Yakub Töre han, a remarkable personality, who put aside any personal ambition and served Yakub bey faithfully, although by descent, learning, and experience he was far superior to his master. Yakub han apparently did not regard Kaşgar solely as his ruler's private preserve but as a rising Muslim nation-state with ties to the wider world. He visited Mecca, Istanbul, India, and even Russia on diplomatic missions and seemed to have become aware of the rising political consciousness of the Muslim masses and of the caliph's potential influence. Yakub han had spent considerable time in Istanbul as the emissary of Alim Kul, the army commander of Kokand, before the fall of Taşkent in 1865. Seeking aid against the Russians, he had presented the Ottoman government with a memorandum describing the political situation of Central Asia. In his later visit (1869) to Istanbul, he met first with the *kapi kethudasi*, the "ambassador of Kaşgar," who acted as the intermediary between the *amir* of Kaşgar and the sultan and was a vital link between the Kaşgaris and the universal Muslim community headed by the caliph. According to the official Ottoman chronicler of the time, Ahmet Lutfi, however, the Ottoman government failed to evaluate properly the significance of the Yakub han's embassy and limited itself to giving the envoy not aid but the usual medal.[48]

The first letter addressed officially by Yakub bey to the Ottoman sultan, announcing the dispatch of an emissary, is dated October 1872—that is, about three months after Yakub bey had concluded the agreement of 22 June 1872 with Baron Kaulbars that gave Russia trading privileges in Kaşgar. Writing in Farsi, Yakub bey stated that he had heard that the sultan, as caliph, had dedicated himself to the good of the Muslims, and asked to be included among the protected people. He described himself as having fought for a very long time for Islam and now was prepared to attach himself to the caliph. Then his letter cautiously pointed out that other details of the mission would be presented orally by Ambassador Seyyid Yakub efendi han who had hastened to the Ottoman capital from Russia.[49]

Yakub han reached Istanbul in Rebiyülevvel (during the late spring of 1873), and was honored this time as the house guest of the caliph, and he requested an immediate interview with the sultan.[50] This was quickly granted, being scheduled for 16 June 1873 at 5 P.M.[51] Indeed, the Russian occupation of Khiva and Buhara had alarmed everybody in the opposite camp and impelled England and its Ottoman ally to use Islam to prevent Russia's advance further south to Afghanistan and India. In private discussion with the sultan Yakub han pledged on behalf of Yakub bey to bring Kaşgar under the suzerainty of the sultan-caliph and to read the *hutbe* and mint coins in his name. In exchange he asked the caliph to confirm Yakub bey as the legal, bona fide ruler of Kaşgar and demanded immediate concrete action to secure the independence of that area. The concrete proof of the caliph's commitment materialized in the form of Ottoman military-technical aid to Kaşgar to replace its obsolete weapons and its archaic military training system and command; these military shortcomings had made the Central Asian hanates easy prey for the Russian forces. The caliph sent four officers, along with six large Krupp cannons, one thousand old and two thousand new rifles, and utensils for the manufacture of gun powder. The four officers belonged to different military branches (infantry, artillery, construction, etc.) and were probably accompanied by another four reserve officers under the command of Murat bey. At least two of the officers, Mehmet Yusuf and Çerkes Yusuf, had graduated that same year from the modern War College (Mekteb-i Harbiye) and had volunteered to go to Kaşgar with Yakub han. (One of them was a Circassian, probably a descendant of the refugees of the 1860s, who nurtured strong anti-Russian feelings.) The caliph also sent Yakub bey letters, gifts, and a medal.[52] There is no question that the Ottoman involvement in Kaşgar took place with the knowledge and support of the British, who claimed that Yakub bey's mission to Istanbul was successful because of their intervention.[53]

A detailed report about the weapons and ammunition and the composition of the Ottoman military mission sent to Yakub bey was provided by Captain Ali Kazim, after he returned home safely.[54] According to the report, the mission went via Suez to Bombay and from there proceeded to Lahore, where it stayed for several months because the British refused to pay further transportation costs. Eventually the Turkish officers and the weapons reached Yarkand and were greeted with joy and honored by a one-hundred-gun salute. Ali Kazim first trained a battalion of artillery, which became very proficient—"like the soldiers of Istanbul"—and then a regiment of three thousand men. However, internecine fighting broke out among Yakub bey's commanders and sons, especially after his death in Korla in May 1877, and the Turkish officers were taken prisoner by advancing Chinese armies. Ultimately the officers were released to the custody of the British in India and returned to Istanbul to tell the sad story of Yakub bey's death and the fratricidal struggle among his heirs.[55]

As one concern of this study is Yakub bey's search for legitimacy as a ruler, it is noteworthy that, in addition to his previous titles of *atalik gazi* and *badevlet*, he took the title of *amir* (emir), indicating that he was subordinate to the sultan in Istanbul who had confirmed him as ruler of Kaşgar. To consolidate further his family's claim to rule Kaşgar, he asked that his title to the emirate be made permanent and be permitted to be passed on to his heirs through his oldest adult (*ekber ve erşad*) son. In great detail, the sultan told the consultative committee considering Yakub's petition that he had faithfully read the *hutbe* and minted coins in the caliph's name and recommended that his oldest adult son be authorized to assume the throne, on the condition that this would be beneficial to the population and the future of the emirate.[56] On the committee's concurrence, the sultan instructed Yakub bey to hoist the Ottoman flag "without any change in its color or emblem" alongside the bey's own banner and to treat the population well.

As the ruler of Yedişehir (seven cities), another of Yakub bey's titles, he acknowledged with gratitude the receipt of weapons and declared that the help provided by Istanbul had given a new life to the Muslims of Central Asia. Moreover, he wrote, he had hoisted the Ottoman flag, read the *hutbe*, and minted coins in the name of the caliph, and he expressed his wish that "Central Asia shall establish relations with the Caliphate and thus . . . create Islamic unity."[57] Yakub bey began regularly to use the title of *amir*, while in his correspondence with Istanbul he referred to the Ottoman ruler as "caliph of the Muslims," but almost never as "sultan of the Turks."[58] It is not clear whether Yakub bey implemented the sultan's other instructions to develop agriculture, education, science, industry, and roads, to open new fields of activity according to the ability and aptitudes of the population, and to establish peaceful relations with his neighbors.[59]

On 30 May 1876 Yakub bey's benefactor, Sultan Abdulaziz, was replaced as sultan by Murad V, who in turn was replaced just three months later by Abdulhamid II. The new sultan recalled an embassy that the Ottoman court had dispatched to Kaşgar shortly before his ascendancy, and later sent his own embassy to Kaşgar. Contrary to his latter-day image as a "panislamist," Abdulhamid did not appear eager to follow the "expansionist" policies toward Kaşgar developed by the bureaucracy and carried forward by his predecessor.

Yakub bey, who was kept well informed about developments in the Ottoman capital, once more dispatched Yakub han to Istanbul via Bombay to congratulate the new sultan and renew the bonds of allegiance—that is, to perform the *biat* as required by Muslim political traditions. Yakub han asked to see the sultan immediately upon reaching Istanbul in 1877, but the cautious Abdulhamid let him wait until the following month before receiving him, the appointment being for the third Tuesday at 5 P.M.[60] While waiting, Yakub han delivered to the Ottoman foreign ministry a letter in which Yakub bey reiterated his allegiance to the Ottoman court. Evidently the ruler of Kaşgar had been advised by his agents in Istanbul about the power and influence of the foreign ministry and the need to gain its favor.[61] (A short time after Abdulhamid assumed the throne, he turned the ministries into powerless clerical offices, however, and the foreign ministry, which during the most of Abdulmecid and Abdulaziz's reigns had been an almost autonomous center of power, came under the sultan's total control.)

In east Turkistan, meanwhile, the Chinese general Tso Tsung T'ang (1812–85), charged with pacifying the areas of Muslim rebellion in the northwest, moved steadily against the forces of Yakub bey. Tso had finally solved his main logistical problem when the Russians decided in 1875 to let the Chinese prevail in east Turkistan, by supplying Tso's forces with badly needed grain. In 1876 Tso attacked and took over the cities east of Kaşgar, and he reached the Tarim Basin in the spring of 1877.

It was in May 1877, during the Chinese offensive, that Yakub bey died under mysterious circumstances. Some claimed that he had been poisoned by one of his enemies (notably Hakim Han Töre), while others said that he willingly took poison after he read a letter from the Chinese asking for his surrender.[62] In any case, Yakub bey's death led to further fragmentation of his forces and supporters. Kuli bey, his oldest son, killed his younger brother, Haj Kuli bey, in front of their father's coffin; and local chiefs such as Sadik bey, the Kirghiz chief who had been defeated some thirteen years earlier by Yakub bey, rose and attacked the Kaşgar forces. Finally Kuli bey sought sanctuary with the Russians in Taşkent. By December of 1877, the Chinese army had entered Kaşgar and put an end to whatever was left of Yakub bey's realm.

It appeared that the relations with the Porte cultivated so assiduously by Yakub han could not assure the survival of Kaşgar and the "pan-Islamic" bridge Yakub bey had helped build between Istanbul and Central Asia. That appearance was deceiving, however, because the links between Istanbul and Kaşgar, long in existence and reinforced in the early 1870s on behalf of Muslim solidarity and mutual political interest, continued to bear fruit of sorts in the years to come. In 1879, almost two years after the Chinese occupied Kaşgar, Eddai Yakub efendi, whom the Ottoman chancery considered the Istanbul representative of the emirate of Kaşgar, addressed a petition to the sultan supposedly conveying the ideas of Mehmet han, the commander of the Kaşgar infantry troops. The petition described the *vilayet* (province) of Kaşgar as rich, inhabited by some five million people, and capable of producing a substantial tax revenue. Then it explained that the Chinese had occupied the city without fight or resistance on the part of its inhabitants as in other Turkistani localities. The petition suggested that the Kaşgaris did not resist the Chinese invaders because they considered themselves to be under the authority of the caliph and somehow outside the main conflict and that the Chinese, in turn, implicitly accepted the special status of Kaşgar, for they left the administration of the entire *vilayet* totally in the hands of the Muslims. In conclusion, the petition asked the sultan to consider sending a special envoy to remind China that Kaşgar "was part of the sovereign imperial Ottoman domains [*memalik-i mahruse-i mulkadari*] and was occupied and conquered [*zabt ve teshir*] without war." The representative of Kaşgar in Istanbul was fairly sure that if the sultan chose such a course of action, the Chinese would acquiesce.[63]

There is no evidence yet available to indicate what the response was to this rather unusual and naive effort to salvage something from the debacle that followed Yakub bey's death and the Chinese occupation of Kaşgar. The Kaşgar drama was not entirely over, however. Yakub bey's son Kuli bey, who had taken refuge in Taşkent with the Russians, sent a confidential letter via a trusted emissary to Molla Mehmet, another Kaşgari representative in Istanbul; he informed the Porte that he had expressed his allegiance to the caliph several times and had taken refuge with the Russians only with the ultimate purpose of going to Istanbul and hoped to arrive there soon.[64] In a subsequent lengthy memorandum, apparently submitted at the request of the sultan after what seems to have been a short face-to-face talk, Kuli bey related the past history of relations between Yakub bey and the Porte and provided information on Kaşgar's relations with the Chinese and the struggle of various native factions.[65] This memorandum provides excellent information on the history of Kaşgar but cannot be pursued further here.

Suffice it to say that Kuli bey professed boundless and permanent allegiance to the caliph, reiterated his desire to liberate Kaşgar, and promised to "relate the important events one by one to the sultan by using the code [*şifre*] given to me." Of course Great Britain was aware of all these developments and had for its own purposes deliberately encouraged the caliphate in its relations with the Kaşgar beys, with the full concurrence of the modernist-nationalist wing of the Ottoman bureaucracy.[66] The relationship did not lead to the liberation of Kaşgar from the Chinese, however. In 1884 the Chinese gave the conquered lands of east Turkistan the name of Xinjiang (Sinkiang, New Province) although the population of the area was almost entirely Muslim and Turkic (Uighur)-speaking.

Despite the lack of ultimate success for his endeavor, Yakub bey of Kashgar appears to have been the forerunner of the incipient political-modernist awakening among the Muslims. Ancient historical and religious ties, including the *hac*, and the similarities of culture, language, customs, and traditions between Central Asia and the Ottoman state certainly played a major part in Yakub bey's offer of allegiance to Istanbul. Nevertheless, those ties had existed for centuries and could not by themselves have brought Kaşgar into the Ottoman fold without a profound political and symbolic transformation of the caliphate in the eyes of the Muslims, however illusory the power of that office. The institution had been dormant for centuries but now was brought to life by the expectations and aspirations of Muslims for independence and modernity and by British manipulations.

The Arab Şeyhs of Bahrain and Arabia: Anticaliphal Subjects

While the Muslims in the peripheral Islamic lands offered allegiance to the Ottoman caliph and sought to enlist his support against the European powers, some of his own subjects in the Arab peninsula did just the opposite. They sought help from or alliance with the British in order to shake off Ottoman authority and gain autonomy, even independence. The Arabs seeking British support were also good Muslims—indeed some claimed to be the best—and, except for the Saudi house, which opposed the Ottoman central authority, they acknowledged to good extent the supremacy of the caliph. Bahrain and the Saudi princes offer the best examples of the centrifugal forces that developed within the Ottoman state along with the centripetal force of

Islam, which brought national interest and faith into an apparent collision course, or concurrence as the case may be.[67]

The island of Bahrain emerged as a major area of contention between the Ottoman government and the British in the second half of the nineteenth century, as the Gulf became vitally important for the British. In the period 1895–97, for example, most of the 2,039 ships that entered it were British. Because British shipping interests called for protection against pirates, including some Wahhabis, operating from the şeyhdoms on the western coast of Arabia, England stationed in the port of Bushire in Iran a political resident, who was also the consul general of Fars and Khuzistan, and placed consular agents in Bahrain, Kuwait, and Muscat. Considerable maneuvering on the part of the British persuaded the *şeyh*s located on the coast south of Hasa (Hassa) to refer their disputes to the political resident, in effect establishing a de facto British presence in the Gulf area. However, the British policy of gaining influence among the Gulf *şeyh*s impinged directly on the suzerainty of the Ottoman sultans, who tried after the 1850s to maintain their authority in Bahrain, Kuwait, Qatar, and the strategically important Hasa province. This Ottoman policy was intensified during the last quarter of the century, and England responded by strengthening further its influence among the coastal *şeyh*s. When Russia, France, and later Germany asked the Porte for coaling stations in the Gulf and railway concessions (France desired to construct a line from Tripoli in Syria to Kuwait), British apprehensions increased.

The already complicated international rivalry in the Gulf was rendered even worse by power struggles among the local potentates. The Saudi princes balanced relations with Istanbul and England, on the one hand, against ties to some of the *şeyh*s of the peninsula and the Gulf, on the other. The latter included the *şeyh* of Bahrain, who had agreed to pay tribute to the Wahhabis after they had taken the island from Muscat in 1801. Bahrain was freed from its obligations to the Wahhabis when Mehmet Ali of Egypt, under orders from Istanbul, invaded Central Arabia in 1811 and then in 1818 destroyed Dariya (Riyadh), the Wahhabi center; but Wahhabi power was reestablished for a while after 1830, thanks in part to England, which prevented Egypt from moving against the rebels. From these events, the Saudis learned the value of British friendship. The Egyptians, having quarreled with the Porte, reoccupied Central Arabia in the years 1838–39 and secured the allegiance of Bahrain, which also accepted the suzerainty of the Persian shah to counteract the Egyptians. When Mehmet Ali finally was forced out of Syria in 1841, by combined Turkish-English forces, the Ottomans were able to restore their rule in Arabia but could not control the Saudis. Faisal ibn-Turki (ruling 1834–38, 1843–65) acknowledged Ottoman sovereignty and paid a symbolic tribute, but he sought British help to assert his authority in Bahrain (based on the 1801 allegiance) and in Qatar, but London refused to supply him with ships lest it affect its good relations with the coastal şeyhdoms. Instead, in 1861 the British compelled the *şeyh* of Bahrain to sign an agreement not to interfere with maritime traffic, to respect earlier agreements of 1847 and 1856, and to abolish the slave trade.

Bahrain and its ruler, Muhammad al-Khalifa, again became the target of Saudi ambitions during the reign of Abdullah, who took power one year before the death of his father, Faisal, in 1866. The correspondence of Şeyh al-Halifa of Bahrain with the Porte, generated during the *şeyh*'s resistance to Faisal's campaign of expansion, tells us much about the inner workings of Arabian politics, the *şeyhs'* attitude toward the Porte, and their relations with the British. The *şeyh* of Bahrain, Muhammad al-Khalifa, reminded the Porte in 1862 that he had not received an answer to an earlier complaint he had addressed to the reformist Sultan Abdulmecid, a great friend of the British, who had passed away in 1861. "Learning now that our lord, the exalted Sultan Abdulaziz, unlike Abdulmecid, is aware of the Muslims around him and of those who are attached to him," the *şeyh* decided to renew his complaint through an emissary who would provide orally additional information on the issue.[68] Feeling threatened by Faisal, şeyh Khalifa asked the Ottoman government for support, promising in exchange to pay taxes and to abide fully by Ottoman laws. The *şeyh* also implied that his renewal of allegiance to Istanbul was inspired by the good Islamic credentials of the new sultan.

The mundane yet powerful motive behind Şeyh Muhammad al-Halifa's renewal of allegiance to the caliph can easily be uncovered, however, by reading the reports of the Ottoman administrators, notably the communications of Mehmet Namik paşa, the governor of Baghdad and the commander of the Iraqi army.[69] (The career of Mehmet Namik paşa epitomizes best the efforts of the Ottoman government to use the European experience of its officials in the administration of provinces. Namik served in the Ottoman embassies in London and St. Petersburg before he became governor of Baghdad.)[70] The governor reported that Faisal bin Saud of Nejd was dissatisfied with the annual tax of four thousand rials paid by Şeyh Khalifa and wanted to replace him with his own son and heir, Abdullah. Faced with this threat, the incumbent *şeyh* of Bahrain had applied to the Porte for protection. Not receiving a satisfactory answer from Sultan Abdulmecid, he approached the British and the Iranians for help against the Saudis and was ready to offer them allegiance, if necessary, to preserve his throne. But Namik paşa stressed that the *şeyh* in reality was loyal to the Porte. He had resorted to foreign help only because the sultan failed to help him.[71]

The plight of the *şeyh* of Bahrain, Namik paşa further explained, was the consequence of the grandiose ambitions of the *kaymakams* (deputy rulers) of Nejd, the Ibn Saud family, and the perennial question of tax payments.[72] Abdullah, Faisal's son, refused to pay the Porte the annual tax (about 200,000 rials) under the pretext that the income of his domain was so low that he could not even meet the expenses associated with tax collection. He further claimed that at one time Abbas paşa, the governor of Egypt, had exempted Nejd from the tax because of its poverty.[73] Asked for his viewpoint, Mehmet Vecihi, the governor of the Hicaz, described Şeyh Abdullah bin Faisal Ibn Saud as "possessing no salaried soldiers and owning only the shirt on his back and eating just rice with meat and having in his presence [and feeding] together with those who came to see him, a total of one hundred to one hundred fifty people." Consequently the governor of the Hicaz felt that Şeyh Abdullah could use much less money than he demanded and that the Ottoman government could get a higher proportion of the taxes collected in Nejd.[74] The governor of Baghdad warned the Porte that Şeyh Abdullah planned to annex Oman and Kuwait and hoped to reach the shores of the Red Sea and Indian Ocean through expansion into Yemen.[75]

Faced with the potential for revolt and disobedience in Nejd—a threat that eventually turned into reality and opened a new chapter in the history of the Arabian peninsula—the Ottoman government did its best to secure the loyalty of the population. It decided to emphasize further the sultan's role as caliph, or "defender of the Muslims," and to win over the Gulf *şeyh*s. The *şeyh* of Bahrain was promised government support and honored in every way possible, and the island was attached to the governorate of Baghdad. At the same time, the notables of Bahrain were assured that the Ottoman ruler, as the caliph of the Muslims, held them in great esteem and affection and would offer them protection. In return, the Porte asked the notables to take individual vows of allegiance and loyalty to the caliph and to the state and to pay no attention to British promises and gifts. All the while, however, the Ottoman government was introducing reforms and institutions of the European type and enforcing them through a centralized authority that threatened the power of the local notables. The caliphal title offered sanctuary to the sultan's reforms.

Conclusion

Initially, the Ottoman sultan-caliphs did not seek the support or allegiance of the leaders of Muslims overseas. Instead, these leaders approached the caliph believing rather naively that he possessed enough military and economic power to assure their independence and protect them against England, France, Russia, and so on, and that his recognition would grant legitimacy to their authority, as was the case for Tipu and Yakub bey. In other cases, caliphal intervention was sought to settle a local power struggle, as in the case of Bahrain, or, to preserve the traditional way of life, as in the Comoro islands. The caliph-sultan obviously did not have the means to satisfy all the demands addressed to him; in fact, one key reason the Muslim rulers appeared so ready to barter away their independence or autonomy in exchange for caliphal aid was that they knew the caliph possessed hardly any means to implement his authority in the faraway lands of Africa and Asia. Nonetheless, their demands greatly enhanced the prestige of the caliphate and drew worldwide attention to it.

The Ottoman sultans seemed reluctant to involve the caliphate in the political disputes of distant Asia, Africa, and Central Asia, but they eventually succumbed to the temptation of the opportunity to gain prestige and influence. First the British, and then the embassies from the Muslim lands, alerted the Porte to the extraordinary political appeal of the caliphate and its potential as a tool of foreign policy. Indeed, England used the caliph in the effort to subdue the Muslims of India, to win the submission of Amir Şer Ali of Afghanistan, and to mobilize the Central Asian believers against Russia—all with very scant success. The caliph began to appear as a potential savior to the Muslims of India, Sumatra, and Central Asia living under British, Dutch, and Russian rule, even while some of his own Muslim subjects in the Arabian peninsula still viewed him mainly as a sultan and sought to escape his temporal authority by soliciting European support. Nevertheless, it should be noted that the correspondence between the Porte and various Muslim rulers did not concern itself with reform or the faith but remained confined largely to political issues, namely the preservation of the Muslim state and all it entailed.

In contrast to the political movement for unity initiated from above, the revivalist movements represented a drive for rebirth from below. Often rising in opposition to the established political order, they were preoccupied with maintaining religious integrity and reviving the faith of society. Thus Sultan Abdulhamid II was caught between two powerful Islamic currents, one at the top and the other welling up from below. He attempted to reconcile the two in accordance with his own intuition, interests, and personal preferences, bending as necessary to the pressure of internal and international events. Because he linked faith in the caliphate and the sultanate to faith in the Empire as a whole, the downfall of one inevitably brought the end of the remaining two. These issues will be studied at some length in the next chapters. However, it should be pointed out that both the Muslim rulers seeking caliphal aid and those rejecting it to seek English or French support had one thing in common: namely, recognition of their regional power and the implicit assertion of local interests and identities—that is, an inchoate nationalism.

3

Russia, Islam, and Modernism

The Legacy of the Past

Pan-Islamism and pan-Turkism were born in nineteenth-century Russia as part of the process of nation formation and the rise of nationalism among the Muslims there. Inseparably linked together, the two movements represented an advanced stage in the struggle of the various Muslim communities of Russia for cultural self-preservation, using their intellectual, cultural, moral, and economic resources to reconstruct themselves, inadvertently perhaps, into a series of new sociopolitical entities. It should be noted that Russia's Muslims were among the first to lose their Islamic political structures—that is, the state government that had had guaranteed their Islamic institutions and way of life: Kazan in 1552, Crimea in 1783, the Azeri and Central Asian hanates in 1806–75. It is not surprising therefore that the most widespread and profound movement of modernist reconstruction started in Kazan, Azerbaycan (Azerbaijan), and Crimea, which had ample time to develop a strong local modern network of leaders and reformulate their Islamo-Turkic identity in a new form. The new forces compelled the community to undergo rapid structural and cultural change and prevented the old traditional culture from withering away.

In this context, pan-Islamism–pan-Turkism constituted a modern, national, and secular process of identity formation among Russia's Muslims. It was stimulated by structural transformation, the market economy, and the relative industrialization of the country. Those structural changes in Central Asia, including the settlement of the tribes roaming its vast steppes, came relatively late but nevertheless helped transform the agrarian and/or pastoral Muslim societies into broader economic units and produced a new type of middle class whose intellectuals, the cedidists (jadidists) led the drive for *tajdid* (renewal) or modernization and, ultimately, nationalism.

Although Russia's Muslim modernists may inadvertently have taken the ethnic nationalism of the Orthodox Christians as a model, they also drew from Ottoman modernism the belief that a Muslim society could change and modernize without losing its basic culture and identity. Indeed, the modernization efforts and political events in the Ottoman Empire profoundly affected Russia's Muslims, notably the intelligentsia, who, in turn, politically influenced their Ottoman counterparts. Substantial areas in Russia had once been part of the sultan's realm, so there were surviving historical, cultural, linguistic, and religious ties between the Muslims of Russia and the Ottoman Empire, and later a developing common modernist-rational pattern of thought shared by the intelligentsia, which facilitated the mutual influence.

It is interesting to note that Russia played a major role in diffusing nationalist ideas among Serbians, Bulgarians, and other Balkan Orthodox Slavs under Ottoman rule but largely ignored, or misunderstood, the rise of nationalism among its own Muslims. The czar smugly assumed that the nationalism of the Muslims was a form of regressive religious obscurantism instigated by the caliph-sultan in Istanbul, while his own brand of Orthodox Christian nationalism and pan-Slavism was a progressive and civilizing ideology.

Modernization, including modern education and, ultimately, ties of ethnicity and nationalism, increased awareness of and gave new meaning and direction to a variety of cultural, political, and religious characteristics that the Ottoman and Russian Muslims had shared for centuries.

These facts may induce the reader to believe that the somewhat common historical and cultural background and similar intellectual and political developments among the Ottoman and Russian Muslims converged naturally toward some sort of ideological fusion—that is, pan-Islamism–pan-Turkism—but the appearance is rather deceiving. Pan-Islam–pan-Turkism in Russia developed independently, without much Ottoman input, despite the existence of a variety of religious ties between Istanbul and Central Asia, Crimea, the Caucasus, and the Volga region. Furthermore, pan-Islam–pan-Turkism in Russia and the Islamism of Abdulhamid in the Ottoman Empire were essentially different. Both were integrative nationalist movements of self-defense, and they looked naturally to each other for support; but each one operated and developed separately in its own sphere of activity. They were actually the result of different historical conditions, and they served different purposes, the appearance of similarity and/or collusion between them notwithstanding (see chapter 13).

Russian Expansion into Kazan and Crimea and the Ottoman Response

The Russian encounter with Islam came about very early, as the Moscovy principality fell under the rule of the Golden Horde—the "Tatar Yoke," as the Russians refer to it—of Cengiz han's descendant, Batu han (d. 1255), in the years 1236–40. The Golden Horde or hanate of Kipçak and, subsequently, the successor Kazan state derived their religion (Islam), culture, and civilization from the ancient Bulgar (Volga) Turkic state in the middle Volga and Inner Asia. (The much debated name "Tatar" belonged to a large eastern Turkic tribe conquered by Cengiz han and subsequently was generalized by the Russians to cover the Muslims of Kazan, Crimea, Astrakhan, Sibir, and Bucak [or Budjak], in today's oblast of west Odessa.)[1] The Golden Horde finally fragmented itself into several hanates in the fifteenth century; the central segment became known as the hanate of Kazan (founded by Ulu Muhammad in 1437) and the southern and southwestern as Astrakhan and Crimea, respectively.

By 1475 the Crimean hanate had accepted Ottoman suzerainty in order to forestall Russian occupation, but it preserved the Cengizid dynasty and political and social traditions; only two of its two southeast provinces on the Black Sea came under the direct rule of Istanbul. Then in 1521 the ruler of Crimea, Sahib Giray, in a desperate act, occupied Kazan and in 1523 tried unsuccessfully to make it an Ottoman vassal. Although the Ottomans recognized Kazan as protectorate in 1524, they did practically nothing to defend it. Subsequently, the endless internecine struggle for power, stoked by Russia among the Kazan pretenders to the throne, continued unabated.

Meanwhile the Moscovy principality had freed itself from the ruler of the Kazan Muslims, seemingly developing a world perspective based on a perpetual confrontation with Islam in the process. Russian Orthodox Christianity, which had its origin in the Church of Constantinople that had fallen under Turkish rule in 1453, played its part. After Ivan III married Zoe (Sophie) Paleologa, the niece of the last Byzantine emperor, he established a legal basis to the throne of the vanquished East Roman Empire with an implicit promise of rehabilitating it. Russian respect for the church in Constantinople was formal, for the Russian clergy and nobility looked down upon Byzantium for, among other things, its having accepted the terms of the Council of Florence in 1439 to submit to and unite with the church in Rome. Russia merely used the Byzantine link to justify its expansionist policy as a crusade aimed at liberating Orthodox Christians from the Muslim "yoke."

The anti-Islamic theme entered early into Russian political thought. By 1521 two religious militants, Maxim the Greek, who came from the Turkish lands, and Peresvetov, who was from the West, had written several pamphlets urging the czar to conquer Kazan, baptize the Muslims, and liberate the other Christians from the "oppression of the foreign Turkish Tsar."[2] The most important prelate in shaping Russian thinking about Islam was Metropolitan Makarij (1482–1563), who claimed that Russia was the leading Orthodox Christian nation and its chief responsibility was to expand Orthodoxy at the expense of Islam.[3] He stressed, among other things, the need to liberate the approximately thirty thousand Russian captives taken hostage by Kazan in 1551; the subject of these hostages still is used to inflame Russian feelings against Muslims. Ivan (IV) the Terrible (r. 1530–84), the grand duke of Moscow and the first to assume the title of czar, captured Kazan in 1552. He banished the Muslims from the city, had the main mosque demolished and the church of Kazan built on its site, while distributing much of the land to Russian colonists, the church, and monasteries. A note written by the Muscovite boyars to the Lithuanian magnates and reproduced by Pelenski expresses well Russia's Muslim policy. It is worth quoting at length:

> The Mussulman nation of Kazan which had shed Christian blood for many years and which had caused our Sovereign much annoyance before he reached his mature age, by God's grace, this Mussulman nation of Kazan died by the sword of our Sovereign; and our Sovereign appointed his viceroys and governors in Kazan, and he enlightened this Mussulman abode with the Orthodox Christian faith and he destroyed the mosques and built churches [in their place], and God's name is being glorified now in this city by the Christian faith, and this land obeyeth our Sovereign, and it hath been united with the state of our ruler; and the Kazan Tsar Yadigar Mehmet, and the wives and children of all *oğlans*, princes and noblemen have been brought as prisoners to Moscow. And we praise God for this, and may God also grant in the future that Christian blood be avenged against other Mussulman nations.[4]

Meanwhile, the Ottoman state had conquered Syria and Egypt in the period 1516–18 and, a few years later, extended its sovereignty over the Muslim holy lands in Mecca and Medina. In the process, it assumed the basic obligation to keep open the road to Mecca for all the Muslims who wanted to perform the *hac*, the pilgrimage that is one of the five basic pillars of Islam. The Ottoman sultan also took the title of "caliph," the successor to the Prophet as the temporal head of the Muslim community.

In 1556 Ivan IV captured the state of Astrakhan at the mouth of the Volga river on the Caspian and, unwittingly perhaps, caused the first major Russian-Turkish clash. The Russians blocked the passage of Muslims who used the road north of the Caspian when making *hac* to Mecca. The Muslims promptly called upon the Ottoman sultan-caliph to perform his religious duty to open the road to *hac*.[5] The sultan eventually organized a massive expedition that failed to dislodge the Russians although the pilgrims' passage subsequently was secured through diplomatic means.

After the conquest of Kazan and Astrakhan, the Russian czars engaged in a series of campaigns—punctuated by interludes of tolerance—to convert the Muslims to Orthodox Christianity. A substantial part of the Tatar nobility converted to Christianity, but the masses, with some exceptions, remained loyal to their faith. The Muslim communities in Kazan, Sibir, and Astrakhan developed Islam as part of their folk culture, wherein ethnotribal identity, the faith, and memories of the imperial past as well blended to create the foundations of a modern identity. Indeed, the ideas of the first modernist Muslim thinkers and precursors of nationalism in Russia— Şihabeddin Mercani (1818–89), Nasiri Kayyum (1825–1902), and Ismail Gaspirali (1851–1914)—revolved simultaneously around Muslim and ethnic revivalism and modern education (see chapter 13).[6]

As Russia expanded to the west and the east, it ultimately confronted the Ottomans in their own lands. Moving south, Peter the Great suffered a crushing and humiliating defeat at the battle of Prut (Stanileşti) in 1711. The Ottoman sultan did not exploit this victory, since Istanbul seemed to attach greater importance to the threat posed by the Hapsburg Empire, whose victory at Vienna in 1683 had turned it into the Ottomans' mightiest adversary. The Russian intelligentsia, meanwhile, continued to elaborate the expansionist state ideology and anti-Muslim message. The works of the father of Russian historiography, Nikolai M. Karamzin (1766–1826), and of Nikolai Pogodin (1796–1826) and N. A. Polevoi (1796–1846), for example, are replete with exhortations and justifications for the czar to occupy the lands of the Muslims in both the east and west.[7]

During the second half of the eighteenth century Russia emerged as the most formidable enemy of the Ottoman state and became the principal cause of its disintegration. By playing on the dynastic ambitions of the Crimean *han*s, Russia engineered the independence of Crimea through the Treaty of Küçük Kaynarca (1774); and nine years later it annexed the peninsula, supposedly in order to put an end to the very civil wars it had instigated.[8] Because the Russian annexation was a devastating economic, strategic, and psychological blow to the Ottoman sultans, they made the reconquest of Crimea a top military priority and tried unsuccessfully for the next two decades to reestablish their authority over the peninsula. At the same time, as the Crimean Muslims grew disillusioned with the civil strife caused by their own ambitious *han*s, they came to regard the Ottoman sultans as the only Muslim sovereigns capable of liberating them from Russian rule. In the process, the Crimeans made the caliph, that is the Ottoman sultan, the focus of their loyalty and submerged their ethnic Tatar tribal identity in their rising Muslim consciousness. From 1783 until 1914 a steady flow of migration brought into the Ottoman state (including Dobruca (Dobruja), which became part of Romania in 1878) thousands of Crimeans (as well and some Muslims from Kazan), enabling them to create a fairly large Crimean community on Ottoman soil.[9] (Some Crimean *han*s lived as refugees in the Ottoman state; their tombs are still standing in the obscure village of Subaşi in Thrace, some fifty miles west of Istanbul.)

The Crimean immigrants remained in close contact with relatives in their native land, intensifying these relations after the 1860s, when the traffic between Istanbul and Crimea and Kazan greatly increased and many young people came to Istanbul for study or business or stopped there on the way to and from Mecca.

The Treaty of Küçük Kaynarca had not only opened the way for Russia to take Crimea but also affected the political consciousness of the Muslims in Russia and enforced their attachment to the caliph in Istanbul. The treaty allowed Catherine II (r. 1762–96) to "make representation" to the Porte on behalf of the Orthodox Christian population, most of whom lived in the Balkan *vilayet*s of the Ottoman state. In time, the Russian bureaucracy transformed this favor into a "right" and used it to interfere in Ottoman internal affairs. Even the Ottoman statesman Mahmud Celaleddin paşa (1838–98), a trusted aide of Sultan Abdulhamid who occupied various ministerial positions and wrote probably the best history of the second half of the nineteenth century from an Ottoman perspective, asserted that the treaty gave the Russian state "extensive rights to protect Christianity [Orthodox] in the Ottoman provinces and exert influence over the Wallachian and Moldavian principalities. Thus the Kaynarca treaty became a strong foundation for Catherine II to promote her expansionist aims in the Ottoman lands . . . and in the year 1781 she entered into an agreement with Austria, to which she left Bosnia and Serbia in order to create a Russian government in Greece."[10] Although his view that Russia actually had a "right" by treaty to intervene on behalf of the Christians in the Ottoman Empire is mistaken, Celaleddin paşa expresses the important and widely held Ottoman opinion that Russians were following Peter the Great's injunction to his successors to use every means to expand southward into Ottoman lands.

By the Treaty of Küçük Kaynarca, the czarina returned the sultan's favor, permitting the Muslims of Russia to use the caliph's name in the *hutbe*, the Friday sermon. This might have been a simple act of courtesy on the part of Catherine II, who occasionally befriended Islam and used the *molla*s—religious men of Kazan—to tame the Central Asian nomads, but it had the unanticipated but far-reaching effect of encouraging the Russian Muslims to think that they had a powerful protector in Istanbul. In fact, odd as it may seem, many Muslims came to view the Russian ruler as the Ottoman sultan's "vassal" because he had "ordered" her to permit her Muslim subjects to swear allegiance to himself as their caliph, something they had not done in the past. (The Muslims of Russia continued to mention the caliph's name in their Friday *hutbe* until about 1892, when the czar asked them to formally mention his own name in their Friday prayer.) The inclusion of the caliph's name in a document signed by Russia gave the Ottoman sultan extraordinary prestige as the protector of Russia's Muslims. Recent studies have claimed that the Küçük Kaynarca treaty brought the caliphate into focus and that the story of the transfer of the title by al-Mutavakkil, the incumbent, to Selim I in 1517–18—was forged by M. d'Ohsson, and perpetuated in his writing.[11] (The truth is that the Ottoman possession of the caliphal title is a fact and the Ottoman jurists justified it as the sultan's rightful title as early as the sixteenth century, as shall be explained in due course.) It should be emphasized, however, that while the caliph appealed only to the Russian Muslims' religious loyalty, avoiding thus any divisive reference to their varied ethnic origins, the Russians used the privilege of representing the Balkan Orthodox Christians to appeal to the Orthodox Slavs' ethnic, linguistic, and territorial attachments.

The Russian effort to promote the Küçük Kaynarca treaty into a carte blanche for activities in Ottoman territory was simply a continuation of its anti-Ottoman offensive began as early as 1770, when their fleet ventured into the Mediterranean with the purpose of inciting a revolt among the Greeks. The revolt did not materialize until 1821, however, and after winning independent statehood in 1830, Greece did not side with Russia, causing Moscow's ire, but chose England as its patron. Finally, the European Christian powers' alliance with Muslim Ottomans to defeat Christian Russia in the Crimean War of 1853–56, spurred Russia to make a crucial shift in its foreign policy. Russia decided to rely predominantly on the Orthodox Slavs of the Balkans, namely the Serbians, Bulgarians, and Montenegrins, to carry out its anti-Ottoman offensive. Pan-Slavism thus was born, primarily as a tool of foreign policy, and the Russian czars used the Orthodox Christian Church, which has always been under the control of the government (at least since Peter the Great), to infuse Orthodox Christianity with an ethnic Slavic consciousness and make it a political ideology for mobilizing the Ottoman Orthodox Christians against their Muslim ruler. In using religion as a tool of foreign policy, the czars set up a model that the English, and then the Ottomans, later tried to employ.

The Crimean War and Opening to Europe

The Crimean War and the Paris Treaty of 1856 changed the nature of Ottoman relations with the West and Russia and altered the course of its modernization. First, the war opened the Ottoman Empire to Europe and overnight produced a multitiered revolution in communications. The successful use of the telegraph in that war induced the Ottoman government to string wires countrywide in 1855, thus connecting the remote provinces to the center, strengthening the authority of the central government, and facilitating communications in general. The war also created a unique opportunity for person-to-person contact between the Ottoman Muslims and Europeans, as the population of Istanbul came to know the large numbers of French officers and soldiers stationed there, and Florence Nightingale (1820–1910), the English nurse who established the first modern hospital service, became a legend everywhere.

The communications revolution that started during the war continued with the introduction of modern newspapers, mainly after 1860. Muslims elites throughout the world were able learn about one another, to acquire new knowledge about Europe and the Ottoman state, and to satisfy their growing curiosity about America. Europe was transformed overnight from a perceived enemy into an ally, and then into a paragon of civilization and model of the future.

However, the popular positive view of Europe was not shared by all Muslims. For instance, during the Crimean War, stories circulated in India that Russia had defeated England and was planning to invade the subcontinent and liberate the Muslims. The British subsequently issued a proclamation describing in glowing terms the success of their troops in Crimea and made a special point to stress that the Ottoman Muslim and British soldiers fought side by side. When the Sepoy Revolt in India occurred in 1857, the British persuaded Sultan Abdulmecid (r. 1839–61) to issue a caliphal proclamation urging the Indian Muslims to cease fighting their British masters, and Britain then thanked the sultan publicly, unintentionally acknowledging that the caliph exercised some authority over the Indian Muslims. Many of the Indian Muslims welcomed London's alliance with Istanbul in the Crimean War and even issued a pamphlet eulogizing the success of the sultan's troops in such exaggerated terms that it implied that Muslim, not European, troops had won the Crimean War.[12]

In accordance with the Peace of Paris (1856), Russia pulled out of the Romanian principalities and the south Caucasus, including the fortress of Kars, and agreed to demilitarize the Black Sea. The Muslims of Russia viewed the allied victory over the czar as proof that the Ottoman Empire's association with Europe assured its survival, had revitalized it, and ultimately would enable it to prevail over Moscow and to liberate them; they ignored the fact that the Paris treaty brushed aside their own claims for autonomy and freedom. Russia, in turn, viewed a strong and revitalized Ottoman state as likely to encourage the Muslims of Russia to struggle for freedom and did its best to ensure its security by expanding into the Muslim lands of Central Asia.

Politics and Islamic Doctrine

The friendly relations developing between the caliph and Europe, chiefly England, in the mid-1850s also helped solve several Islamic doctrinal problems related to the Muslims' status under Christian rule and vice versa. The Indian ulema debated at length whether English rule had turned India into *dar-ul harb* literally, (house of war) and made it subject to *cihad*, for according to a classical Islamic doctrine, Muslims could not live under the authority of a non-Muslim ruler. One side, however, argued that India was part of the *dar-ul Islam* (house of Islam), despite British rule, because the caliph had become England's ally and because London did not hinder the Muslims' practice of their faith. Eventually the ulema in Calcutta concurred that India was *dar ul-Islam* and could not be made subject to *cihad*, in effect opposing the populist revivalist view.

The Crimean War also had a lasting psychological impact on the Ottoman Muslims. The war and the Paris treaty, which appeared for a time as Ottoman victories, came after a long series of Ottoman military defeats and humiliating peace treaties with Russia during the period from 1768 to 1839. The ignoble treaty of Hunkiar Iskelesi of 1833 even allowed Russia to station troops in the vicinity of Istanbul to protect the sultan from his own vassal, Mehmet Ali of Egypt. Mehmet Ali, the commander of an Ottoman military unit, was sent to Egypt in 1801–1802 to fight the French, who had invaded, that country in 1798; but he allied himself with local forces and was recognized as viceroy in 1805. He eventually turned against Istanbul and defeated Sultan Mahmud II's armies, occupying Syria and south Anatolia in the years 1831–39. Sultan Mahmud refused to grant autonomy and hereditary rights to Mehmet Ali and ultimately sought the help of Russia, concluding the Hunkiar Iskelesi Treaty, which allowed the czar to station troops on Ottoman territory to stave off Mehmet Ali's occupation of Istanbul. The British intervened—but not before securing lucrative commercial and economic privileges through a treaty in 1838—and together with the Ottoman troops drove M. Ali back to Egypt. The London agreement of 1840–41 neutralized the Hunkiar treaty, but the conflict with Egypt had inflicted heavy military and economic losses and damaged greatly the prestige of the sultan. England became the de facto protector of the Ottoman Empire; Lord Palmerston's doctrine aimed at preserving the territorial integrity of the Ottoman state as the best policy for serving the British interests in India and the Mediterranean, at least for the time being.

The Ottoman victories in Crimea (on land in eastern Anatolia the Ottoman troops were actually defeated) shattered a prevailing belief among many Ottomans that the Empire was headed toward inevitable doom at the hands of Russia. Indeed, the defeat of Russia in the war of 1853–56 apparently gave many Muslims and leading Ottoman statesmen confidence in the political future of the Ottoman state and led them to view England and France and the other European powers not as the enemies of Islam but as saviors and as trustworthy friends and allies. On the other hand, Europe came, temporarily, to view the "terrible Turk" not as living outside the pale of European civilization but as a "noble" creature sharing the values of the West. This new perception was partly the result of an incident that had helped prepare the European-Ottoman alliance for the Crimean War. In 1849 Sultan Abdulmecid, backed by England, refused to capitulate to Russian and Austrian threats of war and surrender the Hungarian and Polish revolutionaries of Louis Kossuth, who had received asylum in the Ottoman territory.[13] Because of his determined stand on behalf of the Hungarian freedom fighters, Europe viewed the sultan as a noble and courageous defender of Western values and ideals and condemned the Russians as oriental despots and oppressors. Actually, the right to asylum was a centuries-old Ottoman tradition, and many European rulers, including Charles XII of Sweden, had benefited from it in the past.

It is essential to emphasize that the de facto Ottoman alliance with Europe in the Crimean War was the first of its kind in the long, troubled history of Ottoman relations with Christian Europe. It had the side effect of neutralizing the argument of the Muslim conservatives, who claimed that friendship—not to mention alliance—with Christian Europe was impossible. The reformist bureaucracy in response cited the new-found friendship with Europe as proving that religious affiliation had ceased to be an active factor in foreign relations. For example, the relative coolness of Istanbul's attitude toward Şeyh Şamil during and immediately after the Crimean War was partly due to the unease of the Porte in supporting the religious-minded militant *murid*s of the Caucasus while its own Muslim soldiers fought side by side with the Christian soldiers of Europe (although religion was not an issue in either case).[14]

The major by-product of the war was acceptance of the Islahat Fermani (Reform Edict of 1856), which brought the Ottoman Empire into the community of "civilized" nations as a subject and a beneficiary of international law. By granting "equality" to the Ottoman Christians, while giving England and France a certain moral mandate to supervise its enforcement, the *ferman* opened a new phase in the internal and external affairs of the Ottoman state.[15] The edict dealt almost entirely with the rights of the Ottoman Christians. The historian Cevdet paşa, who served in the government during the Crimean War, pointed out in a memorandum addressed to the Palace many years later that "[d]uring the Crimean war circumstances required that additional freedom be granted to Christians since the European states had aided the sublime [Ottoman] state. During the reign of the late Sultan Abdulaziz it became imperative to broaden further this freedom."[16]

The equality granted to the Christians did not amount simply to the enlarging of a set of existing rights; it entailed a basic change in the very legal and philosophical foundation of the Ottoman state. "Equality" for Christians would abolish their status as *dhimmi*—protected people of the Book under Islamic law—and subject them to secular regulations borrowed from Europe. The issue already had been debated in the late 1840s when Ottoman-British relations were at their best. Stratford Canning (first Viscount Stratford de Redcliffe, 1786–1880), the intermittent British ambassador to the Porte and a close friend of Sultan-Caliph Abdulmecid, had presented in person a series of requests for granting "equality" to the Christians.[17] The sultan then submitted Canning's requests to a special committee composed of the leading ulema, who debated the issue from 11 to 27 November 1849 and issued a lengthy report, summarized as follows.[18]

The committee dealt first with the question of testimony by Christians concerning crimes (murder in this case) committed by Muslims and concluded that the acceptance of such testimony would contradict the Şeriat; it recommended only that investigators consult the Christians living in the locality where the crime was committed. The committee ruled that abolition of the *ciziye* (head tax) was unlawful, as was its incorporation into other forms of taxation levied on the non-Muslims, but left the final decision on taxation to the government. As to the employment of non-Muslims in government service, the panel, having stated first that all human groups needed and had the right to justice and to freedom from oppression and intolerance and that all the Christians in the Ottoman Empire enjoyed such rights in accordance with the Şeriat, nevertheless, ruled that non-Muslims could not be placed in a position of superiority over Muslims; thus they could not be given government office and be allowed to command the Muslims. For the same reason, the non-Muslims could be conscripted only for military service that did not conflict with the Şeriat, such as serving in musical bands, construction units, and so on. The committee also expressed its full support for any measures that could bring the Christian subjects closer to the government ("Hristiyan tabaanin taraf-i Saltanat-i Seniyeye bir kat daha isindirilmasi") and recommended that they be given certain commercial freedoms in order to secure their loyalty to the state. (The ulema appeared unconcerned about the political consequences of economic power.)

In sum, the report of the committee of ulema demonstrates that the Ottoman religious establishment opposed, on Islamic grounds, some of the major steps England and France proposed in order to achieve the "equality" of the Christians. Although the committee showed great understanding for the sultan's need to establish friendly relations with the European governments and acknowledged that European ideas were bound to affect the Ottoman Christians, it insisted that the Ottoman state could maintain its Islamic integrity only by remaining faithful to the Şeriat. The committee declared also that forced conversion to Islam was totally unacceptable. It advised the government to investigate whether the conversion of some abducted Christian women or of children fleeing the parents' home was voluntary and whether they were aware of the consequences of conversion and suggested that such converts be questioned in front of parents and local people.[19]

The Reform Edict of 1856 swept away all of the 1849 committee's objections: it accepted the principle that the testimony of non-Muslims had equal value to that of the Muslims; it replaced the *ciziye* with the *bedelat-i askeriye*—a tax in lieu military service, from which the Christians were exempted; and it gave non-Muslims the right of employment in government. Subsequently, many non-Muslims, notably Armenians and Greeks, achieved ministerial positions. Often described as a spontaneous act on the part of the sultan, the Reform Edict of 1856 was drafted by England and France with hardly any consultation of Istanbul and was accepted in its entirety by the Porte as a part of the peace arrangements that ended the Crimean War. The apprehension it raised among Muslims was great. Even dedicated reformists such as Reşit paşa thought the edict grossly violated the Ottoman Islamic principles of government. Many Muslims believed that Abdulmecid had deviated knowingly from the rules of Islam to espouse the edict's provisions, while others claimed that Europe had taken advantage of the sultan-caliph's dependence on the West to dupe, or force, him into acceptance of the anti-Islamic measures. In some areas in the Arabian peninsula the caliph's name was omitted from the Friday *hutbe*.[20]

One immediate consequence of the edict was to split the Ottoman Muslim intelligentsia into ideologically opposed groups. On one hand, the modernists, headed by the Palace and a segment of the bureaucracy, believed that the Edict of 1856 was necessary in order to rejuvenate the state and win the friendship of England and France against Russia. The conservatives, or traditionalists, on the other hand, regarded the edict as an astute European-Christian device designed to undermine the Ottoman state from within. According to Ahmed Cevdet paşa, the conservatives occupying important positions in education, justice, and the administration of the pious foundations believed the foreign ministry and its translation bureau had violated the basic principles of the Ottoman government and abused the power and trust placed in them. The modernists insisted that the edict did not undermine the Islamic essence of the government; they asserted that "esasa dokunulmadi" (the essence was untouched), while their opponents claimed that "*devletin esasina halel getirildi*" (the essence of the state was violated).[21] This ideological split between the foreign ministry, regarded as the most Westernized wing of the bureaucracy, and the other ministries has continued in one form or another until today, although in a diminished fashion.

The reforms ordered by the edict soon were translated into economic benefits for the Christians, with far-reaching effects on social stratification, ethnoreligious affiliations, attitudes toward the ruling government bureaucracy, and growth of the commercial sector, which was dominated by Christians. After Sultan Abdulaziz came to the throne in 1861, he played on the conservatives' suspicions and the fears created by the reforms in order to increase his own authority. Although after the death of reformist ministers Fuat and Ali paşas, in 1869 and 1871 respectively, implementation of the Tanzimat reforms came to a standstill, they had gained enough momentum of their own to prevent the restoration of the old status quo. The reforms were seen by many as basically having strengthened the state, and ultimately that was the winning argument. In the process Abdulaziz elevated the caliphate to new moral, religious, and psychological heights in order to legitimize his own autocracy and dominate the Westernist-reformist wing of the bureaucracy.[22]

All these developments had an impact on Russia's Muslims and on their relations with the Ottoman Empire. Some viewed the modernist measures adopted by the Ottoman sultan as resembling the czar's own policy intended to de-Islamize his Muslim subjects, although the attitude of the intelligentsia educated in modern schools was favorable to reforms. However, disenchantment with the ruling authority in both countries increased the appeal of the community and popular movements as the only reliable upholders of Islamic life; the eventual alienation of the community from state had its roots in this situation.

The effects of the Crimean War on Russia's policy toward its Muslim subjects were deep and immediate, for the war showed that the czar enjoyed little loyalty among them. The Muslims in central Crimea actually had collaborated with the Ottoman-English-French forces, while in the Caucasus Şeyh Şamil's lingering muridist rebellion had the potential to incite other Muslims to rise against the czar and jeopardize the security of the Black Sea. Consequently, the Russian government forced Şamil to surrender in 1859, killing a good part of the Muslim population in north Caucasus and uprooting millions of others. Some were resettled in the Kuban plains, but many fled to Ottoman lands. A large group of Crimean Muslims, afraid of Russian retaliation, had already emigrated en masse to the Ottoman lands in 1856, and this migration continued thereafter.

The Paris Treaty of 1856, which blocked the Russian advance into Eastern Europe and demilitarized the Black Sea, gave the Ottoman Empire some breathing space. Russia remained free to preach panslavism among the Balkan Christians, however; and the Middle East and Central Asia, guarding the approaches to India, remained wide open to its expansion. In fact, the worst fears of the British government in India were about to be realized, as the Russians began the occupation of Central Asia.[23] Anticipating a Russian move southward, the viceroy in India began to prepare plans to occupy Baghdad and Basra in order to establish a British presence there;[24] but the Russians had their own fears that the British might use their ally, the sultan-caliph, to foment trouble among the restive Caucasian and Central Asian Muslims.

The Russian conquest of Central Asia opened a new and a decisive phase in the history of Ottoman relations with the area. Expanding capitalism, the introduction of a modern educational system, the rise of a new type of intelligentsia, and the communications revolution were bound to create a new type of Muslim in Russia and Central Asia. In the context of these profound socioeconomic, cultural, political, and psychological transformations, historical ties between the Muslims of Russia and the Ottoman state intensified and acquired new vitality and meaning.

Historical Relations between the Ottoman Turks and Central Asians

The Ottoman Turks' ancestors originated in Central Asia and, as though attracted by a powerful magnet, migrated steadily westward roughly from the eighth century to the end of the fifteenth century. The Mongol occupation of the Middle East and Timurlenk's (Timur, Tamerland; 1336–1405) march into Anatolia not only gave impetus to these migrations but added a particular religious-cultural element to them; in Central Asia, Timur replaced Persian influences with the Turkic culture, language, and political traditions and weakened further the Mongol political influences in Anatolia.

Timur's victory helped the Turkic popular Sufi orders—which he supported—proliferate further in Anatolia and, ultimately, in the Balkans. He recognized Ahmed Yesevi, whose followers or descendants dominated Anatolia, as a major religious figure, creating the magnificent tomb still standing in Yesi (today's Turkistan) in south Kazakstan; and he rebuilt Samarkand as the center of the Turkic-Islamic civilization in Central Asia.[25] Timur, as is well known, invited many leading Muslim scholars from the Middle East, including Şemseddin Cezeri and other refugees of Central Asian origin, to Samarkand. The subsequent increase in communication between Anatolia and Central Asia resulted in the building of new *tekkes* (lodges) to serve the needs of the Central Asian travelers, many of whom were *hacis* to Mecca, and the repair of the existing ones, such as the Turkistan lodge originally established by Abdullah al-Mencek in 1380 at Tarsus. This lodge served the inhabitants of a total of eighty-four Central Asian localities, including Buhara, Samarkand, Duşanbe, Taşkent, Aksu, Khiva, Fergana, Balkh, Kaşgar, and Hoten.[26] The *vakfiye* (founding act) of a second lodge known as Beyce Şeyh, established in 1381 and still active in 1883, offers true geographic information, including distances between towns in the Buhara region in the fourteenth century.[27] Three lodges in Istanbul provided shelter and employment for months, even years, for Central Asian travelers and *şeyhs* who became part of the ulema of Istanbul and acted as lobbyists and representatives of their han in Buhara, Kaşgar, Khiva, and so on.

The Central Asian centers of learning, such as Buhara, Samarkand, and Khiva, supplied teachers of religion and the positive sciences to the Ottoman sultans. For instance, the sons of Sultan Mehmet I (r. 1413–21) were tutored by Mevlana Ahmed (Muhammad bin Arabshah), who was originally from Damascus but received his education in Transoxiana. Later Sultan Bayezid II (r. 1481–1512) was schooled in mathematics and astronomy by two Central Asians, namely Murim Çelebi and the famous Ali Kuşçu (ca. 1420–74), who was a colleague and friend of Timur's grandson, Uluğ bey. Uluğ bey was himself a leading astronomer as well as the ruler of Samarkand.[28] Ali Kuşçu became a close friend of Sultan Mehmet II (r. 1451–81) and was instrumental in establishing an observatory in Istanbul; it was destroyed in the sixteenth century when the scholastic-minded, conservative ulema gained the upper hand in the Ottoman court over the proponents of the practical sciences.[29]

Probably the greatest Central Asian influence was in the field of religion. At least twenty important *şeyhs*, mostly Nakşbandi from Buhara and Samarkand, settled, preached, wrote, and died in the Ottoman state.[30] The Bektaşi order of dervishes, which changed its orthodox character after the death of the founder, also was established by a Central Asian religious man, Haci Bektaş. (The order included the Janissaries, but it was abolished in 1826, the year the Janissary establishment was destroyed; it still has many adherents in Republican Turkey and Albania. Its main lodge, located in the town of Haci Bektaş in central Anatolia, has become today a sort of national shrine, even though it was closed in the early days of the Republic.)

The historical ties between the Ottoman Turks and the Muslims of Russia acquired a political dimension in the sixteenth century. Shah Ismail of Iran turned Shiism into a political ideology and used it to legitimize his expansionist policy against the Ottoman state and the newly established Uzbek (Özbek) state of the Shaibanids. However, Ottoman Sultan Selim I (r. 1512–20) crushed Shah Ismail at Çaldiran, allowing the restoration of Shaibanid power, and consolidated the hold of Sunnism in Anatolia.[31] This may be seen as part of the reason why some Central Asian rulers regarded the Ottoman sultans as having a special position: not only were the sultans the holders of the caliphate and able conceivably to legitimize these rulers' (often usurped) authority, but they also represented the most advanced and successful branch of the Turks. As late as 1713, Seyyid Mehmed Ömer han, the ruler of Hoten, Kazgan, and other areas, asked the Ottoman sultan to send him a letter, a sword, and other symbols recognizing him as the bona fide ruler of his land;[32] and in 1802 Haydar şah, the ruler of Buhara, asked the sultan to recognize him as the *padişah* (monarch) of Turkistan and of lands of Turan, "Turkistan ve Turan-zemin elhabi tahrir kilinmasi."[33]

The information provided above is intended to place the rise of nationalism and pan-Turkism–pan-Islamism in Russia and the Ottoman Empire into a proper cultural, ideological, and historical perspective. First, we see that Islam in Anatolia developed within the context of Turkic ethnic traditions and was nurtured in good measure by Central Asians; although it remained firmly bound to the basic tenets of orthodox Islam, it had a definitely worldly orientation. This feature of Turkish Islam sets it in a class of its own and is basic to the Turkish form of nationalism. Until well into the nineteenth century, when the Central Asians' need for cultural-religious survival and the Ottoman state's search for the means to oppose Russian expansion forced both sides to turn their long-standing relations toward practical political purposes, the ties between them were apolitical. However, the cultural-religious content of those relations eventually provided the raw material both for the nineteenth-century nationalists' theories of nationhood and for the foreign policy makers' propaganda apparatus.

Cevdet paşa, the noted historian and advisor to three sultans, explained in a memorandum prepared at the request of Abdulhamid II that his first mentor and protector, Grand Vizier Mustafa Reşit paşa (1800–58), had made plans for a Central Asian confederation under the direction of the Porte. To consist of Khiva (*Hayve* or *Hive* in Turkish), Buhara, Afghanistan, and the Türkmen (Turkoman) tribes of the area, it would prevent the advance of Russia into the Maverauneher—the area between the Amu Darya and Sir Darya rivers.[34] According to Cevdet paşa, the project failed to materialize because the Porte did not have direct territorial access to Central Asia and because the British, although agreeing that the project suited their own interests, decided to establish the confederation by themselves. Cevdet paşa observed acidly that the "English could not succeed in uniting so many unorganized and backward Muslim governments because such [unity] could be achieved only by the Great Caliphate."[35] To show that the British did not know how to deal with Muslims, Cevdet paşa refers to three British emissaries imprisoned by the *amir* of Buhara and executed a week before a caliphal message asking him to release them reached him. According to Cevdet paşa, the *amir* stated that if the caliphal request had come earlier "the order of the Commander of the Believers would have been obeyed"; in 1863, three

Italian merchants whom he had arrested on suspicion of spying were in fact freed following the sultan's intervention.[36] Elsewhere Cevdet attributed the English failure to organize the Central Asian confederation to their fear of involving the Ottomans in their Indian affairs, and to their overall "selfishness."[37] In effect, Cevdet paşa's memorandum, as well as scores of dispatches in the Turkish archives, indicate that the Ottoman sultan-caliph and his bureaucracy were well informed about the state of the Muslims in Russia and Central Asia but overestimated their own potential to exert influence on them. Nevertheless, Russian fears of a potential Ottoman-British alliance in Central Asia were exacerbated by the many indications of the Central Asians' regard for the sultans.

In the period 1820–50, Russia established several strongholds in what is today central Kazakstan. Then, in 1855 General M. G. Cherniaev moved from Verny (Almaty) to Yesi (now Turkistan), and in May 1865 he took advantage of the rivalry between the *hans* of Kokand and Buhara to occupy Taşkent, the second largest city of the hanate of Kokand. General Kaufmann, the governor of the conquered lands, brought them into one administrative unit in 1867, and named it Turkistan, or Turkestan. This was the first formal administrative unit in history to bear the Turks' ethnic name. One year later, Kaufmann conquered Samarkand and forced the emir (*amir*) of Buhara to accept Russian protection; Buhara remained nominally independent until 1920, however, and the emir sought help from the Ottoman sultan-caliph (and Persia as well). The hanate of Khiva became a Russian protectorate on 20 May 1873, and all its territories east of the Amu Darya river were incorporated into the governorate of Turkistan. Then, after a rebellion led by the former Russian vassal Han Khudaiar was put down in 1875, the hanate of Kokand was annexed and also made part of Turkistan. This annexation was said to be "in accordance with the wishes of the people of Kokand," a formula devised by the czar and used later by the communist rulers.

Besides the obvious strategic benefits to be gained thereby, the Russian conquest of Central Asia has been attributed to Moscow's economic need for raw cotton to meet the demands of its expanding textile industry (imports of cotton grew from 713,000 rubles to over 6 million rubles in the period 1860–64) and for markets for Russian goods. The Russian expansion was planned in detail by the Russian war minister, D. A. Milyutin, with the full knowledge of the czar, who apparently kept foreign minister M. D. Gorchakov in the dark and instructed him to tell the Europeans that Russia had no desire to annex Central Asia. Later, the foreign ministry apologized to the hapless English and French officials, offering the explanation that the conquest resulted from the Russian generals' personal ambitions and their "unauthorized" campaigns into Central Asia.

Ottoman-Muslim Reaction to the Russian Conquest of Central Asia

The Russian mode of conquest, especially the terror used by the czars' generals to keep the Central Asian Muslims subdued, greatly influenced both the local and the Ottoman reactions as well as the native view of the Russians. The fact that a handful of Russian troops endowed with modern arms defeated large but ill-trained Central

Asian armies with their obsolete weapons boosted the Russians' sense of their own intrinsic superiority over the Asians and Muslims. The Russians saw themselves as the representatives of their superior Orthodox faith and of "civilization"—that is, of European ideas and institutions, which they presented as their own. They remained alien to the liberal spirit of the Western civilization they used as a model, however, and borrowed from it only the weapons, military tactics, and other means necessary to defeat, subjugate, and rule their weak Muslim neighbors. The Russian nationalist Slavophiles, who best represented Russian feelings, rejected the West and its civilization altogether, while the Westernists demanded its acceptance in full. The Muslim intelligentsia sided generally with the Westernists.

Because the Russians knew that their domination of Central Asia would erode rapidly if the natives mobilized their vast human resources and acquired modern knowledge, military tactics, and weapons, General Kaufmann, the governor of Turkistan, stifled innovation and change by supporting the ultraconservative clergy and their brand of dogmatic, devotional Islam, leaving the *vakif*s more or less in their hands. Assured of economic support, the official Russian Muslim establishment rallied behind Russia itself and their own autocratic *han*s, thus alienating the modernist intelligentsia, the cedidists. In addition, Kaufmann prevented the Christian Orthodox missionaries from proselytizing among the Muslims, lest they excite the Muslims to rebel and instill new life in a faith the general believed was doomed to atrophy. He established an efficient administration and brought economic improvements that were well received by the local population; but his successors became corrupt and passive, and their rule caused general stagnation in Central Asia, except in some areas brought under irrigation, which were assigned mostly to Russian colonists.

News about the Russian invasion of Central Asia reached the Ottoman public via private letters, accounts of travelers and eyewitnesses, and personal letters sent by Central Asian leaders to the Ottoman sultan-caliph. As early as 1870 the head of the Türkmen tribes in the Buhara and Khorezm regions sent to Istanbul, through a special emissary named Mehmet Murat, a personal letter asking "the caliph [*hilafetpenahi*] to give me and my people protection and help against the Russian expansionist activities."[38] He referred to the Kazaks as "ulus" (nation) and described in colorful language how "numberless Muslims were martyred, taken prisoners and arrested . . . and mosques, mescids, and inns destroyed or transformed into churches. . . ." In the end the writer placed his desperate hopes "first in God and second, in the protector of Islam and the convent of divine grace [*dergah-i ilahi*]." A variety of other letters describe how the Russians used widespread terror to intimidate the Central Asian natives, already demoralized and cowed by the harsh rule of their own leaders, and how, at the slightest sign of unrest, or merely on suspicion, the Russians engaged in mass slaughter of the natives. For instance, the Yomut tribes near Khiva were first charged enormous fines for minor misdeeds and then, when unable to pay, were nearly wiped out, although the tribes had been friendly to the Russians. The defenders at Göktepe in Türkmenistan were killed to the last man.[39]

Soon the complaints by Russia's Muslims began to appear in the Ottoman press. In a letter published in *Basiret*, the ulema of Orenburg, then the major Islamic center for Russian Muslims, complained that "in addition to numerous forms of oppression against Muslims, the Russians are forcing the Muslim women to dress like Russian women," preventing them from marrying before the age of seventeen, and treating the Muslims as though they had already converted to Christianity.[40] In conclusion, the Orenburg ulema informed the caliph that one million Muslims of the area, unable to endure the oppression, planned to migrate to the caliph's lands. Obviously the migration would impose considerable financial hardship on the Ottoman treasury; already numerous Nakşbandi *şeyh*s, accompanied by their followers, had stayed for months in Istanbul as self-invited guests of the caliph.

Basiret became the most widely read newspaper in the Ottoman capital and, largely as a response to the Russian support of the rebels in Bosnia (1875) and Bulgaria (1876), began an anti-Russian campaign. It disseminated (and exaggerated) the news about the situation of the Muslims in Central Asia and described how the Russians strove to degrade the Muslims' way of life. *Basiret* found that Russia's demand for "equality" for the Orthodox Christians in the Ottoman state contrasted sharply with the czar's oppression and discrimination against his own Muslim, Jewish, and Polish subjects. It reported sarcastically how fifteen-year-old Seyyid Mehmet Necmeddin and ten-year-old Seyyid Mansur, the two younger sons of the *han* of Buhara, had been sent to St. Petersburg to enroll in a unit it described as "the detachment of the czar's servants." The same issue of *Basiret* reported proudly that Abdulmelik Töre han, the oldest son of the *han* of Buhara, who "had strong religious convictions" (actually, this meant strong national feeling) and had been exiled by the Russians, preferred to go to Mecca rather than Moscow; in the holy city he met with another Russian victim, the *han* of Kokand.[41] In June 1877, when Abdulmelik han came to Istanbul, he was received by the sultan with great honor and provided the Porte with extensive information about the situation in Central Asia.

Basiret reproduced a series of letters exchanged by the rulers of Gence, Şirvan, and Karabağ (Penah han) in Azerbaycan, proposing to unite their lands in order to oppose the Russian efforts to convert them to Christianity because "all three of us are Muslims and the Russians who have surrounded us are the enemies of our faith."[42] It implied that the Sunni-Shiite division had come to an end and all the Muslims of Russia were one national group. The flavor of *Basiret*'s sensational journalism can be sampled in the following quotation:

"[T]he mountains of Circassia and Daghestan have been colored red by the acts of those savage beasts, who have killed even the children at the breast of their mothers . . . and the cruel actions of the Muscovites in Central Asia has no parallel. The famous historical places such as Khorezm, and Khiva, which prevented the Russian march toward India and kept their independence as Muslim countries for centuries, have been invaded by Muscovites."[43] One may suspect that *Basiret*'s anti-Russian campaign was financed by the British or some other interested party.

The British Islamic Plan for Central Asia

The British, in fact, had developed a plan to use the Ottoman caliphate to stop the Russian advance toward India and to further their policies in Central Asia. After defeating the Ottomans in the war of 1877–78, the Russians appeared ready to resume their march south to India, despite their agreement of 1873, which accepted the river

Amu Darya as the demarcation line between their and the English spheres of influence.[44] The Russians complained formally that England had urged the Muslims of Central Asia to follow the example set by Yakub bey, the ruler of Kaşgar, and accept the suzerainty of the caliph.[45] In fact, believing that the caliphate commanded widespread loyalty among Muslims in Central Asia, the British officers in Istanbul and in India had in 1876 sent London a plan to use the Ottoman caliphate to mobilize the Central Asian Muslims against Russia.[46] *Basiret* reported that England was intent on establishing a Muslim coalition in Central Asia, that London had stopped the Russian advance further into Central Asia, and that it was improving its relations with Kabul and Kaşgar.[47] Basic to the British thinking was the belief that Muslims were guided only by their religious convictions and that authority of the caliph over other Muslim rulers and ordinary believers was so overwhelming as to make them change their alliances and bring them under British rule.

Eventually, the British ambassador to Istanbul, Henry Layard (served 1877–80), and the viceroy of India, Lord Lytton, agreed to ask the Ottoman caliph to send a mission to persuade the Afghan emir Sher Ali to adopt a friendly attitude towards England.[48] Faced with this proposal, the new sultan, Abdulhamid II, consulted various Central Asian dignitaries found in Istanbul at the time, such as Yakub han, the envoy from Kaşgar, and Abdulmelik, the son of the Buharan *han*, as well as several lesser figures, some of whom resided in Mecca but who regularly visited Istanbul.[49] The sultan-caliph hoped to induce the Afghan emir to join the anti-Russian front; however, he specifically wanted help against Russia in the ongoing war in the Balkans and the Caucasus. The English, on the other hand, wanted the caliphal mission to persuade the emir to block a Russian advance southward into India and to adopt a policy "friendly" toward England—that is, to accept British control. Layard and Lytton believed that the emir would comply with the wishes of the caliph in Istanbul, especially if the sultan sent some person of consequence to Afghanistan.[50]

The issue was debated at great length in Istanbul among Ottoman officials and the ulema, all of whom appear to have agreed that a mission to Sher Ali was useful. The statesman Mahmud Celaleddin, who was intimately familiar with Ottoman affairs, wrote in his memoirs that Henry Layard portrayed Sher Ali as being entirely under Russian influence and asked the sultan to send an extraordinary envoy who could "neutralize the Russian intrigues and in view of the great influence of the caliphate on the Muslims avoid future troubles in the land and leave the English state grateful."[51] Thus, in accordance with "plans to incite the Caucasian tribes against Russia, the English request added weight to the idea of expanding the Ottoman influence into Central Asia so as to create there problems for the enemy. . . . England also believed that sending an Ottoman emissary to Afghanistan via India . . . would quell the anti-British sentiment of the Indian Muslims who had collected money and showed friendly attitudes toward the Ottomans."[52] But Kiamil paşa, one of Abdulhamid II's closest advisors and several times prime minister, advised the sultan that England had remained passive to the initial Russian advance into Central Asia but now, fearing that India would be the next target, wanted to involve the Ottoman state in its own anti-Russian policy in Asia. He advised the sultan to remain neutral toward both the British and the Russians, who were courting ethnic groups such as the Armenians and Bulgarians in the Ottoman state to use in their own foreign policies. Azmi Özcan asserts that Abdulhamid approached the English several times, proposing to use his religious influence among the Afghans to the benefit of the British;[53] but this statement must be qualified: it was only after 1878 that Abdulhamid tried to communicate with the Muslims abroad. Previously he had been reluctant to use his caliphal title in international relations. Even after 1878 he was exceptionally wary of using his caliphal authority to incite the Muslims under French and British rule to rise against their masters.

The foreign office in London opposed Layard and Lytton's pan-Islamic project as well as the idea of establishing a Turkish consulate in Peshavar, for it had begun to develop deep misgivings, worrying that increased caliphal influence in Central Asia would spread to India's Muslims. In fact, a group in the foreign ministry was becoming fiercely anti-Islamic, as it began to regard Islam as the main impediment to the British rule of Muslim lands. London finally approved the mission to Sher Ali because the field officers in Istanbul and India had made commitments that they could not abandon without grave complications. The mission, headed by Şirvanizade Ahmet Hulusi efendi, left Istanbul on 12 July 1877. The Indian Muslims gave the envoy, as the caliph's emissary, a warm and tumultuous welcome in Bombay, a reception that greatly displeased the British; so also did the decision of Hüseyin efendi, the Ottoman consul in Bombay, to accompany the mission to Peshavar and, if possible, to install Şirvanizade Ahmet Hulusi efendi as the representative of the Ottoman government there. The Ottoman mission seemed to be much more interested in bolstering the sultan-caliph's influence in India than in serving the English interests in Afghanistan. In an earlier letter addressed to Khan Molla Khan, the *şeyhulislam* of Afghanistan, and carried there by Esseid Hassan Hayrullah efendi, the *şeyhulislam*'s office in Istanbul stated that the Russians knew that the caliph had great prestige and exerted influence among Muslims and, therefore, they were bent on undermining and destroying the caliphate. The *şeyhulislam* (head of the consultative Islamic council) in Istanbul stated that the English so far opposed the liquidation of the caliphate for the sake of their own interest and advised the Afghans that their friendship with London would translate into further English support for the caliph.[54] The letter did not display any sincere friendship for the English but a desire to strengthen the Ottoman state and the caliphate. London, which had begun to develop some apprehension about both Sultan Abdulhamid and the pan-Islamic schemes concocted by its own field representatives, instructed Lytton to avoid any pomp toward the Turkish mission and not to allow it to stay overnight in areas densely populated by Muslims.[55]

Once in Afghanistan, Ahmet Hulusi efendi, the head of the mission, tried to see the *ahun* (religious head) of Swat, but the *ahun* refused to receive him, deeming the Ottoman mission to be "political." Finally, Hulusi efendi reached Kabul on 8 September and was received with great honors, although his actual talks with Sher Ali did not take place until fifteen days later. The Ottoman envoy apparently portrayed his mission as aimed at establishing a Muslim coalition against Russia—not an Islamic union—rather than at mediating between Afghanistan and the British in India.[56] The *amir*, in turn, advised the Ottoman envoy not to take the English side and told him not to "force Afghanistan to enter under English rule." Thus Sher Ali made it clear that national interests and religious solidarity were not the same. According to reports of the meeting, the *amir* acknowledged that religiously the Sunnis of Afghanistan considered themselves a part of the Ottoman state and wished it all success; however, as the ruler of a separate political entity, he had to accept reality for what it was; consequently, he considered both the Russians and the English the enemies of his country, and the English as the less trustworthy of the two. In conclusion, he told the Ottoman envoy to ask the sultan to persuade the English to evacuate Quetta, which they had occupied in 1876. Thus the mission failed. Hulusi efendi did not hurry back to Istanbul; instead, he sent his report by other means and went to Mecca, where he stayed several months. One year later the British abandoned "diplomacy" and attacked Afghanistan. As for Hulusi efendi, upon his return to Istanbul around 1879, he was first appointed judge to Diyarbehir, then exiled to Amasya, where he died and was buried in 1890; Abdulhamid's efforts to keep him out of the capital are significant.

The mission had ended without producing any of the desired results, despite Layard's exaggerated predictions. In order to counteract London's opposition, Layard had written a letter to Lytton in which among other things, he claimed that the sultan was against Sher Ali's alleged dealings with Russia and ready to ask the *şeyhulislam* to issue a letter excommunicating the *amir*. Layard had boasted, "I think I could get him [the sultan] to do anything you might wish with regard to the Mohammadan states and populations of Central Asia, where the sultan as Head of the Faith has still great influence."[57] The story of the mission demonstrates how the British Foreign Office was ready to exploit, haphazardly, and often as the result of individual whim or inspiration, the most basic Islamic institutions and beliefs for its own imperialist ambitions and was arrogant enough to describe its insipid initiatives as acts of high diplomacy.

The Russian czar was concerned that if the sultan-caliph persisted in his effort to expand his influence among the Muslims of Russia, and England backed him in this, the threat of a Muslim uprising could materialize. The desire to neutralize the caliph's potential influence among Russia's Muslims probably played an important part in the Russian decision to launch the war of 1877–78.

The war of 1877–78 provided the first real opportunity for the Porte to attempt to promote a Muslim uprising. The Ottoman Empire was then harboring over three million Muslim refugees from Russia, including important leaders from the Caucasus and Crimea, who had fled during the period from 1856 to 1876. Many of these leaders longed to return to their homelands, for they had left behind wealth and relatives with whom they communicated frequently. The Porte hoped to use the Caucasian leaders to incite their tribes still residing in Russia to rise against the czar. With great publicity, the older son of Şeyh Şamil, Mir Muhammed, was appointed divisional general and placed at the head of the Erzurum corps stationed on the Caucasian front. Hasan bey, one of the chief Abkhazian leaders, who had informed the Porte that he could easily incite the Circassians to rebel, was sent to join the units stationed in Batum on the eastern coast of the Black Sea, and the navy was instructed to help him. The Porte also decided to make use of one Ali efendi, who had come to Istanbul some years earlier as an envoy of the Dagestanis (Şeyh Şamil's followers). He had asked then for "permission from the caliph of the Muslims" to engage in a *cihad* against the Russians.[58] In 1877, after he had renewed his request and received permission through an imperial *ferman*, along with considerable money, Ali efendi went to *cihad* in

Dagestan. Mehmed Rahim efendi, a former member of the ulema in Orenburg and a tribal chief of the Kirghiz (Kazaks of today), asked for a similar *ferman*; but he was given only a letter signed by the *şeyhulislam*, lest the Russians apprehend him and implicate the caliph-sultan in these anti-Russian activities.[59] The famous General Musa Kondukov, who had given up his commission in the Russian army and then, in an act of solidarity, immigrated with twelve thousand of his Chechen conationals to the Ottoman Empire, was placed in charge of a large detachment and, along with other Caucasian notables, landed in Sokhumkale (Sukhumi).[60]

The result of all the Porte's effort was not very encouraging. Although the port town of Sokhumkale in Abkhazia was conquered, and the Circassians, as well as some of Şeyh Şamil's Dagestanis, rebelled and inflicted losses on the Russian army, the victory was short lived. Unfavorable terrain prevented the Ottoman troops from advancing beyond the outskirts of Sokhumkale.[61] Toward the end of 1877, the Russians quelled the rebellion, then executed hundreds of local leaders and exiled thousands of rebel followers to Siberia, thus reducing further the size of the Muslim population in the Caucasus. Even the Dagestanis, who were well experienced in guerrilla warfare, did not fare better. Faithful to their democratic traditions, the Dagestanis had elected as leader Abdurrahman efendi, one of Şeyh Şamil's heirs (*halife*), only to have the Russians capture and execute him. The resistance to Russia continued, but failure of the organized rebellion taught the incumbent sultan, Abdulhamid, a good lesson.

The plans to foment a Muslim uprising in Russia had been initiated by the bureaucracy, not by the sultan. There was a long list of reasons against it: the great distances separating the Tatar, Kyrgyz, and so on from the Ottoman Empire, the predominantly nomadic character of the tribes and their interminable internal quarrels, the lack of weapons and unity, and the like, but this was brushed aside.[62] When the issue was put before Abdulhamid, he not only was very hesitant to endorse it but even advised his ministers not to call for rebellion because of the great harm and suffering the participants were likely to incur at the hands of the Russians if the initiative failed. Abdulhamid had not then consolidated his authority, however, and so could not effectively oppose his ministers (the reformists-nationalists were still in power), who went ahead with their scheme. They, therefore, were the ones who issued the proclamation describing Russia as the enemy of Islam, out to put an end to the Ottoman state and asking for the Muslims' help.

The Ottoman bureaucracy had tried unsuccessfully on its own to emulate the Russian use of the Orthodox Christians against the sultan. Having seen the Russians use religion and then pan-Slavism with deadly efficacy as ideological weapons, the Porte thought it could do the same; but it was a haphazard undertaking, ill prepared and not grounded in the understanding of the transformation taking place in the mind and society of Russia's Muslims. Russian and Soviet scholars have in turn misunderstood the nature of these abortive movements; they have labeled them all, including pan-Islamism, as reactionary religious uprisings engineered by Istanbul and London, rather than seeing in them the beginnings of a struggle for political and cultural emancipation. Occasionally there is a glimmer of understanding among them. For example, a rather lengthy and, at times, insightful article on pan-Islamism (written in 1911 and dealing with the Young Turks) described all the Muslims as being one nation, as the

Koran ordered. It stressed the view that among Muslims, ethnicity and religion are fused into each other but also stated (wrongly) that the pan-Islamic movement was well organized, that it had several centers and councils, and that it was anti-Christian and anti-European.[63]

Conclusion

Ottoman relations with the Muslims of Russia has a centuries-old history, and until the nineteenth century they were predominantly religious and cultural. Most of the Muslims of Russia shared the same faith as the Osmanli (Ottoman) Turks and were Sunnis, and most of them belonged to Turkic groups and spoke dialects of that language. Until the twentieth century, when the nationality policy of the Soviet regime and language reform in Turkey engendered a variety of often mutually unintelligible "national" languages, travelers from Central Asia, Kazan, Azerbaycan, and so on, found no difficulty in communicating with the Turks. It became a ritual for Muslim pilgrims from Russia, going to or returning from Mecca, to spend considerable time— even several years—in Istanbul. In fact, many of the pilgrims considered the pilgrimage to Mecca incomplete if they failed to visit Istanbul, to pray and preach in its mosques and discuss there the issues of the day. For those Central Asians, the divine hierarchy seemed to consist of God, the Prophet, the sultan-caliph, and then the rest.

There was little variation in the nature of these historical ties between Central Asian Muslims and Ottoman Turks and their political consequences were limited, until modern patterns of social stratification, education, and communications gave them a new political meaning and scope in the nineteenth century. With these changes, there developed a degree of ideological rapprochement between the Russian Muslim elites and those of the Ottoman Empire, and Islam took on a unifying role; but the role differed according to each Central Asian country's circumstances. At the same time, the changes transformed ethnic, tribal, and linguistic affiliations and made them the basis of a new type of political identity that came to, or was made to, conflict with the older religious identity (see chapter 13).

4

The New Middle Classes
and the Nakşbandia

The Genesis of the New Classes

The rise of the new middle classes played a key role in the recasting of Islamic thought, in the modernization of the Islamic societies, and in spurring the involvement of the community in political action. This rise was either accompanied or preceded by the gradual globalization of the capitalist economy and the spread of private land ownership, which undermined the economic foundations of two key Islamic institutions, the *imaret* and the *vakif*. In the wake of capitalism came the occupation of most peripheral Muslim lands by England, France, Russia, the Netherlands, and Italy, although the center—that is, the territorially reduced Ottoman Empire—maintained its political independence. Within Ottoman territory, the passage of state lands to private individuals diminished greatly the economic leverage of the government over the countryside and allowed the community to gain power under the leadership of the new classes—many of whom derived their power and influence from land ownership. By inadvertently contributing to the transformation of the community into an informal political constituency, European occupation and economic influence thus provided the middle classes with a political-economic foundation for promoting their vision of society, culture, and progress and recasting tradition, Islam, and community into a "modern" form.[1]

These new Ottoman "classes" were not classes in the Marxist sense of the word but economic-minded social estates with a strong religious consciousness and liberal economic tendencies. Readily coming together against real or perceived enemies, they displayed little cohesion once the danger disappeared. The largest wing of these middle classes, Muslim and Christian, consisted of people concentrated mostly in agrarian towns or port cities and the fertile valleys and communication hubs of their hinterlands. The agrarian towns came to be dominated by Muslims, while Christians constituted the upper economic group in the port cities and even in some interior cities, such as Damascus, Bursa, Kayseri, and Edirne, occupied influential positions, some being descendants of traditional aristocracies, local notables, and the like. The new Muslim middle classes deserve a profound analysis, with a focus on their communal role.

Lately some scholars appear to have accepted the seminal importance of the land tenure system in shaping the social and political structure of Muslim societies. Hanna Batatu, after citing a number of factors, such as the expansion of communication and growth of towns, claims that "property also assumed a greater significance as a basis of social stratification and in the scale of power," but he adds that it never came into full play because of the British.[2] In Iraq before the revolution of 1958, some 38.8 percent of the land was *tapu*—that is, state land in the possession of private individuals who operated it as their own property, although the title was still nominally with the state. Haim Gerber more recently has stated that the "significance of agrarian institutions has been greatly underestimated" in studying the social changes in the Middle East.[3] European (including Russian) occupation put an end to the rule of the *hans*, emirs, and sultans who for centuries had legitimized their own authority and control of economic resources by relying on the state's supremacy, which they equated with the "Islamic" order of their societies. The established ulema often legitimized the supremacy of the state, thus bolstering the tyranny of the sultans and emirs, and seemed to help perpetuate the existing social and political status quo and the society's material and intellectual stagnation. Control of land helped maintain the status quo.

Foreign occupation destroyed most of the traditional Muslim states, and thus deprived the old elites of their institutional political leverage over the community, leaving the community without the "protection" of the state but free to assert and defend its own Islamic identity and interest, to seek religious and cultural salvation by relying upon its own human and spiritual resources. The community became the source of power for the mobilization welling up from below, as the popular orders, notably the Sufis, increased their following and extended their influence into the urban areas.

Many high-ranking members of the traditional religious establishment sought an accommodation with their foreign political masters, acting as intermediaries between the faithful and the authorities, even though the bond between the community and new European "state" was without the old Islamic essence. Other members of the old religious establishments, usually the lower-ranking ulema or their descendants cast their lot with the community, providing political leadership and reinterpreting Islamic writings in line with their rational and populist orientation. The developing struggle between the traditional establishment and the new classes for the control of the community most often revolved around Islam and land.

Because the Ottoman state maintained its formal political independence and historical continuity and controlled the Islamic holy sites, it had the key Islamic credentials to coopt the new middle classes into its service to "modernize" and be "modernized" by them without seemingly open violation of the faith and culture. The government could claim that it was maintaining the Islamic character of the state-society while, shielded by the legitimizing effect of this claim, it undertook far-reaching reforms, even in the face of mounting criticism that the Tanzimat (1839) and, especially, the Edict of 1856 had undermined the traditional Islamic character of the state. Islamism allowed Sultan Abdulhamid not only to maintain the Tanzimat reforms but also to enlarge greatly the scope and depth of modernization while appearing to maintain the state's Islamic policy and character. The Ottoman middle classes came intellectually and politically into their own primarily during Abdulhamid's reign, as the Muslims enjoyed some support from the sultan and, thanks to the rapid expansion of land privatization, the increase in agricultural production, and the growth of the cities, began to move slowly into the trade and manufacturing sectors.

In the new social-cultural context, the function of the modern educational system and the role of the intelligentsia in the Ottoman state acquired new importance. The idea of catching up with contemporary civilization, or "modernization," became the dominant ideology of the Ottoman elites—even though they were split into groups of modernists, conservatives, and traditionalists—and of the state and even of Islam itself. Although many Ottoman intellectuals were the children of the new middle classes or notables (*ayan* and *eṣraf,* as they were called locally) and were educated in modern schools, often built by their parents, they showed a marked lack of class consciousness—in the Marxist sense—and failed to acknowledge the economic motive of their politics. This attitude derived mainly from the intelligentsia's identification with the ruling order represented by the state; initially most became members of bureaucracy and because of this, asserted the old Ottoman elitist claim that the leader was endowed with special qualities not shared by the masses and served a state that was above mundane interests and dedicated to justice. In fact, however, practicality and pragmatism had always been the hallmarks of the Ottoman conduct of state affairs, and this characteristic was reflected in the intelligentsia's behavior once in power, regardless of what they preached in private or when in opposition to the government. The formal continuity of the Ottoman state, despite the change in its essence, had extraordinary impact in containing the effects of socioeconomic change and popular religious movements. This permitted the rise of the new middle class, which it could mobilize around a "national"—that is, Islamic—axis and give modernization a certain legitimacy and popular acceptance that made it relatively successful, democratic, and lasting in the Turkish state.

In sum, one can state that, in a broad sense, the success of the Turkish modernization and its popular acceptance was due to internal social growth that produced a middle class that—with state intervention at times—learned to harmonize its Islamic culture and ethics with change and some Western modes of life. The pronounced worldly, or *dünyevi,* attitude of this class both in thought and attitude, often described as materialism, was explained, justified, and criticized in Islamic terms until the advent of modern politics. The religious order of the Nakṣbandi played an important role in the Islamist modernization of this new middle class.

The Economic Bases of the New Middle Class: Land Tenure, Private Property

The gradual transformation of the state lands into private property and the de facto control of the *vakif* properties by the Ottoman state had a crucial effect on the rise of a new Muslim middle class. Until the middle of the nineteenth century the Ottoman government controlled most of the economic resources, particularly the land, through its intensively institutionalized and experienced patrimonial bureaucracy. Just as that bureaucracy could use its political power to increase agricultural revenue and direct the economy, it could also, in the process, reshape the society by redefining its own place and function.

The economic basis of the Ottoman Empire, like that of practically all other Muslim states, was agriculture, with most of the cultivable land—in some areas 60 to 80 percent—being *miri*, or state land. Under the traditional system, the *sipahi*s (cavalrymen) had the land in fief (*timar*), collecting the tithe (*öşür*) for the state and for their own salaries. However, the need for more revenue from the land forced the government to amend this system, moving away from the bureaucratic control and management of agriculture toward a system that encouraged individual involvement and sharing in agricultural production. The government began to rely increasingly on the local notables, auctioning off the right to collect taxes and to distribute land to individual cultivators. Thus the notables gained considerable wealth and influence in their respective communities, often in collusion with the top administrators of their districts, sometimes against the central government.

At the same time, the pressure for commercialization of agriculture was increasing, for commodities sold at market prices in the internal free markets yielded higher returns than crops delivered to the state at predetermined prices.[4] Furthermore, the intensified trade with Europe in the eighteenth century increased the drive for the commercialization, bolstering the desire of the land cultivators and tax managers to achieve administrative autonomy and greater control of the land by turning it into private property. Finally, the wars with Russia and Austria in the period 1768–1812 weakened the authority of the central government and allowed the notables (*ayan*s), many of whom were tax collectors, or the administrators, to establish themselves as de facto masters of the land and rulers of their provinces. In 1808 the united *ayan*s ousted the incumbent conservative Sultan Mustafa V (who had replaced the reformist Selim III) and placed Mahmut II on the throne. Then the *ayan*s signed the Sened-i Ittifak (Pact of Alliance), under which the central government recognized as hereditary their rights over the state lands they controlled, and they installed one of their own chief leaders, Mustafa paşa, the *ayan* of Rusçuk, as vizier (i.e., prime minister). The *ayan*s were not "feudal lords" or "usurpers of public property," as Ottoman-Turkish official historiography has branded them. They were, in fact, the precursors of the new middle class that began to fight the bureaucracy for control of land (the economic base of the state's political power) and engendered many of the ideologies of the reform movement in the Ottoman state, including Islamism and nationalism. The sultan and his bureaucrats were the actors who carried out the reforms, but the middle class was the true force, whether the impetus was its own or provided by certain sympathetic bureaucrats, that changed the Ottoman political system from inside. Unlike the upper commercial group, consisting mainly of Greeks and Armenians who served the European economic interests, the agrarian middle class was predominantly Muslim (although the Christians in the Balkans achieved a degree of parity). While the rise of the agrarian middle class affected the economic bases of the emerging social order, the modernist traditionalism of that class affected the structure and philosophy of the surviving old *ilmiye* (ulema) and the new intelligentsia, causing them to split into several groups that often opposed each other on the issues of change, modernization, Islam, and nationalism. In general, the culturally conservative and traditionalist agrarian middle class provided strong support for a modernism of its own brand as well as for Islamism; thus to dismiss the agrarian elements of this new class as "conservative," "traditionalist," or "reactionary" is to ignore the crucial role it played in shaping the modern Ottoman and contemporary Middle East sociopolitical order. Its chief adversary proved to be the state, which the modernist bureaucracy had captured, although the two groups' fundamental views on modernity were not much different from each other.

The key issue dividing the agrarian middle class from the entrenched bureaucracy was the question of government control: the bureaucracy and the sultan wanted to maintain everywhere the supremacy of the center, which guaranteed their own privileged position as a ruling social class. It is this desire to maintain the superiority of the state and themselves as its social basis that inevitably brought them to focus on the control of the land and the economy, which the bureaucracy had refined to perfection during centuries of practice. Thus, the classical battle between centralization and decentralization in the Ottoman state involved not only struggle for political power, as in other empires, but also a fight to control the economy (mostly land) and the culture (religion) of society.

The agrarian groups were not then aiming to achieve political control of the state but rather to *redefining its functions* to make it service-oriented and aware of local needs and the communal good. This exceptionally complex conflict between the state and the agrarian groups continued to gain momentum during Abdulhamid's reign, the Young Turks era, and the Republic and continued to revolve in general around the state's control of the land and the economy. It was responsible in good measure for the rise of democracy in Turkey (which, incidentally, must be judged according to its birth conditions and aspirations rather than solely according to its conformity to general principles of industrial democracy). Suffice it to say that party politics in the Young Turks era was concerned to great extent with statism and free economic enterprise and that the first meaningful opposition to one-party rule in the Republic was organized in 1945 by a group of landowners, headed by Adnan Menderes, who rebelled against the Land Reform Act that intended to nationalize land estates greater than five hectares. The opposition organized itself into the Democratic Party in 1946, and four years later won the elections and opened the era of parliamentary democracy in Turkey. The success of the economic middle class was crowned by Turgut Özal's election to the presidency in 1983, an event that also marks Turkey's first genuine effort to establish a truly broad economic, social, and political democracy.

The Coming of the Age of the Ottoman Middle Class: Socioeconomic Conditions and Political Attitudes

Sultan Mahmud II (r. 1808–1839) abolished the Pact of Alliance of 1808 and, after 1815, liquidated the chief *ayan*s, who had forced him through his grand vizier, Mustafa Alemdar paşa, the chief of the Rumili *ayan*s, to accept what the court described as the "shameful act." In 1831, he abolished the remaining but completely dysfunctional *timar*s, the land fiefs that had been the backbone of the traditional system.

After his brief but utterly unsuccessful experiment with a centralized tax system, Sultan Mahmud II was forced to revert to the old Ottoman system of *havale*—that is, the use of civilian intermediaries (*multezim*s), or tax farmers. Because the centralization policy of the government, often carried out by force, had liquidated many old feudal lords and *ayan*s in Bosnia, Iraq, and Syria, their old networks in the towns now reemerged under the leadership of rank-and-file civilians, who acted as agents of the government in administering state land and collecting taxes, but without the stigma, promoted by the government, attached to the *ayan*s. This new social group, a communal elite, was called *eşraf* (notables), and comprised individuals of local prominence in the mid-size rural towns. The administrative reforms of 1864 and 1870 made these towns district (*kaza*) centers, headed by officials appointed from the center, and created provincial administrative councils. These councils were staffed mainly by the local notables, who thus gained official recognition. The councils, in 1877 and 1878, elected to the Ottoman lower house deputies who provided the first civil opposition to the central government. Political representation was thus de facto associated with decentralization.

Political developments in the international field also promoted the economic ascendancy of the new agrarian middle class. The Treaty of Adrianople (1829) allowed Wallachia and Moldavia, which had produced and sold predetermined agricultural commodities to the Ottomans at set prices, to sell their commodities at market prices to the Hapsburgs and other buyers abroad. The ensuing shortage of food on the domestic markets forced the Ottoman government to use every possible means to increase agricultural production in its remaining provinces. Liberalized control of state lands then induced a fairly large number of people to enter into agriculture and indirectly stimulated the rise of agricultural entrepreneurs.[5]

The liberalization of the Ottoman economy reached milestones in its commercial treaties with England signed in 1838 and 1861. These abolished many of the restrictions imposed on internal trade, for example, the transport of agricultural commodities from one province to another without government permission. The treaties reduced tariffs and opened Middle Eastern markets to the manufactured goods of England, which could be purchased mainly by selling agricultural produce. The result was growth in the number of individuals engaged in agriculture and in the trade of agricultural commodities, which increased the relative influence of the small towns and their notables. At the same time, the ports used for exporting agricultural goods grew rapidly in size, as did the middle-sized agrarian towns that became retailing centers for imported goods and emporia for agricultural commodities destined for export.

A massive influx of millions of immigrants from Crimea, the Caucasus, and the Balkans in the 1856–78 period and afterward added new cultural and social dimensions to the structural changes in the Ottoman economy. These migrants were settled on land given to them as private property and became additional producers of agricultural commodities.

The Land Code of 1858 (Arazi Kanunnamesi) was the first milestone in the movement toward legalization of private land ownership. It was preceded by the Tapu Law of 1847, which was designed to encourage individuals to cultivate state lands that were lying fallow (because of bureaucratic red tape and insecurity) by giving cultivators increased rights. However, the enforcement of the law of 1847 was left mainly in the hands of the local notables, who used it to consolidate their own holdings. The Land Code of 1858 was enforced directly by the government officials and was followed by another Tapu Law in 1859. (*Tapu* today means the deed or property title.) Aimed at improving the economic situation of the peasantry, encouraging initiative to increase production, and codifying more systematically the state's title to the land, it side-stepped the Ottoman agriculturalists' longing for the complete privatization of land and freedom of enterprise. When the state faced a choice between holding tight to its legal title to land and the need to raise more tax revenue through agricultural production, however, it opted for the latter. The Land Code of 1858 was applied mainly in Anatolia, Syria, and Iraq, and somewhat less in Rumili, where the land had already become largely privatized.

The circulation of land in the economy proved to be lucrative. In Iraq (Baghdad), for which we have some hard data, the government collected from *muacele* (down payment made at the time of registration of uncultivated lands in the name of an individual) 299,149 kuruş, or 16.8 percent of the total revenue in March 1869; 2,488,649 kuruş, 63.2 percent of the total revenue in April; and 1,514,181 kuruş in June of that year.[6] Tribes were given land at nominal, or no, fee, the tribal chief often being designated as landowner. The government of Iraq, especially under Mehmet Namik and Ahmet Mithat paşa, parceled out and registered in the name of private individuals all uncultivated land; individuals with valid prior claims were recognized as being entitled to *ukr*—that is, a share of the produce. Although the registrations were stopped in 1883, the land nevertheless continued to change hands. Finally, under Sultan Abdulhamid in 1897, the government amended the Land Code so as to make the possession of state lands almost identical to ownership of them.

The privatized land remained mainly in the hands of Muslims, perhaps an unintended result of the Ottoman government's use of its authority and the laws at its disposal. Foreigners were officially allowed to own land beginning in 1867, but, except in a few places, the provincial bureaucracy worked hand in hand with the local gentry to obstruct the transfer of land to non-Muslims and foreigners. The settlement of the Balkan and Caucasian Muslim migrants in Bulgaria, portions of Serbia and Dobruca, and in Anatolia, where they were recognized as owners or quasi-owners of the state land, helped augment the number of the landowning Muslims.

The emerging Ottoman middle class almost immediately split along ethnic and religious lines into Muslim and Christian groups, first in the Balkans and then, to a lesser degree, in the Fertile Crescent, primarily because the Ottoman state proved unable to maintain the classical social estates and their segregation. The Serbian revolt of 1801, which led to the autonomy of the principality in 1815, started as a peasant reaction to the usurpation of their lands by the *sipahi*s and Janissaries, who seemed now to prefer the security of land ownership to the vagaries of government service and inflation.[7] The Ottoman government sought to control its own officials by seeking the support of the Serbian Christian peasantry, arming them while granting them property rights over the state land they cultivated. Beginning in the 1820s a large number of Balkan Christian peasants, notably in Bulgaria, became owners or quasi-owners of the state land they had worked for generations as tenants.[8] The Tanzimat Edict of 1839 promulgated the idea of "equality" and guaranteed the individuals' rights—especially property rights—with the express purpose of assuring Christian peasants that their land would not be taken away (and in the hope that they would not rebel).

The Reform Edict of 1856 speeded up the cultural, political, and administrative emancipation of the Balkan Christians and reinforced the growing power of their middle classes, while alienating the Muslims from both their own government and their Christian counterparts. The edict was, to a large extent the work of Stratford Canning, the representative of the new Protestantism, who had a very low opinion of Islam and of the Orthodox Christian Church, which he regarded as the tool of Russian foreign policy. In contrast, he considered the emerging Christian merchants and intellectuals educated in the modern schools an alternative to the archconservative Orthodox clergy and a group that, being intellectually and philosophically close to Europe, could serve British economic interest. Some Marxist historians believe the rise of the Christian middle class stemmed from a calculated effort by the British to create an intermediary commercial group between themselves and the natives.[9] It should be noted that the Ottoman Jews benefited less than the Christians from the "equality" brought by the Reform Edict of 1856, entering the modern economic process only toward the end of the century.[10] In any case, the British and French did help train a class of reliable local Christian middlemen—mostly Greeks, Bulgarians, and Armenians—who succeeded in assuming control of the Ottoman external trade, which Europe promoted and which the Ottoman government desired avidly in order to bolster its revenues and meet its constantly rising expenditures. Once they freed themselves from the shackles imposed by their own traditional ecclesiastics, the new Christian elites found themselves, by virtue of their history, social organization, and international protection, as well as their mastery of foreign languages, in a strategically favorable position to benefit from the opportunities created by the market economy and the contact with Europe.[11]

The Christian intelligentsia that arose mostly from the commercial groups and the middle classes took Europe as the ideological model for their nationalism, although the essence of their nationalist thought derived from their own communal-religious culture, including epics of heroism and bravery that mixed reality and myth.[12] The Ottoman government tried to create a balance to the trade supremacy of the Christian middle class by creating a group of Muslim merchants known as Hayriyye Tüccari and then sought to limit the number of *beratli tüccar* (licensed merchants) who worked under the protection of European powers, but it was not successful in this.

The economic and social gulf separating the rapidly growing Christian middle class from its Muslim equivalent widened after 1856 and took on distinct ideological overtones. The Muslims viewed the "equality" brought to Christians by the Reform Edict of 1856 as giving them a freedom of economic activity that was implicitly denied to the Muslims, who did not have a European protector to wrest rights for them from their own government. The Muslims expressed their resentment against the "privileged" status conferred on Christians by the Edict of 1856 in the form of nationalist-Islamist outcries. The Europeans considered this outcry a rejection of Europe and its civilization. The writings of the Young Ottomans (the precursors to the Young Turks), who represented the first organized modern movement of opposition, contain a great variety of complaints related to the economic favors granted to the Christians after 1856. Unfortunately, this side of Young Ottoman thought has been largely ignored by scholars, who have dealt with their ideas outside of their social context.

Immigration and Its Political and Social Effects

The Muslim-Christian ideological split grew wider as masses of Muslim migrants poured into the Ottoman Empire from the Caucasus and the Balkans.[13] Attributing their plight to the discrimination they had suffered because of their Muslim faith, the migrants discovered that the Christians still living in Ottoman lands were relatively prosperous and enjoyed—with European support—rights that the Christians had been denied to Muslims in their old states. The Muslims from the Balkans and Russia increased the Ottoman Muslim population by at least 40 percent in a span of twenty years, from 1862 to 1882, but the country easily absorbed the influx because of the availability of good agricultural land. In fact, the settlement of migrants produced a minirevolution in agriculture, resulting in the introduction of new technology, such as advanced iron ploughs, new crop varieties, and facilities for transportation, including railroads. The resulting urbanization, the growth of agriculture, and the proliferation of new occupations and technological change produced a small social revolution in the period 1860–1900 and underscored religious differences. The change was epitomized by the two-sector development of Istanbul: there arose a relatively modern (mainly Christian) sector—Pera or Beyoğlu—where one could find practically all of the amenities of Europe, next to a dilapidated old city inhabited predominantly by Muslims and some Greeks and Armenians clustered around their historical patriarchates.[14]

The migration and settlement policies of the Ottoman government in the nineteenth century played a crucial role in the rise and cultural-ideological orientation of the Muslim middle class. The migrants consisted not only of rank-and-file individuals but also of traditional aristocratic families, tribal chiefs, religious leaders, and even military officers, some of whom had served in the Russian army. Moreover, those coming from the Danube province (today's northern Bulgaria, Dobruca, and eastern Serbia) had already experienced rapid modernization, for which their province had been a pilot area in the 1860s under Mithat paşa. All these upper-class immigrants, dispossessed of their wealth in their countries of origin, sought new occupations to assure themselves a decent income and position in the new society, thus giving the Muslim middle class new impetus and a distinctly international Muslim coloration. Numerous immigrant leaders had been part of the local Muslim aristocracy, a rank that they tried to maintain through education and economic achievement.

The new Muslim agricultural entrepreneurs and small merchants (local retail trade was in the hands of the Muslims, including the immigrants) abided formally by the established traditional codes of behavior and family affairs, but their thinking was becoming interest-oriented. They retained their conservative and traditionalist outlook in matters of culture, faith, and social relations, but on economic matters they espoused liberalism and local autonomy. Specifically, the Muslim agrarian middle class opposed state interference in agriculture and favored the expansion of private property ownership, intensive economic activity, and material progress, and it wanted the institutional reforms necessary to achieve these ends. Often the Nakşbandi *şeyhs* provided an Islamic justification for these worldly demands, notably for private property, which was regulated by Şeriat; many Nakşbandi *şeyhs* claimed the privatization of state lands and the regulation of *mülk* (private property) by Şeriat was more in conformity with Islam than the state-created and administrated *miri* system. The *miri* lands were basically subject to government regulation only and, hence, outside the jurisdiction of Şeriat.

Indeed, by the time Abdulhamid came to the throne in 1876 the rising Muslim agrarian middle class had become aware of the value of wealth and also of the pragmatic modern education, which they regarded as supplementing their power and influence both in the community and government. Muslim notables, both Turks and Arabs, urged the government to establish mid- and upper-level modern schools and to provide teachers: the notables themselves often furnished the sites and funds for the building and maintenance of the schools. Thus, the traditional *medreses* (religious schools) suffered a loss of popularity, while the modern (*rüşdiye, idadiye*) and professional schools established by the government, mostly during Abdulhamid's reign, were laying the educational basis for the creation of an intelligentsia from the countryside. This group was well able to articulate local grievances, both economic and cultural, against the political center. Martin Strohmeier pointed out that Shayh Husayn al-Jisr in 1880 founded a national school in Tripoli the express aim of which was "to provide an Islamic and 'national' educational alternative to foreign schools by combining religious and secular subjects."[15]

There was, of course, a Muslim intelligentsia of pure urban origin descending from the old state dignitaries, ulema, and so on; but its overwhelming representation in government and its general influence began to diminish as the intelligentsia originating in the new agrarian towns grew in size and importance. Differing from their Westernist counterparts in their ways of understanding modernization, Europe and its civilization, and their own culture, history, and education, the *taşra* (countryside) intellectuals tended to be culturally traditionalist, politically nationalist, economically liberal, and open to change. Most favored constitutionalism and free enterprise, while displaying "nationalist" tendencies in criticizing the Greek, Armenian, and Christian Arab commercial groups for relying on Europe to maintain their monopolistic trade privileges and for exploiting the agricultural sector. They also censured the Ottoman bureaucracy and the statist reformers for "blindly" imitating Europe; instead, they advocated closer relations with other Muslim countries as well as acquisition of the science and technology of the West.

Modern Education and Social-Philosophical Change

The modern educational system played a crucial role in defining the ideological orientation of the new middle classes and spurring their involvement in politics. Promoting upward mobility, it inculcated in the new elites new modes of thought and the inclination and ability to judge social phenomena rationally, in terms of cause and effect rather than as divinely ordained. In the past, when most education was religious, the native terms used to describe the educated were *alim, mutebahhir*, and *mutefekkir* (learned, thinker). The new term for those who attended the modern schools was *münevver* (enlightened—from the Arabic *nur*—light);[16] the Iranians used the term *ruşenfikr* and the Azeris *ziyali* (from *ziya*—light). (Modern Turks use *aydin*, also meaning "enlightened" and denoting the departure from the old concept of *ilim*—

that is, of "sciences" revolving around religion—to one of positive science more in tune with worldly intellectual pursuits.) The new concept of *ilim* from the beginning favored the hard sciences and "positivism," and the extreme reformist intellectuals used to attack religious studies as not being true "science."

The state eventually would use modern education to confer upon its graduates an elite status, including the right to govern and educate those newly labeled as "illiterates"—that is, the traditionalists—and to produce unquestioned unity between the rulers and the ruled in the name of science and progress, replacing the unity that the old *ilmiye* (Turkish for *ulema*) had forged in the name of *din-u devlet*, faith and state. This change occurred after the state attempted, before Abdulhamid's reign, to reform the old traditional Islamic offices and institutions or to create parallel establishments. Thus, while the state still claimed that it was Islamic and was regarded as such by most Muslims, it was at the same time, striving to create new institutional "Islamic" structures with "modernistic" outlook and orientation. For instance, the *mekteb-i nawwab* (or *nüvvab*) was created over the period 1853–62 specifically in order to train judges (*kadi*s), whereas in the past they used to be selected from the graduates of the old *medrese*s. In 1884 such schools were officially renamed *muallimhane-i nüvvab* (schools of judges), and their graduates served in the *nizami* (the new state courts) and also in the religious courts. In 1911, these schools underwent another change in name and purpose, becoming *medreset-ul kuzat* and were restricted to training judges for the religious courts, while the graduates of the Law School served in state courts. Actually, the terms *medreset-ul kuzat* and *muallimhane-i nüvvab* were identical, but the choice of old Arabic form for the first emphasized their Islamic character while the semi-Turkified term for the second stressed modernity. The *nüvvab* schools were retained in the Balkan countries with sizeable Muslim population in order to supply judges for the Şeriat courts; for example, it was agreed in 1913 that a *medreset-ul nüvvab* or *mokhamedansko dukhovnovo uchilishe* (Muslim religious school) would be established in Bulgaria (but it was opened only in 1922–23). The Young Turks, despite their anti-Hamidian views, did not mind having Islam stand for the nationality of the Turks in Bulgaria. Finally, the *ulum-u aliye diniye* (sublime high religious sciences) schools were established in 1900 to replace the old *medrese*s with a new type of modern religious school where religion could be studied in a more rational and detached way. A modernization under Islamic garb was under way.

The basis for modern education in Turkey and the Arab countries of the Ottoman Empire was the Maarif-i Umumiye Nizamnamesi (Regulation of General Education) enacted in 1869 but not enforced until ten years later, when Abdulhamid began his drive for educational reform. It envisioned a school system of three steps: beginning, intermediate, and high. The traditional, semireligious *sibyan* schools, which had been largely financed and administered by the local communities, became the *iptidai* (beginning) schools after 1879 and gradually were taken over and controlled by the government. By 1882 some twenty-five leading *vilayet*s—five of which were in the Balkan provinces—had educational directorates (*maarif müdürlüğü*). Sixteen years later every province, except for Hicaz, had such a directorate and was subject to the supervision of an educational inspector; this bureaucratization was the best indication of the importance attached to modern education. The total number of Muslim schools offering elementary education based on traditional methods was 18,983 in 1892, while the number of modern schools stood at a mere 3,057. By 1905–1906 the number of modern elementary schools had risen to 9,347. That total included 3,388 government schools for boys and 304 for girls, 143 private (community-financed) schools for boys and 36 for girls, and 3,621 government and 567 private coeducational schools. Assuming that each school had an average of about one hundred pupils, the total number of pupils attending modern elementary schools could be estimated to be about one million in a total population of approximately 37 million people. In addition, a number of traditional, or "old method," schools gradually had adopted modern teaching methods or had become "modern" as the government took them over.[17]

The elementary schools prepared students for the *rüşdiye*s, or high schools, which were the foundation for elite formation and the channels of upward mobility. In 1876 there were 22 *rüşdiye*s in Istanbul, 11 in the neighboring provinces, and 390 in the remaining provinces, with a total enrollment of over twenty thousand students. By the end of Abdulhamid's reign, Istanbul boasted nearly 70 such schools, of which 22 were government-run, 39 private, and 6 military; the Empire as a whole had by then a total of 619 *rüşdiye*s, of which 74 were for girls, 57 were private, and 25 military, the rest being government-run boys' high schools. The total enrollment in all the *rüşdiye*s had reached about forty thousand.

Elementary education consisted mainly of religious and ethical courses and initially lasted for three years, while *rüşdiye* education took four years and consisted chiefly of secular subjects, with Arabic and Persian given during the first two years and French during the last two. After 1892, new courses on religion, ethics, Ottoman history, and Turkish were added to the curricula of the *rüşdiye*s, to make them more Islamic and "national." By 1903, the courses on the Koran, ethics, and religious studies were condensed into one single course, and the hours of teaching the Turkish language were increased; however, the trend was toward secularization—that is, less religion—and nationalization. (The nationalistic developments behind this move are examined in the last two chapters of this book.)

The *idadi* schools (from the Arabic *idad*: to prepare, to develop) were a special category between the *rüşdiye* and the university, or *sultaniye*, education. The *idadi*s, according to the law of 1869, were to be established in localities having more than one thousand families and be open to Muslim and non-Muslim children. The initial curriculum in the three-year *idadi*s consisted only of secular courses: Turkish, French, economics, geography, mathematics, geometry, accounting, and so on. Although some 6 or 7 *idadi* schools were opened in Istanbul beginning in 1873, the drive to open new ones stagnated because of a variety of administrative and financial problems, including the local notables' opposition to the government's control of these institutions. However, the main reason for the slow progress in opening the *idadi*s (by 1892 only 34 had been established) was apparently the lack of teachers and students; many graduates of the *rüşdiye*s preferred to enter government service rather than pursue higher studies in the *idadi*s. In time the *rüşdiye*s and *idadi*s were combined, the number of years of education provided was raised to seven, although for financial reasons some *idadi*s continued to offer only a five-year education. By 1906, after the merger with the *rüşdiye*s, there were a total of 109 *idadi* schools in 39 mainly provincial centers, with a total enrollment of about twenty thousand students. In fact, the number of *idadi*s as well as the high quality of education offered there made unnecessary the opening of any more upper-level *sultaniye* schools; the two such schools in existence at that point were the Galatasaray opened in Istanbul in 1869 and the Turkish university, Darulfunun, established formally in 1871 but only opened in 1901 after a hiatus of thirty years.

The Galatasaray was supposed to replace the classical *enderun*, or Palace schools, established in the fifteenth century to train officials for highest government positions. Instead, modeled on the French *lycée*, it became the major source of French culture and influence. In 1878 its director, Ali Suavi, tried to "nationalize" (Turkify) the Galatasaray, but he was eventually ousted.[18] This school initially attracted non-Muslims, but, adding new courses in Turkish, it began to attract Muslims also. In 1869 Galatasaray had 277 Muslim and 345 non-Muslim students; in 1901 it had 724 Muslims and 221 non-Muslims.

In addition, there were teachers' colleges, or *darulmuallimin*, that trained teachers for the three categories of schools and were found even in Arab cities such as Beirut, Damascus, Mosul, Jerusalem, Benghazi (Libya), and in Yemen; there were altogether 32 such schools listed in 1905–1906, although the actual number probably was higher, as some provinces had failed to report their number to the center. Usually, studies on the Ottoman-Turkish educational system do not include the teachers' colleges in their list of professional schools, even though the graduates of these colleges played a key role in the political and ideological training of the Muslim Middle East in general and the Ottoman Empire in particular. The other professional schools, including medical and law schools, war college, and trade and agriculture schools, by 1908 had about twelve thousand graduates, probably two to three thousand of whom were Arabs.

The modern educational system played a crucial role in the political, social, and intellectual history of the Ottoman Empire, especially in the philosophical struggle between the center and the periphery. By permitting the propertied groups of the countryside to educate their children and facilitate their entry into the class of rising new elites, modern education conferred higher social status upon these groups. It also enabled the government to instill its own philosophy into the students in the *rüşdiye*s and *idadi*s and to secure their loyalty to the sultan—although the end result was different from the one envisaged. Despite its numerous shortcomings, particularly the lack of a well-trained teaching staff, the system still was able to disseminate its rationalist philosophical message, and bring people to share in its modernistic goals and its Westernist outlook. The curricula of the *rüşdiye*, and especially of the *idadi*s, which taught mainly secular subjects, often used textbooks that were Western translations. Even the courses on Islam and Muslim ethics had a somewhat causal, rational, and humanistic orientation; and in a few upper-level professional schools European teachers taught in their own native tongues.

Massive growth of the modern educational system during Abdulhamid's reign led to a further deterioration of the *medrese*s, although the sultan did his best to keep them alive and rejuvenate them. It also produced people who, steeped in the rationalist spirit of the modern schools were ready to challenge Abdulhamid for his absolutism and the old Islamic educational system for its dogmatism and parochialism and, as well, the modernists for their blind imitation of the West. In the end, the victory of the modern educational system appeared so complete that by the turn of the century official Ottoman statistics ignored the existence of the traditional *sibyan* schools and cited only the number of the modern schools, which included many of the old *sibyan*s. Ironically, after the Young Turks took over in 1908, they had little to add to the existing educational system implemented by the ousted "obscurantist" sultan.[19]

The debates over establishment of the *rüşdiye*s and *idadi*s in the provinces provide tantalizing insights into both the political attitudes of the new middle classes and the government's efforts to control them. Because the graduates of the *idadi*s filled high-ranking posts in the provincial administration, the central government proposed to enroll students in the *idadi*s free of charge in order to win their allegiance to the state and the sultan. Keeping the *idadi*s as boarding schools financed by the government would enable the government to control them. On the other hand, the educators in the provinces and the local notables wanted to charge tuition for study in the *idadi*s, so that only the children of the rich could attend. They believed that the children of the poor would continue to remain poor even after graduation and then, blaming the government for causing social injustice, would turn to nihilism, anarchism, and socialism—the usual bogies of the upper classes. Bayram Kodaman, who supplied this information based on documents in the Yildiz collection of the Turkish archives, believes that this was an argument fabricated with the purpose of persuading the ever-suspicious sultan to allocate larger funds to the provincial administration of schools.[20] Behind the debate about the financing of the *idadi*s, therefore, was the bigger issue of the state control of the countryside elites and loyalty to the sultan.

The notables, who were willing to finance some of the *rüşdiye*s and *idadi*s to educate their own children, became the main promoters of modern education, seeking thus to control the creation of elites and to influence their thinking. They always sought some way to incorporate into the curriculum their own traditional Islamic values and elements of regional culture. It is essential to stress the fact that family networks played a crucial role in the local or regional opposition to the center. The adoption of the Civil Code in Republican Turkey in 1926 aimed at, among other things, breaking the invisible but ever present control of the notables' families over the local community. Although the local administrators often sided with the notables, in the end, as usual, the government prevailed; the mid-level *idadi*s were given preference over elementary schools and remained under central control.

The changes in the land regime and the rapid expansion of education was accompanied by activity and growth in other areas usually associated with the middle classes and modernization. The number of books printed between 1729 and 1829 was only 180, while between 1876 and 1892 and 1893 and 1907 the figures were 6,357 and 10,601 respectively; the majority of these books dealt with secular subjects. The numbers of newspapers and journals grew from 87 and 144 in 1875 and 1883, to 226, 365, and 548 in 1895, 1903, and 1911 respectively. Civilian associations increased in number from 8 in 1872 to 53, 66, 82, and 132 in the years 1892, 1896, 1900, and 1916. Telegraph centers went up from 93 in 1865 to 223 and 301 in 1869 and 1870, and by 1914 there were 50,000 kilometers of telegraph wires in place. Urbanization increased greatly with the population of six mainly interior towns taken as sample (Damascus, Bursa, Trabzon, Bitlis) growing between 20 and 40 percent. The port cities—Istanbul, Izmir, Trabzon, Beirut, and so on—grew even faster.

The Ottoman Empire meanwhile became wide open to trade with the outside. The number of import-export corporations rose from 20 in 1855 to 30 in 1895; and in the period 1900–1909 there was an even larger increase in export companies. The volume of trade in 1840 and 1845 totalled, respectively 5.2 and 7.4 million pounds sterling. Beginning in 1857, exports and imports were 10 and 12 millions respectively; in 1869, 18 and 24 millions, in 1876 23 and 19 million pounds (note the great jump in exports); in the following years something of a falling-off occurred, but in 1905 and 1912 the figures again climbed above 20 million pounds, reaching 24.1 and 26.1, and 26.6 and 35.2 million pounds respectively, as imports came greatly to overshadow exports.[21]

Behind the quantitative growth in these various areas, there was a massive qualitative change in outlook, which may be fathomed only by an in-depth study of the content of the textbooks used in schools, of the review and journals of the period, of the patterns of socialization among the educated and so on, all of which had their part in preparing the minds of the educated elites for politics.

In sum, the rise of the middle class was a social phenomenon with far-reaching intellectual implications. The modern educational system provided a channel of upward mobility to the children of the middle and lower classes in the countryside and, likewise, presented a challenge to the old traditional modes of thought. It not only supplied the intelligentsia with a new philosophical perspective on Europe and on their own grassroots Islamic way of life and their local and regional ethnic culture but also taught them to use the modern media and new forms of association to express their aspirations and experiences in ideological terms. This transformation, occurring at the individual and communal level, was accompanied by a broader identity transformation in the political frameworks of Ottomanism, Islamism, and, ultimately, nationalism, largely under government initiative and control.

The rise of the new middle class and the growing control of education by the state was accompanied by massive demographic change. Some of the poor peasants, refugees, and various marginal elements of the populace, almost all Muslim, were attracted to the towns and cities along the seashore that grew up not as manufacturing sites but as export outlets. Employment opportunities were few in these towns, but fertility rates began to rise rapidly, both because of the disturbed demographic balance and because of the availability of modern medical care. As a result, the semiurban proletariat emerging in the Ottoman towns and cities was engulfed in poverty, squalor, and experienced a high degree of anomie, a major theme in the nationalist views of Ziya Gökalp.[22] For the peasants themselves, the collapse of the old order was akin to the end of the world. This is fully reflected in the folklore of the nineteenth century, the best example of which is in the work of Hasip, a folk poet from Antep (Aintap). Generally, the masses tended to attribute their problems to their leaders' separation from the faith, while the intelligentsia blamed the leaders for incompetence, corruption, and a "backward" mentality. In other words, alongside the traditional fatalistic view of the masses, who looked for an explanation within their own cultural frame, a more realistic point of view began to emerge. Amid these circumstances, the Nakṣbandia transformed itself from a narrowly based urban religious group into a broad ideological movement, responding in a uniquely Islamic way to the political and ideological needs of the new middle classes, especially their agrarian wing in the small towns.

The New Middle Classes in Politics and Their Ideology

The Ottoman middle classes, Christian and Muslim alike, became involved in politics in the period from 1865 to 1878, first as members of the local administrative councils and then in the parliament, which was an inadvertent party in the sultan's power struggle with the bureaucracy. Mithat paşa, supported by a small group of intellectuals, believed that the sultan's absolutism and autocracy would be curbed by the adoption of a constitution and the establishment of a parliament. In his deposing of Sultan Abdulaziz he received support from the agrarian middle class but also the *softa*s, the students in the religious schools (the potential fundamentalist underclass), many of whom came from various villages and towns in Anatolia and Rumili. Many thousands of *softa*s who studied in Istanbul in the 1870s spent the three months around Ramadan in the countryside, preaching and collecting money. They also conveyed news about the happenings in the capital and disseminated the idea of Islamism —and possibly that of constitutionalism—to the remotest villages of Anatolia and Rumili.

Mithat's considerable success in cooperating with the notables when he was governor of the Danube province had convinced him that the participation of the Christians in government affairs could assure economic success and damp down their nationalism.[23] The members of the House of Deputies elected to the first Ottoman parliament of 1877–78, therefore, included many local notables, most of whom were members of the provincial administrative councils, as well as a disproportionate number of Christians. Once in parliament, these deputies demanded a service-oriented professional bureaucracy rather than an authority-wielding status group.[24] Although Sultan Abdulhamid suspended the constitution and disbanded parliament in 1878, he fully realized that the deputies from the countryside exercised considerable influence in their provinces and that their demands stemmed from genuine needs.[25] Consequently, after 1878 Abdulhamid tried to placate the agrarian middle class with the privatization of land and extensive reforms, including professionalization of the bureaucracy, expansion of education, establishment of an agricultural school, and encouragement of private enterprise and foreign investment. Despite Mithat's expectations for cultural pluralism, however, the parliamentary experiment of 1878 actually alienated the Christians from the government, for the Muslims seemed to regard the Ottoman state and its institutions as Islamic in character and purpose; and after 1878 they followed their own road to modernization and nationhood, widening the split even further.

The idea of progress, or *medeniyet* (civilization), became fairly generalized among the new Muslim middle classes after 1880. There were sharp differences about how to achieve this, but there seemed to be agreement that change was necessary to achieve civilization. The rising agrarian wing and some of its intellectual spokesman had the view that change was likely to be achieved by economic liberalism combined with cultural-historical continuity, communal participation, a degree of local administrative autonomy, and the introduction of facilities for communication and land cultivation. In contrast, the "modernist" intellectuals and much of the central bureaucracy thought progress would stem from institutional change to be carried out under government guidance. From the very start, both the modernists and conservatives seemed to have regarded the achievement of *medeniyet* as the common goal, although they had different ideas what this consisted of and how it should be achieved. The state was, for conservatives, a bulwark, the defender and preserver of society's traditions and identity; for modernists it was more of an offensive force, the only institution deemed capable of changing the society and its culture—possibly after it changed itself and became strong enough to tackle the society. Abdulhamid adopted a middle position between these views: namely, he elected to accept change while maintaining the old institutions and culture, but not their dogmatic spirit. The spirit of the times was elucidated by the Cevdet paşa's argument, "Zamanin tagayyuru ahkamin tebeddülünü meşru kilar," which may be translated "The changing of worldly conditions legitimizes the renewal [amendment] of laws" (*tagayyur* means also "deterioration" and change of essence).

Cevdet sought to harmonize the old Ottoman-Muslim state culture and traditions with views and needs of the new middle classes. A conservative Islamist and an arch-monarchist, he criticized the old ulema for being out of touch with reality and opposing the admission of Christians to government service. A follower of Ibn Khaldun (Cevdet completed the translation of the *Muqaddimah* [Turkish: *Mukademe*]), he rejected absolute historical determinism; hence he believed new measures and reforms could revive the Empire. This view was embodied in his acceptance of *zaruret* (*zaruriyah*—necessity) as legitimizer of change. Cevdet claimed that time and circumstance were the greatest architects of history and had the power to change everything. Thus some of the ulema's conservative opinions could not be considered valid because changed world circumstances required an altered implementation of some of the Şeriat's provisions; nor could the society that had prevailed in the old times be revived.[26] Stressing the need for a moderate stand on religious matters in order to harmonize the society's life with the changed conditions, Cevdet asserted that because a variety of new freedoms already had been accepted during the reigns of Sultans Abdulmecid and Abdulaziz, the ulema was out of touch with reality. Cevdet paşa could cite a large number of Islamic arguments derived from the Koran and the Sunna to support change, and thus he became an important Islamist advocate of reform but without alienating the conservatives.

The change in the classical *vakif* system, that unique Islamic institution, which Cevdet directed for a while as *nazir* or minister, showed how a basic Islamic institution could be "adapted" to new circumstances without causing the sort of popular reaction that arose in India. The government took possession of *vakif* property under various pretexts, and eventually it created the Ministry of Vakifs—Evkaf Nezareti — the very existence of which was a violation of the principle of state noninterference in *vakif* administration. Although a number of *vakifs*, known as *mülhak*, remained under the administration of the *mütevelli* (administrator appointed by the founder), the number of these decreased rapidly. In fact, the continuously changing demands of a market economy could not be reconciled with the "immutable" legal status of the *vakif*. Because the *vakifs* were, economically speaking inert, lawyers referred to them by the European term "estates in mortmain." It was no doubt a point in the government's favor that a good number of the *vakif* lands that became state property were sold or distributed to individuals or were occupied by squatters (see chapter 1, n. 15).

The rise of a Muslim middle class in the Ottoman Empire meant that one new, meaningful center of civil power and opinion was emerging despite fragmentation. The fragmentation of Muslim society into various groups with different political orientations due to social restructuring could be seen even among the ulema, the upper segment of which had always been closely tied to the government. After the 1870s the ulema split openly into upper and lower factions. The upper group, which sided with the government and defended the established order, was represented by the Meşihat Dairesi (Office of Religious Affairs) headed by the *şeyhulislam* and was almost totally dependent upon the government. In contrast, the middle- and lower-ranking members of the ulema tended to identify with and side with the countryside notables and to speak for the conservative populists-modernists (nationalists), as long as the modernists did not question basic Islamic tenets.

David D. Commins has stated that the ulema in Damascus became involved in grain deals and manufacturing, in part because of the changes in the rural economy following the promulgation of the Land Code of 1858. Simultaneously, the "urban notable elite had reconsolidated itself on the basis of landholding and bureaucratic posts by shifting resources into the rural economy and obtaining posts in new government institutions."[27] The statist-populist split of the ulema and the social restructuring opened the way for the reemergence of the Nakşbandia in the role of proponent of modernist-Islamist revivalism. Having undergone profound transformation during the nineteenth century, primarily under Şeyh Khalid, the Nakşbandia provided a new outlet for expression and, although sympathetic to Abdulhamid's Islamist policy, did not openly or fully support his personal rule and absolutism. They became, inadvertently perhaps, the spokesmen for the new middle classes and their brand of orthodox-modernist Islam.

The Middle Classes and the Nakşbandia

Just as the modern educational system produced a new intelligentsia with a modernist-rationalist outlook that was increasingly aloof from its own culture and history, the Nakşbandia, in part under the impact of that modern education, which they adapted to Islamic teachings, searched the Koran and Sunna for an Islamic path to achieve the society's adaptation to the contemporary world without lessening its faith. The popular Sufis were not prepared to respond to the intellectual challenge from the West, while the old religious establishment lacked the emotional appeal of the Sufis and was not enlisting the popular support necessary to form a united front against the outside political and intellectual challenge. The Nakşbandia, therefore, had to offer the emotion of the Sufis and the intellect of rational modernism in order to fill the gap between the elites and masses and achieve a degree of unity and consensus. One day many of these Nakşbandi *şeyhs* will take their place in the pantheon of the Muslim revolutionaries and modernists. With the Kadiris, Rifais, and other orders close to it, the Nakşbandis built the bridge between intellectual and emotional Islam, between the middle and lower strata of society. It did this without adopting an openly militant attitude toward the government and modernist reforms; in fact, whenever possible it sought accommodation between the ruling political order and the new order of society and the challenge to its faith.

The Nakşbandia probably was the most powerful single social, political, and ideological force shaping the cultural history of Asian Islam, in general, and the Ottoman Empire, in particular, during the nineteenth century.[28] In the process, it was unwittingly changing itself from a purely religious, Orthodox Sufi order into the spokesman of the new sociocultural reality by adding a modern component to its traditional religious functions. The Nakşbandia was always predominantly an urban, sightly elitist order dedicated to social and political involvement (*halvat dar enjuman*)—at least since Şeyh Ubaydullah Ahrar's time, and its uniquely advantageous social position and ideological activist tendencies enabled it to influence Muslim leaders of all ethnic backgrounds. Nakşbandis had been advisers to several Baburi rulers in India and enjoyed considerable acceptance in the Ottoman court, especially the Muradi branch at the end of the eighteenth century. Consequently, every fundamentalist-revivalist thinker, militant leader, and populist intellectual mentioned in this study, and many modernists involved in the nineteenth-century Islamic movements seem to have been Nakşbandi or to have had some relation to the Nakşbandia or their close allies, the Kadiris. Indeed, the Nakşbandia in the nineteenth century somehow managed to act both as a regional "nationalist" force and as the agent of international Islamic solidarity and also, indirectly, as an Islamic legitimizer of change and material progress.

The transformation and revival that the Nakşbandia underwent in the nineteenth century was almost synonymous with that of Islam and the Islamic societies as a whole. Although other Sufi orders, such as the Kadiriyya, Rifaiyya, and Tijaniyya, played important political parts in Islamic revivalist movements, none had the political impact of the Nakşbandia, especially in Asia. According to Alkan, in Istanbul alone in 1882 and 1890, the Nakşbandis maintained a total of 52 and 65 lodges, respectively (including about 9 Bektaşi lodges); the Kadiris 45 and 57 and the Rifais 40 and 35, in those two years. The remaining main 13 religious popular orders (Halveti, Sunbuli, Şabani, Cerrahi, etc.) had a combined total of about 110 lodges, combined total of lodges in Istanbul was 260 and 305 in 1882 and 1890, respectively, and 250 in 1920. Many of these lodges served as schools, hospitals, traditional archery training sites, guest houses, and so on rather than being strictly for religious worship. Keeping close to the tradition of study of the Koran and Sunna and believing in the multifaceted role of the Prophet in creating the Muslim society according to God's commandment, the Nakşbandia increasingly emphasized that Muhammad carried out his mission *in this world* and that he transformed the disparate Arab tribes sunk in *cahiliyya* (ignorance, decadence) into a pious but dynamic and resourceful Muslim community. The Nakşbandia believed that a return to the basics of the faith could rejuvenate society if the return and the rejuvenation were properly related to each other. This could be accomplished by remaining anchored in the faith while understanding properly and adapting the Prophet's approach and method of work among living beings. This was a truly revolutionary and humanist approach, for it acknowledged that Islam had worldly aspects, as symbolized by the person of the Prophet—a human being like anyone else. In acknowledging that God chose Muhammad as His messenger and delegated him to reform and upgrade society, Nakşbandis wanted to imbue individual Muslims with a sense of responsibility toward their society and themselves in the light of contemporary conditions. Some organizational aspects of the Nakşbandia that are very important from the vantage point of this study need emphasis.

The Nakşbandia evolved not as a single, rigidly pyramidal Sufi *tarikat* but as a loose organization in which the various *halife*s (successors and disciples) could interpret teachings of their *şeyh* (leader-master) in a rather liberal fashion. Thus a *halife*, upon becoming a *şeyh*, would choose to emphasize and develop certain aspects of his own *şeyh*'s teaching, and his *halife*s, in turn, could further develop those aspects, turning them in particular social and political directions. Needless to say, these social and political elements formally remained subordinate to the basic religious teachings, but they had the potential to challenge the established social and political order and many accepted views.

For instance, in today's Turkey the Nakşbandia are estimated to number about eight to ten million adherents of one sort or another. Necmeddin Erbakan, the head of the defunct Refah Party is a Nakşbandi, as are the Süleymanci, followers of Süleyman Hilmi Tunahan; the Nurcu, that is, Said Nursi's followers; the Işikçis (enlighteners), founded by Hüseyin Işik and led now by Enver Ören, the head of Ihlas Holding, a major corporation; the numerous followers of Fethullah Gülen, a defender of *dün-yevilik* (worldliness) and an exceptionally influential leader, not to mention the Iskender paşa group, established by Ziyaeddin Gümüşhaneli (regarded as central by some scholars) and several other groups. These may differ from one another only in origin (some derive from Said Nursi, others from Gümüşhaneli, etc.) in their approach and doctrinal emphasis, or in their personalities. Lately, however, they tend toward bloc voting for the party closest to their own view (even though they will often split their votes according to the circumstances).

In the nineteenth century, the Nakşbandia remained generally pacifist, nonmilitant, and on good terms with the ruling political authority; but they firmly opposed the European occupation and its threats to the Islamic ethical, legal, and social order. Unlike some of the religious orders—for example, Tijaniyya, which agreed to accept foreign rule if it respected their Islamic way of life and organization—the Nakşbandia opposed all foreign rule, however liberal and accommodating. In addition, some Nakşbandis criticized and fought their own political and religious establishment when it cooperated with and accepted the occupying powers' mode of life.

The lack of reliable in-depth studies on the social and political position of the modern Nakşbandia makes many of the assumptions regarding the place and role of the order within the new middle classes rather tentative. Nonetheless, the historical evidence in hand and insights gained from personal contacts with contemporary Nakşbandi followers indicate that the order's connection with the new middle classes was systemic. Moreover, they spread into the countryside from the provincial towns and cities that were growing both as centers of agricultural production, trade, and education for the notables and as destinations for the Caucasian immigrants.

Some scholars have viewed the Nakşbandia as having promoted a form of ethnic nationalism under the changed conditions brought by social transformation in the Ottoman Empire. This view assumes that, with the elimination of the feudal lords, who had played the conflicting roles of spokesmen for the local culture and ruling instruments of the central authority, the new groups emerged as representatives of the local communities and ultimately voiced their grievances and aspirations in the form of incipient ethnic nationalism.[29] I only partially agree with this view, since the increased cultural and ethnic awareness certainly did not become true political nationalism until late in the Young Turks era, when traditional relationships among the state, faith, and society underwent drastic change, as shall be indicated later. There are, however, a variety of utterances to indicate that a kind of regional ethnonationalism was brewing among Muslim groups. For instance, Ilham baba (Şeyh Abdul Vehhab) of Travnik in Bosnia (he was executed there in 1821), wrote in Serbo-Croatian that the "Turk is not doing well; injustice covered justice." Such "verses expressed both a moral sense and a feeling of nationalism on the part of Yugoslav Muslims," according to Dzemal Cehajic;[30] but this interpretation must be qualified. Cehajic made this assertion during the euphoria of the 1980s, when Bosnian Muslims regarded Yugoslav multiculturalism as having secured forever their acceptance by Serbs and Croats; under these circumstances, they downgraded the Ottoman era of their history as "Turkish."[31]

The Nakṣbandia's Turkish origin became a major theme in twentieth-century Turkish nationalist literature and deserves some elaboration. Fuat Köprülü identified the Nakṣbandis with Turkishness, not only because of the Turkic origin of its founders, such as Ahmet Yesevi and Bahaddin Nakṣbandi, but also because the movement spread initially among the Turks of Eurasia and incorporated some elements of the Turks' old shamanist culture. Bahaddin Nakṣbandi (Muhammad b. Muhammad Bahuaddin Nakṣband [1318–91]) was born in the village of Qasr-i Arifan near Buhara and is buried there. His tomb, at some fifteen miles from the city, was not on the Soviet tourist maps when I visited the site in 1989 and watched hundreds of native people from all walks of life pray at his grave, as did Arminius Vambery in the middle of the last century.[32] In the newly independent republic of Uzbekistan, Nakṣband has become a national figure, being viewed first as an Uzbek and then as a Muslim. Nakṣband's supposed predecessor and "father" of Turkish Islam, Ahmet Yesevi, lived and died (1236?) in Yesi (today known as Turkistan in the Chimkent oblast of Kazakstan). He expressed his ethical thoughts in verse in a pure Turkish, and this was collected by his disciples in his main work, *Divan-i Hikmet*. Yesevi's style, language, and the epic form of religious preaching were designed to appeal to the nomadic Turkic tribes and, therefore, found acceptance mainly among the Kazak, Kyrgyz, and the Türkmen of Anatolia. Köprülü claimed that Bahaddin Nakṣband was profoundly influenced by Halil Ata, later sultan, and Kazam şeyh, both of whom were Yesevi's disciples; thus he regarded the Nakṣbandia as descending from Yesevi.[33] However, in a later study, published in the *Islam Ansiklopedisi* under "Ahmet Yesevi" and "Nakṣbendi," Köprülü changed his position.[34] There he claimed that the Nakṣbandi attempted to take over some features of the Yeseviyya in order to attract more followers, although he insisted on the Turkish character of the order.[35] A recent article rejected his view that the Yeseviyya was a "Turkish order" and instead claimed that the Nakṣbandis sought to absorb the Yesevi, producing literature to support this position.[36]

Historical evidence indcates that the Nakṣbandi had a special relationship with the Ottomans and that their involvement in the affairs of the Ottoman society was active while, in contrast, other Sufis led a life of mediation and seclusion. Most leading Central Asian religious and political figures had some real or symbolic links to Ottoman Turks, it should be noted.

The famous Hoca Nasraddin Ubaydullah Ahrar (d. 1490), whose family dominated politics in Central Asia for centuries, supposedly traveled miraculously in 1453 to help

Sultan Mehmed (1451–81) conquer Constantinople (Istanbul).[37] A large number of Nakşbandi from Central Asia and India and their disciples, who settled in Anatolia, Yemen, Mecca, Damascus, and Baghdad, initiated new disciples and thus came to exert growing influence on the area. The early Nakşbandia in the Ottoman Empire appear to have been pacifist and loyal to the sultanate and its orthodoxy; however, as stagnation and corruption engulfed the Ottoman Empire in the seventeenth century, the Turks came to take a special interest in the reformist-activist Nakşbandis of India. The teachings of Şeyh Ahmet Sirhindi (1563–1624) known as Imam Rabban, found great following among Turks who had been initiated into the Nakşbandia order by Hoja Baqibillah (d. 1603), a spiritual descendent of Hoja Ahrar.[38] Ahmed Jaryani from Yekdest near Buhara translated Sirhindi's *Maktubat* into Turkish. Thus Sirhindi's Nakşbandi branch, the Mucadidiyya, took the upper hand as an almost new school of thought: at once Orthodox, reformist, and antiestablishment, it criticized the Mogul sultan for his excesses and society for its fatalism and superstitions.[39]

Sirhindi's legacy were revived in the Ottoman Empire during the nineteenth century and eventually replaced most of the loyalist legacy of the earlier Muradi Nakşbandis, thanks to the teachings of Şeyh Khalid Shahrazuri Zaruga (1776–1827), who was born in Karadağ in the northern Iraq. Butrus Abu-Manneh has indicated that Şeyh Khalid went to Mecca to deepen his knowledge at the time the Wahhabi occupied the town: "There and then he was inspired to seek enlightenment in India, which is perhaps a sign of a negative attitude towards this [Wahhabi] movement. He could not find a spiritual guide to his satisfaction, either in Mecca or in any other city in Western Asia."[40] He managed to go to India a few years later and there joined Ghulam Ali in his *khangah*, then he returned as the *halife* of Ghulam Ali to establish his own subbranch of Nakşbandia (Mucaddidiyya) under his own name—that is the Nakşbandia Khalidiyya. Şeyh Khalid went eventually to Baghdad and finally to Damascus, where he died in the plague of 1827.

Şeyh Khalid believed that the *ümmet* (community) had gone astray and that, in order to restore it to the right path, the Sunni Muslims should make the period of the Prophet and his Companions their ideal.[41] In his view, the Nakşbandi way was absolutely identical to that of the Companions of the Prophet, and so they had the same rank. In effect Şeyh Khalid accepted, as did Sirhindi, the dictum that the right path for the Muslim was to behave according to the Book and the Sunna and to follow the guidance of the Prophet and the Companions in their own beliefs and behavior. The Nakşbandi further claimed that the virtuousness or corruption of the king was that of the subjects and, therefore, implied that there was something amiss if the government did not act to restore the vitality of society and its virtues. Şeyh Khalid came to express more openly and forcefully *cihad*ist tendencies of the Mucaddidiyya and took an openly critical attitude toward European expansionism and Christian proselytizing. Several Ottoman bureaucrats, intellectuals, and religious men became members of the Nakşbandia-Mucaddidiyya order and involved themselves in the reform movement of Sultan Selim III as Uriel Heyd noted in his much cited article on the "reformist" ulema.[42] The Nakşbandia suffered when the Janissaries and the conservative religious establishment destroyed the reformist programs of Selim III in 1807. The Khalidis, in turn, were forced to leave the capital and spread into smaller towns after Sultan Mahmud II, who initially had been friendly to the order, came to regard their criticism of his "reforms" as a menace to his autocracy.[43] Nevertheless, one of the other Nakşbandi, Pertev efendi, in 1826 drafted the order abolishing the Janissary establishment (followers of Bektaş), which was regarded by reformists as the main impediment to the revival (*ihya*) of the state.[44] The Nakşbandi Khalidis found their way back into the Ottoman Empire in the second half of the nineteenth century as an activist, socially conscious, and ultimately nationalist force, as Muslim immigrants from Russia swelled their ranks and gave the order a strong popular foundation.

Of a total of some five to seven million immigrants from Russia, the Balkans, and the Caucasus who settled in the Ottoman Empire between 1856 and 1914, a large number of the Caucasians were muridist followers of Şeyh Hamza and Şamil, who had been influenced by Khalidi Nakşbandi teachings. Şeyh Ismail al-Kurdumi was Şeyh Khalid's *halife* and was active in Şirvan until about 1817–18; then the Russians forced him to seek asylum in Turkey, where he remained very active. Subsequently, one of Şeyh Ismail's disciples, Muhammad al-Şirvani, took the Khalidi teachings to Dagestan and ordained Şeyh Muhammad al-Yaraghi as his disciple. Al-Yaraghi, in turn, played a crucial role by choosing Kazi (Gazi), Hamza, and Şamil as imams—he apparently named them as his *halifes*—and declaring the *cihad* against the Russians. Şeyh Muhammad al-Yaraghi's nephew, Hasan al-Algadari, who was close to Şeyhs Hamza and Şamil, spread the Khalidi teachings in the Caucasus. It is clear, then, that the muridists are a direct offshoot of the Khalidiyya rather than an independent, or even a non-Islamic, religious movement, as some Russians erroneously claimed.[45] It was after Şeyh Şamil was defeated in 1859 that the Russians forced the millions of Caucasian Muslims to emigrate to the Ottoman Empire; these brought along not only their galvanized faith but also their fierce anti-Russian feelings. The immigrants included many of Şeyh Şamil's immediate followers, as well as his close and distant relatives, who took important positions in the Ottoman military and administrative establishments. In sum, the Caucasian immigrants helped generalize Nakşbandi teachings within the intellectual and cultural life of rural Anatolia.

The influx of thousands of committed muridists, *şeyhs*, and their followers strengthened and radicalized the Ottoman Khalidis and changed the structure and culture of many Anatolian towns. Most of the newcomers engaged in agriculture and trading occupations, while their leaders, many of whom belonged to the tribal aristocracy, quickly became part of their new towns' notables, the *eşraf*. Overnight the migrants made the larger-than-life, heroic image of Şeyh Şamil and his struggle for the faith a model to be followed by all Muslims and also popularized Nakşbandi teachings among the Anatolian masses to an extent hardly known in the past. These teachings not only helped strengthen society's Islamic consciousness but also increased awareness of their material backwardness and the government's inability to cope with it.

The expansion of the Nakşbandia into rural and semirural areas of Anatolia had drastically altered its earlier image as a predominantly urban, even elitist, Sufi order and caused alarm in the government. The case of Şeyh Ahmet Daghestani from the town of Sivrihisar in central Anatolia illustrates both the rapid spread of the Nakşbandi and the depth of the government's fear of their populist appeal. A Caucasian immigrant of thirty-seven or thirty-eight years of age, Şeyh Ahmet was a Nakşbandi-Khalidi (as his seal describes him), who attracted over three thousand followers from Sivrihisar in Central Anatolia and its neighboring villages during his three-year residence in that town. (Some exaggerated reports place the number of his followers at thirty thousand.) The *şeyh* was known as a very pious person, loyal to the government and the sultan. Extensive investigations by several provincial committees and judges exonerated him of any antigovernment intentions. Yet Premier Kiamil paşa reported to the sultan: "A man capable of gathering so many *murids* [followers] in such a short time will assemble many more in the near future. The high respect and acceptance he enjoys makes dangerous this man's residence in the province, and consequently he should be sent (exiled) to another locality and a pension granted to him to assure his existence."[46] The government brought the impoverished, innocent *şeyh* first to Ankara, the provincial capital, and then, in order to prevent his insistent followers from contacting him, exiled him to Damascus in 1886. When large numbers of visitors found their way to Şeyh Ahmet even in Damascus, the government finally brought him to Istanbul and paid him a handsome pension but kept him under constant surveillance.

Sultan Abdulhamid silenced the populist Nakşbandia but courted their middle-class representatives, as in the case of Şeyh Ahmet Ziaeddin Gümüşhanevi (Gümüşhaneli, 1813–93), the founder of the Ottoman-Turkish (Ziayiyye) version of the Khalidi-Nakşbandi order. The son of a local merchant from the small town of Gümüşhane in northeast Anatolia, Ziaeddin accompanied his father on business trips to Istanbul, developing on the side his own business of purse weaving.[47] He eventually remained in Istanbul and dedicated himself to religious studies under el-Ervdi, one of Şeyh Khalid's *halifes*, while he managed a print shop. After he established his own *dergah* (court, convent), Gümüşhanevi trained sixteen or more *halifes*, at least four of whom were from the Caucasus and Kazan. (Much of this early activity took place in Gümüşhaneli's original lodge, located in Cağaloğlu street. The building, just opposite the governor's mansion, was demolished in 1956 and the current Defterdarlik [Accounting Office] was built in its stead.) In addition, he spent several years in Egypt seeking to enlarge his following through the Nakşbandi *tekke* (lodges), constructed by Khedive Abbas I but later overtaken by Muhammad Amin's Khalidiyya.[48]

It is well known that Sultan Abdulhamid, who was cool toward the Khalidiyya, developed excellent relations with Gümüşhanevi and often sought his advice and held him in the greatest esteem. The sultan was represented by a special envoy at Gümüşhanevi's death and, what is even more important, ordered him buried at the entrance to the tomb of Süleyman the Magnificent; few people have ever enjoyed such honor. On the other hand, Gümüşhanevi has been criticized for his social pacifism and for allowing his close relations with and submission to Abdulhamid to undermine his independence. Indeed, Gümüşhanevi supported not only the reforms of Abdulhamid but also the sultan's Islamist policy of unity and assimilation towards immigrants, with whom Gümüşhanevi had close and extensive relations.

Butrus Abu-Manneh believes that Gümüşhanevi tried to develop his own special Nakşbandi order by emphasizing the study of *hadises*.[49] (Gümüşhanevi's two major works are studies of the *hadises* dealing mainly with the Prophet's personal characteristics and habits.)[50] Abu-Manneh also claims that Gümüşhanevi favored the Turks and showed special interest in Russia's Muslims, most of whom were Turks. One of his disciples, Şeyh Zeynullah bin Habibullah, was from Kazan, and Gümüşhanevi's first biography was published by Mustafa Fevzi in Kazan in 1899. Stressing the existence of a strong ethnic national tendency, Abu-Manneh argues that both Gümüşhanevi and Abdulhamid tried to create a Turkish reformist Islam bound to the government, but this contention does not take into account the impact of the Caucasian migrants on the Ottoman Nakṣbandia. It may be said that Abdulhamid was probably concerned with the potential of the militant, populist Sufi Nakṣbandia to polarize the immigrants into opposing religious groups and delay their assimilation into Anatolian society; and he probably did use Gümüşhanevi to prevent any other *şeyh*s from assuming the leadership of the Nakṣbandia and creating division among his subjects. Gümüşhanevi was a sincere and devout Muslim, not an ethnic nationalist, and represented only one of many Khalidi groups active in the Ottoman Empire; but he unwittingly did contribute to the "Turkification" of the Nakṣbandia and re-Islamization of Anatolia.

The Nakṣbandia under Şeyh Gümüşhanevi helped strengthen communication between the Ottoman state and the Caucasus. Four of Gümüşhanevi's *halife*s came from the Caucasus and Russia and were active there at some time. Ömer Ziauddin (1850 or 1851 to 1924) was an Avar born in Çerkaya and wrote a *mevlud* used in commemorating Prophet's birth (among Turks it became a funeral chant, or obituary prayer) in Circassian, in addition to some fourteen other works in Turkish and Arabic. Hasan Hilmi (b. Ali el-Kesrevi in 1829) studied the Western sciences with Suski el-Hac Hasan, who had also been Şeyh Şamil's teacher, then migrated to the Ottoman Empire in 1863 and settled in Düzce. Zeynullah el-Kazani published the Nakṣbandi Turkic literature in Kazan and Caucasia; and Kirimli Mücteba efendi was active in Crimea and Istanbul.[51]

Gümüşhanevi's close relations with Abdulhamid led to the persecution of the Nakṣbandia order by the Young Turks and the Republican governments, even though Musa Kazim efendi, the unionist *şeyhulislam*, was a Nakṣbandi. The order persisted, however, playing important political roles in the recent history of Turkey. For instance, in 1919–22 the Özbek (Uzbek) lodge of Üsküdar, a Nakṣbandi stronghold, helped the Turkish nationalists, including Ismet Inönü, flee English-occupied Istanbul to join Mustafa Kemal's (Ataturk) forces in Anatolia. Eventually Şeyh Ata, the head of the lodge, was arrested by the British, who were astonished that the religious men took such an active part in the resistance movement and carried the population along with them. The names of Bediuzaman Said Nursi (1876–1960), and Şeyh Mehmet Esat efendi, both Nakṣbandi *şeyh*s, have been associated with two supposedly anti-Republic rebellions, in 1925 and 1930 respectively.[52] The main order was able to preserve its continuity: Ömer Ziyauddin, originally from Dagestan, became the *şeyh* after Gümüşhanevi's death; he was followed by Mehmet Zaid; by Abdulaziz Bekkin, originally from Kazan; then, after 1952, by Mehmed Zaid Kotku (the Kotku family is of Caucasian origin); and finally by M. Es'ad Coşan.[53]

Gümüşhanevi's teachings were spread in various forms through the mosques of Istanbul and other cities—the Iskender paşa mosque in the district of Fatih is the main center—until the Nakṣbandi were restored to popularity and official respectability after the late President Turgut Özal and many other politicians declared themselves Nakṣbandi. The contemporary Nakṣbandi show respect for Abdulhamid and advocate his rehabilitation but do not advocate a return to his Islamist and absolutist policies. (They backed the middle-of-the-road Anavatan [Motherland] party before recently switching to the rightist Islamic party, Refah.) Their attitude toward Fazilet, the successor of Refah is not known.

The History Institute of the ILKSAV (the Turkish acronym for the Foundation for Science, Culture and Art) on 2 May 1992 held a symposium to celebrate the 150th anniversary of Abdulhamid's birth. The opening and closing speeches were delivered by Professor Mahmud Es'ad Coşan, the head of the board of governors of the foundation as well as the current (1996) spiritual leader of the Nakşbandi-Khalidi of Turkey. Coşan refrained from either criticizing or eulogizing Abdulhamid; however, he stressed that the meeting should have been held in the sumptuous Palace of Culture (Istanbul's best convention hall) to attract a larger number of people, rather than in the humble mosque attached to the lodge of Selami Mustafa, in the historic district of Eyüb (named after Ayub Ansari).[54] In his writing Coşan has espoused the following view: "The contemporary world is [engaged] in rapid advance and change. As Muslims we are obliged to follow these new developments and take the necessary measures to adopt them [ayak uydurmak—literally "fall in step"]. This is necessary so that we can live in honor and progress." Coşan also believed that there were many people, even among those who were supposed to be leaders—he used the term "guides"—who did not comprehend society's need to adapt itself to contemporary developments. "In addition, the source of our strength is our faith [*iman*] . . . and we feel strongly that we have to engage intensively in good activities in this world as preparation for the next world [*ahiret*]." Enlightenment can be achieved with "qualified personnel, cadres, financial means, proper outlets, modern equipment and plenty of time."[55] In line with Nakşbandi ethics, Coşan attacked acquisitive materialism and advocated a return to spiritualism, first by a purification and enrichment of the soul through a mystic (Sufi) experience and then through love of and conformity to the ethics of the Koran and the Prophet's Sunna. Coşan is a professor of theology at Istanbul University and a prolific writer dealing with the ethical problems of contemporary Turkey. He asserts that Turkey is undergoing Islamization and a return to its roots within the framework of the constitution but that this return should not be viewed as a religious reaction.[56]

Conclusion

The new middle classes in the Ottoman state rose as the consequence of the structural changes caused by the introduction of the capitalist system: the commercialization of agriculture, the conversion of state lands into private property, expansion of trade, introduction of modern education, and other side influences. In the process, the old traditional notables, who had fought the central government for more self-government and recognition of regional interests and cultural peculiarities, were assimilated by the new groups, and wealth, erudition, communal support, modernity, and Islamic orthodoxy became their cultural social marks. There was a high degree of secularization in the court system, symbolized best by the replacement of judges educated in religious *medreses* by professionals trained in modern law schools. Initially, only the Nizamiye, or upper-level modern courts, hired the graduates of the law schools, but gradually the practice extended to all other courts. It should be noted also that the Mecelle, that is, a modernized, updated version of the *fikh* or religious law, was codified by Ahmet Cevdet paşa, but the endeavor could not be finalized. The modernization of the judicial system during Abdulhamid's reign, a subject that deserves far more attention than it is accorded here, was a fundamental departure from the traditional Islamic legal order. It was, however, a truly innovative "Islamic" endeavor in that the West played no part as a model or instigator.

The modern educational system provided an upward channel of mobility for the offspring of the agrarian middle class, who acquired positions in the government bureaucracy and, together with members of the older urban middle class descended from the traditional bureaucratic and intellectual groups, became the new elite class. The migration of millions of Muslims from Crimea, Caucasus, and the Balkans added new social, cultural, and ethnic dimensions to the emerging middle classes. Ottomanism and Islamism became, especially during Sultan Abdulhamid's reign, not only ideologies of political integration and unity, mainly among Muslims, but also sources of identity, values, and ideas that were disseminated through the schools, press, and the new literature. The local community became a religious cultural fraternity with economic interests of its own and could be turned into a political constituency when conditions allowed for it. The achieving of contemporary civilization—or modernity—became the chief goal for modernists, traditionalists, and conservatives alike. But for a small minority, all these groups accepted the notion of change in the social and political institutions—in varying degrees according to their understanding of civilization and of Europe and of identity and value attached to their own culture and history. The fact that the Ottoman state was politically independent allowed its government a considerable freedom of choice in deciding its cultural-educational policies. It should be also noted that despite drastic innovation in practically every field, Ottoman modernization maintained a relatively high degree of historical and cultural continuity, even though such continuity appeared in the eyes of many to obstruct rapid modernization.

In sum, the correct understanding of the structural changes in the agricultural sector is the key to understanding the social, cultural, and political changes in the Muslim world in general and the Ottoman Empire in particular during the nineteenth century. The modernist (Westernist) intelligentsia, to whom researchers have attributed overwhelming importance (probably more out of their own sense of ideological solidarity rather than detached and purely scholarly view) was part of the middle class, though it had its own ideological orientation shaped mainly by its statist-elitist philosophy. However, the bulk of the Muslim middle classes—those who descended from the old ruling aristocracies, the ulema families, and bureaucratic elites and those who rose from humble villages alike—became increasingly dependent for income and position on commercialized agriculture, first at the production end of the process and then at the marketing and distribution level. Their philosophy and modes of thought were affected profoundly by their social position and their economic status. It is, therefore, correct to state that the intensive commercialization of the agricultural sector and privatization of state lands not only played a key role in the restratification of Ottoman society but also oriented it toward a rational mode of thought. The economic regime of Europe that was imposed on or voluntarily accepted by Ottoman society produced a new pattern of social stratification in which some groups were aware of their class interests while others emphasized religious affiliation and loyalty to local and tribal identities. Modern education, new means of communication, including the press and books, easier transportation and relative wealth allowed these new middle classes to develop their own ideas and disseminate them while establishing contacts with their counterparts in other Muslim lands.

The widest impact of the changes in Ottoman society was felt in the second half of the nineteenth century during Abdulhamid's reign. The sultan, to be sure, was hardly aware of the complex sociocultural and economic forces that had transformed the country he was called to rule in 1876. He, like most of his aides, did not have a predetermined plan to cope with the new developments but held to the classical Ottoman concept that the survival of the state had priority over all other considerations and that the ruler was empowered to take whatever measures were necessary to achieve that survival. The agrarian middle classes provided Abdulhamid a strong social base, but diverged sharply in their view of the bureaucracy, which the sultan continued to regard as the state's and the throne's main instrument of power. He tried to dominate, but also to professionalize, the bureaucracy; but that body and its intellectual allies in turn had their own concept of modernity, constitutionalism, and freedom and devised their own ideas and methods to achieve their ends. In the process, they ultimately did away with the sultan and the monarchy but retained the state as the chief instrument of change and legitimacy. The next chapters will deal with these complex and often conflicting issues and trends.

5

Knowledge, Press, and the Popularization of Islamism

After the 1860s, the burgeoning press and the proliferation of published books helped disseminate knowledge, they also played a crucial role in both the rapid spread of Islamism and in its internalization by the middle and lower classes. Direct access to and a near monopoly of new and more diverse sources of knowledge allowed the intellectual strata of the middle classes to carve out a uniquely effective position of power and influence.[1] Students of Muslim intellectual history agree that the bulk of knowledge in traditional Islamic society, being religious, was mastered by the religious establishment, and that "struck right at the heart of person-to-person transmission of [Islamic] knowledge."[2] According to this theory, then, use of the printed word and the spread of secular knowledge broke the monopoly of the ulema.

The Ottoman case, however, does not support fully this sweeping contention. The Ottoman bureaucrats possessed administrative, historical, and literary, as well as religious knowledge, all of which they acquired and transmitted via the schools (*medreses* and the Enderun or the Palace Administrative School) or, later, through the *intisab*, the process of adding apprentices to the households of highly placed officials. High-ranking Ottoman officials often owned libraries of respectable size that contained many books on topics other than religion. Furthermore, although oral communication prevailed at lower levels, the upper religious and administrative establishments wrote extensively, as indicated by the large number of documents in the Ottoman archives, ranging from succinct orders to lengthy reports. While the ulema had a profound and sophisticated knowledge of religion, the bureaucracy had mastered, besides the rudiments of the faith, the political knowledge necessary to rule the society. For instance, *Ahlak-i Ala-i*, a treatise of practical politics by Kinalizade Ali (1510–1572) that was based on works of the same genre by Nasraddin Tusi (1201–1274) and Celaleddin Dawwani (ca. 1427–1502) discussed ethics and economics as well as administration.[3] This exceptionally practical-minded work, which was used as a textbook well into the nineteenth century, shaped the mentality of the Ottoman bureaucracy and stands as proof of the Ottomans' wide use of the written word to disseminate knowledge. Access to religious knowledge through the *medrese* was open to every Muslim, including the children of humble peasants, but the bureaucracy's recruitment system controlled access to the political knowledge essential for claiming the right to rule society. The *ilmiye* (ulema) members wrote and read large numbers of books and tracts on a variety of subjects, many of which can be found in the Suleymaniye manuscript library in Istanbul. The over one hundred thousand manuscripts there provided the material for Bursali Tahir's book on the Turks' contributions to science and the arts (see chapter 16). It is probably more correct to speak about a class monopoly of written knowledge than to depict knowledge as restricted to a small group or to attribute the spread of knowledge to just oral communication. At the same time, the bureaucracy used religion to legitimize this control of political power and knowledge.

The monopoly of religious, political, and administrative knowledge was broken in the early nineteenth century, after the Ottoman government gradually assumed a variety of new functions in education, justice, sanitation, and so on, and knowledge was diversified and percolated down to the lower classes. Formerly performed either by laymen or by religious foundations outside governmental control, or simply nonexistent, these new functions required such a large number of bureaucrats that the government had to open a series of modern schools after the 1830s (a school of engineering had been opened in 1734) and to recruit students from the lower social strata. Consequently, the social bases and qualifications for government service were gradually liberalized, and education became the primary qualifying condition.

Once founded, the modern schools, especially the professional ones, increasingly used printed textbooks; some were translated from French, while a few used directly the foreign-language originals. The public switch to written communication and the proliferation of printed sources of information in the Ottoman Empire, however, took place within the context of established bureaucratic traditions and was less traumatic than in societies relying mainly on oral communication. Moreover, the rational modes of thought prevailing in the bureaucracy made it receptive to new knowledge from outside or from the discovery and reevaluation of developments in the domestic society.

The modern printing press was introduced into the Ottoman Empire in 1727 by Ibrahim Muteferrika (d. 1745); he published some twenty books, a number of them truly unique European translations.[4] Book publishing then ceased until 1783. The low level of literacy, the high cost of printing and printed matter, and, especially, the lack of readers were some of the reasons for the failure of the enterprise to catch on in the eighteenth century. In particular, the lack of a body of readers large enough to sustain a book industry kept the business from developing. By the late nineteenth century, in contrast, there existed increased communication and a new Ottoman middle class that used the new avenues of communication to secure its position and imprint its own intellectual mark on the sociopolitical system. The cost of newspapers and books dropped, internal and world events became known to an increasingly large number of people as literacy spread to the lower classes, and social mobility intensified. (See chapter 4, section on education.)

The bureaucracy-intelligentsia ultimately came to consider themselves both the repository of the new knowledge gathered from reading the printed word as well as the representatives of the future social system they perceived—*imagined* is perhaps a better word—from reading books and newspapers. Oral communication continued to coexist with the printed medium. As mentioned, Sultan Abdulhamid, in his letters addressed to various Muslim rulers, would often inform them that the bearer of the letter would "communicate orally" important matters, probably for reasons of security. Ultimately the religious establishment, and the traditionalists too, began to employ the new knowledge, and the print media defended the sanctity of faith and tradition as they saw them. Eventually the press developed its own sphere of activity and autonomy to become a true political force, which all contenders of power tried to befriend, control, or liquidate, as the case might be.

The intelligentsia made the possession and utilitarian understanding of the new knowledge—mostly borrowed from Europe—the main criteria of modernism (reformism); it became the basis of their claim to high position and, in the twentieth century, their ideology of power. In the nineteenth century the modernist intelligentsia-bureaucracy used the press to create "public opinion," and the Palace, in turn, was compelled to accept the existence of such public opinion (*efkâr-i umumiye*) and seek to win it over by creating its own press. The press popularized the crucial concept of the *millet* (nation), and the constitutionalists of the 1860s tried to portray public opinion as the opinion of the *millet*, which they ultimately viewed as a secular political constituency, while the Palace regarded it as a politicized religious community. Although some constitutionalists, such as Namik Kemal, eventually came to regard the *millet* as a political community rooted in religion, others looked upon it as the product of the state's will and design. In any case, the *millet* acquired a certain political primacy, and the sultan himself had to consider it an entity that, if not superior to him, had some power and will of its own that it could use to oppose actions detrimental to its interest. When Mithat paşa, the driving power behind the Constitution of 1876, was arrested in 1877 by Sultan Abdulhamid II, he told the officials who came to take him away that the *millet* would rebel when they learned of his arrest. He regarded himself as the champion of the people and expected prompt popular support, which did not materialize.[5] The press had not yet acquired political power; but it was on the way toward being able to claim that it was the voice of the *millet*.

The first Ottoman newspaper, *Takvim-i Vaka-i* (Calendar of events) published by the government in 1825, had gone unnoticed; the next, with the explosive name the *Tasfir-i Efkâr* (Expression, or Description of Opinion), published by Ibrahim Şinasi in the early 1860s, dedicated itself to educating and informing the Ottoman public about world events *and to opinion making*. It was quickly noticed, but its readership was limited. The first newspaper to have a large readership was the populist *Basiret*, which became the voice of Islamism and Islamic nationalism.

Islamism and the Press

In the period 1875–80, Islamism changed its scope and direction to become, in fact, a modern type of ideology.[6] As the transformation took place, the press, old classical religious books, and, paradoxically, works translated from Western languages or modeled after Western books not only introduced European ideas but simultaneously disseminated many views of the Islamic revivalist movements, including the idea of popular action to save the faith. *Basiret* (Insightfulness, or Watchfulness, Understanding) emerged in these circumstances to play a major role in the revolution of the printed word and add an international dimension to the Ottoman Muslim political opinion. Starting as a purely entrepreneurial venture, it eventually attracted as writers some of the best-known intellectuals of the time. By 1875 its circulation had soared to 30,000 or 40,000, making it the most widely read popular newspaper of its time. Hilmi Ziya Ülken (1901–1974), the leading Turkish intellectual historian, character-ized *Basiret*, along with the *Tasvir-i Efkar* and *Ibret*, as the "voice of the people" (*halkin sesi*). The development of the people's voice, according to Ülken, was a by-product of the rise of the struggling, small entrepreneurs who appeared after the Tanzimat of 1839. It represented their "desire to conceptualize Westernism or modernism in the form of new ideas and deal with the essence of modernism rather than remain satis-fied with the formal adoption of laws," as had been the case until the 1860s.[7]

The memoirs of publisher Ali efendi (Basiretçi Ali, as he was known) indicate that he was devoid of any firm ideological commitment, although he later described him-self as a modernist and believer in the freedom of the press and the idea that some-how the newspaper was the "voice of the people." Ali efendi, perhaps inadvertently, became the tool of the Ottoman bureaucrats, who looked upon public opinion as the best means to counterbalance the despotism of the sultan. Ali reported in his mem-oirs that he applied for permission to publish a newspaper in 1867 but the bureau-crat in charge of the ministry blocked his request until "normal conditions" prevailed.[8] *Basiret* eventually received its publication permit in 1869, the year the influential reformist premier Fuat paşa died, leaving Ali paşa, as the only surviving reformist-Westernist in the upper ranks of the bureaucracy, to face alone Abdulaziz's drive to restore absolutism. As well as a permit to publish, Ali efendi also received 300 lira from the government for the "good public cause" his paper supposedly pur-sued; although *Basiret* claimed to be independent, it often found itself supporting the government's viewpoint. One year after it began publication, its editorial board, many of whose members were high-placed bureaucrat-intellectuals, sided with Ger-many in the Franco-German War of 1870. The paper's foresight in choosing the win-ner naturally increased its popularity, as did its audacious criticism of some govern-ment officials. It censured Hüsnü paşa, a much disliked interior minister, for his abuse of authority and ill-treatment of the population and thus gained a reputation as the "defender of the people."

After the war Chancellor Bismarck invited Ali efendi to Berlin and rewarded him so generously that he was able to purchase a late-model printing press, which made *Basiret* the best-equipped modern newspaper in Istanbul and, of course, a good friend of Germany. Ali efendi accepted Bismarck's invitation only after he obtained the Ottoman government's permission, and upon returning he reported his impressions and experiences to the authorities. The czar also invited him to St. Petersburg and awarded him a medal, although the newspaper maintained an anti-Russian stance. *Basiret* thus managed to become a newspaper courted by both the Ottoman and foreign governments. The government often "leaked" news to *Basiret*: in 1875 the premier, Nedim paşa, called on Ali efendi and asked him to print the news that the Ottoman government would reduce by half the interest paid to foreign bondholders. The news created a great sensation abroad, and Ali efendi was jailed briefly for dis-seminating "unauthorized" information. In fact, he was a scapegoat who went to jail several times for printing news unfavorable to the government or for inciting public demonstrations, although much of this information was passed to him by govern-ment officials.

The initial editorial staff of *Basiret* included several of the leading intellectuals associated with the Ottoman establishment: Suphizade Ayetullah, Mustafa Celaleddin paşa (a converted Pole), Ismail efendi (former chancery head of Yemen), Hayreddin efendi (this was the name assumed by Karski, also a Pole), and, eventually, Ahmet Mithat efendi, the father of Turkish popular journalism. In contrast to other well-known newspapers, such as *Istikbal* (Future) founded in 1875 by Teodor Kasap, *Terakki* (Progress), *Vakit* (Time), the *Muhbir* (Informer) of Filip (Philip) efendi, and *Sabah* (Morning) of Papadopulos, *Basiret* was an all-Muslim enterprise. There were, of course, several others, among them *Sadakat, Hadika, Hayal* and *Bedir*, owned by Muslims, but none achieved the wide circulation and influence of *Basiret,* which enjoyed both government favor (according to the occasion) and popular support.[9]

The events in Bulgaria, Serbia, and Bosnia in 1875/76,[10] coupled with the return of the Young Ottomans from exile in Europe after Sultan Abdulaziz was deposed, and the relative freedom brought temporarily by the constitution all enabled *Basiret* to adopt a populist Islamist position that increased its popularity and its circulation and deepened its influence. The Islamist position assumed by the newspaper in the years 1876–78 also suited the government's need for popular Muslim support at home and abroad against Russia; so it condoned, if it did actually not encourage, *Basiret*'s appeals to the world's Muslims, especially in Mecca, India, and Central Asia. Indeed, after the deposing of Abdulaziz and the dismissal of his authoritarian ministers in 1876, *Basiret* greatly increased the scope of its foreign news service, posting correspondents in several Muslim countries, thus becoming a truly modern newspaper and gaining financial independence. Inadvertently perhaps, after—and in spite of—years of collusion with the government and the constitutionalists, *Basiret* became truly the "voice of the people." This may be clearly seen from its writings, quoted throughout this study, in the period 1875–78.[11]

Basiret gave increased coverage to questions of change, reform, and Islamic revivalism. Along with other newspapers, it both formulated and expressed in popular terms many of the revivalist views, while defending the rights of the non-Ottoman Muslims. It helped debate, crystallize, and then popularize many of the issues exercising Muslims all over the world, in effect creating a certain broad sense of Islamic identity and solidarity that cut across state boundaries. Namik Kemal, the intellectual guide of the Young Ottomans and a constitutionalist, is credited with mentioning the term *Ittihad-i Islam* (Islamic Union) for the first time in 1872 in his newspaper *Ibret* (Example), but actually the idea was expressed in different forms by *Basiret* several times before that date. It is essential to point out that the idea of establishing a Muslim Union first emerged as a reaction to Russia's pan-Slavist propaganda among the Slavic Orthodox Christian population of the Ottoman Empire and Austria. *Basiret* and *Ibret*, like many other Ottoman publications, proposed to counteract Russia's panslavism with a Muslim version of their own devising, possibly modeled on "pan-Germanic" ideas. Meanwhile, organizations such as *Ihya-i Islam* (Revival, or Reconstruction, of Islam) and the *Society for the Study of the Geography of Muslim Countries* of Hoca Tahsin helped increase the Ottoman awareness of Muslims around the world. Eventually one of the writers for *Basiret*, the famous Esad efendi (d. 1890), authored a pamphlet in which he called for the establishment of an Islamic Union and appealed to Muslims to unite and to fulfill their religious obligations.

By 1875 the partisan attitude of *Basiret* toward Islamic issues became more pronounced, as Europe interfered more in Ottoman affairs on behalf of the Balkan Christians, and it turned belligerent after Russia invaded Ottoman lands in 1877. It described the plight of the refugees in evocative Islamic terms such as "Allah misafirleri, yani muhajir" ("immigrants, that is, God's guests").[12] The paper reported at length the desperate situation of the refugees fleeing the advancing Russian army, the terrorization of the defenseless Muslims and by marauding Bulgarian bands; it described also the poverty, disease, malnutrition, and death among the refugees in a deeply emotional manner that created strong sympathy for the people "whose land was attacked and who were forced to leave their homes and migrate to seek security in the Caliph's House."[13] *Basiret*, like other newspapers, urged the population to aid the refugees and described such aid as the expression of Muslim solidarity and unity.

At the same time, *Basiret* discovered, to its own amazement, an unsuspected dimension to the destitute refugees, who "even if housed in the best mansion cannot forget the deep suffering and sadness, caused by the loss of their *vatan* [homeland]. In their hearts there is always the longing for the *vatan*, on their tongue always the word *vatan*." The refugees' love and attachment for the place of their birth, from which they had been ousted by force, seemed a rather strange, though respectable, feeling to the dwellers in Istanbul, who were meeting for the first time their kin from the countryside. "My God," marveled *Basiret*, "this love of *vatan* is such a great divine gift that even a child in this tragic situation talks with his mother and father only about the *vatan*." This *vatan*, which would become eventually the political fatherland, was initially the actual village or town from which the refugees came and seemed to have a hold on them as strong as their faith.[14] A profound natural human sentiment, publicly expressed, thus became part of the intellectual and emotional patrimony of the new political culture.

Other newspapers, such as *Vakit* (Time), later *Tercuman-i Hakikat* (Truth interpreter), and for a short time *Muhbir* (Announcer) and *Ittihad* (Unity), gave extensive coverage to happenings in the Islamic world. The press described the *hac*, the annual pilgrimage to Mecca, as the epitome of Muslim unity, and it was in Mecca that Esad efendi's pamphlet, *Ittihad-i Islam* (Islamic Union), published in 1872, was printed and widely distributed. The pamphlet has the distinction of providing the first formal and relatively lengthy treatment of Islamic unity. Another pamphlet written in Arabic and bearing the stamp of the muftis of the four Muslims school of law (Hanafi, Şafi, Maliki, and Hanbali) provided *nasihat* (advice) to Muslims in general and to the governments of Turkistan, Iran, India, Morocco, Kaşgar, and Afghanistan, in particular, to beware of the Russians. The *nasihat* urged the Muslims of Central Asia and Afghanistan to unite and oppose the Russian advance southward to India. It also asked the Indian Muslims for help, after telling them how Russia incited the Balkan Christians to rebel against the Ottoman government. Similar calls for help— that is for money—were directed to the Muslims of Hicaz and Morocco, who were urged to join the rest of the Muslims. This pamphlet was reprinted in *Basiret,* which, along with other material published in the Ottoman state, reached India.[15]

The concept of Muslim unity was defined also as the search for progress, modernity, or civilization. Samipaşazade Sezai, a fairly prominent modernist writer associated with the establishment, published a lengthy article on Muslim unity in the newspaper *Ittihad* (Unity).[16] He stressed the importance of education as the source of enlightenment and of unity as stemming from the human need for association. According to Sezai, it was unity that had catapulted Europe to the zenith of progress and civilization. The regress of the Ottoman Empire, the fall of Muslim Spain and even of the Roman Empire was due to lack of unity—by which he actually meant "solidarity." Sezai confessed that without unity and education the Turks could not counter the might of the 200 million people of Europe; for the same reasons, the Arabs, whose civilization and learning had guided the world and produced many skills useful to humanity, now were living in ignorance. Because the 40 million Ottoman citizens were no longer capable of contributing to world civilization, their society needed a rejuvenation through a reappraisal of the Muslims' relations with Europe.

The Ottoman state, in Sezai's view, was the center of the Muslim world because the caliphate was located in Istanbul and because, being close to Europe, it was well positioned to carry to Asia and Africa the achievements of Europe. The Ottoman sultans Selim II and III, Nadir Shah of Iran, and even Timur (Tamerlane) had sought to establish Islamic connections with the West but had failed, for they had resorted to the use of the sword and had spilled blood. "The sword can cut the body," commented Sezai, who obviously reflected the European image of the Turks and Muslims as bent on war and conquest, "but could not produce ideas which appeal to the intellect [mind] and wisdom."

Sezai argued further that Europe had attained a high level of civilization by developing in unity the talents and capabilities given by God to all human beings. In his view the Islamic world could reach the level of European civilization by achieving solidarity and unity and by developing the natural aptitudes of its people as "ordered by the faith." A Muslim Union, according to Sezai, was not the symptom of fanaticism as claimed by some Europeans, but a commandment of the faith and a rejuvenating remedy for society as much as a service to Islam and to world civilization. He remarked sarcastically that the idea of religious unity (the Crusades) was first put forth by the Christians of Europe after the Turks came onto the world scene in the eleventh century but that nobody called the Christians "fanatics."

Sezai particularly urged Muslim leaders to emulate the European model of creativity and civilization by educating their population, implying broadly that civilization was the result of enlightenment and human effort at rationality rather than a divine gift. Sezai also implied that there was harmony between European civilization and human nature—balanced soul and body—as supposedly was the case in Islam in its days of glory, before it was intellectually ossified by dogma and oppression, a truly revolutionary thought. The gist of his argument, therefore, was that Muslims should rely on the natural aptitudes of their peoples, should unite and emulate the European civilization if they wanted to preserve and revive their own Islamic civilization. Sezai's article seems to have created a considerable interest in official circles, for it was stored and preserved in state archives.

The popular *Basiret* and the elitist *Ittihad* represented the two opposite poles of Islamic political thought in the Ottoman capital; but occupying the middle were several other publications, including other newspapers with an Islamic orientation, such as the weekly *Ahbar Dar-al Hilafe*, which initially received British support. In fact, Istanbul in the 1870s became the publishing center of the Muslim world, as thousands of books, pamphlets, and newspapers issued there found their way to Muslims living in Asia and Africa.[17] There were newspapers designed to serve specific purposes, such as *Al-Cevaib* (or *Al-Jevab*), "the first really important Arabic newspaper to be published: the first to circulate wherever Arabic was read, and to explain the issues of the world politics."[18] Published as early as 1861 by Faris al-Shidyaq (1801–1887), a Maronite who took the name of Ahmad upon becoming a Muslim, it appeared until 1884. For a while it received a subsidy from the British, who bought about one hundred copies for distribution in India, while the French banned its sale in Algeria. The newspaper was widely read throughout the Muslim world for its comprehensive news coverage (it had correspondents in many Muslim lands) rather than for its "religious" orientation.

Al-Cevaib did speak on behalf of Muslim causes, but it also praised European civilization and compared the decrepit state of Muslim society to the orderly, industrious, and productive life of Europe. It advocated the separation of religion from politics, women's participation in social activity, and children's education.[19] After coming to the throne in 1876 Abdulhamid gave *Al-Cevaib* money and moral support, not only because it defended the caliphate and Ottoman territorial integrity, but also because it advocated change and education, as well as unity. However, the newspaper alienated the religious establishment after it advised Muslims to learn one another's languages in order to understand one another; the establishment could not envision formal education in a vernacular other than Arabic, but events in the next years disappointed further, as education in Turkish and other languages spread.

To define the sentiment embodied in the concept of Islamic unity as expressed by the press we shall analyze a typical example. In an article titled "Bend-i Mahsusa, Rabita-i Maneviye" (Special bond, spiritual tie), *Basiret* claimed that Muslims were endowed with a special inner bond, *muhabbet-i kalbiye* (profound, heartfelt love), which had a permanent religious essence and compelled all Muslims to move toward central unity and alliance.[20] This sacred bond caused the Muslims to aid each other wherever they were and to fight the enemies of Islam—that is, Russia, at this stage. The newspaper claimed that the "friends" of the Muslims, such as England had no reason to worry about Islamic unity, which was basically a spiritual bond and brotherly feeling among Muslims. *Basiret* asserted that, although Muslims lived in different countries governed by different governments and rulers, their feelings of brotherhood did not challenge or conflict with their political loyalty to their governments, as long as the governments respected their faith.[21] It implied very strongly that the shared feelings of brotherhood among Muslims were religious, not political, and posed no danger to the governments of Europe. In particular, *Basiret* claimed that, faced with the threat of occupation, the Moroccan government, long alienated from the Ottomans, now appeared to lean toward unity and to accept the supremacy of the Ottoman caliph; and it advised the government to send a mission there. Indeed, one year later Abdulhamid did send a mission to Morocco to seek formal diplomatic relations.

The Test: Islamic Unity and War

The influence of the popular press and the politicization of Islam received new momentum in 1876–77, when war with Russia appeared inevitable and the Ottoman government sought to gain the moral and material support of all the Muslims. Ottoman officials in Jedda and Mecca took advantage of the *hac* season, which in 1876 fell in December, at the same time as the Constantinople conference that was pressuring the Ottoman government to grant autonomy to the Balkan Christians. The famous Haci Eyub Sabri efendi (later paşa), who taught at the Naval School in Istanbul, asked Bekir Sitki, the Ottoman military doctor serving in the imperial battalion of the Hicaz, to urge the Muslims in Mecca to unite and to aid the Porte financially. Meanwhile Esad efendi's *Ittihad-i Islam* was given wide circulation, and other Ottoman officers, such as Abdullah paşa and the *amir* of Mecca, launched a campaign to collect money and disseminate the idea of a Muslim Union, which was still aimed at Russia.

In Istanbul, the new sultan, Abdulhamid II, had come to the throne on 31 August 1876. He promulgated the constitution on 23 December 1876 and convened the parliament on 19 March 1877; but his actions did not preempt the Constantinople conference or deter Russia from declaring war on 24 April 1877. Already the czar had stated that it was his Christian duty to end the rule of the Muslims over the Orthodox Christians and even to put an end to Islam, which he regarded as a menace to his authority over the conquered Muslims in Russia and Central Asia. A turning point in the history of the Ottoman state and Islam was fast approaching. The main Russian purpose in the war of 1877–78 was to neutralize, if not to liquidate, the Ottoman state and the caliphate as a political and cultural-religious force. In a letter addressed to the European clergy, *Basiret* told them not to rejoice, since it was impossible to do away with Islam, and not to pay attention to Russia, the "enemy of Islam." Until the winter of 1877 the Islamist propaganda in the Ottoman press was aimed primarily at Russia; the Muslims viewed England as an Ottoman ally and protector. In fact, the press went to some trouble to explain that the anti-Russian Islamic mobilization would help the British in India, despite the fact that the most of Muslim Indians were vehemently opposed to the rule of London. The Ottoman leaders—actually the constitutionalist-modernists—appeared to think at this stage that the relative modernization of the army, the fighting capabilities of the Turkish soldier, and support from other Muslims should enable the sultan to defeat the Russians.

The war provided the first major opportunity for the Porte to make practical use of its Muslim allies in Russia, but the attempt to do so was not successful, as explained previously.[22] Although the war was disastrous for the Ottoman state in every possible way, it helped transform overnight the Muslims' sense of religious brotherhood into a political consciousness, and thus it opened the way for a new sense of solidarity and development of the idea of a new type of political community. True, the homogenization of the population embodied in the idea of Ottomanism, the centralization of authority, the adoption of the European concept of citizenship, and a myriad of other legal, economic, and administrative measures had laid down the material foundations of nationhood, but they had not supplied the psychological force necessary to glue the Ottoman Muslims together into a nation. The war of 1877–78, with the atrocities inflicted by the Orthodox Slavs and the danger of disintegration facing the Ottoman state, gave the Ottoman Muslims a new awareness about themselves and a perception that a new type of sociopolitical organization might be their salvation. This was a mental and psychological transformation that made the Muslims in even the remotest corners of the Empire aware of their position in society and in the world at large.

This was a seminal transformation that will be analyzed later in some depth. Suffice it here to say that both the notion of individual rights and of nation took on a new look. The concept of individual political freedom was almost meaningless to most Muslims prior to 1878 (the rights embodied in the Edict of 1856 were bestowed mainly on Christians); but as more of the public became literate and realized the ineptitude of its leaders, the idea became more general and internalized. The term *millet* no longer referred to a strictly religious congregation or to various non-Muslim groups (*anasir-i muhtelife*) but rather to a political community made up of Muslims. The conservatives viewed the nation as a predominantly religious political community, while the modernists viewed it as potentially a secular and worldly political community. In both cases the prototype differed in essence from the classical *ümmet*, as each intellectual group sought to identify itself politically with the nation on the basis of religion or ultimately of ethnicity. The identification with the "nation," in turn, led each group to develop its own brand of populism, or *halkçilik*, which in 1923–24 joined nationalism as one of the two founding principles of the Turkish Republic.

After 1878 the Ottoman government confronted a mass of individuals awakening to their own humanity and emerging as a new political identity. As a result, the ideas of reform, progress, civilization, and religion took on new meaning and force. Nevertheless, the goal of the early reforms initiated by the Ottoman government was to preserve the state; through them, perhaps unintentionally, the power of the elitist military bureaucratic order that had ruled almost since the state's inception was maintained and augmented. The government's reform movement led to the reorganization of the bureaucracy and the provision of services nonexistent in the past; but it also endowed the government with far more authority than in the past, without noticeably bettering the commoner's life. After 1877–78, therefore, the press criticized the government's failures and the backwardness of society and formulated increasingly individualist demands, including those for political freedom. For the most part, the discussion of all these issues was carried out in an Islamic context, material progress often being described as ordered by the faith. Oddly enough, Islam was increasingly used to criticize statism—that is, bureaucratic supremacy.

The transformation of the religious community into a nation, or protonation, the process of individualization, the spread of new knowledge, the growing dissatisfaction with the ruling order, and the use of the press to articulate and express these developments in political terms all were epitomized in the putsch engineered by Ali Suavi. This event marked a turning point in the intellectual and political history of the Ottoman state and Abdulhamid's life, and consequently it deserves to be studied not as an isolated case of aberration and insubordination but as a seminal development.

Basiret and the Civilian Attempt to Change Sultans

In May 1878 Ali Suavi led a band of Balkan refugees who stormed the Çirağan Palace and attempted to abduct and to restore the constitutionalist-minded Murad V to the throne. Suavi was born in Istanbul in 1838, of parents who had some Caucasian roots, although his father, Kağitçi Hüsnü (Hüseyin), was a paper merchant originally from the village of Çay in the Çankiri district in central Anatolia. Ali studied in both a traditional *medrese* and a modern *rüşdiye*, learned Arabic (then Persian, English, and French) and, like the revivalists, developed considerable insight into the study of *hadis*. Deeply impressed by the Prophet Muhammad's condemnation of tyranny, he called it the "Messenger's first miracle." Suavi taught at the *rüşdiye* in Simav near Kütahya and was later employed in an administrative and teaching position in the town of Filibe (the old Philippopolis, now Plovdiv, in Bulgaria), where he also preached at the mosque and expressed his dislike of absolutism and personal rule. One author has concluded rather hastily that Suavi's force "consisted in being in touch with that large inchoate mass of dissatisfaction which modern political manipulators usually equate with 'the people,'"[23] a pedantic statement that ignores the essence of the extraordinary events of 1875–78 and their creative effect.

From the pulpit of the Yeşiloğlu mosque in Filibe, Suavi talked about a new political order, established a communal organization and achieved a great popularity and following; but he was dismissed from his job for instigating "people to revolt," according to his accuser Ata bey, the well-known historian and defender of the old order. Returning to Istanbul, Suavi worked for the newspaper *Muhbir* and became an effective preacher in the main mosques of Istanbul. In his early writings and preachings Suavi claimed that a healthy government had to rely first on enlightenment and the rule of law and that the relations between the government and the people had to be built on two inseparable principles: freedom and a harmony of views between the government and the people. His articles in *Muhbir* soon caused dissatisfaction in official circles, and he was exiled to Kastamonu; but Suavi's friends secretly brought him back to Istanbul in 1867 and, with the help of French officials in the capital, spirited him off to Paris. There he joined the other Young Ottomans already in exile, practically all of them becoming proteges of Mustafa Fazil paşa, a scion of the Egyptian *khedive*'s family, who used his great wealth to finance the opposition to Sultan Abdulaziz. Ali Suavi eventually went to England and married an Englishwoman.

Returning to Europe, Suavi published the *Muhbir* and then *Ulüm* (1869); the first issues of the latter publication, a total of some 880 pages, were written in longhand by Suavi himself and duplicated for wider circulation. Suavi was initially on good terms with Namik Kemal, the famous leader of the Young Ottomans, but their relations soured after Fazil paşa made peace with the sultan and returned to Istanbul to take a ministerial position. Suavi afterward refused financial assistance from Fazil paşa, whom he described as having embraced the cause of the oppressor, the sultan; but Namik Kemal continued to accept his monthly stipend. After Suavi questioned their political integrity, Namik Kemal and Ziya paşa attacked him in the most abusive terms and depicted him as an unstable, ignorant troublemaker, creating an image that survives to this day.

The difference between Kemal, an elitist in every sense of the word, and Ali Suavi, a populist, stemmed from their social backgrounds as well as their political philosophies. Kemal, from an old bureaucratic family, had a precocious, brilliant mind but was a utopian and a political romantic. His idealization of the Ottoman-Islamic past and glorification of the fatherland (to be discussed later) secured him a lofty position among conservatives and modernists alike. Suavi, on the other hand, was a realist preoccupied with the living society and the material welfare of the individual Muslim as much as with his faith, traditions, and culture. Kemal relied on government and state power to achieve his goals, hence his appeal to the elitist statists; Suavi believed in direct mass action by the community. Sharing the same ideas, aspirations, and methods of action that prevailed in the revivalist movements, Ali Suavi was one of the first Ottoman thinkers to try to give a more systematic and coherent expression to revivalist ideas.

In 1876 Suavi and other opponents of Sultan Abdulaziz living abroad accepted Mithat paşa's invitation to return to Istanbul, and Suavi was appointed head of the Galatasaray—the French *lycée*. Suavi also had attracted the attention of the new sultan, Abdulhamid, who made him a member of the imperial advisory council. Soon, however, he was dismissed from the presidency of Galatasaray, according to some views, for "incompetence."[24] In fact, he was dismissed as the result of pressure from the British ambassador. In a dispatch to London, British Ambassador Layard in Istanbul wrote to Robert A. T. Gascoyne-Cecil, marquess of Salisbury (1830–1903), as follows.

> Your Lordship will no doubt recollect the name of Ali Suavi, and that I succeeded some time ago in having him dismissed from his post as Director of the College of Galata Serai. He was a mischievous intriguer who had, on more than one occasion, endeavored by seditious placards, and by preaching in the mosques of Constantinople, to excite the fanaticism of the Mussulman population, and to produce disorders and disturbances. Although a Softa, he professed very liberal opinions . . . for various reasons I had declined to make his acquaintance.[25]

After his dismissal Suavi preached as usual in the mosques of Istanbul and wrote occasional articles in *Basiret*, using a plain, colloquial Turkish that stood in sharp contrast to the embellished, tortured language of his upper-class contemporaries. Suavi claimed that Islamism, Westernism, and nationalism (Turkism) were complementary; that a state could not be governed on religious principles alone; that general education, the study of modern sciences, and new teaching methods were necessary; that the freedom of assembly guaranteed the rights of the community; that resistance to the unjust was justified; and that industrial development was so essential it should be supported by the government. In addition, he condemned the inertia that seemed to have afflicted the Ottoman and Muslim societies, spoke openly about the Turkishness of some Ottoman leaders, and advocated the use of a pure, colloquial Turkish and the introduction of the Latin alphabet. However, he opposed the adoption of nationality (ethnicity) as a principle of political organization. Suavi further believed that all religions, including Islam, had a spiritual essence and held universal appeal.

On the political level Suavi identified himself with the underprivileged and the oppressed, defending equality among people regardless of their social and political position. In this vein he had great esteem for the wisdom of the simple people and was dismissive of the elite's notion that the masses were too ignorant to understand the intricacies of government. According to Suavi, the Ottoman reforms undertaken so far had not improved people's lives, for they were intended mainly to "deceive" Europe and soothe the fears of the Ottoman Christians. In his view, Islamic principles did not accept the sharp division of society into noble, educated leaders and humble followers, a division that ensured no ideas could be born outside the preserve of a small elite—that is, the state's leaders. Instead, he believed, Islamic principles were more consistent with representative government. People should be taught to take initiatives to better their own lives rather than wait for a mythical savior to deliver them from the tyranny of rulers who acted without responsibility and were interested only in profits. Suavi also claimed the caliphate had no foundation in Islam, thus incurring the wrath of both the sultan and, paradoxically, the English, who wished to use the caliphate for their own political purposes. Extremely critical of European imperialism in all its forms, he called for the unity of the Muslims to fight it and viewed Muslims primarily as individuals whose aggregation formed the community.

The ideas and actions of Ali Suavi cannot be intensively studied here, but especially worthy of attention are his belief in democratic populism and progressism, his search for concrete actions capable of materializing these ideals, and his employment of mass mobilization to achieve his goals. It was precisely these three tenets in his thinking that led to the revolutionary act that put an end to the newspaper *Basiret* as well as to Suavi's own life and to the radical, populist phase of Ottoman Islamism that had flourished from 1875 to 1878. Henceforth Islamism would be promoted from the top by Abdulhamid, minus its element of populist radicalism, although the sultan turned some revivalist aspirations for material progress into state policy and thus was able to contain their political fervor and radicalism.

Suavi was associated with the newspaper *Basiret* chiefly after his return to Istanbul in 1876—that is, after Sultan Abdulaziz had been ousted and the establishment of a constitutional monarchy appeared to be certain. Suavi criticized Sultan Abdulhamid II's conduct of the war, his anticonstitutionalist attitude, the arbitrary dismissal and exile of Mithat paşa (5 February 1877), and, especially, the sultan's refusal to support fully both the Muslim resistance in Bosnia against the Hapsburgs and the Muslims' anti-Bulgarian, anti-Russian revolt in the Rhodope mountains. Although his criticism disturbed many people, he was left in peace. The government and Sultan Abdulhamid II were preoccupied with the ongoing war and probably believed that Suavi's preaching was harmless rhetoric. But they were wrong.

Finally deciding to take matters into his own hands, on 19 May 1878 Ali Suavi announced in *Basiret* that "people" should assemble the next day to hear a very important message and find a quick solution to the country's problems. On 20 May 1878 a group of people, mostly refugees from the Filibe area lost to Bulgaria, with Ali Suavi at their head, marched to the Çirağan Palace, the residence of the ex-sultan, Murad V. Their intention was to re-enthrone Murad V, who had left the throne some eighteen months earlier and was known to support a constitutional system, while, in contrast, Abdulhamid had disbanded the parliament, suspended the constitution, and begun his thirty-year regime of absolutism.

The ill-planned action failed. Suavi was killed in the melee, and his followers were arrested and brought to trial. Eight days later the government closed *Basiret* for good. Ali efendi, the publisher, who had become a defender of the constitution despite his previous closeness to the government, was arrested and sent to exile in the Yemen. Many political exiles returned home after a few years, but Ali efendi came home to Istanbul only after the Young Turks' coup of 1908, although he was permitted to reside in Syria in the meantime. Ali efendi, his *Basiret*, and Ali Suavi had become accomplices in the worst possible crime in the Ottoman political dictionary: the incitement of the ordinary Muslim citizen to rebel against his/her masters, however justified this might seem. The entire power establishment, from the highly placed ulema down to the humblest bureaucrat, rallied to condemn Suavi as an immoral, mentally unbalanced subversive. The establishment teamed up to sully Suavi's memory with half-truths, derision, contempt, and the venomous sarcasm so well employed by Celaleddin paşa, otherwise a sound source.[26] The participants in the putsch, some 100 to 150 people, were brought to trial, the leaders were executed or sent into exile, and the rest were freed but, together with other refugees, signed a pledge of loyalty to the sultan. Among those condemned to death was Hafiz Nuri, a leading *alim* of Filibe, the first active accomplice in the plot. Others, such as Ahmet paşa, Hafiz Ali, Haci Mehmed, and Nuri and Izzet, the sons of Süleyman paşa, to mention just the more important ones, were exiled to various places in the Empire.

The establishment appeared frightened by this Muslim attempted civilian coup, the first of its kind in Ottoman history. The sultan took the unusual step of asking the *şeyhulislam* whether the execution and other punishment of the organizers of the plot were religiously correct. The *şeyhulislam*, then Ahmet Muhtar efendi or Molla bey, as usual obliged; all death sentences needed, in any case, the formal approval of the *şeyhulislam*.[27] Ali Suavi's memory, along with that of Mithat paşa, haunted Abdulhamid throughout his reign, to the extent that anyone associated in the slightest manner with or deemed sympathetic to these two individuals—one a modernist, the other a Muslim activist—aroused the sultan's immediate suspicion and incurred severe retributive action.

The true reasons behind Ali Suavi's putsch were complex and far-reaching. His followers seem to have been mainly refugees from the Rhodope and the Filibe regions, who had been gathered with the promise that they would go to join the Muslim resistance in the Rhodope mountains after receiving the blessing of the sultan and regain their homeland lost to the Bulgarians. A translated extract from *La Turquie* provides a semiofficial and distorted description of the event:

> The so named Ali Suavi, known by the population for his intrigues, his seditious spirit and perfidious activities towards the nation and the State has tried to reach his seditious goals. To this effect he joined some individuals who were incapable of separating the good from the evil and without informing them of his goal went today 8/20 May at four o'clock, Turkish time in the morning, to the Chiragan Palace. Some of these individuals succeeded in entering the palace with the purpose (God preserve us) of provoking a sedition. . . . Ali Suavi, the organizer of this cabal was killed in the collusion, and the principal accomplices whose number is very limited were arrested. This seditious committee did not have any branches, and security and public order which are under the auspices of his Majesty, the Sultan, were not affected at all. His Majesty, the Sultan, had ordered that the case of the arrested be brought immediately to trial and that they be punished according to the law.[28]

A lengthy excerpt from the *Herald Tribune* found in the British Public Records Office gives fuller and more balanced information about the incident and is worth reproducing at some length.

> Among the dead were his Excellency Ali Suavi efendi, late Governor of the Imperial Lyceum of Galata-Serai—formerly well known as a prominent exiled *littérateur* of the "Young Turkey" party—as also a Circassian chief—and some other leaders of the movement. The wounded prisoners, after being questioned by the *binbaşi* (of-

ficer in charge), were, at His Majesty's request, taken before the sultan, who interrogated them in person. They were, they said, from the neighborhood of Philip-
popoli, and had joined a band which had been raised by Ali Suavi and the Tcherkess
chief, with the avowed object of assisting their brethren in the Rhodope. Ali Suavi
had given them arms, and had mustered them near Tcheragan to do homage to the
sultan before they started on their expedition, and the sultan, they had been led to
believe, would furnish them with money. They were not aware that Murad was not
the sultan, or that they were going to the presence of Murad; they thought they were
being led to their Padishah. The sultan expressed his commiseration for them, as
they had been deceived by the instigations and mispresentations of the ringleaders,
and he ordered that every medical attention should be paid to the wounded.

Early in the afternoon, His Majesty summoned Ministers to a special Cabinet
Council at Yeldiz-kiosk, at which some measures were discussed for the prompt
removal of the refugees from the capital, and if our information be correct, it was
decided to charter without delay a sufficient number of steamers to convey them to
some other place. After the Council the sultan sent an invitation to ex-Sultan Murad
to come to the Imperial villa at Yildiz, which that Prince at first declined to accept,
and he was even inclined to resist it when pressed upon him by His Majesty's aide-
de-camp. On being assured, however, that he would be exposed to no sort of in-
convenience, Murad efendi attended the aide-de-camp to the sultan's residence at
Yeldiz-kiosk, and still remains there, the guest of his Imperial brother.[29]

Murat remained there almost to the end of his life. Moreover, Sultan Abdulhamid
refused to issue to Murat's close relatives permission to marry (members of the royal
family could marry only with the permission of the incumbent sultan).

The Suavi incident marked the beginning of self-initiated popular actions for the
defense of the fatherland or for changing the government, which until then had been
beyond the scope of the commoners' thinking. The Rhodope Rebellion provides a
good yardstick for measuring popular involvement in political action.[30] It started in
1877 as a grassroots resistance against the outrages that Bulgarian bands and Russian
soldiers had committed against the Muslims in the occupied areas, but it soon turned
into an armed movement for self-government and independence and brought large
areas under its control. Eventually a Turkish-Muslim government headed by Ahmet
Aga Timirsky (Demir) was established in the Rhodope area. The cease-fire agreement
and then the San Stefano Treaty of 3 March 1878 stipulated that the sultan should
use his authority to end the rebellion in the Rhodopes and a committee composed of
high Ottoman dignitaries contacted the rebels but was unable to persuade them to
lay down their arms. Meanwhile the public opposed any territorial compromise and
urged the sultan to aid the rebels. One Turkish historian claims that Ali Suavi tried
to persuade Abdulhamid II to reject the San Stefano Treaty and fight the Russian army
to the end. The sultan refused, and Suavi, who had been on good terms with him until
then, decided to replace him with Murad V.[31]

For his part, Abdulhamid attempted without success to secure the czar's intervention to stop the massacres of the Muslims. Some of the educated public began to think
the sultan would accept even a humiliating peace treaty in order to keep his throne
rather than fight to preserve Muslim independence and the integrity of their homeland—the *vatan*. Although the Berlin Treaty modified some of the provisions of the
San Stefano Treaty to the advantage of the Muslims, it left most of the rebel areas to

Bulgaria. The resistance there continued until the sultan insisted it stop and used his caliphal authority to persuade the rebels to lay down their arms, an act that cost him much of his prestige and authority. The loss of eastern Rumili to Bulgaria in 1885 further diminished the sultan's prestige. Soon after Ali Suavi's plot was quelled, approximately 180,000 refugees from the Balkans living in Istanbul were sent hurriedly to the interior of the country, lest they stage another massive uprising against Abdulhamid, and the transfer of Murad V to the palace at Yildiz, where he was kept under close surveillance to prevent any other attempt to install him on the throne, was effected.

In retrospect, Ali Suavi, a commoner who had an Islamic and Western-style education, envisioned a modern Ottoman-Muslim society that conformed to existing social, cultural, and political realities. He thought of modernization as a way to build a new society out of an incessant interaction between the traditional society and modern social, economic, political, and cultural forces, including influences from Europe. Yet he never advocated blind imitation of Europe. In effect, he spoke on behalf of an emerging, new Muslim society that was developing its own identity and expectations. The sultan used these same popular expectations to consolidate the power of the state, although in the process he incorporated many revivalist ideas into established Islam. The clash between the Islamist intellectuals, represented by Suavi, and the sultan revolved around their differing vision of the future of Islam, which united them historically and religiously but separated them politically on the issue of individual aspirations and rights. The revivalist Muslim intelligentsia had developed an individualized concept of rights and freedoms and the prerogative to defend them against an absolutist state; at the same time, the political establishment used Islamic arguments to justify maintenance of the status quo, while in contrast, the small, but rapidly growing, modernist intelligentsia adopted an increasingly secular constitutional and liberal perspective. Lying beneath all these developments was a growing yearning for some sort of democracy, although neither the Islamists nor the modernists were able to define it or to overcome their elitist attitudes.

The press played a seminal role in the clash between the intelligentsia and the establishment and became overnight an almost indispensable medium for imparting knowledge and forming opinion. Soon after the closing of *Basiret*, the sultan commissioned Ahmed Mithat efendi to publish a newspaper, the *Tercuman-i Hakikat*, which occupies a vital place in Ottoman intellectual history. The newspaper echoed the sultan's Islamist statist political philosophy but also disseminated masses of new information about every conceivable subject, becoming the most influential modernist medium in the period 1878–1908 (see chapters 7 and 8). After 1878 a large number of books that promoted mass education and enlightenment, along with modernization and the use of the colloquial Turkish, also were published. One of the main representatives of this trend was Münif paşa (1830–1910), who was educated in Damascus and Cairo and spent three years working for the Ottoman embassy in Berlin, where he audited university courses.[32] He believed in the reconciliation of Western and Eastern cultures and, as the minister of education for many years, he implemented widespread educational reforms. Especially during his third tenure, 1885–91, general education and the use of Turkish spread rapidly, and modern libraries were established. Münif believed in the power of ideas and in the supreme leadership roles of the modernist intelligentsia, whom he regarded as the apostles of civilization who should force the "bitter pill of progress," namely science and technology, on the population. He enjoyed the sultan's backing but eventually was dismissed after accusing the sultan of not following Western advice fully.

Ottoman modes of thought underwent profound transformation after the years 1970–78, as realism became its earmark. The best evidence of this is found in the modern literature that developed rapidly after 1860 and reached maturity during Abdulhamid's absolutist reign. Already Namik Kemal, in his introduction to his play *Celaleddin Harzemşah*, although extolling the virtues of Islamic history, decried, by implication, the old modes of thought when he demanded that a writer should conform to *hakikat*, or reality. He stated that progress had produced a modern Ottoman literature and increased by "one hundred times in ten years," the number of readers of modern literature, including women. "Even shopkeepers and servants in Istanbul," he wrote, "read newspapers or at least listen to [a reading of] them. They acquire, thus, knowledge about their *public* rights towards the state, love of the fatherland, military glory, and war events." This introduction deserves to be read by all students of intellectual change in the Ottoman Empire.[33] Namik Kemal wanted people to rely on the intellect (reason), on observation and logic, and to be able to construct mentally future events and situations. One could easily deduce that such "constructions" involved the government and the regime, for the idea of social relativism was spreading. Eventually in 1890, the sultan prohibited the printing and distribution of writings by Namik Kemal, Ziya paşa, the poet Abdulhak Hamid, and even his trusted advisor, Ahmet Cevdet paşa, primarily because they seemed to question the state's— that is, the sultan's—absolutism, even though they remained respectful of Islam and of the ruler.

Conclusion

In sum, the development of the print media, with the increasing availability of newspapers and books at reasonable prices and the growth in the number of readers, permitted both Islamists and Westernists to disseminate a great variety of ideas. Although often confusing and contradictory, mainly after 1878, these ideas prepared the ground for a profound intellectual and political revolution that lasted for generations, if not centuries. Abdulhamid understood very clearly the extraordinary power of the press and tried to cultivate and use it, but he could not prevent it from becoming its own worst enemy and nightmare. The foreign powers used their "free" press to excoriate and condemn Abdulhamid without causing diplomatic incidents except on rare occasions. The French used *Le Figaro*, while the Russians enlisted *Le Nord*, a Brussels newspaper, into their service and financed the famous salon of Madame Olga Novikov in London, in which Turks were described as unfit for Western civilization and as promoters of "Muslim fanaticism." The sultan easily muzzled the domestic press through a special bureau attached to the Ministry of the Interior (a section in the Foreign Ministry dealt with the press abroad), but he could not prevent the dissemination of news. The fact that the Ottoman state did not have its own information organization made all the domestic newspapers dependent on European news agencies.[34]

The sultan's censorship was applied to books and newspapers with a political or openly anti-Islamic content but did little to prevent the spread of ideas on science, modernism, and Europe, which the sultan did not oppose. Some books prohibited from entering the Ottoman state were the following: a brochure titled *Telhis-i Amal-i Vatanperverane* (Summary of patriotic activities) written by one Selim and published in Paris; *History of Eastern Wars, The Secret of Yildiz* by Paul de Regla, published in Paris; *Memalik-i Şahanede Muhaberat* (Correspondence-press in the sublime realm) by Major Osman, published in Leipzig; *Külliyat-i Hikmet* (Hikmet's works) by Abdulhakim Hikmet, published in Geneva; and *Mal d'Orient*, originally published in French in 1887. The author of the last book tried unsuccessfully to blackmail the sultan, asking for 400 liras not to translate the book into English.[35] Among the newspapers prohibited at one time or another from entering the country were *Correspondance de l'Est*, *Petit Parisien*, and *Indépendance Belge*, along with several journals printed in Egypt and smuggled in through various small Mediterranean ports. Calendars likely to contain unfavorable information were also prohibited.[36] Nonetheless, it was during Abdulhamid's time that printed books became a normal accoutrement of the houses of the well-to-do and those eager to learn. Orhan Koloğlu, a former press director in the 1970s, has provided telling statistics on books printed in the Ottoman state in the period 1820–1908 (see table 5.1).

Thus, the Ottoman Muslim public acquired a basic knowledge about modern civilization, Europe, and its own identity—all of which served as the intellectual foundation for the Young Turks movement and the Republic. The true modernistic phase of Ottoman publishing began after 1878 and, especially, after 1880–82, as Ottoman relations with England and France soured and the Ottoman intelligentsia and government placed priority on self-development and self-reliance. Although political freedom was greatly restricted and press censorship heavily enforced, a series of new newspapers and reviews, to be mentioned below in due place, coupled with a rising rate of literacy nonetheless accomplished the widespread dissemination of new and varied information about the progress of contemporary civilization and its formidable force. *Tercuman-i Hakikat* (1878–1922), *Ikdam* (1894–1928), *Tercuman* (published in Crimea, 1883–1917) were among the major newspapers of the new generation that generalized the idea of progress. According to expert opinion, the "foundations of modern Turkish book printing were laid and Western understanding of books and of printing were introduced during Abdulhamid II's reign";[37] but, while the public benefited from the new knowledge disseminated by the press, the sultan became almost a prisoner of the "opinion makers" of the newspaper world and often was prey to their exploitation. He befriended Arminius Vambery, in the belief, among others, that the Hungarian wielded great influence with

Table 5.1. Books Published in the Ottoman State, 1820–1908, by Subject

Years	Literature	Positive Science	Religion	Government
1820–39	56	89	59	13
1840–59	217	230	310	55
1860–76	583	583	372	118
1876–1908	2,950	3,891	1,307	946

Source: Orhan Koloğlu, *Avrupa Kiskacinda Abdulhamid* (Istanbul, 1998), p. 406.

the Western press and would manage to secure the printing of laudatory articles about the sultan. Vambery was allowed to visit the imperial library and honored in many other ways.[38] In another case, the newspaper *Correspondance de l'Est* managed to inform the Porte that it was preparing a pamphlet describing how Murad V had regained his health and would claim the throne. A correspondent for that paper, Theodore Chu, subsequently came to Istanbul and promised to prevent the publication of the pamphlet in exchange for money and favors. The *Correspondance de Wien* also fabricated a story that Reşat efendi, next in line to succeed Abdulhamid, had made plans to take over the throne and then asked for money not to divulge the plan (Reşat did become sultan from 1909 to 1918, after Abdulhamid's abdication).

The press and the modern literature in general preached the virtues of progress, science, and freedom, thus slowly and steadily eroding the foundations of absolutism. The printed word and the spread of knowledge increased greatly the impact of the public schools, which, although controlled by the government, broadened literacy, created their own political culture and methods of indoctrination, and made freedom the chief goal of students. The press and the educational system became in fact the symbol of modernity, if not modernity itself.

Abdulhamid appreciated the power of modern education and engineered its spread to the lower classes both in order to spread his control of his subjects and to create a professional elite, which was to strengthen the state against Europe and to enable him to maintain state supremacy and, ultimately, that of the dynasty.[39] The actual outcome of this complex political-cultural development will be studied in the next chapters.

6

The War of 1877–1878 and Diverging
Perceptions of Islam and Europe

As the ideas of the new Ottoman middle classes and information about the situation of the Muslims in Russia, India, Indonesia, and Africa were disseminated among Ottoman Muslims by the print media and modern education, Islam began to acquire a new international dimension that the West described as "pan-Islamism" and attributed to Abdulhamid rather than to the rising political consciousness of the very middle classes that England and France had helped create.

For a long time the Muslim public had remained aloof from foreign relations and unknowledgeable about their impact on the destiny of the nation. However, anti-French and anti-British public sentiment mounted steadily with the occupation of Cyprus (1878) and Egypt (1882) by England and of Tunisia (1881) by France. These events finally turned the Ottoman public away from England, long regarded as a friend and protector against Russia. The belief that Europe had decided to put an end to the Ottoman Empire increased. Newspapers such as *Basiret* gave wide publicity to popular discontent and generated a degree of anti-European sentiment among the middle classes, who, in turn, communicated their own views to the lower classes. After the 1870s even ordinary Ottomans came to regard Egypt and North Africa as an organic part of their land that had been taken (usurped)—a situation hardly conceivable before the 1860s. Long accustomed to regard the sultan as an absolute ruler who could enforce his authority whenever and wherever he wished, the British and the French could not comprehend that the opposition to them came from a new political force—in fact, a civil center of power that both Europe and the sultan now had to take into account. This was the new middle class that had its own views about government, freedom, and its place in society, and was developing protonationalist ideology akin to anticolonialism. Ironically, the French and the British, who earlier had advocated freedom of expression, complained frequently to the Porte that the hostility of the press and public stemmed from a "fanatical" anti-European sentiment, that needed to be controlled. Although Sultan Abdulhamid was prone to exploit public opinion in his favor, he feared that the rise of anti-European sentiment among Muslims could harm his relations with England and France and often accommodated the two powers by silencing newspapers critical of the West. When the sultan and the Porte proved unable to suppress the criticism completely or to stop Muslims from plotting against

136

the French or English, however, Paris and London came to believe that the anti-European campaign actually was being orchestrated by the Porte and the sultan.

The French in particular believed that the sultan was engaged in "oriental double-dealing" by overtly assuring them of friendship and cooperation while covertly inciting the public against them. In fact, France and Russia both had warned England that efforts to bolster the prestige of the caliph could ultimately prove dangerous to European interests, but London ignored these warnings until their own attempt to use the caliphate against Russia in Central Asia in 1878 failed. In sum, the European powers had compelled the Ottoman state to undertake reforms in the name of progress, civilization, and freedom, yet proved unwilling to face the social consequences of the very changes they had promoted. Instead of accepting as natural the anticolonialism of the new middle classes they had helped create, the Europeans attributed the Muslims' self-consciousness and efforts to defend their independence and culture to religious fanaticism and intolerance.

From the 1870s onward, England, France, and Russia had to contend with a new Muslim middle class that had substantial popular roots and often opposed both its own government and Europe. It is ironic that this new middle class, or at least its modernist wing, opposed its own government in the name of the progress and political freedom it had learned about from Europe, at the same time as it accused Europe of using Western civilization as a symbol of superiority to reject, subjugate, and undermine their own cultures and faith. Also at the same time, the conservative segment of the middle classes, although far more anti-European than its modernist counterpart, was using Western criteria to judge the value of its own culture, faith, and identity. The involvement of the Muslim middle classes in international politics and the European misperceptions of the caliphate as the instigator of this opposition are both illustrated by the Algerian Revolt of 1871.

The Algerian Revolt of 1871 and French Views of the Caliphate

The Algerian revolt clearly demonstrates the revolutionary role of the new middle classes, the politicization of the religious establishment, the growing Muslim anticolonialist attitude, and the French view that all this was engineered by the caliph in Istanbul. The French suspicion that the caliphate was a potential source of opposition to their policy in Africa had emerged shortly after their occupation of Algeria in 1830, when Abdelkader (Abdel Kader, Abdul Khadir), the leader of the Algerian resistance, eulogized the caliph as the leader of the Muslim world and asked for his assistance.[1] These French suspicions abated for a while as a result of the Crimean War and the Paris Treaty of 1856, in which France took a pro-Ottoman stand against Russia and under the soothing Francophile sentiments of Mehmet Emin Ali paşa (1812–71), many times premier and foreign minister. The French suffered a major setback in the years 1870–71, however, after Germany's devastating defeat of France removed it temporarily as a contender for influence in the Ottoman state and Ali paşa passed away.

France had initiated in Algeria a socioeconomic policy that undermined the old traditional economic system and permitted the rise of a new order. The French privatized much of the *beylik* or state lands—called *miri* in Anatolia and the Balkans—giving them gradually to French colonists, and turning the vast, communal tribal lands into private property. These changes, along with the intensification of trade and relations with France, gave rise to a new Algerian middle class in which traditional groups and leaders acquired, for a variety of historical reasons too involved to deal with here (including the lack of a supreme leader), a much more prominent place than in the old middle class in Turkey proper. The first opposition to France came from the conservative wing of this Algerian middle class, made up of various types of traditional leaders and new elites whose relations with their counterpart in Istanbul had greatly intensified since the mid 1850s, in part because of Abdelkader's settling in the Ottoman lands.

The temporary eclipse of France in 1870 and 1871 upset the balance of power in the Black Sea and the Middle East and dealt a costly blow to the Ottoman Empire. Ali paşa, driven partly by his personal sympathy for the French, had made a series of concessions to France in the hope that its military might and diplomatic skill could keep Russia at bay and provide a counterbalance to English designs. Ali died in September 1871 in France, where he had gone to seek medical help, and left a testament the authenticity of which has been long debated. Written in French in the form of a letter addressed to Sultan Abdulaziz, the testament urged the sultan to persist in the implementation of the reforms, the overall spirit and direction of which seemed to favor France.[2] Now the French defeat allowed Russia to change the terms of the Paris Treaty of 1856 and militarize the Black Sea. It also encouraged the Algerians to stage an insurrection with the purpose of driving the French out of the country.

The Algerian uprising, known as the Revolt of Constantine (or Mukrani), eventually spilled out into the Sahara Desert.[3] The revolt then threatened to spread, and fears that the caliphate was behind it were rekindled when Muheddin, the son of Abdelkader, traveled from the Middle East via Malta, Tunis, and Tripoli, to join the insurrection forces in the desert. By 1872, however, the Algerian uprising came to an end because of French counterattacks, the lack of funds, and a fear among the Algerian population that the authoritarian Germans, who were seeking to replace the French, would be even worse masters.

The French came to regard the Algerian revolt of 1871–72 as the result of pan-Islamism and believed that the Porte, through Premier Ali paşa, their trusted friend, had promised monetary help, arms, and ammunition to the rebels. The French suspicion of Ottoman complicity in the Algerian revolt actually derived from rumors circulating in Istanbul and Algiers that the sultan was behind the uprising. A short time after Ali paşa's death on 7 September 1871, two letters written by the Algerian Society of Mutual Help and Preservation of Islam (ASMHPI) to Mahmud Nedim paşa (1817–83), the corrupt Russophile *vezir* or premier (he had been governor of Tripoli in 1867), seemed to substantiate the rumors. In the first letter, delivered to Nedim through the society's two representatives (*vekils*) stationed in Istanbul (both named Mahmud), the society claimed that Ali paşa had urged the Algerians to take up arms against France and had promised them "official and secret help in weapons and money [50,000 guineas]"; in the second letter, the society declared in a much more categorical fashion that "our people have started the insurrection and the war against the French government only on the advice and orders of the former minister Ali Paşa."[4]

Just a brief discussion of the society's claims about Ali paşa is relevant to the viewpoint of this study. That the promise was alleged to have been made orally by Ali paşa, that the society's demand for help came only after his death, and that no help seems to have been delivered to the Algerians all appear to cast serious doubt on the authenticity of the alleged promises. M. Nedim paşa, the recipient of the society's letters, was a bitter opponent of the Tanzimat reforms and might have incited the Algerians to inculpate Ali paşa in the revolt in order to discredit him in the eyes of the French and win their sympathy. On the other hand, it is plausible that the Porte, seeing the collapse of France in 1871, might have tried to reassert its authority over Algeria and win the sympathy of the Algerian leaders by making some vague promises. Evidence in hand, however, indicates that the Constantine Revolt apparently was planned not by the Ottoman government but by middle-class elements of Algerian society with the participation of their Turkish counterparts in Istanbul.

Abdelkader (d. 1883) himself appeared unenthusiastic about the anti-French uprising of 1871. In a letter addressed to the French consul in Tripoli, Abdelkader, who lived in Damascus at the time, claimed that his son Muheddin had undertaken the trip to Tunisia and joined the Algerian rebels in the Sahara without his knowledge or authorization. He then asked the consul to send him news about his son and ensure his safe return to Damascus.[5] It is hard to believe that Abdulkader did not know about his son's plans to join the Algerian rebels; his entourage in Damascus included leading Syrian reformists, many of whom were fully involved in politics and ultimately joined the ranks of Arab nationalists. Meanwhile, some members of Abdelkader's family received pensions from France and acquired French citizenship while his sons Hüsnü and Muheddin became Ottoman citizens and asked the sultan to grant special favors to the Algerian refugees in order to immunize them against French influence.[6]

Years later, France continued to insist that the Algerian insurrection and the Society for Mutual Help were the product of plots against Paris engineered by the North African ulema and the caliph-sultan. For instance, in 1880 after Sultan Abdulhamid II had sent, through Hamdi efendi, a medal (the Mecidiye) to the premier of Tunisia, the French ambassador in Istanbul concluded that this was the sultan's veiled attempt to use Tunisia as a channel of communication with the Algerian tribes and, eventually, to start a general uprising there.[7] The ambassador did express some doubts about his own far-fetched assumptions but insisted that his suspicions were supported by pan-Islamic rumors circulating in Istanbul that the sultan had sent messages to the Muslims of India and had enlisted the support of the şerif of Mecca.[8]

The French fears of a Muslim upheaval in Algeria moved them to intensify their intelligence efforts in Istanbul. As a result, they succeeded in identifying the "two Mahmuds" who had represented the ASMHPI and had sent the letters to the Ottoman premier on its behalf. One was Mahmud Ibn Ali Baba, the other Şeyh Mahmud el-Mufti, son of the mufti of Algiers, who himself was mufti of Alexandria. The French consul, acting on a tip, searched Şeyh Mahmud's house in Istanbul and arrested him there. He then reported triumphantly to Paris that he had found the evidence (the letter sent by the ASMHPI to Mahmud Nedim paşa) to prove that the Ottoman government had been behind the Algerian unrest, that it had established a revolutionary league, and that Şeyh Mahmud and Mahmud Ibn Ali Baba were its agents.[9] Moreover, the consul claimed, the same correspondence showed that the Porte had supplied the revolutionaries with money, arms and ammunition, even though the letters from the Algerians, the last written in 1872, begging the Porte for help prove just the opposite. The French arrest of Şeyh Mahmud in the early 1880s was in fact facilitated by the rivalry between him and Abulhuda and Behram ağa, the chief of Sultan's spies. Actually, Şeyh Mahmud displeased Abdulhamid, not because of rumored plots against the sultan but for an article in which the *şeyh* wrote that the North Africans could rise and defeat the French colonists by themselves—as they did ultimately in the 1950s—implying that they did not need the caliph's help.

The French ignored the elementary fact that the fight was not with Islam but with a growing nationalist-minded Muslim middle class that was embracing Islam as both a faith and an ideological weapon against the occupiers of their land. All this gave the "Eastern Question" a new urgency and ideological dimension.

The Eastern Question and the Changing Image of Islam in England

The Eastern Question acquired an ideological dimension involving the caliphate and pan-Islamism in the years 1860–78, as the Muslim resistance in the occupied areas increased.[10] When Russia and France (and, in the 1880s, England) were unable to use the caliphate to dominate their Muslim subjects, they began to see it and Islamism (pan-Islamism), as a growing threat to their rule. They thus came to believe that "solving" the Eastern Question by disposing of the Ottoman Empire also would halt the threat of pan-Islamism, even though by the end of the century many European statesmen seemed to agree that panislamism was a docile "tiger" and Abdulhamid, instead of being its trainer, was its tamer. Blaming Abdulhamid prevented the European powers from seeing the much more formidable enemy, the new middle classes, that had combined modernism and Islamism into an anti-imperialist ideology of cultural and political self defense.

The Eastern Question first arose in 1774 but took on greater urgency after the 1830s when the growing weakness of the Ottoman Empire inevitably led to the question of how to face its final disintegration. The continuous interference of England, France, and Russia in Ottoman affairs accelerated the disintegration, as the reforms advocated by the Europeans undermined the sociocultural bases of the traditional system. Faced with the Russian landing on the Straits in 1833, Britain decided, at Palmerston's urging, to uphold the territorial integrity of the Ottoman state as the best bulwark against czarist expansion southward to the Mediterranean, the Gulf, and India. It also advocated a series of reforms, supposedly in order to strengthen the Ottoman Empire, the first of which was the Tanzimat of 1839. From 1840 onward, London came to regard the integrity of the Ottoman state as important to the survival of its own empire and sought to play a role in the actual internal administration of the Ottoman Empire. Beginning in 1843, England established consular representatives in key cities in the Balkans, Anatolia, Syria, and Iraq—altogether over thirty-five such offices, which paralleled the Ottoman local administration. In fact, the British consuls and their French counterparts became coadministrators of their respective districts, powerful enough to compel the Porte to remove independent and uncooperative Ottoman administrators from office.

The Crimean War and the Paris Treaty of 1853–56 drastically altered the quality of Ottoman relations with Europe, as the Empire was admitted into the international comity of "civilized" nations and implicitly accepted the patronage of Europe, especially England. London ultimately came to regard the Ottoman Empire as though it was its own colony. However, the negative reactions of both the Muslims and Christians to the reforms after 1856 induced many European intellectuals and politicians to regard the Muslim Turks as unable to absorb Western civilization and its values. The view that the Turks were civilizationally "unfit" and needed to be ejected from Europe persisted among English leaders until 1923. Subsequently, Islam was described as intrinsically opposed to progress and Islamism—and its resistance to European imperialism (portrayed as civilizational)—was said to have proved the point. Few European politicians made any distinction between their civilization and imperialism.

The revolts of 1875 in Bosnia and 1876 in Bulgaria allowed each party to reinforce its own view and clothe the Eastern Question in a unique ideological-religious garb. Whatever may have been the legitimate grievances of the native Christian Orthodox population against the Ottoman administration, their discontent would not have reached the point of rebellion had it not been for the instigation of Russia and Austria. Over the past century a score of scholars, led by the British placed most of the blame on the Ottoman side. Richard Millman, however, in the latest and the most detailed and objective study of this critical period, using a variety of new data, attributes the revolts of 1875–76 partly to misgovernment but chiefly to "Christian Slavic discontent with *any* Turkish or Muslim Government" (emphasis added); he goes on to describe, rightly, the revolt of 1875 as an "overwhelmingly a Christian, if even a Slavic Christian, rising" and detects "aspects of a Christian-Muslim civil war in the rising of 1875 and in the revolt of the Bulgarians in 1876."[11] Although the revolts were really inspired by social causes presented in religious garb, later scholars also were inclined to characterize them as an expression of Slavic nationalism.

Desiring to maintain the sultan's sovereignty over the Balkans for the purpose of preventing Russia from entering the region, the British government agreed to participate in a commission formed to restrain the Balkan insurrection, but the attempt failed. The subsequent Berlin note of May 1876 to the Porte, drafted by Russia, Germany, and Austria-Hungary on the initiative of Prince Alexander Gorchakov of Russia, demanded a change of status in the Balkans; namely, autonomy for the Orthodox Christians. It was followed by the Reichstadt Agreement of 8 July 1876. Under the agreement, if war broke out and the Serbs were defeated, the *status quo ante bellum* would be restored; if the Turks were defeated, however, Serbia and Austria would divide Bosnia and Herzogovina among themselves while Russia would occupy south Bessarabia and the Batum area. In conformity with this, and in order to safeguard British interests, the Conference of Constantinople was convened in December 1876, but it was unsuccessful and gave Russia a pretext to attack the Porte and start the inexorable downfall of the Ottoman state. The events in Bosnia and, especially, Bulgaria created an image of a "cruel," uncivilized Turk. The insurrection in Bulgaria was touched off when a couple of hundred revolutionaries, trained in Russia, put to the torch several Turkish villages and killed some three hundred inhabitants. According to official Ottoman documents, Ottoman irregular forces in retaliation killed 2,100 insurrectionists, including a large number of innocent civilian Bulgarians. Millman points out that "examples of Ottoman brutality were not scarce, but at the beginning of the insurrection the brutalities were perhaps even more on the other side" as rebel chiefs forced their reluctant brethren to join the fight.[12] (Peko Pavlovich, one of the insurrection leaders in Herzegovina, ambushed and killed eighty Turks and skewered their heads on poles at the insurgent camp.) These events had an immediate echo in the domestic politics of England. They provided an opportunity for W. E. Gladstone (b. 1809) and his Liberal Party to attack and discredit the Conservative government of Benjamin Disraeli as being a defender of the Turks. Gladstone, who in his youth seemed to have taken a rather detached view toward religion, eventually became a militant defender of Christian causes in general and Protestantism in particular under the guise of liberalism. In time, he became decidedly anti-Turkish and regarded Islam as reactionary. In a famous pamphlet, Gladstone charged the Turks with engaging in unparalleled atrocities against Bulgarians and exonerated the Bulgarians of all guilt. Specifically he accused the Turks (not the Ottoman government) of killing sixty thousand Christians.[13]

The real target of Gladstone's accusations, of course, was Prime Minister Benjamin Disraeli (1874–80), a Jewish convert, who was suspected of harboring friendly feelings toward Turks and the Muslims. Gladstone wrote, "I was slow to observe the real leanings of the prime minister, his strong sympathy with the Turk"; in a letter to the duke of Argyll, Gladstone claimed that Disraeli hated Christian liberty and reconstruction and supported old Turkey, being lukewarm in his support of "reforms" that would benefit Ottoman Christian and thinking that if vital improvements can be averted, the Ottoman state must break down; and England would then thus have its share without cost or trouble.[14] A very complex man, Gladstone was prone to use the "masses against the classes" but opposed "jingoistic adventures"—for example, the occupation of Egypt—although he did not object when this was accomplished. He had a special affection for the Montenegrins, which added fuel to his dislike of the Turks.[15] Overwhelmed by Gladstone's criticism, Disraeli lost popularity and the elections of 1880. It seemed that his immense service to his country was outweighed by his Jewish origin.[16]

The controversy that erupted in England in 1876 about the "cruelty" of the "barbarous Turks" rekindled an older discussion about the wisdom of England's intervention in the Crimean War in 1853 on the side of the sultan. Many Englishmen had viewed the British action against Russia, a Christian power, as morally wrong and as having granted the Ottoman Empire a twenty-year respite to strengthen itself. In other words, they believed the Crimean War of 1853–56 had given the sultan an opportunity to resurrect his empire without fulfilling his promises to "better" the situation of his Christian subjects, even though the economic situation of the Christians had improved dramatically. By 1876 the English public appeared ready to accept at face value any allegations, however fantastic, against the Ottomans, who were always defined in ethnic terms—that is, as Turks.

England's anti-Turkish feeling was fed by a rather unexpected financial event. On 6 October 1875, the Ottoman government declared that budget deficits forced it to lower to half for the next five years the interest paid to its foreign bondholders, many of whom were Britons. The decision to halve the interest payments was made by the premier, Mahmud Nedim paşa, on the advice of the Russian ambassador in Istanbul.

In effect, this measure deprived the British bondholders of about 2 million pounds a year. The price of one Turkish bond fell from 25 pounds in January to 16.1 pounds in June 1876, causing an enormous outcry on London's securities market.[17] The Ottoman government had spent much of the money it borrowed through these bonds to purchase weapons from Europe, especially to rebuild its navy. The British outcry, however, often focused on the much-trumpeted Palace expenditures, describing it as a lavish oriental squandering of money (although it amounted only to about 5 or 6 percent of the budget, and much of it came from the sultan's own private purse). In any case, while in 1855 the Ottoman foreign debt was practically nonexistent, by 1875 the payment of principal and interest on loans consumed 34 percent of the Ottoman budget. The English ambassador at the Porte knew that the Ottoman default had resulted from a sharp drop in revenues due to drought, which drastically decreased earnings from agriculture, and the government's inability to collect taxes. He was also well aware of the role played by Count Nicholas Ignatiev, a pan-Slavist zealot who was the Russian ambassador at the Porte from 1864 to 1878, in persuading the grand vizier to postpone the interest payment. Nevertheless, he could do little to change the course of events or to stop the rising anti-Turkish sentiment of the British public, which only twenty-six years earlier had hailed Sultan Abdulmecid, the brother of the reigning Abdulaziz, as a friend of Europe and as the champion of freedom for refusing to surrender the Hungarian and Polish revolutionaries to their Russian and Austrian pursuers.

"And thus the English," concluded Cevdet in colorful language, "who regard money as religion and faith [*din ve iman*] turned into the enemy of the Empire. The English government being a constitutional state that follows public opinion, its Cabinet was forced to change its policy toward the Ottoman state though in [certain] matters of common interest it maintained its old policy."[18]

The "matters of common interest" became, from the British point of view, rather fewer in number as the Ottoman society underwent change. Nedim paşa—he who had halved the bond interest rate to the fury of the English—was an advocate of the unity and the involvement of the community in the affairs of the state through a new ideological frame that he termed *gayret-i diniyye ve milliye* (religious and national communal effort) under the leadership of the sultan. The term *milli* (national) had become synonymous with the faith and was frequently used. In line with the populist thinking of some lower-class bureaucrats, Nedim attached importance not to the ulema but to the Sufi *şeyh*s of the popular orders. Nedim paşa, who served as grand vizier in 1871–72 and again in 1875–76, despite his corruption, was well liked by the sultan for his rather systematic support of absolutism; he wrote a book lauding its merits.[19] He was also liked by the ladies of the harem for his romantic, worldly poems and even by some ideologically oriented nationalist Islamists. A Georgian by origin, he had close relations with the Nakşbandi. He expressed the sentiments of the conservative upper elite of the new middle classes, and, unwittingly perhaps, played some role in channeling upward the aspirations, values, and ideas of the lower classes, especially the ideas of Muslim solidarity that so frightened Europe.

The events of 1875 and 1876 echoed abroad among Muslims, notably those in India. The new telegraph and the press informed overseas Muslims that the caliphate was doomed to perish if the Ottoman state disintegrated, for the caliph was powerless without the support of the sultanate. An important example illustrating the emerging international Muslim solidarity was a meeting on 7 October 1876 of the Mohammadan Community of Calcutta, convened in the town hall in order to "express sympathy with Imperial Turkey and gratitude and loyalty to the Queen of England and Empress of India." The list of the sixty-three signatories of the resolutions passed at this and subsequent meetings reads like a who's who of Muslim Bengalis: titles such as "prince," *mirza, syed, moulvie, shayk,* and so on, abound.

The declaration described the events in Serbia and Bulgaria in the years 1875–76 as "civil struggles in Turkey excited by foreign ambition . . . [and] as the most convenient opportunity for renewing the attack on the Mussulman Patrimony in Europe." It criticized the European newspapers for spreading sensational news about the atrocities of the irregular Ottoman police forces in Serbia and Bulgaria while remaining silent in the face of the horrors perpetrated against the Muslims, deplored the "crusade" being advocated by Gladstone against Turkey, and expressed the "sympathies of all Mussulmans throughout the world, who look upon His Imperial Majesty the sultan of Turkey as the Defender of their Religion and Custodian of their Holy Cities and Shrines, and for whom the majority of them are commanded to pray." The following crucial paragraph best expresses the state of mind prevailing at the time among Muslim Indians. "Above all, the anti-Islamite upheaval in Christendom, not only affects the peace of mind of every Mussulman, but is calculated to alarm all Mahomedan Sovereigns in regard to their rights and possessions, and all Mahomedan subjects, wheresoever domiciled as to the future of their Faith in general, and, in particular, of the toleration in their religious Observances and Law." The signatories asked the queen to support the Ottoman sultan and then passed a resolution asking the viceroy and governor general of India to permit district tax collectors to gather subscriptions to support the Ottoman cause, adding that the "war in Serbia is not a religious war between Mohamedans and Christians as such but an ordinary Civil War between the Sublime Porte and its rebellious subjects." It should be noted that this Indian Muslim support for the Ottoman sultan was a spontaneous outburst of solidarity that occurred long before the advent of "pan-Islamism."[20]

The meeting of the Indian Muslims of Calcutta was followed by an incident in Bombay that seemingly further alarmed London about the capability of the Ottoman caliph to incite the Indian Muslims to rise against the Raj. This time, however, the actors were not the rich, pro-British nabobs but a large number of merchants, craftsmen, ulema, and other Muslim members of the middle class. The incident was caused by the arrival of the previously discussed Ottoman Islamic mission to Sher Ali Khan, the ruler of Afghanistan. (See chapter 3, pp. 84–86.)

Şirvanzade Ahmed Hulusi efendi, the head of the Ottoman mission and a descendent of the nobility of the Azeri hanates, sent the sultan a cable from Bombay informing him of his safe arrival (on 28 July 1877), but in a confidential letter he informed the sultan that it was his "duty to convey certain information of events witnessed upon [my] arrival in Bombay." He reported that "more than forty thousand Muslims of India came to meet [me] in order to show their support and love for you as the caliph." Faced with this unexpectedly huge crowd, the mayor of Bombay, a Mr. Grand, decided to whisk Hulusi efendi directly to the Ottoman consulate. An even larger number of Muslims gathered there, but most were not allowed to enter the building.

At night, according to Hulusi efendi, the Muslims showed up again in the front of the consulate bearing candles and lanterns and "demonstrated in favor of and offered prayers for the Caliph." Eventually Mr. Soter, the head of the police (later the mayor of the city), ordered the Ottoman mission to leave the city by train that very day and not to stop anywhere until it reached the border of Afghanistan. Hulusi efendi, in typical Ottoman understatement, wrote, "We deduce from all these circumstances that the English government being apprehensive about the current arousal of Indian [Muslim] public opinion might have become to some extent unhappy about our presence within its borders."[21]

This was, indeed, the case. The outburst of sympathy by the Indian Muslims toward the caliph was reported immediately to London, which, in turn, instructed Lord Lytton, the viceroy of India and architect of the mission, not to permit it to contact the Indian Muslims. This incident had given further credence to and enhanced the popularity among British decision makers of Salisbury's old view that pan-Islamic feelings could turn against England and should not be encouraged. For his part, Sultan Abdulhamid had discovered Britain's Achilles heel—that is, fear of Muslim upheaval in India, a nightmare since the Sepoy Revolt of 1857—and would exploit it in due time, with his usual tact and caution. Meanwhile, the "Turkish Party" in the British government lost influence, giving the Russians a free hand to end the Eastern Question and soothe the fears of their own czar over his restive Muslim subjects. Salisbury's ascendence to power as Premier turned his anti-Muslim and anti-Turkish feelings into governmental policies.

The Wars of 1876–1878

Serbia, using the uprising in Bosnia as pretext, declared war on the Ottoman state in 1876, but its action was short-lived. In October of 1876, the victorious Ottoman troops under Osman paşa—later to become the legendary defender of Plevne—were converging on Belgrade but halted their march and accepted an armistice following a Russian ultimatum. Russia, which had counted heavily on Serbian military success, had to rescue its proxy. In the past, English leaders had officially regarded events in Bosnia, Serbia (still nominally under Ottoman suzerainty), and Bulgaria as internal Ottoman affairs. By the fall of 1876, however, the English favored a joint European initiative to bring better government to the Balkan Christians. The possibility of a joint Russian-Austrian attack on Turkey, foreshadowed by the Berlin memorandum of May 1876, compelled the British to press for a conference to initiate reforms in the Balkans and thus preempt a Russian excuse to attack the Ottoman state. Propounding the view that they were freed from the obligation to uphold the tripartite treaty of 1856, which had guaranteed the territorial integrity of the Ottoman Empire, the British then indirectly pressured the Porte to accept the reforms.

The Conference of Constantinople of December 1876 was attended by the envoys of England (the marquess of Salisbury, who disliked the Turks, the India secretary, and Henry Elliot, the British ambassador at the Porte) and by the Russian, Austrian, German, and French representatives. The reforms proposed ranged from the establishment of a native police to the cession of territory, the grant of further autonomy to the Serbs, and the turning of Bulgaria into a semiautonomous entity. The Porte, which rejected initially the very idea of such a conference, agreed to participate only after the British foreign secretary, the earl of Derby, threatened to withdraw all English support. The fifteenth earl of Derby (Edward Henry Stanley), a hesitant, indecisive individual, had favored in 1864 the breakup of European Turkey and refused to grant arms to Turkey during the war with Russia in 1877. He resigned in March 1878, too late to repair the damage done to the Ottoman military. His wife, Lady Derby, several years his senior, was the mother-in-law of the marquess of Salisbury; she had long private visits with the Russian ambassador, to whom she reportedly passed much confidential information. The British ambassador in Istanbul, Henry Elliot was knowledgeable about Turkish affairs, but he was sick and lethargic and had lost much of his influence in London along with pro-Turkish party. Salisbury expressed grave misgivings about the Turks and Islam and the growing Muslim politicization, especially among Indian Muslims. As early as 1878 up until 1898, Salisbury advocated the peaceful partition of the Ottoman state with Russia, first as foreign secretary and then after 1885, when he served as prime minister through three governments; he remained to the end of his life a critic of everything Muslim and Turkish. What prevented Salisbury from partitioning the Ottoman realm was the opposition of other European powers and Abdulhamid's policies. As Elie Kedourie wrote in his seminal *England and the Middle East* (1956, p. 24), Salisbury saw no "autonomy of young and struggling nationalities" in the partitioned Middle East but at best the promise of good government. In the end, Britain became the chief advocate of Ottoman partition but managed to hide its rapacious intentions behind a façade of friendly advice and occasional propping, until the propitious moment arrived in 1918–22.

The conference began on 23 December 1876. The Ottoman government was controlled by the constitutionalist-nationalists of Mithat paşa and offered stiff resistance to all demands. Salisbury found this Ottoman opposition to what amounted to the dismantlement of the country "infantile" and incomprehensible, and he professed puzzlement that the "Muslim children of India . . . might instinctively desire to maintain their own independence and sovereignty."[22] On the other hand, the Istanbul press, which had become the opinion-making tool of the new intelligentsia, expressed almost unanimous outrage that the conference to dismember the country was being held in the Ottomans' own capital. Europe pressured the Ottoman government to grant autonomy to the Balkan Christians while remaining silent about the political freedom of the Muslims of Russia and India.

The Ottoman Palace meanwhile was undergoing its worst crisis, caused by a military coup that deposed Sultan Abdulaziz on 30 May 1876 (a few days later he committed suicide). His successor, Murad V, known to favor a constitutionalist regime, was deemed mentally unbalanced and replaced three months later by Abdulhamid II. Behind all these events stood Mithat paşa and his group of reformists, populists, constitutionalists, and nationalists. Mithat was also the guiding power behind the Constitution of 1876, which was announced by Safvet paşa, the chief Ottoman representative, the very day the Constantinople Conference opened: 23 December 1876. The coincidence of dates was regarded as likely to preempt the conference's reform proposal, and on 20 January 1877 the conference ended without achieving any lasting result. The Ottoman government, dominated by the constitutionalist bureaucrats, ignored Abdulhamid's warnings and refused to make some of the concessions sought by Europe.

Already, on 15 January 1877, the Russian and the Austro-Hungarian governments had signed an agreement granting Russia freedom of action in the Balkans as long as it did not sponsor the establishment of one single large state (Bulgaria) on the peninsula; in exchange, the Hapsburgs were promised Bosnia and Herzogovina. The last efforts to salvage the conference and avoid the unavoidable Ottoman-Russian war proved fruitless. So did the subsequent London Protocol of 12 April 1877, which made a few changes in the original proposal to favor the Ottoman state. It was rejected by the Porte when the Ottoman nationalists—a new group of political activists—refused to accept any compromise, and on 24 April 1877 Russia declared war on the Ottoman Empire.[23]

The Ottoman public had been informed well in advance that Russia, desiring to expand its territories and eliminate the sources of influence on its own restive Muslim population, was looking for a pretext to declare war on the Porte. *Basiret* pointedly stressed that many European newspapers sided with Russia and looked forward to an Ottoman defeat. It also pointed out that the Ottoman Christians actually enjoyed more rights than Muslims and were not mistreated and asked Russia for proof that the czar followed a policy of equality in his own state toward the Poles, Jews, Azeris, Moldovans, Crimeans, and so on, whom it cited as people deprived of equality. The polemical and emotional tone of *Basiret*'s articles were exceptionally appealing to the Muslims, who saw themselves as victims of European religious prejudice and Russian expansionism.[24] Sentiment in England was now clearly anti-Ottoman and Ponsonby expressed the view that British "pro-Turkish" sentiment had anyway been rather shallow: "I doubt, if any real feeling of friendship ever existed in this country for Turkey. Some persons supported what they believed to be an oppressed nationality—some had material interest . . . some believed that the friendship of the Sultan, the Caliph of the faithful all over the world strengthened our position in India and some were moved by the attitude of rivalry between ourselves and Russia."[25]

Russian and Soviet historians, always eager to justify the czar's aggression, have failed to produce any reasonable explanation for the unprovoked Russian attack on the Ottoman state in 1877. The standard one is that, after exhausting all the peaceful means to "liberate" the Orthodox Christians from Ottoman rule, the czar finally resorted to violent action. This implies that the Russian action was motivated by high ideals, although this was an imperialist war, in fact an anti-Ottoman crusade. A number of Ottoman officials, especially the modernist-nationalist group headed by Mithat paşa, were not averse to a war with Russia, which they believed they could win, and they recklessly isolated the Porte from its European "friends." Sultan Abdulhamid was basically opposed to the war, but he was too new on the throne and was powerless at this stage to prevent it and, as usual, too indecisive to take a definitive stand. One apologist for Abdulhamid wrote that "the Turkish-Moscow war of 1877, known popularly as the '93 war' [from the *hicri* calendar year 1293], occurred at the end of the Tersane conference [the Turkish name given to the Constantinople conference] due to the ignorance of Mithat paşa and his clique," and absolves the sultan of all responsibility "for the war of '93 and its consequences both as a person and as office holder."[26]

The war of 1877–78 was a turning point in the history of the Ottoman Empire, pan-Islamism, and the Ottoman middle classes. It occupies a central position in this study. Soon after crossing the Danube and overcoming, with great difficulty, at Plevne the resistance of Osman paşa, who would later become an adviser to Abdulhamid and an advocate of Islamic unity, the Russian troops crossed the Balkan Mountains. Marching toward Istanbul, the Russian troops and the Bulgarian bands armed by the Russians destroyed Turkish towns and shed rivers of Muslim blood.

The British ambassador to the Porte, Henry Layard, regularly informed London about the Russian and Bulgarian atrocities. Layard's reports were based on numerous dispatches received from the British consuls stationed in Ruschuk (Russe), Sofia, Filibe (Philippopolis-Plovdiv), Burgas, and so on, and their factual objectivity is beyond doubt, although few Western scholars ever bothered to study them.[27] The consular reports indicate that some 300,000 Muslims (mostly Turks) were killed in the Danube province and eastern Rumili, and of the approximately one million forced to flee, only about a quarter returned to their homes after the war. Queen Victoria was so outraged by the atrocities committed against the Muslims that she asked the Cabinet to send the fleet to Istanbul, only to meet with Derby's indecision and procrastination.[28] When the British ultimately did react, it was not because they felt human compassion for the Muslims but because the Russian advance into the Balkans threatened London's interests. By the time the belated British reaction brought the advancing Russian armies to a halt, they had reached the gates of Istanbul. Seeing all this, the average Muslim came to believe that his salvation lay not in the idealistic, but selectively applied, "universal" principles of European civilization but in the self-defensive unity of the believers.

Russia's immediate purpose in attacking the Ottoman state had been to create a Bulgaria entirely dependent on it that could be used as a Russian outpost in the Balkans and an outlet to the Mediterranean through Salonica. Because the Muslim population constituted the majority in the Tuna (Danube) province, which occupied most of the territory of the future Bulgaria, Russia had decided to secure the numerical superiority of the Bulgarians by forcing out the Muslim population. The San Stefano Treaty, concluded between the Porte and Russia in March 1878, created a Bulgaria that included all of Macedonia and the Aegean shores; but the Berlin Treaty of 13 July 1878 returned Macedonia to the Ottoman Empire and cut off Bulgaria's access to the Mediterranean.[29] Serbia, Montenegro, and Romania became independent by seizing territories inhabited by Muslims, while Bulgaria first gained autonomy, then full independence in 1908. Greece, which did not enter the war, was given Thessaly in 1881 and promptly ousted the small Muslim minority residing there. Russia also occupied the northeastern Ottoman provinces of Batum, Kars, and Ardahan, causing the departure of a good part of the Muslim population. England occupied Cyprus as a sort of brokerage fee for the Berlin Treaty and as a downpayment for its defense of the Ottoman Empire against further Russian occupation. Austria occupied Bosnia and Herzegovina. In addition, Russia imposed a charge for war damages—one billion francs—on the already destitute Ottoman treasury.

The war of 1877–78 thus virtually ended the Ottoman presence in the Balkans and led to the liquidation of centuries-old Islamic communities—through forced, induced, and voluntary emigration and its destruction of the Muslim-Ottoman material culture.[30] (The Muslim relocations from the Balkans to Turkey have continued to this day, in the form of migration during peacetime and mass exodus during crises. The latter include the Balkan War of 1912–13, World War I, the Bulgarian forced emigrations of 1951–52 and 1989, the Yugoslav expulsion of Macedonian Turks in 1951, the Serbian "cleansing" of Bosnia in the years 1992–95, of Kosovo in 1998–99, and the forced emigrations of various Muslim groups out of Greece.)

The Berlin Treaty created conflicts and suffering by imposing inappropriate political solutions. It accepted ethnicity as the basis of nationhood for peoples who for centuries had lived in communities organized on the basis of religion.[31] It told the Greeks, Bulgarians, and Serbians that they were, first and foremost, members of a national group and only secondarily Christians. In practice, however, ethnicity and religion remained indistinguishable from one another and became the basis of a communal nationalism specific to the Balkans. The treaty exacerbated Christian-Muslim differences, prepared the ground for the emergence of a secular type of territorial nationalism, and pushed the Muslims' identity to a higher level of consciousness. It created the problems of Macedonia, which became a bone of contention among Bulgaria, Serbia, and Greece, and of Armenia, none of which have been solved.[32]

The Aftermath

By demonstrating the military and economic weakness of the Ottoman state, the war forced the realistic, pragmatic sultan to find remedies to assure its survival. Awareness of the significance of the Ottoman defeat and of the possibly imminent collapse of the Empire also seeped into the consciousness of the Muslim-Ottoman masses and brought about a degree of self-awareness and popular self-defensive mobilization. It created also a certain informal consensus that the survival of the Ottoman state as a Muslim cultural and religious entity required not only a new outlook on society and its affairs but maybe the involvement of the citizens in deciding their own political destiny. The Ottomans lost the war on the battlefield and, together with it, the delusion that they were a *devlet-i muazzama* (great power) and the illusion of *devlet-i ebed müddet* (eternal state); but they won the war of the mind by learning how to think realistically and, if necessary, to take concrete action of their own volition without the prodding of a higher authority. After 1878 Ottoman intellectuals actively searched for the causes of and remedies for the weakness of their state in society itself rather than lamenting helplessly its misfortunes of their state as God-ordained.[33] Educated in the modern schools, the Muslim intellectuals became increasingly concerned with the revival of their society. Many advocated the emulation of the victorious West, while others turned toward the fountainhead of their own culture. However, unlike the Muslim revivalists of the late eighteenth and early nineteenth centuries, who had sought the revitalization of society through the renewal of the faith, after 1878 there was a material element added to their search for religious-moral revival.

For the first time in Ottoman history the civil sector began to contemplate changing the political system to bring it somewhat in line with popular expectations and respect for the society's culture. Emphasizing the practical instead of the ideal, their answer to the European challenge, although Islamic in name and purpose, stemmed from a pattern of thought and view of the world that was markedly different from the classical Muslim model. It was, in fact, a European type of response garbed in Islamic attire. A fundamental cultural and political change was taking place in the Ottoman mind, and its catalyst and its chief channel of expression as well, paradoxical as it may appear, was Islamism. It was both culturally self-preserving and conservative and change-oriented and progressive.

The multifaceted change in thinking and attitudes was seen not only among the educated Muslims of the middle classes but also among the masses, as documented by field reports of European observers. As one of many such reports noted, the Turkish-Russian war of 1877–78 had triggered a series of events "which will bring about the metamorphosis of the Orient and will make the Mediterranean the center of a political and economic competition."[34] British vice-consul Biliotti's report from Trabzon (Trebizond) describing the state of mind of the average citizen is worthy of quotation.

> There are among Turks at large unmistakable signs of genuine patriotism and delirious enthusiasm, two sentiments which are always blended in the hearts of the Muslims. Religion being, therefore, the basis of patriotism among the Mussulmans at large, it is natural for them to imagine that the same feeling actuates the Europeans. So long, therefore, as one or more European Powers were, in the opinion of the Turks, siding with them, their patriotism could not attain full development, but it reached its highest pitch the moment when they have been under the impression that all Christian Powers had abandoned them. In their minds something like a conspiracy has been concerted against them, and as it always happens in similar cases, they closed their ranks to resist the supposed onslaught. It would seem as if no better means than the measures which have been practiced could have been devised to obtain the revival of the Turks. *Most likely the realization of the gravity of their situation and the isolation in which they found themselves, have worked wonders with them.*[35]

On the psychological level even the humblest peasant began to wonder about the human roots of the tragedy that threatened the political existence of the Ottoman state and the fate of their own Islamic community. For instance, the French consul in Trabzon, conveying information he received from Batum, reported that the military commander of the city, Dervish paşa, dressed in his gala uniform and followed by a large group of Muslims, went to surrender the flag of the city to the Ottoman governor, who, in turn, was to leave the city to the Russians under one of the provisions of the Treaty of Berlin. The consul emphasized that the Shiite Persians in the city until then had not mixed with the Sunnis, but they participated in the flag procession because the surrender of the city was an "act [which] represented in the eyes of the population not so much a defeat of the Ottoman Empire as a setback for Islamism."[36]

The British consul, Herbert Chermside, one of the most knowledgeable observers of Turkey, upon returning from a trip to Asia Minor in the spring of 1878 reported that he had been struck by the definite expression of public opinion, often most revolutionary, that has permeated to the most out-of-the-way hamlets, and that is, *in many points opposed alike to the traditions and religion of the Turks.*

There is a strong feeling of resentment against the Constantinople Government and the Pashas in general. It really seems to have come home to the nation, that with a brave and devoted soldiery and a magnificent country, they are yet in a hopeless state of ignorance, poverty, and disorganization; in fact *they seem to have somewhat realized their own condition* and to have an idea of what reforms and improvements are wanted. . . . I used the words above "revolutionary" and "opposed to traditions and religion". By this I meant that the people of Asia would go to war with England against Russia even if the sultan was at peace with Russia and did not order them.[37]

The population seemed to have gained enough self-confidence to decide its own future. In fact, Chermside said, that population was asking, "What has our Padişah done for us?" and showed a willingness to follow England not only in war with Russia but also in securing help to build roads and railways, while they criticized their own government for not accepting reforms. These feelings were shared by the "governing classes, officials, mollahs, zaptiehs and peasants alike"; Chermside concluded: "I have been asked many questions as to the troops coming from India, and also about [the English] rule over Mohammedan races. Of course among themselves there are differences of opinion, and I have heard several discussions showing a tamer appreciation of things, than . . . I should have expected."[38] This report, it should be noted, was written in May 1878, at the time when England was pressuring Russia to change the harsh terms of the San Stefano Treaty and appeared as an Ottoman friend. Soon the friendly feeling toward England turned into animosity, when England took possession of Cyprus in 1878 and occupied Egypt in 1882.

Another report from French sources stated that the Muslim refugees from Thessaly, mostly small farmers who had sold their possessions to the Greeks for a low price and emigrated almost penniless to the Ottoman lands, questioned the human causes of their plight. "Ni cette émigration de correligionnaires, ni le fait grave dont elle est la conséquence, n'ont excité les passions des turcs soit contre les héllènes ou les étrangers; l'effet a été autre, c'est à dire de discréditer profondément à leurs yeux leur propre gouvernement."[39]

The mistrust of the Ottoman Muslims toward their own government went hand in hand with a search for support that turned into a feeling of political solidarity with Muslims in other parts of the world and to a call for concrete popular action. The British ambassador in Istanbul reported:[40] "The natural desire for national preservation has risen to such a pitch as to lead in all probability to important and combined action on the part of the Mohammedan races of European Turkey, the object of which would be determined resistance to the proposed extension of Bulgaria, by means of a protracted guerilla warfare to which south and Central Albania, as well as the Rhodope mountains . . . would be peculiarly adapted."

The ambassador added:

Information received from various parts of European Turkey fully show the general determination of the Mohammedan populations for a national defence against what they consider to be unjustifiable and cruel treatment, as regards life, honour and property experienced by their co-religionists at the hands of the Bulgarians and

Russians, and since it is held the sultan's government is powerless in obtaining the guarantee for the protection of . . . its Mohammedan subjects . . . it is only fair that they should provide for their own safety even if the government were to oppose the attempts.

The new "nationalism" stemmed from the new social stratum that took over the representation of Islam and the cause of the Muslims. Indeed, the government's signing away of the lands inhabited by Muslims resulted in three separate movements of popular resistance to occupation in which the Islamic sense of solidarity and self-preservation was used to mobilize the local population. In Bosnia, the Muslims, aided by some Serbs, battled the Austro-Hungarian occupation troops for several months. The Albanians gathered and organized the League of Prizerin, which marked the beginning of Albanian nationalism and independence, with the participation of Mehmed efendi, the mufti of Tashlik, who had played a prominent role in the Bosnian uprising. In the Rhodope Mountains the Muslims long resisted the Russian and Bulgarian troops and grudgingly laid down their arms only after the sultan asked them repeatedly to do so, although resistance in some areas continued into the twentieth century. Most of these rebelling groups were not ethnic Turks but Slavs and Albanians, who nonetheless considered themselves Muslims, Ottomans, or "Turks," as all these terms meant the same thing. Many of them eventually emigrated and settled in Turkey. Ali Suavi's effort, mentioned before, to reinstall Sultan Murad V on the throne was both a move against the established political order that especially frightened Sultan Abdulhamid and the first example of populist activism. The religious upheaval from below materialized in political revolt. The masses learned how to mobilize themselves.

The ground was thus well prepared for the emergence of a new ideology. A lengthy British consular report written after the British occupied Egypt in 1882 summarizes best the state of mind among the Ottoman Muslims and the psychological-political atmosphere that nourished Islamism after 1878.[41]

Some years ago the Mohammedans were kept in ignorance of all political upheavings, and appeared indifferent to their results; but the progress education has made among them, the development of a native press, the introduction of Western civilization, and the growing facilities of communications with the principal centers in Europe, have gradually awakened a spirit of inquiry among this people.

They now take a keen interest in national and foreign political affairs, and follow up and ventilate events which affect their country and religion.

The usurping views of Austria on Bosnia and Macedonia, our occupation of Cyprus, the action of France in Tunis, and our proceedings in Egypt, are all burning questions now eagerly discussed among the higher as well as the more ignorant and fanatic classes at this place.

The European public does not hear much of this, as the Turks, unlike the Christian nationalities, have not the same hold on their own press, nor the means of propagating their views abroad through foreign newspapers.

Nevertheless, judging from what I observe and hear, it is manifest that Mohammedan feeling here, and chief centers in the interior, is much moved by passing events in Egypt.

Influenced by the ideas and sentiments of the "Terdjumani Hakikat" and other Turkish newspapers, whose circulation has increased in these parts, the people in general look upon England and France as enemies of their religion and existence.

This feeling finds expression not only among the ignorant, but also among members of the *ulema* and army.

The latter talk very high and in a tone of defiance about our proceedings in Egypt, and lead the simple-minded to believe in the realization of coming great events in which Islam is once more to be called upon to stand its ground against the combined forces of Christendom, when much blood will be shed and great miseries follow.

Superstition worked up by religious zeal also contributes to foster and strengthen such ideas to which every passing event gives a certain significance.

Hence the strong sympathy the people feel for Arabi [Urabi] Pasha and his insurrectionary movement. He is considered the *beau ideal* of a good Mahommedan, and his acts are glorified and magnified in harems as well as in cafes.

What tends to enhance his prestige and popularity is the deep-rooted conviction among high and low that the sultan, as caliph or Head of the Mahommedan world, is in tacit connivance with him and the so-called National Party in Egypt.

I should also add that Mahommedan feeling at this place is very adverse to England, and that our influence, no longer considered friendly, is suspected and run down.

Conclusion

In sum, the state of mind described in this report from an observant British consul came to prevail in the Ottoman state after 1878. The political and social-cultural events of the succeeding years, including the development of Sultan Abdulhamid's own policies, were nurtured by this state of mind, which was profoundly different from that of the Ottomans of all the previous centuries.

The war of 1877–78 and the Berlin Treaty constituted the most important historical, cultural, and psychological watershed in the history of the Ottoman Empire. For the first time, both Ottoman statesmen and the public realized that the total collapse of the Ottoman state was an imminent possibility. True, the Ottoman state had suffered a series of defeats and had lost territory for more than a century prior to 1878, but those losses occurred at the periphery. Because the core, that is, the Balkans, and Anatolia (and the Arab provinces) remained almost intact, some Muslims seem to have thought that the Empire had a magic power to revive and survive indefinitely. The war of 1877–78 destroyed once and for all this "Ottoman phoenix" myth. Henceforth the fate of the Empire was to be seen not as predetermined by divine will but as determined by economic, psychological, cultural, social, and demographic forces.

The defeat in the war was also a defeat for the modernist-Europeanist constitutionalist wing of the middle classes—especially of the urban bureaucratic, liberal intelligentsia that had made Mithat paşa its spokesman and representative. The conservatives portrayed the defeat as the result of the "modern" leaders' lack of wisdom and foresight, while they described Sultan Abdulhamid as a wise leader who opposed the war but could not prevail upon the modernist-nationalist hawks. The sultan now was free to argue that the throne had held the Empire together for six hundred years and could continue to do so in the future if ill-willed modernists did not challenge its power and authority. The agrarian and conservative wings of the Ottoman middle classes supported him, for the maintenance of the territorial integrity and independence of the state was the condition that guaranteed their own position and interest.

The sultan thus had found a social base and a justification for turning Islamism into an ideology, although his understanding of *ümmet* differed from that of the middle classes, who tended to view the *ümmet* as a sociocultural religious entity embodying worldly aspirations and expressing their own regional-cultural background and interests while paying lip service to universal brotherhood. Abdulhamid accepted the view that the public desired material progress in all its forms and that that progress would also strengthen the state. He ignored the essential fact that the public's desire for material progress was accompanied by an inchoate demand for the recognition of the individual as the ultimate object of progress and that individual freedom was an indivisible part of progress. Abdulhamid's development policies after 1878 were dictated by these social-political imperatives. As the agrarian middle classes gained popularity with Abdulhamid, gates opened for the upward mobility of the regional and local cultures, for the expansion of modern education to the lower classes, and for a new, realistic understanding of the situation of the Ottoman state. The stage for the emerging confrontation was thus set: the individual versus the omnipotence of the state.

7

The Making of a Modern Muslim Ruler
Abdulhamid II

The Legacy of the Past

Few leaders in world history have played such a crucial role in their societies and yet have been so maligned and so despised, not only by outsiders but even by their own successors. European literature has portrayed Abdulhamid (r. 1876–1909) as the "red" sultan who harshly put down internal revolts by the Armenians, as a reactionary who opposed Western civilization, and, especially, as an intriguer who concocted panislamism in order to subvert and undermine "civilizing" European rule over Muslims. He also was more or less generally condemned in Turkey during the Young Turk period and the Republic. In the Arab world, Abdulhamid was accorded a friendlier treatment than in the West and Turkey. The easing of government controls over the Turkish press in the 1950s, however, brought forth an avalanche of pro-Hamidian writings and gave new exposure to several friendly books published in the previous decades.

Sultan Abdulhamid obviously did not create the ingredients that entered into the making of Islamism, but he synthesized those forces under the pressure of events and gave the resulting Islamism (pan-Islamism) a specific political-ideological aspect, making it appear to be his own personal creation. A brief study of his life and background is appropriate here.

There appear in Abdulhamid's life and policies a series of baffling contradictions which, at first sight, are difficult to explain. For instance, he is seen as a religious conservative, yet he was the most Europeanized sultan with respect to his own daily living habits, and his promotion of modern reforms in education, government, and communication affected the inner fabric of the Ottoman society far more profoundly than the Tanzimat reforms. Similarly, although he was an Islamist, many of his close personal associates were non-Muslims: his banker, Zarifi, and his physician, Mavroieni, were Greeks; his friend Arminius Vambery was a Hungarian Jew. During his tenure a large number of Christians entered government service and occupied high positions over Muslim subordinates, thus placing Muslims under non-Muslim authority. Yet the sultan remained to the end of his life a devoted Muslim and a firm believer in the superiority of Islam and Islamic practices, helping to build

155

mosques and repair holy sites in Mecca, Medina, and elsewhere. Although occasionally government facilities were used in religious ceremonies and displays—for example, the *hac*—the traditional separation of executive functions from faith were maintained and strengthened.

Abdulhamid occasionally drank a glass of champagne before his meals as a sort of tranquilizer. In 1888, after Kiamil paşa, the grand vizier, wrote the sultan proposing to lower the export duties on wine and to make up the resulting loss of revenue by charging fees on certain legal transactions, Abdulhamid agreed. The export of wine was beneficial to the "state," even though the state was "Islamic" and he was the caliph.[1] This was not hypocrisy or use of a double standard but the consequence of a traditional, practical "secularism" that gave priority to financial matters and left the state free to pursue its own interests as long as it did not openly violate the faith. A discussion between Mehmet Namik paşa (b. 1804), a former ambassador to London and governor of Iraq, and the Palace secretary Ziya paşa is significant. Namik told Ziya that it was inconceivable for a *beytulmal-i Muslimin* (Muslim community's treasury) to collect taxes (*rüsum*) from the sale of wine and pigs. Ziya replied that the state treasury was not a *beytulmal* and that Namik paşa's own salary contained a portion of wine and pig taxes. Abdulhamid subsequently told Namik not to get involved in such controversy.[2]

Some eight years earlier, when the Greeks and Bulgarians in Edirne fought each other trying to take possession of the same church building, the sultan decided to let the Greeks have it, but, overlooking the fact that Bulgarians had massacred tens of thousands of Muslims in 1877–78, offered the Bulgarians a land parcel that belonged to the municipality as well as 50,000 kuruş to build their own church.[3] It was state interest that made Abdulhamid arrest the popular Şeyh Ahmed efendi Daghestani and exile him to Damascus, for he feared that grassroots revivalism would turn against the government.[4] If one looks at Abdulhamid's internal and external policies in a detached way, one is bound to conclude that these policies did not stem from dogmatic, religious principles but from certain Ottoman historical practices and pragmatic state considerations.

The Ottoman imperial tradition of statehood made it a sacred duty for a sultan to assure the survival and integrity of the state inherited from his predecessors. However, unlike his predecessors, who had believed in the state's miraculous ability to survive for ever, Abdulhamid realized that the Empire was economically weak and torn by internal strife and that a resurgent Islam could not alone overcome the country's material backwardness. He initiated a variety of remedial administrative, economic, educational, and similar measures without even developing a formal theoretical, philosophical, or ideological explanation for his "modernism," which was simply a de facto *dünyevilik* (worldliness)—that is, an interest in the material aspects of human life.

The sultan believed that he had the authority (*hüküm*—to command and decide) to undertake any measure necessary to assure the survival of the state for the good of the community. That right was rooted in the old Central Asian Cengizid-Turkic *töre* (tradition), which was secular in essence and practical in intent. It constituted a special feature of the Ottoman political philosophy that regarded government or rulership an exercise in the manipulation of power relations decided and determined by the ruler himself, limitations imposed by religious code and precedent notwithstanding. The absolute authority lying with the sultan permitted the development of an extraordinarily rich body of government legislation known as *kanunname*, a secular body of laws, parallel to the *urf* (*adat*, or customary law) and the Şeriat. Although in theory the Şeriat was supreme and all other laws conformed to it, in practice the *kanunname* could circumvent its restrictions and were the most important laws as far as government affairs were concerned. The formula allowed the government to adapt to changing circumstances but retain its Islamic character, as argued by Cevdet paşa. The sultan was the ultimate decision maker and was responsible not to any popular or ecclesiastical forum but only to God. Sultan Abdulhamid was first, and above all else, an Ottoman sultan, and he made extensive use—more than all his predecessors—of the state authority entrusted to him, as the enormous body of decrees, orders, and discreet instructions stored in the archives indicate. Unlike his predecessors, Abdulhamid found his authority challenged almost from the beginning by the Constitution of 1876 and the "modernist" bureaucracy, although the challenge had been initiated during the latter part of Abdulaziz's reign.

Established by the House of Osman at the end of the thirteenth century as a small principality on the eastern shores of the Sea of Marmara, the Ottoman state in less than a century had grown into a giant empire. The founders of the state, Ertuğrul and his successors Osman and Orhan, belonged to one of the Turkish tribes that had been pushed westward by the Mongol invasion of Anatolia, but they rejected from the very start any tribal affiliation or denomination.[5] The state was "internationalized" and fully bureaucratized mainly during the rule of Mehmet II (1451–81), in part in order to allow the Islamized and Ottomanized ethnic groups access to power; the government remained in the hands of the Muslims, although the Turks, as an ethnic group, had no priority in control of the state. Yet, the Empire retained its Turkishness—in language and in a variety of traditions of government and authority and in a special social order that was uniquely Muslim and Ottoman but also "Turkish." Some of these "Turkish" characteristics of the Ottoman culture and state were rooted in the original folk religious culture of the Turks of Central Asia but others derived from Islamic, regional, and local and ethnic cultures, which had changed and reshaped themselves throughout centuries. No consideration was given to this issue until late nineteenth century, mainly during Abdulhamid's reign, when a number of new forces, including the concept of modernism, interacted with the Ottoman-Islamic-Turkish historical factors and produced new syntheses.

The sultan played an inadvertent but seminal role in these developments. He, like his predecessors, considered the preservation of the Ottoman state, the patrimony (*mülk*) of the dynasty, his most sacred duty. In order to fulfill this sacred obligation, the sultan used every available means, including the introduction of new laws, reforms, and the like. In the sultan's eyes, and those of some supporters, the survival of the state was a sufficient reason to legitimize his absolutism, and he could always buttress this with some religious arguments. In fact, the first systematic efforts to formulate an Ottoman theory of absolutism were made during the latter part of the nineteenth century by Mahmud Nedim paşa in his tract, already mentioned, and by Ahmet Mithat efendi's article in *Tercüman-i Hakikat*. The gist of these writings was that *istibdat* (absolutism) was not *zülüm* (tyranny), which was religiously condemned, but a traditional Ottoman-Islamic form of authority suitable and necessary in circumstances of the time. Obviously, the reverse argument, if supportable, could deprive the sultan of this legitimization. In other words, if the state's survival could be assured by other means, such as constitutionalism, then absolutism had no reason to exist. The modernists and constitutionalists implied exactly that in 1876, when they proposed a constitution and a parliament as a new political order supposedly better suited to the survival of the state. The secularist implications of this position are obvious.

Abdulhamid considered his absolutism divinely sanctioned and labeled any opposition to it as heresy and a source of evil and degeneration. Yet the sultan never explained convincingly why and how his absolutism was sanctioned by Islam, especially since many ulema disagreed with him. In fact, Abdulhamid's despotism was an act of desperation; but it never degenerated into personal, bloody personal reprisals, as in the case of his fierce, unpredictable, and vengeful grandfather, Mahmud II. Abdulhamid had a quiet temperament, seldom becoming angry or abusive, although his quelling of revolts in Armenia and Macedonia and the fierce attacks of his adversaries obscured his better side.

Abdulhamid came to regard centralization as a corollary of absolutism and as a major administrative instrument necessary to counter all the internal and external challenges to his administration. From the start, Abdulhamid's policies met with resistance from various groups, each with different reasons for opposing him. These included the agrarian wing of the middle classes, the modernists in the bureaucracy, and part of the religious establishment. As Abdulhamid strived to preserve the integrity of an Ottoman state and strengthen it militarily, the gap between absolutism and tyranny was often narrowed; against the enemies of the state, selective tyranny was applied.

Abdulhamid's Life

In view of Abdulhamid II's pivotal role in the rise of Islamism and in shaping the last decades of Ottoman history, the remainder of this chapter will be devoted to a study of his life, personality, political ideas, and religious views, based mainly on official documents, his own memoirs, and the reminiscences of the people who worked for him. Much of this material has not been used before. The existing works on Abdulhamid, notably those written in the West, are subjective and negative, while many appearing in the last twenty years in Turkey and the Arab world tend to be excessively defensive and laudatory.[6]

Abdulhamid II was the thirty-fourth Ottoman sultan and the twenty-sixth caliph. He was born on 21 September 1842 in the Çirağan Palace, the traditional summer residence of the sultans, the son of Sultan Abdulmecid (1823–61) and Tir-i Müjgan. His mother, a beautiful woman whom Abdulmecid married in 1839, was the daughter of one of the Shapsih (Circassian) chiefs of the Ubikh tribe. (The Ubikhs were one of the least numerous of the Circassian groups in Turkey and even in Caucasia, and their language is now extinct. The last speaker of Ubikh in Turkey became the subject of a prize-winning documentary film by Ismet Ersan, ca. 1986.) From his early childhood, Abdulhamid was subject to family losses. He was the second and only surviving child of Tir-i Müjgan. He was about eleven years of age when she died of tuberculosis in 1853, soon after giving birth to her third child. Tir-i Müjgan had been very fond of her son, and he had responded to his mother's affection with a deep and warm attachment to her; he cherished her memory in many ways, including special treatment accorded to the members of her Circassian tribe. Her early death deprived him of affection, and he became taciturn, introspective, and secretive—which in turn isolated him from the rest of the royal family.

The changes in the Ottoman Empire were paralleled by a profound transformation in the lifestyle of the sultans, the most ostentatious change being in the royal residences. For centuries, since the conquest of Istanbul in 1453, the Ottoman sultans and their families had lived mostly in the Topkapi Palace (and in a few summer palaces such as Çirağan and Beylerbeyi), and the architecture, traditions, organization and spirit of Topkapi provided a model for the entire Ottoman Empire. It was at the Topkapi Palace that the Turkish culinary art, which connoisseurs place on a par with the Chinese, supposedly the most sophisticated cuisine, was developed. However, each of the last three Ottoman sultans in the nineteenth century had built a new palace on the European shore of the Bosphorus, each one larger than the Topkapi Palace. Abdulmecid built Dolmabahçe on land reclaimed from the sea, as the name indicates. Abdulaziz tore down the ancient imperial summer residence at Çirağan, near Beşiktaş and built in its stead a gigantic palace. Neglected and damaged by fire, it has been restored and now has become a luxury hotel. Abdulhamid himself built the Yildiz Palace, made mostly of wood with a huge park on several hundred acres. Occupied for a long time by a military school and greatly damaged, Yildiz Palace was restored and serves now as the headquarters to IRCICA (Research Center for Islamic History, Art and Culture). In 1994 the center opened a museum dedicated to Abdulhamid, while other sections of the palace, including the harem, are slowly being restored.

Dolmabahçe Palace, which Abdulmecid began building on the Bosphorus in 1853–54, was modeled by its architect, Balian, scion of a well-known Armenian family long in the service of the sultans, on the palace at Versailles. Today a museum, the Dolmabahçe became overnight the symbol and model of modernity, bringing European court habits and lifestyles, including brilliant diplomatic receptions and dinners, to the Ottoman court and upper society. The building of Dolmabahçe represents the Ottoman opening to everything European: institutions, architecture, dress, city planning, arts and literature, as well as new concepts about women (marriage began to be seen as a partnership) and romantic love. Sultan Abdulmecid seemed to take special interest in the new concept of love, as various European ladies apparently won his favor, to the detriment of the women in the harem. When the venerable palace at Topkapi lost its primacy to Dolmabahçe, the consequences of this seemingly trivial development were far-reaching. In the ensuing battle between the "old" and the "new," many of the sultan's early favorites and their aides were left to live in dire poverty in the Topkapi Palace, while the new ones congregated at Dolmabahçe. Abdulhamid was reared in both palaces and seems to have preferred the Dolmabahçe.

After the death of Tir-i Müjgan, Abdulmecid entrusted Abdulhamid to his fourth wife, Perestu ("swallow" in Persian), a daughter of one of the Circassian chiefs, and charged her with his upbringing. Perestu, a pious, mature woman, was childless. She took charge of Abdulhamid and treated him as her own son. One may assume, however, that Abdulhamid efendi, as the palace attendants called him at that time, shared the feeling of abandonment and rejection felt by the incumbents of Topkapi Palace. This feeling of rejection deepened when Abdulmecid began to show an open preference for Murad, his elder son, whose vivacious and warm personality contrasted sharply with the cold aloofness of Abdulhamid. After Abdulhamid became sultan in 1876 Perestu received the coveted title of *valide sultan* (mother of the sultan) and headed the harem, a particularly influential institution, but Abdulhamid told Perestu categorically not to involve herself in state affairs.

Abdulhamid received his early education, in the customary imperial tradition, from private teachers who were known for their erudition and knowledge of state affairs. He was exceptionally intelligent, possessed a prodigious memory, and showed considerable interest in practical things, but not in learning and study, although he asked Münif paşa to teach him political economy. In his memoirs, he openly acknowledged that "when enthroned I did not find much time for regular study and research. My [earlier] days as heir to the throne, like those of my brother were spent [doing] vain things";[7] presumably this was because he was a remote third in line for the throne. His life of pleasure, including drinking and amorous pursuits, ended after his doctor—the Greek Mavroieni (or Mavroiani)—warned him that the consequences of such a free life might be disastrous for his health. Thereafter, Abdulhamid abstained from alcohol and led a very healthy life. However, the fierce and unscrupulous power struggle going on among the various factions of the bureaucracy and of the palace personnel taught him not to trust anybody. He became extremely secretive and almost pathologically suspicious of everyone and everything that affected vital government decisions, producing negative results.

Following the long-established Ottoman imperial tradition of learning a practical trade, Abdulhamid became a good carpenter and built some excellent pieces of furniture; carpentry was his means of relaxation and a hobby he practiced almost to the end of his life. He was addicted to work. His regular day consisted of fourteen hours during which he personally read and answered much of the voluminous internal and external correspondence. The huge Yildiz collection in the Turkish archives is testimony to Abdulhamid's extraordinary capacity for work; it certainly does not support the Western image of the Ottoman sultan as a lazy despot dedicated to harem pleasure. The contrary was in fact true: his life as a ruler was dedicated to the duties of his office, while his relaxation consisted of meals with his family, watching plays, and listening to opera music performed mainly by European artists.

The sultan was an introverted pragmatist who relied on observation and experience rather than on reading and reflection in dealing with the problems of life and state. He was handicapped by a lack of resoluteness and firmness, as well as by his predilection for temporizing with piecemeal measures and the use of various intermediaries. He cultivated, for practical reasons, the good will of many people, both natives and foreigners, such as Arminius Vambery (1831–1913), whom he tried to use as a public relations agent in his dealings with the European press.[8] Abdulhamid knew some French, but his "Turkish was closer to the colloquial and free of the intricacies of the Ottoman spoken by the elite."[9] In temperament, behavior, and taste,

Abdulhamid was similar to his uncle Abdulaziz: both seemed to be closer to the average Muslim Ottoman than to the upper-class elites. This populist streak might have been entered their makeup from their mothers, who were commoners (as were the mothers of most of the sultans), but also may have been the result of the gradual penetration of the folk culture into the upper establishment.

Abdulhamid believed firmly that his authority as sultan was of divine origin. "The *padişah*," he said, "is accountable only to God and History." He therefore considered the forced abdication of his uncle, Sultan Abdulaziz, to be the gravest insult brought to Ottoman royal traditions and prerogatives and feared that it had set a precedent for his own dismissal. The subsequent suicide of Abdulaziz, which Abdulhamid later treated as an assassination, only increased his mistrust of the constitutionalist wing of the bureaucracy.[10] Tahsin paşa, his long-time personal secretary and one of his few trusted aides, relates in his memoirs that Abdulhamid feared all the bureaucrats but especially those in the *şeyhulislam*'s office, the Meşihat Dairesi, whom he kept under continuous surveillance.[11] As the sultan knew too well, the *şeyhulislam* alone could issue the *fetva* (religious opinion) sanctioning the sultan's dethronement. He mistrusted the *softa*s, the students of the religious schools, whom the dissident *ulema* and the constitutionalists could mobilize against the ruler as they did against Abdulaziz.

In 1889 rumors circulated in the Ottoman capital, and were reported in the European press, that Ömer Hilmi efendi, a protegee of Cevdet paşa (who was minister of justice at the time) and high official of the Meşihat, held in his house a series of meetings attended by the *ulema* and other learned figures who criticized the sultan's policies and acts. Moreover, Kiamil paşa, the grand vizier, had reportedly distributed large amounts of money to the *softa*s. Although the palace initiated investigations showed that the rumors were just that, Kiamil paşa was eventually "neutralized" by being sent to govern the Aydin province, and the *softa*s were placed under surveillance.[12]

Abdulhamid knew very well that most of the job seekers around him were interested not in service but in a high income and that at the first opportunity they would betray him. In a talk with the British ambassador, the sultan complained that in Turkey the only way to make money and live in luxury was to hold government office, the higher the office the better the reward. Consequently, the competition for office was intense and unscrupulous and produced few truly qualified officials. The sultan believed that this struggle for position resulted from the Ottoman state's being a classless society. In contrast, England was a class society that allowed people to secure income from business, and seekers of government jobs there acted out of love for the country rather than a desire for a prestigious and lucrative means of existence.

Abdulhamid was firmly in favor of material progress in all forms, and at the very start he seems to have sided with the practical-minded administrators—provided they did not question the state's political traditions and the throne's supremacy.[13] It is significant that throughout his life Abdulhamid showed profound respect and deference toward his rather neglectful father (Abdulmecid) and uncle (Abdulaziz) and praised their reforms and alliances with Europe; but he refrained from eulogizing their rapprochement with the West in matters of culture.

The economic policies of Abdulhamid, which have received only scant and, for the most part, negative attention, must be reevaluated. A true Ottoman middle class, rooted in economic occupations and displaying distinct cultural characteristics of its own, arose mainly during Adbulhamid's reign. The crucial Land Code of 1858 was reconsidered and amended to facilitate the passage of state lands into private hands, mostly Muslim. Private enterprise, if not encouraged, was not obstructed, while foreign capital—mostly French—penetrated the Empire and, along with a rising group of local Muslim and Christian entrepreneurs, established an industrial basis for future development. The Ottoman Bank (a French institution serving as the state bank) and the Debt Administration (est. 1882) brought about the rudiments of systematic modern financial administration, although at a high political and social cost. The import-export policies, especially in agriculture, where the competition of American crops on European markets posed serious threats to Ottoman produce, acquired increased weight in government decisions. It can be safely stated that the Ottoman economy underwent major changes during the reign of Abdulhamid and that these affected the cultural, political, and social developments. Abdulhamid did not appear to have acquired a full understanding of the capitalist transformation taking place around him, but he seemed to have accepted it as inevitable. His economic policies consisted, on the one hand, of a laissez-faire attitude toward business and, on the other, of efforts to build, in the name of progress, an infrastructure of railways and roads, which helped greatly in establishing the foundations of a cosmopolitan, although somewhat primitive, capitalist system. The new middle class that developed as a result of these policies proved to be the key agent of change in the Ottoman Empire. Interest in technology and the practical sciences arose with it, as indicated by various projects undertaken by the government or private Western companies and by the introduction of science subjects in mid- and upper-level text books. Abdulhamid's economic policy led to dependency on the West;[14] but it produced also an Ottoman commercial bourgeoisie (mostly Christian) and an Ottoman-Muslim agrarian elite. The "national" economic policies of the Young Turks and the statism of the Republic were both a continuation of the economic policies developed mainly during the reign of Abdulhamid and a reaction against them, notably against foreign private capital.

A basic characteristic of Abdulhamid's personality was his religiosity. He was sincerely attached to Islam and praised its past grandeur: "If we want to rejuvenate, find our previous force, and reach our old greatness we ought to remember the fountainhead of our strength. What is beneficial to us is not to imitate the so called European civilization but return to the *Şeriat*, the source of our strength. . . . Mighty God, I can be your slave only and ask only your help. Lead us on the right path."[15] He understood "civilization" as social behavior and family customs. However, he was fully aware that his piety would not suffice to protect him against the religious establishment or the intruding forces of change, including the growing attraction of worldly things and facilities which the sultan openly accepted. The previously mentioned notion of *dünyevilik* (worldliness), which occupied a central place in Abdulhamid's thinking and was accepted as a natural part of man's attitude, clashed with the religious establishment's austere view that material welfare and pleasure, especially if originating in the West was sinful. Actually, the issue of *dünyevilik* had wide ramifications; it was part and parcel of the popular notion of progress (and secularism), although the modernist intelligentsia was not able to define and explain it satisfactorily, and the religious establishment viewed it as materialism and atheism.

During Abdulhamid's reign, the gulf between the religious establishment affiliated with the state and the new "free" ilmiye developing among the new middle classes widened further, as seen in the politicization and subservience of the *şeyhulislam*. Mithat paşa used as an accomplice the *şeyhulislam* Hayrullah Hasan efendi (1834–98) to dethrone and enthrone three sultans in a span of three months in 1876.[16] In a lengthy handwritten note summarizing the events of 1876–79, Sultan Abdulhamid refers sarcastically to Hayrullah efendi as *şerrullah* (evil of God).[17] Once firmly established in power, Abdulhamid first appointed Hayrullah efendi to a post in Medina and then exiled him to Taif in today's Saudi Arabia, where he died in dire poverty. Then he appointed his "own" *şeyhulislam*, Mehmet Cemalleddin efendi, who served the sultan faithfully and made himself indispensable—even to the Young Turks for a while—for he knew how to deal with the troublesome *softas*.[18] He was a dedicated monarchist but also an Islamist who enjoyed a degree of respect among the conservative ulema and the population, largely because of his erudition and patriotism (nationalism). After the Union and Progress Party seized power through a coup in 1913, Cemaleddin, known as "Abdulhamid's *şeyhulislam*," went to Egypt, where he lived to the end of his life and wrote his "memoirs," a bitter censure of the Young Turks' policies of 1908–1913. The Young Turks' own *şeyhulislam*, Kâzim Musa, was a champion of modernism and Islamic identity. In a series of articles published in the Islamic review *Sirat-i Müstakim* (Straight path), he discussed the limits of Westernization and reform of the methods of teaching religion with the unification of the four Muslim legal schools. Known as a dedicated supporter of the Committee of Union and Progress (CUP) of the Young Turks, he escaped the arrests and trials that followed the fall of the Unionist government, the subsequent occupation of Istanbul by the British of 1918–19, and the internment of the leading figure in the CUP to the island of Malta.

The personal family life of Abdulhamid is relatively well known and was not greatly different from that of his predecessors. His daughter wrote in detail about it. According to her, Abdulhamid had four *kadinefendi*, that is, legal wives, and eight *ikbals* or favorites. (The title *kadinefendi* was given only after the husband became a sultan.) A very sensual man, Abdulhamid had also many concubines and love affairs of one sort or another.[19] He had seventeen children altogether, many of whom died abroad while the imperial family lived in exile from 1924 to 1952. In private life, Abdulhamid showed an open preference for European music, liked theater, and appreciated the comfort of modern amenities such as gas, electricity, railroads, and street cars, which were introduced mainly to Istanbul during his reign; he dispensed with the traditional *hamam* and opted for the European bath; and he replaced the old heating system in Yildiz Palace with a modern one.[20] He built a private theater within the Yildiz compound, where he staged European plays, and he wrote, or commissioned someone else to write, plays about incidents taking place in the Yildiz Palace. Some of the leading singers of Europe were invited to perform in his theater for European ambassadors and his own friends. He also appeared to prefer the Gregorian calendar, later adopted officially by the Young Turks, rather than the old lunar one.

The sultan was deposed in April 1909, accused of inciting the anti-CUP uprising of 1909, although there is no evidence that he had anything to do with it. The uprising, led by some fundamentalists such as Derviş Vahdedi and his newspaper *Volkan*, was fueled by economic and social discontent, dissatisfaction with the military's involvement in politics, and the "betrayal" of constitutionalist ideals. Abdulhamid was deprived of his throne by a *fetva*—as he had fearfully anticipated all his life—signed by a new *şeyhulislam* selected by the Unionists. He was forced to live under house arrest in Salonica, guarded by a special military unit first headed by Fethi Okyar. In addition, the Unionists subjected him to considerable pressure to surrender his portfolio of European stocks. During the Balkan war, Abdulhamid was moved back to Istanbul to live in Beylerbeyi Palace under the supervision of the Union and Progress Committee and the care of a doctor. He died of natural causes on 18 February 1918.

Abdulhamid, the Bureaucracy, the Constitution, and the Centralization of Authority

Abdulhamid's political views and his policies were profoundly affected by the modernist bureaucracy's ascent to power and its struggle to increase its own authority to the detriment of the throne. The Tanzimat of 1839 created a growing need for trained personnel to man new offices and services. Although the process had started during the reign of Mahmud II (1808–1839), the bureaucracy began to take control of state affairs chiefly during the reign of Abdulmecid. Abdulhamid had spent his childhood watching helplessly as the new bureaucrats usurped the prerogatives and authority of the old imperial bureaucracy and the sultan. Sultan Abdulaziz made some attempts to reassert his power by enlisting the support of the conservatives and expanding the caliphate's authority, especially after the death of the reformist ministers Fuat and Ali paşas in 1869 and 1871. In response, the bureaucracy-intelligentsia began promoting constitutionalism in its effort to restrict the throne's power. Specifically, the constitutionalists of 1876, headed by Avni (head of the army) and Mithat paşas, sought a new source of legitimacy for the throne's authority in a consensus of the people, or *millet*. The constitution also aimed at generalizing Ottomanism, giving the non-Muslims representation in the government. Life and property were seen no longer as the fruit of imperial benevolence but were considered birthright of all Ottoman subjects—something promised in the Tanzimat Edict of 1839 but not yet fully implemented.

The palace viewed the constitutionalists' efforts to involve the population in the political process as self-serving. As the important Ottoman bureaucrat, M. Sait Halim paşa (1863–1921), a descendent of Mehmet Ali paşa of Egypt, put it, "The reformists, in order to change and improve the oppressive administration, decided to make use of a third element, that is, the people, who until then appeared to have been forgotten and neglected."[21] In its effort to counteract the constitutionalists, the palace enlisted the support of the traditionalists within the bureaucratic-religious establishment. Their appeal to the Muslims' attachment to Islam and allegiance to the caliph received an unexpected boost in the decade 1865–75, after the modernists and constitutionalist bureaucrats also appealed to Islamic unity and solidarity to oppose the Russian expansionism. The bureaucrats (and some Islamist nationalists) portrayed the failure of Abdulaziz to put down the rebellions in Bosnia and Serbia in 1875–76 (he actually succeeded, but Russia intervened) as unwillingness to defend the Muslims' rights. This played a part in encouraging the *softa*s, who normally supported the caliph, to demonstrate against Abdulaziz, giving psychological help to the constitutionalists' efforts to oust him.

At the very start of his reign, therefore, Abdulhamid saw an ongoing struggle between the palace and the modernist bureaucracy. As he also developed great suspicions about the loyalty of the religious establishment, he felt the need to win the support of the masses against both the liberal bureaucrats and the religious sector, the monarchy's search for alliance with the masses was something unprecedented in the past. In response, the bureaucracy offered the population constitutional rights and vague promises of material betterment to counter the throne's appeal to the Muslim masses' traditional loyalties and faith.

Sultan Abdulhamid had several confidential talks with Mithat paşa prior to taking over the throne late in the summer of 1876. Acting from a position of weakness, he agreed to promulgate the constitution but refused to accept the Europeans—especially the English—as its guarantors, as Mithat supposedly demanded. All along, the sultan had considered Mithat's effort to introduce a constitution a bureaucratic device intended to infringe the throne's inalienable sovereign and divine rights. Mithat, on the other hand, had agreed to enthrone Abdulhamid in the hope that the sultan's formal acceptance of the constitution was sufficient to bind and limit his power. In order to secure Abdulhamid's agreement, Mithat accepted a series of amendments to the proposed constitution, including Article 113, which empowered the sultan to exile whomever he deemed to be a danger to state security. The constitution was proclaimed in December 1876 and the parliament convened in March 1877. The sultan's worst fears then appeared to materialize: the bureaucracy-intelligentsia now presented itself as the self-appointed voice of the "people" and sought to use the parliament as its tool to curtail the sultan's imperial rights and prerogatives. The "people" that the bureaucracy claimed to represent were not envisioned in terms of class, wealth, occupation, or other concrete characteristics but consisted of the undifferentiated totality of those under the government's authority. In the end, the "people" were what the ruling elites, the only social group conscious of its position and interest, defined them to be.

The deposing of Sultan Abdulaziz on 30 May 1876, through a coup engineered by Mithat and his military allies and sanctioned by the şeyhulislam, aligned the three key forces of the Ottoman state—namely, the religious establishment, the army, and the bureaucracy in favor of the constitution and, implicitly, against the sultan. The "new rulers" was a "junta consisting of the ulema, army and intelligentsia," according to one writer, who opined that a country in which "the teachers, students, military and intelligentsia united in order to control the government was doomed."[22] Sultan Abdulhamid never forgot or forgave Abdulaziz's ousting, and he regarded his subsequent suicide as a murder contrived by Mithat and Avni paşas.[23]

The group engineering this coup was different from past ones, however, for it sought not only to replace one ruler with another but also to institute a new political order. Abdulhamid was allowed to replace Murad V on 31 August 1876 because of the latter's insanity, but only after he agreed not only to promulgate the constitution but also to appoint as palace secretaries two well-known advocates of constitutionalism, Ziya paşa and the poet Namik Kemal. Thus the sultan proclaimed the constitution on 21 December 1876, but shunned the festivities celebrating its adoption. He convened the parliament on 4 March 1877 with a lengthy speech, simply in order to satisfy the consitutionalists at home and the demands for reforms from abroad.[24] He had already dismissed Mithat on 15 February 1877, and he subsequently closed the first parliament because of its sharp criticism of the executive. Mithat was arrested and put on a ship destined for Brindisi, Italy. Eventually he was invited back, then was appointed governor of Syria. Finally, he was arrested and tried in 1881 for the "murder of Abdulaziz." His death sentence was commuted to life, but Mithat and other leaders of the coup of 1876 were murdered in prison at Taif in 1884.[25] In 1878 Abdulhamid finally closed the second parliament and suspended the constitution indefinitely, partly by reacting to strong criticism and accusations that his intereference in military command had been responsible for the defeat in the war of 1877–78.[26]

The sultan had suspected all along that the reformist bureaucracy would use the constitution to legalize the European involvement in government decisions and help achieve its own supremacy. Several Turkish and European scholars have claimed that the constitution issued in December of 1876 was a deceptive maneuver aimed at undermining the Constantinople Conference meeting then in Istanbul;[27] but Sir Henry Elliot, the British ambassador, wrote that the preparation of the constitution took place "more than a year before its promulgation, when it was declared to have been invented only to defeat the Conference then sitting at Constantinople."[28]

According to the sultan, the constitution could be enforced only in a country in which the people had achieved political maturity; otherwise, it would easily be abused to oppose the legitimate ruler and create confusion. In any case, the sultan sincerely believed that because he was responsible only to God, not to any persons, he could not be reined in by a constitution. An elitist at heart, like most of the Ottoman ruling stratum, he regarded the common people as unable to understand the refinements of government and politics. He noted sarcastically that "the silence of the *avam* [lower classes] and the thanks of the *hava*s [elites]," which followed his summary dismissal of Mithat paşa, showed that the people did not care for politics. In Abdulhamid's cynical opinion, the very "people" whom Mithat claimed to serve by providing them a constitution and granting them freedom had shown by their silence "how little they deserved and appreciated a constitutional regime."[29]

Throughout his life, however, Abdulhamid remained fully aware of the existence of a public capable of action, regardless of whether it was properly organized and motivated or misled by ill-intentioned leaders. In explaining his acceptance of the Constitution of 1876, he stated, "Since the nation, this time, wanted to experiment by taking its destiny in its own hands, I agreed that the nation should have its way. I accepted and promulgated, with minor changes, the constitutional text proposed by Mithat paşa . . . because it was necessary to give to a sick people who saw Mithat as 'the savior of the state' the very solution [the constitution] he proposed. I could not dismiss him otherwise." In defending censorship of the press, he claimed that the Ottoman population "was ignorant and innocent and so we are compelled to treat it like children for indeed they are no different from bodily grown-up children."[30] He was constantly aware that the "people" could be manipulated by his opponents, like Mithat, whom he regarded as motivated only by personal greed and desire for vengeance rather than by principle.[31]

The specter of "people," as a political constituency with Mithat (or someone like him) as its voice, remained Abdulhamid's nightmare to the end of his life, and he used a variety of devices to counter their appeal by courting popular support for himself whenever necessary. A sympathetic Turkish historian described Abdulhamid's court-ing of the people as being motivated by sincere "democratic" motives.

> Sultan Abdulhamid began his reign with good intentions and engaged in democratic activities unprecedented in Ottoman history and in a short time won the hearts of the soldiers and the population. His first act fifteen days after investiture was to take his evening meal together with officers and dignitaries in the General Military Head-quarters. . . . [F]our days later he went to shipyards and met the navy personnel and ate there the ordinary soldier's meal. After visiting and distributing gifts to the wounded in the war with Russia, he and his ministers prayed in various mosques attended by the ordinary people.[32]

Actually, within one year of his enthronement Abdulhamid became a near recluse. Indeed, after Mithat's ousting, the sultan lived in fear of dethronement, exile, and death. Ali Suavi's failed coup, which occurred in 1878, well after Mithat was neutral-ized, and another attempt staged by the Scalieri-Aziz bey committee in July 1878, reinforced Abdulhamid's fear that the "people" could be persuaded, bought, or co-erced at any time to act against their own ruler. These attempted coups pushed the sultan to the brink of insanity and near physical collapse, as described in the dispatches of Ambassador Layard, with whom Abdulhamid developed (at least for a while) good relations.

In sum, the Ottoman constitution and parliament of 1876, which many dismiss as a flimsy political stopgap, played a crucial role in the internal developments of the country and affected profoundly Abdulhamid's personality and state policies. The sultan's propensity toward loneliness, secrecy, suspicion, and fear of assassination was raised to pathological levels. He therefore did not travel outside Istanbul after becom-ing sultan, although he previously had visited Egypt and in 1867 had accompanied his uncle Sultan Abdulaziz during a visit to France and Germany, where he seemed to observe everything as closely as possible and to have learned a great deal about Europe. Abdulhamid's seclusion, which won him the name of "hidden sultan," seemed to have resulted from a sense of insecurity, not a calculated move to create an aura of superiority and mysticism around the throne and the caliphate.[33] He was in-satiably curious about his subjects and their thoughts, as well as about the physical features of his lands; consequently, he charged a group of specialists with photograph-ing the people, the main towns, and the natural views of his realm. By 1893 they had taken a total of 1,819 phytochrome pictures, and the resulting fifty-one albums were deposited in his library (now the library of the University of Istanbul), while copies were sent to the "National" Library of the United States (Library of Congress) and to England.[34] These albums today constitute a unique and invaluable portrait of the traditional life, customs, architecture, and so on, of the Ottoman Empire at the end of the century.

The sultan's desire not merely to know but to control his subjects and his fear of enemies led him to establish a very sophisticated spy network, which reported directly to him. The spies, who became corrupt overnight, operated mainly in the capital and kept the sultan's potential enemies under surveillance; state security and the sultan's safety thus became synonymous. In addition, Abdulhamid encouraged his subordinates to spy on each other, and a letter accusing a high official of acts, words, or merely ill thoughts against the sultan would have a fatal effect on his career.

Abdulhamid and his small staff in the Yildiz Palace assumed all executive and legislative authority, leaving direct executive prerogatives only in minor matters to the prime minister and other ministers. The sultan also assumed direct authority over the *vali*s, or provincial governors, notably in critical areas such as the Hicaz, Africa, and the Balkans. As mentioned before, the centralization of authority during Abdulhamid's reign reached the highest possible level, the greatest in Ottoman history. A description of Abdulhamid's self-defined role and the functions of his palace staff are remarkably similar to those of the president of the United States and the White House staff, except that Abdulhamid was not elected and did not have a "congress" to balance his authority. Tahsin paşa, who was the chief palace secretary and a sort of chief of staff from 1894 until 1908, has provided one of the most detailed descriptions of the organization and operation of the executive in the Yildiz Palace.[35] The key ministries, such as defense and finance, reported directly to the sultan, using their own letterhead and, as entitled, receiving replies from the sultan; this correspondence is classified as *resmi maruzat*, or official petitions or memoranda. Ministries of secondary importance also reported to the sultan, but he would answer them only selectively, this is known as *hususi maruzat*, or private petition or memoranda. The ministers became, in fact, the chief clerks of their respective departments, while the premier, or grand vizier, who was called by the Persian title *sadrazam* for much of Abdulhamid's reign, lost most of his traditional prerogatives. Abdulhamid changed his grand vizier thirty-nine times; Sait paşa, served at least seven times; Kiamil paşa, one of the most capable and well-educated administrators, also occupied the position several times. Meanwhile, the sultan kept the lesser ministers in place for as long as possible in order to increase their degree of specialization and proficiency. In any event, Abdulhamid's palace staff was relatively efficient, especially after he personally took charge of both internal and, particularly, foreign affairs.

Abdulhamid tried to depoliticize the bureaucracy and increase its efficiency by professionalizing it. He established a civil service commission in 1878 and a personnel committee to reform the bureaucracy. He also opened or enlarged a series of professional schools, which, paradoxically, became the training ground for a new generation of liberal intellectuals and the source of opposition to the sultan. Among them were the famous elitist Mülkiye, or School of Administration (today's Political Science School, part of the University of Ankara), and the Schools of Finance, Trade, Higher Education, Law, Navy, Agriculture, Fine Arts, and Mining, as well as the School for the Deaf and Blind and industrial schools for women. The three-tier modern educational system discussed elsewhere in detail (chapter 4), which was greatly expanded during Abdulhamid's time, increased the rate of literacy and increased greatly the readership of the press and of modern-style literature—to the detriment of the dogmatic conservatives. A modern statistical system and population surveys modeled after the American system were introduced during Abdulhamid's reign: the head of the first American census, Samuel S. Cox, who was appointed ambassador to

Istanbul, provided the sultan with necessary information.[36] In addition, the first Turkish University (Darulfünun) was opened (the attempt in 1870 had failed), as were a series of museums, modern archives, and a library, which became and still is the central library of the University of Istanbul.

The history of Abdulhamid's library at Yildiz Palace, along with information about the background of some of the directing personnel, provides insights into sultan's attitudes toward science, the West, cultural continuity, and the endless ideological battle over Turkey's own past. The library was rich by the standards of its time: it had approximately 90,000–100,000 items of all kinds, including rare Turkish, Arabic, and Persian manuscripts as well as important Western works on history, literature, and philosophy. In 1908 some "revolutionaries" were thwarted in their efforts to acquire the rare books from the library, which later, as the library of the University of Istanbul, was used by those accusing Abdulhamid of obscurantism to educate the Republican youth. In the 1940s the library acquired many new books and became qualitatively the best library in Turkey. The library personnel represented at once both the historical-social continuity and the cultural-political dichotomy of Turkey. Nureddin Kalkandelen, the son of Sabri bey, who had thwarted the attempt to rob the Yildiz library in 1908, became a director in the 1950s, replacing Fehmi Karatay, an expert on old manuscripts. Nureddin, in addition to his knowledge of manuscripts, had special expertise on the Ottoman-Arabic script. His assistant, Ali bey, who knew Arabic, Persian, and French, was a pious Muslim, praying five times a day. In his old age he married the cleaning woman in the library in order to take care of her and her five children after the woman's husband suddenly passed away. The other assistant, Naci bey (of Konya), a well-known poet, atheist, and bonvivant bachelor, a materialist by philosophy, spoke perfect French and was an authority on Persian poetry. Ali and Naci were very good friends and both provided invaluable help to students, including this writer, seeking to decipher hand-written manuscripts or to clarify obscure Arabic and Persian words and sentences or translate French or English words into Turkish. After the military takeover in 1960 a group of "progressive" politicians tried to close the library by dividing its books among various other institutions, supposedly in order to achieve a "balanced representation" of books but actually to eliminate an embarrassing monument to Abdulhamid's memory. Nureddin Kalkandelen mobilized support and successfully opposed the dismantling of the library. Other attempts to close the library also failed. Republican dogmatism promoted in the name of science and progress was worse than Abdulhamid's Islamic conservatism.

Abdulhamid continued the effort to deprive the religious establishment of influence over the judiciary. In the 1850s, the Tanzimatists had established special schools designed to train *naibs* (assistants or deputies to judges), usually members of the *ilmiye* or ulema, to help implement the newly adopted laws that were often copied from Europe. Abdulhamid enlarged and modernized the curricula of these schools (*mekteb-i nüvvab*) in 1884 and had the future judges trained as a professional class rather than a religious group, despite their Islamic credentials. The *mekteb-i hukuk* (law school), *dava vekili* (advocates), and their associations all have their roots in these *nüvvab* (plural of *naib*) schools.[37]

The first efforts toward modern and national architecture and fine arts (calligraphy, book binding, sculpture, decoration, carving) were initiated during Abdulhamid's reign. A memorandum addressed to the sultan criticized the architecture of the Valide mosque and other "modern" buildings (e.g., the Bayazit Library erected before and during Abdulaziz's reign), as having little to do with the *real* Ottoman architecture or with European styles. These buildings, called "alafranga" (French) according to the memorandum, betrayed ignorance of both Ottoman models and minimum Western professional standards. The memorandum advocated a return not to the old Arabic, Persian, or even Selçuki architectures but to the styles of authentic Ottoman artists, such as the architects Kasim, Musa, and Sinan, who "are our ancestors . . . and combined Roman and Byzantine with Arab and Persian styles and created a new Ottoman architectural style science." It also recommended that the government take an active role in repairing "all mosques, museums, *medreses*, libraries, in a word, all *national* old buildings in the capital and provinces . . . and expand the school of fine arts"[38] It should be noted that the first national museum—today Turkey's chief museum of archeology—was established during Abdulhamid's reign by the celebrated Osman Hamdi (b. 1842), the son of Ibrahim Edhem, director of foreign publications and an European educated and sophisticated aide to Abdulhamid.[39] The new small group of modernist traditionalists also began to attack the notion of "alafranga,"— not in rejection of change, Europe, or modernity, as construed by some scholars, but as a criticism of shabby, low-quality innovations and goods promoted merely because they were "Western." What both the old Ottoman elite, with its deeply rooted sense of traditional palace culture and exquisite sense of esthetics, and the well-educated modernists were looking for was *authenticity*—that is, for a meaningful relationship between the material culture introduced in the name of modernism and the society's own roots, tastes, needs, and culture.

The increasing rejection of everything Ottoman as backward, useless, and shameful by most of the upcoming "modernist" intelligentsia trained in the very schools established by Abdulhamid was a consequence of the traditional split of society into elite and the masses and the lack of facilities to initiate the rapidly growing number of bureaucrats into the niceties of the traditional elite culture. Political liberalism would become the dominant ideology of most of the new elite, which soon came to regard Abdulhamid's absolutism and rejection of the blind imitation of everything European as tantamount to a total rejection of modernity and contemporary civilization. Lurking behind these rather extreme positions was a growing confusion about the meaning of "civilization" and "modernity" and the place of the old in relation to the new. The conflict between *alafranga* and *alaturka* was actually a conflict between images of the "new" and the "old" as perceived by their respective apologists. These images had little to do with reality, but nonetheless they were treated as reality and provided a basis and background for the emergence of nationalism, which could claim to represent, under the guise of *authenticity*, the "real" Turkish self. One of the severest critics of the *alafranga* was Hüseyin Rahmi (Gürpinar, 1864–1944) whose works, along with those of Ahmet Mithat, provide one of the best pictures of the inner conflict caused by modernization of the Ottoman society from 1880 to 1918.[40]

The search for a redefinition of identity and reconciliation of the traditional with the modern inside the framework of the old culture also took place among non-Muslims, although the literature on this subject is rather limited. One little-known work, by a Karamanli (Turkish-speaking Orthodox Christian) Evangelos Misailidis

(1820–90), was a novel titled *Temaşa-i Dünya* (Watching the world) and published around 1871–72; it is an excellent study of the clash of identities and the search for modernity among Christians and of the ultimate reconciliation with one's own ethnoreligious group. The author, incidentally, proclaimed that ethnicity among Christians was stronger than unity based on religion, because "an Armenian cannot become a Greek and a Greek cannot become an Armenian," although both are Christians. He also stated courageously that "I am not mistaken if I say that the Turkish order has changed into European order" thanks to the Tanzimat. The hero in Misailidis's lengthy novel is the lawyer, Favini (the son of a depraved European father and Greek mother), who travels throughout Europe looking for the best country in which to settle and assimilate or become "modern." He becomes an "Englishman," a "Frenchman," and so on, in turn but at the end decides to settle in Greece, which, though not perfect, he considered better than Western Europe. It should be noted that Misailidis was a good Orthodox Christian, who studied in Greece and worked for the Greek patriarchate in Istanbul. He published, to the end of his life, the review *Anatoli*—in Turkish but using the Greek alphabet—in Istanbul; and he fought against the efforts of the Greek government and the Patriarchate to Hellenize his Turkish-speaking Karamanlis—most of whom were exchanged in 1926 for the "Turks" of Greece, many of whom were Greek-speaking Muslims.[41] A variety of other changes in identity and ethnicity occurring in 1890–1908 and the publication of classics such as *Seyahatname* of Evliya Çelebi, by *Ikdam*, the moderate Turkist newspaper, will be studied in a different context.[42]

Under Abdulhamid the military establishment was professionally upgraded, the curriculum of Harbiye (War College) was specialized further to train staff officers in the European style, and the school's name was changed to Mekteb-i Fününu Harb (School of War Science). The sultan respected the army's military traditions, and he did his best to cultivate the friendship of the upper-ranking officers, including Osman paşa, and to modernize the army. However, late in his reign Abdulhamid began to distrust the regular army because of the officers' alleged positivism and support for the opposition, and he relied instead on the palace regiment, whose soldiers and officers were often drawn from among the non-Turkish groups, especially the Albanians. However, although the consensus that Abdulhamid favored the modernization of the Ottoman army and the professionalization of the officer was fairly general, it seems that he neglected the military during the last fifteen years of his reign, and he also cut down the military budget.

The truth is that Abdulhamid attached utmost importance to the reorganization of the military. As early as 1880 he sought, and two years later secured, German assistance, which culminated in the appointment of Lt. Col. Kohler and, finally, Colmar Von der Goltz as military advisors. It was during his reign that the officers' training was upgraded and regularized, starting with the mid-level military *rüşdiye* and *idadi* schools and culminating in the Mekteb-i Harbiye (War College) or, for the most capable, in the Erkan-i Harbiye (Chiefs of Staff). The last, as a concept and an organization, was largely the work of von der Goltz. The problem with the army (numbering ca. 700,000 at the end of the century), besides the officers' constant opposition to field exercises, was the growing number of underpaid officers, and the lack of a proper retirement system. The annual army expenditures were some 7,756,000 liras out of a total national budget of 18,927,000 liras for 1897; when the Debt Administration claimed 6,483.000 liras, little was left for investment in economic development. Eventually the sultan, with his customary lack of resolve, instead of retiring the surplus officers and downsizing the standing army in favor of the reserves, started economizing by cutting down military supplies and procrastinating on the payment of officers; this aggravated further the grievances resulting from the unbalanced pay scale, which saw the top generals getting 9,000–13,500 gold kuruş while a colonel was paid 3,600 and a lieutenant only 250. Moreover, the tension between the *alayli* (officers coming from the ranks) and *mektepli* (those educated in schools) and the growing tension in Macedonia called for increased military expenditure and the stationing there of large number of troops and officers, making worse an already bad financial situation.[43] The roots of the revolution of 1908 that started in Macedonia must be sought not only in the liberal ideas of the Union and Progress Committee, but also in the financial grievances of its military members.

The sultan was basically a pacifist who tried to avoid war at all costs and seemed uninterested in titles other than sultan and caliph. He was given the title of *gazi*, to conform to some old Ottoman war traditions, after the Ottoman armies stopped (temporarily) the Russians in Plevne in 1877; but he did not make use of it. Abdulhamid favored compromises such as granting some autonomy to the Balkan Christians in order to avoid war with Russia; he acquiesced in the occupation of eastern Rumili by Bulgaria in 1885; and he did not gloat over his decisive victory against the Greeks in the war of 1897, which he had tried to avoid to the end. He had a rather clear and realistic view about the nationality problem in the Ottoman state, but aside from a few economic and cultural incentives, he failed to produce any lasting solution to that problem. Obviously, his increasingly autocratic stance provided no remedy but, on the contrary, worsened the already tense intraethnic national conflicts, and he became the target of attacks by non-Muslim groups, notably the Armenians.

Abdulhamid's centralization of all power, including religious authority, in the palace appears at first sight to be in line with the Ottoman sultans' traditional absolutism, which was in fact fairly limited. Close scrutiny reveals that Abdulhamid's policy featured unprecedented changes. Because the palace staff was expanded and organized into a bureaucratic apparatus that could control the rest of the executive and the population as a whole, Abdulhamid had, in effect, in the name of *istibdat* (absolutism), established the organized nucleus of a modern totalitarian government, which his Young Turk successors and then the Republic expanded and refined. True, the sultan increased the authority of the center, but in order to win the support and confidence of the countryside notables, paradoxically he actually granted them considerable economic incentives, autonomy, and cultural freedom, which they used to strengthen their control of the community—which, ultimately, they turned against the political center.

Between Modernism and Islam

The information that helps explain Abdulhamid's anticonstitutionalist policy, his efforts at centralization, and, ultimately, his one-man rule does not explain the sultan's

Islamist philosophy. Instead, an entirely different mixture of internal conditions and international circumstances were combined with his own personality and view of Islam to produce his Islamism. Abdulhamid believed that Islam was not the backward faith described by Western writers but a religion that had brought light, peace, progress, and happiness to people who previously had lived in the darkness (*cahiliye*). Its past achievements convinced him that Islam was open to progress and science. Although the sultan accepted the view that the Muslim societies had stagnated for centuries while the West advanced, he believed that the basic principles and spirit of Islam remained intact and that the awakening detected among Muslims during the past few years showed that it was open to evolution.

Islam, according to Abdulhamid, abided by dogma, as did Christianity and Judaism, but it also honored virtue and respected freedom of thought. For instance, after Polish and Hungarian revolutionaries were accorded asylum in the Ottoman Empire in 1849, his father, Abdulmecid, was prepared to go to war with Russia and Austria to protect the right of asylum. Likewise, to show that Islam was a tolerant religion, Abdulhamid cited the many national groups living safely within the Muslim states. He noted also the converts to Islam who reached high positions in the Ottoman government: for example, Tevfik paşa and Rifat paşa, ambassadors to London and Paris respectively, and the several German-trained army officials whose Christian wives were fully accepted by their husbands' Muslim families. Abdulhamid's policy on government officials' marrying foreigners was more liberal than that of the Republic, which explicitly forbade them to marry "foreigners," that is, non-Muslims. (This prohibition was abolished only in 1995.) The sultan, of course, considered conversions to Islam, especially by educated Europeans, proof of Islam's superiority. He honored with the title "şeyh" Abdullah William (Henry William) who became a Muslim in 1887 while traveling in the Ottoman state; William took an active part in introducing Islam in England and was a critic of the British expedition against Sudan.

According to Abdulhamid, Islam never accepted fatalism. The Prophet stated that "God is great and merciful, but He cannot deal with the individual's everyday problems. Everybody is duty-bound to think and work. 'Those who do not sow cannot reap, those who do not work cannot find bread to eat.'" The sultan noted that Christianity, too, accepted the omnipotence and omnipresence of God, but "Christians are nevertheless thinking, working, and progressing while we [Muslims] remain spectators [to world progress]."[44]

Abdulhamid charged that many Christian leaders nurtured dogmatic prejudices against Islam, even while they preached open-mindedness and impartiality toward progress, civilization, and culture. He based these accusations on a number of concrete events, such as the efforts of the French missionaries, who incited the Maronite peasants in Lebanon to rebel against their Druse landlords in the 1860s, and the conflict among various Christian denominations about jurisdiction over the holy sites in Jerusalem. He was critical of the one-sided and subjective report about the Bulgarian events in 1876 by E. Schuyler, an American missionary, and held the Christian clerics responsible for creating the Europeans' negative attitude toward Muslims. As the sultan put it, "This clergy has attributed to the Muslims all the outrages committed by the Crusaders against the people of our country and did not hesitate to slander the Muslims in every way in order to incite the Christians to rebellion."[45]

The sultan claimed that slavery in Islam had no economic motives (unlike that institution in the Americas) and should be viewed and judged according to the circumstances; in fact slavery had been officially abolished in 1857, although it was still practiced in some remote areas of the realm, where any precipitate effort to abolish it would have caused unrest.[46]

Like the rest of the Ottoman sultans, Abdulhamid never went on the *hac*, as every Muslim is required to do at least once in a lifetime if at all possible. However, as a sincere believer and a practicing Muslim, he became a member of two popular brotherhoods. He did not join the elite Mevlevis, favored by many of his predecessors and his brother Murad. Rather, in his youth he joined the Şahzeliye (Shadhiliya) because of his friendship with Şeyh Zafir efendi, who had predicted that Abdulhamid would become sultan and later was made an advisor; and he also joined the Kadiriyya, through the offices of Abdullah efendi, the *şeyh* of the Yahya efendi lodge. Abdulhamid's sincere belief and daily practice of Islam secured him deep respect among believers throughout the Muslim world. Moreover, he tried to open up his country to the world and to inform Europe and the United States about Ottoman society. For instance, following the invitation of the United States, he ordered his government to participate in the Chicago (1893) world's fair, where it built a model "Turkish"— not Ottoman—village with a mosque and covered bazaar that sold Ottoman products; but he opposed the show of whirling dervishes or public display of Muslim prayers as demeaning to Islam.[47] Nowadays, dervishes are sent on periodic trips to Europe and the United States to display "Turkish" culture.

Abdulhamid's view of Islam as a progressive and dynamic religion open to science and progress reflected the reformist, progressive beliefs of the new Muslim middle classes and of their intellectual spokesmen. According to his daughter, Abdulhamid often said that "religion and science both are faiths," implying without intending to that one can be substituted for the other.[48] The sultan unwittingly also made a sharp distinction between faith and deed (action) and never directly or indirectly advocated the involvement of religious men in politics or government, except for himself as caliph (which, incidentally, is not a religious but a political position). Indeed, there is not an iota of evidence in Abdulhamid's, his daughter's, or anyone else's memoirs or writings to indicate that the sultan ever defended *theocracy*, meaning a form of government run by a religious elite, which was an accusation often made against him. That he turned Islamism into a modern type of ideology and used it to hold together the Ottoman Muslims was part of his political plan, not the consequence of his faith. The sultan considered the Muslims' attachment to their religion and the Europeans' love for *patria* as being identical and political in nature: "The love which they [the Europeans] have for their motherland we [Muslims] nurture for our religion. Our enemies call the love for our religion fanaticism. . . . Prophet Muhammed's doctrine, to which we are attached with a profound love, defends equality among people, protects the weak, values the good and orders obedience to law. We are ennobled by the great love we feel toward our faith."[49]

Personal opinions about Abdulhamid tend to be very partisan. Fortunately, we have two descriptions of him by men who dealt personally with him after his abdication, when he was no longer able to reward his supporters and punish his enemies. These descriptions were provided by Fethi Okyar, an army officer who stayed with Abdulhamid during the first three months of his exile in Salonica, and Atif Hüseyin, the doctor who cared for him from 1908 until his death in 1918.

Fethi Okyar (1880–1943), who belonged to the inner circle of the Young Turks and then became minister and prime minister in the Republic, was a very close friend of Atatürk—until his Free (Liberal) Party, established in 1930 to provide loyal opposition to the government, turned against the establishment and was abolished. Okyar, a major in the army, was entrusted by the Young Turks' high command to take Abdulhamid to Salonica after the latter's forced abdication in 1909. During a three months' stay with Abdulhamid in Salonica, Fethi, who was a Turkified Albanian from the town of Pirlepe in Macedonia, held long private and frank talks with Abdulhamid and won his confidence and friendship. It was Fethi Okyar who brought the sultan back to Istanbul during the Balkan war because the former ruler did not trust any one else. Okyar directed that his memoirs be published long after his death, as his honest, forthright, and objective observations conflicted with the negative official view and dark portrait of Abdulhamid.[50] According to Okyar, Abdulhamid was balanced, intelligent, dignified, modern-minded, wise, and well-informed. Profoundly attached to his country and his faith, he also was aware of the capabilities and limitations of his people and government. Abdulhamid believed that only the maintenance of the political status quo would assure the integrity and survival of the Empire, because giving the ethnic groups, including the Albanians, extensive autonomy, positions in the government, and exemption from taxes only led them to demand ever more autonomy and possibly independence. He had to win the goodwill of the provincial notables and tribal leaders by giving them positions of responsibility, establishing the tribal schools and the Hamidiye regiments, and appointing Arabs to high positions.

According to Okyar, Abdulhamid was keenly interested in discovering how the Balkan states, freed from Ottoman rule in 1878, became in such a short time so powerful and resourceful as to challenge their old masters. Fethi bey told the sultan that nationalism was the key to the Balkans' social and political rejuvenation, explaining that the Bulgarians, considered a primitive group even by their Russian patrons, enlisted the support of the village priests who used patriotic-religious sermons to rid their conationals of ignorance, teach them practical skills, and orient them toward concrete goals. Abdulhamid complained that the Muslims in the Ottoman Empire did not have the benefit of properly trained religious men. In fact, they had promoted ignorance by telling Muslim pupils that they would become infidels if they attended the courses given by European teachers at the medical school opened by Abdulmecid, his father. Later, non-Muslims rushed to enroll in the modern professional schools that he himself opened, while Muslims, and especially Turks, were kept aloof by religious propaganda. Even current members of the clergy were mostly incapable of understanding not only the contemporary world but also the virtues embodied in their own faith such as reliance on intellect, science, logic, and spiritual unity. (It is interesting to note that Atatürk held the same opinion about clerics in Turkey.) In contrast, Abdulhamid considered Abdurreşid Ibrahim, the Tatar Islamist, as the ideal type of modern, learned Islamic leader who knew several languages, traveled extensively, and had high political ideals; and he also praised Cemaleddin Afghani as a "great thinker with free thoughts." While ruling as a sultan, however, Abdulhamid had treated both men with suspicion.[51]

Abdulhamid explained and justified his anticonstitutionalism in a rather unusual way. He told Okyar that he never abolished, but merely suspended, the Constitution of 1876, for "national" reasons. The constitution as promulgated would have perpetuated the superior economic, commercial, and educational position of the non-Muslims and would have kept the Turks, the *asli* (basic) group of the country, forever in an inferior position. (Raising the Turks' status was a key ingredient in the Young Turks' nationalism.) The Arabs, Albanians, Jews, and Christians, according to the sultan, had aspirations and goals "specific to their nation and race"; the Christians and Jews wanted to reach these goals by establishing free nations. The Turks and other Muslims, despite their numerical superiority, were less developed than the Jews and Christians and "painful as it is to express it so openly this is the truth."[52] It was therefore essential to maintain the supremacy of state in order to thwart the rise of ethnic and national consciousness among the various minority groups, to prevent individual freedom from undermining the integrity of the state, and to give the government time to raise the economic, cultural, and political level of the Muslims, particularly the Turks. Abdulhamid openly declared himself Turkish and claimed to be honored to be a member of the Turkish nation.

According to Okyar, Abdulhamid volunteered to advise the Young Turks on foreign policy but was turned down. Finally their leader, Talat paşa, who seemed to have developed considerable respect for the ex-sultan, did consult him about how to get out of the impasse caused by the Ottoman entry into World War I on the side of Germany but was told that it was too late.[53] As far as Muslim unity was concerned, Abdulhamid regarded it as a means to thwart Europe's imperial ambitions over Ottoman lands.

The other relatively objective source about Abdulhamid, Doctor Atif Hüseyin, cared for the sultan in his last years and reported regularly to the CUP. His reports describe Abdulhamid in a positive light as open-minded and progressive, while bound to his faith and traditions.[54]

The Caliphate, the Fate of Muslims, and Foreign Policy

Sultan Abdulhamid was aware of the unique position of the Ottoman state and of the caliphate in the Muslim world. The Muslim population of the Ottoman Empire consisted of only about twenty million people, but, he claimed, the eyes of most of the other Muslims living in countries subjugated by foreign powers were turned toward Istanbul. "Our relations with countries inhabited by Muslims," wrote Abdulhamid,

> must be expanded and we all must strive for togetherness. As long as the unity of Islam continues, England, France, Russia and Holland are in my hands, because with a word [I] the caliph could unleash the *cihad* [holy war] among their Muslim subjects and this would be a tragedy for the Christians. . . . [O]ne day [Muslims] will rise and shake off the infidel's yoke. Eighty-five million Muslims under English rule, 30 million in the colonies of the Dutch, 10 million in Russia . . . altogether 250 million Muslims are beseeching God for delivery from foreign rule. They have pinned their hopes on the caliph, the deputy of the Prophet Muhammed. We cannot [therefore] remain submissive in dealing with the great powers.[55]

As caliph, Abdulhamid managed to identify himself with the cultural and religious aspirations of large groups of Muslims and to introduce a series of reforms that produced widespread material changes; but he failed to understand the innovative spirit and individualistic aspirations embodied in the popular revivalist movements that he feared so much. He was especially irked by the politically active popular movements, whose demands ranged from economic development to recognition of their ethnolinguistic and territorial identities. In his memoirs Abdulhamid strongly condemned, as the greatest threats to Islam and to the Ottoman Empire (and also to his own throne), *kavmiyet* (ethnic-tribal nationalism) and *vatan sevgisi* (love of the territory of the fatherland). Realizing that the Ottoman state consisted of a variety of Muslim and non-Muslim nationalities and that the non-Muslims were striving to break away, the sultan advised the Muslims to emphasize their common faith, which united them as a family, rather than their ethnic identity, which tended to separate them. "For this reason one should not give priority to the idea of an Empire [identified with Turks] but on the contrary stress the fact that we are all Muslims. The title of Amir-ul Muslimin [caliph] should be given priority everywhere and every time. The title of "Ottoman ruler" should take the second place because the state's social structure and politics is built on religious principles."[56]

The sultan believed that the idea of an ethnic "nation" and "race" were preached by the English in order to divide the Turks and Arabs and incite uprisings in Arabia, Albania, and possibly Syria. Likewise, the concept of the territorial fatherland, or *vatan*, advocated by some youths who had been influenced by a "superficial understanding of Europe," was used by England to undermine the sultan's influence in Egypt. Consequently, he urged the Muslims to "give priority to the faith and to the love for the caliph and relegate the *hubb-ul-vatan* [love of the territorial fatherland] to the second plane."[57] Actual developments in the Ottoman Empire, meanwhile, were leading toward the intensifying of ethnic awareness.

The sultan acted with justice and magnanimity toward non-Muslims as long as they did not challenge his authority or engage in bellicose acts, like those of the Armenian nationalists who once nearly killed him as he was leaving the mosque after Friday prayer. The Jews enjoyed during Abdulhamid's time unprecedented economic and cultural development as well as protection against the Greeks' animosity and frequent use of the nefarious blood libels. Nevertheless, while respecting the religious and cultural rights of the non-Muslims, as indicated by the proliferation of their churches and ethnic schools, the sultan defended the view that the state's dominant culture was Islamic, for Muslims constituted an overwhelming majority of the population.

Abdulhamid did not suspend or abolish any of the Tanzimat reforms but actually prepared reform plans far more comprehensive than those of his predecessors. British ambassador Layard reported to London that during a dinner on 27 May 1879, the sultan produced a series of proposals to reform the entire government structure. These affected the military, the central administration, the provincial administration, the courts (including the Islamic ones), the legal system, finance, trade, agriculture, municipalities, public education, and other institutions. Moreover, the sultan succeeded in carrying out many of them, despite the extraordinary financial burden of Turkey's foreign debt. The foreign debt, now collected through the Debt Administration Office, established in 1882 and headed by Europeans (although most of its employees were Muslim Ottoman subjects), was a major economic burden, but did help in systematizing the financial affairs of the Ottoman state. The sultan, however, stabilized the foreign debt situation by setting limits on borrowing from abroad and increasing state revenue enough to finance some of his reforms.[58] By the very extent of his reform proposals, Abdulhamid unwittingly played a major role in showing Islamic society the depth of its underdevelopment—even as he was upholding the virtues of the faith and giving the Muslims a new perspective on their own potential strength.

The Impact of International Events on Abdulhamid

Islamism might not have been born and evolved as it did if the Ottoman state had not faced the danger of imminent destruction through the war of 1877–78 and the subsequent loss of English support. Because England had showed some concern for the opinion and welfare of India's Muslims, Abdulhamid's immediate predecessors apparently concluded that English friendship toward Muslims, including the Ottomans, was genuine and everlasting. Abdulhamid thus had started his reign in 1876 with belief in the permanency of British support, for he saw Russia as their common enemy. Although he appeared to have inherited his father's reliance on the British, unlike his father, he was not ready to comply with every request from London. Abdulmecid once asked his son, a child, but still of royal blood, to kiss the hand of the "büyük elçi" (ambassador) Stratford Canning, as a sign of respect, but Abdulhamid would not do so.

Abdulhamid's confidence in England's support and in Europe's impartiality was shattered by the events of the years 1876–78. Already the French defeat by the Germans in 1870–71 had led the British to agree to amend some of the provisions of the 1856 treaty and allow Russia to militarize the Black Sea. After a large section of the English press and many statesmen had become openly anti-Turkish and anti-Muslim during the Balkan uprisings of 1875 and 1876, the British cabinet defied Queen Victoria's express wishes by refusing to provide or sell weapons to Turkey, under the pretext of maintaining "neutrality" during the war of 1877–78. Then, on 4 June 1878, Ambassador Layard, following London's instructions, compelled the unwilling sultan to sign the Cyprus Convention, ceding that island to Britain. The sultan's prestige suffered, while his anger at the humiliations—some calculated—inflicted upon him by London increased. During the Constantinople Conference in the winter of 1876–77, the sultan repeatedly invited the British delegate, the marquess of Salisbury, to dinner but was rebuffed. Meanwhile, Salisbury met frequently with the Russian ambassador at the Porte, and shared lavish dinners. During the war of 1877–78, the sultan had viewed with sadness and profound indignation the indifference of Europe to the plight of the millions of Muslims in the Balkans and the Caucasus. Although the European press had magnified beyond any realistic measure the atrocities committed by the Turkish irregulars in Bulgaria in 1876, it seldom mentioned that hundreds of thousands of Muslims, including children and pregnant Muslim women, were murdered and disemboweled by Bulgarians, Serbians, and Russians in 1877–

78. Paradoxically, the best information on these atrocities are in the British consular reports from Varna and Ruschuk.[59]

The efforts to liquidate the Muslims were often the consequence of fierce anti-Muslim ideological literary writings that had nurtured Balkan nationalism. For instance, the classical poem "Mountain Wreath" by Petar Petrovich Njegos, "the Shakespeare of Serbia," who was a bishop and ruler of Montenegro (1830–51), denounced the refusal of converted Muslims to return to their old faith, Orthodox Christianity, and advocated the eradication of Islam from Montenegro. Njegos's poem has been described by Serbian historians as a part of their ideology of national liberation from the Turks' rule. However the main target of the poem are Slavs who converted to Islam, whom the author views as "traitors." Although the Muslims plead that the two faiths can "live together in this land of ours" and urge the Christians to "let us all as brothers live," the "hero" in the poem, Bishop Danilo, replies that this is not possible since his land reeks of "this False Religion"; he tells them that they will be treated like other "traitors" in the past. So there would be "no single seeing eye, no tongue of Turk . . . we put them all into the sword . . . and all their houses were set ablaze, of all their mosques, both great and small we left but accursed heaps."[60]

The sultan was well informed about the fate of the Muslims in the Balkans, but he could not help them. He limited himself to providing food for tens of thousands of the Muslim Balkan refugees from his own funds, and he urged his ministers to do the same. The plight of the Muslim refugees appears to have strengthened Abdulhamid's feeling of solidarity with believers and politicized his pious nature, causing him to see his position of caliph as having a global, missionary-like dimension. Whatever trust and friendship the sultan might have harbored toward England vanished entirely after he read Article 61 of the Berlin Treaty, which appointed England supervisor of reforms to be undertaken in the eastern provinces, where the Armenians amounted to a bare 20 to 35 percent of the population. The appointment of Lord Rosebery—an avowed pro-Armenian and a plotter with the Young Turks—to head the supervisory body, increased further Abdulhamid's suspicions about London's intentions toward him and his country.[61]

By 1878 England already had begun to act as if it were the ruler of the Ottoman state. A memorandum, probably dictated by Abdulhamid, asserted, "At the conclusion of the Cyprus Convention, England appeared intent to use and administer the Sublime State as its own possession and colony. Consequently, it is essential to take the necessary measures and actions that would oppose and render ineffective the ill-intentions of the aforementioned state."[62] It is known for certain that after 1878 Salisbury, the British foreign minister, attempted to administer the Ottoman state as a colony. The sultan asked the Porte to hasten to bring in finance officers from Germany, as already agreed, and to sign new contracts to hire additional military, fiscal, and administrative officers from the same country. It also recommended that the administrative reforms contemplated for Anatolia should not lead to or encourage ethnic divisions but strengthen solidarity among Muslims. The widespread administrative, economic and fiscal reforms taken by the Ottoman government after 1878 can be linked to this basic directive issued by the sultan.[63]

Coming to power in 1880, the Gladstone government forced the sultan, through the display of naked naval power ("gunboat diplomacy"), to cede, as stipulated by the Berlin Treaty, Dulcingo on the Adriatic Sea to Montenegro and, one year later, Thessaly to Greece. Finally, the British deprived the Ottoman state of its most precious jewel by occupying Egypt in 1882, under the pretext of "protecting" European lives against the revolt of Colonel Urabi. The occupation was followed by long discussions in which England tried to persuade the sultan to denounce Urabi and agree to a joint occupation of Egypt. The occupation of Egypt crystallized Abdulhamid's Islamist thoughts, which had been stimulated by the previously mentioned European and Russian aggressions and insults and by Europe's partiality toward the Ottoman Christians and its indifference, veiled in high-sounding rhetoric, to the massacre of hundreds of thousands of Muslims.

Joan Haslip has admirably captured Abdulhamid's state of mind, showing that it resulted from the plight of the Muslims and from England's apparent readiness to partition the Ottoman Empire at the most opportune moment and that it led to his intention to use the caliphate as an instrument of domestic and foreign policy. Haslip's description of a meeting held in 1877 between Layard and the sultan and based on Layard's report clearly portrays Abdulhamid's position:

> The sultan rarely allowed his bitterness to transpire, though many of his ministers spoke openly against what they considered to be the defection of a former ally [England]. Only on one occasion did he show how much he resented the attitude of Europe. In discussing the question of the atrocities committed by the Russians in the Caucasus, he asked whether the raping of Moslem women and the murder of their children would stir up as much resentment in England as the alleged Turkish atrocities in Bulgaria; or was it, he asked, a matter of Christian against Moslem?
>
> Layard had never seen the sultan angry before. 'We are accused in Europe,' he said, 'of being savages and fanatics, but we are not the savages who brought on an unjust and horrible war which will lead to the sacrifice of innumerable human beings, nor are we the fanatics who have incited Greeks, Armenians and Bulgarians to exterminate those who differ from them in religion.'
>
> For the first time the future leader of Pan-Islam hinted at the large spiritual forces at his command. 'Unlike the Czar, I have abstained till now from stirring up a crusade and profiting from religious fanaticism, but the day may come when I can no longer curb the rights and indignation of my people at seeing their co-religionists butchered in Bulgaria and Armenia. And once their fanaticism is aroused, then the whole Western world, and in particular the British Empire, will have reason to fear.'
>
> The sultan spoke, knowing that the Ambassador was watching apprehensively the coming and going of emissaries from Afghanistan and Russian Turkestan, all of whom were treated by the sultan as favored allies. Ostensibly their intrigues were directed against Russia, but England had too many interests at stake to ignore any form of religious agitation on her Indian frontier.[64]

Indeed, England, which had tried to use pan-Islamism to further British interests in Central Asia and India, would soon begin to fight it. The sultan now was without the protection of England, which he had cherished, although not to the extent of becoming London's docile client. Instead he would use his caliphal title to build unity within the Empire and solidify the support of overseas Muslims—even against Europe, if need be.

Conclusion

The political reforms that Sultan Abdulhamid inherited and implemented had been adopted by his predecessors under considerably different internal and international circumstances. Under British influence and the security offered by Palmerston's policy of maintaining the territorial integrity of the state, the Tanzimatists apparently had accepted the universality of Western political ideas and believed that administrative, military, and economic efficacy would naturally flow out of them. They did not have to deal with opposition groups or a critical press to explain and justify the reforms to the masses. The ruler's power was absolute as was the belief in his righteousness; the *fetva* of the compliant *şeyhulislam*, if needed, could be easily secured to provide the necessary religious legitimacy. The ruling elite—that is, the imperial bureaucracy—thus immunized against popular reaction, could engage in any reform deemed necessary for the state's survival.

The Ottoman alliance with Europe and the successful war against Russia over the period 1853–56 not only increased the influence of Great Britain but also opened the door further to massive cultural, economic, and social influences from Europe. The changed patterns of social stratification and acquisition of wealth, the modern educational system, and other factors produced two seemingly conflicting results: first, they undermined the traditional social order and mobilized the masses in populist religious movements that appeared to advocate a return to the old order but actually sought to accommodate change within a traditional Islamic social framework; second, they precipitated the rise of a new and increasingly individualistic middle class, with its own pragmatic values and modernist Islamic identity. The political impact of these reactions, which began to materialize in the 1860s in the Young Ottoman movement, was contained largely because of the Tanzimatists' close and friendly relations with Europe, especially England. The political system of Europe had provided the Young Ottomans a source of inspiration for revitalizing the Empire, while its military might protected the state against Russian attacks and its diplomacy defined the unrest and autonomy demands of the Balkan Christians as the sultan's "internal matter," largely in order to forestall the czar's interference in Ottoman affairs. This protection allowed the Ottoman state to regain a degree of health and vitality and rebuild its confidence that it was a world power. (The Tanzimat period resembled the period of unprecedented modernization and Europeanization of Turkey between 1947–95, which was result in large measure of the international protection provided by the North Atlantic Treaty Organization and the economic help and cultural and political influence of the United States.)

All delusions were shattered by the devastating defeat of the Empire in the war of 1877–78. Because a change in the old European balance of power led to the need for a new one that favored Russia and the French ambitions in North Africa, to the detriment of the Ottomans, opinion in England no longer held that the integrity of the Ottoman Empire served London's interests, and it underwent a definite ideological shift in favor of Christians. Thus, after 1878 Sultan Abdulhamid was left alone and unprotected in the international arena, while facing at home the enormous tension created by populist-democratic yearnings and demands for material betterment, the quest by the elites to increase their own influence in the political system, and the political demands of the Armenians and Greeks. Underlying this was the rise of regional, ethnic, and interest consciousness among various groups.

A truly modern society with an interest-oriented concept of self and many new aspirations, as well as a yearning for a new collective identity, came into existence mainly during the reign of Abdulhamid. The sultan closed the parliament and suspended the constitution of 1876–78 with little protest from Europe or even his own populace and assumed all power for himself. He curtailed political freedom and controlled the press, but he maintained, intensified, and broadened the reforms of his predecessors. He sought to consolidate the unity of the Ottoman Muslims by making the caliphate their rallying institution, while using it not only to justify and legitimize (in traditional Islamic terms) his temporal authority but also to facilitate the introduction of a great variety of changes cloaked in Islamic garb.

Abdulhamid was the first Ottoman sultan to become aware of the enormous power of the masses, and he employed all means at his disposal to use, control, contain, or repress them, as the case seemed to warrant. Paradoxically, he also played a key role in preventing Muslim outrage against Europe from taking a militant, destructive direction. Abdulhamid opposed European colonialism and imperialism in all its forms, especially its mistreatment of Muslims and denigration of Islam, but he acknowledged the material and intellectual achievements of Europe, which he often contrasted with the regressiveness of Muslim societies. He showed a special interest in the United States for its progress in science, the prosperity of its population, and its secularism, which he believed to be akin to Islam's outlook on religion and government.

The uprising of 1909 that cost Abdulhamid the throne stemmed from changes in the very meaning of "state" and in the relations between government and the individual that took place during Abdulhamid's rule. Formal Islamism was Abdulhamid's creation, but he did not believe in a theocracy, and least of all in the involvement of religious leaders in government. It has been said of Atatürk that he became a dictator so that there would be no other dictator after him. Abdulhamid may be said to have become a religious potentate in order to exclude future Muslim Savanarolas from taking control of the government. He presided over the most meaningful phase in the formative period of a modern Turkish nation-state, but the Empire he left behind was stagnant, weaker, and disunited despite the numerous development measures taken by the sultan. *Hürriyet* (freedom) had become the principal yardstick for measuring all progress. In fact, freedom of expression and association was regarded as the true elixir of intellectual and social life and totally incompatible with autocracy. The discourse of the opposition revolved not about Abdulhamid's achievements in matters of education, administration, and so on, but about his destruction of political "freedom"—a concept that only two generations earlier was basically unheard of.

8

The Sultan's Advisers and the Integration of Arabs and Immigrants

The war of 1877–78 and the Berlin Treaty of 1878 were instrumental in determining the fate of the Ottoman state and the policies and ideological views of Sultan Abdulhamid. The loss of the Balkan provinces deprived the country of over one-third of its population and of substantial revenues, reducing the once mighty Empire to a second-class power, with its main strength now in Asia and in its Muslim population and its survival dependent upon England. Even worse, the Berlin Treaty introduced the concept of the nation-state as the new principle of political organization. As the Greeks had before them, the Serbians, Romanians, and Montenegrins declared independence and the Bulgarians autonomy and went on to form states based on a communal nationalism that blended ethnicity and religion and was bolstered by various myths of glorious historic pasts.

If the principle of the nation-state had been applied to the Muslims, and if the Muslims had accepted ethnicity as a foundation for nationhood, the result would have been total disintegration of the Ottoman state. Yet, by signing the Berlin Treaty, the Ottoman representatives (who were not even allowed to participate in the debates over its terms) and, by implication, the caliph accepted the legitimacy of the nation-state. Central Islamic principles, the *ümmet* (universal community) and the *tevhid* (unity), were left open to the centrifugal force of the vision of the nation-state and its underlining principle of ethnicity.

The treaty left outside Ottoman authority and responsibility most of the Orthodox Christians in the Balkans, who had been a source of continuous political problems and rising nationalisms despite the Ottoman government's efforts to accommodate their demands. Now, after the Berlin Treaty, the Muslims formed the overwhelming majority (about 80 percent) of the population left in the Ottoman state, and the remaining non-Muslims, such as the Arab Christians, Armenians, and Greeks, lived in enclaves without direct territorial connection to any European state or Russia. Political logic dictated that the sultan had to maintain at all costs the unity of the dominant group, namely the Muslims, and seek to bind them together to assure the state's survival. The seeds of Abdulhamid's Islamist policy and of the move, however unintended toward an Ottoman-Muslim protonation, were sown in these circumstances.

The new demographic situation of the state also called for integrative policies. Muslims of various ethnic backgrounds, ranging from primitive tribes and tribal nobility to well-educated urban dwellers from former Ottoman territories who were migrating into the state experienced problems in integration and adjustment. Moreover, the Shiite-Sunni conflicts in Iraq and Yemen gave Iran and England good opportunities to separate those two territories from the Ottoman state. The English and French after 1881–82 encouraged the rise of ethnic Arab nationalism and promoted the idea of an Arab caliphate, using the Christian Arabs as ideologues and Cairo as their publishing center. We shall look briefly at some of the integration problems facing the Ottoman government.

Migration

The immigrations of the second half of the nineteenth century occurred at a crucial stage in the structural transformation of the Ottoman state from a multiethnic political system into a unitary nation-state, a transformation that culminated in the establishment of modern Turkey. True, migration and settlement were common occurrences throughout Ottoman history. What made the nineteenth-century migrations unique was the timing, the number of people involved, and the ideological-political motivation behind them. The movement of about 500,000 Tatars from Crimea in 1856 was followed, after 1862, by that of over 2.5 million Caucasians, practically all of whom were Muslims. The migrants were settled in the Ottoman domains in the Balkans, Anatolia, northern Syria, and Iraq. Subsequently, in 1877–78, the Caucasians previously settled in the Balkans were moved again to Anatolia, along with some Jews and approximately one million native Muslim residents of the Balkans—mostly Turks. Then, from 1878 to 1914, some 2 million more Muslims immigrated to the Ottoman state; for example, there was a huge exodus of Muslims from Macedonia during the years 1911–13, not to speak of Cretans and other fringe groups.[1] In addition, about one million nomads (Turkomans, Kurds, Arabs) were settled in Anatolia, Iraq, Syria, and even the Arabian peninsula. The new settlers, though united by their faith and the Ottoman political culture, were divided into diverse linguistic, ethnic, and tribal groups.

Abdulhamid became aware of the problems posed by the immigrants, some of whom were rather unruly, as soon as he came to the throne. In 1877–78 he had provided out of his own funds shelter for about 200,000 refugees who flocked to Istanbul; but several hundred of the refugees from the Balkans still helped Ali Suavi stage his attempted coup to oust Abdulhamid (see chapter 5). Soon afterward, the sultan, having learned his lesson, ordered all the refugees out of Istanbul, dispersing them to the four corners of the Empire. From 1878 until the end of his reign, Abdulhamid revamped and refined the existing policies for settling and incorporating immigrants and refugees into the Ottoman state. Because of the large number (equaling some 30–40 percent of the population in 1882) and diverse ethnolinguistic background of the refugees, however, the sultan's effort to assimilate them into the Ottoman social body actually amounted to a socioethnic restructuring and caused society to update its old identity, in accordance with the new circumstances.

Literally thousands of new villages and scores of new towns were established in Anatolia and the northern Arab provinces, and millions of acres of uncultivated land were brought into service, tripling agricultural production, so that the amount of tithe collected after 1880 was almost three times higher than in the 1840s. The immigrants and refugees were given title to a farm of about twenty-six acres on average (about ten to eleven hectars), making them small landowners. In contrast, the traditional Ottoman land cultivator had been a sort of tenant on state (*miri*) land, although the land was held in perpetuity by the family. The transition of state lands to private ownership was eventually finalized during the era of the Young Turks, consolidating the rise of the new middle classes, as either producers and sellers of agricultural commodities or small merchants.

In the process of structural transformation, some of the old Ottoman elites formally preserved their positions, but their sustaining social bases and cultural outlook changed dramatically. The influx of Muslims of diverse ethnic background (Circassians, Bosnians, Albanians, etc.) was turning the Ottoman state into a predominantly Muslim state while producing a high degree of ethnic diversity. The government tried to overcome the ethnic diversity by creating a political culture based on common characteristics and expectations of its dominant Muslim sector. The rapid expansion of the modern school system after 1880 and the use of textbooks glorifying the Ottoman-Muslim past aimed at consolidating internal unity and the sense of a common past. That all this inadvertently appealed more to the Anatolian and Rumilian Muslims than to Arabs helped to shape their identity as a distinct ethnocultural entity.

In 1893 the sultan announced a new immigration policy that favored Muslims, mostly those from the Balkans.

> The time when we embraced intimately those of different religions is long past. We shall accept only immigrants who are our conationals [Ottoman Muslims] and those who share the same religious beliefs. We must pay attention to strengthening the Turks. We should see to it that the surplus Muslim population of Bulgaria, Bosnia, and Herzegovina is systematically brought and settled here. . . . We must strengthen the Turkish elements in Rumilia and especially in Anatolia and mold the Kurds and make them part of us. My predecessors who occupied the Turkish [Ottoman] throne committed a grave error in not Ottomanizing [converting] the Slavs.[2]

Consequently, in 1894 Ibrahim Derviş paşa, an assistant to the sultan, issued a detailed memorandum intended to encourage the immigration of the Balkan Muslims and provide them with the best settlement conditions in the Empire. The memorandum, which mentioned the efforts of the Austrians to stop the emigration of the Bosnians and even to recall those already settled in Turkey, revealed that the Austrians had induced the mufti of Tuzla, Mehmet Tevfik efendi, to write a religious comment designed to discourage the emigration. The sultan personally studied the draft of Derviş paşa's memorandum and ordered measures to preempt the Austrian efforts "by giving the utmost care and attention to immigration problems in order to increase the size of the Muslim population [in the Ottoman state] by permitting the Muslims living under the authority of neighbor governments to come here."[3]

Behind the sultan's "Islamist" immigration policy was a deeper concern that the Western powers would pressure the Ottoman government to admit as immigrants their own subjects and then use the defense of their subjects' welfare as a pretext to interfere in Ottoman affairs. Already Russia had officially asked that some 200,000 Russians be allowed to join the several thousand who previously had come to the Ottoman lands on their own to trade or to pursue other purposes. Moreover, Russia claimed jurisdiction over all these immigrants. Then, after the Russian government began to persecute its Jewish subjects in the early 1880s, thousands of Jews fled for their lives to the Ottoman state, notably to Palestine. Russia soon claimed that those Jews were still its subjects and wanted to register and "protect" them. (Eventually the Russian Jews came under the protection of the British.) In addition, in 1898 the German Settlement Society of Hannover debated the idea of settling one million Germans along the Anatolian railway and of securing for them a special administrative status, so as to create there a "new German homeland."[4] The Greek population in the Izmir area also engaged in suspicious actions: a report prepared by Mehmet Şakir paşa called the sultan's attention to the fact that the Greeks, aided financially by the nationalist society Ethniki Hetairia (est. 1894), were purchasing land around the Gulf of Izmir and smuggling arms. He advised the stationing there of a military unit.[5]

The measures designed to expedite the adjustment of the Muslim immigrants, such as giving them land, building houses and schools for them, and coopting their leaders into the system, were part of the same "politics of unity" aimed at the communal, tribal, and religious leaders of Anatolia, Syria, and the Arabian peninsula.[6] Kurdish leaders, for example, were given gifts and appointments to various offices, including the command positions in the Hamidiye regiments charged with maintaining security in their areas. Guests at the Yildiz Palace over the years included thousands of tribal leaders, notables, communal chiefs, and, naturally, religious figures. Abdulhamid's daughter recounts in her palace memoirs how the sultan invited, through the intermediation of Şeyh Abulhuda al-Sayyad, one of Abdulhamid's advisors, about one hundred tribal chiefs from Yemen in order to persuade them to maintain peace in that turbulent province. The guests wore their colorful local dress and, after listening to Abulhuda's speech delivered in Arabic, were hosted either in the special headquarters built for the purpose adjacent to the *tekke* (lodge) of Zafir al-Madani efendi or in Abulhuda's own house. They, like other communal and tribal leaders who were impressed with the gifts and attention they received at the Yildiz Palace, swore permanent allegiance to *halife-i resul* (successor of the Prophet), as they preferred to address the sultan.[7] The sultan reminded his guests of the dangers facing the state (he always used the Islamic term *devlet-i Islam*—Muslim state) and the faith. He also promised the guests whatever practical assistance they seemed to want, such as roads, better administrators, relief from or postponement of taxes, schools, and the like; usually the demand for modern schools was paramount. In return, the leaders were asked to display in their home mosques the carpets, candles, and other religious artifacts and to mention that the items were the caliph's donations. Often, however, the promises made by the sultan in the Yildiz Palace for tax relief and other benefits later would become subject to a tug-of-war between local notables seeking to increase their power and wealth and the Ottoman officials holding their ground. The officials were generally opposed to the local notables and in some cases arrested and exiled them to other provinces. In one case Abedin paşa, the governor of Diyarbakir, arrested and sent to Albania some one hundred Kurdish *ağas* (landlord notables), but the sultan intervened and they were returned.[8]

In order to expedite assimilation—and to forestall organized opposition—the sultan encouraged both the leaders of the tribes immigrating from the Caucasus and the notables from the Balkans to settle in cities; the most important ones were urged to stay in Istanbul, where they received government pensions as well as various *nişans* (medals), as expressions of royal attention. To maintain his influence, the sultan also awarded pensions and medals to tribal and community leaders in the faraway corners of the realm. For instance, he gave such gifts to several Nogai leaders, originally from Crimea and Bucak, who settled in Dobruca in the nineteenth century, in order to dissuade them from returning to their native lands, now under Russian rule, and he ordered an end to the discrimination by their own upper-class coreligionists.[9] The sultan-caliph sought to maintain his influence even in the outlying districts of his extensive domains, thus increasing the influence and prestige of the central Ottoman government and discouraging the appeal of regional and ethnic nationalism among the Muslims.[10] The Arabian Wahhabis and the Zaidis of Yemen remained a constant threat to internal unity, however, as did the Shiites of Iraq. Egypt, the most populous Arab country, gave the English a platform from which to encourage separatist tendencies as well as ethnic nationalist aspirations and to challenge the legitimacy of the caliph's title.

To summarize: after 1878 Abdulhamid's chief goal was to maintain the territorial integrity of the Ottoman state. Realizing that attainment of this goal required internal unity, the sultan sought to create a new sense of political solidarity based on the Muslims' common faith. He used his central authority and employed the faith as an ideological tool to unify and unwittingly transform the religious community into a political one—that is, into an Ottoman Muslim entity or a protonation.[11] The integration policy of the sultan and his use of religion for political purposes, however, produced unforeseen consequences for society and the character of the state itself. In trying to save the Ottoman state inherited from his ancestors, Abdulhamid actually turned it into something different. The classical Ottoman state did not have a official political Islamic ideology of state and did not attempt to establish a monolithic Muslim nation; but it was "Islamic" in the sense that it was ruled by a Muslim dynasty in accord with Islamic laws. The "nation" that was to emerge out of the sultan's endeavors was a new type of political entity. Amalgamating the diverse Muslim ethnoreligious groups into a single Muslim political nation required using forces that could produce dissension as well as cohesion and solidarity and thus mold a political entity far different from the obedient, politicized religious community envisioned by Abdulhamid. The sultan, moving society into the era of modern politics, was to become one of its victims.

Unwittingly perhaps, Abdulhamid employed some of the ideas and mobilization tactics used by the revivalist (*ihya*) Islamic movements. He also effectively used the communications media, from newspapers to special brochures, to convey his message of solidarity to the masses in simple but religiously appealing terms. In many of these publications Abdulhamid spoke not as a potentate but as a believing Muslim, who happened to be the caliph and was acting to fulfill his unifying mission on behalf of the faith. The sultan was using Islam to build a Muslim nation in the modern sense of the word, retaining and reviving Islamic traditions, loyalties, and symbols at the very time he was changing and creating a new "whole," still as part of the "true Islam." To introduce innovation and concern for the living world in the name of the faith and its "preservation" was indeed a new approach.

Clearly Islamism (or pan-Islamism, as the Europeans called it) was used in the interior of the country as an ideology to forge a unity that inadvertently created a new Muslim identity under the guise of the old. In the past, although the state identified itself with the faith, in reality it did not define or enforce the articles of the faith; this task was left to a variety of formal and informal organizations. After 1878, however, the caliph and those involved in the discourse defined Islam in precise political terms suitable to the emerging Ottoman-Muslim—and ultimately Turkish—nation-state, as shall be indicated later. In this context, the state formulated at least four major ideas which were new, some historical roots notwithstanding:

1. All Muslims are part of one community, the head and commander of which is the caliph.
2. Muslim communities all over the world face the danger of subjugation by Europe. The enemies of Islam have gained the upper hand and have occupied Muslim lands not because of the inherent inferiority of Islam, as Western missionaries and agents claim, but because the members of the *ümmet* remained disunited, ignorant, and unaware of the progress registered by the Western world.
3. The weakness of Muslim society has resulted also from the weakness of *iman* (faith) and the believers' failure to understand properly and obey their faith. Muslims, therefore, should properly interpret Islamic principles in the light of reason and science. Predestination should not be interpreted as fatalism, and Muslims must attach importance to worldly aspects of their existence, such as material progress, rather than solely to the dogma of the faith.
4. The rejuvenation of Islam is possible through a return to its basic principles, and that, in turn, depends first and foremost on achieving the unity of the *ümmet* under the guidance of its leader, the caliph, or emir ul-Muminin.

Abdulhamid's use of advisors may be understood better in the light of the ideas above.

The Sultan-Caliph's Advisers

Sultan Abdulhamid made wide use of advisers. They have been regarded mainly as pan-Islamic advisers, although their chief task was to provide ideas to help the sultan carry out his policy of political and cultural integration, strengthening the state and maintaining the tradition. He selected his aides for their knowledge of Ottoman traditions and Islamic law, as well as current affairs, and for their practical intelligence and innovative capacity. He also chose some charismatic heroes who could be trusted to carry out delicate missions without stirring up adverse reactions. All of them came from the higher ranks of the Ottoman political-military and Arab-intellectual establishments; no true religious figure was included in this group.

The most prominent adviser to the sultan was Ahmet Cevdet paşa (1823–95). Endowed with a phenomenal memory and a critical spirit, he was educated in a classical *medrese*, where he developed a keen interest in the study of history as well as education. Cevdet was very familiar with Ibn Khaldun's *Muqaddima* and appears to have been deeply influenced by its political relativism. He eventually became the official chronicler of the Empire and produced the multivolume classic, *Cevdet Tarihi*, which covers Ottoman history from 1774 to 1826. He was the head of the Mecelle Cemiyeti (Society of Mecelle), established in order to adjust the Şeriat legislation to the "requirements of the time," as demanded by the Edict of 1856. The Mecelle was a modern Islamic legal code based on the Şeriat but including various new provisions designed to accommodate the changing circumstances in the law of contracts, family, property, and so on. Yet this truly innovative legal work is hardly known despite its extraordinary importance for understanding Ottoman thinking on modernity. Cevdet paşa wrote almost the entire Mecelle. The code is divided into sixteen chapters and was published first in 1868 and finally in 1876.

Before writing the Mecelle, Cevdet had entered the service of Reşit paşa, the architect of the Tanzimat reforms, who was looking for someone well versed in Islam but open to new ideas and flexible of mind. Cevdet actually lived in Reşit's house until the latter's death in 1858. He then went on to occupy various high government positions, such as minister of justice (divan of juridical ordinance) under Abdulaziz and various offices under Abdulhamid. He thus worked for three sultans during the most turbulent era of Ottoman history, becoming intimately familiar with the affairs of the court. Although a very good Muslim, he did not hesitate to propose the amendment of various government practices, regardless of their Islamic origin, if they did not suit the requirements of the time; he criticized the ulema for ignoring the need to adapt their thinking to changing circumstances. In short, Cevdet possessed all the basic credentials, traditionalist and modernist, for gaining Sultan Abdulhamid's trust and respect.

Cevdet paşa had enjoyed the protection of Mithat paşa but had turned against him, for Mithat's constitutionalism conflicted with Cevdet's firm belief in the absolutist sultanate as a basic feature of the Ottoman government. He participated in the tribunal that condemned Mithat and his associates to death for allegedly plotting the death of Sultan Abdulaziz, for Cevdet considered the forceful ousting of a sultan an act of lèse-majesté. (This is a facet of his life that even one of grandsons found deplorable.) Although the sultan dissolved the Mecelle committee headed by Cevdet in 1888, he remained on good terms with the historian; both were Islamists and modernists in their own way. Cevdet possessed so much confidential information that, when he died in 1895, the sultan ordered all his papers brought to Yildiz Palace. However, much of the basic advice he furnished the sultan is unpublished and scattered piecemeal in the Yildiz archives; I have used these documents to a considerable extent throughout this work. Cevdet paşa's views are analyzed in other chapters in different contexts.

Cevdet paşa was Abdulhamid's chief advisor on all doctrinal, political, historical, personal, and international matters, so presumably his interpretation of events and advice had a deep effect on Abdulhamid's decisions. For example, Abdulhamid's information about the events of the period 1839–76 probably derived mainly from the factual-interpretive history that Cevdet wrote at the sultan's request, known as *maruzat* (expositions), it is an excellent source for the period.[12]

Cevdet believed the Ottoman state rested on four foundation pillars: (1) the dynasty (sultanate), which was Ottoman; (2) the government, which was Turkish;

(3) the faith, which was Islam, and the caliphate; and (4) the capital, Istanbul. The state could not survive if any one of these pillars was destroyed or weakened. Cevdet paşa of course, was echoing the ideas of his mentor, Mustafa Reşit paşa, who had declared:

> We do not possess the necessary [military] power to maintain the territorial integrity of our state. Consequently, it is our [geographical] position which shall help us preserve [that integrity]. [In order to do so] we must build a good administration. The foreign states shall not leave us in peace. All states aspire to possess Istanbul but the city is indivisible. If we are not able to produce a good administration [the foreign powers] will establish a joint administration [in Istanbul] too.[13]

For his own part, Cevdet paşa recognized the incompatibility of interests among the European powers and advised the sultan to play one state against the other without siding permanently with any power. At the same time, he criticized the Ottoman bureaucracy for being ill-trained and unscrupulous. Cevdet believed that the foundation of the European states was the "nation," which was created and sustained by love of the fatherland, Europe having replaced religion with the idea of the fatherland. Because this had created a concrete, material anchor for their thoughts, beliefs, and sentiments and a basis for unity, European children grew up with the idea of the fatherland as an inseparable part of their identity. For the Ottomans, in contrast, the *vatan*, or fatherland, was the square in the middle of the village. To hold together the state and create the fatherland attachment as the foundation of a new political entity—a nation—the Ottomans had to use religious sentiment, the most widely spread and commonly shared feeling.

According to Cevdet, all Muslims constituted an inchoate *nation*, but a variety of policy errors and philosophical misconceptions had prevented that nation from becoming a reality. Chief among the "errors" noted by Cevdet was the creation of the *millet* system, which allowed each major non-Muslim group to preserve its identity and culture and then emerge as an independent nation in the nineteenth century. Cevdet preferred a unitary form of state and a well-amalgamated Muslim nation forged by properly using the unique Muslim institution, the caliphate. He believed that the caliphate was the only agency that could create a relatively united Ottoman-Muslim entity with Islamic unity as its ideological foundation. Consequently, whoever opposed the caliphate (and its temporal basis, the sultanate) was an ill-intentioned subversive. Cevdet's views, only a few of which are summarized here, were adopted in various forms by Abdulhamid as his state policy and personal philosophy (see chapter 4).

Mehmet Sait (Küçük) paşa (1838–1914) occupied the post of grand vizier seven times under Abdulhamid and twice under the Young Turks. He was a very good administrator, one whose practical intelligence and perseverance secured him power and wealth, although Abdulhamid personally detested him.[14] A dedicated Anglophile and a firm believer in centralized government, Sait was also vain, ambitious, corrupt, and loyal only to his own position and interest. He has been accused of institutionalizing Abdulhamid's despotism, but Sait actually was behind some of the main reforms carried out during Abdulhamid's time, including the vast expansion of the educational system, the creation of a chamber of commerce in Istanbul, the modernization of the civil service, and the systematization of the budget.

Sait was exceptionally suspicious—like the sultan himself—and dreaded Abdulhamid to the point that he once took refuge in the British Embassy lest the sultan execute him. Sait paşa got back at those who derided and humiliated him in his memoirs; unfortunately the memoirs lack political weight and are essentially a vengeful criticism of Kiamil paşa, his chief enemy, and of the sultan.[15] Abdulhamid realized that whereas Ahmet Cevdet was attached to the sultan out of historical and philosophical considerations, Sait paşa's loyalty was conditional and self-interested. Nevertheless, Sait paşa was also the sort of Turkish nationalist and reformist who believed in a centralized effort to absorb and integrate the Arab provinces through reforms and education. Hence one may consider him the first enforcer of the Islamist policy of Abdulhamid.

The sultan's third advisor was Kibrisli Mehmet Kiamil paşa (1832–1913), who also served several times as grand vizier. A dignified person of integrity and a well-educated, polyglot reformist who enjoyed the respect of the Europeans (while he was visiting Egypt, British royalty invited him to tea), he was the exact opposite of Sait paşa, his rival and critic. Kiamil was dedicated to the sultan's Islamist policy and had a correct understanding of the precarious international situation of the Ottoman state. Being less doctrinaire than his contemporaries, he searched for practical means to preserve the Ottoman state but seemed less dedicated to the survival of the dynasty; thus, Abdulhamid mistrusted him—especially after he wrote a memorandum suggesting a redefinition of ministerial responsibility and a new approach to the Armenian question. The sultan ousted Kiamil as grand vizier and sent him as governor (*vali*) to the Aydin (Izmir) province, where he stayed for over eleven years. Nonetheless, he continued to advise the sultan, on request, as shown by various memoranda used in this study. His numerous memoranda indicate that he had not only an independent way of judging events but also an excellent grasp of world affairs. The Young Turks twice made him grand vizier in the years 1908–1913 despite his past association with Abdulhamid. Kiamil's papers are often a copy of the documents in the Yildiz collection, but some are unique.[16]

The last and probably the most charismatic of Abdulhamid's major advisors was Gazi Osman paşa (1832–97), who served as commander of the military garrison in the Yildiz Palace and as yaveran-i ekrem, the chief of the sultan's aides. Traditionalist-minded and deeply religious, Osman paşa enjoyed popular support to the point of adulation (the "Osman paşa March" is still one of the favorite martial songs in Turkey). His fame derived from his legendary defense of the fortress of Plevne in Bulgaria in the war of 1877–78; during this defense his outnumbered army inflicted severe losses on the Russian troops and held up their advance toward Istanbul for several months. He surrendered only after he ran out of ammunition. Welcomed as a hero by the population upon his return to Istanbul, Osman paşa received the title of *gazi* ("victorious"). He became the spokesman for the anti-European views of the traditionalist wing of the army and the conservative establishment and fierce apologist for Muslim causes. Immensely popular with the Muslim masses, he was sent by the sultan as a trouble-shooter to areas of Muslim unrest and sat next to Abdulhamid every Friday in a horse-drawn carriage during the public procession to the weekly prayer.

At the same time, Osman paşa played an important role in supporting the modernization of the army and in, *inadvertently*, shielding the nationalist transformation of the new officers' corps from public scrutiny and government control. In some ways he became the patriarchal symbol of unity and continuity between the military glories of the old Ottomans and the expectations of the new. For reasons too complex to be dealt with in detail here, the military in Turkey have generally imagined themselves as being the only continuous institution with historical roots bridging the Ottoman Empire, Young Turks, and the Republic and as being responsible both for change and continuity. As such, they feel free to venerate successful Ottoman commanders, from Orhan Gazi to Atatürk, as much as to accept technological and scientific progress and modern military instruction. (For instance, Atatürk kept as his chief of staff Marshall Fevzi Çakmak, a practicing Muslim and distinguished soldier, and honored him—he never consumed alcohol in his presence—even though the younger officers complained among themselves about Çakmak's old-fashioned military doctrines and tactics.) Osman paşa and the rest of the military agreed, after the devastating defeat suffered in the war with Russia in 1877–78, that the Ottoman army needed not only more weapons but, especially, well trained commanders and a stronger motivation. It is in this context that General Colmar Freiherr von der Goltz (1843–1916) began training a new brand of officers, aiming to create in them a self-respecting image as "Turks" and raise their optimistic belief in the destiny of their "nation" and in their exalted mission is worthy of mention.

Von der Goltz came in 1883 as an advisor and inspector of the military schools, after modernization of these schools and up-to-date training of the officers appeared an unavoidable necessity. It seems that the idea of including systematic ideological and philosophical dimensions in the army's training was confronted then, although the issue needs further investigation. Initially von der Goltz—a major figure in German military history—had a low opinion of the country; but when he left in 1895, he had not only trained (superbly, it is said) a group of high-ranking officers but also changed his own opinion about the country. He would return in 1908 and then, during World War I, he commanded the First and Sixth Ottoman Armies and died of natural causes on the Middle East front. Von der Goltz believed that Turks had the basic ability to understand and absorb Western civilization and that common Turks possessed high moral capabilities, fearlessness, discipline, self reliance, and respect for authority—all stemming from their traditional way of life and Islamic beliefs. He believed that the spread of modern education and the rise of a new elite (that is, the army officers whom he appreciated as national leaders) attuned to contemporary civilization could revive the Ottoman state and that a change of regime would positively affect the army. Von der Goltz served as adviser to the military training schools and wrote their textbooks, thus increasing the impact of his ideas. The Ottoman victory over Greece in the war of 1897 for which Abdulhamid took immense credit, actually was a vindication of von der Goltz's effort and theories. After the German's departure, however, Abdulhamid's mistrust of the military showed itself in budget cuts and other unfriendly acts, to the extent that, in 1908, when von der Goltz returned, he found the army in deplorable condition. By this time, von der Goltz had become an advocate of an Ottoman-German alliance. As a bitter enemy of England and France, he supported pan-Islamism, which he viewed as a Turkish-Arab partnership; but he regarded a joint German-Ottoman attack on Egypt as impossible as long as Abdulhamid was in power. With the Young Turks' revolution of 1908, von der Goltz's choice pupils, such as

Mahmud Muhtar Izzet, Mahmud Şefket, Pertev Demirhan (who wrote, in German, an excellent biography of his teacher), and others came to occupy high and influential positions.[17] Thus Osman paşa, whom Abdulhamid trusted as loyal to the sultan as a defender of Islam and the Muslim world, proved to be a shield behind which his younger colleagues in the military schools and the army were turning against caliph-sultan, without Osman's knowledge, and becoming the self-appointed servants of the "nation" (the Turkish nation) rather than of the sultan.

In addition to named advisers, Abdulhamid had another twenty-five to thirty high-ranking officials, including province governors, whom he trusted personally and used in sensitive areas for delicate missions. These highly educated officials, some of whom had served the predecessors of Abdulhamid and had European experience, conveyed their views directly to the sultan. Their opinions were open and, if necessary, critical (except of the sultan), and provide the researcher with the best yardstick for gauging Abdulhamid's aims and understanding his methods of ruling. Many of them came from ancient Turkish families of Anatolia, associated with the state. Of the many who had served Abdulhamid's predecessors and thus provided continuity, we mention very briefly only three. Ahmet Şakir paşa (1838–99) was a descendant of the feudal lords of Yozgat's Çapanoğullari family. Educated in the traditional schools, he had served as ambassador to Russia and other places abroad (he married a Romanian woman) as well as governor of Crete. He took an active part in the reform movement in eastern Anatolia, including the areas inhabited by Armenian minorities, and in the organization of the Hamidian regiments, whose unit commanders were appointed from among the Kurdish tribal chiefs. Another, even more prominent example, was Mehmet Namik paşa (1804–1895). Born to an ulema family from Konya, he served as ambassador to London, occupied several high positions in government, and was instrumental in devising the first land measures to serve as the basis for the Land Code of 1858. He implemented the code during his second tenure in Baghdad in 1861. Namik paşa opposed the Constitution of 1876 (an important credential in the eyes of the sultan) and was highly critical of certain "un-Islamic" measures of the government; but as the French poet Lamartine described him, he was, like his colleagues, "thirsty for enlightenment and progress." He translated Ibn Battutah's travelogue into Turkish, along with the Redhouse dictionary.[18] The third example was Gazi Ahmet Muhtar paşa (1839–1919; mentioned in different contexts elsewhere). He came from a merchant family in Bursa, originally from Kastamonu, and, despite his military and intellectual achievements, his independent mind and temperament aroused Abdul-hamid suspicions; he was eventually "exiled" to Egypt, where he served as Ottoman High Commissioner (1885–1909).

A second group of outside advisors to Abdulhamid consisted mainly of Arabic-speaking dignitaries who served as intermediaries between the palace and their respective provinces and also as publicists and propagandists. Keenly interested in securing through them the support of the Arab masses, the sultan tried to recruit these advisors and advocates from the religious orders with a large popular following. Certainly chief among them was Şeyh Abulhuda al-Sayyadi (d. 1909), the head of the Rifai brotherhood, which was influential in Syria.[19] Abulhuda was an eloquent speaker, an excellent pamphleteer, and a dedicated advocate of Islamic unity under Ottoman patronage. He occupied high positions in the Ottoman government, such as chief judge of Rumili and *şeyhulislam*. Abulhuda believed that the Islamic unity promoted by Abdulhamid would best serve the Arab interests, for he feared that without the Ottoman military and political shield the Arabs would be fragmented into a variety of groups and be occupied by foreign powers. He acted as intermediary and interpreter between Abdulhamid and visiting dignitaries, tribal and religious chiefs, and lay leaders from Syria, Iraq, and the Arabian peninsula. In fact, he drafted some of the letters in Arabic sent by Abdulhamid to various chiefs in Mecca, North Africa, and elsewhere. Abulhuda also wrote altogether over two hundred works in which he described the Ottomans as the God-sent saviors of Islam. Abulhuda's role has been exaggerated, however, probably because of his closeness to the sultan and his free access to the palace. He does not appear to have been as involved in policy-making decisions, as were the advisers in the first group. Rather, he was consulted about Arab and Islamic issues and richly rewarded, but his advice was only selectively followed. On balance, Abulhuda seems to have been more of an Arab patriot, who used his closeness to the sultan to promote the regional interest of the Arabs in the belief that the Ottoman rule, though deficient, was preferable to European domination.

Şeyh Muhammed Zafir al-Madani was both an adviser and confidant who enjoyed the deep respect and affection of Abdulhamid, for he had predicted that Abdulhamid would become sultan. Zafir was the head of the small Madaniyya branch of the Şazeliye (Shadhiliyya) brotherhood. The order, established by Ali b. Abdullah (d. 1258), flourished mainly in Algeria, Tunisia, and Morocco and eventually played a leading role in the struggle against the French occupation. Şeyh Zafir, his brother and other relatives carried the sultan's messages to the Sanusi, the tribal chiefs and notables of Libya, and various other North African notables, tribal chiefs, and dignitaries and urged them to remain faithful to the caliph and the Ottoman state. This brotherhood became established in Istanbul only in the nineteenth century but became popular during the reign of Abdulhamid, who joined it at the urging of Şeyh Zafir and Şeyh Mahmut Ebu Şemmat of Damascus. Şeyh Muhammed al-Zafir's lodge, located just a few hundred yards from the Yildiz Palace, is next to the mansion he shared with his brother, Hamza. Known today as Ertuğrul Tekke Camisi (Ertugrul Mosque of the Lodge), it harbors Zafir's *türbe* (tomb) with the inscription: "Şazili Tarikati Şeyhlerinden Kutbul Arifin, Tunuslu Şeyh Muhammed Zafirin Türbesi" (The tomb of the most learned Şeyh Muhammad Zafir of Tunisia, one of the *şeyh*s of the Shadhiliyya brotherhood). The year of his death was 1321 (1905).[20]

Abdulhamid apparently was a dedicated member of the Şazeliye order; after being deposed and forced to live in Salonica in 1909, he wrote letters that were carried to Ebu Şemmat by one of his guards, who also was a member. In reply to a letter from the *şeyh*, in 1911 the sultan wrote:

> I kiss your sacred hands and beg that my prayers be accepted along with my greetings. . . . I read and follow day and night the Şazeliye writings and rites . . . [and want to inform you] that I have never given up voluntarily the Muslim caliphate. I did so under the pressure and threats of the members of the Union Society known as Young Turks. [Political to the end, Abdulhamid continued:] The Unionists insistently asked me to agree to the establishment of a national fatherland for the Jews in Palestine, but I refused categorically to accept their demands . . . and later I turned down the 150 million English pounds [offered for Palestine]. I told them . . . for over thirty

years *I served the Muslim Nation and the ümmet* [*millet-i Islamiye ve ümmet-i Muham-mediye*]. I preserved thus unspoiled the legacy of all the Muslims and of the Otto-man caliphs.[21]

Two other Arab advisors to the sultan were Şeyh Fadl al-Sayyid of Hadramut (1820–1900), of whom there will be some discussion in another context, and Şeyh Ahmad Esat (Asad)—Esadefendi. Fadl was born in Malabar, India, to parents from Muscat, and became both a pan-Islamist ideologue and a Muslim nationalist who dealt pri-marily with the politics of Yemen, Aden, and Muscat. Meanwhile, Esadefendi was involved with the problems of the Hicaz, notably Mecca and Medina, where he often distributed caliphal literature to pilgrims. Fadl fled to Mecca in 1853 to avoid pros-ecution for anti-British activities in India. He became temporarily the governor of the Zafar province, thanks to the support of the unruly al-Kathiri tribe, and declared the province an Ottoman possession. Fadl wanted the sultan help him remain gover-nor of the Zafar. The sultan did not do so, but he retained Fadl in Istanbul to provide extensive information on south Arabia and serve as intermediary between the digni-taries from south Arabia and the sultan.[22] Fadl even wrote several books, for example, *Tarikat al-Hanifa* (The path of the Hanifi, or the brotherhood of Hanefis) (1899), calling for obedience to the sultan.

Learned religious leaders, largely of Turkish and Caucasian origin, constituted a third group of Abdulhamid's outside advisers. Well versed in contemporary practi-cal issues and society's problems, they seem to have formed the sultan's inner brain trust on local (Turkish-Caucasian) affairs. Again, the Nakşbandi played a key role, and among them was Ahmet Ziyaeddin (Ziyaettin) Gümüşhaneli (Gümüşanevi), mentioned previously.[23] However, we have only limited information about their activities.

Ahmet Mithat Efendi and the Tercüman-i Hakikat

Abdulhamid also had a variety of associates chosen either because of their impact on the population and their loyalty or simply because their stand on political issues cor-responded with his. The journalist and writer Ahmet Mithat efendi was the most important example of the sort of associate who could work to create solidarity among the Muslim population, uphold the virtue of absolutism, and oppose the liberal con-stitutionalists while advocating change, progress and Western civilization. Lurking beneath the discussions on constitutionalism was Mithat paşa's alleged intention of separating the caliphate from the sultanate. In order to separate the two offices, Mithat paşa supposedly advocated a certain autonomy for the Arabic-speaking provinces that would place them under the authority of a caliph descending from the Prophet's fam-ily, the *şerif* of Mecca.[24] To counteract these ideas of Mithat paşa, Abdulhamid had to convince the public that constitutionalism, ostensibly aimed at curbing the sultan's personal autocracy, in reality intended to undermine the sultanate and especially the caliphate, then ultimately the Ottoman state and Muslim society.

Abdulhamid considered the press vitally important for the dissemination of the imperial doctrine of absolutism and the Islamist ideology of unity. As noted previ-ously, the press had emerged as a political force in the early 1870s and had become the medium for opinion making, political indoctrination, and (lastly) the dissemination of news. A stringent press law had been introduced in February of 1877 in order to control the news about the debates in the parliament, scheduled to be opened the following month. The sultan seemed very concerned about the effect that press reports of these debates might have on the population, especially in light of the abortive coup engineered by Ali Suavi through the newspaper *Basiret*. About a month and a half after closing *Basiret*, the sultan launched his own newspaper to promote absolutism and Islamic unity and to put to rest the rumors that the old constitutionalists were planning to proclaim the Republic. He chose for the purpose the *Tercüman-i Hakikat* and its publisher, Ahmet Mithat efendi, a disaffected protegé of Mithat paşa.

The new *Tercüman* began to publish on 28 June 1878, and for the rest of the century it remained the most influential medium for educating and indoctrinating the masses in modernism and Islamism. Ahmet Mithat efendi (1844–1912), a commoner born of Caucasian parents, had a precocious intelligence; he had been on the staff of the *Ittihad* (Union), the newspaper that supported Mithat paşa, until he decided Mithat's constitutionalist ideas were leading to a republic. Ahmet Mithat believed that a European-type parliament was incompatible with the traditions and philosophy of the Ottoman state, and even Islam. Soon he won the sultan's friendship by publishing his well-known book, *Uss-i Inkilap* (Origin of reform), criticizing the manner in which Abdulaziz was ousted and Abdulhamid was compelled to promulgate the constitution. The sultan helped Ahmet Mithat finance publication of the *Tercüman*, but the assistance quickly became unnecessary, as the newspaper became very popular (though Ahmet Mithat continued to receive a stipend). The *Tercüman* conveyed the sultan's views to the public in popular language. For example, a series of articles titled "Istibdat" (Absolutism), begun in July 1878 and written by Ahmet Mithat efendi himself, made a distinction between oppression (*zulüm*) and absolutism or autocracy. The latter was described as a means of government designed to benefit society, for the ruler (sultan) did not use it for his own personal gain. Citing the Arabic root of the word, *istibdat*, Ahmet Mithat claimed that "absolutism" actually freed the ruler from any group pressures or influence in making his decisions. Ahmet Mithat further distinguished between *kanuni hürriyet* (legal freedoms), given to the public by the ruler in the form of laws, and the *political* freedom demanded by dissidents in high office which could neutralize the good to come from "legal"—that is, state-given—freedoms. The gist of the articles was that absolutism was a good form of government if applied by the right person, the sultan-caliph, who by the force of faith, history, and tradition had the right to do so. (Behind this discussion there was obviously the much more basic question of natural rights versus state-created, or given, rights.)

Ahmet Mithat also wrote of individuals as capable of judging and deciding by themselves the extent of their freedoms. He did not condemn the abrogated constitution outright but described it as a vehicle used by the enemies of the state to usurp the powers of the sultan.[25] At the same time, he was probably one of the few intellectuals—perhaps the only one—to express the idea that Ottoman society and, presumably, its (Islamic) identity were changing. In fact, Ahmet Mithat declared insistently that a new Ottoman-Muslim, Turkish-speaking nation—*yeni bir Osmanli milleti*— was being born before his contemporaries' eyes and that its essence was the attachment to the sultan;[26] the first part of his statement was correct but not the last.

Some time after the publication of the articles on absolutism, freedom, and government functions, all of which give an excellent picture of the Palace's frame of mind, Ahmet Mithat was given another mission. A *muhtira-i seniye* (imperial note) asked him to explain to the Muslims the policy of the European powers toward the Porte. This undated memorandum (ca. 1882) stated that Gladstone's policy had hurt the Ottoman Empire and that England and Russia had become its worst enemies. England, according to the sultan, had tried to divide the Ottoman Empire into a series of small states and planned to move the caliphate to Egypt or to Jeddah and use it to rule all the Muslims at will. Appalled that some people known as "Young Turks" were supporting the English, the sultan expressed his view that the survival of a state and a nation depended first on preserving their religion (even with a little fanaticism, which meant dedication and attachment). "The Christians in our country," wrote the sultan, "are reasonably educated and are believers in their faith, and fanatical enough to assure [the survival] of their religion" and thus preserve their national consciousness. (The sultan used the term *milliyet*, which is normally translated as "nationality." Actually he meant "consciousness," because in his view the source of nationality was religious consciousness.)[27]

Following the sultan's directive, Ahmet Mithat wrote a series of editorials, "Islam and Civilization, or the Current Relations with England," in which he stated that Europe used its distorted view of Islam to interfere in Ottoman affairs, officially turning the Eastern Question into a debate on Islam versus civilization.[28] Europe, in the writer's view, condemned Islam as condoning savagery without allowing it the right to refute the allegation. He contrasted the fate of Muslim Spain with the protection Islam gave to Christians and Jews, and he claimed that Muslims' attachment to their faith, state, and fatherland did not preclude respect for Christianity. The Europeans' biased attitude toward the Turks was just the opposite of the Ottoman writers' universal view of civilization and humanity, as they translated and read Victor Hugo, Voltaire (banned later), and other European writers. Ahmet Mithat criticized England for subtly encouraging the Ottoman state to enter into war with Russia in 1877 but then failing to provide it with any help, for remaining silent about the atrocities committed against Muslims in Bulgaria, and for depriving the Ottoman state of its possessions, such as Cyprus. In Ahmet Mithat's opinion, the Muslims viewed the reforms advocated by Europe as their own and essential for progress, provided they were not used to promote the political hegemony of Europe or as a means to liquidate the Ottoman Empire. He warned England not to take for granted the friendship of the Ottoman public, for the Turks "could be induced directly and effectively to forget the past and the old unproductive alliances [with England], and be persuaded to develop new friendships abroad beneficial to the Ottoman interest."[29] England thus was put on notice that the sultan could seek the friendship of other European powers, as he eventually did with Germany and Russia.

In another editorial, describing an interview with an Iranian, the *Tercüman* claimed that the English- and French-led European campaign against Islam had awakened the Muslims to reality and generated in them a sense of solidarity and a keen interest in renovation-revival (*teceddüd*). He urged Iranians and the Ottomans to put aside their old quarrels, and unite for their own good to "create" the long-contemplated *ittihad-i Islam.*[30] The *Tercüman-Hakikat* newspaper, however, made clear that it advocated a panislamist foreign policy only as a means of self-defense, at last resort. In reality a reform-minded publication, it gave far more space to disseminating its publisher's reformist views, populist-communalist philosophy, and deep conviction that religion was a source of values and a means for individual moral education and spiritual nourishment. For Ahmet Mithat, Islamic unity was a political necessity, not a religious goal. He was not an opportunistic puppet of the sultan.

Although Ahmet Mithat was a convinced monarchist who believed sincerely in the righteousness of Abdulhamid's Islamist policy, he was also a dedicated reformist and a crusader for general education, enlightenment, progress, and even women's rights.[31] In sum, he was the intellectual spokesman of the new Muslim middle classes. He published sixty-eight novels (twenty-nine of which were translations from European languages, mainly French), six plays, a very popular book on his travel to Europe, and a large number of books on history (including a thirteen-volume work on the history of various European countries), philosophy, and science, as well as numerous books and pamphlets on religion, especially Islam. Ahmet Mithat believed that education, delivered in every way possible, was the key to the rejuvenation and salvation of the Ottoman state. There is no question that he was responsible for single-handedly popularizing Western science and literature in the Ottoman Empire while upholding the virtues of religion in general, and of Islam in particular.

Seeking facility in communication in order to impart knowledge to the population, Ahmet Mithat led the trend toward Turkishness in language. This ultimately produced a sort of ethnic awareness, although he condemned unequivocally any form of ethnic nationalism. He used the vernacular Turkish in all of his writings, and he conveyed to his readers an image of the Ottoman Empire that was Islamic in form but reflected the Turkish cultural characteristics of Rumili and Anatolia rather than the traits of Arabia. Ahmet Mithat efendi is not often included in lists of major Turkish writers. The elitist evaluation of him is epitomized by the view of Ahmet Hamdi Tanpinar, the doyen of Turkish literary history.

Ahmet Mithat was not guided by a given moral [intellectual] standard but by the needs of the market, the desire to assure the stability of the [social] group from which he came, and by his own low level [of intellect]. The market always needs stability, and [consequently] places its security above everything else. Behind Abdulhamid's coup [closure of the parliament] there were [those] involved in this market [economy] whose money and security had been destroyed several times by street [mobs].

Ahmet Mithat, [our first Turkish] novelist . . . implanted his views into the urban population. He did not start from a desire to uphold [the virtues] of Duty, or from great idealistic ambitions, but from [the need to glorify] the middle man's natural instinct to flee [Duty]. Namik Kemal and his peers regarded learning as a natural [tendency]. Ahmet Mithat made leisure and dreaming [of wealth] a habit and [virtue]. His books introduced for the first time into the life of the working man the idea of leisure [and] the hour reserved for reading. . . . With him the small people's life changed. The hours spent around a lamp in a wooden house acquired a new meaning and new life. The entire family gathered around someone who knew how to read and debated what was read. . . . Ahmet Mithat taught the Turkish public to [like] the novel. . . . To the end of his life he fed the public, which he considered his family, novels, journal article, stories, popularized science.[32]

Indeed, Ahmet Mithat, under the patronage of the sultan, was publishing his newspaper and a very great number of books. By his choice of subjects and use of a language designed to appeal to and please the public, he was both creating and giving publicity to a popular culture. The culture involved values, likes and dislikes, habits and preferences, heroes, rituals, entertainments, psychology, and religion and was shaped as much by inherited tradition as by the new urban and political forces. This dissemination of the popular culture was a significant step toward democracy, if democracy is to be viewed not only as a matter of elections and polls but as an expression of tastes, idioms, aspirations, and visions of past and future shared by a large public and, ultimately, by the leaders. This was the culture of a nation that was already taking shape through a dialectical interaction of a variety of demographic, cultural, political, historical forces, and so on, before the nation builders took over the process.

Thus, for thirty years Ahmet Mithat served the Islamist policy of Abdulhamid, while disseminating, in his own simple but effective way, his middle-class vision of a national Turkish homeland and the ideals of dedication to progress and science and attachment to one's faith and identity. He, more than anyone else, is responsible for awakening the Turks' intellectual curiosity about everything European and for acquainting the Ottoman pubic with Europe's history, civilization, and the humanist traditions. Ahmet Mithat was a Turkish-Muslim humanist and, politically, a traditional modernist; he and his literary works deserve a much more comprehensive study than I have given here.

Abdulhamid's relations with the press became increasingly complicated as his desperate efforts to coopt both the foreign and domestic press increased. *Vakit* (Time) gradually replaced *Tercüman* as a more militant outlet for Islamism and pan-Islamism and for virulent opposition to England, devoting considerable space to the affairs of the Muslims under British rule. *Tercüman*, meanwhile, became a moderate reformist, modernist, Islamist publication dedicated to spreading knowledge. *Al-Hilafa*, begun in 1881 by Louis Sabuncu with English help, proposed to deal mainly with the issues concerning the caliphate, but in 1890 Sabuncu ceased his activities in exchange for a high-paying job in the service of the sultan. The *Al-Gayret* (Effort), an Islamist publication started in London in 1881, was apparently financed by the sultan himself. Its opposite was *Al-Basiri* published in Paris by Halil Ganem, a former deputy in the Ottoman parliament of 1876, who was a bitter enemy of Abdulhamid. (Other newspapers, such as the famous *Al-Cavaib* and *Al-Ittihad* have been mentioned in different contexts.)

Cemaleddin Afghani, Adviser on Islamic Unity and the Shiites

Shiites of all varieties probably constituted about 20 percent of the total Muslim population in the Ottoman state; but, supported by Iran and England, Shiism appeared to be spreading in Iraq and the south of the Arabian peninsula, undermining the unity sought by the sultan. After Cevdet paşa prepared a memorandum on the question, a committee was convened at the sultan's order to discuss ways of ending the Sunni-

Shia rivalry.[33] Cevdet had pointed out that the majority of the Ottoman Shiites consisted of Imamites (Twelvers) in Iraq and Zaidis in Yemen; the warlike Ismailis in Behran-Yemen and the Mutevali in Sayda-Lebanon were only small minorities. Moreover, the Zaidis actually were closer to the Sunnis, for they recognized the legitimacy of the first two caliphs (Abubekir and Omar). The Twelvers (so called because they held that the line of succession from the prophet stopped with the twelfth imam, who would return as the Mahdi), on the other hand, were opposed to both the Sunni caliph and the Iranian shah for usurping the authority of the *mujtahid* (Shiite religious leaders). Cevdet stressed the political importance of the Shiite Imams "in Arabic [-speaking] Iraq, where they are in abundance and located in the vicinity of Iran." According to Cevdet, the Sunnis and Shiites had no real doctrinal differences, the rivalry between them arising during Shah Ismail's reign in the sixteenth century for sheerly political reasons. Now that European occupation threatened the entire Muslim world, including the Shiites, they were under religious obligation to unite (*tevhid*) to oppose the domination and oppression of the Christian states ("duvel-i Nasaranin tagallup ve tahakkumlerine karşi"). The Ottoman caliph, as the bona fide head of the Sunnis, had a legitimate claim to be the leader of all the Muslims and to use the Ottoman state apparatus to undertake the necessary measures for unity. In contrast, the shah of Iran did not possess the religious legitimacy or the actual power to become the head of the Muslims. In fact, instead of fighting the enemies of Islam, the shah was trying to convert the Sunnis of Iraq to Shiism by using the *mujtahids*; the majority of these being Ottoman citizens, many living in Karbala and Najef, they could be won over to the caliph's cause. In the end, Cevdet paşa recommended that the sultan try to win the Shiites' sympathies by repairing the *türbes* of the Prophet's family in Medina and Karbala (*Atabat-i Aliye*), by making donations to the Shiite shrines in Karbala, Necef, and so on, and by inviting the *mujtahids* to his palace and giving each special attention according to his rank in the Shiite hierarchy (though not in such an ostentatious way as to offend the Sunni ulema).

Taking Cevdet's advice, a committee chaired by the caliph decided to repair the *türbes* of the Prophet's family at Medina along with those of Hüseyin (Ali's son) and others at Necef and Karbala. It politely rejected the request of the shah, originally sent in 1886, to be allowed to repair the Necef tombs, but the sultan promised to carry out the repairs himself exactly as desired by the shah. In line with the committee's decision, Abdulhamid used his own funds to repair the abode of Seyyid Ali Pak, a descendent of Imam Zeynelabidin, near Hims (Homs), donated money to the *vakifs* in the area, and honored various Shiite and Sunni communal leaders in Iraq with gifts and medals.[34]

Despite all the sultan's efforts, Iranian influence and Shia activities in Iraq continued to increase. Ali Galip, the Ottoman ambassador in Teheran and a dedicated Islamist, reported that, on instructions from Istanbul, he had tried to enlist the *mujtahids* in the caliphal drive for Muslim unity. The *mujtahids* agreed that it was the duty of every Muslim to pray for the sultan and to refrain from dividing the faithful, but the Iranian government had taken advantage of the friendly policy of the Ottoman government toward them and tried to spread Shiism. The Shia *ahunds* (preachers, low-level clergy), who entered Iraq under the pretext of offering educational services to the Iranian citizens actually for long periods preached their Shiite doctrine in the villages and among the tribes. The *ahund*s were known as theologians, preachers, and schoolmasters in Iran. In Ottoman Iraq they became missionaries and penetrated even into the ranks of the Ottoman Sixth Army. They won the hearts of the Iraqi peasants by acting as intermediaries between the local population and the government officers, often using special emissaries known as *karperdar,* and persuaded the Shiites not to send their children to Sunni schools. The ambassador recommended that stern measures be taken in order to limit the access of the *ahund*s and other Iranian citizens to the Iraqi villages and to prevent the Iranian consuls from acting as "though they were in their own country."[35]

The caliph's efforts to court the Shia religious men displeased the Sunni ulema. The latter had lost their lands—actually state lands left temporarily to their private use—to the central treasury. Now they saw that the Shia *mujtahid*s, of whom in Necef and Karbala alone there were about 2,200, enjoyed wealth and prestige while the Ottoman teachers and officials were so miserably paid they could hardly make ends meet.[36] The Ottoman government responded to the Shiite challenge in Iraq by placing reliable Sunni religious men in responsible positions there: Alusizade Şakir efendi volunteered to administer the *zaviye* (lodge) of Ali and eventually rose high in the Ottoman hierarchy; and Şeyh Taha efendi established a *medrese* in Karbala that attracted many students, including several Shiites.[37] In addition, the ensemble of buildings known as the Külliye of Hüseyin in Baghdad, which had been repaired some three decades earlier by Shah Nasireddin of Iran, was subjected to a thorough renovation. Kiamil paşa, emulating the methods used by Protestant missionaries to convert the Armenians, proposed to recruit young Shiites to study in the major Sunni centers of learning.[38] A dozen or so Shiite children were indeed recruited for this purpose, but only about three finished their studies and went back to Iraq. Meanwhile, the sultan had decided to appoint a leading Sunni scholar, Şeyh Said efendi, to work in Samarra, which had become a major center of Shia propaganda. However, the Iranian influence and Shiite proselytizing continued unabated in Iraq.

The dangers of the Shiite expansion in Iraq seems to have induced the sultan in 1892 to invite Cemaleddin Afghani to Istanbul. A number of scholars have attributed various motives to sultan's invitation: to help him plan his "pan-Islamist" policy, to prevent Afghani from joining the advocates of an Arab caliphate, and to control his anti-European activities.[39] It was true that the sultan did not like Afghani's antimonarchist views, his advocacy of parliamentarianism, and his revolutionary panislamist ideology, although he admired his intellect and dedication to Islamic causes. One defender of Abdulhamid, the publisher of his memoirs, wondered why the sultan, himself an Islamist, disliked a fellow ideologue dedicated to Muslim causes.[40] Others such as activist nationalist-Islamist poet Mehmet Akif (Ersoy) (1870–1936) have praised Afghani, while secularists have condemned him. In reality Abdulhamid's attitude toward Afghani was dictated by practical considerations. As early as 1885, Afghani wrote the sultan a lengthy letter, which is a masterpiece of both eloquence and dedication to Islamic causes, proposing to preach Muslim unity in India and Central Asia. While that letter remained unanswered, a shorter, more matter-of-fact letter that Afghani wrote the sultan in 1892 promptly resulted in the invitation to Istanbul.[41] Abdulhamid had no interest in Afghani as a worldwide pan-Islamic crusader and did not fear his potential support for an Arab caliphate. Correspondence between Cevdet paşa and the sultan indicates that Abdulhamid wanted Afghani's help to counteract the shah's propaganda in Iraq and win the loyalty of the Ottoman Shiites, possibly even convert them to Sunnism.[42] Before inviting Afghani to Istanbul, the sultan asked Ahmet Cevdet paşa about Afghani's background and the reason he had been forced to leave Istanbul in 1870. Cevdet, as minister of justice at the time, knew the situation firsthand and had read the famous sermon that prompted Afghani's ousting. Cevdet replied that Afghani was a capable person who knew Arabic and Persian (Farsi) well, but he had to leave Istanbul in 1870 because of semantics. The ulema had objected to the terms Afghani used in a public talk: in discussing prophecy, Afghani used the term *sanat* (manipulation, art, a human creation) as an equivalent to "prophecy" and thus seemed to have denied the essence of prophethood (*nubuvveti ta'dad eyledi*). Cevdet paşa claimed that Afghani did not lack respect for or question the Prophet's revealed mission; rather, he simply was unfamiliar with *sanat*'s connotation among the Ottoman ulema. Cevdet then went on to describe Afghani's struggle with the British in Egypt, his involvement in the Tobacco Revolt in 1891–92, and his activities against the Iranian ruler. Cevdet did his best to assure the sultan that Afghani was not "opposed to the caliphate, and once the Iranian problem had been solved, he obeyed the Sublime command and came to Dersaadet (Istanbul)."[43]

Probably the decisive proof that Afghani was invited and came to Istanbul in 1892 to help the sultan win over the Shia of Iraq can be found in a letter addressed by the chief secretariat (*başkitabet*) of the palace to a "member of the ulema." The letter, written on behalf of the sultan, is undated, and the name of the *alim* to whom it was addressed is not mentioned. The content of the letter makes clear, however, that the *alim* was Afghani, for it describes him as someone who had "traveled in most of the Muslim countries, who had lived a long time in Iran and who knows the Sunni [*ehli sunnet*], who had studied the differences among various Shia groups, who had learned about the general situation in the world by living in Europe and defended [and desired to see] the unity of Islam."[44] Obviously nobody but Afghani fits this description. The first part of the letter describes the efforts by the Catholic Church to convert the Orthodox Christians and Armenians to its own creed and accuses the Armenians of luring the Muslims of Bitlis to their own faith and of attempting to infiltrate the army units sent to Crete by posing as Muslims. Emphasizing the Muslims' need for unity and claiming that such unity could be achieved more easily among Muslims than among Christians, the letter finally tackles the central theme—the Shia-Sunni difference. According to the letter, the difference arose from Shah Ismail's political ambitions, and interested parties in Iran were exploiting the ignorance of the inhabitants of Iraq and Baghdad proper in order to perpetuate the shah's ambitions. Furthermore, the main activities undertaken by the Ottoman government to prevent the Shia infiltration of Iraq had failed. Although the difference between the Shiites and Sunnis was minimal—the *kibla* of both was the Ka'aba—the Shiites persisted in maintaining their own sectarian views and worked against the Porte by supporting, among others, the dissident Armenians.

The letter stressed, in conclusion, the absolute necessity of achieving the unity of all Muslims by creating an association (*cemiyet*) headed by two or three Sunni ulema and two or three Shia *mujtahid*s who believed in Muslim unity and caliphal supremacy. Thus formed, the committee would try to neutralize the influence of those

Iranian *mujtahids* who persisted in their Shia beliefs. At the same time, it would try to bring the Iranian military forces under the command of the caliph (the shah would retain executive power) and abolish sectarian differences among the Muslims living in the Ottoman state. After citing suras from the Koran supporting *tevhid* (unity), the sultan asked the recipient of the letter to express his opinion freely about these matters but *ordered* him in the name of the caliph to keep the correspondence absolutely secret. Afghani's answer is not available but it certainly exists somewhere, and we do know from Mirza Aga Khan Kermani's biography of Afghani that the latter managed to persuade some Shia ulema to collaborate with the caliph.[45] We also know Muzaffareddin şah visited Istanbul as Abdulhamid's special guest, and that only Halil Rifat paşa also attended the two-hour confidential discussion between them.

In addition to the question of unity there were other technical problems discussed, such as the law of 6 October 1874, which forbade Ottoman women to marry Iranian men lest the children born from these mixed marriages refuse to serve in the Ottoman army.[46] The total number of such people was estimated to be around 22,000. Meanwhile, Iranian intellectuals living in Istanbul, who were led by Afghani according to Mirza Aga Khan Kermani, engaged in activities to achieve the unity of the Shiites and Sunnis and the assassination of the Iranian shah by Afghani's followers. The sultan refused to deliver Afghani to Persian authorities, and he died of cancer in Istanbul in 1897. However, the relations between Afghani and the sultan had deteriorated by the mid-1890s; Afghani's Shiite mission had failed, and he was accused of plotting against the sultan. His defender, Cevdet paşa, passed away in 1895.[47]

The Shia-Sunni rivalry in Iraq, although appearing to be grounded in the usual religious reasons, actually had simple, mundane causes. In a comprehensive report of 1893, the inspectorate of the Sixth Army bluntly pointed out that the spread of Shiism and tribal unrest in Iraq and the Arabian peninsula was due not to a lack of Islamic zeal but to bad administration. The report ominously forecast that England and Iran could separate these areas from the center if the necessary practical measures were not enacted soon. It further suggested that Seyyid Cemaleddin (Afghani) efendi along with Abulhuda and other Sunni ulema be consulted for theological arguments to counteract the teachings of Seyyid Selman and his brother Seyyid Abdurrahman, who preached "heresy," and it recommended that the brothers be interned at Bursa (where Khomeini was briefly interned in the mid-1960s). Ironically, the two brothers were Kadiri şeyhs not Shiites.[48] Several other reports, some issued as late as 1908, proposed a variety of measures to deal with the danger of Shiism in Iraq. Ahmet Şakir paşa recommended the establishment of a mobile ulema committee—*seyyar muderris*—composed of the highest religious dignitaries in Iraq to travel to the areas most exposed to Shiite propaganda;[49] but a staff major, Ali Riza, who spent three years as consul in Iran, claimed that the spread of Shiism in Iraq was due to ignorance and recommended the establishment of various schools to combat it.[50]

The reports suggest very strongly that local people were not against Islamic unity but wanted first to end the stagnant economic situation of the area and the corruption and maladministration of Ottoman officials. These failings had fueled the rise of a local Arab consciousness, a form of regional nationalism that used Shiism as a channel of self-expression. Already the fear of Arab nationalism had left a deep impression on Abdulhamid's mind, and he objected to Kiamil paşa's suggestion to send Shiite children to study at Al-Azhar in Egypt, the highest institution of Sunni learning, lest they be affected by nationalist ideas spread by the British.[51] In short, the desperate efforts to stem the tide of Shiism and nationalism, or regional nationalism, were largely unsuccessful; instead, these new forces increased in strength, not only because of British efforts to bolster them but also because they expressed the particularism and local self-consciousness engendered by new historical conditions and structural changes.

After the Imamites of Iraq, the Zaidis were the second largest Shiite group to be subject to the effort to achieve unity. When Ottoman relations with the British began to deteriorate and pan-Islamism appeared to threaten the British hold on Indian Muslims, London involved the Zaidis of Yemen in its campaign against the Ottoman caliphate. Istanbul had to respond immediately. The Zaidis, despite their relative closeness to Sunnism, presented a far greater political challenge than the Twelvers because of Yemen's distance from Istanbul and the very thin, ineffectual presence of Ottoman bureaucracy in contrast to the strong British influence there. The sultan did his best to accommodate the Zaidis, who were the followers of Zaid bin Ali Zeynelabidin and accepted the existence of different imams in different countries, thus coming very close to the acceptance of territorial separateness. The Ottoman state faced great difficulty in subduing Yemen from the time of its initial conquest, which took thirty years, from 1539 to 1569, and thereafter. The already shaky relations between Yemen and Istanbul deteriorated very rapidly in the 1870s, not only because the centralization drive threatened the autonomy of various chiefs but also because a substantial part of the tax revenues once spent locally were now diverted to the central treasury.[52]

Abdulhamid did his best to cultivate the local notables and tribal leaders of Yemen; he invited many to Istanbul, assigned some to head the local administration and appointed others as assistants to the governor. The sultan also invited about one hundred religious leaders to Istanbul; each was given 1,500 liras, and their children enrolled in the *aşiret mektepleri* (tribal schools). Nevertheless, revolts led by Şeyh Yahya and Imam Hamideddin broke out in 1889–90 and 1891, respectively, the latter in north Yemen. Unable to understand the real reasons for these revolts, the sultan sent to Yemen, in addition to military units, Namik efendi, who was entrusted with studying the situation and seeking to secure the loyalty of the local *şeyh*s and other leaders through gifts of various sorts, but the effort produced limited results. When a new revolt broke out in 1895, the sultan renewed his effort to win the sympathy of the local population, opening a series of first- and second-level schools designed to train a local pro-Ottoman elite. All this again produced limited results, and in 1905 still another revolt (led by Imam Yahya, who saw himself equal in rank to, if not above, the Ottoman caliph) was mounted. A reform commission consisting mainly of members of the Şura-i Devlet (State Council) was established in 1907, and better communication with the imam—through Şerif Abdullah and Şeyh Ahmet efendi, both of whom were from Yemen and lived in Istanbul—was initiated.[53] The sultan decreased the tax burdens of the poor, built a series of schools, and generously distributed the usual medals and gifts, especially bound Korans. Having appointed the Arabic-speaking administrators, the sultan then staffed the local councils with members of the ulema and local notables, whom he asked to advise the central government. By the time the Young Turks came to power in 1908, Yemen had gained a de facto autonomy that the new government found it prudent to respect. In exchange, Yemen agreed to remain under Ottoman jurisdiction. The sultan never seemed to realize that the trouble that arose in Yemen stemmed from real shortcomings such as poverty, maladministration, unjust distribution of taxes, and economic stagnation.

Sultan Abdulhamid's drive to integrate the Muslims of his realm into a tight Ottoman Muslim union also involved marginal groups, such as the Yezidis in eastern Anatolia, where Armenian nationalism posed the most dangerous threat to Ottoman authority. The government tried to bring the Yezidis into the fold of orthodox Islam by opening mosques and schools in their villages and towns and by sending there Sunni ulema and teachers. The usual method of conferring medals, titles, and pensions on the group's leaders was practiced as well. The first experiment began in the *vilayet* of Bitlis in 1887, apparently at the request of the Yezidis inhabiting the village of Batarvan. The second became necessary in 1891, in the Mosul area, when a group of military men who did not know the local language inflicted harsh treatment on the population and alienated them from the government.[54] It appears that these efforts were partly successful, even though several Yezidi leaders went back on their earlier vow to help "Islamize" their people (probably under French instigation). In any event, the Yezidis of the villages of Şihlik and Sincar in the *vilayet* of Mosul were brought into the fold of Sunnism.[55]

In addition, some Nestorians became targets for Sunni propaganda. The Ottoman Nasuris—as they were known—had adopted a friendly attitude toward Islam, in part because of their peaceful cohabitation with Muslims in mixed villages and towns. Moreover, they were relatively uninvolved in the confessional sectarian struggle that had gripped other groups in Syria and Iraq; furthermore, they had withstood the massive French effort to convert them to Catholicism. In the last decades of the nineteenth century their stance rapidly changed to favor Islam. Several villages in the *sancak* of Lazkiye, in the *kazas* (subdistricts) of Merkab, Ceble, and Sahyun, apparently asked the *mutasarrif* (head) of the *sancak*, as the caliph's representative, to provide them with schools and mosques and to teach them the essentials of Islam; fifteen schools and an equal number of mosques were thus built. Some Nasuris of Alexandria and Antioch likewise converted, and a total of thirty-eight schools were built in their villages.[56]

Conclusion

The Islamic drive for unity within the Ottoman state aimed at countering the efforts of England and France to exploit ethnoreligious differences among various Muslim groups, in the same way that Russia had used Orthodoxy to politicize the ethnonational groups of the Balkans in the period 1855–78. Although the means and methods the Ottoman administration used to achieve unity did not address the problems that had alienated Sunnis and Shiites, the Shiites of Iraq and Syria supported the unity of Islam against European expansion; and even some *mujtahids* acknowledged, at least formally, the caliph's leadership. In fact, respect and support for the caliph as the religious head of the Muslim community and for the caliphate as a central Islamic institution were quite high. The Tobacco Revolt in Iran indicated that the Iranian revolutionaries were prepared to accept unity, in the form of an alliance between equals, with the Ottoman Empire. They did not, however, envision the fusion of Iran into the caliph's realm. The key issues alienating the people of Iraq from the Ottoman administration and drawing them toward the shah and Shiism were centralization, taxation, administrative inefficiency, and the extension of the military draft to the Arabic-speaking provinces. To the Iraqis, these were local problems of sufficient importance to undermine the effort to achieve the unity sought by the sultan. Centralization increased the presence of Ottoman administrators and army units and posed a direct threat to the de facto authority and tax privileges of the local leaders. Taxes then became the principle cause of friction between the central government and the Iraqi notables, tribal chiefs, and ulema—the very groups whose support Abdulhamid relied on in the countryside. (This was also the case in Syria and Yemen, but there were no agents of the shah proselytizing in those areas.) Yet its growing need for revenue and the drying up of many tax bases led the Ottoman government to revise and curtail many exemptions and impose new taxes. The basic Ottoman principle was that everybody and all production of goods were subject to taxation. The exceptions, for high religious dignitaries, government officials, the *vakifs*, most religious lodges (*tekke*s) and establishments, and a few other special cases, had been created to win the submission and support of local leaders and their groups. The loss of territories in the Balkans, in however, curtailed tax revenues, while war reparations paid to Russia and the Debt Administration increased the need for more such revenue. Meanwhile, the Land Code of 1858, enforced widely by Mithat paşa while he was governor of Iraq in the early 1870s, had expanded the scope of private property and created—to the detriment of the state—powerful proprietied groups demanding a high degree of self government. Consequently, when the Ottoman administration sought not only to eliminate or limit tax exemptions but also to assert the government's rights over lands with dubious exemptions, the *vakif* lands, and state lands cultivated by local dignitaries and ulema, it antagonized the beneficiaries, usually local notables or ulema but sometimes also peasants, who were always suspicious of the central government anyway.

The establishment of a central *vakif* administration had changed the classical Islamic status of the *vakif* as an autonomous social institution and deprived many local ulema—the usual administrators of the *vakifs*—of income, position, and prestige and brought them to raise questions about the government's commitment to upholding Islamic principles. Yet a cursory look at the *irade*s for 1894–1918—that is, the imperial orders—for expenditures met previously by *vakif*s indicate that approximately 4,600 mosques, *medrese*s, lodges, graves, and the like, located in every corner of the state, such as Istanbul, Jerusalem, Bolu, Bengazi, Batum, and Salonica, were repaired. The state *vakif* administration also financed the building of new mosques for immigrants, payments for imams sent to teach Islam to various tribes, and a variety of other religious activities.[57] Traditionally such activities were left to the discretion of the *mütevelli*—that is, the *vakif* administrator appointed by the donor. The state ignored all this tradition and replaced the individual administrators with its own bureaucrats.

In the ultimate analysis, Iraq and Syria came to regard the central government's drive for Islamic unity and the fuller integration of the Arab provinces into the Ottoman Empire as likely to increase their burden of taxation and administrative red tape. As they did their best to undermine that drive, without opposing it openly, their political and ethnic consciousness increased. The Arab-speaking territories were entities with unique histories, cultures, and personalities that, despite their profound attachment to Islam—or maybe because of it—had a "national" flavor of their own. Although the Arab provinces had absorbed a high degree of Ottoman influence, de facto self-government had preserved their cultural and social characteristics. Abdulhamid's Islamist policies and educational system, promoted through an increasingly powerful central authority, actually encouraged the reaction of local and regional particularism. Clearly, religion alone could not satisfy the demands for local self-assertion, education, welfare, and progress in the new Muslim society that emerged in the second half of the nineteenth century; centralization and monolithic ideology threatened local autonomy and the established folk culture of the Arab areas of the Empire, resulting, after 1880, formation, under the aegis of Islamism, of two ethno-national entities, one Turkish and the other Arabic. Both were modern and Islamic, each in its own "national" way.

9

Ottoman-European Relations and Islamism

The Aftermath of the Berlin Treaty: Gladstone's Policy and the Ottomans

After the signing of the Berlin Treaty in July 1878 there was a waiting period of some twenty-one months during which adverse British foreign policy actions vis-à-vis the Porte were held in abeyance. There was no let up in the anti-Ottoman, antisultan propaganda war, which only intensified. For the Ottomans, this period was simply the calm before the storm. In April 1880 the Liberal Party won an overwhelming election victory over the Conservatives in England. The election had been fought largely over the issue of Lord Beaconsfield's (Disraeli's) foreign policy—that is, the policy of cultivating the friendship of the Ottomans and helping to maintain the territorial integrity of the Empire, which had been initiated by Palmerston some forty years earlier. The Ottoman leaders were well aware of the anti-Turkish views of William Ewart Gladstone (1809–1898). He had caused irreparable harm to the Empire when he was prime minister in the 1876–78 period; now he had been elected to the post once again. Musurus paşa, the Ottoman ambassador in London, cabled the results of the election to Istanbul but reassured the sultan that the "GOM" (grand old man) would not necessarily make the Eastern Question a partisan issue.

However, England's foreign policy priorities had changed. London had become as worried about the growing power of Germany as it had been about Russia, and it now viewed the disintegration of the Ottoman Empire as probably imminent and even as desirable. It therefore decided to occupy the strategic points of the Empire and encouraged France to do the same in Africa, in order to strengthen Paris against Germany and cast a blight on the imperial ambitions of Germany and Italy in North Africa and along the Red Sea littoral. The reaction of Sultan Abdulhamid was to issue veiled threats to play his "pan-Islamic" card and to seek to forge stronger links with Germany—which, of course, caused Britain and France to become more worried and to raise the volume of their anti-Ottoman polemics a notch or two higher. Having come to agree that the caliphate and Islamism (pan-Islamism) threatened their interests, Britain and France engaged in a ruthless campaign to undermine the Ottoman caliph, questioning his legitimacy and seeking to replace him with an Arab caliph of their own choosing. At the same time, France launched a crusade of its own to convert various Christian groups in the Middle East to Roman Catholicism.

The British attitude and Gladstone's policies toward the Ottomans were determined not only by diplomatic considerations but also by domestic conditions. English public sentiment had taken a strong anti-Turkish, anti-Muslim turn. In fact, a strange mixture of secularism, populism, and religious fervor had come to possess the Europeans as a whole and was fueling the machinery of imperialism. Secularism in Europe had made religion a subordinate element of "civilization," on the basis of which Europeans claimed superiority over non-Westerns, especially Muslims. Paradoxically, the "secularist" Europeans felt a proprietary interest in the Christians of the Middle East, the view being that they should not be the subjects of a Muslim authority that was not as "civilized" as Christian Europe.

Ambassador Henry Layard had been generally sympathetic to the Ottomans; but as the Conservatives sensed that they were losing popularity and would probably lose the next election, they attempted to win over the British public by adopting the same sort of protective attitude toward the Ottoman Christians that had so greatly increased the appeal of Gladstone and the Liberals after 1876. Layard tried to act tougher. Using a rather minor issue to make his point, in April 1880, just before he was recalled, he asked the Porte to guarantee "freedom of religion"—that is, freedom to proselytize—to a German missionary named Kohl; he also wanted the Porte to act against Ahmet Tevfik efendi, a member of the ulema, whose militant preachings he cited as proof of growing "Muslim fanaticism." Although Layard threatened the severance of diplomatic relations if he did not receive immediate satisfaction, his demands were turned down, the Porte acting as though it were quite unconcerned that relations with England might be severed: the Ottoman officials knew Layard was bluffing. This was, however, one of the worst British-Ottoman confrontations in twenty-five years.[1] Layard was removed as ambassador almost immediately after this confrontation, and he was replaced by George Goschen, who proved to be a rather impetuous and immature hawk.

Gladstone attempted, immediately after taking over the government, to enforce Article 61 of the Berlin Treaty, which provided for "reforms" in the six provinces of eastern Anatolia, where the bulk of the Ottoman Armenians lived. The Ottoman government was charged with protecting the Armenians against the attacks of Kurds and Circassians. Article 61 of the Berlin Treaty was almost identical with Article 16 of the earlier San Stefano Treaty, which had empowered Russia to oversee the "reforms" in the east Anatolian provinces; the difference between the old article and the new one was that England now was given the supervisory authority. The Porte saw the so-called reforms as aimed at creating a sort of administrative autonomy for the Armenians, to be followed possibly by independence. The ratio of the population in the six provinces was one Armenian to either three or five Muslims, depending upon what statistics one used, and the Muslims feared the Armenians would embark on a drive to exterminate them or force them to flee their ancestral homes. (This was the strategy the Russians and Bulgarians had used with impunity in 1877–78 in order to secure a Christian majority in the autonomous principality of Bulgaria in advance of the San Stefano and Berlin Treaties.) Before 1878 the Armenians in the Ottoman state had been so friendly to the Ottoman government that the Porte referred to them as the *millet-i sadika* (faithful nation). As late as 1895 a total of 2,633 Armenians still were in Ottoman government service (a high proportion of their total number), but the rapid disintegration of the European section of the Ottoman state and the emergence of autonomous Bulgaria had convinced the Armenian leaders to advance their own national claims. The Armenian patriarch Nerces (Nerses) of Istanbul, who had issued fervent vows of loyalty to the sultan at the start of the war in 1877, changed his position overnight and asked the Berlin congress to recognize the autonomy of Armenia. Although he claimed the number of the Armenians in the Ottoman state amounted to "two and a half million" people, British confidential reports, Ottoman official records, and estimates by various Armenian bishops and officials all placed the total number of Armenians in the Ottoman state at 1.2 million or 1.4 million at most.[2]

The Armenian patriarch himself soon admitted he had manipulated the population figures. Before proposing concrete reforms, the Gladstone government wanted to ascertain the exact number of Muslims and Christians in eastern Anatolia. Ambassador Goschen, who had arrived in Istanbul on 28 May 1880, invited several capable British consuls stationed in the area to discuss "the relative numerical proportions of the different populations inhabiting Asia Minor, and available means for testing the statistics which have been put in by various persons."[3] Major Henry Trotter, a very highly regarded consul in charge of the *vilayet*s of Erzurum, Diyarbakir, Muş, and Van (the area claimed by Armenian nationalists), duly examined the Armenian claims and declared that he could not "admit the accuracy of the statistics shown in the enclosure" (presented by Armenians), which were the same "as those submitted to the Congress of Berlin."[4] According to Trotter, the total number of Muslims living in the *vilayet*s of Erzurum, Van, Diyarbakir, and Harput came to 1,490,500; of Christians, only 649,000. Even after Trotter had added 40 percent by including, in addition to the Armenians, the Nestorians, Syrians, and other Eastern Christian denominations, the number of Christians amounted to only 908,600, a figure originally put forward by Consul Taylor, the predecessor of Trotter. At the same time, the population figures for Muslims did not include many of the nomadic Türkmen, Kurdish, and Arabic tribes roaming the area. Trotter and the other British consuls in Anatolia, such as Chermside and Wilson, could not come up with a total of more than 900,000 Armenians in eastern Anatolia or of more than 1,200,000 in all of the Ottoman state. These totals were far lower than those that Patriarch Nerces had submitted to the Congress of Berlin.[5] Eventually the patriarch confessed that he had counted the Armenian population of a given district several times, including that district each time he counted the population of a new province. He also admitted that he had left out of his count the nomadic Muslims, notably in the districts where the Turks were in the overwhelming majority.[6] His admissions, however, were not made public by the British or the other Europeans.

Because he attributed the British and European acceptance of the patriarch's false data, along with their support of the Armenian minority and their disregard for the rights of the Muslim majority, to their pro-Christian biases, Sultan Abdulhamid asked his advisers to provide him with confidential reports about the ethnic composition of the population in the six provinces in question. Those confidential statistics, present in the Prime Ministers' Archives, show that from 1878 to 1897 the ethnic-religious ratio of the population in the six provinces remained more or less stable at around 78 percent Muslim and about 17 percent Armenian; only in the district of Van did Armenians represent as much as 41 percent of the population; but Van accounted for only about 10 percent of the total population of the region.[7]

The Armenian question played a major role in the worsening of Ottoman-British relations, as each side considered it a yardstick to measure the other's intentions and true feelings, and it added new weight to the festering nationality question in the Balkans. In 1878 the Albanians established the Albanian League at Prizren (in today's Kosovo province) to protest the provisions of the Berlin Treaty, which had left some of their territory to Serbia and Montenegro, and to oppose the future loss of territory; some of them even contemplated the establishment of an autonomous Albania. Meanwhile, in Bosnia and Herzogovina some popular preachers and members of the establishment, such as Mehmet efendi, the mufti of Taşlica, led the Muslims in a guerilla war that, with the help of Serbian partisans, for three months prevented the Austro-Hungarian army from occupying the country. Nevertheless, the new British ambassador at the Porte not only ignored grievances that had created the Muslim fervor in the Balkans but went as far as to accuse Istanbul of fomenting the unrest that, in fact, Abdulhamid was doing his best to contain. The sultan had already incurred the dissatisfaction of many Muslims for persuading the rebels in the Rhodope Mountains of Bulgaria to lay down their arms. Yet Ambassador Goschen continued to believe that Istanbul had organized the Balkan unrest and was delaying implementation of the Berlin Treaty provisions. He persuaded London to display its naval force in front of Dulcingo to make the Porte cede it to Montenegro, another humiliation of the Porte at the hands of its "protector."

British-Ottoman mutual suspicions continued to escalate. The anti-Turkish faction in the British establishment regarded the procrastination of the sultan in undertaking "real reforms" in eastern Anatolia as evidence of his ill will and bias against the Christians. At the same time, the sultan regarded the British insistence on "reforms" as designed to create an autonomous Armenia and to fragment further—then ultimately put an end to—the Ottoman state. The sultan, with his suspicious mind, was inclined to see in every British and European move a sinister design aimed at him personally as well as at the existence of the Empire as a whole. England, in turn, interpreted the sultan's suspicions and his self-defensive measures as the devious maneuvering of an "oriental despot" bent on keeping all authority for himself. Actually, the attitudes of the British and of the sultan reflected the new urgency the Eastern Question had acquired after the war of 1877–78 that made the total collapse of the Empire an imminent possibility.

The British Fear of Pan-Islamism

The British suspected that the frantic efforts the sultan made after 1878 to bolster his image and influence among Muslims could be used to subvert their rule in India; London saw in the Indian Muslims' displays of friendship toward the sultan an ominous threat. Relatively trivial incidents in 1877–78 had already increased English suspicions about the Ottoman ruler's intentions to use his influence against the British in India. Shazada Sultan Ibrahim, a descendant of the Delhi sultans acting as the head of the Muslim-Indian refugees in Istanbul, received from the Ottoman government a monthly stipend of 500 kuruş, as did hundreds of other Muslim refugees with some social ranking as a matter of traditional royal benevolence and hospitality. British suspicion intensified when Nusrat Ali Khan (Moula Bukhsh), publisher of *Peyk-i Islam* (Follower, satellite of Islam), who was a militantly anti-British and an active supporter of the caliphate, came to Istanbul; he had played a leading role in collecting funds in India for the Ottoman war effort in 1877–78 but left India for the Ottoman capital after the authorities in India closed the newspaper he published there. According to British intelligence, he supposedly had brought with him to Istanbul a memorandum signed by some seventy Muslim princes of India, who expressed their willingness to recognize the caliph as their leader and promised to help him financially.[8]

Nusrat Ali married a Turkish woman and in 1880 began to publish the newspaper *Peyk-i Islam*, in which he propounded the view that the Ottoman sultan was the caliph of all the Muslims in the world, including the Indians. A small group of Indian Muslims, who were supported by the British, challenged the legitimacy of elevating the Ottoman sultan to the caliphate, initially with little effect. The bulk of the Indian Muslims, many of their newspapers, as well as papers published in the other Muslim lands (to the consternation of the British) appeared, however, to have accepted the Ottoman sultan as the bona fide universal caliph.

These developments revolving around the caliphate seem to have given Ambassador Layard a new excuse for the failure of the caliph's embassy—planned by Layard—to persuade the *amir* of Afghanistan to turn against Russia and befriend the British as explained in detail elsewhere. In the end, Layard apparently attributed the failure of the mission not to his own exaggerated opinions about his ability to manipulate the caliph and the Muslims of Central Asia against Russia, but to the duplicity of Hulusi efendi, the Ottoman emissary to the Afghan *amir*, and possibly of the sultan himself. Layard then tried to rehabilitate himself in the eyes of the Foreign Office by treating the *Peyk-i Islam* affair as the tip of the iceberg of a major anti-British conspiracy concocted by the Indian Muslims in Istanbul, possibly with the sultan's support. Thus blown out of proportion, the affair caused several English newspapers, including the *Statesman*, to open a virulent campaign against panislam that, in turn, compelled the Muslim press in India and the Ottoman state to respond.[9]

Ottoman documents indicate that the *Peyk-i Islam* matter resulted from Ottoman bureaucratic carelessness and disregard for the possible implications of the decision to help Nusrat Ali publish his newspaper. Nusrat Ali and his copublisher, another Indian Muslim, submitted a memorandum asking the Porte for permission to publish the newspaper in Istanbul and stating that, sooner or later, the British would be forced out of India and that the forty-odd million Muslim Indians would need a new ruler. If their ruler were to be the Ottoman caliph, this would more than compensate for the loss of a few million Muslims left in the Balkans as a consequence of the Berlin Treaty of 1878. The two apparently also offered to use their newspaper to spread pan-Islamic views among their coreligionists in India and to uphold the supremacy of the caliph. At any rate, their request for publishing permission was sent routinely by Premier Sait paşa to the minister of interior, who provided 2,000 kuruş to the publishers as a matter of benevolence. The paper began publication in May 1880, with one edition in Urdu and one in Turkish.[10] Layard, eager to correct his image as a friend of Abdulhamid, chose to regard the allocation of money to the publishers as an act of Ottoman ill will toward England. He managed to obtain copies of the newspaper and the bureaucratic correspondence and sent all of them to London, provoking outrage, as Cevdet paşa, the confidant and adviser of the sultan, recalled:

> The Gladstone group came to power and the [*Peyk-i Islam*] correspondence was given to them. The anger and hatred of Gladstone, who did not like the Turks anyway, increased further. Consequently, both the conservative and liberal ministers believed that the sultan [Abdulhamid] was engaged in inciting the Indian Muslims against England. [The reason] for their belief is that the [sultan's own] prime minister and the interior minister's offices, realizing their error, accused each other of granting the money. They finally placed the blame on the sultan ... [S]uch a betrayal [of the sultan] occurred for the first time [in the history of] the Porte.[11]

The issue was a tempest in a teapot. The newspaper had a very limited circulation— only eighteen copies reached India—and it quickly ceased publication.

After the *Peyk-i Islam* episode, the British decided to keep an eye on the Islamist newspapers in Turkey and abroad and often accepted at face value the sensational reports in the Muslim press about Islamic political activities.[12] The "activities" range from secret anti-British committees supposedly established in India at the sultan's orders, through Osman paşa's pan-Islamic conspiracies, to the activities of the Turkish consul in Bombay, and other similar exaggerations based more often on rumor than fact. There is however a bizarre and unusual case which indicates that, when necessary, Abdulhamid could make adroit use of disinformation. Şeyh Süleyman efendi (1821–90) the head of the Uzbek lodge in Istanbul, the "ambassador" of the Bukharan hanate at the Porte since 1847 and a very learned man (he authored a Çagatay-Ottoman dictionary), was well trusted by Abdulhamid. (The *şeyh* had been charged with diplomatic missions to Hungary.) The British suspected Şeyh Süleyman of being a Russian agent and eventually secured his intelligence services by paying him a salary that was insignificant in relation to the *şeyh*'s personal wealth and expenditure. Şeyh Süleyman gave the British some accurate information about trivial incidents in the imperial palace and also long lists of Indian Muslim notables who had supposedly agreed to serve as the sultan's Islamic agents in India. The British authorities in India, alerted by London, found no trace of Ottoman pan-Islamic activities and regarded the people named as "Islamic" agents by the Şeyh Süleyman to be above suspicion.[13]

Moreover, a secret British investigation by P. D. Henderson, the head of the secret police in Bombay, found that Nusrat Ali had little following in India. Henderson concluded that he was unable to express an opinion about the existence of a panislamic conspiracy in India. In fact, in 1881 the judge of Rae Bareb, Sayid Mahmud, the son of famous reformist and pro-British Muslim scholar Sayid Ahmad Khan, wrote two letters to Henderson stating that the Indian Muslims felt sympathy for their Turkish coreligionists and regarded the sultan as the greatest Muslim monarch but did not owe allegiance to him. Only in a few places did they even mention his name in the Friday sermon (*hutbe*), and they did not strive to join a Muslim union. According to Henderson, Sayid Mahmud "held that recently Muhammedanism in India had taken a nationalistic tendency, which would prove conducive to British rule," though in the end this view proved untrue. Sultan Abdulhamid declared on several occasions that his activities were part of his religious responsibilities as caliph and were not directed against England; but he could not convince the British. London continued to view Istanbul as the source of all evil, in line with Gladstone's view that Muslims were not trustworthy. Thus, within the span of a few years the British, who had been steady promoters of Muslim allegiance to the caliph, came to fear that Istanbul had turned the tables and was using panislamism against them in India and elsewhere.

The change in the British opinion about panislam and the caliph's role in it brought England solidly into line with the Russian and French views on the question. Earlier the Russians had warned England not to incite Muslim religious passions, lest London become their target. (Years later the Bolsheviks convened the Baku Congress in 1920 with the specific goal of inciting the Muslims to rebel against the British.) France, for its part, regarded the British reversal of opinion as a vindication of the policy of neutralizing the Ottoman caliphate that France had applied in North Africa since the conquest of Algeria in 1830.

French Reaction to the British Change of View on Pan-Islam

French suspicions toward the caliph had been aroused by the Algerian Revolt of 1870–71, and they regarded the Algerian Muslims' sympathies for their maltreated co-religionists in the Balkans in 1877–78 as more anti-French sentiment inspired by the caliph. Consequently, the British change of opinion about pan-Islam and the caliph, as well as London's desire to see France compensated for the loss of Alsace-Lorraine to Germany in 1871, gave new impetus to France's intention to occupy Tunisia. Indeed, Paris considered the occupation of Tunisia vital to preserving Algeria, as a diplomatic memorandum stated clearly: "La possession de Tunis nous est indispensable si nous tenons a conserver l'Algérie. C'est un axiome, une verité qui s'impose par son évidence même a quiconque sait lire une carte. Deux moyens s'offrent à nous pour attendre ce but: un protectorat ou une prise de possession pure et simple. Je n'hésite pas a me prononcer pour cette dernière solution."[14] Now France could justify, partly at least, the occupation of Tunisia as a step toward preventing the spread of pan-Islamism, although its real goal was to consolidate the French hold on North Africa. France considered opposition to its imperialism in North Africa as stemming from sheer fanaticism, Muslim bigotry, and opposition to the spread of "civilization." It leveled the accusation, based on false intelligence, that Tunis was attempting to draw up a "manifesto"—that is, a proclamation—intended to create a political entente among all Muslim groups living in the area extending from Morocco to India.[15] This plan, according to the French, was conceived by Khayreddin paşa of Tunisia (he was Abdulhamid's premier for a short time) and was supported by Italy and Germany in order to hurt French interests in Tunisia and Algeria; already many Tunisian tribes, at the "sultan's urging," were attacking the French posts in Algeria. Despite the Porte's denials, Paris continued to insist that this "manifesto" was evidence of the sultan's wish to use his caliphal prestige to regain authority over North Africa and thus compensate for the loss of territory in the Balkans.

Fearing that a worldwide "pan-Islamic conspiracy" was afoot, the French decided to prevent some seven hundred totally innocuous circular letters signed by Abdelkader from arriving at their destination in Algeria.[16] The French somehow believed that Abdelkader's letters were the follow-up to an earlier letter written by Said paşa, the Ottoman premier, which had been distributed among the Muslim *haci*s in Mecca. Actually the premier's letter merely extended greetings to the believers and asked them to support the incumbent caliph against the French and English efforts to promote the idea of an Arab caliph. However, French sensitivity on the issue was exacerbated when Islamist writings that regarded North Africa as being under the caliph's authority appeared in *Vakit, Osmanli, Tercuman-i Hakikat* and *Ceride-i Havadis,* Ottoman papers receiving occasional monetary support from the Palace.[17] The truth is that all these newspapers, following popular pressure, began to promote openly the idea of an Islamic union as a possible means to save whatever was left of the once-mighty Ottoman Empire after 1878, even though the Ottoman government itself opposed the radical proposals aired in the press. Abdullah Kiamil, the spokesman for the government, dismissed the Western outcry concerning the Islamic Union and described it as contrived to preempt Muslim opposition to Europe's own designs to subdue all the Muslims in the world. The spokesman added that if a Muslim union ever were established, it would have the peaceful, self-defensive purpose of building internal solidarity among Muslims, for the Porte had no intention to conquer North Africa or attack the West.[18]

In 1881 France occupied Tunisia on the basis of the Treaty of Bardo, which the bey (dey) had signed under duress, and appeared determined to extend French rule further east into Tripolitania and south to Fezzan. They met resistance, however, and, failing to consolidate their occupation quickly, began to fear a North African popular uprising directed from Istanbul. Their fear was reinforced after the Porte sent two thousand troops to Tripoli to maintain order, despite its prior assurances that it would not send any military force there.[19] A series of other incidents increased suspicion that the Ottoman caliphate was striving to undermine France's rule in North Africa. When a group of notables from the Tunisian tribe of Urgama, which harbored many from the holy city of Qairawan who had bitterly fought the French, came to Tripoli asking for Turkish help, they were believed to be plotting new action. French fears were intensified when a number of dissident families from Tunisia took refuge in Tripoli and kept in close touch with both the Ottoman authorities and their constituencies in Tunisia;[20] and when el-Arabi Zarruq, the former governor-mayor of Tunis, stated in a letter to the Porte that Tunisia and its citizens considered themselves a part of the Ottoman state, it was considered further confirmation of the French view.[21]

Algerian dissidents, as usual, did not stay peaceful either. Ali ibn al-Zahir, known as El Loute, had close relations with the Moroccan royal family and had gained fame by preaching in the major mosques of Algiers.[22] According to the French, al-Zahir had cited Koranic verses to the effect that the Muslims were obliged to fight the infidel and that war was the best form of obedience to God; he called upon all Muslims to unite under one ruler and sought to cultivate the friendship of the Wahhabis in Arabia. The French were cheered by the thought that the anti-Ottoman Wahhabis would not mind seeing the Turks defeated and the caliphate taken over by an Arab. To their disappointment, however, they found out that Ibn Saud's followers were ready to support the caliph if the threat to Islam became a reality; and most Arabs living on the Red Sea littoral actually held the caliph in great esteem.[23] France was so concerned that the Muslim reaction to its occupation of Tunisia would generalize throughout the Arab world that it confidentially instructed the French consuls in Damascus and Mosul to provide information on the politically active Muslim groups in their areas and to find *concrete* proof that Sultan Abdulhamid engaged in panislamic activities there. In reply the French consuls in Syria reported at length that the sultan had close relations with various Muslim *tarikat*s (Sufi orders), religious leaders, and the like, but they failed to produce concrete evidence that the sultan engaged in panislamic activity as imagined by the Europeans.[24] (The long report is also notable for having produced a list of the *tarikat*s active in the Mosul area.)

The British Occupation of Egypt

The British occupied Egypt in 1882, allegedly in order to protect the European lives endangered by the revolt of Colonel Urabi (Arabi) paşa, but really in order to pre-empt French designs on the country. They thus added new fuel to the fires of pan-Islamism; even the Arabs, who were well disposed toward London and Paris, came to suspect that England, France, and Russia had decided to end Muslim independence everywhere in the world. The surge of friendly Muslim feeling that arose toward England in 1878, engendered by the British efforts to change the San Stefano Treaty in favor of the sultan, vanished entirely. From 1882 onward, a new chapter in the history of Ottoman-Turkish relations with Muslim intellectuals began to unfold. In the past, the Porte had ignored, and sometimes silenced, Muslim intellectuals and journalists who too harshly criticized the British, French, or even the Russians. After 1881–82, as these intellectuals rapidly gained fame and public support, the Ottoman government often had to go along with them; but the sultan remained deeply suspicious of militant intellectuals and popular movements. For example, a group of people in Izmir demonstrated in support of Urabi and criticized the sultan for allowing the British to land troops in Egypt and for having failed to send Ottoman soldiers to fight alongside the Egyptians;[25] the sultan eventually ordered the arrest of these pro-Urabi demonstrators for creating unrest. However, public sentiment in Egypt and in North Africa, which had not been friendly toward Istanbul, reversed itself. After 1882 many Egyptian intellectuals gave priority to fighting British imperialism and colonialism and looked upon the caliph as a potential savior. Even Colonel Urabi, who had opposed both the Ottoman and the British presence in Egypt, adopted a friendly attitude toward the Porte. Eventually Mustafa Kiamil and his nationalist Vatan (Homeland) Party became the proponents of panislamism, Ottomanism, and caliphal supremacy.[26] At the same time, the public seemed inclined to judge the sultan on the basis of a new criterion—namely, his actual performance in maintaining the independence and territorial integrity of Muslim lands. This was in fact a function that had not hitherto been considered in assessing his performance as caliph.

The escalating animosity between the Porte and the British and French produced a series of new alignments. The sultan now sought to better his relations with Russia and Germany in order to counterbalance the French threat in North Africa and pressure England to revert to Palmerston's protective policy of helping check French ambitions. In addition, as the English and French actions negatively affected the Ottoman Muslims' attitude toward Christians, many Christians, in turn, began to sympathize with French and British policies toward the Muslims, including the occupation of Egypt, and offered their services to Paris and London.[27]

The coincidence of the Muslim millennium of A.H. 1300 (A.D. 1882) with the occupation of Egypt further increased the excitement among Muslims and aggravated the fear of panislamism in the West. Muslim newspapers forecast great events of universal scope, such as the resurgence of the Ottoman Empire and the revival of Islam.[28] A reckless activism seemed to grow out of the atmosphere of pessimism, frustration, and despair caused by the events of the years 1878–82; a particularly sore point was the award of Thessaly to Greece in 1881, although Greece had not entered the war. Now Muslims began to think that "even an unsuccessful war would be better than a tame submission to the encroachment of the European Powers."[29]

By the end of 1882, and increasingly afterward, the reports of the British consuls came to resemble those of the French, suggesting strongly that Sultan Abdulhamid had launched a worldwide pan-Islamic movement and that the Muslims as a whole nurtured a deeply rooted, permanent animosity against all Christians. In a matter of a few years the British consular reports from Anatolia, following London's mood and its need to justify its anti-Turkish policy, showed a drastic change of tone. British consuls harped incessantly on the dangers of pan-Islamism and the Muslims' supposedly atavistic anti-European and anti-Christian attitude. Even the sober-minded consul C. W. Wilson reported from Anatolia, "Agents have been actively engaged in Anatolia in preaching panIslamism and in exciting those feelings of dislike or hostility towards Christians which are always more or less latent in the mind of every Muslim."[30] Similarly, Consul General J. E. Blunt, one of the most knowledgeable British officials, wrote from Salonica in the European part of the empire:

> The usurping views of Austria on Bosnia and Macedonia, our occupation of Cyprus, the action of France in Tunisia, and our proceedings in Egypt are all burning questions now eagerly discussed among the higher as well as the more ignorant and fanatic classes at this place. . . .
>
> [P]eople in general look upon England and France as the enemies of their religion and their existence . . . and believe in the realization of coming great events in which Islam is once more to be called upon to stand its ground against the forces of Christendom. . . . [S]trong sympathy [is felt] for Arabi Paşa [the leader of the anti-British revolt in Egypt] and his insurrectionary movements. He is considered the *beau ideal* of a good Mohammedan, and his acts are glorified and magnified in harems as well as in cafes.[31]

As Blunt goes on to say, the British had come to believe "that the Sultan, as Caliph or Head of the Mohammedan world is in tacit connivance with him [Urabi] and the so-called National Party of Egypt."

As for the change of Ottoman sentiment toward England, Consul General Blunt stated that a Turkish admiral and general of division had told him, "A few years ago the name of England had a magic influence and was honored and loved in the smallest village of Empire; now, we, your friends, regret to say it is mistrusted by all." England, however, did not look for the cause of Muslim animosity in its own occupation of the Muslim lands; rather, England turned its anger against the caliph for not using his caliphal prestige and authority to assuage the Muslim resentment against British expansion.

A series of new developments not only dashed Ottoman hopes of a reconciliation with England but also raised the specter that the events of the years 1876–78 were about to repeat themselves. Armenian unrest in eastern Anatolia was on the rise, as the Hunchak (Bell) student organization, established in 1886 in Geneva, and the Dashnak association, founded in 1890 in Tiflis, Russia, engaged in a variety of nationalist activities, including acts of violence. This provoked counterterrorist actions that were given wide and negative coverage in the European press. The harsh quelling of the Armenian uprising in Sasoon and the court acquittal of Musa bey, portrayed as a persecutor of the Armenians, created outrage in Europe. Meanwhile, the Greeks in Crete, who had been temporarily calmed by extensive Ottoman concessions in favor of local autonomy, again took up arms and asked for *enosis*, that is, unity with Greece.

It was in these circumstances that the voice of Gladstone was once again raised and sent shivers down the spine of the sultan, who remembered how the GOM had turned English public opinion against the Turks in 1876, and won the elections of 1880 by using the "Bulgarian horrors" to accuse his Conservative Party opponent, Benjamin Disraeli, a converted Jew, of insensitivity toward the fate of the Christians. Gladstone had been forced out of office in 1885, in part because of the debacle suffered by General Gordon in Sudan and the unrest in India. The British public, which admired Gordon, turned against Gladstone and reversed the acronym of his nickname GOM to MOG (murderer of Gordon). Gladstone tried to make a political comeback in 1889, and he once again chose the Ottoman treatment of its Christian subjects as his main theme. In a speech in the House of Commons on 12 February 1889, which was a rehearsal for full attack later, Gladstone complained in rather temperate language that "mistreatment" of the Armenians, the acquittal of Musa bey, and the events in Crete showed that the situation in the Ottoman Empire was deteriorating, and he expressed his hope that the incumbent government of Lord Salisbury and its ambassador in Istanbul, William White, would not cover up the Ottoman "misdeeds" as in the past (a reference to Disraeli's alleged cover-up of Turkish acts in Bulgaria). Although he still managed to praise the sultan for "statesmanship" in agreeing to cede Thessaly to Greece in 1881 and for acquiescing meekly to the Bulgarian annexation of eastern Rumili in 1885; he failed to mention the Bulgarians' open violation of the Berlin Treaty defining the Muslims' rights. By this time, however, England had lost its influence at the Porte and could not affect the sultan's policies.

Faced with the indifference of the Porte, the GOM turned belligerent. In a precampaign speech delivered in Manchester early in November 1889, Gladstone attacked the Conservatives in the words he had rehearsed a few days earlier before a Liberal Party caucus. Claiming that atrocities similar to those committed in Bulgaria in 1876 were now taking place in Armenia and that the Porte had rejected all allegations against it, as it had in 1876, he threatened to arouse the public to the injustice done to the Christians and accused Salisbury (prime minister in 1885, 1886–92, 1895–1902) of remaining indifferent to their fate. Gladstone praised the *Daily News*—the newspaper he used in 1876 to wage his anti-Turkish crusade—and expressed his wish that it would perform the same mission now, if need be. He did not hesitate to use contemptuous, even insulting, language in referring to the Ottoman government, and he reminded the Salisbury government that it could expect to receive the same treatment (loss of election) as had Disraeli in 1880. Finally, Gladstone dealt the coup de grâce to Ottoman thoughts of reconciliation when he stated that the Porte's treatment of the Armenians and Cretan Greeks had freed the British government from any obligation to honor the provision of the Cyprus Convention of 1878 that called upon England to defend the Porte against a Russian attack.[32] The Gladstone speech was promptly translated and published in the Russian press, and the government newspaper, *Novoye Vremya*, also used the occasion to praise the Russians for "liberating" the Orthodox Christians in the Balkans from Ottoman rule and to remind the world that there were still Christians suffering under the "yoke" of the Muslims and Turks.[33]

The sultan, therefore, became apprehensive that Gladstone's criticisms might again compel the Conservative government, lest it lose the forthcoming elections, to undertake decisions detrimental to Turkey. Although some spokesmen for the Conservative Party and some newspapers, such as the *Morning Post*, tried to answer Gladstone, the Porte found their defense to be rather hesitant, sterile, and on the whole, ineffective, although the fact was that Gladstone had lost much of his influence upon the British public. The British consular reports from the field turned acerbic and abusive toward Abdulhamid II, while describing in euphemistic terms the good intentions of their own government toward Turkey. The following lengthy excerpt is an example:

Guiltily conscious that his personal fears and narrow-minded bigotry can never reconcile him to England's policy of the regeneration of Turkey, on broad statesmanlike lines, Abdul Hamid has opposed to that policy one of the revival of Islam, and has chosen to imagine England his personal enemy.

Relying solely on Mussulman fanaticism, which Abdul Mejid and Abdul Aziz had recognized as a political danger, and had in great measure rendered dormant, the present Sultan has reawakened and fomented that fanaticism. In his policy of the revival of Islam he has spent large sums, chiefly drawn from his State domains, which like the former Khedive Ismail, he has greatly enlarged by methods fair and foul, on Moslem schools, medressehs, mosques and tekkehs, while his whole administration is directed towards strengthening the Moslem element to the prejudice of non-Moslems, who, during his reign, especially in remote regions, have been subjected to a policy of slow, but certain, impoverishment and elimination (this policy has undergone alarming developments of late); he has gradually removed all Turkish statesmen of influence and liberal views, in whom he scented opposition to this policy of his, more worthy of a seventh century caliph than a nineteenth century Sovereign, and has surrounded himself by a set of Khojas, Sheikhs, and similar fanatics attracted from Arabs, India, Afghanistan, Egypt, Wadai, Bornu, Sokolo, the Cape, &c., upon whom he lavishes large sums of money, and whom he uses as his emissaries in furtherance of his Panislamic movement in those countries.

England happens to be, directly or indirectly, the civil ruler in most of these places, and, as the Church and State are inseparably mixed up in the principles of Islam, England again happens to be the silent and passive, though not active, opponent of his personal Panislamic scheme.[34]

The report provided a view of Abdulhamid that has lasted to this day.

The British clearly realized that both pan-Islamism as an ideology and the Ottoman Empire as a political entity no longer served British interests after the sultan ceased to follow policies decided in London. Unlike his predecessors, Abdulhamid faced an increasingly rebellious intelligentsia and a new middle class prone to dissect and criticize the politics of the sultan and the British alike in their search for ways to better their own political and social position. Because the sultan now had to satisfy all these conflicting interests, which could coalesce anytime into one single opposition voice and depose him, internal pressures on him threatened to become stronger than those emanating from outside. Yet, while the new intelligentsia criticized France, England, or the West in general for political designs on the Ottoman state, they kept turning more and more to the West for intellectual and philosophical nourishment. Indeed, the intellectual, philosophical, and political influence of Europe upon the Ottoman Empire greatly intensified, paradoxically, during Abdulhamid's reign, because of the improvements in modern education, literacy, and newspaper circulation.

France, the most feared and detested colonialist power until England replaced it in 1882, became the almost exclusive inspiration in matters of literary tastes, political ideas, and modern living for the Westernist wings of both the intelligentsia and the middle classes. In spite of half a century of close Ottoman association, the British influence on the Turks in language, ideas, dress, and tastes, remained minimal, although by temperament and social-political tradition Ottoman society was closer to the British than the French. The French triumphed over the English as the main source of inspiration for the new Ottoman intelligentsia, above all because of their ability to influence the Ottoman intellectuals. The French analyzed and put before the intellectuals, who now were flocking to France at the ratio of about twenty to every one going to England, both their own subjective views on Islam and the Turks and their anti-British clichés; and a large group of these intellectuals rapidly internalized the French propaganda and made it part of their "Western" outlook and "national" culture. France supplied and shaped the worldview of these intellectuals as seen clearly in the case of the Young Turks, whose French friends often worked for their intelligence services. The anticlericalism of the French radicals became antireligion in the Ottoman Westernists, with positivism serving as its scientific explanation. Many Ottoman intellectuals alienated themselves from traditionalism, including their own culture and history, and avidly absorbed everything "new," all packaged in French colors and serving France's foreign policy. Finally, the French inculcated in the minds of the Ottoman intelligentsia, by a rather unique use of rationalist arguments that glorified Western civilization (in French garb), an image of Islam as the cause of Ottoman regression.

In search of a liberal regime, a humanist philosophy, and their own identity in a changing world, the anti-Hamidian Ottoman intelligentsia embraced everything French, including the French rage at Ottoman-British relations. The French consul in Aleppo reported that England had

> an interest to let vegetate a state [Ottoman] which supplied them a market where they could exchange their manufactured goods against the raw material indispensable to their industry. It is this policy which inspired the coalitions against the viceroy of Egypt in 1840 and the czar in 1854. . . . The last Turkish-Russian war [of 1877–78] broke down the power of the sultan and destroyed his prestige and thus speeded up the division of the heterogeneous elements which composed the Ottoman Empire.[35]

Commenting on the consequences of the weaknesses of the Ottoman Empire, the consul stated further: "The Turkish weakness has created among the neighboring states a lust which must necessarily lead to the total ruin of a country already reduced to pieces . . . England had to change tactics; she is trying to reserve for herself the best possible morsels. . . . [S]he has started by seizing Cyprus to assure herself an observation post which commands Syria and Egypt." In consequence, the consul asked Paris to strengthen and expand the "bases of French influence," meaning the Catholic religion, in the threatened area. Specifically, he asked Paris to intensify religious (Catholic) propaganda in the Ottoman state and to expand the French school system.[36]

The consul's reports seem to have produced the desired result. Subsequent French diplomatic correspondence from the Middle East shows that the money allocated to Catholic missions and to French-language schools increased several times, and by 1891 the effort had reduced the number and influence of the existing Italian schools to insignificance. Thus the Italian language, which had been the lingua franca of the Mediterranean since the fourteenth century, rapidly lost its place after the 1880s to French. Paris then mounted a massive campaign to convert every Christian community in Syria and Anatolia to Catholicism, dispatching special missions into the mountains to find the "lost" Christians, mainly the Nestorians, but also the Orthodox Greeks and the members of the old Eastern churches.[37] The French missionaries reminded the Christians of their historic ties to Rome and, using money and educational incentives, urged them to convert to Catholicism. At the same time, in France, the French intellectuals—including some agents of the French Security Office—were indoctrinating the growing number of Ottoman political refugees, mostly Muslim intellectuals known as Young Turks, in the antireligious positivism that eventually came to be known as "secularism."

Conclusion: The Consequences

The uses of religion for propaganda purposes by Europe and by the Ottoman sultan may be sharply contrasted. Whereas Christianity was used as the ideological weapon of colonial expansion, Islam was used in defending against colonialism. France censured pan-Islamism while conducting the most bigoted of religious campaigns in Syria and elsewhere. Though the English government did not adopt or finance openly a pro-Christian campaign in the Ottoman state, it subtly backed the Armenians and Greeks, especially after its relations with the Porte cooled. Ottoman foreign policy, which had been holding a course friendly toward England from 1878 to 1880, began to shift rapidly toward Germany. A few days after Gladstone delivered his speech in Manchester in 1889, the sultan hurriedly invited Kaiser Wilhelm to visit the Ottoman Empire, despite the inclement weather prevailing in November, to "strengthen and consolidate the unity and harmony" between the two nations. After the kaiser and the empress had visited the country and the kaiser had declared himself to be a "friend of the Muslims," the sultan insistently asked the Ottoman diplomats in Europe to appraise the international effect of his visit.[38] The Ottoman ambassador in Vienna reported that the emperor, during his passage through the Hapsburg capital, though affected by a severe cold, had expressed deep satisfaction with his visit in Istanbul.

The Germans already had studied the possible use of Islam in their foreign relations in the Middle East and were more than ready to try the *cihad* on their British and French adversaries.[39] Baron Max Von Oppenheim had spent more than three decades in the Middle East, including his appointment to Cairo in 1885, and had written voluminously on pan-Islam. Oppenheim believed that if Turkey participated in a war against England, it could incite other Muslims to rebel and tie down much of the British army and navy.[40] The German ambassador at the Porte in the late 1880s was also a believer in the power of panislam and looked for an opportunity to use it to solidify German political influence at the Porte. Nevertheless, although the German military advisers and capitalists had greatly increased the kaiser's influence in the Ottoman Empire after 1878, they had not ended the long-standing Ottoman ties to England. The Ottoman government began its drift toward Germany only after Gladstone's anti-Turkish speeches in 1889.

Despite his growing pro-German tendencies, however, Sultan Abdulhamid chose neutrality as his basic stand on foreign policy.[41] He seemed to think that the European powers were headed toward a violent confrontation and that neutrality would best serve Ottoman interests. The opponents of Abdulhamid, including the leaders of the Young Turks, on the other hand, believed that England and France were determined to divide and occupy most of the Ottoman lands in the Middle East, regardless of the government's policy and of Abdulhamid's hopes to preserve a degree of British friendship. The mutual vituperation and accusations had torn to pieces that friendship—if, indeed, it had ever really existed and isolated the Ottomans from their British and French "friends." Ultimately, in order to avoid total isolation from Europe and falling prey to Russian occupation, the government of the Young Turks concluded a secret military alliance with Germany on 2 August 1914. It was dragged into the First World War on 3 November 1914. Britain and France had wanted the Ottoman state to become their enemy formally, so that they would then be justified in partitioning its lands—as they in fact did, in 1918–22.

10

Continuity of Form, Change in Substance
Dynasty, State, and Islamism

Abdulhamid's efforts to intensify the unity of the Muslims living within the Ottoman boundaries and to increase his influence among Muslims living abroad have been cited by the sultan's admirers as proof of his dedication to Islam, and by his critics as evidence of his subversive pan-Islamic designs. It should be emphasized that Sultan Abdulhamid's "Islamic" and "pan-Islamic" activities remained confined mostly to religious matters, although their ultimate purpose was political; and Abdulhamid, as had his predecessors, used religious rituals of authority to secure popular acceptance for and loyalty to the emerging territorial (national) state. Indeed, the crucial process of acculturating the Muslim masses to a hitherto nonexistent territorial statehood (nationhood) would not have been possible without the manipulation of traditional symbols of authority through the medium of Islam. This chapter, therefore, will demonstrate how European symbols of territorial statehood were assimilated into the Ottoman political culture and will provide a synopsis of the sultan's main "Islamic–pan-Islamic" activities designed to adapt the cultural system to new conditions.[1]

As early as the 1830s, the Ottoman modernists felt the need to redefine the relationships among the ruler, the dynasty, the state, and the citizens. In order to depersonalize the state and authority and centralize the fragmented classical Ottoman Empire into a unitary type of state, the bureaucracy helped persuade Sultan Abdulmecid to manipulate the old symbols of authority, rulership, and faith in a way that would shift loyalty away from the sultan to the state. As this process of limiting the ruler's authority continued under Abdulhamid, despite his absolutism, it gradually made the sultan the representative, rather than the master, of the state.

At the same time, "Islamic" propaganda was used to strengthen the bonds of unity among the believers, to consolidate their loyalty, first, to the state and, ultimately, to the "nation." Islamic orthodoxy and propaganda was used to lay the groundwork for the acculturation of tradition to modern statehood, turn the *din-u devlet*—faith-state unity—into *din-i millet* or, national faith. The reformist sultans Mahmud and, especially, Abdulmecid did not pay much attention to the psychological dimensions of the reform—that is, the internalization of change. Sultan Abdulhamid, on the other hand, not only maintained the institutional (state) innovations introduced by his predecessors and accelerated the modernization of the community-society, but he also promoted internalization of the changes by labeling them "Islamic" and sanctioning them with his caliphal authority. He tried to enhance further the quasi-sacred position of the dynasty, the state, and the sultanate—without whose prestige he could not have carried out his reformist policies. Abdulhamid's efforts at modernizing the society were far more widespread and successful than those of his predecessors. Ultimately, however, he has been judged mainly on the basis of his absolutist rule, including his suspension of the constitution and the parliament of 1876; political (subjective?) judgment had superseded facts.

Harmony of Dynasty, State, and Faith

Almost half a century before the Tanzimat of 1839 brought about a drastic transformation in the meaning and function of the state, the process of change had begun under Sultans Selim III (r. 1789–1807) and Mahmud II (r. 1808–1839). Traditionally the state territory and all the objects and living creatures on it were considered to be the property of the dynasty, with all rights embodied in the incumbent sultan. Mahmud II expanded the ruler's prerogatives, making the state and the dynasty-sultan inseparable, both in theory and practice, from each other. He turned a legal fiction into a practical principle of government and personalized absolutism to a degree unknown in the past: the only instance to fit Max Weber's definition of "sultanism." In the process, perhaps inadvertently, he deprived the state monolith of its religious legitimacy and exposed all change in government to accusations of "heresy." Subsequently, all Ottoman reformers had to prove that they were not violating the faith. The situation thus created was in fact more prone to be affected by religious influence than the old system. The truth is that, in the classical Ottoman state, despite the fact that the *din-u devlet* theory made the state appear inseparable from religion, in practice the state had always acted freely as its interests dictated and, when necessary, used the faith to legitimize its acts. The spokesman for the faith was not the caliph but the *şeyhulislam*, who was theoretically free to act within his own sphere—although ultimately that freedom could be exercised only for as long as he did not challenge the state. Any group controlling the state could use the şeyhulislamate to legitimize its political supremacy, as did Mithat paşa and the Young Turks by asking the *şeyhulislam* to legitimize as ruler the sultan of their choice.

Abdulhamid tried, by neutralizing the *şeyhulislam*, to restore outward harmony between faith, state, and society—assuming that the absence of conflict, a result of the believers' failure to grasp the state subversion of official religion that had deprived the faith of creativity and resourcefulness—might be considered the criterion of harmony. The use by the state of the religious establishment for its own purposes hampered religious freethinking and ossified official Islam, rendering it dogmatic, rigid, formalistic, and lifeless. The state ignored the historical tradition of according the faith its own sphere of autonomy—a basic purpose behind the establishment of the şeyhulislamate in the fifteenth century. The internal disturbances, the destructive Celali revolts (1546–1655), and the military defeats and territorial losses in the period from 1596 to 1718 needed a popularly acceptable explanation; thus all these misfortunes were attributed to deviation from the faith, which in turn resulted in emphasis on ritualism and formal conformity.

The Köprülü period, lasting from the middle to the end of the seventeenth century, was marked by an increase in state power and arbitrariness and a subtle violation of Islamic precepts, even as the state was proclaimed the servant of religion. The Kadizadeler movement, the first fundamentalist Ottoman movement seeking to purify society (it condemned as *bida* tobacco, coffee, dancing, visits to saints' graves, etc.) was, among other things, a reaction to the state's inability to live up to its role as defender of the faith and its violation of the basic tenets of the faith. Ultimately, the difference between *ifta* (opinion on religious grounds) and *kaza* (legal opinion) became blurred; it disappeared in 1836–37, when the *kadiasker* (chief judge responsible to the grand vizier) was placed under the authority of the *şeyhulislam*. Thus the nineteenth-century reforms helped reveal the festering relations between the state and religion that had existed since the end of the seventeenth century and to redefine the caliph's position with regard to the state, dynasty, and community.

Abdulhamid placed the dynasty in the service of the state, and he went on to make the caliphate the representative of the Ottoman religious-political community. This de facto uncoupling of the caliphate from the sultanate was, in fact, the first step toward recreating autonomous spheres for the state and religion, leading to a sort of secularism in reverse—that is, freeing religion from state domination rather than the other way around, although that was not his intention. He tried to strengthen both the state—through a series of reforms in administration, education, and so on—and the community (*millet*)—through Islamic endeavors. (The discussion of this issue was the key debate taking place in Turkey in the 1990s.) The caliph now was free to act as the representative of all Muslims and to mold them into a new sociocultural whole, a sort of political community or protonation that would in turn call for a redefinition of the role of the state. The state could no longer claim to be the embodiment and agent of the faith, and it gradually began to function as a service organization, though without being able to shed its aura of supreme authority. Mithat paşa perceived these subtle changes in the meaning and function of the sultanate and caliphate, and he planned the formal separation of the two institutions; but Abdulhamid wanted to use the latitude gained by the caliphate to further strengthen his authority as sultan, despite the contradiction between the two polities. Abdulhamid declared, therefore, that the caliphate had priority over the sultanate, knowing that loyalty to the caliph in practice strengthened the sultan's position as the head of the dynasty and of the state, the structure and function of which had been broadened, diversified, and implicitly "secularized." The march toward liberating religion from its traditional subservience to the state had begun, despite claims to the contrary. In the next sections I shall analyze this process.

Old Rituals to Assure Loyalty to the Modern State

The Ottoman sultans recast traditional, often Islamic, symbols of authority and invented new ones in order to secure popular acceptance of the modernized state and its institutions. Preserved, yet changed, were old Islamic *biat* (acknowledgement of authority or allegiance to the new ruler) and the "coronation," the *kiliç kuşanmak* or *taklid-i seyf* (sword girding) of the sultan, which were among the oldest rituals of investiture. Sultan Abdulhamid paid special attention to the *biat*, which usually had taken place in the Topkapi Palace immediately after the old ruler's death or deposition. The *biat* eventually became *yemin*, or an oath of loyalty not to the sultan but to the state, even though the ruler was its recipient.

The sultans immediately preceding Abdulhamid had given the *kiliç kuşanmak*, which followed (several days or, in one case, a month) after the *biat*, a greater degree of pomp than in the past and turned it into a real coronation. An old Turkic tradition, it was basically a quasi-religious ceremony investing the sultan with the necessary sovereignty to rule the realm. The swords used belonged to the Prophet, or to Osman, the founder of the dynasty, or to Omar al-Khattab, the second caliph—the choice was significant only in the eyes of the beholders. The sword ceremony took place in the district of Eyüp on the Golden Horn at the tomb of Eyüb Ansari (Halid ibn-i Zeyd Ebu Eyyub al-Ansari). Because Eyüb was the Prophet's companion and standard-bearer, who died during the Arab siege of Constantinople in 672, he linked the Turks to Islamic history and stood for continuity with the past. The *kiliç alayi* (sword-girding procession, which included state dignitaries, ulema, and military personnel) used either a sea route going from the sultan's palace to Eyüp, returning by land, or vice versa, but it never followed the same route twice. The person who performed the girding could be the *nakibül eşraf* (the official in charge of the Prophet's descendants), the Çelebi of Konya (descendants of the mystic Maulana Rumi), or the *şeyhulislam*, but he was usually one of the first two. The ritual was retained to the end of the Empire, and Sultan Abdulhamid, who was "crowned" in this customary fashion, had the *şeyhulislam* do the girding.[2]

The adoption of an Ottoman "coat of arms" in the nineteenth century is a good measure of the changed nature of the relationship between the state, the dynasty, and the sultan. Some of the early Turkic groups and states had a sort of coat of arms, typically consisting of weapons and the usual lion, eagle, or wolf. For instance, that of the Turkic Cumans (Kipçaks) featured a lion with a star above and full moon below and was incorporated into the Magyar coat of arms after the Cumans settled in Hungary and were baptized as Catholics. The traditional Ottoman state, however, did not have a coat of arms or a state flag because the state could not be envisaged as an independent entity separate from the faith and the ruler. The search for a proper coat of arms in the late Ottoman state and even the early Republic proved to be difficult. During the era of the Young Turks the nationalist organization Türk Ocaklari (Turkish hearths) organized a competition to design a "national" coat of arms, and a similar competition was organized in the Republic by the education ministry in 1927. After considerable difficulty and changes of the original model, a Republican coat of arms finally was adopted.

Some scholars have described the *tuğ* (horsetail) as a sort of Ottoman coat of arms, but the *tuğ* actually designated ranking in the bureaucracy; the sultan's hat had five horsetails.[3] In the pre-nineteenth-century Ottoman state the *tuğra*, that is, the seal or monogram bearing the name of the ruling sultan, was used to stamp all documents and correspondence; each sultan had his *tuğra* (monogram) drawn by the *tuğrakeş* (master of *tuğra*s, or employee of the monogram service), who was part of the *nak-kaşhane* (inscribing-engraving-minting service) of the palace. The *tuğra*s appear on all official documents (*fermans*, called *irade*s after 1839) and on coins minted during a sultan's reign and, after 1856, were constantly changed by adding to them new decorative elements, such as scrolls and flowers. The term *tuğra* is of Oğuz Turkish origin. Its continual use among Turkish dynasties since the ninth century proves its rather unique Turkish character.[4] The *tuğra* epitomized the personal nature of the traditional state, in contrast to the coat of arms, which indicated that the state had acquired its own sphere of autonomy and was distinct from the sultan.

The idea of a coat of arms—*arma-i Osmani*—for the Ottoman dynasty was borrowed from Europe, along with its Italian name, by Sultan Mahmud II. This first Ottoman coat of arms had a *tuğra* as its centerpiece, supplemented by symbols of both religious and modern laws, signifying the state's continuity between the old and the new, and by other designs, such as sabers and roses, representing the sultanate and the caliphate. Sultan Abdulhamid retained this Ottoman coat of arms but embellished it further. The flag (*sancak, bayrak*), which in the past had had martial, religious connotations and a rather unique evocative power of its own, was also discreetly incorporated into the coat of arms, although the population long continued to regard the flag (a green one) mainly as the sacred symbol of the faith-state.

A similar process resulted in the adoption of military marches as the "national" hymn or anthem. The nineteenth-century sultans, commissioned the best-known European composers to produce "official" state marches, each of which bore the name of the commissioning sultan, while the old *mehter*, the traditional Ottoman military music, was all but ignored. The first march, commissioned by Mahmud II and known as the Mahmudiye, was composed by Giuseppe Donizetti (who was made a *paşa* and died in Istanbul in 1856) and expanded by Franz Lizst. The march Johann Strauss wrote for Abdulmecid in 1849 also was modified later, by Calistro Gualelli, who became a court musician in 1856 and, with the help of other European musicians, organized the Mizika-i Humayun (Royal Music) and the Harem Fanfari (Fanfare of the Harem). The former eventually became the Mizika-i Makam-i Hilafet (Music of the Caliphal Office) and was renamed the Riyaseticumhur Filarmonisi (Philharmonic of the Presidency) when it was moved to Ankara in 1924. Even though the caliphate was abolished in 1924, its official band thus survived. (The irony embodied in a Muslim caliphate with modern European music band is rather obvious.) Today the *mehter* has been revived in Turkey as the true expression of the national culture, while the sultans' marches are museum pieces. It has been asserted that all of these activities were intended to revive the old traditions of authority.[5] Actually, all of them, including the commissioning of marches, can be linked to the efforts of the dynasty to define its place in the new state structure.[6]

The introduction of medals (*nişans*) for "service and loyalty to the state" replaced the old idea that one served the faith and therefore was rewarded in the next world. The term for *nişan* can be translated as "mark," "seal," "engagement," "distinction," "chosen for approval," "target," and the like. The *nişanci* in the classical Ottoman bureaucracy was a high official in the correspondence department, chosen for his knowledge of the law, who legalized state documents on behalf of the sultan by placing the *tuğra* on them. In practice, however, deeds of bravery on the battlefield and loyalty to the ruler had been honored through some sort of remuneration, a fief (*timar*), a purse of money, and so on. A sort of gold medal called *madalya* (from the French *medallion*) seems to have been introduced in 1728, but it was retired twenty-three years later. The first *nişan*s offered as the symbol of state honor and gratitude for service were introduced by Sultan Mahmud II in 1832 and usually were granted to bureaucrats. In 1852 Abdulmecid introduced the *mecidiye* medal, of which there were five classes (the *mecidiye* was also a silver coin worth 20 kuruş [piasters]); and in 1862 Abdulaziz introduced the Osmani medal. Sultan Abdulhamid not only used the *nişan*s of his predecessors to reward followers, subordinates, tribal chiefs, communal heads, and foreign dignitaries, but also introduced a series of new medals, such as the Hanedan-i Ali-i Osmani (Ottoman Dynasty), Ertuğrul (the father of Osman, the dynasty's founder), Imtiyaz (Privilege), Şefkat (Gratitude-Affection). In addition, the sultan often supplemented the granting of these medals with gifts and periodic or regular pensions. Altogether there are about fifty-four categories of "Ottoman nişans."

The awarding of pensions, with or without a medal, became one of the most effective forms of royal patronage employed by Abdulhamid to secure loyalty to the state and enhance his influence as sultan-caliph. He also used imperial letters and invitations to the palace to reward individuals for services rendered to the state. As a result, there are in the Turkish archives approximately twenty-five catalogues known as Irade-i Taltifat (or Taltifat Iradeleri Kataloglari, in current Turkish) covering the period from 1876 to 1916. Because each of these registers lists an average of about 2,300 (for roughly a total of 100,000) letters of promotion, awards of medals, and other types of *taltifat* (honors, compensation) given to government officials, tribal leaders, and the like, an in-depth analysis of them could provide excellent insights into both the Ottoman state efforts to secure the citizens' loyalty and social-political ranking.

The medals granted were occasionally supplemented by jobs in the government, although Abdulhamid eventually tried to shrink the size of the bureaucracy, which had outgrown the treasury's capacity to support it. In the period 1777–97 the Ottoman scribe service had numbered just about two thousand, and the total bureaucracy probably consisted of no more than six thousand to eight thousand officials. In contrast, by Abdulhamid's time the total number of bureaucrats had reached seventy thousand, but this was reduced by about half by 1900.[7] Some of these new "bureaucrats" were actually the recipients of state (the sultan's) pensions, and they included Christians, for the largest number of non-Muslims entered government service during Abdulhamid's tenure.

The *aşiret mektebi* (tribal school), which deserves extensive study, was part of the sultan's effort to secure the loyalty of the Arab notables and tribal chieftains and to disseminate the new concepts of government among them. It was established in the Kabataş district of Istanbul in one of the imperial palaces in 1886 and was upgraded in 1892; its purpose was to train the children of notables and tribal chiefs—Arabs, Albanians, Kurds—in modern methods of administration, teach them Turkish, Ottoman history, and geography, and foster their loyalty to the state and the caliph.[8] The school was closed in 1907, however, after students started to show increased interest in politics, especially in national issues. The more capable graduates were allowed to enroll in the Mülkiye, the school of administration established in 1859 and upgraded into elite status in 1877, while others were enrolled in the Harbiye, the war college.[9] Abdulhamid admitted students from the provinces and overseas countries to the Mülkiye as a special royal patronage and assigned them the best positions upon their graduation. However, he did not want to undermine the school's quality, so he made certain the candidates were fully qualified for an institution that drew four or five candidates for each available place.

In sum, the Ottoman sultans' manipulation of the traditional emblems of authority and their adoption of new ones apparently was designed to increase their visibility among and acceptance by the population at large. On closer examination, however, it may be seen that these activities divested the dynasty of its traditional position as the absolute owner of the territory and all that lived on it and subordinated the dynasty to the state. This change was, in fact, the beginning of constitutionalism.

"Religious" Activities to Strengthen and "Nationalize" the Community (*Millet*)

Sultan Abdulhamid's religious activities, often described as "pan-Islamic" endeavors, were so many and varied as to defy easy generalization or a complete listing. Many revolved around ancient rituals that had been carried out routinely for centuries by governments, religious men, *vakif*s, and individuals as acts of piety or religious obligation. The sultan simply upgraded in scope and visibility the politically suitable rituals, turning some obscure ones into grandiose ceremonies and helping consolidate his influence on the community and consolidate Sunnism and the Hanefi legal school to which most Turks belong. At the same time, the sultan did his best to "sanctify" the memory of the founders of the Ottoman dynasty and portray them as the "fathers of the nation," although the ethnic implication was outwardly ignored. He furthered Abdulmecid's repair of the tomb of Ertuğrul Gazi, the father of Osman, at Söğüt and turned it into a religious-national shrine, while the tombs of Osman, Orhan, and other early Ottoman rulers in Bursa, the first Ottoman capital, also became shrines and the Muradiye cemetery in the same city became a sort of informal national monument. History was thus being subtly nationalized, idealized, and Turkified through religious acts by the most Islamist sultan to rule over the Ottoman state. These activities, hardly noticed or properly interpreted until now, appear to have been engaged in to assure the believers' loyalty and to enhance the religious stature of the sultan as the *amir al-muminin*; they in fact fostered a new image of society and state and facilitated the identification of the Muslim Turks, with their Ottoman past. Inadvertently, all these activities became part of an unplanned process of identity change, the beginning of ethnic Turkism and, ultimately, nationalism.

Sultan Abdulhamid's goal being the preservation of an independent Ottoman state, which, in turn, guaranteed the independence of the nation (the emerging Muslim *millet*) and perpetuated the dynasty and the faith, many of his "pan-Islamic" activities were aimed at preserving and perpetuating the Ottoman material legacy under the color of the religion. Thus the repair of the holy places in Mecca, Medina, and Karbala and of the mosques and *türbe*s (tombs) of dignitaries throughout the Ottoman Empire enhanced the caliph's position and influence but also Ottomanism; this was equally true for activities such as the upkeep of the holy places and the feeding of the population of the Hicaz, which Abdulhamid updated and regularized through administrative changes. The state won some recognition for repairing mosques, schools, and the like, a job performed in the past by the privately endowed *vakifs*. A random search of the *irades* (orders) issued by the Vakif Ministry, itself a "modern" reorganization of an old Islamic institution, for the repair of religious buildings over a twenty-four-year period reveals, among many others with varying purposes, orders pertaining to following establishments: the Mahmudiye school in Istanbul; the *medrese* of Tetimme-i Rabia, built by Mehmet II in Istanbul; a mosque in Jerusalem; the Beni Zekerya mosque in Nablus; the cobblestone pavement of the Haram of Mecca; the Beyazid mosque in Bolu; the Haydarhane mosque in Baghdad; Sofiyye tombs in Damascus; the Yazici Mehmed mosque of Yenice-Vardar; the Isahk paşa school; the wall of the cemetery at Eyüp-Istanbul; the Kuyucu Murad *medrese* in Vezneciler-Istanbul; and the Great Mosque at Benghazi. One order donated a piece of land that belonged to a Muslim *vakif* to Saint Mary's Church in Istanbul, since both the *vakif* and the church were religious and one should not be preferred over the other).[10]

Sultan Abdulhamid, of course, took a well-publicized leading role in the repair of the most prestigious—and politically sensitive—holy sites. He personally ordered the repair of the Ka'aba and the mosques in Medina, Karbala, and Necef, including the Atebat-i Aliye, the family tombs of Ali, the fourth caliph. When the incumbent shah expressed in 1890 a wish to repair Husein's tomb at Karbala, as his predecessor had done in the 1790s, the Ottoman government quickly allocated 162,000 kuruş to the project and gave credit to the caliph for the repair.[11] In other instances, the repair of holy places, such as the Haram in Mecca and Medina, was undertaken by the premier's office after due consultation with the *şeyhulislam*.[12] (Sometimes Abdulhamid provided funds from his own rich purse. The real estate of Sultan Abdulhamid, which today is claimed by his heirs and is subject to litigation in the Turkish courts, consisted of approximately 750 pieces of property, ranging from modest houses, through rows of apartments and stores, to extensive farms.) Although the sultan ordered that all Muslims be treated equally, in practice the bureaucrats of the *Vakif* Ministry gave preference to the Sunnis and to the Hanafi legal schools, appearing to discriminate against the Alevis—that is, Turkish Shiites. Often, religious unity and national interest clashed in the form of individual disputes. For instance, the custodian of Imam Abbas's tomb in Karbala, Seyyid Murtaza (whose mother was a close relative of Shah Fethali of Iran), was replaced by Seyyid Hüseyin on the advice of the Ottoman governors of Baghdad, Namik and Abdurrahim paşas. The two governors believed that the custodianship of important religious sites should not go to Iranians. Seyyid Murtaza, in a petition addressed to the sultan, claimed that he was a loyal Ottoman citizen and a member of the reserve forces, and he obtained redress.[13]

The Hicaz and the *hac*, as explained in the next chapter, acquired a central place in Abdulhamid's caliphal policy of securing worldwide Muslim support for his policies and primary of the Ottomans. Consequently, in order to preserve the caliph's visibility, the Ottoman governors prevented overly generous donations for the Hicaz by non-Ottoman Muslims and controlled the expenditures of funds provided by other Muslim rulers. In fact, the government declared in 1882 that the Hicaz was the only Ottoman possession in which foreign citizens, including Muslims, could not own real estate as they otherwise were entitled to do by a law passed in 1867. In Mecca, the clothing of the Ka'aba yearly in a holy mantle (*sitare-i şerif*) with the sultan's name embroidered on it took place amid pomp and publicity. The new cloth was taken to Mecca and the old brought back to Istanbul by a huge caravan of pilgrims, the *sürre alayi*, often consisting of as many as sixty thousand people from all over the world. For approximately fifty-five days the caravan proceeded on foot from Damascus to Mecca under the supervision of the *sürre emini*, an official appointed by the central government, spending each night in a *menzil*, a station for overnight stay. Much of the expenditure for the defense of and for a variety of services to the pilgrims was borne by the Ottoman government.[14] Under Abdulhamid the holy lands became a major center of communication as the Ottoman officials in Mecca and Medina distributed books, brochures, and specially printed Korans to the pilgrims.

The authorities paid special attention to the printing and distribution of the Koran, but not for the political reasons assumed by some scholars. Rather, as early as 1860 the government had imposed a prohibition on the import of Korans from Iran, Egypt, Kazan, and other places because of the possibility that they would have serious printing errors. After printing presses became reasonably priced, individual entrepreneurs without much education had sought quick profit by printing and distributing the sacred text; but in the process they had misprinted or sometimes had omitted material, thus altering the basic meaning of the text. The most widely used and officially authorized version of the Mushaf (Koran) was a lithograph copy by Al-Hajj Muhammad written at the order of Mahmud II (ca. A.H. 1249). In 1897 a total prohibition on unauthorized printing of the Koran was instituted, and the government established a monopoly on the sale of the holy book, only to see it abused by unscrupulous officials. The notorious Osman bey, who made a fortune from his monopoly on the sale of the approved Koran, invested his money in real estate in Istanbul in the fashionable district bearing his name today. Ultimately the Matbaa-i Osmaniye, a special press, was charged with the printing of holy texts rather than the Matbaa-i Amire, the official government printing house. (It is interesting to note that this official press, known initially as Takvimhane, is still functioning in Istanbul as Milli Eğitim Basimevi, the printing press of the National Education Ministry. It is another proof of institutional continuity from the Ottoman into modern Republican period.) (A new preoccupation with the accurate printing of the Koran emerged in the late 1980s in the Soviet Union, after the Soviet government granted its citizens freedom of worship. The four existing Soviet muftiates lacked the technical facilities and expertise to provide sufficient copies of the Koran to satisfy the huge popular demand. Many people refused to buy "communist" Korans and asked for Korans from Turkey, and Saudi Arabia, which donated one million copies. In the 1970s, Libya had furnished the Koran to Muslims in the Balkans and the Soviet Union; most copies were quickly sold on the black market at astronomical prices.)

A variety of other religious activities have often been cited to prove the sultan's support of "obscurantism, superstition, fetishism," and the like. These practices included the ostentatious display of objects supposedly owned by the Prophet or other Muslim Fathers and vesting deserving officials with the robe of honor (*hilat*) in the name of the state and the sultan. Conversions to Islam were encouraged, and converts in need of material help were provided assistance—a fairly modest effort to counter the efforts of European missionaries who had engaged in a massive campaign to show the "right Path" not only to the oriental Christians but also to the Muslims.

Christians and Jews were never forced to convert however. In fact, fourteen Arabs from Damascus, who had tried to force a priest to convert to Islam in about 1868, were punished with exile to Fezzan in the central Sahara. Even fifteen years after the sentence was passed, Abdulhamid hesitated to grant clemency to the culprits, despite his minister's argument that fifteen years of exile was enough of a punishment. The government did not prevent the missionaries from proselytizing but tried to regulate and restrict their activities and urged Muslim pupils not to enroll in missionary schools.[15] Nonetheless, after the 1890s a growing number of Muslims did enroll their children in foreign schools, including those of the missionaries, which offered a practical orientation and superior teaching techniques. Even in the Ottoman capital, Roberts College (now Boğaziçi University) became the preferred school of the Turkish elites. Again, the idea of worldliness and of material progress embodied in the state policy sanctioned by Abdulhamid as sultan had more effect than the religiosity he promoted as caliph.

The caliph's most effective and widespread endeavor to promote Islamic solidarity and attachment to the throne was undertaken in schools, for he believed that the individual's basic identities and loyalties were developed first in the family, then in the schools. The Ottoman sultan wanted to develop in the pupils a sense of ethics and their own religious identity but not to inculcate in them any feelings of hostility or hatred toward other religions or nationalities. The introduction of religious courses occurred chiefly after 1890 to counter the spread of nationalism and foreign missionary activity. This policy of using religion to teach ethics rather national hatred stands in sharp contrast to the practice in Balkan schools, as this writer, who received his primary and secondary education in a Balkan country, can testify. Celal Nuri, a well-known liberal could not understand how the Balkan Christian nations could use their religion to justify the cruel treatment inflicted on Turks in the Balkan War of 1912–13. He became a fierce nationalist and advocate of *milli kin*, or "national hatred," to mobilize the Turks for self-defense, but his advice went unheeded.

A long memorandum submitted to the sultan showed that the Muslim pupils were becoming alienated from their religion and growing uninterested in religious rituals and traditions. Sultan Abdulhamid believed this loss of interest in religion resulted from the inadequate teaching of Islam in schools and that the Muslim students attending foreign schools—in this case the Mekteb-i Sultani or Galatasaray in Istanbul, which used French as the language of instruction—were being brought up without attachment to their own faith. Moreover, he understood that Muslim students in the (American) Roberts College were praying together with Christian pupils under the direction of a *papas* (Turkish does not have a counterpart for "minister"; the usual term is "Protestant *papas*"—that is, "Protestant priest").[16] In an effort to counteract this growing indifference to the faith, the sultan ordered the establishment of a twelve-man committee to examine school curricula and propose changes likely to strengthen the students' religious feelings and their attachment to the caliph. He stated firmly that Islam was the "only bond that united so many [ethnically] different Muslim groups" and promoted unity, solidarity, and attachment to the state. In the same memorandum, however, the sultan expressed his respect for all the reforms undertaken since the early 1800s and reiterated his belief in the power of education and science to achieve progress.

The weakening of religious sentiment and attachment to traditional institutions affected not only sections of the modernist intelligentsia but also the general public. The Yildiz archives contain a large number of documents describing how Muslims let many mosques and other religious sites decay, while Christians were able to build churches and schools even in the remotest villages, thanks to their growing economic power. Many Muslims in the provinces actually regarded many public ceremonies such as *iksa-i hilat*—the undressing one and dressing the other dignitary with the kaftan (robe) donated by the sultan or vizier—as outdated or superfluous, though the central authorities insisted that they be continued. The intelligentsia, many government officials, and the public appeared to agree that the root of this Muslim lack of interest in religion lay in economic backwardness, the inability of the government to cure it, and traditional Islam's own aversion to "worldliness" and contemporariness.[17] Actually the phenomenon reflected a change of identity from religious to political Islam and a worldly, materialistic understanding of the faith. (Hi'at, killut, and khelaut from Arabic have the meaning of robe of honor.)

Overseas "Pan-Islamic" Activities

The sultan's relations with the Muslims in India, Sumatra, Java, Africa, Japan, and China have been subject to intensive debate for over a century and have often been described as part of Abdulhamid's "subversive" pan-Islamic endeavors. In fact, his relations with the Muslims in Asia and Africa, and especially in India, were purely religious in character, although overseas Muslims regarded these relations in a political light. They cannot be equated with his efforts to establish political unity and solidarity among the Ottoman Muslims.

The Indian Muslims, the heirs to the brilliant Mogul Empire, morally and financially supported the Ottoman state and the caliph throughout the nineteenth and early twentieth centuries in the hope that the caliph would help them maintain their Muslim way of life (see chapters 1, 7, 9). Nevertheless, the British administration in India feared that the Indian Muslims would turn their religious allegiance into active resistance if the sultan issued the call to *cihad*. They seemed to ignore the crucial fact that the Indian Muslims' frustration stemmed from poverty, lack of education, colonial rule, and the oppression of their own rich, "modernized" elites rather than from any lack of "freedom of religion"—which London had generously granted them. Sultan Abdulhamid was fully aware of the revolutionary potential of India's Muslims and London's fears, as he made clear in the following revealing statement.

> Everyone knows that a word from the caliph, the head of the Muslims, that is I, would suffice to inflict a great harm to the English authority in India. One does not need great intelligence to realize it. If Germany, Russia, and France had accepted my help [suggestion] during the Boer War in Transvaal, they could have destroyed the fictitious English castle in India, but they failed to act on time and thus missed the opportunity. That was the best time to ask England to account for its oppression of the Indians and for the violent, stern action undertaken against other nations. It was a pity that nobody used this [excellent] occasion. But there will come the day of revenge when the Indians [the sultan does not use the term *Muslim*] shall break the

English yoke and free themselves. India, which has a population of millions of people, shall easily oust the few thousand English who have oppressed them, the moment they truly desire to do so.[18]

The sultan had expressed his views only in the presence of palace intimates, but his words reached the ears of the British, who had managed to bribe and to use as a spy one of Abdulhamid's oldest and most trusted servants, Haci Ali paşa.[19] So, the "Islamic" threat widened further the rift between the sultan and the British.

Despite his potential to create trouble for the British in India, the sultan refrained scrupulously from becoming politically active there. He knew that the threat of *cihad* was more effective than the call itself. When the Ottoman government received permission to open consulates in Calcutta, Peshawar, and Karachi, in addition to the one in Bombay, it sought to appoint as honorary consuls local dignitaries who were good Muslims but loyal to the British. Some Indian Muslim publications eulogized the caliph; a number of mosques cited the caliph's name in the Friday sermon; Indian Muslims furnished continuous monetary assistance to Istanbul and celebrated the Ottoman victory over Greece in 1897; but there were practically no other pan-Islamic activities in India organized by Istanbul. The impact of the medals many Muslim dignitaries in India received from the caliph was actually rather insignificant. One unscrupulous official even offered the medals in exchange for 300-rupee donations. As a result, by 1895 many British statesmen, including Lord Curzon, came to believe that the caliph's political influence among England's Muslim subjects could be ignored as a foreign policy factor. However, many British remained firmly attached to their stereotype of Muslims so indoctrinated in their faith as to follow blindly the orders of their caliph.

This view survived into the twentieth century and influenced British policy toward the Turks in the Middle East. David Fromkin believes that Lord Kitchener's deficient understanding of the Muslim world and the misinformation supplied by his lieutenants has "colored the course of political events ever since." Thinking that Islam was a centralized and authoritarian religion and that Muslims obeyed their leaders and regarded religion as being everything for them, Kitchener and his followers assumed Islam "could be bought, manipulated, or captured by buying [or] . . . manipulating its religious leaders."[20] Consequently, he regarded the Turkish sultan-caliph as a continuing threat to the British position in British India and Egypt, and one that could undermine the Indian army, much of which was Muslim. This view prevailed also among some United States officials, although they viewed the Muslims as allies and asked the caliph to intervene on America's behalf in the Philippines. Abdulhamid had a keen interest in scientific developments and in the special constitutional status of religion in the United States. Because the sultan believed that American prosperity had resulted from a good accounting of the population and management of the national resources, he asked Samuel Sullivan Cox, the American ambassador in Istanbul and the organizer of the first modern U.S. census, to initiate the Turks into the study of modern statistics, one of the first of the exact sciences to be introduced in the Ottoman Empire.[21] This friendly Turco-American entente was followed by a more serious political one.

Oscar S. Straus, a Jew who was appointed U.S. ambassador to Istanbul in 1897 and served three times as minister and ambassador to Turkey, contrasts, in his memoirs, his own friendly acceptance by Istanbul with the Austro-Hungarian rejection of A. M.

Keiley as minister to Vienna "because Mrs. Keiley, being of Jewish parenthood, was *persona non grata.*"[22] Straus writes that in the spring of 1899 he received a letter from Secretary of State John Hay informing him that since the Turco-Greek War of 1897 the sultan had regained authority and respect among Muslims throughout the world. Furthermore, Hay suggested that because "his advisors thought the time propitious for him, as the religious head of Islam, to make known his authority to the Mohammedans of the Philippines, Java and neighboring islands . . . the Sultan under the circumstances might be prevailed upon to instruct the Mohammedans of the Philippines, who had always resisted Spain, to come willingly under our control." Straus then obtained an audience with the sultan and showed him Article 21 of a treaty between Tripoli and the United States which read:

> As the government of the United States of America is not in any sense founded on the Christian Religion; as it has in itself no character of enmity against the laws, religion, or tranquility of Musselmans; and as the said states never have entered into any war or act of hostility against any Mehomitan [*sic*] nation, it is declared by the partners that no pretext arising from religious opinions shall ever produce an interruption of the harmony between the two countries.

Pleased with the article, the sultan stated of the Philippines that the "Mohammedans in question recognized him as khalif of the Moslems and he felt sure they would follow his advice." Two "Sulu chiefs," who were in Mecca, were informed that the sultan and the American ambassador had reached a definite understanding that the Muslims "would not be disturbed in the practice of their religion if they would promptly place themselves under the control of the American army." Subsequently, Ambassador Straus wrote, the "Sulu Mohammedans . . . refused to join the insurrectionists and had placed themselves under the control of our army, thereby recognizing American sovereignty."[23] His account is supported by an article published in the *Journal of Race Development* (April 1915) by Lt. Col. John P. Finley, who had been for ten years the United States' governor of the district of Zamboanga Province in the Philippines. Finley wrote:

> At the beginning of the war with Spain the United States Government was not aware of the existence of any Mohammedans in the Philippines. When this fact was discovered and communicated to our ambassador in Turkey, Oscar S. Straus, of New York, he at once saw the possibilities which lay before us of a holy war. . . . [H]e sought and gained an audience with the Sultan, Abdul Hamid, and requested him as Caliph of the Moslem religion to act in behalf of the followers of Islam in the Philippines. . . . A telegram to Mecca elicited the fact that they not only visited Mecca in considerable numbers, but that at that very time there were Moros from Sulu in the Sacred City. . . . The Sultan as Caliph caused a message to be sent to the Mohammedans of the Philippine Islands forbidding them to enter into any hostilities against the Americans, inasmuch as no interference with their religion would be allowed under American rule.
>
> President McKinley sent a personal letter of thanks to Mr. Straus for the excellent work he had done, and said its accomplishment had saved the United States at least twenty thousand troops in the field. If the reader will pause to consider what this means in men and also the millions in money, he will appreciate this wonderful piece of diplomacy in averting a holy war.

The sultan's interest in America remained constant. For instance, he developed special concern for the American Indians because he was told that they were of ancient Turkic stock. Abdulhamid was the first foreign head of state to receive an invitation to the Columbian Exposition of 1893, held in Chicago to honor the four-hundredth year of America's discovery. Although the sultan did not personally attend, from Jerusalem alone a total of one thousand people came to visit the exposition and take advantage of the opportunity for Middle Easterners to become acquainted with America. The World's Parliament of Religions held its inaugural meeting at the same time in Chicago, so the sultan's officials, besides exhibiting a large number of Ottoman wares at the exposition, built a miniature mosque in Chicago to demonstrate in a concrete fashion what Islam was.[24] (The centennial meeting of this parliament was held on 29 August 1993, also in Chicago, but accomplished little.) The sultan had shown similar interest in celebrating the centennial of American independence; the Ottoman exhibit at Philadelphia contained a large number of books which were later donated to New York University, though in the 1960s the books still remained in their crates at the library.

An authentic "pan-Islamic" move aimed at establishing a sort of Muslim union was initiated, paradoxically, by the shah of Iran. After the Ottomans signed the Berlin Treaty in 1878 and ceded a substantial area in east Anatolia bordering Iran to Russia, the shah feared that Russia would soon move into Iran. Consequently he discussed with the Ottoman envoy in Tehran the need to establish a sort of league of Muslim states under the joint leadership of the sultan and the shah.[25] Subsequently the sultan sent to Tehran a supposedly secret emissary (though the English quickly learned about it). However, Iranian complaints that the Ottoman government gave support to such anti-Iranian rebels as Şeyh Ubaidullah, who in 1881 issued a call to *cihad* against the shah, and the Ottoman apprehension about Iranian-backed Shiite propaganda in Iraq put an end to the unity talks. National interest thus prevailed over religious solidarity.

Ottoman "Islamic" activities in South Asia were rooted in a variety of local economic, social, and political factors, and Islam conveniently provided the necessary legitimization and gave a universal dimension to local grievances; Istanbul's Islamic activities were a mere catalyst. Galip bey, the first Ottoman consul in Batavia in 1883, was a truly dedicated pan-Islamist. He asked that the caliph's name be cited in the Friday *hutbe* and established closer relations with the local ulema and notables; however, when Galip attempted to treat the local Muslims as though they were the subjects of the caliph, Istanbul reminded him that citizenship was a matter of international law and asked him to tone down his activities. (He was eventually replaced by Sadik bey, who was himself recalled after local Muslims accused him of being indifferent to Islam.) Istanbul did not allow the warship *Ertuğrul* to stop in any South Asian ports en route to Japan for an official visit, despite insistent demands by local Muslims and the extraordinary opportunity for the caliph to enhance his prestige and influence. Moreover, the much-heralded project to bring the children of South Asian notables to Turkey for study in Ottoman schools ended in fiasco; language difficulties and the lack of funds for educational facilities limited participation to just a dozen or so. Even the attempt to establish commercial relations with the area produced meager results.[26]

Japan was another country often described as the scene of pan-Islamic activities. These were limited to the individual efforts of some Muslims who went to Japan for a variety of reasons, including Abdurreşid Ibrahim, the Russian pan-Islamist, who wrote a book on the subject. The truly meaningful Ottoman-Japanese relations were nonreligious and were initiated at governmental level by the Japanese before Abdulhamid's enthronement. These relations were intensified after 1876, in part at the suggestion of England, and again in the period 1878–79, as a consequence of the Ottoman government's need for new international support. After Prince Kato-Hito visited Istanbul in 1881, improving Ottoman-Russian relations impeded the development of further rapprochement, beyond visits and the usual exchange of medals, until 1887. In 1889, the old warship *Ertuğrul*, repaired and equipped for a sea voyage, was sent to Japan, ostensibly in order to deliver the chief Ottoman medal to the emperor. The warship stopped briefly in Bombay and Colombo, where it was warmly hailed as a "free" Muslim territory, and in Singapore (for some repairs) but not in Java and Sumatra, in order to avoid either antagonizing the Dutch or appearing to endorse Dutch sovereignty over the Muslims. Upon reaching Japan in June 1890, the crew spent three months as the emperor's guests, but on the way back to Turkey the warship sank in a storm near the Japanese coast. All but seventy crew members were lost.

The Ottomans greeted the Japanese victory over Russia in 1905 with extraordinary enthusiasm, not only because it weakened the Empire's traditional enemy but also because it proved that Asians, including Muslims, could master modern science and technology. Abdulhamid showed considerable interest in Japanese Islam but opposed Ottoman participation in an international conference held in Japan, at which the conversion of the country to one of the monotheistic faiths was to be discussed.[27]

The involvement of Istanbul in China, where Islam had a long history and Muslims were numerous, began in 1900, largely at the request of Germany. Because Muslims played an active part in the Boxer Rebellion, the hard-pressed kaiser asked the caliph to use his religious influence to advise the insurgents to lay down their arms. The sultan accepted the proposition but asked to study the situation on the spot and dispatched a committee comprised of one representative each from the religious establishment, the military, and the administration and headed by Enver paşa (a descendant of Polish converts, he was known in the European circles of Istanbul as "Edward"). The mission reached China late in 1901, well after the rebellion had been put down and German concern had dissipated. Facing grave financial constraints in China, Enver paşa had to be repatriated overland through Russia. Much later, in 1906, a leading Chinese Muslim, Wang Kuan, was invited to Istanbul, and, at his request, four members of the local ulema were sent to teach Islam in China; and thanks to their efforts, after they returned to Istanbul, the Daru-l Ulumu-Hamidiye (Abdulhamid School of Science—House of Learning) was opened in 1908 in Beijing. The religious school flew the Turkish flag and had an initial enrollment of one hundred pupils. This activity in China, and similar sorts of missionary activity on the part of local Muslims or new settlers (in South Africa, for example) partly aided by Istanbul, are now cited as evidence of Abdulhamid's international "pan-Islamic" endeavor.

The caliph's activities among the Muslims living under European authority were mostly limited to purely religious matters. Furthermore, he often advised his diplomats and agents serving in Asia and Africa to refrain from political involvement in the affairs of the countries where they were stationed. There is no evidence that the sultan ever tried to organize or promote any sort of worldwide Muslim union. Much later a Muslim in England did attempt on his own to establish such a body but was unsuccessful. Even Eraslan, who is sympathetic to Abdulhamid's pan-Islamist activities wrote, "He used his caliphal title in the conduct of religious affairs but in administrative matters one can say that he made use only of his sultanate attributes."[28]

On the other hand, Sultan Abdulhamid was genuinely concerned about the Muslims' religious rights and the West's respect for Islam. For instance, he tried to dissuade the Comédie Française from staging Voltaire's play *Mohammad*, which portrayed the Prophet in a negative manner, and he asked the British government to repair the damage done by Christian zealots to a house used for worship by a group of Muslims in Liverpool. Likewise, the sultan demanded that the Romanian government punish a customs officer who had thrown into the sea a Koran found in the luggage of a Muslim. Nevertheless, when he sent a very respected scholar to Spain to rescue the manuscripts of the Cordoban caliphate, the sultan was accused of using the mission as a cover for pan-Islamic propaganda because his special emissary stopped in Morocco en route to Spain.

As caliph, Abdulhamid met with simple mullahs, dervishes, popular religious men, and even ordinary citizens from overseas, but he gave preference to traditionalist-minded notables, tribal chiefs, and religious scholars who did not pose a challenge to the existing political-social order or to his title as caliph.

He disliked and mistrusted the revolutionary popular revivalist orders, other revolutionaries, and freethinkers, knowing too well that they posed the most dangerous challenge to his elitist sociopolitical order. For instance, he treated the revolt of the first mahdi in the Sudan with suspicion, for he believed that the mahdi was an English agent; and he kept his distance from Urabi paşa of Egypt. He remained cool toward Ismail Gaspirali, probably the greatest Muslim modernist thinker and political activist of his time. He would not receive Gaspirali, who asked to see the sultan when on his way to Cairo to organize a Muslim international conference to study the economic, social, and educational conditions of the Muslim world. Abdulhamid befriended and decorated Mehmet Nureddin, the revolutionary mufti of Taşlica in Bosnia, who had taken a leading part in the populist uprising and resistance to the Austrian occupation of Bosnia and Herzogovina in 1878 and had participated in the League of Prizeren. After the Austrians complained about the mufti's revolutionary activities in Kosovo and Yeni Pazar (Novi Bazar), the sultan invited him to Istanbul, where he was received as a hero by the population and was decorated with a medal. When the Austrians complained that the mufti still continued his seditious activities in Istanbul and asked that he be neutralized by sending him into exile in Anatolia, the mufti, in an impassioned letter of loyalty and obedience answering a query sent secretly to him by Abdulhamid, assured the caliph that he remained at his orders and would not do anything unauthorized.[29] Always cautious, Abdulhamid categorically tuned down elaborate plans to celebrate the four-hundredth year (Muslim calendar) of the Ottoman assumption of the caliphate in 1517, lest this act antagonize the Arabs and bring forth a debate about the legitimacy of the Ottoman caliphate.

In truth, the political fervor in the Muslim world that helped the Ottoman caliph enlarge his influence overseas had a populist origin rooted in the structural transformation of the old order and the emergence of a new middle class represented by the modernist nationalists and revolutionaries such as Gaspirali, Urabi, Afghani, and their like, who increasingly opposed Abdulhamid's autocracy and, more significantly, his conservative view of Islam. Also among the opponents of Abdulhamid's absolutism were the Arab modernist-Islamists, such as Rashid Rida, Abdallah al-Nadim, Kassem Amin, Abd al-Rahman al-Kawakibi, Şekip Arslan, Ahmad Amin, Abul Kassem al-Shabi, to mention only a few. A new generation of Muslim intellectuals, created partly by the sultan's own schools were rapidly superseding him. They promoted the idea of an Islamic renaissance based on national and patriotic ideals, scientific education, individual awareness, respect for natural love, attachment to the land of one's birth, and a variety of similar sentiments and thoughts.[30] In Damascus, for example, a new body of nationalistic, reform-minded, religious thinkers, the intelligentsia of the new middle classes, who preached *ictihad* while attacking *taklid* (imitation, acceptance of precedence in toto) and the exclusive reliance on the four schools of law were on the rise.[31] Some prominent Damascenes, such as Abdulhamid al-Zahrawi and Tahir al-Jerzairi, a relative of Abdelkader, criticized the caliph for converting the caliphate (sultanate) into an instrument of oppression—as did Rashid Rida, whose *Muhawaret al-Muslih wa'l-Muqallid* (Conversations of the innovator and the imitator) was banned by Abdulhamid. (It was translated into Turkish in 1916 by Hamdi Akseki, a respected Islamist scholar who occupied high positions in Turkey.) Abdulhamid never came to terms with the new middle-class activists. Regardless of whether the new groups invoked European liberalism and modernism, Islamic reformism, or regionalism-localism to justify their position, the only legitimate elite in the eyes of the sultan was comprised of the religious establishment, the notables who accepted his authority, and the government bureaucracy—provided all were loyal to him.

To summarize, in the short run Abdulhamid's "pan-Islamic" activities popularized his name and greatly enhanced his prestige among Muslims overseas. At home, however, they helped ultimately provoke challenge from a new brand of opposition consisting both of intellectuals educated in the modern schools and of liberal, progressive, but also revolutionary, Islamists. A number of Nakşbandis, such as Şeyh Mehmed Esad of Erbil and Şevki Celaleddin, and many more Bektaşis, Kadiris in Syria, and even Mevlevi leaders became critical of the sultan's absolutism despite his Islamist policies. Abdulhamid managed to maintain in appearance a degree of cultural and political continuity in the Ottoman state, which enhanced his religious prestige and which proved in the end incapable of preventing the political revolution that he helped prepare and that ousted him.

Conclusion

The disparate and seemingly disconnected activities analyzed in the preceding pages actually revolved around two goals, the first of which was to create new symbols redefining the identity of the state on the basis of territory. As newly defined, the name *Ottoman*, for example, symbolized that the state no longer belonged to the house of Osman but represented the land, its people, and their collective political identity. The coat of arms, marches, and medals signified that the territorial state had become the supreme locus of loyalty and allegiance and that the sultan was its representative. In order to maintain a sense of continuity, various traditional symbols and practices were amended and incorporated into these new ones, although their function and meaning changed substantially. The *tuğra*, which had been unique to a specific sultan, now was encompassed in the state coat of arms, just as the sultanate-dynasty became a hereditary institution, part of and subordinate to the state rather than its absolute master and personification. The allegiance to the territorial state, that is, Ottoman patriotism, shifted the duty of sacrifice and devotion from Islam to the fatherland by describing them as being one and the same.

The second goal of Abdulhamid's activities was to preserve the integrity of the Ottoman state and of the faith by uniting the Ottoman Muslims in a religious bloc centered on the caliph. It was his actions pursuant to this goal that added a political dimension to the Muslims' religious consciousness. Religion in the hands of the state became an ideological means of political mobilization. Because the sultan used his authority as caliph—the head of the *ümmet*—to disseminate this politicized Islamic identity, it was internalized as the de facto political identity of all Muslims and of the state but not by Christians who were formally part of the state but not of the nation.

Problems arose because the sultanate, as the representative and chief executive office of the state, became separated from the caliphate. This separation created a true dilemma as to whether the territorial state or the faith was the primary source of the citizens' political identity and loyalty, for the original theory of caliphate did not recognize duality in either the sultan-caliph or the state-community. The Ottoman sultans had avoided conflicts between state and religion until the sixteenth century, when the House of Osman assumed the title of the caliph as an accessory to that of the sultan and along with the title, a variety of practical obligations toward Muslims. However, the state remained supreme: it preserved the caliphate but made it politically powerless. The political revival of the caliphate under Abdulhamid created de facto state-caliphate duality and brought the faith into potential conflict with the reformed territorial state, which was, in fact, the material foundation of the caliphate.

The irreconcilable conflict over demands for loyalty and allegiance between the territory-based state and the community-nation rooted in religion soon became apparent. The state assumed an increasingly material and territorial orientation—that is, a "secular" attitude—as the new elites began to regard modernization, science, and progress as its true goals. In contrast, the basis of the community was still religion, the spiritual essence of which could not be reconciled with either the "secular," territorial-material character of the state or, ultimately, with the absolutism exercised on behalf of modernity. The de facto separation of the faith and state that prevailed during the early Ottoman centuries and had begun to reemerge during Abdulhamid's rule was finally eliminated completely when the state assumed control of the faith in the name of secularism.

Although Abdulhamid used his caliphal authority to defend the dignity of Islam and the religious rights of Muslims, the effectiveness of his actions actually depended on his position as head of state. In this capacity, he observed the norms of international law by respecting the sovereignty of other states, and his so-called pan-Islamic endeavors abroad were largely symbolic personal gestures.

11

The Harameyin, the Caliphate,
and the British Search for an Arab Caliph

The New Roles of the Caliphate and the Hicaz

After 1880 the Hicaz became crucial, both practically and symbolically, to Sultan Abdulhamid's policy of integrating the Ottoman Muslims into a cohesive community and expanding his religious influence overseas. As the holy sites for the annual Muslim pilgrimage, Mecca and Medina (nineteenth-century neo-Sufism made the latter especially important) both became centers of indoctrination and legitimization of the sultan's efforts to turn the caliphate into a de jure universal Ottoman Muslim institution. More efficient and less expensive transportation increased the number of pilgrims in the second half of the nineteenth century, while the availability of written information and more advanced education had enhanced the *hacis'* intellectual development and political awareness. As a result, Abdulhamid now faced a new generation of politically awakening Muslims.

An enlightened, critical audience could find reason to question the legality of Abdulhamid's own title to the caliphate. Indeed, the British, the French, and the khedive of Egypt all questioned the Ottoman sultan's claim to the office. Thus the caliphate was subjected to historical and theological scrutiny, which showed that the meaning and function of the original office had undergone profound change. In order to understand the change—and the Ottoman sultans' holding of the caliphate—it is necessary to examine the institution from the Ottoman vantage point.

The term *caliphate* is derived from the Arabic *halifat rasuli-llah* (the successor to the Prophet); but the caliphate was a strictly political institution, not based on any commandment, despite some vague allusions to some such institution in the Koran, but on the sheer practical necessity of appointing a leader to head the Muslim community after the Prophet's death in A.D. 632.[1] Discussion of whether the original caliphate was an elective office, an inheritable monarchy, a special type of prophet-kingship, or an administrative office created by the free will of the community is outside the scope of this study.[2] In any case, the Ottoman sultans became the holders of the office during the reign of Sultan Selim I (1512–20). The conqueror of Syria and Egypt, Selim I is supposed to have accepted the title officially from the Abbasid caliph al-Mutawakkil, in a ceremony held in the mosque of Aya-Sophia (church of Hayia

Sophia) in Istanbul; but there is absolutely no record of this event, despite the Ottoman government's claim that it occurred. Several other Muslim rulers, including the
Baburids of India, and even the imam of Yemen, also claimed to be caliphs, largely
on the basis of their protection of and service rendered to Islam and the Islamic cause.
Their claims, and those of earlier Ottoman sultans such as Beyazid II (r. 1481–1512),
who stated that he was entitled to be caliph because he was the best fighter in the cause
of Islam (*afdal al-guzat wa'l-mujahiddin*), were all weak, however, as none of these
leaders controlled the Hicaz. Beyazid's son, Selim I, however, was on his way to
becoming the actual protector of the two Muslim holy sanctuaries (Khadim al-
Haramayn al-Sharifyan).[3]

The Ottoman claim to the caliphate became truly meaningful when Suleyman the
Lawgiver (r. 1520–66) established his sovereignty over the Hicaz and, thus, actual
custody of the holy cities. Over the course of the sixteenth century, service to Islam
and to the Muslim community, including the power to guarantee the safety of pilgrims
and access to Mecca, emerged as the chief legitimizing condition for the claim to the
caliphate, supplanting the view that the caliph should descend from the Prophet's
tribe—the Qureyish. In other words, practical considerations now took precedence
over genealogy and became central to Ottoman arguments for the legitimacy of their
hold on the caliphate. Jalaladdin Dawwani (ca. 1427–1502), whose views found great
favor at the Ottoman court, argued that the real caliphate lasted only thirty years
after the Prophet's death and that circumstances afterward were such that a righteous
ruler could hold the caliphate if he governed with justice and enforced the Şeriat as
the law of the community. This theory marked an important departure from the
orthodox views on the caliphate put forth by al Mawardi (974–1058), the *kadi* of
Baghdad, in his *Kitab al-Ahkam-Sultaniyye*.[4]

The Ottoman historian and grand vizier Lutfi paşa (d. A.H. 970/A.D. 1562) asked
whether "it is permissible to apply the name of Imam and Xalifa to the sultans when
they are of other than Quraish" descent and proposed to answer his own question in
order to achieve "cessation of doubt and acquisition of certainty." According to Lutfi
paşa, "What is meant by the Xalifa is he who commands to the good and prohibits
evil. If the conditions mentioned above are combined in one person, to wit, conquest
. . . [,] maintenance of Faith with justice, command to the good and prohibition of
evil, and the general leadership—then he is a Sultan who has a just claim to the application of the name[s] of Imam and Xalifa and Wali and Amir without contradiction." In Lutfi paşa's opinion present circumstances called for the use of criteria other
than membership in the Qureyish tribe—namely, the maintenance of the faith "in
the requisite manner over all the peoples subject to him, and the Osmanis were blame-
less in the maintenance of the Faith and Equity and the Jihad."[5]

During the era of the Young Turks, Şeyhulislam Musa Kazim defined the caliphate as a position bestowed on someone who met certain conditions and thus was
charged in the name of the Prophet with the protection of the faith and the governing of worldly affairs. Moreover, he said, the Muslims had the absolute obligation to
obey the caliph (but were excused from so doing if he failed to fulfill his duties).[6] The
revival of the caliphate is attributed to the Treaty of Küçük Kaynarca, signed in 1774
with Russia, which included a provision that the Muslims under Russian rule would
cite the caliph in the Friday *hutbe*.[7] In the twentieth century some Muslim writers,

such as Ali Abdul Raziq (1888–1966) claimed that the monarchs spread the belief that the caliphate was a religious institution "so that they could use religion as a shield protecting their thrones against the attacks of rebels."[8] The Young Turks abroad published in Cairo in 1896 a pamphlet entitled *Imamet ve Hilafet Risalesi* (reissued in 1908), which used Islamic arguments to challenge the sultan's violation of the caliphate's functions, much in line with Wilfrid S. Blunt's argument that Abdulhamid managed to reconcile Islam with an Ottoman caliphate thanks only to his political power. In any event, by the end of the nineteenth century, although few people noticed or seemed to care, the sultan had ceased to be the caliph of the Ottomans and had become the caliph of the modern-age Muslims.

The transformation in the meaning of the caliphate resulted both from the sultan's own political decision and from the Muslims' yearning for a central Islamic institution to speak on behalf of all Muslims and, possibly, to mobilize them around common goals, assure them political independence, protect their cultural and religious integrity and dignity and, above all, to oppose European occupation. In the eyes of many Muslims, the survival of the caliphate became synonymous with the existence of the faith itself.

The pressure to change the caliphate into a central, universal Muslim institution was first felt as early as the reign of Abdulmecid (1839–61), but he seemed rather unwilling to stress his caliphal authority or extend it to non-Ottoman Muslims. The next sultan, Abdulaziz (r. 1861–76), became more interested in the potential of the caliphate to enhance his imperial authority, especially against the liberal constitutionalist wing of his own bureaucracy—notably the powerful Tanzimat group ensconced in the foreign ministry and its intellectual offspring, the Tercüme Odasi (Office of Translations). But initially it was the reformist bureaucracy that, eager to enhance the international standing of the Ottoman state, adopted a positive attitude toward pan-Islamic appeals from non-Ottoman Muslim leaders. They turned against Sultan Abdulaziz and covertly discussed the separation of the sultanate from the caliphate after the sultan began to use the caliphate to bolster the throne's authority. Thus, the so-called separation of religion from politics in the Ottoman Empire did not originate in questions of philosophy and dogma but, rather, in the mundane desire for power. In the process of supporting their own positions, both the sultan and the bureaucracy devised ingenious, often fictitious, arguments that distorted the meaning of the caliphate, secularism, and religion and culminated in the abolition of the caliphate in 1924.

Sultan Abdulhamid II's use of the caliphate as a means of domestic and foreign policy was not a planned action. A committed Muslim, he was determined to preserve the Islamic character and survival of the Ottoman state and dynasty by enlisting the support of the community, revitalizing the state, and curtailing European interference in Ottoman affairs. Abdulhamid sought to weaken the argument that the caliph should descend from the Qureyish tribe by reviving Lutfi paşa's argument that service to Islam was sufficient to legitimize the caliph's position. In his view, the service to Islam did not consist solely of keeping the holy sites in good condition and assuring the safety of the *hac*, as his ancestors had done; it entailed the worldwide defense of Islam and of the religious rights of Muslims living under foreign occupation. Şemseddin Sami, in accordance with this view, defined the caliph as "Deputy of the Prophet and the imam and emir [head] of all Muslims, who has the sacred duty to protect the Islamic şeriat";[9] and Cevdet paşa claimed that "it was an Islamic requirement to obey and submit to whomever has the power and majesty" ("şevket ve kudret sahibi her kim ise ona itaat ve inkiyad teraiz-i islamiyedendir").[10]

Once Mecca had become the center for propagating the caliph's new image as the spokesman for and defender of Islam as a whole, maintaining Ottoman sovereignty over the Hicaz at all costs acquired primary importance. Consequently, the maintenance of peace and harmony between the two administrators exercising authority, respectively, over Mecca and the Hicaz as a whole became critical. The administration of the holy sites in Mecca was in the hands of the *şerif*, or *amir* (emir), of Mecca, who was descended from Prophet Muhammad's family and exerted considerable influence on the Hicazi people, particularly on the tribes. The emirs came from the Awm (Abadile), Zeyd, and al-Berakets families, who competed with one another for the post. The province itself was administered by the *vali* (governor) bound to Istanbul. The Ottoman *vali* stationed in the Hicaz, therefore, represented the temporal or administrative power, while the emir, although appointed by the sultan, represented what may be called the spiritual dimension of authority. Thus, the most apparent area for an Ottoman clash with the Arabs, from a doctrinal and historical viewpoint, was the Hicaz. Eminent scholars claimed, erroneously, that the "usurpation" of the caliphate by the Ottoman sultans was the principal cause of the Arab-Turkish rift.

The Arab Emir and the Ottoman Vali in the Hicaz

The loyalty of the *şerif* of Mecca to the caliph appeared essential, not only for assuring the Ottoman rule over the Hicaz but also for providing de facto legitimation of the caliph's title. Many Arabic-speaking people in the Hicaz, as well as in Syria and Egypt, regarded the emirs/*şerif*s, who descended from the Prophet's tribe, as the true and legitimate rulers of the holy cities. In fact, many Arabs from the Hicaz, where tribal ties remained strong, were aware of the special place of their province in Islam and tried to maintain a sort of "purity," resisting assimilation into the Ottoman elite by refusing to attend Ottoman schools or to enter the Ottoman civil service.[11] The Ottoman government, in turn, treated the Hicaz (and especially Mecca) as an autonomous entity and showed the emirs of Mecca vast respect. For instance, the sultan stood while receiving the emir to signify deep respect for his ancestry; but, unlike some of the harem women, not a single Ottoman sultan ever performed the *hac* during the tenure of the dynasty, which lasted for over six centuries (1286–1922). Only Sultan Osman II, who was killed by Janissaries because of his reformist intentions, expressed a desire to go on the *hac*. Mehmet II, after conquering Constantinople in 1453, sent emissaries with gifts to Mecca. His heir, Beyazit II, followed the Mamluk model by creating the office of *naqib-ul eşraf*, whose main responsibility was to keep the records of the *eşraf* (plural of *şerif*), the descendants of Hasan and Huseyin, the Prophet's grandsons. The punishment of the *eşraf* (not to be confused with the *ayan-eşraf*, or notables) was the responsibility of the *naqib-ul eşraf*, even for ordinary crimes.[12] The sultan appointed the emir through a special document known as the *mensur* (lit.

prose), which included a series of perfunctory phrases of praise for the emir but, with the exception of some general advice, did not contain instructions.

The special status of the Hicaz was maintained roughly from 1601 until its conquest by the Wahhabis in the early 1800s. When Mehmet Ali's son Ibrahim defeated the Wahhabis and subdued the Hicaz, he appointed a military officer as the *vali* of Mecca and reduced the emir to the role of a simple functionary. After the restoration of Ottoman rule in the Hicaz in the 1840s, Istanbul returned both the *vali* and the emir to their old positions and granted the latter the traditional respect and honored him with the title of *paşa*. Some members of the emir's family who had taken refuge in Istanbul during the Wahhabi occupation of Mecca continued to live in the Ottoman capital. Some were given a handsome stipend and later occupied positions in the government, including a seat in the Council of State, Şura-i Devlet.[13]

The emir's main income came from half of the customs revenues collected at Jeddah, and he derived additional profits from the annual Ottoman subsidies for the maintenance and repair of the holy sites, as well as from the import and distribution of wheat to the Hicaz. The relations between Mecca and Istanbul were thus buttressed by mutual dependency: the emir received economic and military support from the sultan, who gained legitimacy and acceptance by having the emir acquiesce to his political authority and help assure the pilgrims' safety, access to the holy sites, and the tribes' loyalty. Besides certain religious jurisdiction over Mecca, the emir also had the authority to appoint some officials in the city, such as the market inspector (*muhtasib*) and the heads of the guilds and of the city quarters.[14] Aware of his potential political influence, the Porte often instructed the appointed *kadis* (judges) of Medina and Mecca to report on the emir's activities. Every year the sultan confirmed the emir in office, leaving no doubt as to the primacy of the political power—and of the purse. The buildings and offices of the two holy mosques (the Haram-Harameyin) in Mecca and Medina were administered by two *şeyhs*; the *şeyh*, or *muhafiz*, of Medina was often the Ottoman governor of that city, and the duty of management of the mosque in Mecca was merged with the governorship of the Hicaz in 1864. The imams (prayer leaders), muezzins (announcers of prayer) and the heads of the maintenance personnel were responsible to the *şeyh* of the Haram. There were also some muftis (experts or interpreters of religious law in the technical sense) appointed by Istanbul for both holy cities.

Just as Abdulhamid knew that the Hicaz offered him a unique platform for the advancement of his influence in the Muslim world, it also could imperil the legitimacy of his claim to the office. The British knew that they could undermine Abdulhamid's caliphal legitimacy, prestige, and influence if they could establish the principle that Abdulhamid was not a bona fide caliph, since he did not descend from the Qureyish. As a result, after the Porte's relations with London deteriorated around 1880, it was British policy to promote the ethnonationalist view that the *şerif* of Mecca, an Arab, was the rightful caliph, while the Ottoman sultan, a Turk, was a usurper. The first British plans to manipulate the caliphate surfaced in 1877, some five years before Wilfred S. Blunt (1840–1922), a foreign ministry official from 1859 to 1868, who has been given undue credit for his efforts to separate the Arabs from the Turks, launched the idea of an Arab caliphate and published his views on the subject.[15] In any case, through a representative in the port of Jeddah, some forty miles west of

Mecca, the British had secured a unique strategic advantage that they utilized to control the Indian pilgrims, to gather information, and to influence the emir and the local *şeyh*s. A series of documents in the Ottoman archives indicates that Abdulhamid was fully aware of British intentions and the means at their disposal and did his best to counter their propaganda.[16]

The Ottomans did not have the economic and military capacity to oppose the British. The sultan knew that a miscalculated *cihad* could backfire, triggering European reprisals that the weak Ottoman state could not withstand; but he divined that the threat of *cihad*, if properly manipulated, could produce suitable results. The threat would remain credible, however, only so long as the sultan maintained intact the integrity of his credentials as caliph and kept Harameyn under his full authority. There were domestic critics also who questioned his use of the caliphate to augment and legitimize his temporal power. Some constitutionalists had already advanced the view that if the caliphate were separated from the sultanate and transferred to the emir of Mecca, the *şerif* would become the spiritual head of the Muslims, and the sultan would be compelled to use constitutional means to legitimize his authority. Gabriel Charmes, who traveled through the Ottoman state and spoke with many constitutionalists, claimed that Mithat paşa wanted to consolidate the constitutional regime by granting a large degree of autonomy to the Hicaz and even to other Arab provinces and possibly to appoint the emir as caliph, thus separating the caliphate from the Ottoman sultanate.[17] As mentioned previously, Mithat paşa was known to maintain relations with British and was suspected by Abdulhamid of wanting to depose him. Mithat's relations with the British continued even after his death sentence was commuted to life in Taif prison. Attempts to poison him there were thwarted after the British embassy in Istanbul informed Mithat's family about these plots. Mithat regarded the French as the idealistic champions of individual freedom and contacted their diplomatic representative in Jeddah on 4 January 1883, asking for help for himself and two friends to escape from prison. On instruction from Paris, the French in Jeddah turned him down. It should be noted that Mithat had initially sought asylum in the French consulate in Izmir in May 1881 but had been persuaded to surrender to Ottoman authorities. Eventually he was arrested, with the promise of an open and "fair" trial, which ended by condemning him to death for planning Abdulaziz's murder. The truth is that neither the French nor the English and nor, least of all, the Russians liked Mithat paşa, because of his nationalism and reformism.[18]

The ousted khedive (*hidiv* in Turkish) Ismail of Egypt decided to avenge his dismissal by Sultan Abdulhamid (in agreement with the British) in 1879 by challenging the sultan's right to the caliphate. Ismail used *Al-Khilafeh*, published in Naples by his former secretary, Ibrahim al-Muwailihi, to challenge the sultan's caliphal title, and he financed the publication of *Al-Ittihad* in Paris for the same purpose; but he did not propose an Arab to replace the sultan. The Ottoman embassy in Paris confidentially informed the foreign minister that a brochure, written by Ibrahim bey Melhi (Muwailihi) and questioning the sultan's caliphal title, was being shipped secretly to the Hicaz for distribution among the pilgrims. The Ottoman government alerted the customs authorities in the Hicaz to confiscate the material if the first attempt to do so in Naples failed.[19]

The Emirs and the British

By 1880 the British had concluded that the Hicaz was becoming a major power base that the caliph could use to incite the Muslims of India to revolt. As early as 1876 the British resident in Aden had been instructed to keep a close eye on the pilgrims from India. Subsequently, James Zohrab was appointed as the British consul in Jeddah, and, treating the emir as a true sovereign, Zohrab persuaded him to send a mission to advise Sher Ali of Afghanistan to come to terms with Britain because "Islam needed the British protection." Zohrab believed that the *şerif*'s word carried a greater weight among Muslims than the sultan's, for the *şerif* was a direct descendant of the Prophet and represented the spiritual side of Islam, while the sultan embodied its political aspect. As Ram Lakhan Shukla explains, "While preparations for the mission [to Afghanistan] were under way Zohrab exploited the disaffected Arabs to promote the scheme of detaching the Arabs from Turkish rule and bringing them under British influence in collusion with the pro-British Şerif Hüseyin Pasha." In Zohrab's view, Turkey had ceased to regard England as a friend—meaning that Turkey refused to comply with British instructions—so London had to use a new weapon to compel the sultan to adopt a pro-British policy.[20] Zohrab believed a British protectorate over the Hicaz would put the *şerif* outside Ottoman control and allow Britain "to guide the whole Mussulman world."[21] British ambassador Henry Layard in Istanbul shared Zohrab's views but advocated caution. All the preparations came to a halt, however, after Şerif Hüseyin paşa was assassinated in March 1880 by an Afghan resentful of his support for Britain's policy in Afghanistan. In Hüseyin's place, Abdulhamid appointed as *şerif* Abd al-Muttalib (Abdulmuttalib or Muttalib) from the rival Zeyd clan. Muttalib was ninety years old, fiercely anti-British, incorruptible, and independent.

Muttalib had held the position of emir from 1851 to 1855, but he had been ousted for his antigovernment, antireformist activities, including a revolt he started to oppose the abolition of the slave trade. In order to ingratiate himself with the sultan, Muttalib informed Abdulhamid that members of the Aun (Awn) family had plotted with his liberal enemies in Istanbul to secure Abdulaziz's ouster in 1876.[22] During his short tenure (1880–82), Muttalib managed to secure the dismissal of two *valis*, Naşid and Saffet paşas, and the appointment and then dismissal of Haci Izzet paşa to the same position. He accused the *naib* of Medina, Tahsin ağa, of mistreating the ulema and then censured the *şeyhulharem* (the custodian of Medina), Hayrullah efendi, a former *şeyhulislam*, for lacking modesty and *adab* (ritual courtesy) and for failing to take proper care of the holy buildings.[23] In his offensive against the Ottoman-Turkish personnel in the Harameyn, Muttalib appeared emboldened by the fact that the pilgrimage in 1881 took place without major incidents and the epidemic diseases remained under control; he took credit for both.

Indeed, an outbreak of cholera in September 1881 caused 157 deaths the first week but only 42 deaths in the second week of the pilgrimage, thanks, not to Muttalib's prayers, but to the measures taken by Nuri efendi, a major in the Ottoman army.[24] Already following the recommendations of the Mixed Sanitary Conference held in Istanbul in 1865, the Ottoman government had established a health commission in the Hicaz, put in effect a quarantine in Jeddah, and installed a permanent doctor in Mecca. In 1881 the government cautioned the British and the French about the health danger likely to result from the increase in pilgrims from their lands. This warning played into the hands of the French administration in Algeria, which tried to limit the numbers making the pilgrimage, allegedly because the pilgrims returned with weapons and appeared prone to challenge French rule; but the French Foreign Ministry supported the pilgrimage so that the pilgrims could compare the relative security and prosperity of Algeria with the dire poverty of the Ottoman lands.[25]

Eventually the *vali* of Hicaz decided to settle scores with Şerif Abd al-Muttalib. Osman Nuri paşa, *vali* for over ten years, from 1881 onward, ousted and jailed Muttalib for "plotting" with the British to instigate a new revolt against the Porte, on the evidence of some "intercepted" letters. The move was not unwelcome. The Hicaz population was so pleased to learn about the dismissal of Muttalib that in Naka, one of the quarter of Mecca, the excess of joy resulted in the death of some sixty people when the firing of their rifles ignited some ammunition.[26] British dispatches from India show clearly that Muttalib's so-called letters of sedition were actually prepared by British officials, who managed their "interception"; Osman paşa himself used a fake *ferman* (decree), supposedly sent by the sultan, to depose Abd al-Muttalib but was not reprimanded for his actions. The British simply wanted their archenemy, Muttalib, replaced by the more docile, pro-British Awn al-Rafiq (1852–1905). The British took seriously the emphatic advice of Consul Zohrab that "England having at least 60,000,000 Muhammedans under her rule must feel deeper interest in the man who is supreme in Mecca than [does] the sultan who has but 16,000,000."[27] Once installed, al-Rafiq remained in power for over two decades and managed to maintain excellent relations with the British, the Porte and the Ottoman *valis*, especially Ahmed Ratib paşa (1893–1908). The Ottoman officials, however, remained highly suspicious of the emir. Osman Nuri paşa tried to reduce the authority of the *şerif* to insignificance, but Awn al-Rafiq protested and moved from Mecca to Medina, while the notables and the tribes of the Hicaz prepared to rebel. Osman paşa was removed to another post but remained in the good graces of the sultan. Meanwhile, Muttalib, who was over one hundred years old, died in 1887 in his well-guarded villa in Medina.

From 1886 onward the new emir and Sultan Abdulhamid remained on friendly terms, although al-Rafiq developed increasingly close relations with the British and lost much of his local support because of incompetence, maladministration, and tyrannical behavior. Butrus Abu-Manneh believes that Abdulhamid kept al-Rafiq in this influential position for so long just to show the Muslims how indispensable the sultan was to the Islamic world so that they would come to disregard the saying that "imams are from Qureyish."[28] In other words, the astute sultan was making the point that he served the Muslims better than the Prophet's own descendant. Abdulhamid's main reason for keeping al-Rafiq as emir, however, was the latter's disinclination to challenge Abdulhamid's credentials as caliph. The Ottoman officials serving in the Arab lands, including the high commissioner of Egypt, Ahmet Muhtar paşa, advised the sultan in 1894 to abolish the emirate and concentrate all authority in the *vali*'s hands, but the sultan refused since the emir played an important role in the ruler's relations with the tribes. As usual, Abdulhamid tried to avoid any unrest in the Hicaz that would give the British a pretext to occupy the province. At the same time, he himself sent four well-trained battalions and five warships to the Hicaz and reinforced the fortifications.

The British continued to support publication of anticaliphal newspapers and tracts, such as the *Bayannamat-ul-Ummat al-Arabiyah* (Narrative of events of the Arabs), *An-Nahlah* (The bee), *Al-Mirat* (The mirror), and, especially, *Al-Khalifah*, published by the Rev. John Louis Sabunji. In the end, the native leaders of the Hicaz and Hadramut feared European expansion more than Istanbul's rule, especially after Italy and France had occupied areas in East Africa and seemed bent on expanding into the Hicaz. The emir of Hadramut, the famous Seyyid Fazil (Fadl) paşa, who was a dedicated supporter and adviser of Abdulhamid, advised the sultan to assert the Ottoman presence in south Arabia by sending warships and by posting officials in the area to confer medals and to remind the local notables that they were still Ottoman subjects. Believing that the coastal lands of south Arabia, which "being linked to Hicaz, the center of Islam, and to other Arab centers, which, if occupied, could result in all kinds of evil," Fazil even advocated the incorporation of Oman into the Ottoman sphere of influence.[29]

By the end of 1880s, India became another locus for the British campaign against the Ottoman caliphate. The *Punjab Times* questioned the legitimacy of the Ottoman caliph and compelled Istanbul to secure from Lord Salisbury a statement that the British government opposed the views expressed by the *Punjab Times*. In a rebuttal published in the *Morning Post*, the Ottoman government claimed that the last Abbasid caliph had indeed transferred his title to Sultan Selim I in 1517 and that this act of renunciation was both public knowledge and confirmed by the existence of a written document that was available for inspection (although, as mentioned, there is no evidence that such a document did exist).[30] The Porte further stressed that the Ottoman sultan was a "padişah," or "ruler of the sovereign, sacred, Islamic country"—that is, the Ottoman state which included the Hicaz—and he also possessed the "illustrious title of custodian and defender of the holy lands."[31] The *Punjab Times*, presumably read by Indian Muslims, seems to have deeply worried the Porte, as did other Indian newspapers that also questioned the legitimacy of the Ottoman caliphate and criticized Abdulmecid's collaboration with the British. *Akhbar-i Am*, a newspaper published in Lahore, denied that the "Sultan of Rum is the Caliph of all Muslims" or that the Indian Muslims owed him allegiance and support; it added that the English "should not forget that the revolt in India in 1857, was quelled thanks to the friendship and alliance that existed then between England and the Caliph."[32] As though to counter these attacks with concrete action, the government issued an order to all the Ottoman authorities in the Hicaz to treat the pilgrims with the utmost courtesy and to help them in every way possible so as to preempt any complaint.[33]

In Egypt a number of newspapers, such as *Al-Ceziret ul-Misiriye* and *Al-Kahire*, referred to their own khedive as "malik" and even as "caliph," further increasing the sultan's anxiety about the Arabs' loyalty to him.[34] There were also a great number of writings in the Egyptian press upholding the Ottoman sultans' title to the caliphate.[35] Kiamil paşa, the former premier who was governor of Aydin (Izmir), informed the sultan that a large number of Egyptian newspapers questioning the legitimacy of the Ottoman caliphate were being smuggled into his province and were being read by the population, which would, however, side solidly with the sultan in a showdown over the caliphate. To maintain this popular allegiance, the governor advised Istanbul to deal equitably with dissidents and critics rather than exiling them arbitrarily to faraway lands.[36]

Sultan Abdulhamid's growing autocracy had created dissidents and critics not only among the elites but also among the lower ranks of the population of Arabia and Egypt. Some mahdis acting as popular preachers took an openly anti-Ottoman stand. Seyyid Safir efendi of Yemen, who belonged originally to one of the Hadramut tribes, attracted a large number of followers from among the natives after he settled in the Medina area and established good relations with the tribes there. Apparently he criticized the sultan's government and refused to obey the decisions of the court, the officials, and even the caliph. Seyyid Safir took possession of the income of various *vakif*s and did not hesitate to attack physically the members of the progovernment religious establishment, such as Şeyh Halil Harputi efendi; he was eventually sent back to Yemen.[37] The number of self-proclaimed mahdis and mystic preachers who enjoyed great popularity increased markedly toward the end of the century. The sultan befriended those who did not challenge the political-social status quo or the sultan's rule and caliphal title and punished (usually exile with a pension) those who appeared dangerous. In 1884 Şeyh Muhiddin, who claimed to be the Mahdi, was brought from Damascus to Adana and then sent to Silifke, where he backed his claims by citing passages from the Koran. He was later sent to one of the small Mediterranean islands so as to render him harmless.[38] Finally, opposition began to surface from within the religious establishment itself. After the Young Turks established their associations in Europe, some religious men in Istanbul also joined their organization or voiced open criticism of the caliph. For instance, Hoca Muhiddin efendi declared that the Ottoman sultans had usurped the caliphate, so it was practically a sin to address Abdulhamid as "caliph."[39]

Ottoman Reactions to British Designs on the Caliphate

Sultan Abdulhamid followed closely the British and French efforts to promote the cause of an Arab caliphate. The Ottoman government claimed that it had sound information that England had sent several *mutemehdi*s—or "mahdis"—to Arab lands.[40] Various actions designed to counter these presumed efforts were undertaken. For example, a *mutemehdi* was closely shadowed in 1883 by the Ottoman police in Jerusalem and Syria, but no evidence that he had incited the people to revolt was obtained; special measures were also taken at the Syrian border with Egypt to apprehend the English-trained "mahdis." Dispatches were sent with instructions to officials to watch out for popular religious agitators. Similar instructions were sent to the *vali* of Tripoli after the agents of the mahdi of Sudan apparently tried to recruit the tribes of Fezzan to their cause.[41] The sultan's suspicion was reinforced by the reports of his diplomatic envoys. In particular, a lengthy report from the Ottoman vice-consul in London, Halil Halit, provides valuable insight into Ottoman perceptions about the British designs on the Middle East, Arabia, and the caliphate.

The vice-consul reported that the British interest in Iraq, Basra, and Arabia had increased to such a degree that they were likely to spur England to take direct possession of the area without waiting for the disintegration of the Ottoman state. According to Halit, who was echoing Lord Curzon's views, the British would not mind if

Russia occupied the Ottoman lands, provided that the result was an expansion in British foreign trade, as already had occurred in the former Ottoman lands now under the czar's rule. Halit believed that because the British favored everything Christian, they instinctively desired to see the end of Turkish rule, even in Istanbul. Considering the Russian occupation of Ottoman lands inevitable and desirable, the British anticipated it would silence the caliph forever, draw the 75 million Indian Muslims closer to England and "bring Christian civilization to the savage lands." It also would allow England to establish full sovereignty in Egypt, to occupy Arabia and the Gulf area, and to build railroads through Iran to connect these areas with India. England was very apprehensive that an Ottoman military, political, and economic revival would have an electrifying effect upon the Indians, Indonesians, and other Muslims, who had reacted enthusiastically to the Ottoman victories in the war with Greece in 1897. The Ottoman diplomat flatteringly informed the caliph that his moral and spiritual influence among the Muslims in the world was the main deterrent to British designs in the Gulf and Arabia. Consequently, he suggested Abdulhamid do his best to retain the good will of the Arabs, by expanding trade and establishing an efficient administration in their areas. The Arabs, according to Halit, should be treated with justice and respect and should have their freedoms upheld and the wealth of their notables protected against covetous Ottoman officials. A successful administration in Arabia would increase love for and enhance the authority of the caliph everywhere in the world so that even the "emirate of Oman could be persuaded at the proper time to join the caliphal state, and its ruler could become the *vali* of the Porte."[42]

Sultan Abdulhamid, fully aware of London's plans to install an Arab caliph in Mecca, believed the "English are the most dangerous of all the great powers because for them promises have no value."[43] To Abdulhamid, Gladstone and Pope Pius IX were of the same mind and followed the same road of religious prejudice, although neither had a true knowledge about the actual situation prevailing in the Orient or about the good treatment accorded to the Christians there. The sultan believed that the British would not hesitate to name the khedive of Egypt as caliph, or "in case of need one would expect the English to appoint even Lord Cromer as caliph." In 1900 Abdulhamid wrote that the English press was advocating that

> Arabia should become an English protectorate for it was natural for England which had 56 million Muslim subjects to take possession of the Muslim holy cities. It is regrettable that the influence of England in Arabia is very strong. Now the English have started to create difficulties for us in Yemen. They have incited the Arab tribes to rebellion. Aden is the general headquarters of the English campaign in Arabia. . . . We are in a difficult situation there. We are trying to defend ourselves against the English intrigues by giving presents and money [bribes; the term used is *bahşiş*] to the tribal chiefs. . . . Aden is the Gibraltar of the East for it commands the east coast of Africa.[44]

Concern about the British threat induced the Ottomans to try to win over the Muslims by making their pilgrimage to Mecca as comfortable and as safe as possible and to ensure proper food supplies by calling upon Egypt to send regularly the wheat earmarked for Mecca and Medina. Subsequently, a letter signed by 132 *haci*s from Java praised the *vali* of Hicaz, Nafi paşa, for ending the perennial abuses inflicted on the Javanese pilgrims by the local merchants and so-called guides. For example, Nafi paşa had closed a "travel" company operated by one Ibrahim Iraki, who asked each pilgrim to pay the cost of a return ticket upon arrival in Jeddah, charged twenty mecidiyes more than other travel companies, and extracted additional payments for being the *kahya* (superintendent) of the rather large number of pilgrimage guides who helped the *haci*s properly perform the religious rites.[45] The *vali* had also ordered the camel drivers to not overcharge the pilgrims traveling from Mecca to Medina and had forbidden the tribes to collect more than their due share of taxes from the pilgrims; he also prevented the infamous Osman bey from obliging each pilgrim to buy a copy of the Koran for two and half rials. In 1883 the sultan made his presence more visible in Medina by repairing the southwestern walls of the city and erecting there the Hamidiye Gate, which, adorned by special lamps sent from Istanbul, displayed the sultan's *tuğra* (seal).

The protective measures taken by the caliph, combined with falling maritime transport rates, helped increase sharply the number of *haci*s—and the sultan's prestige as well. According to an official report sent by the grand vizierate to the sultan, 450,000 pilgrims came to Mecca in 1888, several times more than in the 1850s.[46] The English countered Abdulhamid's efforts by cultivating the friendship of the emir of Mecca, the Gulf *şeyh*s, and the Omanis, and by attempting to persuade the ulema of Al-Azhar to write a pamphlet questioning the sultan's title to the caliphate.[47] The sultan, in turn, continued to cultivate the goodwill of the notables and *şeyh*s of Arabia (establishing the tribal school, granting them aid, tax exemptions, medals, etc.), but he also strengthened the Ottoman military presence in Mecca by turning an unfinished building scheduled to be a *medrese* into a barracks and stationing troops there.[48] The struggle over the caliphate, despite minor setbacks, ended in the favor of the sultan. Even the Saudi princes, who had sought British help against Istanbul throughout the nineteenth century, refused to support London against Abdulhamid.

The rather significant success of Abdulhamid in containing and deflecting the British and French assaults on his caliphal title and the many favorable ramifications of that success stemmed from the fact that most Sunni Muslims regarded the sultan as the sole ruler capable of maintaining the territorial integrity of the Hicaz and defending the Muslims' rights. Muslims who had collaborated with the French and British in their country of origin still refused to do so in the Hicaz. The failure of the British and the French to undermine Abdulhamid's legitimacy as caliph not only enhanced his prestige among Muslims but also increased European fears that the caliphate enjoyed the support of Muslims all over the world and was thus a permanent threat to their rule over Muslims. This Muslim attachment to the caliphate produced a perverted image of the Muslims and their faith among many Europeans, and influential British officials came to regard the caliphate as the linchpin of Muslim resistance to their ambitions in the East. Horatio Herbert Kitchener (first earl) believed sincerely that the Indian mutiny in 1857 was engineered by Muslims and that a major European power, such as Germany, could manipulate the caliph against England. His fear of a German-backed *cihad* was eventually dramatized by John Buchan in his novel *Greenmantle* (1916), the plot of which has Germany use a Muslim prophet to destroy the British.[49]

The Hicaz Railway

The Hicaz Railway, began just after the turn of the century, probably offers the strongest evidence of the effort the sultan made to maintain his control of the Hicaz and thus to serve the holy sites and validate his caliphal claim to be the spokesman, defender, and representative of all the Muslims in the world.[50] There were other considerations also. The sultan was able to point to the Hamidiye-Hicaz Railway as proof that Islam permitted the coexistence of science and religion and that Muslims could become masters of technology. An eternal pragmatist, Abdulhamid also used it to help market agricultural commodities from Syria and to enable the Ottoman government quickly to dispatch troops to Yemen and the Hicaz. The decision to build the railway was finally made after rejection of a variety of earlier proposals, dating back over thirty years to 1864. The original advocates of a railway from Damascus west to the Mediterranean ports were powerful Syrian and Lebanese families such as the Azms and Sursuk, who possessed large tracts of land and produced sizable quantities of exportable agricultural commodities. Many of these families descended from the old Syrian aristocracy, but others had risen as part of the new middle classes created by the market economy. In any case, they and other producers in south Anatolia needed a rapid, safe and inexpensive means to carry their products to the Mediterranean ports, for the relative growth of agricultural production in Anatolia, Syria, and Iraq after 1860 had increased the surplus of agricultural commodities and put a premium on rapid marketing and exports. The Baghdad Railway (1888), built by German capital, partially solved the transportation problems in central Anatolia and ultimately in northern Syria and Iraq, but not in southern and western Syria, including Palestine, where the economy was developing at a rate faster than in Anatolia. By 1895 the French already had completed a line running via Hawran, but the English, unable to build the Acre Damascus Railroad, sold it to the Ottoman government, which completed it as part of the Hicaz Railway project in 1906.

The northern section of the Hicaz Railway was financially feasible and desirable, but the Ottoman government was keenly interested in reaching the southern region. Because the arid, poorer areas of Tabul or Madain Salih (the point beyond which the non-Muslims were not admitted) in the south offered little economic reward, the railroad's northern section was built first. It then proved so successful that the revenue derived from freight carried from Syria to the Mediterranean ports sufficed to finance the deficit-ridden southern section. The sultan believed that it was essential to "build the railroad between Damascus and Mecca in the shortest possible time. Thus in case of trouble we can rapidly send troops there [the Hicaz]. The second important point is to strengthen the bond among Muslims to such a degree as to shatter English treason and cunning on this solid rock [of Muslim solidarity]."[51] The sultan made a special point of praising Abdulaziz Ibn Saud, who "dreamed once of becoming the strong ruler of a free Arabia, [but] realized that the independence won with the help of the English amounted to accepting their rule. The emir of Kuwait, Mubarak, has freed him of English influence and [helped] turn him toward us." In the sultan's opinion the railroad would help secure the loyalty of the Arabian *şeyh*s and keep the British at bay. History proved the sultan wrong in both cases.

In 1906 the sultan wrote that his dream of building a railroad to the Hicaz was becoming a reality and gave credit for securing the necessary funds from "all Muslims but especially the Indians" to his Arab secretary, Izzet al-Abid bey. "The Mecca [*sic*] railroad has demonstrated that we [the Muslims] still have the capacity for development and the ability to thwart the English, who have used every means to oppose this initiative." It would enable the Ottomans to avoid using the Suez Canal and "in case of need permit us to send [to the Hicaz] troops in [full] security."[52] The various opponents of the railway understood full well the advantages it would bring the Ottomans, both militarily and commercially. Its construction of the railroad increased the tensions between the emir of Mecca and his Ottoman masters and between London and Istanbul. The British opposed the railroad because, by giving the Porte direct land access to the Hicaz, it would curtail the advantages they derived from controlling the sea passage to the area. The British did their best to discourage the Muslims of India from contributing money to the railway fund, and they successfully obstructed the full implementation of the construction plan. The sultan had to abandon plans to build a subsidiary railroad branch to the Gulf of Aqaba when London, fearing that the sultan would use the port of Taba to transport troops to Yemen, resorted to its usual "gunboat diplomacy" to compel the Ottoman government to recognize Taba as part of Egyptian territory, although the sultan was nominally Egypt's sovereign. Taba, at the northern tip of the Red Sea, was located on deep water suitable for the docking of large sea-going vessels. In the spring of 1906, Ottoman troops occupied Aqaba and Taba, and that prompted an English ultimatum on 3 May 1906, requiring the sultan's troops to evacuate the Sinai peninsula in ten days. Abdulhamid refused to comply with the British demand, and subsequently a commission decided (on 1 October 1906) to leave Aqaba to the Ottomans and Taba to Egypt. (Taba is in the Sinai peninsula; the Israelis built a hotel there after 1967 and long refused to return it to Egypt, even after signing a peace treaty.)[53]

It was not only the British who objected to the railway. One of the strongest opponents was the emir of Mecca, Ali Ibn Abd Allah (r. 1905–1908), but the docile Awn al-Rafiq had also opposed it, lest it give the Ottoman government easy military access to dominate Mecca. Ultimately, the emir was instrumental in preventing the Ottoman government from constructing a separate branch from Jeddah to Mecca, a mere 45 to 50 miles, and from extending the line from Medina to Mecca, across about 270 miles of relatively flat land. Ironically, the Ottoman presence in the Hicaz outlasted the Empire and Abdulhamid (both expired in 1918). The Ottoman garrison in Medina surrendered in 1919 under pressure from Istanbul, a point duly noted by Muslims eager to see something symbolic in Abdulhamid's Islamist policy. The tribes, as well, were opposed to the railway because it threatened their lucrative camel transportation business, especially during the *hac* season. (Today a superhighway links Mecca, Medina, and Jeddah; ironically, it was built by a Turkish company on contract to the Saudi government.)

Sultan Abdulhamid announced the start of construction on 2 May 1900, but actual work on the railway did not begin until the first of September. To emphasize the Islamic and Arabic dimensions of the enterprise, the sultan placed his secretary, Izzet al-Abid paşa, at the head of the project. A small board of supervisors in Istanbul reported directly to the sultan, while the key financial responsibilities were entrusted to the Damascus Central Commission. The commission's secretary, Muhammad Fawzi paşa; Adib Nazmi, the editor of the local journal *Suriyah*; and Abd al-Rahman, all prominent Syrian-Arabs, along with many other landlords involved in commodity exports, were the moving forces behind the project. Kazim paşa was general director of the Damascus Central Commission until he became the governor of the Hicaz in 1908, but the actual construction was initially in the hands of Heinrich Meissner (later paşa), a capable German engineer. Meissner's sympathy for the Ottomans and confidence in their basic abilities facilitated his relations with his employers and subordinates and the success of the construction. Most of the engineers working for the railway administration were graduates of the Istanbul Engineering School. The work force of about five thousand consisted of both Turkish soldiers, many of whom were drafted specifically for this purpose and paid special wages, and Arabs. An assortment of Muslim and non-Muslim craftsmen cut stone and built more than nine hundred bridges and ninety-three stations. Christians were employed mostly at the beginning to train the Muslims, as the avowed purpose was to make the railroad a Muslim enterprise. The railroad was financed in its major part by donations from Ottoman Muslims, starting with Sultan Abdulhamid and his ministers; some Ottoman Christians also contributed. The Indian Muslims contributed heavily through some 150 committees they established for this purpose, although practically all Indian Muslims came to *hac* by sea. All the donations amounted to 417,000 lira in 1900; in the period 1903–1908 donations rose from 651,184 to 1,127,894 lira, and the total income, including taxes and operating income, rose from 1,033,465 to 3,975,445 lira.[54] The railway carried freight and some 30,000 passengers, mostly pilgrims, per year; it became profitable after 1910. Its operating profit rose from 70,246 liras in 1910 to 93,368 in 1914, while its capital rose from 3.8 million to 4.5 million liras in the same period. Ochsenwald estimated that the total cost for construction of the main line and branches at the end of March 1912 came to 4,283,000 liras including rolling stock, or 2,800 liras per kilometer, which compares very favorably with 7,440 liras for the Anatolian railroad and 4,780 liras for the narrow gauge of the Jaffa-Jerusalem branch.[55] The rate of construction was expected to reach about 500 kilometers per year, but the actual mileage fell below this. Progress was expedited greatly in 1903, when about 250 kilometers had been built; another 247 kilometers were added in 1904–1905. The construction continued after Abdulhamid lost power in 1908, as the Union and Progress Party was quick to recognize the many benefits offered by the railway. Most of the sections south of Maan were destroyed by the Bedouin tribes after 1916; they were repaired, but only to be destroyed again.

The railway was not really a piece of "political propaganda," as Jacob Landau casually defined it, but a well-thought-out project with economic, military, and political purposes. It was to replace the caravan road from Damascus to Mecca that had been followed by pilgrims practically since the inception of the regular *hac*;[56] and it also symbolized the reconciliation of Islam with science, technology, and modern management. Probably one of the most successful projects undertaken by Abdulhamid, it proved to be ephemeral; it was Muslims who destroyed the railway, out of ignorance or greed or because divisive nationalism proved to be stronger than unifying Islamism.

Conclusion

The fate of the caliphate was decided late in the nineteenth century in the struggle between the British and Sultan Abdulhamid. The British, acting on the stereotyped notion that whoever controlled the caliphate controlled the Muslims, promoted the cause of an Arab caliph, questioning the legitimacy of Ottoman sultan. Abdulhamid countered the British by reviving the sixteenth-century Ottoman argument that service to Islam, rather than Qureyish descent, was most important to the legitimacy of the caliphate. He went so far as to claim that the caliphate had precedence over the sultanate, although he knew all too well that it was the sultan's temporal power that assured the caliphate's role among Muslims.

Abdulhamid's actions had far-reaching consequences derived from the nature of his arguments and the audience he addressed. He asked the individual Muslim believers to support and obey him as caliph, promising in return to uphold the primacy of the faith. He created, in effect, an unwritten contract between the ruler and the individual Muslims, regardless of their rank, and changed drastically the connotations of both state and religion; in fact, the first step toward recognizing separate autonomous sphere of activity for the state and faith, a situation that existed in practice at the inception of the Ottoman state, had been taken. The state was a concept born of the intellect, while the faith stemmed from the emotions; the two could coexist but one could not substitute for the other unless forced from above, as the Republic attempted to do.

Abdulhamid never made use of the call to *cihad* except in the war with Greece in 1897. However, after the Young Turks ousted Abdulhamid, they brought to the throne Mehmet V Reşat (r. 1909–1918), who dutifully issued, on 11 November 1914, the call to *cihad*, in order to incite the Muslims to rise against England and ensure victory for Germany. This elicited a very limited Muslim response, however, for the obvious reason that they had no compelling interest in fighting for one European power against the other; furthermore, the call did not emanate from a free caliph dedicated to the faith but from a small clique who controlled the state and acted in concert with their German ally. Since the state violated some basic tenets of the *cihad*, the *ümmet* now was free to seek by itself the proper action and organization to retain its faith and assure its worldly existence of the community. Paradoxically, Mustafa Kemal (Ataturk) assumed that role in 1919–22 while the caliph-sultan was a British prisoner in Istanbul.

The British tried to launch an Arab caliph subject to their own wishes. Şerif Hüseyin, the emir of Mecca who engineered, with the British, the "Arab Revolt" of 1916, claiming that he was the "king of the Arabs and the caliph of all Muslims." Despite his excellent Qureyish credentials, including descent from the Prophet, he found few followers.[57] The Muslims of the world continued to regard as caliphs the Ottoman sultans, who had served Islam equitably for centuries and kept Hicaz open to pilgrimage to all of them. The Turkish National Assembly abolished the sultanate in 1922 and replaced the outgoing sultan-caliph, Vahideddin, with Abdulmecit II, who retained only the title of caliph. Two years later, in 1924, Turkey abolished the caliphate also, against widespread opposition, and exiled the incumbent, whose fate has been related elsewhere in this work.

Şerif Hüseyin formally claimed the caliphate in 1924 and promptly tried to use it and the *hac* to further his own personal political ambitions. Specifically, he tried to pressure the British and French to abandon their mandates in Syria and Iraq, which they had obtained despite promises of independence for the Arabs if they would rebel. But he was recognized as caliph only by his two sons, Faisal and Abdullah. Although the British had promised to uphold the rule of the *şerif* in Mecca, they did nothing to help when the Saudis resumed their efforts to conquer Hicaz after World War I. The Saudis' claimed that the *şerif* should be deposed for having used Mecca and the *hac* for "secular" political purposes, asserting that the holy sites and the *hac* were purely religious—a view held by the Ottomans during most of their rule. (Since World War II the Saudis have turned the holy lands into a national Wahhabi shrine, even though they do not insist any longer that Muslims conform to Wahhabi views and rites. Ultimately, in 1987, King Fahd took on the Ottoman-devised title of "protector of the Holy Lands.")

The efforts of some leading Muslims to revive the caliphate, which included the convening congress under the chairmanship of Rashid Rida in Cairo 13–19 May 1926, proved unsuccessful. Only a few leaders, such as Shawhat Ali of India, proposed to proclaim as caliph Abdulmecit II, who was waiting in Paris. Instead, each participating delegation wanted to make its own ruler caliph, signaling the ascendancy of national identity and interest over religious loyalty. Abdulhamid, the last true Ottoman caliph to freely exercise its prerogatives, politicized it beyond the permissible limit and thus undermined its religious symbolism. The Young Turks merely certified that fact by issuing a hollow cihad.

12

The Caliphate and Ottoman
Foreign Policy in Africa

The maintenance of authority over the Hicaz was dependent on controlling the land and sea approaches to this vital province. Although the north was securely in Ottoman hands, the east and even the south consisted of wide stretches of desert; and the western border, formed by the Red Sea, remained very vulnerable to outside attacks. Defense of the Red Sea acquired greater importance after the French occupied Tunisia in 1881 and the English occupied Egypt in 1882, especially as Paris seemed determined to move further south and east toward the Hicaz. North and Central Africa then emerged as a primary line of defense for the Ottoman possessions in the Middle East, especially Arabia. Ottoman strategic interests in Africa and Abdulhamid's Islamist policy, therefore, became mutually interdependent and inseparable.

The overall direction of Abdulhamid's policies in Africa was set by his predecessors as early as the 1830s, when France occupied Algeria and manifested its expansionist ambitions. The Ottoman bureaucracy tried, during the reigns of Mahmud II, Abdulmecid, and Abdulaziz, to revive the Turks' ties to the rulers of Central and East Africa, reasserting the sultan's title to those lands and, whenever possible, establishing there an actual Ottoman presence. Sultan Abdulhamid developed his policy in North Africa amidst conditions totally different from those his predecessors confronted, however, for he faced a combined threat from the major European powers. He thus tried to devise new ways to halt French intrusions into the Sahara, to oust the British from Egypt, to thwart budding Italian ambitions in Libya, and to restrain Germany from making inroads into the area and yet remain on good terms with all.

The loss of Tunisia to France left Istanbul with almost insurmountable strategic, economic, and psychological difficulties in Libya. Libya, the one secure Ottoman territory remaining in Africa after 1882, was governed from Istanbul; it was divided into three provinces, Tripoli (Tripolitania, Trablusgarp), Benghazi, and Fezzan (Fizan) deep in the south Sahara. It was Istanbul's communication line to the south Sahara and Central Africa and its defense line for the approaches to the Red Sea and, ultimately, to the Hicaz.

Abdulhamid's policy toward England in the Mediterranean and the Red Sea remained basically unthreatening despite the British occupation of Egypt, for England was still the only power that could effectively oppose the French advance into Tripolitania and Central Africa or discourage budding Italian ambitions. The Porte also knew that France was determined to promote its own ambitions in Egypt and disrupt British-Ottoman relations. The Ottoman ambassador in Paris advised the Porte that "prudence . . . dictated [them[not to adopt an openly antagonistic policy toward England, which has occupied Egypt and is in a position to raise difficulties for us in the Red Sea (*Bahrahmer*)."[1]

The Africa policy devised by the Porte after 1882 aimed to strengthen the Ottoman influence in the Sahara and Central Africa and to win over the native population and their leaders through tax incentives and increased authority granted to local government. Supplemented with appeals to religious solidarity and allegiance to the caliph, Ottoman policy in North Africa relied heavily on the participation of the local population in government and was quite assertive, innovative, and dynamic, contradicting the image of the Ottoman state as the "sick man of Europe."[2] The involvement of the native population in the administration and defense of their country was accompanied by the liberal and anticolonialist ideas spread by many Ottoman dissident intellectuals exiled to Fezzan, or elsewhere in the area.

Algeria-Tunisia

The French occupation of Algeria in 1830, based on such flimsy pretexts as the nonpayment of certain commercial debts and the humiliation of the French consul, made North Africa friendly toward Istanbul. No doubt the Ottoman effort to oppose the French invasion, despite the grave threats to its own survival posed by the Greek revolt of 1821, the war with Russia in 1828–29, and Mehmet Ali's occupation of Syria, convinced many North Africans that the Ottomans' good will and desire for solidarity were real and sincere. The popularity of Sultans Abdulmecid and Abdulaziz in North Africa increased steadily, especially after French ambitions in Tunisia and Central Africa, including Sudan, became more obvious. With the help of this burgeoning native good will, Istanbul was able to put an end, as early as 1835, to the rule of the Karamanli dynasty in Tripoli (est. 1715) and to expand its influence further to the west and south. In Tunisia, France used the modernist policy of Ahmad bey (in office 1837–52) to increase its influence over his successors and the "modernist" elites, thus alienating many of the Tunisian leaders and Muslim conservatives—especially after Archbishop Lavigerie, appointed by Paris in 1867, undertook a crusade aimed at Islam,[3] Paris also sought to control the trans-Saharan trade route and that antagonized the local merchants and the tribes.

The balance of European interests in the Mediterranean was disturbed by the French defeat at the hands of Germany in 1870, the collapse of Ottoman power in the Balkans after the war of 1877–78 (which resulted, in part, from the inability of France to counterbalance Russia), and the British occupation of Cyprus in 1878. England now appeared willing to compensate France for its territorial losses in Europe and to strengthen it against German ambitions by allowing it to take territory in North Africa.[4] Lord Salisbury, whose dislike for Africa was well known, is reported to have told the French foreign minister William Henry Waddington in 1878, "You cannot leave Tunis in the hands of the barbarians."[5] Bismarck also appeared to hope that compensating France with Ottoman territory in North Africa would, temporarily at least, direct France's energies overseas and quell its desire to avenge the defeat of 1870 and retake Alsace and Lorraine. France landed troops in Tunisia in April 1881, ostensibly to punish the Khumiri tribe for attacking Algeria, and forced Muhammad al-Saduk (Sadik), the bey of Tunisia, to sign at his Bardo Palace a treaty that the French Foreign Ministry had drafted years before the invasion.[6] Soon after signing the treaty, which gave France the right to post a resident minister and advise the bey, Paris moved most of its forces out of Tunisia, leaving the impression that it was not serious about holding on to its new possession. The Tunisians rebelled, hoping for possible aid from Istanbul.[7] Sizable French units then entered Tunisia a second time in October 1881, and, after inflicting considerable damage, consolidated their protectorate, claiming that it was the obligation of a superior civilization to aid the "underdeveloped."[8] When Saduk bey, Istanbul's friend, died on 27 October 1882 and was replaced by Ali bey, resident minister Paul Cambon had the opportunity to tighten further the French hold over the country.

The Porte responded to the events in Tunisia by seeking closer cooperation with the Tunisian tribes that had taken refuge in southern Tripolitania. Among those tribes was the Vurgama and its subordinate clan, Tevazin, together numbering about 100,000, who had left their original places of Makati and Feran under French pressure. The Vurgama and Tevazin sought the help of Şeyh Ali bey bin Khalifa, the anti-French tribal leader at his camp in the *kaza*s of Festo and Nalut in the Ottoman *sancak* of Cebelgarb. Bin Khalifa, already supplied with arms by the *vali* of Tripoli, decided to attack the French, but the *vali* told him to engage in armed action only if ordered to do so by the sultan.[9] The tribes then stopped in the no-man's-land between Wadi al-Fasi and Tripolitania as the frontier between Tunisia and Tripolitania was not drawn until 1910, even though a French-Turkish commission was formed to look into the problem as early as 1889. The *vali* of Tripoli, Ahmet Rasim paşa, knew that the French were looking for a pretext to advance into south Tripolitania and punish the fierce Tevazin tribe.[10] A very resourceful administrator and a relative and supporter of Mithat paşa, the *vali* kept his position from 1881 to 1896 despite Abdulhamid's morbid fear of anyone associated with Mithat, for the sultan's pragmatism, as usual, prevailed over his prejudices.

The *vali* believed that the French intended to occupy Tripolitania and stated that he needed 200,000 rifles and a battalion of regular troops, to supplement the local militia, and a detachment of Kuloğlus. The Kuloğlus constituted a higher social group descended from Turkish soldiers and native women; their armed total number in the area in 1881 consisted of 1,200 cavalry and 2,800 infantrymen; the Kuloğlu received no payment but were exempt from taxes. Meanwhile, following French promises of leniency, a large number of tribesmen returned to their original homes in Tunisia. The *vali* had already acknowledged that the "love of the fatherland was so strong among these tribes that sooner or later they would return to their abandoned homes."[11] In fact the tribes would have returned home even earlier if Şeyh Hamza Zafir, the brother of the influential advisor to the sultan, had not urged them to stay. The French quickly seized the opportunity to describe the refugees as being the prisoners of the Ottoman government and of Şeyh Hamza, its agent. Ahmet Rasim paşa finally suggested that Şeyh Hamza be recalled from Tripoli, for the French calumny had damaged his prestige.[12] Meanwhile, Ali bin Khalifa fought the French throughout the winter of 1882–83 but his success was limited. Istanbul thus learned that the influence of the caliph among the rank and file was without effect unless they were properly indoctrinated and their leaders' devotion to the sultan firmly secured. While a number of lower-ranking Ottoman officials had tried to please the sultan with glowing reports about the miraculous appeal of the caliphate, the realistic Rasim paşa had pointed out that caliphal exhortations were not enough to unite the tribes or overcome geography, climate, and logistics. Events proved him right and prompted Istanbul to mobilize the natives for self defense.

Following the opinion of the *mutasarruf* (governor of a *sancak* or district) of Fezzan, Istanbul directed the army commander, Zeki paşa, to occupy the vital salt mines at Gavur, but Zeki refused.[13] Accused of insubordination, Zeki paşa explained his reasons for failing to comply: the distance between Tripoli and the salt mines was 393 hours (almost 1,500 miles), the Anatolian and Rumilian soldiers could not withstand the desert heat, and the transport of four thousand soldiers and their food from Tripoli would be prohibitively expensive. Instead, Zeki paşa advised his superiors to organize the local people of Fezzan and the Kuloğlus into special units to accomplish the same task at minimal costs. The eventual outcome was that Istanbul found it convenient to entrust more of the defense of the land to the native population and to limit its own role to providing military training, arms, and leadership. The native troops that were so trained and armed later formed the nuclei of the national military and local paramilitary units in the anticolonialist struggle against the French and Italians.

Ottoman Relations with the Sanusiyya

The Ottomans developed close relations with the Sanusiyya after the events of 1881–82. In order to establish a common front against the French advance into Central Africa and the potential Italian intrusion into Libya, the Porte devised new forms of collaboration and alliance with local elites who could effectively use the prestige of the caliphate to mobilize the population, especially the tribes. Ultimately, the Sanusiyya became, under the Ottoman auspices, the catalyst of the alliance between the urban ulema, the tribes, and the trading oasis dwellers.[14] It should be duly emphasized this type of broad alliance for self-defense based on a coalition of popular groups and middle-class elites occurred only in Libya after 1881, and in Anatolia in 1919–22 in the Turkish War of Liberation. Sultan Abdulhamid's improving relations with the Sanusi and the transformation of the Sanusiyya from a purely religious revivalist order into a populist resistance movement must be seen in this context. Nevertheless, in developing ties with the Sanusiyya and some African Muslim rulers, Sultan Abdulhamid—a great believer in the binding power of international agreements—sought to buttress his claims to south Sahara and Central Africa with legal, historical, and diplomatic arguments. As early as 1884, when England and Germany convened the Berlin West Africa Conference to decide the future of Africa, the sultan instructed his ministers to defend there the "historical rights, the important material and moral interests of the Sublime [Ottoman] state and the sacred rights of the great Caliphate against all secret ill intentions."[15]

As noted before, the Sanusiyya had not been initially friendly to the Ottomans (see chapter 1). Yet, by the end of the nineteenth century, the sultan and the Sanusiyya were such close allies, that the French described—with exaggeration—the Sanusi as being the caliph's most faithful religious agents. Actually religious affinity and practical considerations were complementary rather than mutually exclusive.[16] Ottoman documents and various other sources show that the sultan decided after 1881 to improve his relations with North Africa by sending there some of his trusted advisers from the Zafir family—Seyyid Hamza and Beşir. The view that Şeyh Muhammad bin Zafir al-Madani, a protege of Grand Vizier Mahmud Nedim paşa, was a rival of the Sanusi became inconsequential after 1881.[17] He also instructed Sadik al-Mueyyed, a member of the Azm family of Syria, to contact the local leaders of North Africa, including the Sanusi, and later gave the leaders pensions and hosted them in Istanbul.[18] In 1885 the Porte decided to establish a *kaymakamlik* in Kufra, and in 1895 this became a Sanusi stronghold. Al-Bayda, the initial Sanusi center close to the Mediterranean, had been replaced by Jaghbub, the major headquarters of the *tarikat*, some 500 kilometers southeast of Benghazi and half the distance to Kufra. The view of some scholars' that the Sanusi moved southward in order to distance themselves from the Ottoman centers of power (as well as to proselyte among the Central African tribes) must be placed in the larger frame of Ottoman-Sanusiyya relations.[19]

Abdulhamid was interested in increasing Ottoman authority and visibility in Central Africa, buttressing Ottoman relations with the friendly rulers in the area, and, incidentally, using their help to collect taxes. The sultan did his best to please the North Africans, not only by listening to the recommendations of trusted emissaries, but also by removing unpopular administrators. When Ali Kemali paşa, the *vali* of Benghazi, used a special military unit made up of infantry, cavalry, and artillerymen to collect taxes and pacify the tribes of Cidabi, Zawiye, and Magarib, the *naib* (the regent judge of Benghazi, Seyyid Mehmet Şavki) expressed the outrage of the tribesmen in a letter to the *şeyhulislam*, who dutifully sent it to the caliph.[20] The *naib* pointed out that the *vali*'s heavy pressure forced the tribes to migrate to Tripoli so the "promises of reforms and guarantees given amounted to nothing."[21] Ali Kemal paşa was removed and replaced by Haci Reşid paşa as the governor of Cyrenaica. Eventually Musa Kazim paşa, a dedicated Islamist, was appointed *vali* of Cyrenaica and served from 1885 to 1888.[22] The *vali*s of Tripoli in particular were selected with special care for the delicate tasks of maintaining Ottoman rule in North Africa and consolidating the caliph's prestige while mobilizing opposition against the French. They sent regular confidential reports to the sultan about both the state of affairs and the activities of the Sanusi, including Şeyh al-Mahdi.[23] One of the most successful governors was Nafiz paşa, who recommended the most trustworthy and influential Tunisian notables and *şeyh*s to the sultan for special attention and the award of the ubiquitous medals and pensions. He served also as a very effective channel of communication with the Muslim rulers of Central Africa, until French pressure finally forced Istanbul to remove him from his post in Tripoli.

Because the Sanusi solidified their own power and influence among the tribes and lower urban groups while harnessing popular support for Istanbul, the French began to fear that this, along with the broadening German-Ottoman friendship, threatened their hold on Algeria and Tunisia. (The French press published reports about German officers and scholars traveling in disguise among Saharan tribes and inciting them to rebel against France.) Paris came to regard the Sanusi as the obedient tool of Istanbul, and possibly of the Germans, and as the greatest obstacle to their own advance into Central and East Africa—especially after the French-British declaration of 1890 limited the French sphere of influence south of Tunisia and Algeria and recognized the British protectorate over Zanzibar. Meanwhile, the Porte defined the area south of Tripolitania as its own "hinterland," heightening French fears that the Sanusi and the Porte had concocted a "pan-Islamic" conspiracy against Paris. Existing evidence indicates that the Sanusi did their best to avoid a confrontation with France by engaging mainly in religious activities, especially in the area of the Chad. Yet the French remained unconvinced. In 1902 the French Ministry of Interior asked its embassy in Istanbul to report on the pan-Islamic activities in North Africa. In response, the embassy portrayed the caliph as dangerously influential and enjoying high prestige in North Africa because the Muslims considered him the sole defender of their rights, while harsh treatment by the French led the lower classes to join the popular religious orders in self-defense.

The French consul in Tripoli attributed the pan-Islamic activities in North Africa to the native notables, whom he regarded as the chief channel of caliphal influence and as the main supporters of the Sanusi. Then he went on to describe the opposition to French imperialism as born not from patriotism but from "Islamic fanaticism and regression," although he gleefully noted that the anti-French coalition among Muslims produced little practical result due to the notables' personal rivalries and intrigues.[24] The French consul also reported that the Turks had laid claims to a large section of Central Africa. Indeed, in a note addressed to the Powers in November 1890, the Porte claimed Waday, along with Bornu, Borku, Kanem, Kuwar, northern Congo, and Nigeria. The consul recommended that the French occupy Waday and dislodge the Sanusi as a preliminary measure and then proceed to occupy forcefully the areas left to France through the second English-French agreement of 21 March 1899.[25]

After 1900 the French intensified their efforts to annihilate the Sanusi in Central Africa. As a recent book states, "La Sanusiyya est ainsi devenue, aux yeuz des Français, la confrérie maléfique par excellence. L'histoire des relations entre la France et la Sanusiyya est donc entre 1850 et 1920, celle d'une longue hostilité entrecoupée d'explosions violentes et d'acclamies passagères."[26] (There was an alliance between the Sanusiyya and Sultan Ali Dinar, although this was long denied by the British; it was couched in religious terms, but it was basically a defensive agreement to oppose European occupation.)[27] In 1901 the French attacked and liquidated the Sanusi stronghold of Bir Alali (est. 1899) deep in Central Africa, despite the Sanusi effort to avoid a confrontation at all cost. Throughout these years, the Sanusi remained in contact with the Ottoman authorities in Benghazi, who supplied them with food and weapons.[28]

Abdulhamid appeared sorry that the French ambitions in Tunisia, Sudan, Somalia, and ultimately in the Red Sea had forced the Porte to change its traditional pro-French foreign policy. The "reforms carried out during the rule of my illustrious predecessor Abdulaziz and my father Abdulmecid in the army, schools, transportation [etc.]," the sultan acknowledged, "were inspired by France."[29] Somewhat regretfully, the sultan wrote, in 1898:

The French do not like my preference for the Germans. There are reasons for my sympathy for the Germans. [First] the person of the kaiser . . . who inspires confidence and natural liking. . . . The Germans are actually more likable than the French and in temperament they resemble the Ottomans. The Germans like the Ottomans move slowly into action and are trustworthy and loyal, hard-working and tenacious. The French are also hard-working but lack the tenacity of the Germans. They waste time with their disorganized politics. [True], the French lack the tenacity of the Germans but they have enthusiasm which is like a straw fire [burns out fast]. . . . We like the French now less than in the past because they have usurped Tunisia and have adopted the Republican form of government.[30]

In any event, it was the replacement of France with Germany as the source of Ottoman reforms and diplomatic support in general that put the philosophical core of Turkish modernism under German statist-nationalist influence and made the Ottoman Empire a tool of Germany's militarist ambitions in 1914.

The Ottoman-Sanusi cooperation became closer after the Triple Alliance in 1887 agreed to consider Tripolitania and Cyrenaica part of the Italian sphere of influence.[31] One year later, the Ottoman government gave the Sanusi *şeyh* weapons and ammunition and supplied the Tripolitanian tribes, which were under attack by the French-controlled Tunisian tribes, with ten thousand rifles. As the Italian pressures increased so did the Ottoman reliance on the Sanusi. In a note in his memoirs written in 1902, the sultan stated that the Italians had offered him 4 million liras in exchange for Benghazi; but, believing that the Sanusi were determined to defend the area to the end, he vowed to help them.

There is nobody but Mahdi Şeyh Sanusi who is capable of defending our rights in Banghazi. He is in a position to assemble in case of need an army of thirty thousand people. He has no intention to leave Benghazi to the Italians without a struggle. Moreover, al-Sanusi is in contact with various dervish [*sic*] orders throughout the world whose numbers are in the hundred of thousands. If the Sanusi decide to fight they will force the Italians into a bloody war far worse than the war of the mahdi of Sudan [against the English]. We have provided the Sanusi with sufficient weapons and cannons and this makes them a redoubtable enemy to be taken seriously.[32]

All these events followed a logic of their own. The caliph's influence in Libya increased greatly after 1888, mainly because the interest of the center and the periphery coincided. By the end of the century, the Sanusi had acquired a pivotal role in the Ottoman strategy to defend North Africa and the Sahara against the French and Italian advance and to protect the approaches to the Hicaz. Ottoman assistance helped the Sanusi to strengthen their social position in Libya and become the dominant political group there; the Sanusi, in turn, helped the caliph-sultan maintain his authority in North Africa and assure Istanbul's communication with the Chad, Bornu, and so on. This cooperation was based both on a mutual interest and certain ideological Islamic affinity, which had long-range consequences for the future.

The occupation of Libya by Italy after 1911 was never completed, thanks to a guerrilla resistance organized by a handful of Ottoman soldiers and the Sanusi. The Turco-Italian agreement of 17 October 1912 contained a secret provision according to which the sultan would be recognized as caliph, the spiritual head of Libya, but would be represented by someone residing in the country. Later that same year, however, the caliph recognized Libya as independent and the Sanusi as its leaders and entrusted the people to defend the independence of their country. Enver paşa, commander of the Libyan forces in Derna (and engaged to the caliph's niece Naciye), conveyed the messages personally to Ahmad al-Şerif, the new Sanusi leader. Enver paşa also arranged for over three hundred sons of Libyan şeyhs to be trained as officers in Turkish military schools.[33] Ahmad al-Şerif was invited to Istanbul in 1918 and, unable to return home, remained there and eventually joined the Turkish nationalists in the War of Independence in Anatolia. He was greatly honored in Turkey but was disillusioned by the abolition of the caliphate and left the country for Syria. Şeyh Suleiman al-Baruni, who had been imprisoned before 1908 for accusing Abdulhamid of usurping the caliphate, became a deputy in the Ottoman parliament and one of the major leaders of the anti-Italian struggle. After Ottoman officers and troops formally retired from Libya in 1912–13—following the Ottoman-Italian agreement and the Balkan War—Istanbul still continued to provide limited help to the local resistance forces. The Libyan experience gave the Ottoman officers training and experience in guerrilla warfare that they put to excellent use against the invading Greek, French, and Italian forces in Anatolia from 1918 to 1922.

Rapprochement with Morocco

The Sanusi also played a role in the establishment of relations between the Ottomans and Morocco in the attempt to stand against European—notably French—expansion. The Moroccan leader, Mawlay Abderahman (r. 1822–59), had supported Abdelkadir of Algeria against the French, but after the defeat of his army at D'Isly (1844), he agreed to their demands, while looking for ways to preserve his country's independence.

The effort to establish a rapprochement between Istanbul and Morocco, provides excellent insight into the attitudes and foreign policy of two important Islamic dynasties: the Alawite Serifian dynasty (est. 1659) and the Ottoman (est. 1286). The two rulers first attempted timidly to gain information about each other. As early as 1852 the Ottoman *vali* of Tripoli sent Mahmut Faiz efendi to Fas-Fez (the Muslim name for Morocco), ostensibly to buy horses but actually to find out what the Moroccans thought about the Ottomans. Mahmut efendi reported that although he traveled as an ordinary person, apparently the Moroccan leaders knew about his mission, for they gave him audience and showed him great respect, chiefly because he came from the Ottoman state.[34] In the end, the Moroccan leaders told the Ottoman "secret" emissary that they were very eager to enter into communications and establish relations with "a large and illustrious Muslim power such as the Ottoman State." They also expressed profound disappointment that an earlier diplomatic initiative undertaken by Sultan Abdulhamid I (r. 1774–89) and Moroccan ruler Abdullah (r. 1757–90) to reestablish relations had been fruitless. That initiative failed because the Ottoman sultan had asked for financial assistance for his forthcoming war with Russia, while the Moroccan ruler had hoped to acquire Algeria and Tunisia. Faiz made it clear that the Moroccans were more than eager to enter into some sort of relations with the Ottoman state.[35]

Some years after Faiz's mission, the newspaper *Basiret* started a campaign in favor of relations with Morocco, which it described as a far more important contributor to Muslim unity than some smaller nations. It urged the Ottoman government to send a mission there promptly.[36] Earlier, *Basiret* had published the summary of a letter supposedly addressed by Mawlai Muhammad IV (r. 1859–73), the ruler of Morocco, to Ismail paşa, the khedive of Egypt. The Moroccan ruler told the khedive that "the path to happiness and security lies in implementing and enforcing rapidly all the laws of the esteemed Devlet-i Ali-i Osman [Sublime state of the Ottomans] to which Egypt is legitimately bound," otherwise the consequences would be unpleasant.[37] Soon after *Basiret*'s appeal, a letter by Mawlay Hasan I (r. 1873–94; *Mevla* in Turkish) was brought by Seyyid Ibrahim Sanusi to the sultan in Istanbul. In it the Moroccan ruler proposed that he and the Ottoman sultan help each other and work to unite the Muslims.[38] Obviously pleased, Sultan Abdulhamid personally answered the letter, while the Meşihat, the office for religious affairs headed by the *şeyhulislam*, wrote to its counterpart in Morocco.[39] The first section of the sultan's letter was a long, flowery panegyric extolling the greatness of God, the Prophet, the first four caliphs (*rashidun*), and the ancestors of the Moroccan dynasty. Then the sultan humbly described how he came "to sit on the podium of the great caliphate and the adorning throne of the imamate" ("calis-i kursi-i hilafet-i kubra ve erike pira-yi imamet-i kubra") before he advanced his claim that although Muslims lived in both the east and west (*masriq ve magrib*) they all had the duty to defend the caliphate against the ill intentions of the foreigners. After stressing the view that all believers were brothers and backing it with the proper paragraphs from the Hujurat sura of the Koran, the sultan pointed out that blasphemy (*kufr*) was on the rise and that it was the duty of all Muslims to unite and fight the polytheists (*muşrikin*). The letter provides an excellent sample of Abdulhamid's epistolary and argumentary style, which is preserved in the translation.[40]

The Ottoman *şeyhulislam*'s short letter addressed to his Moroccan counterpart, which accompanied the sultan's, stressed the importance of establishing unity among Muslims and urged all Moroccans to maintain communications with the Ottomans. Actually the main purpose of this letter was to emphasize the importance of the Ottoman sultan so that the Moroccan ulema would persuade their ruler to accept the supremacy of the Ottoman caliphate.[41] Indeed, the chief goal of both letters from Istanbul was to convince the Moroccan ruler to recognize Abdulhamid as the caliph of all Muslims.

The Ottoman-Moroccan hopes of establishing formal relations were revived in 1882, when the Spanish ambassador to Morocco informed his superiors in Madrid that the establishment of Ottoman-Moroccan relations would undermine the French penetration of Morocco. Spain, supported by Italy, hoped that the Porte could provide Morocco with military personnel to replace French officers in training the native troops.[42] That this initiative also apparently produced no results did not discourage Istanbul from pursuing its courtship of Morocco, and in 1887 the Porte decided to send two religious dignitaries there but was unable actually do so because of a series of troubles in the Magreb.[43] In 1889 the Ottoman ambassador in Madrid again informed Istanbul that the Moroccan envoy to Spain had visited him and highly praised the caliph. Sharing the envoy's anxiety about the growing danger of foreign

(European) influence in Morocco and the ultimate fate of the millions of Moroccan Muslims, the Ottoman ambassador suggested that establishing relations between Fez and Istanbul could thwart the anti-Islamic influence of the foreigners and prevent the steady deterioration of living conditions in Morocco.[44] A Moroccan dignitary Mawlay (Mevla) Omar, who was visiting Istanbul, informed the Porte that Mawlay Hasan was now following the advice of the foreigners and discouraging his subjects from taking any interest in the Ottoman state. In fact, the visitor claimed, his ruler had acquired European instructors for the army and engaged in warfare to subdue the tribes, while upper-class Moroccans were flouting Islamic rites and traditions. For instance, the *şerif* of Tangier (*Tanca* in Turkish) had always socialized with Europeans, had married a non-Muslim woman, and now ignored the Islamic way of life. Even more alarming was that the townspeople accepted as normal the *şerif*'s deviation from Islam and still continued to support him. Mawlay Omar therefore urged Abdulhamid to establish regular diplomatic relations with Morocco as soon as possible so as to thwart the de-Islamization of the population. The sultan sent Mawlay Omar's information, along with his own opinion, to the Council of Ministers and asked it to debate the issue and recommend action; but apparently no concrete results came from those exchanges. Instead, France persuaded the British, Spanish, and Italians that they would have much more difficulty dealing with the Ottomans if they established a bridgehead in the western Mediterranean than they would coping with a weak Mawlay Hasan dominated by his pro-European governors.[45] Mawlay Abdulaziz (r. 1894–1908) and his brother, Abdulhafiz, became involved in a variety of domestic disputes and did not pursue the dialog with Istanbul.

At first glance it would seem that Sultan Abdulhamid's efforts to achieve some sort of rapprochement with Morocco had no effect on the course of African history. France acquired the northwest quadrant of its African empire, thanks to both imperialist adventurers such as Eugène Étienne, a *colon* born in Algeria, and private interests that saw Africa as a vast domain to colonize and exploit. The entente signed on 8 April 1904 between Paris and London gave France a free hand in Morocco and the British similar rights in Egypt. Infuriated beyond measure, the kaiser intensified German relations with Istanbul and also with Morocco, visiting Tangier himself on 31 March 1904. The Algeciras Conference of 1906, held in order to prepare a program of reform and quell the storm over Morocco's sovereignty, recognized Germany's freedom of trade there but put the country squarely into the Spanish-French sphere of influence. After Mawlay Abdulaziz abdicated in 1908, his brother, Abdulhafiz, remained the sole ruler of Morocco, but he was ineffective. By 1912 France had occupied Morocco—giving Germany in exchange part of the French Congo and Spanish Rio de Oro—while Abdulhafiz took a pension offered by the French, joined the Tijaniyya, and wrote poems praising the Sufis. European historians of modern Africa, such as Thomas Pakenham, treat the Ottoman Empire as a nominal power and Abdulhamid's efforts to form a united Muslim front against European expansionism as a mere nuisance and a political gesture. However, a close and critical scrutiny of the literature, including the documentary material used in this work, indicates that Istanbul provided substantial moral support to Morocco's anticolonialists and nationalists, to the point that the British and French were so concerned about an alliance between Istanbul and Morocco that they did their best to prevent it. Turkish-Moroccan relations became closer after anticolonial nationalism superseded—or absorbed—panislamism in both countries. The Young Turks established close relations with Moroccan nationalists almost as soon as they came to power in 1908; by November of 1909 they managed to send twelve officers to Morocco to train the local units. Although the officers left the country in 1910 under intense pressure from France, some returned after 1912 and took an active part in the resistance against the French occupation. A considerable number of Moroccans studying in Egypt joined or established their own panislamic associations which were, in fact, anticolonial nationalist organizations.[46]

The thirty-one-year interval between the French occupations of Tunisia and Morocco was due not only to the squabbles among the European powers but also to French concerns over the internal resistance that could arise from the unity between the two Muslim rulers. The best proof of such a possibility came from Libya, where the Ottoman-Sanusi alliance mobilized and provided guerrilla training for the local population in a protracted war that the Italians never won. In Algeria and Tunisia, as well as in Morocco, the Ottomans' overt and covert support for various groups opposed to France kept the resistance alive.

Urabi of Egypt and the Mahdi of the Sudan

Ottoman policy in Africa took a special form in Egypt and the Sudan. Egypt became part of the Ottoman state in 1517 by right of conquest. Centuries later the Sudan was incorporated into Egypt by Mehmet Ali, a Turk from Kavala who commanded an Albanian unit and became viceroy of Egypt in 1805; the Sudan became part of the Ottoman realm only because Egypt was formally under Ottoman suzerainty. The English occupation of Egypt in 1882 brought about a marked change in the relations of the khedives and the Ottoman sultans; each depended upon the other to oppose the British, when it seemed needful, but at other times each tried to use the British against the other. The fact that the sultan and khedive were ethnically related had little practical value, except to some Egyptian Christian nationalists and Sudanese fundamentalists, who articulated their opposition against the ruling order of Egypt by calling it "Turkish."

The events leading to the British occupation of Egypt and Sudan began in 1881 with the so-called Officers' Revolt led by Colonel Urabi (*Arabi* in Turkish), and the fundamentalist revolt of 1881–82 in Sudan led by a self-titled mahdi. Urabi's revolt, aimed chiefly against the Egyptian ruling order, was thus implicitly against the Ottomans; the Sudanese revolted mainly against the occupation and rule by Egypt, which they saw as a British proxy and labeled *Turkiyya*. The Ottoman sultan thus appeared the long-range target of both revolts, although his government bore little direct responsibility for the events taking place in either country. Nevertheless, the revolts provided Sultan Abdulhamid with some leverage, not only to reassert the Ottoman presence along the shores of the western Red Sea but also to increase greatly the caliphate's influence and politically mobilize the population. Both the British and Abdulhamid opposed the radical nationalism of Urabi and the religious militancy of the mahdi—the two future ideological trends of the Muslim world—for different reasons, of course; the British interpreted any kind of opposition to their expansionism as an impediment to "progress," while the conservative sultan viewed all radical and revolutionary movements—Islamic or non-Islamic—as a threat to the established social and political order.

The sultan initially regarded the Urabi uprising as a subversive movement that could threaten his caliphal seat. He feared that the English had used Urabi to promote Arab nationalism and had engineered the "revolt" in order to end Ottoman rule in Arabia and Iraq and allow the Arabs to take possession of the caliphate. These fears were magnified when he learned that the Anatolian Turkish population had demonstrated in favor of Urabi and hailed him as a Muslim hero. He instructed the Ottoman interior ministry to suppress the propaganda of some "people who roam Anatolia, and especially Arabia, and describe the action of Arabi [Urabi] paşa as a legitimate struggle, and thus deceive and instigate to malfeasance the simple-minded people. The harmful activities undertaken and the conditions being created by Arabi paşa would bring actual foreign intervention."[47] The sultan ordered the immediate arrest of anyone who engaged in seditious talk centered on Urabi's action, especially in Arabia, which was seen as likely to believe in Urabi's propaganda. He also ordered his administrators to prevent any conflict between Muslims and Christians, and he consistently rejected English proposals to land troops jointly in Egypt to pacify the country.[48] The sultan knew that any open action against Urabi would gravely damage his prestige as caliph and chief spokesman for Muslim causes. In fact, he always suspected that the English were planning to involve him in some joint action against Muslims in order to undermine his influence among those who viewed the caliphate as the symbol of Muslim unity and freedom and the Ottoman state as its political-military protector.

Despite his personal aversion to Urabi, therefore, the sultan refrained from intervention in Egypt and was the ultimate beneficiary of the rising anti-British sentiment there. Indeed, Abdulhamid eventually conferred the title of *paşa* on Urabi and awarded him a decoration in the hope that he might drive the British out of Egypt and facilitate the return of the Ottomans. The British occupation of Egypt, however, also allowed the sultan to rid himself of a growingly troublesome person, Ahmet Gazi Muhtar paşa, upon whom the sultan had conferred the title of *gazi* in the Russian war in 1877. Son of a merchant family from Bursa, Ahmet received a good modern military education to become both a very capable officer and a distinguished mathematician and astronomer; he authored the table of conversion, covering the years 1830–1925, of the Muslim lunar calendar to the solar calendar in a widely used reference source, *Takvim Us-sinin* published in A.H. 1331 (A.D. 1915). But as Ahmet Muhtar became somewhat critical of sultan's absolutism, Abdulhamid appointed him Ottoman commissioner for Egypt in 1885–1908.

The mahdi revolt in the Sudan may have provided the best opportunity for assessing not only Ottoman policy in the Red Sea and Abdulhamid's concern over control of the Hicaz but also the sultan's attitude toward radical Muslim religious movements.[49] The mahdist movement, one of the most militant fundamentalist Islamic movements of the nineteenth century was led by Muhammad Ahmad Ibn Abdullah (1844–1885), a Sufi who rose in 1881–82 (the millennial year for the *hicra*) to deliver Islam from the corruption of the "Turks," meaning the Sudan's Egyptian rulers, and the English. The uprising was a reaction to the changes in the traditional social order

caused by the emergence of the ulema as the dominant religious group and its association with the ruling Egyptians. It was also a local movement that sought to maintain the traditions of Sudan as embodied in the lower classes, for whom the mahdi
became the spokesman. After defeating the Egyptians, the mahdi attempted to establish a government based on Islamic principles. In Istanbul, Sultan Abdulhamid first
viewed the uprising as British-inspired and led in part by Urabi's followers, who had
escaped to the Sudan. The mahdi's basic goals, Abdulhamid thought, were to establish an Arab government, to control the Hicaz and Arabia, and to establish an Arab
caliphate. In F. A. K. Yasamee's words, Abdulhamid was very concerned that the
mahdist revolt "might easily spread across Red Sea into Arabia. The Red Sea was a
conduit, not a barrier: its African and Arabian shores were bound by numerous trading
links. . . . [T]he Ottoman government's first concern was to prevent the insurrection
from spreading into neighboring regions, and above all into Arabia."[50] However, the
sultan categorically refused to become involved in the Sudan. He would not even
permit the khedive to recruit an army from the Ottoman Empire to fight the mahdi,
lest such an act appear to serve the British. He was also rightfully apprehensive that
the Ottoman troops might join the mahdi's army or Urabi's revolutionaries, as many
Ottoman intellectuals and army officers sympathized with Urabi. In addition, Abdulhamid turned down a proposal by the British offering to abandon Sudan and to establish a form of self-government there if the Ottomans agreed to occupy the country, despite the urging of his counselors, including Seyyid Fadl of Hadramut, and
ministers, who hoped to use Sudan to bar the British and French penetration of Arabia.
He expressed fears that any military action abroad might degenerate into a greater
war and allow the British to implicate him in an action against Muslims that would
damage his caliphal credentials. In any event, by 1885 Italy, with the tacit support of
Britain, had occupied Massawa (Massuwa), indicating thus that London cared little
for Ottoman interests.[51]

   The mahdi defeated and killed General Gordon, occupied Khartoum, took possession of the British arsenal, and appeared ready to march toward Arabia as he had
threatened to do. In England, Gladstone resigned after a show of force that was, rather,
an empty gesture of bravado, and the English decided to retire from Sudan—temporarily, as it turned out. The mahdi unwittingly had helped rid the Porte of Gladstone,
its worst enemy, but the deep fear that the British would try to occupy the Hicaz remained. Istanbul reinforced its military units in the Hicaz and Yemen—it had already
dispatched warships to the Red Sea—but refused to send troops to Suakin (Sawakin)
as demanded by the British to prevent its occupation by the Italians. As early as 1851
the Ottoman government had decided to reassert its sovereignty over Massawa and
Suakin, which administratively depended on the *vilayet* of the Hicaz.[52] But by 1874 it
had agreed to leave the ports of Seyla, Massawa, and Suakin to direct Egyptian rule,
while retaining formal sovereignty over the Red Sea littoral all the way to the Horn of
Africa. Still hoping to force the sultan to collaborate with them, the British threatened to conclude an alliance with those tribes of the Sudan and Arabia that nurtured
hostile feelings toward the caliphate, but the sultan-caliph remained adamant.[53] In
the words of Gazi Osman paşa, the sultan's adviser on Islamic military issues, joint
operation with the British forces against the Islamic population was impermissible.[54]
The mahdi died in June 1885, and his successor, Khalifa Abdallahi, seemed less an-

tagonistic to Abdulhamid, in part as reaction to French advance in Central Africa. This led the sultan to honor the new Sudanese mahdi with letters, envoys, and favors, including a medal; but the new mahdi refused the invitation to visit Istanbul, lest he become a "perpetual guest."

After Salisbury replaced Gladstone as British prime minister, a fresh start was made in the Anglo-Ottoman negotiations concerning the fate of Egypt. Gazi Ahmet Muhtar paşa and Henry Drummond Wolfe, the Ottoman and British high commissioners respectively, began discussions in 1885 and concluded the Anglo-Ottoman Convention on 22 May 1887, agreeing to set a date to discuss the British evacuation of Egypt, but Drummond Wolfe left after one year and was not replaced. Ahmet Muhtar paşa remained in Egypt as Ottoman commissioner until 1908. The British tolerated Ahmet Muhtar's stay in Egypt because, as Drummond stated it, his presence gave the British regulation of Egyptian affairs an indirect caliphal blessing. The commissioners also contacted the successors of the mahdi in the Sudan, but all their efforts failed when the sultan refused to consider in a single package the British evacuation of Egypt and the Sudan and a joint action with London in the Red Sea. The sultan, acceding to the British negotiator believed that the English intended to establish an independent Arab government in opposition to the Empire, the caliphate, and the sultanate and to transfer the Islamic caliphate there.[55]

Sultan Abdulhamid's hesitant policy in the Sudan may be attributed to his insufficient military and economic means, to his well-known fear that small local conflicts could easily degenerate into large-scale wars that would give Europe opportunity for interference, and, above all, to his firm decision to insulate the Hicaz from any conflict there or in its vicinity.[56] Despite pressure, threats, promises of territory, and other inducements, he never engaged in hostile action against other Muslim rulers or rebels, although he disliked many of them and condemned their radicalism. This feature of Abdulhamid's foreign policy came to be idealized in the Middle East, mainly after the 1960s, as he was increasingly glorified as a true-believing Muslim ruler dedicated to the cause of Islam.

The Muslim Union in East Central Africa

While Ottoman foreign policy in North Africa tried to prevent the European occupation of the area and to consolidate defense of the Hicaz by reasserting Ottoman sovereignty, suzerainty, and influence, in the rest of Africa the sultan tried to resurrect old friendly ties and past relations. It should be noted that the first attempts to establish relations between East-central Africa and Istanbul were initiated by the native rulers and religious leaders of East Africa who faced the English and French threat. As early as the 1860s, the leading ulema of Henzevan in the Comoro Islands had asked the caliph to advise their own sultan not to "sell" the islands to the Europeans (see chapter 2). The famous *şeyh* of the Comoro Islands, Şerif Muhammad Maruf (1853–1905), was a disciple of the Tunisian Ali Nureddin Yashruti (d. 1893), whose teacher had been Muhammad Ibn Hamza Zafir al-Madani, Abdulhamid's trusted adviser. After Maruf criticized Sultan Ali bin Umar, the ruler of Grand Comoro, for his unIslamic attitudes and for his collaboration with the French, he had to flee Grand

Comoro (but returned shortly before his death). Istanbul apparently had established some relations with the Yashrutiyya order in the Comoro Islands, and especially with Zanzibar, where the old Ottoman ties to the ruling dynasty and the influence of the Kadiriyya brotherhood gave Istanbul considerable leverage.[57]

The complex history of relationship between Istanbul and the imams of Oman received a special twist in the eighteenth century after Ahmad bin Said, the founder of the Abusaid dynasty, forced the Persians out of Oman. The Ottomans, grateful to them for securing Arabia against the Persian threat, sent the imams of Oman (which was never an Ottoman possession) an annual subsidy that significantly bolstered Omani finances. Ahmad bin Said died in 1775, and his son and successor, Seyyid Sultan bin Ahmad, was killed by pirates in 1804 as he was returning from Basra, where he had gone to claim the subsidy. Ahmad's son and successor, Seyyid Said, paid special attention to Zanzibar and turned it into a major political and Islamic cultural center. Seyyid Said (r. ca. 1807–1856) initially ruled both Oman and Zanzibar, and early in his reign he fought the Wahhabis in Oman, gaining further Ottoman gratitude. Afterward he turned all his attention to his possessions in Africa, and in 1832 he made Zanzibar the capital of his African domains. Zanzibar then became the political, commercial, and cultural center of central East Africa, as a large number of Arabs accompanied Seyyid Said to Zanzibar and spread Islam into the interior. Meanwhile, against European advice, the sultan introduced clove cultivation and made Zanzibar prosperous and famous. Seyyid Said remained on friendly terms with the English throughout his reign, as did his successor, Seyyid Majid (r. 1856–70), whose reign was marred in 1859 by the attempt of Seyyid Barghash (his brother) to oust him. Barghash sought the aid of the French but was eventually banished to India by the British. Nevertheless, when Barghash finally came to the throne after Majid's death, he remained on good terms with the British, even visiting London, as well as Paris and Berlin.[58]

Barghash (r. 1870–88) was a devout Muslim and a very good administrator and diplomat. His special agent, Abdullah Salim el-Kheimiri, was resident at times and active in both Istanbul and Cairo. During Barghash's reign, and probably thanks to him, the Uwaysi branch of the Kadiri brotherhood established a strong presence from Zanzibar all the way to Somalia. Faced with European designs on his land, Barghash used his ties to the Kadiri order to strengthen his influence on the mainland. However, during his final years in power Barghash began to lose his possessions in East Africa to the Germans, who in 1885 declared Zanzibar to be their protectorate.

Istanbul seems to have decided to approach Seyyid Barghash sometime in 1877, after the Porte learned that the Zanzibari ruler planned to perform the pilgrimage to Mecca. When Barghash (*Bergoş* in Ottoman documents) failed to come to Mecca in 1877 or 1878 as expected, the Porte instructed its agent in the Hicaz to send the famous Mecidiye medal and the sultan's letter directly to Barghash so that "the spiritual ties bounding together the Muslim community [camia-i Islamiye] would be strengthened."[59] Emin bey, one of the high Ottoman officials serving in the Hicaz, who spoke Arabic well, was delegated to take the medal and Abdulhamid's letter to Zanzibar. Upon learning that Sultan Barghash had died and that his brother Khalifa bin Said (r. 1888–90) had taken the throne, Istanbul immediately dispatched to Zanzibar Şükrü efendi, the chief scribe of Hudeyda, with the sultan's congratulatory message. Encouraged by the warm reception the Ottoman embassy received in Zanzibar, the sultan sent a more important emissary, Abdelkadir efendi in 1889, the chief judge of the trade court of Beirut.[60] The sultan, in his letter deplored the interference of foreign powers in Zanzibar's affairs, including the blockade of its coast intended to stop the slave trade. Abdulhamid firmly stated that, as the holder of the "glorious caliphate which is a unique attribute of the sultanate . . . and in view of the [world] position of the Ottoman state, and having in view the well being of the faith and the ultimate goal of achieving the happiness and progress of the Muslims," he could not remain indifferent to the events in that part of the world.[61] After enumerating the special attributes of envoy Abdelkadir efendi, the sultan stressed that he had been sent to study events on the spot and that "his oral communications should be given full credence."[62] As usual the sultan preferred to convey his most intimate thoughts and feelings through his emissaries rather than transcribe them in the *humayuname* (royal letter), which served as formal introduction and official sanction for embassy.

The embassy to Zanzibar seems to have had a wider scope than just formal diplomatic contact. It included Sami bey, an army officer, who was to provide military advice to Zanzibar. The available evidence indicates that Istanbul wanted to sabotage Germany's designs in Zanzibar, but the French still claimed that the mission was devised to serve German interests and would cause political harm to Istanbul. Sureyya bey, chief Palace secretary, read about the French view in the *Journal de Débats* and advised the Porte not to send the mission, even though France had not raised official objections yet. He was overruled: the sultan insisted on sending the mission.[63] Meanwhile, ironically, the Germans, who were blockading Zanzibar, asked Istanbul to help them recruit a few hundred Sudanese to perform police duties there to avoid antagonizing the natives with the presence of European policemen; the Porte answered that it would consider such a request only if it came from the rightful ruler of Zanzibar.[64]

The impact of the sultan-caliph's diplomatic activities in East Africa can only be surmised. Roland A. Oliver has indicated that the Arabs of Central and East Africa turned against the Europeans between 1884 and 1888 and sought to drive them out, and he has implied that Sultan Barghash bin Said played an important part in these developments, which appear to have been directed "from a center."[65] Actually anti-European insurrections began in Buganda in 1877–78 and were led by "Muslim leaders"—that is, the "Arabs"—and the Kadiriya and seemed directed against both the Christian missionaries and earlier Egyptian attempts to establish influence in East Africa. In sum, the local native resistance to foreign occupation began much before Istanbul's initiatives and the correspondence of Sultan Abdulhamid with Seyyid Barghash and his successors. Rulers of Zanzibar continued to remain staunch friends of Istanbul for approximately two decades after Britain established a protectorate over the country in 1890 (with the agreement of the French, who in exchange took Madagascar). Seyyid Ali bin Hamud (r. 1902–11), despite his British education, nurtured "strong sympathies for the Pan-Islamic movement."[66] He not only visited Istanbul and was received with great honor by Sultan Abdulhamid, whose name was being mentioned as caliph in the Friday *hutbe* both in Zanzibar and on the mainland, but he also was very close to Ahmad bin Sumayt, a leading *kadi*, who had spent a year in the Yildiz Palace in the 1880s and received a medal from the sultan. For reasons that remain obscure, Seyyid Ali bin Hamud abdicated in 1911, while in England to attend the coronation of King George, and he died in Paris in 1918. His successor, Seyyid Khalifa II, remained loyal to the British and was very pliant to their demands. After the Ottoman state went to war in 1914 on the side of Germany and the Young Turks issued the call to *cihad*, Seyyid Khalifa II sent a letter asking all the leading Muslims in East Africa not to follow the "call of the Turks."

Ottoman relations with the rulers of Bornu in Central Africa complemented the initiative in Zanzibar. Bornu (*Bernu* in Ottoman documents) once had been under Ottoman rule, and the Porte attempted to maintain relations through the *vali*s of Tripolitania. In 1848 the ruler of Bornu, in a gesture of obedience, sent to the Ottoman *kaymakam* of Fezzan some gifts, along with ninety men and women slaves to be offered to the sultan in Istanbul. When the slaves who survived the trip arrived in Tripolitania, the sultan instructed Mehmet Ragip, the *vali* of Tripoli, to free them. The remaining thirty-seven men and thirty-four women appeared so disoriented, however, that one Ziver efendi persuaded them to pair up and marry and then dispatched them to work on the sultan's estate in Mihaliç in Central Anatolia or at the state agricultural station near Istanbul. Everything was properly registered and dated, and the liberated slaves were placed on a ship commanded by Akhermani Süleyman, but there is no indication whether they arrived safely in Istanbul.[67] It is interesting to note, however, that there are at present two or three villages in the Aegean region of Turkey whose population is definitely of African origin. The villagers claim that their forefathers came to the shores of today's Turkey many years ago after the ship transporting them from Africa sank in a storm. (There were also large numbers of Egyptian *fellahin* [villagers] brought to work in the cotton fields of Cilicia [Adana], and their descendants form a distinct group known as *fellah*, though they are Turkified. It is not clear whether the Aegean group came from Egypt or from Bornu.)

After Sultan Abdulhamid came to the throne, notably after Ottoman-French relations deteriorated, he tried to revive relations with Bornu and Kano, instructing the Ottoman *vali* in Tripoli to enter into communications with the new rulers of Bornu, and to report the results.[68] The sultan wrote a letter to Ibrahim al-Kanimi, whose conservative predecessor was opposed to the revolutionary movement of Umar Tal, proposing to strengthen the political and commercial ties between the two countries. The sultan also discreetly mentioned his title as caliph and stressed the need to establish a united Muslim front and awarded al-Kanimi the Mecidiye medal.

As the Porte strove to maintain its position in Central Africa, it issued, late in 1890, a declaration restating the Ottoman claims over Sokoto, Bornu, Kanem, Waday, and Baquirimi. Its aim was to forestall a French advance into the area and, indirectly, to thwart the Italian plan to occupy Tripolitania, for Italy backed the Ottoman claims to large tracts of land in Central Africa in order to prevent France from capturing them. However, the Ottoman policy in Bornu was unsuccessful, as late in the 1890s Rabih Fadl Allah conquered Bornu and Baquirimi and put a virtual end to the trade of Central Africa with Tripolitania. While the Ottoman government proved unable to defend its friends and allies against either Rabih or the Tuareg tribes, France, in contrast, successfully prevented Rabih from molesting the petty rulers in Chad, which was under its sway. After the Fashoda (now Kodok) incident of September 1898 demonstrated that the French dominated Central Africa and could easily threaten the British positions on the Nile, the French and the British signed the accord of 21 March

1899, which left the hinterland of Tripolitania and Cyrenaica south of the twenty-second parallel to France. Meanwhile Italy moved towards an agreement with France "in order to save what remained of Italy's colonial options."[69] Although the Porte continued its active policy in North Africa, at times displaying military muscle, it did not prevent further French moves into Sahara or Italy's occupation of Libya in 1911.

An interesting sidelight on Sultan Abdulhamid's African initiatives was a special mission to South Africa. The well-known Ebubekir efendi (d. 1880) went to South Africa at the request of the British government to teach Islam and conduct prayers for the Indian Muslim workers imported there by Britain. Ebubekir efendi arrived in South Africa in 1862 and fought to overcome the superstitions and folk rituals the workers had brought with them from India. He became chief consultant for Muslim affairs for the area as far away as Mozambique, and he kept Abdulhamid informed about these affairs and about the African Muslims' high regard for the caliphate. Ebubekir married the daughter of Jeremiah Cook (grandson of the famous Captain Cook) and had children who became active in South African politics (as his grandchildren are in the present day). Ebubekir's son Ataullah was appointed Ottoman consul to Singapore in 1900.

Conclusion

The impact of the sultan's diplomatic-religious activities in North and Central Africa can be summarized in a few lines. Relatively smooth relations between Istanbul and Africa resulted from the absence of tensions or of any major conflict of interest between the center and the periphery. Istanbul honored local autonomy and, in places, supported it with tax exemptions and recognition of special privileges. The Ottoman military and police forces, used to consolidate the local resistance against European occupation and to establish a power balance between the urban population and tribal areas, thus became the main guarantors of peace and security in the settled areas; but in the ultimate analysis, the Porte lacked the economic and military means to meet fully the African Muslims' expectations. The grand Muslim alliance in Africa did establish, however, some solid ideological and cultural foundations for the movements of resistance and revival. Indeed, the idea of resistance to European imperialism used to mobilized the upper layers of the population for the defense of the fatherland nurtured the rise of local nationalism. Thus were sown the seeds of the African liberation movements of the twentieth century.

13

Formation of Modern Nationhood
Turkism and Pan-Islamism in Russia and the Ottoman Empire

Identity Redefinition among Muslims of the Russian and the Ottoman Empires

Pan-Islamism, pan-Turkism, and nationalism in both the Ottoman and Russian Empires were the consequence of the interactions between modern education, the new social classes, and political liberalism, which operated within specific historical settings and preexisting relations that accounted for both the similarities and the differences between the two empires. This chapter proposes to study how new forces of change during the latter part of the nineteenth century not only helped engender Islamism (pan-Islamism) and nationalism in the Ottoman and Russian Empires but also to reveal how the different historical, cultural, and social circumstances and government policies prevailing in each county, produced a different type of Islamism and nationalism in each.

The overwhelming majority of Russia's Muslims considered themselves to be of Turkic origin and spoke a variety of closely related Turkic languages. Among themselves they shared a unique imperial political heritage under which lineage, along with language, furnished the ingredients necessary to reconstruct, in a new national format, their ethnic identity in the nineteenth century. Specifically, Cengiz han, and especially his descendants, had provided Russia's Muslims with a unique, lasting ethnopolitical and historical and cultural legacy and identity framework. That framework was the *ulus* (nation), which comprised all the ethnic groups and tribes that lived under one *han*, the son or grandson of Cengiz. The *ulus* was an imperial, Central Asian type of nation with the initial bond of unity in allegiance and loyalty to the *han* and, ultimately, to Cengiz han. Thus, it may be seen as a kind of extended political family in which the ruling *han* provided the vital link that bonded its subjects to the mystical father figure of the nation, Cengiz han. The Cengizid origin gave the ruling *han* his legitimacy and authority and created a sense of relationship between him and his subjects.

Charles J. Halperin has noted that of the initial four *ulus* established by Cengiz's descendants, only Batu's, known as the Golden Horde (est. 1236), escaped assimilation and obliteration by the conquered peoples and maintained existence in its own state and the successor states of Kazan and Crimea until the sixteenth and eighteen centuries respectively.[1] Extending north of the Caucasus and the Black Sea and east of the Urals, Batu's *ulus* consisted mostly of Turkic groups, such as the Kipçaks (Kumans-Polovetsy) and Karakalpaks (Cherny Klobuky), who later changed names and reemerged in the fourteenth through the sixteenth centuries as Tatars, Uzbeks, Nogais, and so on. Conversion to Islam added a new dimension and strength to the identity of Batu's *ulus* by making its members part of a large universal community of believers with an advanced civilization. However, unlike many other converts, who submerged their previous ethnic culture and identity into the universal religious identity of Islam, the members of Batu's *ulus* and its successors fused and preserved their clan identities and nomadic customs within the broader Tatar or Uzbek (etc.) identity. The prevailing folk Islam and their unique form of Islamization gave the identity of the Russian Muslims—especially those living in the Volga and Ural regions— a unique coloring and vitality.

The rulers of the Golden Horde, Berke han (r. 1257–66) and, especially, Özbek han (r. 1313–41) made Islam the religion of the state. Indeed, the conversion of Özbek han carried an extraordinary symbolic value in the association of his subjects' new Islamoethnic identity with the state and the Cengizid dynasty. The conversion cemented the association of the *ulus* with the idealized dynasty and made attachment to the faith and loyalty to the dynasty synonymous; it also gave the emerging Islamic-tribal-ethnic (Turkic) communal identity unique regional and ethnoreligious characteristics that survive until today. Nowhere in the Islamic world did faith, dynasty, and ethnicity blend in the way they did in the Golden Horde and its successor states. Devin DeWeese, in a ground breaking study, dismisses the old Russian and Western views about the "light" attachment of the inner Asian tribes to Islam and points to the seminal role played by the epic tradition, both in reporting the conversion of Özbek han and in the Islamization of society from the fourteenth to the twentieth centuries. The Islamization and Turkification were simultaneous. As DeWeese says, Baba Tükles, the person who supposedly converted Özbek han, appears in the classical work of Ötemiş haci in multiple roles—as Islamizer, nation former, mystic ancestor, and the like, linking Islam with indigenous Inner Asian values and, most important, with Inner Asian concepts and formulas for sanctifying the origin and legitimacy of human communities. This oral epic, cherished by most Turkic peoples of Eurasia more than any other, asserts the centrality of Islam in their own conceptions of communal origin, identity, and solidarity that are incorporated, along with the native culture and their original ethnic identity, into their new identity.[2] One must also stress the well-known fact that, while the power holders and army commanders in Cengiz's empire were mainly Mongols, the local rulers, officials, fighting troops, and, toward the end of the *han*'s life, his advisors were predominantly Turkic and Muslim. The total number of Mongols in the Batu's army was not more than four thousand. The overwhelming number of the Turkic tribes present in Batu's *ulus* had its share in converting and turkifying the Mongols, who became part of "us."[3] Thus, Russia's Turkic groups achieved political and economic preeminence but also inherited from Cengiz—who was not Muslim—certain secular principles of statehood, including the idea of the supremacy of imperial law (*yasa*), the sense of hierarchy, and criteria of leadership that became part of their political culture.

The ethnization and popularization of Islam among the Turkic tribes gained new momentum under Timur (Tamerlane), who identified himself with Turkic traditions and folk Islam and took a special interest in the mystical Yesevi order, while the urban areas followed the orthodoxy of Sunnism and the Persian culture.[4] Timur, who did not descend from Cengiz han, not only assured, unwittingly perhaps, the cultural, linguistic, and political preponderance of the Turkic groups but also strengthened, reshaped, and perpetuated their ethnic identity, always in association with folk Islam. Thus, the Uzbek, Kazak, and other tribal dynasties formed after the disintegration of Timur's empire derived their distinct political identity from their ethnicity, which stood on a Turkic tribal and linguistic foundation, and from Islam. The large part of Russia's Muslims had established many of the prerequisites of modern nationhood, such as a political state, association with a territory, common faith and similar culture, and a body of law, before the emergence of the Ottoman state as a major power at the end of the fourteenth century. Thus historical circumstances raised and maintained the importance of ethnicity as an identity source and secularizing force among Turkic peoples of Eurasia in a manner not seen among Ottoman Turks, despite their common devotion to Islam. In this context it should be noted that the Muslim literature treats the conversion to Islam of the Ilkhanid ruler Ghazan (Abu Said, r. 1316–35) as hardly a seminal event. The Ilkhanids were descendants of Hülagü, who ruled the Middle East, and Ghazan was the ruler of a thoroughly Islamized society; his conversion merely removed a cause of friction between himself and his Muslim subjects. Whereas Ghazan took the faith from the ruled, Berke and Özbek were the ones who disseminated it among their subjects. (The Bulgars, who had converted to Islam in the late tenth century, also played an important role in the Islamization of the area but this is outside our immediate interest.)

The Cengizid legacy, the conversion to Islam, the Turkification process, the role of folk Islam in the early nomadic life of the Turkic tribes, and so on, played a special role in defining the Turks' identity and gave their modern nationalism special ethnic and "secular" features. Charles Warren Hostler, who wrote one of the first studies on Turkism stated: "The Turkification of Anatolia indicates, then, that the Islamization of the Turks (which preceded Turkification of Anatolia) was not a denationalizing force. A deep feeling of national and linguistic separateness existed, and no outside cultural elements attracted the Turks."[5] Hostler claims that the Turkification of Anatolia in the eleventh through fifteenth centuries was greater than that of the Kemalist period. The modernist-nationalist intellectuals of Russia—and some Turkists in the Ottoman Empire and the Republic—defined Cengiz and, especially, Timur as their common ancestors and the patriarchs of Turkism and incorporated them into their nationalist pantheon (hence an overabundance of children bearing these names).[6] The memory of Cengiz han and Timur has survived in the epics and stories of the nomads and tribesmen of Central Asia regardless of their ethnic and religious background, for they welcomed, among other things, the law and order and the security of life and trade brought by these rulers. Today, after seventy years of communist rewriting the histories of Central Asian states, Azerbaycan, Kazan, Sibir, and so on, are being rewritten again by a variety of newly created national institutes or by individuals who are replacing the Russian-Soviet versions with national ones.[7]

In chapter 3 I indicated how the small Orthodox-Russian principality of Moscow revived and grew into an empire by expanding, mainly east and south, into Muslim lands, first Kazan in 1552 and then Crimea in 1783, and how its history became intertwined with the Ottoman one. From the very start of its conquests in the sixteenth century, Muscovite Russia attempted to convert its Muslim subjects, notably the Tatars, by force or through inducements, oscillating between repression (as during the reign of Peter the Great, Nicholas I, and the communists), tolerance and accommodation (as under Catherine the Great), and, beginning in 1855, relative temporary freedom under the Alexander II, Alexander III, and Nicholas II. The Tatars' centuries-old struggle for ethnocultural survival and a search for an adaptation to changing political and cultural circumstances was finally resolved. In the ultimate analysis, Islam provided Russia's Muslims a universal frame of identity and also considerable freedom to retain their old ethnolinguistic identities. This historically conditioned symbiosis between ethnicity and faith enabled Russia's Muslims to preserve a high degree of cultural, historical, and ethnic continuity and transform it into modern national identity.

A few Russian intellectuals were aware that the ethnic factor played a special role in shaping the identity of their Muslims, that urban and folk Islam were not the same; but the ruling circles continued to depict Islam as a regressive, obscurantist force that justified their own drive to assimilate the Muslims and destroy their cultural and historical legacies. A special section of the Kazan Orthodox Seminary was charged with studying Islam and proselytizing among Tatars. Influential writers, such as Mikhail Alexeyevich Miropiev, described the Muslims as subhuman creatures who had lost their human attributes, such as the ability to think rationally and understand nature. The Russian anti-Islamists compared the "fanaticism" of the Uzbeks and Tadjiks—that is, the inhabitants of the urban area where classical, ("degenerated," in the Russian view) Islam dominated—with the relative freedom of thought and "natural" behavior of the "children of nature"—that is, the tribal nomadic Kazak or Kirghiz—and called for the protection of the latter against the "barbarism" of established Islam. Viewing Islam as transnational, unitary, homogeneous, and as an inveterate enemy of Russia, these imperialist writers called for Russia to maintain permanent military superiority over the Muslims and to destroy or dominate the Islamic centers of power and culture.[8] Russian policy in Transcaucasia in 1816 has been summarized as one of keeping the natives aware of Russian power, of generating new economic needs, of encouraging dissension among various ethnic groups, of introducing Christianity, and of preventing the formation of links with Turkey and Iran.[9] The anti-Islamic literature appearing in periodicals such as *Pravoslavnii Sobesednik* (1855–1917), published by the Kazan Theological Academy, has been subject to various studies. Suffice it to mention once more that there was a high degree of continuity and consistency in this official negative view of Islam in both the czarist and the communist periods; and one of the basic goals of both these regimes was to do away with the outside sources nurturing the culture and identity of Russia's Muslims: chiefly, the Ottoman Empire and Iran.

The Ottoman state, although established late in the thirteenth century by a conglomeration of humble Turkic tribes without the leadership of a recognized tribal dynasty (the Kayi ancestry is debatable), developed from the very start as a nontribal political entity; and despite the existence of a great variety of tribes on its territory, it remained immune to tribal or ethnic influences and affiliations. The state acquired a distinct identity of its own apart from the ethnic identity of its subjects. The Ottoman sultans were not related by blood to either the Cengizids or the Timurids, although they still respected their legacy. The Crimean *hans*, the last to be conquered by Russia, had become vassals of Istanbul in 1475, were related to Cengiz and supposedly were designated heirs to the Ottoman throne, if the House of Osman became extinct. The Kazan *hans*, governing the central lands of the Golden Horde, also were descended from Cengiz; they looked condescendingly upon the Ottoman sultan's lack of illustrious imperial pedigree and resented also the vassalage of Crimea—a former territory of the Golden Horde—to the Porte.

It should be noted that the bulk of the early Ottoman Empire was established first in the Balkans. Almost from the beginning it was a predominantly an East European state, especially after it incorporated the Bulgarian and Serbian principalities in 1397 and 1459. Sultan Mehmed II (r. 1451–81) regarded himself as being not only a *han* but also a caesar, heir to the East Roman Empire or Rumili; the Turks referred to the Balkans as Rumili (Romanland). The Ottomans granted to the Orthodox Christian population in 1452 (and later to the Jews in 1495) absolute freedom of religion and the right to retain their body of family law, to be implemented by their own clergy under the direction of autonomous patriarchates. From the mid-sixteenth century to the last quarter of the eighteenth, Peç was the seat of the patriarchate for the Serbs and Ohrida for the Bulgarians and Macedonians. This was the Ottoman *millet* system, under which the religious community had a legal status, stemming directly from basic Islamic principles, according to protection to the peoples of the Book, that could not be altered by the government. The rights of Russia's Muslims, on the other hand, stemmed from the czar and his government and could be broadened or restricted at will. Nonetheless, the number of Muslim converts to Orthodoxy in Russia was far smaller that the number of Christian converts to Islam in the Ottoman Empire. Despite the freedoms they enjoyed as Christians, a fairly large number of Slavs, Boşnaks (Bosnians), and Albanians converted freely to Islam for a variety of economic, cultural, political, and historical reasons. These converts preserved their ethnic identity and language to an extent not seen among many other Muslims, even though the Balkan Christians ultimately called the Balkan Muslims "Turks," while Russia called its Muslims "Tatars."

In sum, the historical evolution of the Ottoman and Russian Muslim societies followed different patterns until developments in the nineteenth century produced a realignment that seemed to converge on religious—cultural level and diverge on the linguistic—ethnic level.

Economic-Social Change, Modern Education, and the Intelligentsia

Deprived of political power, the Muslims of Russia could fend off cultural and religious assimilation by retreating into isolation, thus remaining outside the events transforming the czarist society. The isolation and underdevelopment of Russia's Muslims persisted for as long as Russia itself remained underdeveloped and unable to devise new means to assimilate or change the Muslim society from within. In the nineteenth century all this was changed. First there was the introduction of capitalism. As the century unfolded, the Russian czars promoted a type of capitalism designed to strengthen their state, initially without much regard to religion or ethnicity. Capitalism in Russia undermined the patriarchal Muslim order, producing a leadership vacuum and a crisis of identity; but it also created the conditions for the rise of what Miroslav Hroch might have called the small subject nation: an ethnic intelligentsia identified with the ruled, a literary language, and a unit of administration coinciding with the territory of the subject ethnic group. The upper groups of the Volga Tatars, Crimeans, and the Azeris, who had been long under Russian rule, had attended Russian schools, and learned foreign languages, were among the first to develop a new awareness of their own cultural and ethnic identity. Some of them actually had been in the employ of the Russian government. For instance, as early as the eighteenth century, Catherine the Great used the Volga Tatars as traders and Muslim missionaries and teachers to establish commercial relations with and convert to Islam the natives of the northern Central Asian steppes, in order to facilitate Moscow's rule. In the nineteenth century, the Tatars used their position as intermediaries to assert their own ethnocultural identity and interest, and educate the less developed Muslims of the steppes in modernism and nationalism. These "enlightened" Muslim teachers, who were the first beneficiaries of Russian reforms, used the Tatar language as the vehicle for converting, re-Islamizing, and assimilating some of the peoples of the steppe into the Tatar nation, itself in the formative stages. Finally, in 1906, the Russian authorities prohibited the use of Tatar as a language of instruction and instead mandated the use of the Kazak language, in addition to Russian, in the steppe schools so as to stop the spread of "pan-Islamism-pan-Turkism," which served as a convenient shelter from which Tatar teachers could disseminate their own nationalism. Thus the Russians facilitated the spread of the Kazak language and also sowed the seeds of a Tatar-Kazak conflict, which still survives.

The modern school system was the tool for producing and reshaping knowledge and identity rather than for simply transmitting centuries-old religious knowledge to future generations, as had been the case with the traditional Muslim schools in Russia and elsewhere. Capitalism in Russia produced Muslim middle classes, with new elites such as entrepreneurs, merchants, industrialists, and intellectuals, who were active in large centers, notably in Kazan and Azerbaycan, and open to the idea of change. The elites, although varying in makeup and influence from one Muslim group to another, seemed to share the idea of *cedid* (newness-modernity), which became in fact their common philosophy and produced their modernist-nationalist ideology. In Kazan, the elite was modernist-traditionalist, while in Crimea the leadership consisted of an intellectual elite who descended from the dispossessed traditional elites— including the *mirza*s (middle noblemen)—and were less interested in economic enterprise than in the modern intellectual professions and learning. In Kazakstan, on the other hand, instead of capitalism there was colonialism, for the Russian administration, beginning in the period 1860–80, dispossessed the nomads of millions of acres of grazing pastures and settled in their place large numbers of Russian colonists. It also settled many tribes, educating the children of the tribal nobility in the modern educational system or enlisting them in government or army service, in order to create a pro-Russian elite. In sharp contrast, the Uzbek oasis states, occupied only in the 1860s, had a large, traditional middle class of craftsmen, artisans, and sophisticated ulema deeply immersed in their Islamic culture and the traditions of classical Islamic learning. The Russian (and Soviet) regimes gradually replaced this native Uzbek-Tadjik middle class with an army of Slavic functionaries, teachers, and agricultural experts specializing in cotton cultivation and, in the communist era, in industrial management. They became also the leading urban social stratum. Deprived of access to meaningful and lucrative government positions, the resentful natives sympathized with and followed their own conservative traditional leaders until challenged by a small group of intellectuals seeking renewal. Throughout Russia most of the upper ulema had easily acquiesced to the czar's authority as long as the latter did not tamper with their leadership positions and allowed them to use religious properties and retain control of the community. The political leadership and the upper bureaucracy and the control of the economy was in the hands of a Russian elite.

In the Ottoman Empire, the introduction of capitalism was preceded by a two-century tug-of-war between the state (the titleholder of a substantial part of the arable lands), the tenants (who were the commodity producers), and, especially, the merchants (who were outside the direct state control and wanted some sort of commercialization of agriculture). The actual introduction of capitalism resulted from pressure by England and France in the nineteenth century and manifested itself, first, in the liberalization of trade and then in the expansion of private landholding and rise of a commercial bourgeoisie consisting first almost exclusively of Christians. The splitting of the Ottoman classes along ethnic-religious lines has been analyzed elsewhere and need not be repeated here. Suffice it to say that while among the Christians the entrepreneurial groups became de facto leaders of their respective ethnic communities, among the Ottoman Muslims the bureaucracy and its ally, the modernist intelligentsia, occupied the dominant position. The Muslim landlords and merchants, although influential in their respective local communities, had little influence over the government or society at large until almost the end of the century. The Ottoman government provided economic incentives to Christians in order to secure their political loyalty.

It may sound odd to state that by the end of the century, the "oppressed" Christian merchants and professionals in the Ottoman Empire became superior in wealth, knowledge, and prestige to the Muslims, while in Russia the bulk of the Muslims continued to be underdogs, despite the substantial progress registered by their small, modern elite class. It should be noted that overshadowing and affecting the elite developments was the fact that both Russia and the Ottoman Empire, absolutist monarchies, were attempting to modernize themselves by using a form of bureaucratic centralization to transform their multiethnic empires into unitary states. Thus political unitarism called for both empires to undertake the cultural and, especially, the political homogenization of their populations. Russia, under Peter the Great, initiated a series of reforms one century before the Ottomans and thus produced a powerful Russian state that eventually embraced Russianism—a form of imperial Orthodox nationalism—as a unifying and assimilating device.

Indeed, Russia's intelligentsia undertook, in the nineteenth century, a reappraisal of its culture, nationality, identity, and the ideas of progress and Westernization. As a result, P. Y. Chaadayev, in his *Letters* (influenced by Karamzin's *History*), A. I. Turgenev, Pushkin, and other writers gave Russian identity a new meaning, dynamism, and direction. This process, in addition to the government's expansionist policies, encouraged the Slavist views of N. Y. Danilevsky, R. A. Fadayev, and others who believed that Russia and the Slavic (Orthodox) nations of Europe were indissolubly linked to one another, that Western Europe (read Catholics and Protestants) was permanently hostile to them, and that the Ottomans served the West's interests. Obviously, the emerging panslavism was partly a response to the Ottoman alliance with the West that resulted in the Russian defeat in the Crimean War (1853–56) and put an end—temporarily—to the principle of Christian unity in the solving of the Eastern Question—that is, the dismemberment of the Ottoman Empire.

Active in the Slavonic Benevolent Committee, formed in 1858 in Moscow to support cultural and religious activities among the Ottoman Slavs and to award scholarships to Balkan students, were dedicated pan-Slavists such as Konstantin and Ivan Aksakov. Ten years later, when a branch of the society was opened in St. Petersburg, one of its members was N. P. Ignatiev, who had been appointed Russian ambassador to Istanbul in 1864 and who later played a crucial role in supporting the nationalist movements of the Orthodox Christians and the Slavs of the Balkans and in launching the unprovoked war of 1877–78 in order to "liberate the Orthodox brothers." At the same time that pan-Slavism's messianic message became part of the elementary school curriculum, however, it also became something of a reverse guide to the new Muslim intelligentsia of Russia, who developed immediate sympathy for and solidarity with the Ottoman Muslims. The war of 1877–78 was a watershed for the internal and international policies of the Ottoman government and for Russia's attitude toward its Muslim subjects.

Russia's Muslims and Ottoman Policies after 1878

Relations between the Muslims of Russia and the Ottoman Empire developed at two levels: first, at the government level, through the exchange of information between Ottoman diplomatic offices and local native leaders and, second, at the popular level, through newspapers, visits, and person-to-person relations. The relatively good relations developing between Istanbul and St. Petersburg after 1882, as a reaction to Ottoman alienation from England and France, resulted in intensified trade and communications and made the Ottoman and Russian Muslims more susceptible to each other's influence. The Porte sought to gather as much information as possible about Russia's Muslims in the hope of maintaining the caliph's *religious* influence there, although it scrupulously refrained from engaging in political or subversive action. The caliph's initiatives met initially with considerable support from the modernist- and traditionalist-minded Muslim elites in Russia but also, paradoxically, with some opposition from the upper ranks of the Muslim religious establishment, which had entered the service of the czar and became increasingly alienated from the modernists (nationalists).

The Ottoman embassy in St. Petersburg and the consulates in the Caucasus regularly informed the Palace about the major events involving Russia's Muslims and the czar's policy toward them.[10] Istanbul devoted special attention to Muslim dignitaries from Russia who visited the sultan's lands; Premier Kiamil paşa, for example, personally informed the sultan as soon as he received a cable from the Ottoman consul in Tiflis (Tibilisi) that the uncle of the *han* of Khiva was coming to Istanbul and should be received with proper honors.[11] Just as the consular reports helped form Ottoman perceptions of their coreligionists in Russia, they now provide historical insight into the situation of Russia's Muslims during this period. For instance, a rather lengthy consular report from Tiflis informed the Porte that the villages of Tatareskiya Oyi, Novayadon, and Enada in the Simbirsk district had asked for authorization to build mosques in their localities, but that the Russian Council of State had informed them that permission would be issued only to localities with a minimum of two hundred taxpaying Muslim inhabitants. According to the same report, the permission to build mosques was further subject to approval by the highest local Orthodox priest, and localities had devised a variety of devious measures to compel the Muslims to convert to Orthodox Christianity. The Porte was particularly upset to learn that the Russian government had made special efforts to turn the Muslims "away from the caliph," by closing their native schools and enrolling their children in Russian schools "even before they had a chance to learn their mother tongue"; but the majority of children attended no school and "lived in ignorance and savagery like their parents."[12]

The Ottoman government and the press were additionally alarmed to learn of Russian efforts to draft the Muslims into the army and to bureaucratize the Muslim religious establishment, in order to use it to enhance the Muslims' loyalty to the czar. The initial "muftiate," that is the chief administrative office of the Muslims, modeled after the Orthodox bishoprics, was established by Catherine the Great in Ufa (known as the muftiate of Orenburg because Ufa was at the time part of the province of Orenburg). Later other muftiates were established in Crimea in Bahçesaray and in Mahaçkala and in Azerbaycan. The same arrangement prevailed during most of the Soviet regime. The system had some success in coopting the upper Muslim religious establishment; for example, the mufti of the Caucasus, Hüseyin efendi Gaybev, who expected to receive the order of St. Vladimir from the czar, wrote to the imams of the Muslim villages that "it is a duty to obey the ruler [*padişah*] and [his] Judges . . . be they just, or oppressive, Muslim or non-Muslim, or . . . even slaves." The mufti cited passages from the Koran and examples from the *hadis*es trying to prove that it was acceptable for Muslims to obey a non-Muslim ruler. He described how some early Muslims of Mecca went to Ethiopia and accepted the authority of its Christian (Nasara) ruler. Hüseyin efendi concluded his letter by asking a vital question: "Is there any religious reason, custom, and tradition which prevents us from living in our own original homeland under the protection and care of the merciful, just, brave and illustrious emperor Alexander Alexandrovich?"[13] After complaining that religious men from "foreign countries"—that is, the Ottoman Empire and Iran—roamed the Caucasian provinces as teachers, Sufi mystics, and dervishes and that the inhabitants accepted them with open arms and fell under their influence, the mufti ordered the imams to keep such preachers out of their villages.

The usual tension between the religious establishment and folk religion thus gained new intensity as the representatives of the former became identified with Russian rule. The mufti was particularly incensed by the steady emigration to the Ottoman state of many Caucasians, who left Russia to avoid being drafted into the czarist army and so face the risk of having to fight their own coreligionists in the caliph's forces. He accused the emigrants of abandoning their *vatan* (fatherland) and of having violated the advice of the Prophet, who had affirmed that the "love of the fatherland was part of the faith" ("hubb-ul vatan min al-iman"), according to a *hadis*. He assured the emigrants who desired to return to their fatherland that they would be wholeheartedly welcomed back. Hüseyin efendi told the imams that God gave his human creatures the mental faculties to acquire education, science, and technology and that they were obligated to sharpen their intellect. He urged the Muslims to attend the lay schools of the czar as much as they attended their own religious schools, to love the *vatan* the way they loved their own mothers, and to be good citizens. Among the many characteristics of good citizenship, according to the mufti, were love of the country, a meek disposition ("like a lamb" ["kuzu tabiatli"]), a strong body, refusal to engage in intrigue and political debates, and the ability to transform oneself into a "lion" when enemies attacked the *vatan*. The mufti concluded, "[T]he fatherland is not only the place where one is born but also the land of the state of which one is subject. All people living in one country under one single authority are considered to be its citizens and share the same fatherland without difference of sex and religion."[14]

The mufti obviously was an "apparatchik" whose concept of government, morality, and obedience to authority, though backed by koranic verses, reflected the Russian political philosophy and Orthodox Christian teachings and was designed to serve the czar's government. However, the mufti was promoting also the idea of a territorial fatherland by appealing to the natives' sense of patriotism, their love for their own land, which was now occupied by Russians. Obviously, the Russian government, in ordering the mufti to eulogize the *vatan*, sought to secure the loyalty of the Muslims and deter them from developing any allegiance to the Ottoman caliph or to the shah of Iran and from migrating to the Ottoman state. There were, of course, three "fatherlands" that the colonized Muslims might think of: the territorial tribal land, the historical fatherland remembered by the elites, and the Russian fatherland, promoted by the state. The love for the first of these, defined in religious terms, survived after the Caucasians migrated to Turkey, and thus the desire to return to the original *vatan* became a characteristic of their culture in diaspora.

The Porte's representative in Tiflis responded to Hüseyin efendi's letter by having his own friends and allies in the community propagandize against the mufti. The newspaper *Keşkül* (pub. 1884–91), an advocate of ethnic national identity and Azerbaycani Turkishness, which was published in Turkish, and other papers were induced to print articles supportive of the Ottomans, Islam, and the caliph. The consul also announced his intention to visit several towns in the Caucasus to counteract the mufti's views and asked for travel funds, which Istanbul approved immediately.[15] The sultan-caliph thus was siding with the Muslim nationalists—the anti-Russians—in the Caucasus against the traditionalist Islamic establishment that was one of the bases of his support within the Ottoman Empire. Most of the traditional religious establishments seemed ready to obey any state, Islamic or Christian, as long as it was allowed to remain in charge of the community and its leaders were recognized and paid by the ruling government.

The sultan's effort to counter the effects of pro-Russian propaganda is considered by some as evidence that he had launched a secret pan-Islamic campaign; however, the more reasonable view is that the Porte's effort to counteract harmful propaganda was natural for any government wishing to retain the goodwill of citizens in another country. The Russian and Soviet views on this issue varied greatly. Charles Hostler makes note of the secret czarist Turkistan Security Office report, which defined the pan-Islamists as aiming toward the "national self-determination of the Muslim," and, despite their religious appearances, as actually seeking national self-determination. Gabidullin, who wrote one of the basic books on panislamism, though affected by conventional Russian views, agrees that the pre-Revolution documents concerning pan-Islamism speak more about pan-Turkism. The Tenth Party Congress of 1921 treated pan-Islamism and pan-Turkism as forms of bourgeois democratic nationalism. Stalin's initial views were more or less the same. In contrast, however, the Great Soviet Encyclopedia defined pan-Islamism as a religious political doctrine advocating the unification of all Muslims in one state under the leadership of the caliph and claimed that it was influenced by C. Afghani, that the muridists of the Caucasus and Sultan Abdulhamid exploited it, and that the Germans used it for their imperial purposes.[16]

In any case, the battle between the caliph and the czar for the loyalty of Russia's Muslims was won by neither, for Islamism and nationalism in Russia followed a course determined by internal factors rather than by St. Petersburg's decrees or Istanbul's wishes. There is an apparent contradiction between the view that the Turkic-speaking Muslims of Russia and those of the Ottoman state had long-standing linguistic, ethnic, religious, and cultural affinities and the claim that Islamism and nationalism, including pan-Turkism, in Russia had little connection to Istanbul, at least until the Young Turks took over the government there in 1908. The truth is that the special historical considerations and socioeconomic conditions prevailing in Russia and the Ottoman Empire dictated different routes for the Islamist-nationalist movements in the two countries. The Russian and Ottoman governments were sovereign entities pursuing different goals and policies in different social environments. To be sure, both were multiethnic, traditionalist, and absolutist monarchies that were undertaking modernization primarily to rejuvenate the state and, only secondarily, to improve the welfare of society. However, the Russian state was "national," bearing the Russian ethnic label and possessing a well-developed Russian culture, while the Ottoman state was truly *anational*, resting on culturally semiautonomous religious communities that had subsumed ethnic identities under those of the Islamic or Orthodox Christian religious universalism. Capitalism and industrialization also were far more advanced in Russia and had produced there a relatively large middle class and a group of professionals more numerous and better organized and trained than their Ottoman counterparts. The Ottoman peasantry was economically better off than the Russian mujiks, as were its Christian subjects in comparison with the Muslims; but the debt-ridden Ottoman Empire was under constant threat from foreign powers, including Russia, and its sparse middle class was divided into antagonistic Muslim and non-Muslim sectors, rooted mainly in agriculture and commerce respectively.

Acting from a position of strength, Russia continuously sought ways to assimilate its Muslim subjects, even as it defended the national rights of the primarily Slavic Orthodox Christians in the Balkans and encouraged them to rebel against the ruling Ottomans.

Social Change and Identity Reconstruction among the Muslims of Russia

In the nineteenth century, Russia used at least three means in its effort to coopt its Muslim subjects into state service and, ultimately, to assimilate them. The first was to recruit the children of the top Muslim leaders into the Russian army, a policy that was enforced until recent times.[17] The sons of the Muslim tribal chiefs, in particular, were trained in a subordinate capacity as officers in the Russian army. Referred to sometimes as *emanet* (given in trust), these cadets were in reality hostages who received a typical Russian military education. As a result, many acquired new ideas and some were Russified to the extent that they no longer felt at ease in their native society.[18] For instance, after one of Şeyh Şamil's sons returned from Moscow, as requested by his father in a peace agreement signed with the czar, he often complained of alienation from his own society and asked to be sent back to St. Petersburg, causing his father—the symbol of resistance to the czar—great grief.

Sometimes, however, the *emanet* interpreted the knowledge and new beliefs learned from the Russians from the perspective of their own ethnic group. Chokan Valikhanov (d. 1865), a descendant of the Kazak *hans*, served the Russians faithfully, for he believed in their modernist mission; but he was soon disillusioned by the Russian hegemonic practices and dedicated the rest of his short life to collecting the literary treasures of his own nomadic people, now part of Kazak national culture. Musa Kondukov, the son of a Caucasian (Chechen) feudal chief, although a general in the Russian army, turned against the Russians and emigrated with his tribe (statistics put their total number at twelve thousand) and fought in the war of 1877–78 in the Ottoman army against the Russians. The same was true for Eyüp Sabri paşa, who belonged to the Russian gendarmerie in the area of Revan yet fought on the side of the Ottomans in 1877–78. After the war, Eyüp Sabri, along with eighteen subordinate officers and his entire tribe (called Zeylan or Zilan; he was its chief), emigrated to Anatolia and asked to be employed in the gendarmerie of Erzurum where the group settled.[19] Abbaskulu Agha Bakuhanli (1779–1846), descended from an aristocratic family of Kuba (Azerbaycan), served in the Russian army and even fought the Ottomans in the war of 1828–29; but then he became an early leader of the Azeri modernist movement. He established the literary "Gulistan" society, wrote books on history and literature, and promoted the establishment of modern schools to teach Islam and Western sciences. He also went on the *hac* to Mecca and stopped in Istanbul. Mehmet Ali Mirza Kazembey (1802–1870) collaborated with the Russians but also advocated the development of a common language for all the Muslims of Russia long before Gaspirali tried to create an actual language.

However, there were many Turks who served the Russian government willingly and faithfully, when the czar allowed them to retain their Islamic faith and support it. Such was the case of Yusuf Tahir bey, a general in the Russian army originally from the Caucasian region of Derbend, who in 1879 bequeathed 10,000 rubles for the maintenance of the holy places in Mecca and Medina, a bequest that was delivered by the Russian embassy in Istanbul to the Ottoman Foreign Ministry, only to be pocketed by an unscrupulous official, who was apprehended and severely punished, on the orders of the sultan.[20] Moreover, many Muslim officers in the army became thoroughly Russified, converted, and assimilated and, in a number of instances, were set to rule their own kin in the newly conquered areas of Central Asia and, as teachers, used school textbooks, such as the *Ustad-i Awwal* (1902), that defined Russia as the Muslims' fatherland.

Capitalism, Social Change, and Education

I have already mentioned that the rapid development of capitalism in Russia permitted the rise of a Muslim entrepreneurial class in Azerbaycan and Kazan, the areas that played decisive leadership roles in the Muslim national revival.[21] The Huseyinof brothers of Orenburg (theirs was a true rags-to-riches story), the Akçurins (Akçora) of Simbirsk (Uliyanov) in Kazan, Zeynulabidin Tagiev, Murtaza Muhtarov, the Sultanovs, Nagievs, and Asadullaevs of Azerbaycan are just some of the best-known Russian Muslim entrepreneurs. The issue needs further elaboration.

   In Azerbaycan the discovery of oil created overnight a small but rich class of entrepreneurs. By the early 1860s, 80 percent of the oil wells were in the hands of Muslims, although twenty years later they owned less than 20 percent. Nevertheless, the Azeri Muslim entrepreneurs maintained control over the real estate market, silk spinning, and some other fields despite the growing competition of the Armenians and Russians, who received preferential government treatment. The city of Baku grew from a small town of 15,000 people in the mid-1850s to an industrial-financial metropolis of more than 200,000 at the end of the century.[22] It was this oil city, gripped by social and ethnic tensions stemming from rural immigration and economic inequality, that became the intellectual cradle of Azerbaycani modernists and nationalists who eventually affected their Ottoman counterparts. The Azerbaycani entrepreneurs are now becoming the subjects of interest in Azerbaycan itself. The *New York Times* (22 March 1997) reported that the life of Timurbek Asarbekov, a herdsman who became an oil tycoon, is a subject of study in contemporary Baku. (When I visited Baku in 1990, an Azeri scholar showed me a manuscript dealing with the history of the Muslim oil magnates of Baku, which he had been unable to publish under the Soviets.) The newspaper *Kaspy*, a Russian language periodical owned by Tagiev and published by Ali Mardanbey Topçubaşev, became the voice of the Azeri liberals as well as of European political ideas; many of the liberals eventually associated with the Kadets (the party of the Constitutional Democrats).[23] The wealth acquired by the Muslim entrepreneurs assured their loyalty to the Russian government and, at the same time, furnished them the means to finance the modernist institutions that led to the national redefinition of their own ethnic group and enabled them to acquaint themselves with the West. A good part of the first group of modernist Muslim intellectuals remained loyal to the Russian state, believing that modernity and democratization could be achieved within Russia.[24] However, the next generation lost hope and assumed radical positions, especially after Alexander II (r. 1855–81) resumed the authoritarian rule and the anti-Ottoman policy of his predecessors. For instance in Azerbaycan, the initial passive modernism of Abbaskulu and Hasan Melikzade Zardabi (1837–1907) took an activist form as they openly defended the establishment of national (*milli*) schools to train the *milli ziyalilar* (the national enlightened elites) and adopted pro-Ottoman attitudes.

The spread of modern education among Muslims was in part financed by their own bourgeoisie and produced the most lasting results. It began essentially as a counter to the efforts of the Russian religious establishment to use the modern schools as means of assimilating of the Muslims, especially in Kazan, the citadel of ethno-Muslim historical consciousness and resistance to russification. In the best-known case, Nikolai Ilminskii, a professor at the Orthodox Academy of Kazan—the former capital of the Tatar hanate and now the center of the anti-Muslim crusade—launched a campaign to use the educational system both to convert Muslim Tatars to Orthodox Christianity and to prevent the Kreshchennyetatar (Tatars who had converted to Christianity) from joining the thousands of their group who already had returned to Islam. Ilminskii established a modern school in 1863, hired a group of converted Tatars who were also fluent in Russian to use their own Tatar language to educate and convert their kinsmen by promoting the virtues of education, enlightenment, and progress subtly presented as elements the Christian faith. Ilminskii converted over 100,000 Tatars (by the lowest estimate) and inspired among the Kazan Muslims an unprecedented effort to find a means to avoid conversion and assimilation.[25]

The educated Muslims of Kazan began to establish their own European-type schools—often against the opposition of their traditionalist leaders. Such schools imparted a multifaceted knowledge, unlike the old Islamic schools, the curriculum of which consisted mostly of rote instruction on religion. According to one report, at the turn of the century the modern Muslim schools offered about 180 hours of secular courses, 168 hours of Russian language and literature, and only 24 hours of religious teaching.[26] The language of the new Tatar schools was native, their orientation national, and their spirit modern, inquisitive, and secular. They developed a dynamic understanding of Islam as well as a "national" vision of the faith that was rooted in their own historical experience and the coexistence of faith and ethnicity. Ilminskii, of course, opposed the modern schools run by native Muslims. He wished to keep Islam stagnant, so that Muslims would have to convert to Christianity to achieve progress.

The victory in the war of 1877–78 relieved Russia's exaggerated fears of Ottoman pan-Islamism and permitted the czar to subject the Muslim educational system to further modernization designed to undermine the traditional bases of Muslim culture. The traditional system consisted of the *mektep* (school), which was usually located in the mosque and was headed by the imam, who served also as teacher. The *mektep* did not provide any secular education, but it played a major role in familiarizing the pupils with Islam and in engendering a sense of Islamoethnonational identity, shared by most of the Muslims of Russia. Concerned with this situation, the Russian government had sought, as early as 1870 to challenge the educational monopoly of the *mektep*-mosque by creating the Russo-Tatar schools, which offered instruction in Russian and some secular subjects but also Islamic religious instruction presented by Tatar and Russian teachers. The number of the Russo-Tatar schools remained limited, probably numbering not more than three hundred. In 1874 the Ministry of Education took control of all Muslim schools, made mandatory the teaching of Russian and some secular subjects, and opened Tatar teacher-training seminaries in Kazan, Ufa, and Bahçesaray. The purpose behind these measures was to replace the "fanatical" Tatar *mollas* (religious teachers) with more liberal teachers open to the ideas of "modern civilization" as preached by Russia. The native opposition to the Russo-Tatar schools weakened considerably in the early 1880s, as did the influence of the traditional *mollas*, for the new generation of Muslims began to regard modern education as a means of advancement and emancipation. It seemed that Muslim modernist intellectuals and the Russian government were united against the conservative *mollas* in promoting the cause of modern education, which culminated eventually in the opening of community-supported *usul-u cedid* (new method) schools devised by Ismail Gaspirali.

The new school system modernized and partly Westernized (in a Russian style) the rising Tatar Muslim intelligentsia. The subjects taught reflected the Russian concepts of state, society, motherland, and human beings, but they also included general ideas and knowledge dramatically different from that prevailing in either the classical Muslim societies or in traditional Russia. Modern education awakened the Tatars' Islamic consciousness, giving Islam new functions as a source of secular national identity and a means of cultural self-preservation. In other words, the education provided the Muslims with the intellectual means both to understand the causes of the material and political backwardness that had brought them under Russian rule and to seek remedial action. Thus they used Russian cultural facilities to advance their own national cause. It bears repeating that the Muslim intellectuals' search for change or modernization (cedidism, or "renewal" as it was called) was also a form of political and national emancipation. The European-inspired scientific spirit, positivism, and progressivism of the Russian renaissance of the late eighteenth century were all to some extent embodied in this Muslim movement, as were some elements of Russian pan-Slavism, which served as the model for the Muslims' pan-Turkism.[27]

The Muslim modern school system that arose alongside the Russian one often copied the structure and spirit of the Russian nationalist schools, simply replacing the term Russian in the textbooks with Muslim, Tatar, Kazak, and so on. Thus, the so called national awakening among the Muslims of Russia became associated from the start with ethnic-religious identification. Muslim pupils in the new schools appropriated and incorporated into their own nascent political culture the concepts of religion, ethnicity, history, and fatherland, as formulated by Russian textbooks, and took pan-Slavism as model for their own pan-Islamism–pan-Turkism. Eventually they used those concepts as antidotes to the Russian nationalist propaganda, giving the Islamic and native themes taught in the Muslim modern schools an increasingly nationalistic color as the Muslim-educated elite came to consider the czar and his regime as the chief obstacle to social and political emancipation. This trend in Muslim thinking accelerated greatly after the Russian government in 1910 sought to use Islam to stem the cedidists' influence. A meeting backed by Prime Minister Petr A. Stolypin and headed by Alexei N. Kharuzin, director of religious affairs in the Interior Ministry met to find some ways "to counteract the Tatar-Muslim influence in the Volga region." The speakers accused the cedidists of turning the new method schools and the *medreses* into centers of nationalist indoctrination and friendship for Turkey, which they defined as panturkist-panislamist. The policies that followed on the report issued at the end of this meeting sought to isolate Islam supposedly in order to preserve its "spiritual purity" from secular learning and gave the traditionalists (kadimists, from *kadim*: old, ancient) official support. This was just the opposite of the policies followed in the 1880s, and the measure antagonized the Muslim modernists and pushed them closer to the Young Turks government in Istanbul, which had made modernization the supreme goal, with nationalism as its instrument.

As previously noted, the defeat of 1878 spurred the Ottoman government to turn to education to modernize and raise the political consciousness of its Muslim subjects. Consequently, the educational system envisaged by the law of 1869 was implemented more rigorously. The number of elementary schools increased as did that of higher-level professional schools modeled mainly after their Western counterparts. The Ottoman professional schools attracted to Istanbul a considerable number of Muslim students from Russia, who considered these schools both modern and "national"—that is, respectful of their Muslim identity and proof that Islam and modern science were compatible. Moreover, in the Ottoman Empire "modernity" was acknowledged as being of mostly European origin, and the students from Russia got the opportunity to go to the sources of modernity, for they had ready access to European philosophy and literature through the press in Istanbul, which was much more cosmopolitan than that of St. Petersburg and enjoyed publishing freedom as long as it did not criticize the ruler. Thus these students discovered how false were the Russian claims to be the creators of the "modern" civilization they imposed on Muslims. From the late 1880s to 1917, a fairly large number of such students from Russia came to study in the Ottoman professional schools, and they introduced the Ottoman intelligentsia to the pan-Slavist, nationalist, populist (*narodniki*), and socialist ideologies of Russia and informed their own conationals about the Islamist-populist-constitutionalist views developing in Istanbul and the rest of the Muslim world. The reformist, anti-imperialist ideas of Muhammad Abduh and C. Afghani thus became well known among Russia's Muslim intellectuals, thanks at least in part to the students from Russia in Istanbul.

Ottoman education ignored ethnicity and differences of language and emphasized the unity of faith in order to keep the Muslim ethnic groups—Turks, Arabs, Albanians, and others—together. Its aim was to preserve the Muslim-dominated, multiethnic, multinational Ottoman state, which lacked the sort of ethnonational core that was the foundation of the Russian state and of the emerging nationalism among Russia's Muslims. (Such a core was finally developed by the Turkish nationalism that emerged after 1908. See chapters 16 and 17.) One may postulate that the official endorsement of modern education by the head of the Muslim community, that is, the Ottoman caliph, had some part in breaking down the resistance of conservatives. At any rate, by the end of the century most Muslims in Russia seemed to have realized that going to modern schools and learning Russian did not necessarily bring about Russification but actually provided them with greater intellectual power to understand their rulers and defend their own culture.

The frame of mind among Muslim Ottoman intellectuals was different from that of their Russian counterparts, especially after the debacle of 1877–78 and under the fear of the imminent disintegration of the Empire. They were concerned first with assuring the survival of their state rather than with asserting the identity of their specific ethnic group. Once they came to regard modernization as capable of saving that state, they pursued it as their chief goal. Because the main problem was to hold together and mold into one social unit the various Muslim groups, the Ottoman school system officially continued to de-emphasize ethnicity, language, and Turkishness, stressing Islam as the fountainhead of identity and solidarity and Ottomanism as a political-historical integrative principle. Finally, some 150 years after the Russians accomplished this change, historiography in the sultan's lands was altered to become Ottoman and then definitely Turkocentric.

Historiography, needless to say, plays a crucial part in national indoctrination. The classical Ottoman history was written as history of the dynasty rather than of a people. For example, Ahmed Lütfi efendi, who chronicled the events from 1825–26 to 1878, continued to view Ottoman history from a purely dynastic point of view; eight volumes of his chronicles, known as *Tarih-i Lütfi*, were published during his lifetime, and the remaining eight volumes are being published now. In contrast, Abdurrahman Şeref (1853–1925), the last official Ottoman chronicler, attempted to introduce a new, vaguely Ottoman "national" approach, expressed in a series of biographies of the statesmen of the period. These appeared in two dailies (*Sabah* and *Vakit*) and were eventually gathered in a book.[28]

The issue of how to view the history was ever present in Namik Kemal's mind. He wrote a two-volume *Ottoman History* (a small section was published in 1888, the entire work in 1911, and it was reprinted in 1971–74), in which he defined the writing of history as the transfer of past information to the future in order to teach the government how to rule. He eventually referred to Turks as the architects of Ottoman history and praised Islam as their guiding principle. Kemal also wrote a series of biographies of Ottoman and Muslim statesmen, who were portrayed as, among other things, nation builders. The question of whether the history to be written was Islamic, or Ottoman, or Turkish, was revived during the period of the Young Turks. In 1909 the new Sultan Reşat appointed a committee headed by A. Şeref to write history from an Ottomanist viewpoint. There were other histories of the Ottoman state that took a different approach, such as the *Netayic ul-Vukuat* by Mustafa Nuri paşa (1824–1890) of the Mansurizadeler family. He occupied several high positions in the government, as his title indicated, including the Ministries of Education, Vakifs, and Defter-i Hakani or Archives. Citing Ibn Haldun's view that all states periodically change and renew themselves, in his four-volume work he divided Ottoman history from its start to 1824 into six sections, each one with its own special institutional characteristics.[29]

The Russian schools, in contrast to the uncertain Ottoman historiography teetering between dynastic and "national," used a well-established Russian "national" historiography to portray their history as a unilinear, victorious struggle of the Russian Christian nation against Western and Eastern [Islamic] enemies bent on destroying that unique creation, the Russian state.

The educated offspring of the Christian Ottoman bourgeoisie, that is, Greeks, Armenians, and so on, sure of their identity, increasingly portrayed the Muslims as devoid of a national spirit and consequently unable to understand and absorb Western civilization. They equated nationalism with civilization, a view echoed later by Yusuf Akçura. They held that Christianity was their "national" link to the West and its superior civilization. In response to this religion-based concept of civilization, the Muslim intelligentsia of Russia, and a few in the Ottoman Empire, sought to view Western civilization in secular terms as consisting of science, while religion was viewed as a private, individual matter. They opposed religion if it impeded the acquisition of scientific knowledge and civilization but acknowledged Islam as part of their "national" culture and history. They may not have realized that their secular concept of civilization and their politicized and nationalized understanding of Islam had turned them into a new type of Muslim. For Russia's Muslim intellectuals, Islam was part of their national culture and was subordinate to it, while the official government position in the Ottoman state was just the opposite. This changed in the twentieth century as the modernist nationalists in the Ottoman state came closer to their Muslim counterparts in Russia. Whereas their parents had seen the Ottoman state mainly from the perspective of their common faith, the representative and symbol of which was the caliph, the new intellectuals viewed the situation of both the Ottoman and the Russian Muslims from the perspective of modernism, progress, nationalism, and populism. Eventually, most of these intellectuals came to regard political freedom and modernism as inseparable and as guaranteeing the survival of the faith as well. When Sultan Abdulhamid, in contrast, continued to view the political unity of the Muslims, including their acquiescence to his absolutism, as a basic condition for ensuring the survival of the Ottoman state, many of the liberal-minded Muslim intellectuals, and later the socialists in Russia concluded that the sultan-caliph—like their own reactionary and absolutist Alexander III (1881–94)—was just another despotic czar, albeit clad in Muslim garb.

In sum, the modern schools in Russia imparted to the Muslim children knowledge about their own faith and their civilizations and taught them to think rationally and dialectically.[30] Through education, the Muslim intelligentsia of Russia discovered that the might that enabled Russia to conquer their lands originated in science and technology that had its roots in the West. Arminius Vambery, the Hungarian observer who spent considerable time in Central Asia, remembered that as early as the 1850s the Russian Muslims were criticizing the intellectual and material stagnation of their societies and voicing the need to emulate the sciences of the West.[31] Following the introduction of the modern schools, the rate of literacy among the Muslims of Russia living west of the Urals increased greatly, and, by the turn of the century, was higher than that of the ethnic Russians, at least in certain areas;[32] it was distinctly higher than that in the Ottoman Empire, where efforts to generalize primary education had just begun.

Leaders of Muslim Emancipation in Russia and "National" Characteristics

The movement for intellectual social and political emancipation among Russia's Muslims was led by a number of well-known personalities. The most towering figure was Şihabeddin Mercani (1818–89), a Tatar theologian and historian from Kazan who attacked traditional Islamic teaching methods and advocated in his numerous works scientific, critical, and world-oriented research on Islam and on the history of Kazan and its people. Specifically, he promoted *ictihad* (individual free opinion), the return to the foundations of Islam (the Koran and the Sunna), the acquisition of European knowledge, and the learning of Russian. It was his use of the term *Tatar* as a national category resting on ethnicity and language that gave the term its contemporary meaning. Largely unknown in the West, and ignored by scholars of the Islamic reformation, Mercani was a true innovator as much as a nationalist and a dedicated Muslim. Rizaeddin Fahreddin (Fahreddinoğlu; 1859–1936) followed Mercani's method and achieved high distinction; Hüseyin Feizkhani (1826–66) was educated in Europe and advocated the Westernization of Tatar culture; Musa Jarullah Bigi (1875–1949) first had hope of working with the Russians and communists but became disillusioned, moved to Turkey, and eventually died in Cairo after producing some of the most outstanding theological works of the century. The names of Ayaz Ishaki (Idilli; 1878–1958) and the great, charismatic Abdullah Tukay (1886–1913), who galvanized the Tatar national awakening in Kazan with the power of his poetic imagery rooted in the folk culture of his people, also need special mention. These important figures sought the roots of their society's renewal in enlightenment, folk culture, faith, and history as much as in the power of intellect and the will of their coreligionists. The Muslim intellectual awakening in Russia appeared simultaneously as modernism and nationalism. Nationalism was regarded as a "political objective to be achieved by spiritual and cultural renaissance. From then on nationalism found itself inseparably bound up with reformism."[33]

The creation of "national" languages played a vital role in the rise of ethnic nationalism among the Muslims of Russia. A linguistic orientation toward the vernacular gave modernization its ethnic content and identity and led soon to discussions about the choice of script most suitable to Turkic phonetics. In Azerbaycan, Crimea, and Central Asia the creation of a literary language using the Arabic script but based on an idiom spoken by the masses went hand in hand with the establishment of modern schools and the idea of renewal. In Kazan, Abdul Kayyum Nasiri (1828–1904), who taught the Tatar language at the Russian Orthodox Seminary there, rejected the use of Arabic and Ottoman Turkish words alike when he created the literary language for the Kazan Tatars (whose literati previously had used Çagatai). Among the promoters of Nasiri's new Kazan Tatar language were the brothers Ahmet, Gani, and Mahmud Huseyinof, wealthy businessmen from Orenburg, who established the Huseyiniye Cedidesi Medresesi (new Huseyiniye mosque) in that city and financed the publication of some reviews, possibly including the nationalist *Türk Yurdu*, published in Istanbul by their close friend Yusuf Akçura. Similarly, Fatih Kerimi first published in Orenburg in 1907 the *Şura*, a journal known for its coverage of a wide range of subjects. The Kazan Muslims called themselves Tatars mainly in defining themselves in relation to Russians but also in expressing their own emerging ethnonational identity. Within their own ranks, some preferred to use the term *Şimal Türkleri* (northern Turks) in order to disassociate themselves from the Mongols, as the Russians used the term *Tartar* or *Tatar* as synonymous with *Mongol* and even applied it to the Azeris and other Muslims. Later, in the Soviet period, the term *Tatar* was applied to the Muslims of Kazan and Crimea. G. Ibragimov was the advocate of

Kazan identity based on the history of the area called Tatarstan (and of the Tatars) today.

In Azerbaycan, Türki, the folk language, slowly began to replace the Farsi (Persian) spoken by the upper classes. This change was supported by the Russians, who were eager to dilute the Persian influence in the Caucasus. The movement for the use of Türki was led by Ahunzade Mirza Feth Ali (1812–78), the Tatar Molière, who used drama to criticize superstition and ignorance, and by Hasan Melikzade-Zerdabi who published the *Ekinci* (from 1875 to 1887), considered the first Turkish newspaper in Russia. Zerdabi emerged as a pillar of Azeri linguistic nationalism; he advocated the unity of all Turks and also individual freedom as part of civilization. The brothers Unisizade, Celal and Sait, published *Ziya-i Kafkasya* (1881–84), while Hasan Ali Hüseyinzade (1864–1941) and many others pushed the idea of modernism and national revival to new heights. It is interesting to note that Ahunzade, a pupil of Mirza Sefi Vazih (1799–1852), who was a dedicated advocate of modern education, used the colloquial Azeri Turkish for educational plays and comical stories; overcoming his early opposition to the sultan, he came to Istanbul in 1863 and put before Premier Fuat paşa and, apparently, Sultan Abdulaziz a project to adopt the Latin alphabet. A respected government official, Ahunzade was close to Iran and wrote also in Persian (he is considered the founder of modern Persian literature); but eventually he opted for Azerbaycani Turkish after Shah Nasreddin (r. 1848–96) of Iran failed to meet his reform expectations. The Azeris established in Baku the Yeni Türk Elifba Komitesi (the Committee for the New Turkish Alphabet) in May 1922, and four months later published the *Yeni Yol* (New path) review in the Latin alphabet. This was six years before Turkey adopted it. The new alphabet would be called Turkish, although they used *Elifba*, the Islamic name for the alphabet.

In the land that is today's Kazakstan, the great Abai Kunanbaev and Ibrahim Altinsarin created a literary Kazak language out of the many tribal dialects and a new school system that competed with the traditional schools dominated by Tatar teachers friendly to the caliph.[34] Meanwhile, in Crimea, Ismail Gaspirali (of whom there will be further discussion), simplified the old Arabic alphabet and used it in his modern school system; he subsequently tried to devise a lingua franca for all Russia's Muslim elites based on the language spoken in Istanbul.

Creation of all these written "national" languages did not begin as part of the nationalist drive but as a part of the search for a means to disseminate knowledge among the lower classes. The language and literature created for the sake of enlightenment and modernization united the tribes, attracted new converts to Islam in the Caucasus, Kazan, and Kazakstan, and helped assimilate various smaller ethnic groups into the larger units that became the national prototypes, headed by their respective elites. Those elites then assumed leadership of the "national" cause that was enunciated in the tongue chosen by them as their "national language." Thus various related ethnolinguistic groups were reassembled into a new entity, the modern (or premodern) type of nation that scarcely existed in the past, despite frequent references to the "reawakening of a long subdued historical identity," especially among Kazan and Crimean Tatars. By an entirely new process, intellectuals acting on behalf of a particular ethnic group ultimately used history, language, religion, and territory interchangeably to construct their "national" edifice. (Years later, Soviet nationality policy unwittingly consolidated this development, giving it a totally secular—even atheistic—orientation, by stressing ethnicity and language as the chief elements of group identity and territory as its locus.) Even the Crimean students in Istanbul, who linguistically and culturally were, after the Azeris, the closest to the Ottoman Turks, established their own association and published in their own dialect brochures dealing with events in their country. The same was true for Muslims coming from other areas of Russia. In 1910 a group of cedidists from Bukhara, led by Osman Khoja, N. N. Burhan, and Hasan Şeyh, likewise came to study in Istanbul; so did Abdurrauf Fitrat, the leading Bukharan nationalist-modernist, who later wrote there his famous *Munazara*, the debate between a French and Bukharan scholar about the merits of modern education. These were followed by many others. By this time the upper classes of Central Asia, particularly those of Bukhara and Khiva, had made it a matter of distinction to send their children to study in Istanbul, and at one point Bukhara had thirty-eight students in the city. As the students were supplemented by hundreds of merchants and travelers, the Bukharans became numerous enough to found in Istanbul (in 1911) the Buhara Tamim-i Maarif Cemiyeti (the Bukharan Society for the Development of Education).[35]

Islamic affinity played a major role in facilitating the relationships between the Muslim intellectuals of Russia and those of the Ottoman state, but what really brought them together was their common interest in modernization and whatever it entailed. For many Muslim intellectuals, notably those from Russia, Islam did not consist solely of prayer five time a day, fasting, and the reading of the Koran. In fact, they considered the reclusive life of prayer and meditation, cherished as an ideal by the pious members of the traditional society, as a betrayal of their worldly duties; and they regarded their political subordination to Russia the result of ignorance and social disorganization rather than of any shortcomings of the faith. They accepted and respected Islam as a fundamental source of their identity and culture, and as a bulwark against the ruling czar, but not as the guide of their political or social life. In the Ottoman Empire, on the other hand, because Islam was used by Abdulhamid to legitimize his absolutism, modernist liberals saw it as an impediment to progress, especially after the positivists declared science and religion to be mutually exclusive. The Russian Muslims did not accept the religious Islamism promoted by Abdulhamid but developed their own modernist, nationalist version of it, which became known as pan-Turkism. This ideology, had as its two inseparable facets, nationalism and Islamism and, as its main exponent, the well-known Ismail Gaspirali.

Ismail Gaspirali and Nationalism

Ismail Gaspirali (Gaspirinskii; 1851–1914) achieved a synthesis of Islam, modernism, and nationalism that he used along with tradition to revitalize the Crimean intelligentsia, and his views affected Ottoman intellectuals as much as the Russian Muslims.[36] Born to a family of *mirzas*—mid-level nobles—in the village of Gaspir in Crimea, he was educated first in a military school in Moscow, where he seems to have fallen under the influence of Slavophile thought and wrote articles friendly to the Russians. He was awakened to reality by the chauvinism of Slavophiles such as Katkov, who defended the Greek atrocities committed in Crete against their own kin who had converted to Islam, considering it fit punishment for traitors to their faith—a point of view similar to that of the Serbs who, in the 1990s, callously killed Muslim Bosnians. Gaspirali then decided to go to Istanbul, when he met some of the leading Ottoman intellectuals. Disenchanted with the sultan's autocracy, he later went to Paris and he worked as an assistant to Ivan S. Turgenev. Upon returning to Crimea he dedicated himself to the affairs of the Crimean Tatars, and served as the mayor of Bahçesaray, the capital of the defunct Crimean hanate.

Gaspirali's basic goal was to conceive and implement a modernism that was responsive to the observable, concrete intellectual and material needs of the Muslims of Russia, especially the Crimeans. Central to Gaspirali's thought was the idea that in the past Crimea had its own civilization, a well-defined territory, and its own illustrious state and government that was linked dynastically to the Golden Horde and Cengiz han. Gaspirali campaigned against emigration, which was a marked departure from the traditional tenet that Muslims were obliged to emigrate (*hicret* [Arabic—*hijra*]) from lands not under Muslim authority. Gaspirali's views appeared to be in accord with the goals of the Russian government, which, under Alexander II, experienced one of its sporadic phases of liberalization and modernization. He managed to retain the friendship of the next czar's administration by portraying his version of Islamic modernism in Crimea as compatible with Russia's policy of weakening the hold of the traditional *mollas*. Gaspirali combined the ideas of a liberal, progressive nationalist with a capacity for synthesis and the ability to materialize his ideas. The established ulema of Crimea headed by Mufti Adil Mirza Karaşaysky, who, like his counterparts Sultanov in Ufa and Ahunzade (not the writer) in Baku, was appointed by the czarist government, was opposed to practically all of Gaspirali's reformist endeavors, terming them threats to Islam. Gaspirali, in turn, demanded that the mufti and his Spiritual Board be elected by their constituency rather than be appointed by the Russian governor of the province.[37]

After Gaspirali opened his first modern school in 1883 in Bahçesaray, the number of such modern schools supported by their respective Muslim communities multiplied rapidly throughout Russia, including Central Asia, reaching a total of about five thousand by 1914. His *usul-u cedid* (new method) reduced the learning of reading from two years to mere forty days. Gaspirali's greatest political contribution to the national and intellectual awakening of the Muslims of Russia, however, may have been his newspaper *Tercüman* (Interpreter), which he began to publish in Bahçesaray in 1883 under the motto *Dilde, fikirde, işte birlik* (Unity in language, thought, and work). The paper used a simplified Turkish that Gaspirali had devised from that spoken in Istanbul with the addition of words borrowed from other Turkic dialects; it was comprehensible to intellectuals speaking any of the Turkic dialects of Russia. Indeed the *Tercüman* was read throughout Russia and the Ottoman Empire for its liberal, progressive approach, and the great variety of topics it covered appealed to a variety of people. Sultan Abdulhamid prohibited the entry of the *Tercüman* into the Ottoman state from 1896 to 1908, but that did not stop it from being regularly smuggled in and easily obtained in the capital. Although in order to entice Gaspirali to support his policies, the sultan offered him a large sum of money, the publisher rejected this, accepting only one of the medals Abdulhamid regularly presented to selected personalities.

The position of Gaspirali on the question of nationality was simple and lucid. While interested in the fate of all the Muslims, he chose to concentrate his efforts first on the situation of his Russian conationals. He believed that there was no such thing as a Crimean Turk (Tatar) who was not a Muslim. Russia had Christian and Jewish subjects (the Gagauz, Chuvash, and Karaim) who were linguistically and ethnically Turks or Tatars, yet were not regarded as such. Rather, according to Gaspirali, the common ethnonational identity of the Muslim peoples of Russia was rooted in their Islamic ethos, which could unite them as one nation. Initially using the term *Tatar* instead of *Turk,* in order to soothe the fears of the Russians, he really addressed his teachings to all the Turco-Muslims of Russia. He published in 1882, in Bahçesaray, the first yearbook of Russia's Turks, *Salname-i Turki.*[38] Gaspirali came to believe, toward the end of his life, that the Muslims of Russia had successfully incorporated modernism into their Islamic identity and progressed intellectually to the point of being able to provide leadership in the drive for modernist emancipation to the rest of Muslims in the world.

After a degree of freedom came to Russia around 1905, Gaspirali at last began to speak openly of "one Turkish nation" made up of groups who spoke different dialects of Turkish and were ruled by different potentates, and he declared that all the Muslim nations called Tatar or other names by the Russians were in reality Turks.[39] This was the beginning of Gaspirali's "pan-Turkism." Gaspirali probably was aware that the Tatars of Russia, although claiming to form one single ethnic group, were actually splitting, despite frantic efforts to bridge over the fissures, into three main ethnonational groups—Kazan, Crimean, and Başkir—which would eventually be given different administrative status by the Soviets. The same was to happen among other Muslim groups. In other words, the pan-Islamic–pan-Turkic movement toward unity went parallel to the growth of regional ethnic nationalism among the people who claimed to be both Muslim and Turkic. Gaspirali recognized that each Muslim group of Russia had its own ethnolinguistic identity, but he believed that as modernization nationalized and politicized the elites, it created a perception of a broader Islamo-Turco entity above their regional ethnic identities. This realization led Gaspirali to view the Muslims of Russia as one nation speaking dialects of Turkic but not to espouse publicly the unity of all the Turks in the world. The view that the Muslims of Russia formed their own Turco-Islamic nation that followed its own separate path of development emerged long before formal appearance of pan-Turkism in the Ottoman Empire. It should be noted that emergence of a modest amount of freedom in Russia after 1905 also encouraged many Muslims to return to their homeland, as did Hüseyinzade Ali, who was teaching at the medical school in Istanbul and disseminating his Turkist ideas. In Baku, Hüseyinzade Ali became involved in the publication of *Hayat,* a newspaper that advocated progress for Muslims of Russia, in accordance with the conditions of the Russian state. The newspaper also wished progress and happiness for all Turks in the world but avoided any talk of pan-Turkist union. (Hüseyinzade eventually returned to Istanbul and became engaged in Young Turks politics.)

Gaspirali's idea that Muslims of Russia constituted a single nation inspired plans for an All-Russian Muslim Congress that were aired openly after 1905. The congress itself was the work of Abdurreşid Ibrahim (1853–1944), a Siberian Tatar. He was a reformist, a follower of Cemaleddin al-Afghani and probably the most dedicated pan-Islamist of the Turkic world; his first work, *Çolpan Yildizi* (Venus), was a criticism of the injustices suffered by Russia's Muslims. Abdurreşid traveled extensively—and repeatedly—to Istanbul, the Hicaz, India, Indonesia, Japan, Central Asia, and Europe. He published his impressions in books and articles, describing Muslims everywhere as willing to fight for liberation and progress and as holding the Ottoman caliph in great esteem and hoping that he would come to their rescue. He published in Russia the *Tearuf-i Muslimin* (1910–11), which dealt with Islam in Russia. After 1908 Abdurreşid became involved in the politics of the Young Turks and was close to Eşref Edip and Mehmet Akif, the publishers of the Islamist review, *Sebil-ül Reşat* (1908–1912), the former *Sirat-i Mustakim*, which defended Islamic orthodoxy and modernism. He had been a close collaborator of Rizaeddin Fahreddin and a member of the *Tatar Cemiyeti Hayriye*, an Islamic association established by Tatar Islamists who were growingly upset by the positivistic (*imansizlik*, or faithless) leanings of some of the Young Turks. Abdurreşid criticized also the servility of the religious men toward the government. He eventually left his village of refuge in central Turkey and went to Japan, where he died.[40] After studying in Medina and then residing for a long time in Japan, Abdurreşid came to Istanbul, where he contacted Sultan Abdulhamid. He returned to Russia in 1904, where he joined the Russian liberals and petitioned the interior minister to provide special (*helal*) food for Muslim soldiers, to establish a new *vakif* administration, to allow the Muslims to own land, and to give the Muslims rights at least equal to those accorded the Christian minority groups of Russia. Reacting favorably, the minister encouraged Abdurreşid and the Muslim leaders of Volga and Crimea to organize delegations and to petition for formal recognition of their rights and freedoms. When they then came to St. Petersburg, the leaders of the various delegations of Russian Muslims, such as Ali Mardan Topçubaşi(ev), the Azeri editor of the newspaper *Kaspi*, Bunyamin Ahmetov, Ismail Gaspirali, and others, decided to convene the All-Russian Muslim Congress, which met on 28 August 1905 in Nijni Novgorod on a ship supposedly rented for a cruise. The main issue debated and decided by the congress was the establishment of a Muslim Alliance (Ittifak al-Muslimin) to promote the political and social rights of the Muslims and to establish cooperation with the Russian liberals, and even with the monarchy.[41]

On 13 January 1906 the Second All-Russian Muslim Congress convened in St. Petersburg, with 108 delegates in attendance. It decided, over the opposition of Gaspirali, to change the Muslim Union into a formal political party and to collaborate with the Kadets. At this same meeting, however, a group of young participants criticized the congress and its views as obsolete and espoused socialism, thus sowing the seeds of ideological dissension in the Muslim community. The third All-Russian Muslim Congress was held from 29 August to 3 September 1906 only after Abdurreşid and his colleagues obtained permission by assuring the interior minister that the congress would warn the Muslims against the evils of pan-Islamism, socialism, and anarchism.[42] Attended by some 800 delegates, this congress was openly dominated by "pan-Turkists," advocating unity among Russia's Muslims.

The ideas put forth in the three congresses focused almost entirely on securing social, political, and economic progress for Russia's Muslims. Thus the Muslim Union appeared to be an interest group as much as a nationalist organization and attracted the modernist-nationalist elite of all the major Muslim ethnic groups of Russia, including Ayaz Ishaki, M. E. Resulzade, Sadri Maksudi, Fatih Kerimov, Ilyas Alkyin, Cafer Seydamet, Ibrahim Ahmedov, Hasan Ata Gavesi, just to mention a few of the main participants. They debated and recognized the rights of women, electing a woman—Muhlise Bubi, scion of a famous family of scholars teaching at the *medrese* in the village of Bubi—as *kadi* (judge), an unprecedented act, and recommended a federal form of government as best assuring the future of Russia's Muslims. There was not yet any open discussion of separatism. An outgrowth of the second congress, the Muslim Union Party, entered the First Duma with twenty-five deputies and the Second Duma with thirty-five, and it looked to attain its goals through legal means. Its hopes dwindled, however, when the number of its deputies fell to ten and then to seven in the Third (1907–1912) and Fourth (1912–1916) Dumas, as the result of internal conflicts and the rise of regional ethnic nationalism that superseded the principles of Islamic unity.

The Russian government had watched with considerable anxiety the relentless growth among its Muslim intellectuals of a nationalism (Turkism) that it regarded as identical with pan-Islamism. Because Stolypin feared such nationalism would give a strong, pan-Islamic Turkey a profound influence over the Russian Muslims, he promoted an Anglo-Russian agreement to deter the development of a worldwide pan-Islamic movement, which England feared too. Speaking with Sir Arthur Nicolson in favor of an Anglo-Russian treaty, Stolypin warned that both England and Russia had "millions of Mussulman subjects [who] . . . would doubtless feel the effect which the new development would create."[43] The Russian government believed to the end that pan-Turkism and pan-Islamism were Istanbul's creations. The czarist regime sent its own Muslim emissaries to the Ottoman state to preach a "right" "true" (nonpolitical) Islam, encouraged the printing of the Koran and Islamic books in Russia, and offered protection to its Muslim citizens in the Ottoman Empire in order to retain their loyalties and, if necessary, to use them against their own caliph. Finally, in 1907, Peter Stolypin restricted the activities of the Muslim Union and caused many Muslim leaders to flee to Istanbul.

During the First World War the Muslims of Russia formed a special group of Islamic believers that divided into distinct ethnolinguistic-national categories; but even as the czar's officials were becoming aware of and fostering the separation of the Muslims into those ethnolinguistic subgroups, they could not understand how the Muslims' faith managed to survive such national differences. The Soviet regime, following on the footsteps of its czarist predecessor, failed to grasp the unique relation between ethnicity and faith among Russia's Muslims and so attempted to emphasize the various ethnolinguistic peculiarities of its Muslim subjects while trying to liquidate their faith. In the process it inadvertently secularized Islam and turned its rites, rituals, and beliefs into key cultural features of the national culture of the Tatars, Uzbeks, Azeris, Kazaks, and others.

Modernism and Nationalism in Central Asia

On the vast Kazak (Kyrgyz) steppes east and north of the Aral Sea, the Kazak intelligentsia formed in the second half of the nineteenth century initially was interested, above all, in modernization that followed closely the Russian model. Their pro-Russian disposition was soon drastically reversed, however, by the Russian colonization of the Kazak lands and the forced settlement of the nomads carried out between 1860 and 1900. In the wake of the Kazak uprising of 1916, staged ostensibly to protest the military draft but actually to express accumulated resentment, the czar's reprisals caused the death of a large number of Kazaks and turned the survivors further against the Russians. The memory of their nomadic society with its complex and deeply internalized culture, now destroyed by sedenterization, became one of the main focuses of resentment against the czar's government, and, along with a new sense of Islamic identity, fed the rise of modern Kazak nationalism. To knowledgeable observers it became apparent that the nomad's "indifference" to Islam, so touted by Russian and Western scholars, was a myth.

The modernism of the Tatar merchants, clerics, and intellectuals who dominated the Kazak schools and religious establishment was a second source of Kazak nationalism that strongly influenced their feudal nobility and intelligentsia. The Tatar *mollas*, or popular preachers, succeeded in disseminating Islam among the remaining Kazak animist tribes; and in the towns many of the *medreses*, often manned by Tatar teachers, promoted pan-Islamism sometimes to the point of preaching allegiance to the caliph in Istanbul. V. Popov, an education curator, reported in 1888 that the Kazak students in the *medrese* of Novoi Kazanska run by Tatars answered Inspector A. F. Alektorov's question, "Which is our capital and who is our czar?" by saying, "Our capital is Istanbul and our czar is the sultan." According to the report, the pupils were purposely taught to believe that the caliph was their ruler.[44]

Underlying the national question in the heart of Central Asia (Kokand, Bukhara, Korezm-Khiva) was the fragmentation of the society into nomadic tribal and settled urban elements.[45] The tribal culture of the countryside had a strong ethnic character, being linguistically Turkic and religiously Sufi mystic, while the culturally Persian-dominated urban community was orthodox Islamic, deriving its identity mainly from the urban environment and the faith. The political power in Khiva and Bukhara belonged to the traditional political, religious, and cultural cadres, who regarded the small groups of modernist cadidists as the enemies of their own rule and portrayed them as opposed to Islam. Meanwhile, the Russians in St. Petersburg did not consider Central Asia an organic part of their national territory, as they did Kazan, Crimea, and Azerbaycan, and instead, they saw it as a colony to be exploited and a strategic outpost to be used either as a jumping-off point to India or as a buffer zone to prevent a British advance northward.

Islam in Central Asia presented a picture different from that in the rest of Russia. The faith came to heartland of Central Asia in the eighth century A.D. and influenced its urban institutions and way of life to a degree unknown in the north. Bukhara became one of the a major centers of orthodox Islamic learning in the world and produced some of the towering philosophers and scientists of Islam. By the nineteenth century, however, the autocratic *han*s, relying on a stagnant *medrese* system and fighting each other for power, had opposed reform and abused their political power to such a degree as to reduce the Maveraunnehir, the heartland of Central Asia between Amu Darya and Sir Darya (Seyhan and Ceyhan), to a shadow of its former brilliance.

The effort to establish a modern system of education in Turkistan, as the Russians named Central Asia in 1867, was started by intellectuals who had attended either Russian or their own few modern schools, and their main focus was on modernization. In Central Asia, modernism was equated with education and idealized to a degree not seen anywhere else among the Muslims of Russia; one of the most successful pieces of modernist propaganda was Mahmud Hoca Behbudi's play, *Padarkush* (Killer of Father, or Patricide), subtitled *Okumagan Balaning Hali* (The fate of the uneducated son). However, early in the twentieth century their modernism, too, evolved into ethnic nationalism. This was due in part to the struggle with their own traditionalist religious leaders, who relied on Islam in rejecting change and continuing to maintain control of the community, often with the support of the Russians. Indeed, the struggle to control the community and propagate modern education and political change led even the cedidists of Central Asia to identify themselves openly as "Turks," as in Taşkent following the Bolshevik revolution.[46] In Turkistan, the concepts of modernity, nationality, and *vatan* took a unique shape. Modernity, for many of its advocates, was primarily a form of enlightenment and anticonservatism, and nationality was an identity that resulted mainly from membership in the urban community and Islam rather than language, and/or ethnicity. Abdurrauf Fitrat (1886–1947), the leading Bukharan cedidist, thus could write in Persian, Uzbek, or Türki about the problems of his beloved city while specifically promoting the Uzbek cause.[47] These historical circumstances predisposed the Central Asian modernists initially more toward panislamism than towards the pan-Turkism-pan-Islamism favored by Muslims west of the Urals, who had long been under Russian rule and were accultured to ethnic nationalism.

In the end, however, although following different routes of cultural and political evolution, practically the entire modernist Muslim intelligentsia of Russia, accepted, including those of Central Asia, in varying degree, ethnic criteria for self-identification but without rejecting Islam. Between 1922 and 1936 the Soviet regime reorganized Central Asia, dividing Turkistan into a number of autonomous republics and national territories on the basis of ethnolinguistic identities and affiliations, such as Uzbek, Türkmen, Tadjik, Karakalpak, and so on. This association of territory with a national-ethnic group was a truly revolutionary development for the area, and it speeded up the process of nation formation and raised the questions of modernity, ethnicity, and national identity to a new level.

Conclusion

Modernism was the starting point of the transformation that produced two different versions of Islamism (and panturkism) in the Ottoman and Russian empires due to the different historical, social, and political circumstances prevailing. The Ottoman state was an independent Muslim state whose institutions, culture, and identity showed a certain continuity. In Russia, the Muslims had lost their independence, statehood, and political institutions to a government representing a different religion, culture, and language; their remaining, but fast deteriorating institutions, such as the old *medrese* and *vakifs*, functioned primarily in cities and towns, while the tribal areas were left to rely only on their nomadic and/or tribal culture and folk Islam.

The Russian government's ability to assimilate the Muslims remained limited as long as the societies of both conqueror and conquered remained at an economic and cultural standstill. However, the socioeconomic and cultural developments of the late eighteenth and nineteenth centuries enabled Russia to use modern education, service in the army and government, conversion to assimilate its Muslim subjects, especially in regions long under Russian rule, such as Kazan, Crimea, and Azerbaycan. The Muslims for the first time were unable to isolate themselves in their protective cultural and religious shell; they began therefore to use the same type of European education to fight the ruler and, in the process, to revitalize their communities. The entrepreneurial Muslim middle classes, especially their intellectual wing, became the new agents of change. Modernism for them always meant the rejuvenation *of their own society* rather than the reform of the culturally alien Russian government.

One of the key differences between Ottoman and Russia Muslims concerned the distinction between reform of the state and reform of society. In the Ottoman Empire, modernization was essentially a drive to strengthen the state, as well expressed by its slogans: "Bu devlet nasil yaşar" (How can this state survive?) or "Bu devlet nasil kurtulur" (How can this state be saved?), and initially it involved mainly the ruling institutions and their bureaucrats—a status group. In Russia, in contrast, Muslim modernizers did not seek to modernize the state (which they viewed as Russian), but sought for means to revitalize their respective communities by redefining their identity based on ties to territory, culture, language, and aspirations. The community (the future nation) came first and the state came second among Russia's Muslims; in the Ottoman state the reverse was true.

Sultan Abdulhamid openly and repeatedly condemned ethnic nationalism, believing the *hubb ul-vatan* (love of the fatherland), Turkishness (ethnic identity), and Turkism or (ethnic nationalism), were the antitheses of his brand of universal Islamism and likely to have a divisive impact upon the Muslims. Yet, even on this issue he was, as usual, rather ambivalent. He openly opposed the ethnic Turkism of the Russian Muslim intellectuals (and appeared to encourage the development of a kind of Anatolian-Turkish nationalism as its antidote) mainly to placate the Russian government, but he offered asylum to any Muslim from Russia. He tried to maintain close and warm relations with the traditional Muslim rulers of Bukhara, Kaşgar, and Khiva; but he distanced himself from the younger generation of nationalist modernists, even when seeking to coopt them into his service, as in his unsuccessful effort to recruit Gaspirali, and many others. In short, the sultan seems to have been torn between the admiration he felt for the intellectual courage and creative spirit of Russia's Muslim modernists and his fear of their antiabsolutism.

Many of the cedidists of Russia turned against Sultan Abdulhamid, not so much because of his Islamist policies but because of his autocracy and political conservatism, and their antiabsolutist and antitraditionalist tendencies increased as time progressed. The second generation of cedidists in Russia was more nationalist and less traditionalist than the first. Although they remained interested in Islam as a source of culture and panturkic unity against Russia's domination, they paid more attention to their specific *vatan*, became more identified with their own ethnic group, and stressed class differences in their communities. Abdurreşid Mehdi, the leader of the Young Tatars, having become the advocate of a purely Crimean national identity and homeland, by 1905 criticized Gaspirali for taking up the cause of a large Turco-Muslim nation and trying unsuccessfully to convene international panIslamic congresses instead of pursuing Crimean interests. Eventually the Young Tatars became advocates of Tatarism, a form of narrow Tatar nationalism, and hoped to assume the leadership of all the Turanian peoples of Russia. The Milli Firka (National Party) emerged in 1917 to proclaim the independence of Crimea, just as the Kazan nationalists tried to proclaim their own independence and statehood; but this independence lasted only a short time. It should be noted that a group of Crimean revolutionaries, established in Istanbul in 1906, was instrumental in creating secret underground cells throughout the peninsula and in founding the Milli Firka. There is no indication that they were supported by the Istanbul government.

Crimea first became a union republic, then lost even that status; finally, Stalin exiled the Tatar population of Crimea to Central Asia (in 1944).[48] Azerbaycan followed a different path. Its pan-Turkism was more pronounced than pan-Islam and it came close to a "union" with the Ottoman state ruled by the Young Turks. Ottoman troops under the command of Nuri paşa, the brother of panturkist Enver paşa, entered Baku in 1918 to put an end to the Bolshevik Commune. Well-received initially by the population, soon the Ottoman army was regarded as an occupying force; by the time it pulled out a few months later as part of the armistice that sealed the Ottoman defeat in World War I, the dream of pan-Turkic unity with the Ottoman Empire had all but evaporated.[49]

As the case of the Tatars indicates, stress on the vernacular, adherence to local customs, and devotion to a specific territorial fatherland had the potential to separate the Muslims from each other, even though they continued for practical reasons to support some sort of inter-Muslim unity in Russia. Deprived of common political institutions and a common modern civic culture that could bring them together in the name of a single nation, the Muslims of Russia came to rely on Islam as their only common link. The late Alexander Bennigsen, in an essay that summarized his views on pan-Turkism and pan-Islamism, stated that "Panturkism, the unity of all Muslims, was the key to survival. It was a practical and vital necessity not a politicophilosophical exercise as it was at this same time in the Ottoman Empire or in the rest of the Arab world."[50] In the last analysis, it can be seen that Russia's pan-Islamists–pan-Turkists were not aiming at the political unity of all the Muslims in the world but just at an inter-Muslim alliance in Russia to force the government to grant its Muslims equal rights and a degree of self-government.[51] The scope of the Russian pan-Islamic–pan-Turkic movement was regional, as local idioms were turned into literary languages and used to write the local history. It is evident that Abdulhamid's pan-Islamism, developed mainly for domestic purposes, had limited impact, or none at all, on pan-Islamism–pan-Turkism in Russia, despite a variety of indications to the contrary. Resulzade argued that panturkism was a cultural movement rather than a political program and that Azeris had to make their Caucasian neighbors their priority.[52]

Russian liberalism and Muslim hopes for rights and development came to an end in 1907, when Stolypin embarked upon his oppressive policies. One year later the

Young Turks put an end to Hamidian rule in the Ottoman Empire and made their own brand of modernism the priority, upholding the virtues of science, positivism, and, ultimately, ethnic nationalism of the sort understood by Russian Muslim intellectuals. The Young Turks revolution was a vindication of the views of most of Russia's cedidists and played a major part, at least for the Azeris, in causing them to turn away from Iran and embrace wholeheartedly the cause of ethnic nationalism and also liberalism. Meanwhile, following the return of autocracy, most of the leading Muslim modernist intellectuals of Russia fled to the Ottoman state: Yusuf Akçura, Ayaz Ishaki (Idilli, 1878–1954), Ali Hüseyinzade (1864–1941), Ahmet Agaoğlu (1869–1939), Ibrahim Abdurreşid, and, after the Bolshevik Revolution, Zeki Velidi Togan (1891–1970) and Mehmed Emin Resulzade (1884–1955) were among the hundreds who came to Istanbul. Many of those who stayed in Russia, even including socialists such as Stalin's one-time assistant Sultangaliev were subsequently liquidated for promoting, among other evils, "bourgeois nationalism."

After 1908 the emigré Muslim intellectuals from Russia found in the Ottoman state not the former disoriented but pluralist-minded Tanzimat society but a determined Ottoman-Muslim nationalist ruling elite. The Young Turks, faced with nationalist demands for equality and independence from the Armenians, Greeks, Bulgarians, Zionists, and Christian Arabs, sought to define their own Turkish identity and to create a core Turkish nation on which the Empire could rest. The Muslims from Russia, Hüseyinzade Ali, Yusuf Akçura, Ahmet Ağaoğlu, and others, brought with them a conceptual Turkism based on ethnicity-race.[53] The ethnic nationalism of Russia's Muslims was so useful for converting the multiethnic Ottoman society into a Turkish nation that the intellectual, historical, and cultural similarities between the Ottoman and Russian Muslim intellectuals were emphasized, while differences were ignored. However, transforming Islam into an ingredient of ethnic culture, a process that seemed so easy and natural for Russia's Muslims, proved far more difficult for the Ottomans, whose ethnic and religious identities had evolved and become related to each other in a different manner.

That the Russian Muslim Turks were the ideological precursors of Turkish ethnic nationalism has been acknowledged by the most authoritative of Turkish sources, namely, Ziya Gökalp, the father of Turkish nationalism. In an article written about 1922, Gökalp points out that the first "Turkism," the French "turquerie" (interest in things Turkish), was followed by Turcology or the study of the ancient Turks, Huns, Mongols, and so on.[54] According to Gökalp, that, in turn, was followed by Ahmed Vefik paşa's (1823–91) linguistic Turkism, specifically by both his translation of the *Secere-i Turki*, a genealogical work by Khivan ruler Abu Bahadir han (1603–1663), and his compilation of the lexicon *Lehçe-i Osman-i* (Ottoman dialect). Then, Gökalp noted, when Süleyman paşa introduced the use of Turkish books in the military school in about 1875, he stated that "the term 'Ottoman' is only the name of our state, while the name of our nation is 'Turk.'" Finally, Gökalp claimed, while Abdulhamid was suppressing the nationalist "holy movement" in Turkey, "two great Turkish nationalists were growing up in Russia. One of these was Mirza Feth Ali Ahundov [the satiric dramatist from Azerbaycan] . . . the second was Ismail Gaspirinsky."[55]

The real Turkist movement, in Gökalp's view, began to be stirred up toward the end of Abdulhamid's reign, thanks to "Hüseyinzade Ali bey who had come to Istanbul from Russia [and] taught the principles of Turkism at the Military Medical School, and [to] his poem, 'Turan,' [which] was the first manifestation of the ideal of pan-Turanism." Moreover, Gökalp stated, Hüseyinzade had become "converted to Turkism under the influence of the nationalist movement in Russia; as a college student he had been inculcated with the love of the nation."[56] Even the title of one of Gökalp's major works, *Türkleşmek, Islamlaşmak, Muasirlaşmak* (Turkification, Islamization, modernization—though the last term can more accurately be translated as *contemporariness*), written in 1918, was first coined about 1905 by Hüseyinzade Ali and published in the newspaper *Hayat* in Baku as *Türkleştirmek, Islamlaştirmek, Avrupalilaştirmak* (to Turkify, to Islamize, to Europeanize). In 1910 Hüseyinzade and Akçura became members of the powerful Central Committee of the Committee of Union and Progress, the real governing body of the Ottoman Empire. Thus the idea of ethnic Turkish nationalism, which came from Russia, began to be accepted and implemented by the Young Turks government in contravention of the specific identities developed by the Ottoman Turks under the aegis of Ottomanism and Islamism.

The national movements in Russia subsequently followed their own course. The younger generation of Muslim nationalists and socialists supported the Bolshevik Revolution because it rejected czarism and, supposedly, Russian nationalism. Azerbaycan, mainly under its Musavat (Equality) Party, enjoyed a brief independence (1918–20) as did Crimea; the Kazan Muslims proclaimed the Idil-Ural republic in 1917. The Bolsheviks put an early end to these independence movements. The Kazaks of the Alash Orda established their own government for two years, and their army fought on the side of the Russian revolutionaries, only to be suppressed shortly after the victory over the White Russian armies. In Kokand (Taşkent) the natives aided the Russians to achieve early victory and establish the first Bolshevik government, but the Russian inhabitants promptly turned against them and re-established their domination under the label of communism, while the native resistance known as the Basmachi movement resorted to guerrilla tactics. (After 1920 the communists in Moscow incorporated into the Soviet Union the protected emirates of Bukhara and Khiva, which had been nominally independent until then.) However, the drive for national rights continued under the early communist regime, and the call for a united Turkic front to support that drive continued to be heard. Mirza Sultan Galiev was a Tatar Marxist, but his brand of "national communism," in which Islam and the national aspirations of Russia's Muslims were given wide recognition, had more to do with nationalism than with Lenin and Stalin's Marxism.[57] He advocated the creation of Turkic republic for all Russia's Muslims and asked for the end of "oppression of a nationality by the other." Many of the Turkic communist leaders in 1920–25 opposed the division of Central Asia into national territories, and, under the leadership of Turar Ryskulov, asked for a unified Turkic republic and a single communist party for the Turkic peoples of the Soviet Union. Unable to stamp out these national demands coming from "reactionary bourgeois," who were at the same time dedicated communists, Stalin initiated the purges of the 1930s; but these had only temporary success.[58]

Turkey emerged as an independent state following the disintegration of the Ottoman Empire in 1918 and the bitter struggle against Greek, French, and British occupying forces from 1919 to 1922; but relations between the Turks of Turkey and the Turks of the Soviet Union were cut off entirely from 1920 to 1991, even though Turkey officially and persistently denounced pan-Turkism. For seventy years there was no communication between the two sides. In 1991, however, history eventually began to repeat itself as all the Turkic republics of Central Asia—Kazakstan, Kyrgyzstan, Uzbekistan, and Turkmenistan, along with the predominantly Persian-speaking but Sunni Tajikistan, and Azerbaycan in the Caucasus—declared their independence. At the same time, the Crimean Tatars, exiled to Central Asia in 1944, began struggling to return to their native peninsula, which simultaneously had become a bone of contention between Russia and Ukraine (Khrushchev had ceded Crimea to Ukraine in 1956); by 1997 about 300,000 Crimeans—half of those who still resided in their places of exile in Central Asia and Caucasus—had returned to their homeland, only to meet with violence from the Slavs quartered in their houses. Meanwhile, Kazan remained in the Russian Federation in exchange for a large degree of autonomy.

Turkey was one of the first countries to recognize the newly independent Turkic states of the former Soviet Union, and it immediately entered into economic, cultural, and political relations with them that were both quantitatively and qualitatively unprecedented.[59] Pan-Islamism or pan-Turkism is not mentioned. Those currents of thought, having played their historical role, have become part of the past. They may be resurrected, though only in a changed form, as a defensive tactic, should Russia again become a threat to the independent existence of either Turkey or the newly sovereign national states.

14

The Reconstruction of State, Community-Nation, and Identity

Sultan Abdulhamid developed and implemented his Islamism with two key purposes in mind. His first goal was to achieve unity among Ottoman Muslims and thus prevent the fragmentation of his country into national territorial states. Domestically, therefore, he employed every economic, educational, and financial means available to strengthen the Ottoman state internally, although in the process he inadvertently accelerated its structural transformation and helped change the very meaning of "state." His second purpose, to maintain peace at all costs, stemmed from his knowledge that both the integration of the Muslim population and the maintenance of the Empire's territorial integrity were vitally dependent on peace. In his foreign policy he tried to remain on friendly terms with the big powers, yet prevent their interference in Ottoman domestic affairs, even accepting the loss of eastern Rumili to Bulgaria in 1885 in order to avoid a possible war and subsequent Russian or English interference. At the same time, the sultan constantly, though subtly, used the threat of *cihad* to prevent such interference and balanced the ambitions of one European power against another.

Sultan Abdulhamid achieved both his goals; he prevented the further fragmentation of the Empire, and he built a degree of political unity and solidarity among Ottoman Muslims. During his thirty-three-year reign the Ottoman state avoided involvement in international wars (the Greek War of 1897 was of short duration, and the Ottoman victory bolstered the sultan's reputation), while the international political impact of the Armenian and Macedonian nationalist uprisings remained limited. However, although Abdulhamid held the Empire's loss of territory to a minimum, he was not able to forestall the development of the ethnic nationalism among both Christians and Muslims, and this ultimately led to the disintegration of the Ottoman Empire in the years between 1912 and 1918. The relative peace that prevailed during most of Abdulhamid's reign, from 1878 to 1909, and afterward until 1912, permitted the various internal processes of change to mature. Most of the changes had begun long before Abdulhamid's reign; the sultan's social and economic policies only accelerated them or, occasionally, altered their course. Because the sultan had unparalleled full control of the state power, he could give direction to some of the political and cultural changes that came out of his policy of unity. Nevertheless, in trying to direct these, he undermined further the traditional forms of religious and social organization and created, unwittingly new forms of association. The rise of the civil society gained momentum, as did the realization of ethnic identities. Abdulhamid was vehemently opposed to ethnic and territorial nationalism, considering them divisive forces; but both ethnicity and attachment to the territorial fatherland gained so much ground during his tenure that they played a key role in reshaping the Ottoman Muslims' political identity. In short, the sultan used state power and institutions to maintain the integrity of the state but could not prevent the change in the political identity of his subjects in ways and to degrees that were not intended or foreseen.

Identity Change and the State

Charles F. Keyes has argued that radical change in the economic and political structures of a society affects its primordial identities, which then can be "manipulated for the purposes of group, or nation, formation and for mobilization." Specifically, the cultural, religious, tribal, and other types of primordial identities can be used to establish new organizations or to restructure old ones for protest, defense, and other purposes.[1] Structural reorganization, in turn, along with change of state boundaries, evolution, and migration all can contribute to radical identity change, according to Keyes.[2] Moreover, the identities themselves can be adopted, or created deliberately, to mobilize a group and unite it to achieve a predetermined purpose, such as to defend independence, some cultural legacy, or some other common interest, and so on.[3] N. Poulantzas, on the other hand, clearly shows how the state can allocate incentives and opportunities and initiate social and cultural policies in areas such as education and language in order to restructure society according to predetermined schemes. Furthermore, the state can also turn religious solidarity into a reason for social action and employ it to rationalize that action as advantageous to the collectivity and its supreme creed.[4] The state can then use the reformulated or redefined collective identity for mobilization purposes. Mustafa Kemal used Islam to mobilize the population against the Greeks invading Anatolia from 1919 to 1922, and the subsequent victory helped him to convert the Islamic identity gradually into a Turkish national one, although the regime never acknowledged this change. Nevertheless, even when changes are initially introduced or sanctioned by the government, the state cannot direct or control subsequent developments resulting from the dialectical interaction of economic, cultural, social, and religious forces that occur in the society at large. The changes in the Ottoman Empire were both natural, caused by the pervasive influence of the capitalist system and migration, just to name the main ones, and state-directed, the results of intentional efforts to create new institutions and identities. These subsequently stimulated the evolvement of various secondary identities, some traditional and others newly formed, which gained new political meaning and potency and became the distinguishing marks of the various groups in the Ottoman comity, replacing religion as the chief mark of identity.

Ethnicity, one of the dormant secondary identities, was the first to acquire political importance, first among Christians and later among educated Ottoman Muslims. Defined in cultural terms, "ethnicity" is the sum total of lineage, language, religion, customs, traditions, forms of association, tastes in food, and the like, shared by members of a group that use them to identify with one another and to differentiate their group from others. It is always possible for one group, at a given historical moment, to emphasize a particular characteristic as its main mark of ethnic identity. Prior to the late nineteenth century, the revival of ethnicity in the Ottoman Empire implicitly led to a reappraisal of the classical Islamic definition of identity. The Koran states that Muslims are part of one universal religious community (*ümmet*) but are divided into tribes and nations, and it forbids any nation or tribe to claim superiority over others on the basis of its peculiar tribal-national-ethnic characteristics (Koran 49.13, Sura al-Hujurat). Historically this was an admonition to a deputation that came to Medina to see the Prophet around A.D. 631 and was rather arrogant in its behavior and tribal pride. Nevertheless, it may be claimed that the Koran does not prohibit Muslims from forming association among themselves on the basis of linguistic or other ethnic characteristics, as long as they do not assert those characteristics to dominate or claim superiority over others.

Although not viewed formally or officially as the distinguishing mark of a ruling ethnic group, in practice language played exactly that role among the Muslims. Arabic, the language of the Koran, defined an ethnic category known as "Arabs" and remains the chief identity mark of today's Arabs. Persian was the literary language of the Persian upper classes, which used it to assimilate a variety of ethnic groups—including numerous Turks—to make them part of the Persian, nowadays dubbed *Iranian*, nation. Turkish, on the other, hand had no universal recognition among Muslims as the idiom of religion or the distinguishing cultural mark of an elite class. It was the language of the Ottoman state, in a version created by the bureaucracy, and of the Turkish folk. This became a crucial issue as the Ottoman government sought after the 1850s to create a nation suitable to its needs. There was no political difficulty as long as the nation, the state, and the language were not identified with a specific, politically dominant ethnic group—that is, with the ethnic Turks. The Turks had not yet developed as an ethnic nation, as had the Christians, nor did they possess the keen linguistic consciousness of the Arabs and Persians. However, the structural changes and government policies of the Ottoman state gradually raised ethnicity to the status of a major identity characteristic, first among Christians, then among Muslims, especially the Turks, and as the basis of nationhood.

The emergence of ethnicity as the major form of identity was essentially the acknowledgment of an existing reality, as well as a reflection of change. Underneath the main, traditional religious identity promoted by the state, Muslims and Christians alike had always possessed secondary identities defined by ethnicity, tribe, history, region, and language. The Ottoman government had never denied or proscribed these but, through the patriarchate for the Orthodox Christians and the state for the Muslims, it had tried to supersede them by religion to the extent possible. The official identity for non-Muslims in the Ottoman state was determined by membership in one of the three culturally autonomous religious communities, or *millet*s; the Orthodox one included the Western Christians, mostly the Slavs in the Balkans; the Armenian *millet* represented the Eastern Christians; and the Jews belonged to their own *millet*. However, in addition to faith, the Christians identified themselves profoundly with their own ethnic communities. Although the Muslims were not formally organized as a *millet*, in practice they acted as such, especially after the office of the chief mufti (*şeyhulislam*) was created in the fifteenth century and charged with issuing the *fetvas*, the religious opinions that sanctioned government acts as being in conformity with Islam. It was this office rather than the sultan that could claim to represent the faith. However, the *örf* (customary law) and *kanunname* (the sultan's decrees with the force of law) provided the state with legal avenues to circumvent the dogma of the faith and to control the society and the *şeyhulislam*, who was appointed by the sultan. Ethnic identity remained far stronger among the village and tribal folk than among the ruling strata, and the *soy* (kinship group) formed the basis of the tribe. The nineteenth-century development of ethnicity and Ottomanism—that is, the state-sponsored process of creating a nation—led ultimately to the revaluation of history and the search for the ethnic origins of the Ottoman state.

Structural Transformation, the New Bureaucracy, and Identity Change

Geographically and culturally the Ottoman state was at the junction of several major literate cultures—Roman-Byzantine, European, Islamic, and Central Asian. Its bureaucracy therefore inherited notable political, historical, and intellectual assets, which it used rather effectively, to develop a rational understanding of the phenomenon of power as the determining tool of state, along with creative ability and an unusual flexibility to adapt the innovations of others to their own system. The Ottoman Turks preserved the Arabic alphabet, took gunpowder and the big cannon from Europe and China, and adopted their land system, literature, philosophy, and concepts of authority and administration from Islam, Persian, and Central Asian Turco-Mongolian practices. The Turkish tribesmen who established the state in the thirteenth century assimilated all these elements into a new format that was not Arab, European, or Persian, but Ottoman; it was a bit of all of them but also something apart. As a further consequence of geographical position, when the market economy, technology, and new modes of organization from the West spread to the rest of the world, they impacted the Ottoman Empire first. Then, the fact that the Ottoman system was originally a meritocracy, having no aristocracy of the blood and egalitarian in outlook—except with regard to the state and its representatives—proved to be helpful in the long and painful transition to modern nationhood and statehood.

The sharp division of the population into four estates—rulers, scribes, merchants, and peasants—regardless of their faith, allowed the state to control the major economic resources and prevented the formation of social coalitions against the ruling elite. A Muslim peasant, although a member of the Islamic community, was still a *raya*, a food producer and a husbandman belonging to the fourth social estate along with his Christian fellow peasants. The key aim of the state bureaucracy was to prevent the emergence of economic elites that could challenge its primacy. Even state dignitaries returned the state property held during their tenure in office and could not easily accumulate cash, since the state forced them to build mosques, bazaars, and wells, or used minor pretexts to dispossess them of their "illicit" wealth. High officials also were prevented from passing to their heirs the land given to them at their investiture in office. As the result of these social policies, the Ottoman state, with some exceptions, developed neither an aristocracy of wealth nor an independent civil class of freethinking writers and intellectuals strong enough to challenge the "state," that is, the ruling bureaucratic order or promote the cause of an ethnic group. The capitalist system, and the nineteenth-century reform movement carried out by the bureaucracy in order to assure its own survival, to put it in Weberian terms, undermined the traditional socioeconomic and political order and permitted the rise of landed groups that challenged the state's omnipotence. It is essential to note that as the state began to lose its grip on the basic economic resource (land) and faced the challenge of a proprietorial group rooted in the community, it sought to create for itself a new human foundation, the nation, to consolidate its power by opposing the sultan's supremacy only to face the combined opposition of the proprietied group and community. The struggle of the modernists, bureaucrats, and propertied middle classes prepared the historical-social foundation for the rise of democracy in Turkey. Needless to say, this democracy must be understood in accordance with its birth conditions rather than by solely abstract principles.

Until the reign of Selim III (r. 1789–1807) the traditional Ottoman state apparatus had consisted of a small, well-organized bureaucracy of military origin tied personally to the sultan, who was the God-sanctioned master and personification of the state, the owner of all its main resources, including land, and its chief executive officer. The state—that is, the sultanate and the bureaucracy—were an organic whole, dependent on each other and able to limit each other's authority under the panoply of various Islamic principles of government. The sultanate's outwardly absolute authority was curtailed by the system's internal controls. The state claimed to safeguard the highest human virtues, as defined by the faith that formally legitimized its authority, while in practical matters such as defense, tax collection, the land system, the maintenance of law and order, the state acted more or less independently. All this internal balance system was undermined during the reign of Mahmud II (r. 1808–1839). Mahmud destroyed the major institutions—the Janissaries, *timar*s (land fiefs), *ayan*s (notables), and the like—which had both sustained the traditional system and limited the sultan's absolutism. In building his autocracy, Mahmud, the only sultan who came close to fitting Weber's definition of *sultanism*, ousted the bureaucracy from its "partnership" with the sultan in ruling the state and sought to make it a functional group totally subordinate to the sultan. The new "modern" centralized system of administration and taxation introduced by Mahmud did not work, for the bureaucracy felt deceived and threatened and refused to become the "servant" of the people it had been for centuries accustomed to govern. (Mahmud commonly practiced the summary dismissal and execution of bureaucrats; he condemned Reşit paşa, the future architect of the Tanzimat, to death in absentia.) Mahmud II destroyed the traditional system but was unable to create a new one, hence he brought the state to the brink of total collapse. The Tanzimat (1839) was forced to create new institutions to replace those destroyed by Mahmud. The sultan also inflicted a devastating blow to the religious institutions and some of the religious orders, and thus created a long crisis of identity that Abdulhamid attempted to cure by "reviving the old order" (which, in fact, turned out to be a new one).

When the benevolent Abdulmecid (r. 1839–61) came to power, the bureaucracy initiated a series of reforms in education, sanitation, and state administration; it turned from being the servile tool of the sultan to the actual master of the state in all but name. Thus the Tanzimat Edict of 1839 assured the political ascendancy of the bureaucracy, which turned the state into its vehicle of power and made the reforms, or modernization, its justification for supremacy. It still used the sultan, however, to provide the old form of religious legitimacy, so Abdulmecid kept his nominal position as the supreme holder of authority. Power actually was concentrated in the hands of the modern bureaucracy, which controlled chiefly the Foreign Ministry, while other ministries remained in the hands of the traditional conservatives. Abdulaziz (r. 1861–76), partly in reaction to his father's reforms, which had limited the ruler's absolute power, tried to re-establish the sultanate's old authority by emphasizing his position as caliph—that is, as the head of the *ümmet* rather than the state. The bureaucracy fought back. To retain control of the people or community, it introduced in 1876 a European-type constitution, which was intended to make the sultan a constitutional monarch and help the bureaucracy to broaden and legalize its authority.

The bureaucracy had prepared the ground for its promulgation of the constitution through various administrative moves over a number of years. Using the ever-expanding telegraph system, begun in 1855 during the Crimean War, it sent direct orders out to the countryside in the name of the sultan, thus centralizing power and demoting the local lords and tribal leaders, who had controlled the local communities and been the sultan's link to them. In order to create a degree of uniformity in political outlook and enhance administrative homogeneity, the bureaucracy eliminated, over the years 1862–65, the *millet*s, the religious communities, as informal cultural-administrative bodies. The increased centralization of government created a need for more trained personnel, so the number of modern schools was increased also. All of these actions, without intent on the part of the bureaucracy, promoted the rise of a new middle class. The local notables whose power had diminished were incorporated into the system as members of provincial and municipal councils, while education in the modern schools provided a channel for entry into government service of the middle classes in the countryside. Notably, families in provincial centers were able to place more of their members and friends in government service and secure access to political patronage. The diary kept by Aşçi Dede (his Arabic name was Ibrahim Halil, 1828–1910), who long served as a finance officer in Damascus, provides an excellent inside picture of the intrigues and struggles of those families, mostly Arabs, to penetrate the local government, then use it both to promote their own interest and, indirectly, to insinuate regional considerations into the exercise of authority.[5] Thus the government authority that had been used by the bureaucracy to consolidate its own power began to be used by the elites of the new middle class to promote family interests and, eventually, the interests of their economic and ethnic group, regions, and localities. This produced a crisis in the perception and sense of the purpose of "state" authority.

As long as the ruler and the ruled appeared to operate within the framework of uniformly binding religious commandments, the masses accepted the superior economic and social position of the ruling personnel as the consequence of divine will. Some change had been favored by many of the conservatives, but they saw the bureaucracy's domination of the sultan and the Ottomanization (secularization) of the society, as a deviation from the principles of the traditional state and, hence, from the fundamentals of Islam. (It should be noted that some Arabs referred to Abdul-mecid as *al-Khain*—traitor—derived from his other title—*han/khan*). Realizing that the reforms were separating the state from the religion, they viewed the bureaucracy as the culprit and the sultan as the victim of his own servants, just as Abdulaziz's religious advisers described him. Like the sultan, they deemed attempts to attribute the Constitution of 1876 and the parliament to "public opinion" or the "voice of the people," to be no more than a plot by the bureaucracy to gain an independent legitimacy and free itself from the restrictions of the faith and the sultan's authority.

The concerns of the conservatives had some validity. The constitution introduced secular and individualistic concepts of citizenship, human rights, and so on; yet the bureaucracy that was to put it into effect was hardly aware of the existence of such rights, let alone prepared to implement them. The conservatives' feared that the bureaucracy, freed from the constraints of Islam and the sultan's supervision, would make the modernism embodied in the constitution its overriding criterion of legitimacy—as it ultimately did—disregarding the wishes, culture, and aspirations of the individual Muslim. Because Islam was the only generally accepted vehicle capable of protecting the freedom of the individual, according to the conservatives, once the traditional *din-u devlet* was abandoned, the "godless" state would be free to undertake anything it wished in the name of the new GOD called modernity. Obviously, the more extreme of these fears were unfounded, but what counted was the conservatives' perception of the bureaucracy's unbridled authority rather than of the ultimate benefits of the reforms for society. One example of this kind of outrageous thinking, although expressed well after these issues emerged, was provided by Mustafa Sabri efendi, *şeyhulislam* for a while during the time of the Young Turks. In the 1930s he published in the Egyptian newspapers a series of scathing attacks against Mustafa Kemal and his government, whom he accused of taking control of the state by deceiving Sultan Vahideddin (r. 1918–22), who allegedly instructed him to start the liberation struggle in Anatolia. "Mustafa Kemal," claimed Sabri efendi, "is everything in new Turkey. He is not only the foundation of the nation and everything which is sacred but the personification [of the nation and religion]." Sabri efendi ignored history and distorted events to prove his thesis that the modernists needed to abolish the sultanate and the caliphate in order to deprive society of its Islamic safeguards and establish their godless, materialistic dictatorship;[6] this literature was reprinted and circulated freely in Turkey in the 1990s. What is true is that after the 1860s the bureaucracy, notably the reformists, actually did see themselves as the true masters of the country and its people.[7] For example, the chief reformer, Reşit paşa, ended up possessing such vast estates that in the 1960s his descendants still owned some of the choicest building sites around Istanbul, west of the resort town of Büyük Çekmece.

Ottomanism and Modern Nationhood

To create a "nation" as underpinning for their "reformed" state, the Tanzimat reformers promoted "Ottomanism." Ottomanism produced a series of social and cultural changes that, paradoxically, increased the sense of common culture among Muslims and, at the same time, stimulated the rise of ethnic and regional consciousness. Its main ideal intent, however, was to turn hundreds of disparate ethnic, religious, social, and regional groups into one homogeneous political bloc—the nation—by making all the subjects of the sultan Ottoman citizens and equal before the law, regardless of faith, origin, and language. Before the enactment of the Citizenship Laws of 1864, no one outside the dynasty had legitimately been called *Osmanli* or (in the Western version) Ottoman. The very concept of unitary territorial state-nation made homogeneous by common lay citizenship had no precedent in Ottoman or Islamic history. The traditional Ottoman state consisted of a very large number of religious, tribal, social, and ethnic groups with no single common ethnic or political identity except for the faith. If they had a quasi-secular common view, it was that they (or their leaders) saw themselves as the subjects (servants) of the ruler whose dynasty owned the state, the Devlet-i Ali-i Osmani, or the Sublime State of the Osmanlis. By contrast, Ottomanism implied that the country belonged, or should belong, to its citizens and that their ownership of the state was based on their citizenship status as "Osmanli" or Ottomans, regardless of religious affiliation.

The government did its best in the late 1860s early 1870s to popularize the new Ottoman identity, occasionally defining the country as an Ottoman Union (Ittihad-i Osmani) and even talking about pan-Ottomanism as the alliance of its many nationalities. The newspaper *Basiret*, often the sounding board for Ottoman statesmen, asserted in 1870 that the term *Ottoman* covered all Muslims and non-Muslims, not just the Turks, and that pan-Ottomanism was the only way to oppose pan-Slavism as well as to prevent the fragmentation of the Empire into Greek, Armenian, Arab, Kurdish, and other entities. *Basiret* further claimed the Ottomans formed a nation that shared the same *vatan*, so the Christians now employed in government offices should not pay attention to divisive views.[8] In order to dramatize that all the Ottomans had become part of one nation, the press generally, with the government's prodding, gave wide publicity to the establishment of a military unit consisting of Muslim and Christian volunteers, which had the crescent and the cross side by side as emblems on its flag (some saw it as insulting the crescent). *Ittihad*, as the name implies, was a newspaper published in order to promote the unity of Muslims and Christians. It gave extensive coverage to examples of Muslim-Christian cooperation to prove that they had embraced wholeheartedly the idea of an Ottoman union and had rejected the separatism embodied in the Eastern Question.[9]

The constitution and the parliaments of 1876–78, although originating in the struggle for power between the sultan and the bureaucracy, were also part of the drive to establish Ottomanism. Mithat paşa and the constitutionalists believed that, somehow, making the parliament the representative of the governed would assure popular "participation" in government decisions and strengthen the unity of the land. Midhat even thought he had tangible evidence that "popular participation" produced good practical results. As the governor, in the period 1864–68, of the Danube province chosen as a pilot area for reforms, he had secured the participation of the local notables, many of whom were ethnic Bulgarians, in the reform and administration of the province, with brilliant results. The "popular participation" he used as an example involved only the upper echelons of the new middle classes and the local administration, but Midhat paşa believed that the same sort of participation of all the countryside notables, regardless of faith or nationality, would quell the demand for autonomy not only from the Balkan Christians but also from the Arabs, who apparently had tired of maladministration and exclusion from government decisions. The parliament, in Midhat's view, had the potential to integrate the Christians politically into the emerging Ottoman nation. His ultimate vision seemed to be of a secular state that was basically a federation of mininations with no power; this was pseudofederalism designated to reinforce and "mask" the strong unitary state, similar to the "federalism" of the USSR in 1936–91.[10]

The constitutionalists believed that the multireligious Ottoman state could be turned into a cohesive political unit if the population were properly informed about the advantages of Ottomanism. They tried to convince the Muslim population that constitutionalism and the parliament actually conformed to Islamic principles and institutions, such as the *cemaat* (local congregation), *şura* (council), *ijma* (opinion of the community) and *meşveret* (consultation-deliberation). It was also necessary to convince the sultan that they had grassroots support, so they touted public opinion as the voice of the *millet*, or "people" a certain amount of cynicism notwithstanding. According to a popular anecdote, Namik Kemal and several of his journalist friends took a pleasure trip on a small boat. When a sudden storm threatened to sink the boat, Namik Kemal reportedly said, "There goes Ottoman public opinion, to the bottom of the sea." They managed to survive, as did "public opinion."

Eventually the constitutionalists, especially Mithat paşa, would be accused of taking their political ideas from Europe and fabricating the Islamic equivalents; and one could easily question the sincerity of the constitutionalists in seeking popular participation in government. They continued on the path of the Tanzimat, imposing wholesale change from above without consulting the community, since it was too "ignorant"; this was a view held by both the bureaucrats and, especially, the sultan. From the viewpoint of this study, probably one of the most important but neglected aspects of the constitutional experiment was that it sanctioned the existence of an entity called the "people" as the source of authority and, second, because of its recognition that the "Ottoman people, that is, nation," consisted of a variety of ethnic groups including non-Muslims. The parliamentary debates were monopolized by the Muslim deputies, who acted as the true "representative of the nation" and did not miss any opportunity to affirm the Islamic character of the state and the "sacred" rights of the sultan-caliph, and to criticize bitterly the bureaucracy for its professional deficiencies. Without a grounding in any organic, psychological and cultural roots shared commonly by the entire population and without any widespread economic success to point to, Ottomanism merely helped raise to a conscious level the existing—and in some ways unbridgeable—ethnic, religious, and economic differences between Muslims and Christians. These differences became even more important because class differentiation appeared to follow ethno-religious lines.

Ottomanism, being the absolute antithesis of the religious and social segregation that prevailed in the classical Ottoman state, rendered meaningless the "art of government," by which the classical bureaucrats achieved group balance, the practical *raison d'être* of the state. Ottomanism is regarded today by almost all students of Ottoman history as a failed principle, chiefly because it did not prevent the disintegration of the Empire and, as an ideology of unity, died along with Empire. This judgment is true if one views Ottomanism solely as an instrument devised to accommodate the Christians and keep them in the Empire; but if Ottomanism is viewed from the perspective of the Muslims, one can say that it implanted the modern political concept of nationhood into their existing religious-community society and gave it a new form, increased vitality, and a new lease on life. By the end of the 1870s, when the Christians had rejected Ottomanism as a plot to keep them subjugated to the sultan, most Muslims had reacted by embracing Ottomanism as an expression of the *tawhid* (unity), which was a cardinal point of Islam even though Ottomanism derived from non-Islamic principles. The Arabs remained staunch supporters of Ottomanism, at least until World War I. The truth is that Ottomanism helped create a series of new Muslim groups that were very different in essence from both the traditional religious communities and from the ideal envisaged by the Tanzimatists or Islamists. It is worth elaborating this point.

Centralization, Ottomanism, and Localism

Assorted centrifugal effects, such as localism, ethnic awareness, and group interest, were stimulated by Ottomanism in direct contravention of its unifying intention. This fragmentation—or subdivision of identity—resulted from an individualistic philosophy that permeated Ottomanism, as well as from cultural, social, and administrative changes that helped stimulate the rise of ethnic and regional awareness. The upwardly mobile middle- and lower-class representatives brought with them their disparate local cultures, customs, and aspirations, which they hoped to see become part of the nascent "national" culture or, at least, to be accorded some respect. Indeed, the emergence of ethnicity and the rise of nationalism in the Ottoman Empire would have been unthinkable without the recognition won by the folk culture of the "people" and the ascent to power of representatives of the lower classes. In this section we deal with the rise of localism and regionalism that was a part of the process of ethnic identification and nation formation among the Muslims, all stimulated by Ottomanism.

The classical Ottoman Empire did not tamper with the culture of its provinces, towns, and villages, because the principal tool for changing identity—that is, education—was in the hand of the community not the state. The centralization drive of the nineteenth century was concerned mainly with expanding the political authority of the center to the detriment of the periphery. Ottomanism served to undermine the autonomy of the people who had helped the center maintain its control over the provinces. The Bosnian lords, the tribal leaders in the Taurus Mountains stretching from Adana to Mosul, the şeyhs of Arabia and Syria, and such well-established dynasties as the Karamanlis in Libya were among the traditional leaders gradually replaced by individuals appointed from the center or by local people compliant toward the center's policies; often these were members of the new middle and lower classes, whose stature derived from education and economic achievement rather than family status.[11] These new local leaders, in turn, backed the government's reformist efforts, not only to neutralize the local traditional notables and discredit their allies but also to cultivate the loyalties of the people who would become their own supporting constituencies.

Ottomanism-cum-centralization thus deprived the central government of some of its old traditional allies in the countryside but created for it another set of "modernist" friends from among the new local elites.[12] Appearing to side with the center, out of self-interest and because of their modernist philosophy, the new leaders also were bound close to their local communities by culture and family ties. Among them were members of the popular religious orders as well as people educated in the modern schools and others who had achieved prominence in the community, not through ascriptive titles, but by initiating some change and reform, or at least telling the local people that a good government could better their fate. Thus new notables from the lower groups who had identified themselves with the local population and with modernist—ultimately nationalist—aspirations could become the allies of the center if the government met their expectations. Thanks to the Empire's division into smaller administrative units—the *vilayet* (province) and its subdivisions, the *sancak* and *kaza*—long-ignored towns were turned into regional power centers for the agrarian wing of the middle classes: Konya, which had been the capital of the Selçukis; the old Zulkadir principality of Diyarbakir, the home of the Kurdish notables; Sivas, considered the center of the Turkish Alevis; Erzurum, the gate to Iran; Adana, the old fief of the Ramazzanoğullari; and many others became new cultural, administrative, and commercial centers, developing with their own local identities and interests and searching out the roots of their pasts. The provincial administrative bodies, in which many local notables served, not only promoted, when suitable, the reforms ordered by the center but became the avenue for advocating local interests and expressing their cultural particularities. Enough literature was produced in these regional centers to enable scholars to reconstruct the social history of various Anatolian towns[13] and their notables and the history of prominent families and their relations with the center. Like the many other valuable local histories, these have been ignored by most scholars, but they often provide a view of the reforms and social and political changes that is markedly different from the picture presented by the central government. The literature also provides considerable information on the families of notables and their participation in the struggle for Independence from 1919 to 1922.[14]

The English consular reports from Anatolia in the late 1870s, cited in various sections of this work, indicate also that many local people who had become conscious of their social position did not hesitate to voice their aspirations and criticize the central government for ignoring the countryside. An incident illustrative of the new self-consciousness of the countryside is the encounter between Sultan Abdulhamid and Said Nursi (Bediuzzaman, 1876–1960), whose teachings now give direction to one of the largest and most influential religious orders in contemporary Turkey, the Nurcular. A Nakşbandi *şeyh* and ethnic Kurd from the province of Bitlis, Nursi was a self-appointed spokesman for his countrymen, but he rejected Kurdishness as a basis for political allegiance and advocated Turkish statehood and Islamic nationhood.[15] He was granted an appointment with Abdulhamid in 1902 to 1903 and presented the following petition:

> The easterners [of Anatolia] are an important part of the Ottoman nation. Although the government knows their situation, I still beg permission to convey some wishes and demands about some needed . . . services. Some modern schools have been opened in eastern Anatolia, but only those who know Turkish can benefit from them. Those who do not know Turkish regard the sciences [*sic*] taught in the *medrese* [religious school] as sufficient for their progress and advancement. The children are

thus deprived of [modern] education and learning because the teachers in these [modern] schools do not know the local language. . . . [The solution to this problem] is for the government to open in eastern Anatolia in Bitlis, Van, and Siirt, at its own expense, [modern] schools [that can register] at least fifty pupils and have them study the positive sciences in addition to the religious ones. Thus the religious and positive science taught in the [proposed] Eastern Academy [the name appears as school and university] shall become the foundation of the national education. This foundation in turn shall be the basis of unity and togetherness. . . . Thus [the people in the east] will become a strong part of our fatherland . . . and give proof of their natural abilities and capacity for civilization.[16]

Sultan Abdulhamid received Nursi in the imperial palace at Yildiz, where the Nakş-bandi *şeyh* arrived dressed in his coarse native clothes. After describing the dire economic situation of eastern Anatolia, Nursi urged the caliph to use his authority to satisfy not only the spiritual but also the material needs of the Muslims. He told the sultan that because Islam did not permit tyranny, individuals suspected of disloyalty should be tried by regular courts rather than summarily punished and exiled on the basis of secret denunciations.

Arrested and tried for his criticism of the Hamidian regime, the *şeyh* claimed in the court that his basic identity was Ottoman, while his Kurdishness was a subidentity derived from the "name given to the people who inhabit the area where I was born and grew up." Still, he insisted on respect for local customs and dress.

> I was born in the mountains of eastern Anatolia. You must view my coarse appearances with the "glasses" of that region and not according to the refinement of Istanbul. If you do not so [respect our cultural peculiarities] you will alienate us from Istanbul. . . . My dress and behavior is contrary to the accepted norm [prevailing in Istanbul]. Your criterion should not be based on appearance but on something lofty and permanent such as spirit [faith] and what is right.[17]

Nursi's remarks demonstrated that Ottomanism transformed the Muslims into a sort of political community while increasing consciousness of their local identity and custom. Peter Hardy, who cannot be accused of defending the Muslim cause, after a survey of Bareilly's life made a similar trenchant observation about India: "The reform movement of Sayyid Ahmad Bareilly and the Fara'izis contributed to the gradual . . . transformation of the Indian Muslim community from an aggregate of believers into a political association with a will for joint action. . . . Ahmad's message appealed not to the higher but to the humble strata of Muslim society in India."[18]

The rise of ethnoregional consciousness amidst the tendency toward uniformity and homogenization pursued by centralization could be seen even among the state elites, as the government's need for personnel rapidly propelled upward officials who remained attached to their regional culture. The notoriously pro-Russian Mahmud Nedim paşa, a Nakşbandi sympathizer who served as premier in 1875, often sought the company of his Caucasian fellows and delighted in the local lore. Sultan Abdulhamid showed special sympathy to his mother's humble Circassian group, the Ubikhs, although he later identified himself openly as an ethnic Turk while upholding the primacy of his Muslim identity. The Tanzimat Ottomanists had tried to transform the state from a small, narrowly based, and segregated administrative apparatus into a broad political association based on a new popular foundation. Sultan Abdulhamid broadened and infused the Ottomanism he inherited from the Tanzimatists with the cultural and psychological ingredients of Islamism. Thus Islamism as an ideology helped integrate the local religious communities into a larger political unit, the Ottoman protonation, at the same time it competed with the revival of local, ethnic, and other subidentities that challenged and/or sought accommodation with the wider Islamic and Ottoman identities.

Islamism and Nationhood

The Islamist policy of Abdulhamid speeded up, redirected, and gave new content to Ottomanism. The Tanzimat government had implemented centralization, common citizenship, and other measures to create a degree of homogenization in society but had not interfered with the religious, ethnic, linguistic, and local identities of Ottoman subjects. Those identities, instead of submerging themselves into a common Ottoman identity, became stronger, however; Ottomanism appeared not only as a threat to those subidentities but clearly lacked the psychological and cultural strength to manage the forces awakened by the effort to form a united Ottoman nation. The Christians, in particular, became almost totally estranged from the Empire, as they regarded Ottomanism as a Muslim ideology of unity, despite the fact that some upper-class non-Muslims apparently did accept it. Islamism sought to counter the idea of the nation-state introduced under the Berlin Treaty and serving as the justification for the separation of various Christian entities in the Balkans from Europe. The "nationalism" of these groups was mainly religious in nature. One can argue convincingly that the nationalist movements among the Balkan Christians in the nineteenth century did not start as movements of liberation from the "colonial" rule of the Ottomans, who aside from taxes had no interest in the area as a colonial market or source of raw materials but as social protest movements against the consequences of the breakdown of the traditional order that soon became movements of liberation from the political domination of a religiously and ethnically alien group—that is, the "Turks." The five-hundred-year Ottoman rule in the Balkans had taught the Christians to see everything, as did the Muslims, in religious terms. The strongest "national" feature of the modern political identity of the Balkan Christians derived from their membership in their Orthodox *millet*, which combined with ethnicity to create pressure for nationhood among Bulgarians, Serbs, and others. The "national" histories of the Balkan states were written mainly after they attained independence in 1878 and, naturally, did not reflect actual events; they were, instead, subjective reinterpretations of the past aimed at gratifying the national ego. The culprit for national failure was, of course, the "Turks," their faith, and their "five-hundred-year yoke." In reality, it may be seen that the Balkan Christian political movements in the nineteenth century sought "liberation" from a government that had suddenly begun to interfere with citizens' everyday lives, thanks to the centralization that had resulted, paradoxically, from European-type reforms.[19] However, the imaginary Turkish-Muslim nation conjured up by the writers of after-the-fact "national" histories was depicted as the obstacle to the acquisition of Western civilization by the people of the Balkans. (Ironically, today, in 1998, Muslim Turkey is more Westernized and advanced economically, politically, and culturally than the Balkan states that were formerly part of the Ottoman Empire.)

The independence of the Balkan states, Abdulhamid rightly believed, could be followed by the secession of the Arabs, and possibly lead to the loss of Anatolia—to the Armenians, the Greeks, and possibly the Kurds. Islamism was designed to prevent the Arabs from breaking away, and it invoked the threat of *cihad* to prevent further interference in Ottoman domestic affairs on the pretext of protecting the "rights" of the other groups. As a devout Muslim and caliph, the sultan believed sincerely in his basic obligation to defend the honor of Islam and the rights and independence of all Muslims, regardless of their ethnic differences, but he also knew full well that the Arabs would secede if their *survival as Arabs* was jeopardized by either the government's domestic policies or international developments. Thus by combining Islamism with Ottomanism-Islamism, Abdulhamid had devised an ideology that was likely to serve the interests of the Arabs far more than the Turks. Therefore, the Arabs' "national" movement, initially, was not separatist at all. A large number of Arabs regarded their Ottoman rulers not as a foreign colonial power but merely as a ruling dynasty of non-Arab origin, which they obeyed as long as the Ottoman state and the dynasty remained Islamic, respected the Arab way of life, promised to fulfill their aspirations, and shielded them against European occupation. It was the Christian Arabs, educated in modern schools, who first remembered, or imagined, past glories and strove to produce a modern versions of their history. The nationalist literature of these Christian Arabs did not much bother the sultan; he was, however, exceptionally apprehensive about separatist tendencies among Muslims. He was informed, for example, that a Syrian leader, Ahmad al-Sulh, with the support of Abdelkader, the Algerian leader living in exile in Damascus, and some Syrian notables and tribal leaders, had held a meeting in 1878 to plan the secession and independence of Syria if the Ottoman Empire were to disintegrate.[20] Later he also learned of activities by Şeyh Tahir al Jazairi, an advocate of Arabism and close associate of Abdelkader.[21]

To counteract possibly secessionist plotting, the sultan courted the Arabs notables. He tried to enlist the support not only of Syrian religious leaders such as Abulhuda but also of powerful lords such as the Azm family, and Izzet paşa al-Abir (the sultan's secretary), and he encouraged the Arabs to become officers in the army. Arabs eventually constituted about 15 percent of the Ottoman officers. As the officer corps grew from about 10,000 officers in 1884 to 18,000 in 1896, this meant that about 2,700 officers were Arabs.[22] Arab notables and dignitaries were made members of the local administrative bodies and honored with titles, medals, and pensions, and their *vilayet*s were placed at the top of the protocol lists. Consequently, many Arabs considered themselves bona fide Ottomans—as long as the center did not threaten their Arabness, position, or interests. At the same time, the specter of secessionist nationalism in Syria, followed by similar stirrings among the Albanian Muslims, including the formation of the League of Prizerin, strengthened the sultan's resolve to foster unity among all Muslims. In addressing Muslims, Abdulhamid seldom referred to them as *ümmet*, and even less often as *cemaat* (the local religious community and congregation), but usually as *Müslümanlar* (Muslims). The sultan did not deny the existence of the *ummet*, rather, he visualized it not as embodying a religious ideal but as an actual community composed of living individuals. He was a *dünyevi* (worldly) Muslim. He therefore asked the individuals to use their intellect and reason to understand rationally both the world in which they lived and their faith, so as to secure the survival of the community in this world, not the next.

The mode of rationalistic thinking that Abdulhamid promoted proved to be truly revolutionary, even if revolution was the last thought in the ruler's mind. Throughout most of the existence of the Ottoman Empire, the state, while appearing as the instrument of faith, actually had primacy over both the religious establishment and the individual. Theoretically, the state was supposed to conform to and serve the faith, but the entire traditional Ottoman institutional structure, as well as the political culture, was created on the basis of state supremacy. Sultan Abdulhamid appeared to place the state in the service of the faith, but if examined closely his supposedly "theocratic" measures are seen to be merely cosmetic and designed to maintain the old appearances. What he did—and this is key to understanding his approach—was to recognize priority of the community (the aggregate of individuals) over the state and to give the caliphate priority over the sultanate in its relations with the community— paradoxically, in order to preserve the state and his own supremacy. There is no question that Abdulhamid tried to mobilize the community partly as a shield against the bureaucracy, which he could not fully control. Thus the community became the foundation of the state and, in a way, equivalent to the "people" that the constitutionalists had sought unsuccessfully to mobilize to support their own power. In acknowledging the supremacy of the community and its head the caliph, Abdulhamid inadvertently stripped the state of the religious-mythological aura that enabled it to exploit the faith. He exposed the state for what it was: a worldly, man-made organization that served its masters' pleasure. In exposing the state's purely political nature, Abdulhamid exposed also his own absolutist rule as being a worldly occurrence that the caliphate could not legitimize. Indeed, without a supporting state, the caliphate had little political credibility unless it was turned into a depoliticized religious office, if that was at all possible. (The fear that this could not be achieved led to its abolition in 1924.) Although the mystique of the state as a superior creation beyond the individual's grasp would endure, Abdulhamid's Islamist philosophy was undermining the statist philosophy, ironically at the same time that he was increasing state authority to the maximum (see chapters 7 and 8).

Contrary to the view of the late Enver Ziya Karal, long the head of the Turkish Historical Society, and various other scholars, Abdulhamid did not create a theocracy. Giving the caliphate theoretical primacy over the sultanate, as Abdulhamid did, had the result that the two offices became separate institutions, each of which could be affiliated with the faith and with the state but only in a new way. Thus the path was cleared for the development of a system under which the state and the faith acted independently, each in its own sphere of autonomy. That this sort of system never actually evolved was due to entrenched ideas of statist supremacy and misconceived notions of modernity that put the state and religion on a collision course. This is why, after Abdulhamid was removed from power in 1908, the ideological disputes of the Islamists versus the statist-nationalists erupted violently into the open. Sultan Abdulhamid, whose real intention probably was to restore the arrangement that predated Mahmud II and to consolidate his own power, opened the door that allowed the faith to break free of state tutelage and freed the state from the pretention that it was serving the faith; but the process was not completed. The state continued to use the faith for its own purposes, often in the name of secularism.

Abdulhamid did not ask for an Islamic constitution to redefine the functions of the state because another man-made constitution, like that of 1876 (which he had suspended), did not appeal to him. He preserved and expanded the Tanzimat reforms, but the ideological-cultural chaos created by Mahmud II and the Tanzimatists worsened under his rule, a result of the mishandling of relations between state and faith; he was unable to put in theoretical terms a de facto situation. However, there was a bright side to the picture: society began to free itself from its total subservience to the state and sought to create its own culture in collaboration with, or opposition to, the state as the case might be. A nation would thus be created, partly according to the blueprint of the state but mostly according to the dialectical interaction of society, culture, faith, ethos, and the desire for self preservation.

The Nation

The identity of most modern nation-states derives from a political awareness of language, faith, ethnicity, history, and so on as the common bond(s) that hold together the members of a nation. All or most of the elements that enter into the making of modern nation might have existed for centuries, unnoticed and constantly changing. In other words, national identity and nationalism stem from the subjective perception, collective awareness, and internalization of both an identity emanating from one or more sources and of the supposedly unique and superior nature of that identity. Although Sultan Abdulhamid opposed the idea of a nation defined by attachment to a territorial fatherland and/or to ethnicity or language, his Islamism, when grafted onto Ottomanism, yielded a sense of nationhood that was anchored both in Islam and in various historical, regional, and ethnic particularities. As caliph, he led and sanctioned, through religious manipulation, the rise of a redeeming Muslim nationalism that was, in fact, a normal process of political-intellectual, or national, "awakening." He used the state to raise the Muslims' religious identity to a very high level of consciousness and to confer a high value upon it by trying to make that Islamic identity a source of self-esteem, dignity, and pride—that is, to paraphrase Liah Greenfeld, turn it into a Muslim nationalism.[23] Abdulhamid's nationalism gave the Muslim society a realistic understanding of its human nature and worldly needs. That it was articulated through religion—an approach that occasionally worked against established Islam and those that lived from exploiting it—was a matter of method rather than essence. Indeed, the emergence of nationalism throughout the Islamic world, as indicated in the discussion of the Russian Muslims, was a process of enlightenment or a blend of rationalism and political activism that at times appeared indistinguishable from what came to be mislabeled *Islamic reformism.*

Abdulhamid's preaching of Islamic unity and, especially, his praise of Islam as a noble faith that was fully compatible with science and civilization was psychologically uplifting for the Muslims. It reassured them that the economic and political backwardness of their own society was not the fault of their religious culture and identity and freed them to seek the roots of regression in the social, political, and economic environment surrounding them. This was a form of modernist rebirth in religious guise that the Russians and Europeans were at a loss to understand, pejoratively labeling it "Muslim fanaticism." A more serious observer would have realized that this "Muslim fanaticism" resulted from the intellectual and emotional tension generated by the transformation of an old religious identity into a modern one through its politicization. The sultan had to tend to material progress, which he, like the "infidel" Mahmud II, believed essential to the security of the state and the welfare of the community; faith alone would not suffice. Paradoxically the innovations he introduced in the effort to better society in a material way made individual Muslims aware of their own interests and their differences with the Ottoman center.

While the sultan was able to maintain in the thirty years from 1878 to 1908 an environment of relative quiet and unity, during which the processes of identity transformation and social restructuring intensified under the umbrella of Islamism and Ottomanism, various social, cultural, and economic forces emerged to change the direction of the nation formation. Modern education played a major role, for it involved the choice of a specific language as the medium of instruction and government communication. The sultan Turkified the expanding educational and judicial systems, although the Arabs, Greeks, and Armenians were free to publish books and newspapers in their own languages. Language became a determinant of identity only after the state gave up its national neutrality and used the language to identify itself with an ethnic group—the "Turks," as shall be discussed later. Beginning after the mid-1880s, the interest in native language manifested itself mainly as a search for enlightenment and knowledge, only later becoming the criterion of national-political identity. The Muslim groups with established languages, such as the Arabs, opened their own schools in their own languages and were free to promote their own ethnic cultures and identities, as long as they did not advocate separatism. This relatively benevolent policy toward ethnicity derived in part from the sultan's respect for the old Ottoman traditions of cultural and religious pluralism. It also was rooted, however, in his erroneous view (or hope) that ethnic nationalism was something specifically Christian and that, because the loss of the ethnic Balkan provinces in 1878 had greatly reduced the number of Ottoman Christians, nationalism would not contaminate the Muslims. This view is expressed clearly in Ottoman censuses of the nineteenth century. The classical Ottoman population surveys (*tahrirs*) had classified the population into Muslims, Christians, Jews, and Gypsies. The census of 1877–78, following Mithat paşa's Ottomanist dream of creating a unified nation, abandoned the old classification based on religion and counted the entire population as individuals. The censuses of 1882 and 1914 adopted language as the basis of ethnonational identity and classified the Balkan Christian population as Greeks, Bulgarians, and so on, while the Middle Eastern Christians were classified under such categories as Armenians, Latins, Protestants, and Syrians. All the Muslims, however, were counted as a single religious category to the end of the Empire, regardless of their ethnic and linguistic characteristics.[24]

Christian groups within what was left of the Ottoman Empire continued to assert their ethnic separations. The Armenians, who had been essentially a religious-ethnic community with a corresponding identity, soon espoused nationalism and made separatist claims.[25] Similarly the Greeks remaining in Anatolia, Thrace, and Macedonia vastly expanded the activities of their *syllogues*, the political organizations they dubbed "literary and scientific" associations. With financial support from the Greek government and rich Greeks, including Abdulhamid's own friends, G. Zarifi, the banker, and Christaki efendi Zographos, the *syllogues* sprang up in all the major Ottoman localities inhabited by Greeks and added political momentum to the cultural awareness disseminated by the existing Greek educational institutions. In the Istanbul area alone the Greeks had over one hundred schools as early as 1878, and the number had nearly doubled by the end of the century.[26] New non-Muslim nations even began to appear. For example, the drive for formation of a Macedonian nation—still under Ottoman sovereignty—accelerated after the 1880s, despite the efforts of Bulgaria, Greece, Serbia, and, for a while, the British to deny the existence of a separate Macedonian nationality and identity.[27]

Abdulhamid's hope that this virus would not spread to his Muslim subjects was not fulfilled. Ethnic consciousness also spread among the Muslims, chiefly as the result of education (enlightenment) and, sometimes, because the Ottoman government encouraged it to balance that of other groups. The kind of ethnic national awakening taking place under the aegis of Ottomanism could be clearly seen among larger Muslim groups, such as the Albanians, who will be discussed in a different context, and the Bosnians, who were in a rather special category. The Bosnians, unlike the Albanians, did not display much interest in developing and organizing their own ethnic community, although they maintained the awareness of their identity throughout the Ottoman period.[28] There were stirrings of ethnicity also among smaller, more marginal communities. Thus the Yezidis in the *vilayet* of Mosul, numbering altogether about 68,000, agreed to register in the *sicil-i nufus* (population registers) if their identity as "Yezidis" was mentioned specifically on their identity cards (*tezakir-i Osmaniye*). The term *Yezidi* actually was inserted in the column identifying the card-holders' faith, the Ottoman government agreeing to recognize the identity in order to prevent missionaries from converting them to Christianity.[29] In Syria and Lebanon the so-called Muslim-Christian conflicts and riots of 1901–1903, many manipulated by the British, Russian, and French consuls, and the unrest among the Druzes, was caused by the usual reaction to taxation and conscription and, especially, the breakdown of old forms of authority and the assertion of a sort of "ethnic" consciousness.[30] As a British agent explained, "Druzes would not listen to advice, for they are no longer under the control of the Sheikhs," and "the Ottoman government has allowed the Druzes to have their own way."[31] The Ottoman government preferred at the end, to the great annoyance of the British, not to fight the Druzes of Hauran but to settle the dispute through a mixed commission.[32]

Ethnic-national fervor in the Ottoman Empire reached a peak during Abdulhamid's reign, both despite and because of Ottomanism-Islamism. Sultan Abdulhamid protected the Christians, as Ottoman citizens, and enhanced their already good economic situation; but this stirred up further Muslim resentment and Christian animosity as well. The Ottoman Jews, toward whom Abdulhamid had a friendly disposition in spite of his opposition to Zionism, likewise achieved rapid emancipation and modernization mostly during Abdulhamid's reign. The opposition to Abdulhamid's rule took organized form after 1885—ironically, because of his unwillingness or inability to enforce a "real" Ottomanist policy. Restoration of the constitution and the parliament was the main platform of the opposition, which considered both these institutions indispensable to true Ottomanism. Constitutionalism, in fact, unified the members of a great variety of often antagonistic ethnic groups, who joined the secret Union and Progress

Society, dedicated, as its name indicates, to the preservation of the Ottoman union. During the latter part of Abdulhamid's rule, when Ottomanism thus came to be regarded as an embodiment of constitutionalism and a state principle guaranteeing each group its own future national existence, every ethnic group with political aspirations believed it also embodied a principle of freedom and of ethnic (national) development under the protection of the very government they were soon to defy.

The Young Turks revolution of 1908 succeeded so well and so swiftly that Catholic, Orthodox, and Muslim clergymen, and even Bulgarian and Greek *komitacis* (guerrillas), were embracing each other as Ottoman "brothers." This joyous outburst collapsed in less than a year, however, as the Christians expectations of Ottomanism proved to be unrealizable. Each non-Muslim group that wanted independence or union with its mother country, for instance, expected the government to allow and even aid separation and thus preside over the dismemberment of the Empire in the name of Ottomanism.[33] The Armenians, Greeks, and Macedonians all anticipated that the "Turks" would use their control over the government and the army to help them further develop their own ethnic culture and language to restore the "national" institutions of their vanished past. As disillusionment set in, the Arabs were willing to stay in the union if they were granted additional administrative autonomy and cultural freedom and were defended against European occupation.

The Tanzimat reformers believed that a state with a well-integrated population was the best avenue for the cultural survival and modernization of its citizens; they used citizenship as a means of integration while Abdulhamid used the faith. As mentioned elsewhere, the Ottoman modernizers—who later became "Turks"—were essentially a status group or a statist class of various ethnic backgrounds. Once the Young Turks came to power, they too viewed a modernized and strengthened Ottoman state as the guarantor of political and social survival of their class and the only instrument capable of revamping society to create a human basis—ultimately in the form of a nation—for the state itself. They ultimately chose ethnicity but not before experimenting with the old ideologies. A new definition of Ottomanism—actually an assimilationist idea—was developed that asked the Arabs, Armenians, Macedonians, Greeks, and others to see themselves as equal, individual members of one homogenous Ottoman nation (state), rather than as members of mininations based on autonomous ethnoreligious communities. The Christian ethnic groups, however, wanted the state only to act as a "gendarme," enforcing the law and maintaining security in the name of "Ottoman patriotism" so that they could freely develop their own separate ethnic cultures and identities. They thus shaped the context in which the Young Turk leaders eventually began to portray themselves as the friends of the most oppressed and underdeveloped group—the Turks, the last ethnic group to discover its ethnicity. Tekinalp described how the non-Turks were grouped around their strong communal organizations and developed their national and mutual-aid associations and schools, bought land, revived the local industries and engaged in trade, achieved remarkable prosperity, and left economically behind their "master," the Turk. He described (exaggeratedly) the commoner Turk as "subject to all the oppression and miseries. . . . Jails and exile were imposed on the better and strong [Turk]. . . . He did not have clubs or newspapers. . . . His schools, besides being few, were a deceit and taught him nothing that formed personality, forged character, and compelled him to action."³⁴ After 1910, Turkism, or Turkish nationalism (not to be confused with Turkishness or ethnicity), therefore, developed as a corollary of Ottomanism—not as its antithesis, as it was later interpreted to be.

Conclusion

The Ottoman modernization policies in the nineteenth and early twentieth centuries were undertaken exclusively by the state-government without consultation with or input by civil-private groups, who expressed the viewpoint, feelings, or aspirations of groups at large. Expression of opinions other than those approved by the government in power were regarded as subversive or hostile and treated as such.

It should be noted that the decision makers in the state-government consisted of a very small ideology-inspired minority of civil-military bureaucrats who once acquired control of power with the sultan's blessing (Tanzimat reforms of 1839–76) and especially violence; Mithat paşa's coup of 1876–78; the sultan's dismissal of the Parliament and abrogation of the Constitution in 1878–1908; and the Committee of Union and Progress "revolution" in 1908–18. The pattern has continued in Turkey to the present day, although with considerable refinement. Modernity was the common goal of all these changes, ensuring a degree of social-cultural continuity, although the methods and justifications used by each power-holding minority conflicted with and negated the policies of the previous one, creating extraordinary confusion and unease in society. It also made a scholarly study of the period extremely difficult.

It will be argued at length in the following chapters that since 1908 there has been a rather one-sided understanding of Islamism, Ottomanism, and Turkism. Many scholars claim that, after trying and failing to reform the state through Ottomanism and Islamism, the Turks decided to abandon both for nationalism. In reality all three concepts coexisted and evolved together in constant interaction. Ottomanism and Islamism nurtured Turkishness, were absorbed by it, and survive in it today. When Ziya Gökalp differentiated "artificial" Ottomanism from the "real" one that was likely to save Turkism and Islamism, he knew that all three of these ideologies were so deeply embedded in one another that they were inseparable, as a proper reading of his famous article on the subject makes clear. Gökalp's criticism of Ottomanism grew vehement after the Empire disintegrated in 1918 and the leaders of the Turkish nation, defined as a nation-state that emerged in Anatolia in the years 1919–23, turned their backs on their Ottoman and Islamic heritage and proceeded to advance their own Turkish nationalist interpretation of history and national culture. Turkish nationalism emerged, first, from the search by state elites for a suitable means to reform the state; then from the realization by those elites that a strong state needed the cohesive, unitary, social basis of a nation that was sure of its ethnic identity, and, finally, from the belief that the national territory set the boundaries of the nation and its identity. Turkish nationalism has unique strong points, such as an orientation to the future, pragmatic solidarism, lack of historical hatred, and lack of romantic nostalgia for the past and irredentism. It also suffers from parochialism, xenophobia, materialism, the savior—or great-man—syndrome, and an artificially created state mysticism that could be implanted in the national ethos provided the community's memory of its Ottoman and Islamic past had disappeared.

15

Ottomanism, Fatherland, and the "Turkishness" of the State

In the era of modernization, the sultan and the Ottoman elites made use of both traditional and newly introduced concepts, institutions, and titles in order to recast the multiethnic and multilinguistic traditional Ottoman comity into a relatively homogeneous united political body. Usually referred to as "reform," this effort was neither undertaken according to a well-defined plan nor carried out by an organization created specifically for the purpose but resulted from the belief that change was better than preserving the status quo. The Tanzimat reforms of 1839–56 created a momentum that led to a great expansion of their initial scope. After 1870, a small but constantly growing number of both modernist and Islamist intellectuals, educated mostly in the modern schools, expanded their interest beyond political institutions to the social, cultural, and philosophical aspects of society. Despite growing dispute about its nature, there was a basic agreement that change was inevitable and would have to include the acceptance of *dünyevilik*, or the worldly aspect of human and social life. The Hungarian Arminius Vambery, who had followed events in the Ottoman Empire for forty years, claimed that Ottoman society had changed in a very fundamental manner and achieved a high degree of progress toward diversity of thought, lifestyle, and patterns of organization.[1] He failed to note that Ottoman change was not a predetermined, unilinear absorption of solely Western concepts but a multidimensional evolution that incorporated values and ideas of the traditional culture and history as well. Indeed, changes in the social structure and emerging forms of association based on ethnicity, government position, profession, and the like were shaped also by traditional ideas that blended with new aspirations and ideas into one concept, namely, *medeniyet*, or civilization. This was accompanied by a growing interest in the sociopolitical framework in which civilization would develop, that is, the nation; the state would guide the nation to civilization. The community would be molded into a nation whose main axis was Islam.

However, the various elements of modern nationhood, such as fatherland, or territory, ethnic identity, language, and so on, that entered into the making of the nation were alien to the religious community. The question was to internalize these elements of modern nationhood without creating a conflict with Islam or the accepted version of Ottoman history. Notions of ethnicity and, to a somewhat lesser extent, of territory and the secularized understanding of the nation created fierce controversies during the Young Turks era, but not during Abdulhamid's reign, mainly because of his adroit use of Islamism. Since, for the mass of Muslims, Islam provided the only legitimate avenue for accepting change, including the reshaping of the Islamic identity into a national one, Islamism was the route Sultan Abdulhamid took to turn Islam into a dynamic worldly force that would not only integrate the multiethnic Ottoman Muslims of Anatolia and Rumili into a relatively cohesive political unit but also gradually change their old modes of thought and identity. This occurred mainly as the consequence of a variety of developments outside the sphere of the government for which Islam provided legitimacy and from which the absolutist government prevented dissent. The remainder of this chapter will be dedicated to studying the complex process of acculturation to modern nationhood both through and despite Islam, as the case may be. It is essential to emphasize here that while Abdulhamid did not tolerate political opposition, he was open to almost everything associated with "civilization."

The Territory, the Fatherland, and the First Perceptions of Turkishness

Territory played a seminal role in determining the "worldliness" and the scope and "character" of the nation. The rise of a territorial-political concept of the fatherland helped solidify not only the individual's ties to the state but also to the nation that would inhabit the territory of the fatherland and become the basis of the state. The individual's natural feelings of attachment and love for his/her own place of birth were broadened into political loyalty to a broader territorial unit, the fatherland, inhabited by people sharing the same culture (mostly deriving from Islam), language, and history—that is, to *patria*. Ultimately, the existing individual sentiment of attachment to the land, which was part of the commoner's culture, would become part of the national culture; but to the traditionalist conservative, bondage to a territorial fatherland seemed an alternative to the attachment to faith—that is, something akin to the sacrifice of the spiritual God to a material, man-created deity. The territorial fatherland could be accepted and the attachment to it internalized only if it were proven to be part of the faith. The frequent quotation of the *hadis* "Hubb-ul vatan min-el-iman" and Namik Kemal's play *Vatan* (discussed below) were aimed at promoting such internalization.

Muslims throughout the world had the notion of a natural birthplace, or the "small" homeland, and expressed it in such terms as *memleket* (for the Turks), *bilad* (for the Arabs) or, later, and more commonly *vatan/watan*, to cite just a few. Although the literature of the Muslim peoples contains innumerable examples of great writers and poets, including Sa'adi (1184–1291) and Hafez (1325–89), as well as lesser figures, who expressed eternal love for their birthplace or the city in which they lived, this attachment carried no political meaning. Indeed, in Islam this natural feeling for one's birthplace never became the general basis of political allegiance until the nineteenth century, despite a few exceptions. Bernard Lewis states that Mirali Esseyyid Ali efendi, who served as Ottoman ambassador in Paris in the late eighteenth century, used the term in a political sense, as in the French *patrie* and that such usage "is clearly due to

European influence and example."[2] It is my contention that, while some Europe-oriented Ottomans may have adopted the European usage of the term *fatherland* as applied to a political entity, they did not—could not—simply adopt, through example, the emotional content implicit in the European usage: that came later, after the internalization process. True, the question of a physical homeland was touched upon by Muslim leaders such as Caliph Umar, who reportedly told his followers, "Hicaz is your home only in as far as it is a pasturage," and Ibn Khaldun referred to the nomadic peoples as "savages who have no homeland" (and thus made no distinction between their own and others' territory). Furthermore, the much debated question of *hudud*, or frontiers between states, suggests that territory did enter somehow as a practical issue into classical Muslim thinking, but without being a principle of state.[3] The expression, "My homeland is wherever the Şeriat rules," expressed best the traditional concept of Muslim "fatherland."

Territory emerged as the foundation of the fatherland and as the object of allegiance in the Ottoman Empire out of necessity of finding a safe locus for the perpetuation of Muslim faith and culture. When millions of Muslims from Crimea, the Caucasus, and the Balkans were forced out of their original *vatan*s between 1856 and 1878, primarily because they were Muslim, they seem to have realized that if the Ottoman state disintegrated, their cultural and religious existence was in jeopardy. The first issue debated and settled consequently, was the change in the meaning of the well-established principle of *hicra*, the obligation to migrate to the lands under Muslim authority. Ismail Gaspirali openly defied the call to *hicra* in his exhortations to the Crimean Muslims, and so did the Caucasian mufti, when they appealed to their coreligionists not to migrate to the Ottoman state (see chapter 13).

For most of the refugees, "ethnic cleansing" was the experience that dramatized the need for a secure territory where their culture, religion, and values could develop in full freedom. However, for some Balkan refugees the love of their original territorial *vatan* was so strong they would rather live there under non-Muslim rule than remain under the sultan's authority, and a number of refugees actually did go back to the Balkans and Russia. Likewise, Ahmet Rasim, the *vali* of Tripoli, reported in 1882 that some hundred thousand members of the Vurguma tribe, originally from Tunisia, showed "through words and behavior that they wanted to return to their fatherland, because the love of the fatherland was a natural necessity" ("muhabbet-i vatan emr-i tabii bulunduğundan"), even though the caliph in Istanbul did not favor their return.[4]

It was in these circumstances that the *hadis* of unclear origin mentioned earlier, "hubb-ul vatan min-el-iman" (Love of the fatherland is part of the faith), found wide acceptance, especially among Russia's Muslims. In the Ottoman state, the *vatan* and the attachment and love for it was defined and shaped by Namik Kemal in his seminal play *Vatan yahut Silistre* (Fatherland, or Silistre). To this day this play remains a source of patriotic inspiration to many in Turkey and was probably the work that consecrated N. Kemal's place in Turkish history and literature. (He was accused of plagiarizing the play *Patrie* by Victorien Sardou, which was staged in 1869 at the time N. Kemal was in Europe; but the two are different.)

A leading constitutionalist, Namik Kemal (1840–88) accepted the love of country as a God-given, superior sentiment derived from faith and history. He attempted to convert the individual's personal attachment to his birthplace to an attachment to a "national" territory, or *vatan* in the defense of which martyrdom was a sacred duty. In his view, the fatherland was the source of duties and demands for sacrifice and, in exchange, provided glory and inner contentment: only lastly was it a place in which to live and achieve happiness. This play, with its multisided, evocative psychological power, and populist appeal, revived memories of Ottoman historical greatness and provided a vision of a free life for people having common legacy and living in ancestral lands. It deals with many of the issues discussed in this study and thus deserves a detailed analysis.

Namik Kemal wrote *Vatan yahut Silistre* in haste for the theater season in 1873 and issued it as a supplement to the newspaper *Siraj*, published by Tevfik Ebuzziya, a well-known literary critic and historian. Although lacking in literary and technical quality, the play was staged on 1 April 1873 and just once afterward.[5]

The symbolically named hero of the play, Islam bey, is a patriotic intellectual who falls in love with Zekiye, the daughter of Ahmet bey, an army officer presumed dead because he has not been heard of for fifteen years. Islam bey hears Zekiye bemoaning her love for him and enters her room through a window (the romantic audacity was itself a novelty), only to tell her that he must leave immediately for the battlefield to defend the *vatan*. Zekiye decides to follow her beloved secretly, dressed in a man's uniform. The two lovers meet but do not recognize each other, in a besieged fortress at Silistre on the Danube, known for its heroic defense against Russia in the Crimean War. There they encounter Sitki bey, the deputy commander of the fortress. Eventually Islam bey and the disguised Zekiye volunteer to go into the enemy's camp to blow up its ammunition; but before the mission can be carried out, the Russians lift their siege and retreat in the face of the defenders' staunch resistance. Nonetheless Islam bey, assisted by Zekiye, defeats scores of remaining Russian soldiers. The two volunteers eventually return to the Ottoman camp to report the victory to Sitki bey, who turns out to be Ahmet bey, Zekiye's long-lost father. Although a graduate of the War College, Ahmet bey, it is revealed, lost his commission in the army in a case involving his family's honor when a corrupt court sided with his opponent. Assuming the new name of Sitki bey, he rose again through the ranks from a simple enlisted man to become *miralay*, or colonel. As Zekiye also divulges her true identity, Ahmet bey assumes his traditional position as the beloved and undisputed head of the united family and convinces Islam bey and Zekiye to marry that same day, the defense of family integrity and honor being an essential subtheme of the play.

The *vatan* is portrayed from the very start in terms of, above all, personal and family considerations: it is a sacred entity requiring devotion, allegiance, and sacrifice. Islam bey tells Zekiye at their first encounter that regardless of his burning love for her, he has to leave her, maybe forever, because

[t]he state has declared war. The enemy is trying to trample under its feet the bones of our martyrs on the frontier [*serhat*, which has a powerful mystical connotation of martyrdom; lit. "first line" or "document"]. How can I stay in comfort at home when the fatherland is in danger. . . . Fatherland! Fatherland! I shout that the fatherland is in danger, don't you hear me? God created me, the fatherland reared me. God nurtured me for the fatherland. . . . I feel the bounty of the fatherland in my bones. My body [is part] of the fatherland's earth, my breath [is part] of the fatherland's air. Why was I born if I was not to die for the fatherland?

332 *Politicization of Islam*

When Zekiye acknowledges, "If what is involved is the fatherland . . . then what can I say? Go, my Lord, go [to defend the fatherland]," Islam bey joyfully declares, "If I die, I shall not be regretful . . . because . . . to know that a girl like you is living in the fatherland, in my view, is better than to actually have you . . . but I shall not die." The play is full of declarations that martyrdom for the fatherland is a duty for Muslims and Ottomans.

Namik Kemal's effort to define the fatherland as being synonymous with the duty to defend and die for it was actually motivated by practical considerations. The literature of the period indicates that the traditional martial spirit of the Ottoman Muslims was being eroded by newly emerging individualistic and materialistic concerns. "The fatherland, which safeguards everybody's rights and life," Islam bey complains;

> when in need of defense, it has to be defended by forcing [*whipping*] the children of the fatherland [*evlad-i vatan*] to go to the frontier to fight. The fatherland is everybody's real mother, and yet many people try to exploit it in its good and bad days and aren't willing to shed even two drops of tear for it. The fatherland is nurturing forty million people and, yet, now it has not found even forty souls to volunteer to die for it. In the past, this fatherland kept alive with its sword several states while now it is preserved with the help of a few other states [the English and French, who supported the Ottomans against Russia].

Like many of his contemporaries, Namik Kemal believed that the love of the fatherland was deeply imbedded in the hearts of the Ottoman Muslims but needed an occasion and a leader to evoke it. "Our men," asserts Islam bey, "do not know what the meaning of the fatherland is, and our women have never heard its name. . . . Consider it whatever you may, be it conceit, pride, or craziness—*I see the fatherland as a necessity for you and me*" (emphasis added). In effect, Namik Kemal declares through the mouth of Islam bey that the love of the fatherland lies in an undefined, unformed state in everybody's heart, waiting for the proper occasion to express itself. That was provided when the enemy invaded the fatherland:

> Then the people are transformed [*halka bir başka hal gelir*] and there is no difference between me and the most miserable peasant. Then those [village] Turks dressed in heavy woolen dresses, those soft-spoken, mild-faced villagers, those helpless poor whom we regard as being no different from plow oxen, then and there they shed aside their [indifference] and reappear as the personification of Ottomanism and as the spirit of bravery. . . . [Remember] they had to whip the soldiers to force them to face the enemy. But once the [villagers] saw the enemy, you could not stop them even if you used the sword, bayonet, and stick.

The play has several subthemes, such as Ottomanism, which express fairly well the intelligentsia's spirit and the preoccupations of the time; for "Ottoman," in Namik Kemal's thinking, was already synonymous with "Muslim" and "Turk" and excluded the non-Muslims. Although the heroes represent various sections of the Empire—for example, Baghdad, the Hicaz—Rumili is given the first place; all the main protagonists are from Manastir (Bitola) in Macedonia. (Zekiye appears in the first scene dressed in the local Albanian dress, possibly a sentimental acknowledgement of Namik Kemal's own ancestry and advocacy of Ottomanism.) Consequently, Namik Kemal's fatherland has rather well-defined geographical boundaries, at least in the northwest. Islam bey tells the volunteers under his command,

Comrades, we shall go to the shores of the Danube. The Danube is the elixir of our life [*ab-i hayyattir*]. If the Danube is lost the fatherland cannot survive, and nobody can live on. . . . [A] human being [*insan*] cannot live if he sees his fatherland trampled underfoot. . . . Allah has ordered [that everybody] possess the love of the fatherland. . . . [O]ur fatherland is the Danube, the two are synonymous. If you search the shores of the Danube you will find there a bone either of your father or brother. . . . [T]he Danube was crossed several times [by the enemy] . . . but never taken.

While Islam bey and Zekiye speak for Ottomanism, the two other principal characters, Sitki bey and his aide, Abdullah Çavuş, are portrayed as "Turks," through their informal behavior, straightforward talk, friendliness, belief in honor and justice, and use of the colloquial—all of which the Ottoman elite considered the Turks' "national" characteristics. In his name as well as traits, Abdullah symbolizes the loyal, hardfighting squad (*manga*) commander or sergeant considered to be the backbone of the army and symbol of Turkish military prowess. The çavuş (sergeant, squad commander), it should be remembered, were mostly ethnic Turks of village origin, who earned their rank among the conscripts by their intelligence, loyalty, and hard work and who did most of the fighting. Moreover, unwittingly perhaps, the play portrays Sitki bey (Ahmet bey), the commander, and Abdullah, the fighter, not only as ethnic Turks but also as the most important people in the defense of the fatherland. The Ottoman Empire thus was on its way to becoming a Turkish homeland, in the view of intellectuals such as Kemal.

The play was also a voice for "populism." As one of the future architects of the Constitution of 1876, the poet wanted to say—very cautiously—that the Ottoman public was "awakening" and that the government should respect it. "How many people," asks Islam bey, "would have fulfilled their duty if you did not lead them?" Sitki bey responds modestly, "You too do not know our people. They have that virtue [the determination to defend the Turks' fatherland] in their blood. . . . But, it [the nation] is in need [of a leader]. *It is in need because it believes or is made to believe that it is in need of a leader.* . . . [S]trange thing! Everybody's after pleasure and amusement [*zevkinde safasinda*] while here we are discussing very serious matters" (emphasis added). This dialogue and the play as a whole can be seen as apologies for rooting the idea of an Ottoman fatherland among Muslims, and especially Turks, although emphasis is placed not on their ethnicity but on their historical relationship to the Ottoman state. Essential to note is the fact that Namik Kemal's fatherland was a concrete deity to which the poet sought to transfer all the loyalty, the sense of solidarity, and sacrifice commanded hitherto by the faith. The latter obviously sought to retain its privileged position either by rejecting every innovation or by learning to coexist with ethnic nationality and other competing identities. Finally, Namik Kemal's love of the *vatan* had transcended—in fact, absorbed—the mystical, personal, and warm quality of the Sufis' love of God, which ultimately helped turn Turkish nationalism into a religion and popularized it among the masses far more than it is assumed.

Commenting on the furor created by the play, Nuri bey (later one of the Palace secretaries) claimed that the people had realized, partly thanks to this play, that they were identified with the fatherland and could do something effective and concrete to perpetuate its existence. Murat bey, the Islamist publisher of *Mizan*, hailed the play as showing the way for the future, "like those who contemplated the light while liv-

334 Politicization of Islam

ing in the darkness [of oppression and ignorance]" and stated that it had wide impact, because "it was written in the new style which accords better with our national character [*mizac-i milliyemiz*]"—that is, in the simplified colloquial Turkish spoken by the masses. Many young Turks echoed Namik Kemal's patriotic sentiments.[6]

Indeed, the concept of *vatan*, as articulated and expressed in the play, became such an inseparable part of Ottoman, and later Turkish, culture that today Namik Kemal is remembered by rank-and-file Turks as *vatan şairi*, the fatherland's poet, or the poet who wrote *Vatan Şiiri* (Fatherland's poem). This is martial poem, sung in chorus by all the protagonists of the play, which concludes:

> Wounds are medals on the brave's body;
> The grave [martyrdom] is the soldier's highest rank;
> The earth is the same, above and underneath;
> March, you brave ones, to defend the fatherland.

In the ultimate analysis, the fatherland for Namik Kemal was the territory of the state (*devlet*) and the nation (*millet*) was the community of Ottoman Muslims, led by Turks or by those closely identified with Ottoman history. The events described and the historical evocations indicated that Namik located the core of the fatherland-state mainly in Rumili and Anatolia. Thus, even though the play was translated into Arabic and enjoyed popularity in Arabic-speaking lands, its thrust is mainly Ottoman and Turkish.

Namik Kemal's admirers viewed him a dedicated patriot, while a handful of religious conservatives criticized him as a nonbeliever. Actually, in his play the faith was not the goal but, rather, the means to mobilize patriotic zeal. He invoked history, faith, myth, and pride to sanctify the fatherland, perhaps ignoring the fact that, according to the main argument of the archconservative Islamists, this desecrated the faith. Bernard Lewis believes that ultimately, for Kemal the real national bond was Islam and that his Ottoman fatherland rested on the feelings of Islamic brotherhood and loyalty; there "was no Ottoman nation," he said, and the old dynastic allegiance "was indeed being undermined by the new ideas of nationality coming from Europe."[7] My own analysis leads to a somewhat different conclusion. Terms such as *millet* (nation), *kavim* (ethnic-national group), *kavimiyet* (nationality-nationalism), and *cinsiyet* (stock, sex) were already being discussed as early as the mid-1860s. *Millet*, previously used to refer to the Christians, was appropriated by the Muslims as the "national" name of all those who shared Islam. For the Ottoman Muslims, it first denoted a *religious-national* identity and only later acquired ethnic connotations; but Russia's Turks from the start gave *millet* mainly a national-ethnic and territorial meaning. The issue came out also in a dispute between Şemseddin Sami (also known as Fraşeri) and Rifat Samih; the latter emphasized the nonreligious content of the term *millet* as understood by the younger generation.[8]

For centuries the Ottoman Muslims (actually, Turks) had fought and died at the call of the sultan for the faith, not the fatherland, but now Namik Kemal placed the fatherland, and implicitly the nation, which he never fully defined, at the focus of loyalty and received overwhelming popular support. Even when Sultan Abdulaziz and his conservative entourage exiled Namik Kemal and suspended the play, they could not prevent the idea of fatherland from gaining popularity. Yet Abdulhamid showed respect and consideration for Namik Kemal. Abdulhamid's Muslim "nation" and the poet's idea of *millet* were not really that different from each other, although the sultan gave the love of the fatherland secondary rank because he saw it as a device used by the British to undermine his primacy as caliph. The relevant passage in the sultan's memoirs is worth quoting:

> Some youths who received a little intellectual polish in Europe make at times speeches claiming that the love of the fatherland should come first. The love of the faith and the caliph should be first, and love of the fatherland, *hubb ul-vatan*, second. Is it not the same among the Catholics of Europe? The Christians place first loyalty to the Catholic Church, and then to the pope and then, third, to their fatherland. England is spreading in the Muslim lands the idea of the fatherland in order to undermine my authority. This idea has advanced substantially in Egypt. The Egyptian patriots, without realizing, are accepting the English ideas and are undermining the power of Islam and the prestige of the caliphate.[9]

Cevdet paşa, on the other hand, believed that Europe had replaced religion with the fatherland: "The sentiment of attachment to the fatherland, which divides the nations and inspires them with a sort of selfishness is something specific to Europe. . . . The situation with us [Ottomans] is different. The *vatan* reminds the soldiers of the square in the middle of their village. Even if the fatherland sentiment strikes roots among us . . . it cannot replace and be as strong as religious exhortation."[10]

The rise and development of the *vatan* concept, including the role of Rif'a Badawi Tahtawi (1801–1873) in generalizing its spread and potential for impact on the Ottomans, would be worth a special study. According to Albert Hourani, who echoes Tahtawi's views, the love of the country—*hubb ul-vatan*—appears to have the "specific meaning of territorial patriotism in the modern sense, and the mother-country—la Patrie—becomes the focus of those duties which, for Islamic jurists, bound together members of the umma and that material feeling which, for Ibn Khaldun, existed between men related to each other by blood." Hourani claims that the *vatan* envisaged by Tahtawi was Egyptian, not Arab.[11] The idea of a purely ethnic nationality, defined initially in Turkish and Arabic as *qawmiyah-kavmiyet* (from the Arabic *qawm*), gained the upper hand mainly in the twentieth century, as shall be indicated later.

From Fatherland to Nationality: The Turkishness of the State

At the beginning of Ottomanization, there was no deliberate effort to create a nation-state based on the cultural characteristics of the Turks, the dominant ethnic group. But as the state ceased to be the patrimony of the House of Osman and became theoretically the property of its citizens, there developed an interest in the nature and origin of the state. There was need for a name and symbol with which the citizens could identify and decide who they were. The first discussions having ethnic overtones took place among the top Ottoman administrators, as they began their efforts to Ottomanize the state—that is, to turn the subjects into a "nation" and make it the foundation of the state.[12] The first major statement in the nineteenth century concerning the Turkish character of the Ottoman state—still viewed as the preserve of a status group—has been attributed to Mustafa Reşit paşa, former ambassador to London, author of the Tanzimat Rescript of 1839, and the moving force behind the reforms that followed. According to the historian Cevdet paşa, Reşit, and then Fuat paşa, claimed that the Ottoman state rested on four basic foundation pillars: Islam, the dynasty (which was Ottoman and embodied in the caliphate), the hükümet (government, the executive or administrative branch, which was Turkish), and the permanent capital of the state (Istanbul). This formulation appears in a variety of Ottoman documents, though the order varies.[13] Apparently, Cevdet paşa told Abdulhamid about Reşit and Fuad paşas' views about the foundations of the Ottoman government, and the sultan asked Cevdet to write down the information. Orally and in writing, Cevdet paşa often repeated Reşit paşa's view that the loss of any of these four principles would lead to the downfall of the state. Fuad paşa (d. 1869) told British ambassador Stratford Canning the same, but turned the "Turkish administration" into "the Turkish state" "devlet-i Türkiye" and ranked it second to Islam.[14] Cevdet paşa himself, in his classic history covering the late eighteenth and early nineteenth centuries, pointed to the Turkishness of the Ottoman fathers, although without attaching to it political significance. Sultan Abdulhamid himself claimed that

> [t]he great Ottoman state was founded on faith, after Yavuz Selim absorbed the caliphate. But since the original state was established by Turks, in reality this is a Turkish state [*devlet-i Türkidir; Türki* in the sense of "Turkish," not "Turkic"]. Since the exalted Osman established this sublime state it has stood on four principles; the ruler [dynasty] is Ottoman, the administration is Turkish, the faith is Islam, and the capital is Istanbul. The weakening or dismissal of any of these principles will affect the foundation of the state.[15]

The memorandum, which reflected the sultan's dynasty-centered, ambiguous views, further stated that the caliphate and Islam were holding together the Arabs, Kurds, Albanians, and Bosnians, but

> in fact the Turks constitute the real strength of the state. As long as the Turks survive, the rest will [follow] and sacrifice themselves for the dynasty as part of their absolute [religious] obligation. This is the reason for which the Sublime Sultanate should place on a higher level the national fate [*kadr-i millet*] but also respect the Arabs, with whom we share the language of our faith . . . instead of addressing them as "fellahs" as our ignorant officials insult them in Arabia. . . . [All this] naturally makes the Arabs hate the Turks.[16]

In the memoirs he wrote after his dethronement Abdulhamid recalled that in his own search for ways to "save the state," that is, to prevent the war of 1877–78, he offered Rüşdü (Rüşti) paşa, one of Mithat's friends, the premiership. After inviting Rüşdü to his private quarters, a sign of deep trust and respect, the sultan appealed to Rüşdü's ethnic pride by saying, "You are a Turk from Anatolia. . . . I knew you even before my enthronement as a person with experience [and integrity] and you know the high degree of my regard for you."[17] It seemed that only the Turks could be trusted to save the state.

Language and Communication as Sources of Ethnicity

The Turkishness of the Ottoman state became more evident in the last quarter of the nineteenth century, thanks to increased use of the Turkish language. First, there was increased communication between the center and the provinces. Probably more than half of the total of the huge volume of the nineteenth- and twentieth-century correspondence stored in the prime minister's archives was written in Turkish. The officials appointed from the center, or to represent the center, were predominantly Turkish-speaking. In the past, some of the lower-ranking officials in the provinces were either natives or outsiders who spent lengthy terms in the provinces, learned the local tongue, intermarried, and became assimilated into the local population—all the while maintaining superior social status. Such was the case, for example, of the Kuloğlu in Libya and Algeria, who were the offspring of Turkish soldiers and local women. After the 1860s, however, appointments to provincial positions from the center were of relatively short duration, so many officials completed their service and returned to the center without gaining much knowledge of the local tongues. After the loss of the Balkan provinces in 1878 and 1912–13, practically all the government officials whose main language was Turkish were relocated to Anatolia, Syria, or Iraq, where they increased the perception that the central administration was "Turkish." In many places, the officials now communicated with the local people through interpreters, and many local notables and dignitaries soon found it useful to learn Turkish to facilitate bureaucratic transactions.

The elementary schools in the Arab provinces and all levels of the religious schools used Arabic as their main language of instruction, but Turkish increasingly prevailed in the higher modern schools and in government. For instance modern *nizamiye* courts chiefly used Turkish, as did the mid- and upper-level professional schools. Arabic was introduced into the curricula of the *rüşdiye* and *idadi* during Abdulhamid's reign, not as an instructional medium, but as a foreign language, like French. By the Turkification of the curricula and government communication, Abdulhamid hoped to increase administrative efficiency through the use of a single language, rather than to spread the use of Turkish. Turkish thus appeared as the language of the state and of higher education and the professions and, therefore, as a symbol of power, modernity, and progress—in a word as the medium of enlightenment—even though Ottoman Turkish was not as developed as Arabic. At the same time, Turkish became the language of the Ottoman modern elites, who saw Arabic solely as the language of religious studies and as an ethnic provincial idiom. The development of modern newspapers and a modern literature after 1860 became the other major factor in spreading the use of Turkish and generating a sense of linguistic consciousness. The printed word rapidly became both the means of enlightenment and, secondarily, a source of ethnic awareness. As the colloquial Turkish of Istanbul took its place as the language of communication and of modern literature, this increased the awareness of Turkishness and facilitated communication between the educated and the lower-class urbanites.

The dominant preoccupation of the twenty-year period from 1870 to 1890 was "enlightenment"—that is, the spread of knowledge—and knowledge helped create ethnic awareness. The best example of the link between language and enlightenment is provided by the *huzur dersleri*. The *huzur dersleri* (lessons in "royal" audience)—officially recognized in A.H. 1172 as part of the state activity—consisted of debates conducted during the month of Ramadan in Arabic (which only the educated understood) in the presence of the sultan in the principal mosque of Istanbul. There, up-

and-coming scholars, mostly from the provinces, freely challenged the established ulema with questions derived from the Koran, and the winner of this scholastic debate gained not only some monetary reward but also recognition by the religious establishment. In the latter part of the nineteenth century, the public interest in these religious discussions increased to the point that several other mosques began holding similar debates on religious matters and occasionally on daily issues. When Sultan Abdulhamid ordered that the *huzur dersleri* be conducted in Turkish, to accommodate the large proportion of listeners who did not know Arabic, it was clear that the rational understanding of the text had acquired priority over its rote memorization. Now the audience could understand the questions, and the sophisticated answers, counteranswers, and criticism, all of which shed a great deal of light on the level of Ottoman intellectual development and religious thinking during the last decades of the nineteenth century. The Turkish texts of the debates were also published, "in order to secure some [practical] benefit from these debates rather than have them published in Arabic only because the latter is the 'language of [religious] science.'"[18] I have checked the lists of the participants in the debates for A.H. 1200–1341 (ca. 1795–1925), but I could not find many Arabs or the names of Ebulhuda or Muhammad Zafir, two Arab advisors of Abdulhamid and learned scholars of Islam. Instead, the list is replete with Turkish names, which also indicate the participants' provinces of origin, such as Antalyali Muhammad Said, Dagistani Muhiddin efendi, Vodinali Ömer Hulusi, Konyali Elhac, Maraşli Murtaza, and so on. They seem to have come overwhelmingly from the Anatolian and Balkan provinces, indicating that the "Turkification" of Islam in Anatolia and Rumili was well under way.

It is quite easy to conclude that the outcry for the use of Turkish and its simplification was a form of nascent Turkish nationalism and populism. Yusuf Akçura, in his classic work on the evolution of Turkish ethnic nationalism or Turkism, published originally in 1928, claimed rather arbitrarily that the early Ottoman modernists were the defenders of *dilde türkçülük* and precursors of political Turkish nationalism.[19] They included such figures as Ibrahim Şinasi, Ziya paşa, and, especially, Ahmet Vefik paşa and Süleyman paşa (1838–78); Süleyman was author of *Sarf-i Türki* (Turkish grammar) and *Tarih-i Dünya* (World history)—the first part of which was published in 1876 and sold rapidly, although Abdulhamid later banned the publication of some sections. David Kushner, like Akçura, similarly sees the development of Turkish nationalism as a unilinear movement from the linguistic stage, through a historical-literary stage, to a political ideology.[20]

There is also a communication, which gained some notoriety because it belonged to the well-known Turkish historian Fuad Köprülü, about a letter supposedly sent by Sultan Abdulhamid to a teacher in Manastir (Bitola), Macedonia, in 1884, recommending that the language of instruction be Turkified by eliminating Arabic and Persian words and that authentic Turkish words used by the local population be collected, thus "displaying a high level of national consciousness."[21] In addition, there is the much repeated story that Abdulhamid overheard an Albanian officer in his palace guard shouting, "You stupid dirty Turk!" to the gardener, who had spilled water on the officer's uniform while watering the palace garden. Abdulhamid reportedly admonished the Albanian officer, "You must not forget that these humble Turks have created and are the main sustainers of this state," adding "I am a Turk." These examples indicate a sharpening of the sultan's ethnic awareness, but certainly this was not nationalism. All needs to be placed in proper perspective.

Turkish—highly stylized and using many Arabic and Persian words—had always been the language of the Ottoman administration, but with limited, if any, national-ethnic connotation. It was later designated as the state language in the Constitution of 1876, and it was retained after the Young Turks' takeover in 1908; deputies who did not speak Turkish were given four years to learn it. The Arabs and other Muslims saw the language used by Ottoman officialdom mainly as a means of communication for the state and, perhaps, denoting the social status of the rulers, but not their ethnic or national superiority. In fact, this lack of a "national" imprint enabled a variety of Muslim Arabs, Circassians, Albanians, Georgians, and others associated with the Ottoman elites to adopt Turkish as their main language because it was the language of the state and modernity. The lurking danger was, however, that at some moment the ruling group might make the language the mark of the state's ethnic-national identity and use the language to indicate the ethnic group that mastered the state. Namik Kemal, while in exile on the island of Lesbos, would write to his friend Menemenli Rifat that linguistic diversity was a barrier to the assimilation of the non-Turkish-speaking Muslims and, if politicized, would undermine the unity of the state and of the nation. Yet politicize it is what Turkish nationalism ultimately did, or, to be more exact, was forced to do, perhaps by historical and ethnic circumstances beyond its control.

The lack of nationalistic or political significance attached to the Turkish language and the concern for improving the communication and educational capacity of the tongue are clearly indicated by the case of Şemseddin Sami (Fraşeri, 1850–1904). Born to an Albanian feudal family, he went to a Greek school in Yanya (Joanina). Coming to Istanbul in 1872, he entered government service, meanwhile publishing short stories and plays, such as *Besa* (Oath), which portrayed Albanian life, translated books from French, and worked for various newspapers, notably the *Sabah* (Morning). His main and lasting contribution to Turkish culture was *Kamus-i Türki* (Turkish dictionary) of 1901. In *Türk Yili* Yusuf Akçura described Şemseddin Sami as a Turkish nationalist, but a careful reading of his famous article "Lisan-i Türki-yi Osmani" (The Ottoman Turkish language) clearly shows he was an Ottomanist. Moreover, he authored an Albanian dictionary and a Latin alphabet, known as the "Istanbul alphabet," which was adopted in 1879 for the purpose of increasing literacy among Albanians.[22] The Fraşeri family is portrayed in Albania as the architects of Albanian modern nationhood and nationalism and honored as such; yet Sami considered himself a "Turk" because he was member of the Ottoman state elite, and he saw no conflict between his Ottoman political identity and Albanian ethnicity.

State and National Identity

The issue of the separate identities of the state and the nation is crucial to understanding the Muslim nation-formation process, the roots of Arab separatism, and the ultimate disintegration of the Ottoman Empire. Throughout Ottoman history, as in that of other Muslim states, the basic identity of the elites was determined by their association with the state, which accorded them superior social and political status and brought them high income. In the last decades of the nineteenth century, thanks to the large number of modern schools, the children of the middle classes and the offspring of the countryside notables of diverse ethnic backgrounds were able to become part of the government elite and use Turkish as their language of communication. By the end of the 1880s this intelligentsia—a social class—also increasingly adopted modernism, including liberalism and populism, as the ideology to save and rejuvenate "their" state, with which they were so intimately identified. At the same time, the intelligentsia came to view the state as a potential instrument of progress and civilization (and populism) provided that it was controlled, not by an autocratic sultan and his servile aides, but by an idealistic, "illuminated" (*münevver*) group dedicated to the good of the *vatan*, as they liked to visualize themselves. The intelligentsia's advocacy of progress, civilization, and freedom was a convenient slogan for criticizing the sultan and a justification for their own claim to power through the domination of the government-state. In opposition to the elites, civilian countryside groups advocated decentralization, local autonomy, and private enterprise but did not want to change the traditional "Islamic" character of the state. The increased prestige of the state as the instrument of civilization (modernity) attracted thousands of ethnic non-Turks into government service and facilitated their assimilation as "Turks," whether or not they retained any original ethnic awareness. The number of Arab, Bosnian, Albanian, and Kurdish intellectuals who became Turkified because of their association with the state in the period 1870–1912 was probably several times greater than in any corresponding period of the past. Some of them even became the leading exponents of Turkish nationalism and members of various political movements, including the Union and Progress associations.

Still, Ottomanism, although rapidly being infected with the rising ethnic consciousness, was still functioning at the turn of the century. Sati al-Husri (b. 1879) was initially an exponent of modernism and Ottoman nationalism; however, in contrast to S. Sami, who remained a "Turk" to the end of his life, al-Husri became ultimately a major exponent of Arab nationalism.[23] Istefanaki Musurus, a Christian Greek, whose written and spoken Turkish were so poor that he needed interpreters, could become the Porte's ambassador in London (1902–1907) just like his father, Kostaki Musurus (1851–85), who had been fluent in Turkish.

To summarize, the multisided transformation of the Ottoman state along with rising ethnic consciousness, in the second half of the nineteenth century provoked criticism and opposition among some Muslims but not rebellion. The masses and their leaders acquiesced in the decisions of the state under the archaic but tenacious view that the state still conformed to the commandments of Islam and was the trustworthy custodian of the believers' faith and traditions. Although the Tanzimat reforms had created some suspicion that the leaders had tampered with established Islamic political norms and traditions, the masses' habit of obeying while staying aloof from the government was too deeply entrenched to be discarded overnight. The situation only began to change after events and reforms began to alter the believers' modes of social organization and, eventually, affected their perception of their identity and ethnicity.

The Emergence of a New "Turkish" Society: Migration and Sociocultural Restructuring

The traditional socio- and ethnolinguistic structure of Anatolia and Rumili gradually disintegrated as a result of capitalism and migration, a process that led to a reintegration that in turn facilitated the reshaping of an Ottoman-Muslim and eventually Turkish nation. The Ottoman Empire had never been a nation in the modern sense of the word but, rather, the conglomeration of various ethnoreligious groups. There were three main groups who in general occupied well-defined areas of the Empire: the Orthodox Christians, living mainly in the Balkans; the Turco-Islamic group, which also lived in the Balkans, and in Anatolia; and the Arabo-Islamic group of the Middle East. The other smaller ethnoreligious groups, such as the Jews and Armenians were dispersed throughout Anatolia and the Middle East; they did not have much in common with one another culturally, linguistically, or religiously. By 1878 the Orthodox Christian *millet* had disintegrated into a series of nation-states or emerging ones (such as Macedonia) and undermined the universal orthodoxy preached by the ecumenical patriarchate in Istanbul (and the Hellenization it was subtly promoting). The Arabo-Islamic group, which consisted mainly of Syrians, Iraqis, and Egyptians, and also North African and the peninsula groups (Yemenis, Hicazis, etc.), were aware of their separate regional identities as well as their Arabness; they also recognized the common Islamic bonds that tied them to the Ottoman state and provided for a degree of unity between them and the rest of Muslims.

The Turco-Islamic group in the Balkans consisted mainly of ethnic Turks, who were roughly 60 percent of the total number of Muslims there from 1860 to 1878. Turkic tribes came into the Balkans in three waves. The first came from the north in the ninth through eleventh centuries. They were known as Pechenegs, Cumans, Uzes, and so on, and most were animists, converted to Christianity, to become eventually "Bulgarian," "Romanian," "Magyar," and the like, and (a few) to Islam. The second group of Turks migrated into the Balkans from Anatolia in the thirteenth century and settled mostly in today's western Bulgaria and Greece. They were Muslims and had been the subjects of the Selçuki sultans. Many of those who settled in Dobruca on the western shores of the Black Sea between 1265 and 1275 converted to Orthodox Christianity; known today as the Gagauzes, or the people of Keykaus (their royal leader), they preserved their Turkish language, and a large part of them migrated again and settled in Bessarabia (today's Moldova) in the early 1800s. The largest group of Turks migrated and settled in the Balkans during Ottoman rule in the fifteenth and sixteenth centuries.

The third category of Muslims in the Balkans consisted of converts such as Albanians, Bosnians, and smaller groups of Greeks, Vlahs, Serbs, and so on, who accepted Islam in the fifteenth through seventeenth centuries.

The converted Balkan Muslims, while intermarrying and mixing with one another and with the Turks, retained their own language, customs, and traditions and mainly continued to inhabit their original places: Bosnia, Herzogovina, northern Montenegro, southern Serbia, and Macedonia. (It is interesting that the Muslims of Serbia rebelled against the Porte in 1830, in part because of the support the government gave to its vassal, Milos Obrenovich, the head of the autonomous Serbia. Sultan Mahmud II actually empowered Milos to punish the Muslim rebels, who were eventually massacred or forced out of their towns and villages. This first Serbian "ethnic cleansing" of the Muslims was thus carried out with the approval of their own caliph-sultan because they had defied the state's authority.) However, the Muslims drew closer to one another and to the Ottoman government after the 1860s, partly in response to Ottomanism and Islamism but mainly to form a united front against the mounting nationalism of the Balkan Christians. A large number of Turks in the Balkans were killed or uprooted, along with the Circassians who settled there in the 1860s, during the Turco-Russian war of 1877–78. The rest suffered the same fate in 1912–13. Fear of reprisals from their own ethnic "brothers" brought many non-Turkish Muslims in the Balkans to sympathize with the Ottoman government and the caliph-sultan, and many migrated and settled in Ottoman lands. After 1856, and especially after 1878, the terms *Turk* and *Muslim* became practically synonymous in the Balkans. An Albanian who did not know one word of Turkish thus was given the ethnic name of *Turk* and accepted it, no matter how much he might have preferred to distance himself from the ethnic Turks.

At the same time, the Muslim intelligentsia in the Balkans began to attach a special importance to the role of their region in the establishment and then the expansion of the Ottoman Empire into Anatolia and the Middle East.[24] The term *evlad-i fatihan* (sons of conquerors), which appears in Ottoman documents as an objective description of the offspring of the first Turkish settlers, now acquired symbolic meaning, for the new generation of Balkan Muslim intellectuals used it to portray themselves as the defenders of the Ottoman legacy, in the manner exemplified by Namik Kemal's play *Vatan*. Many of the proponents of this incipient Balkan Muslim nationalism were ethnically non-Turks, but they were now identifying themselves with the Ottoman-Muslim nation emerging under the auspices of the state—which was increasingly called "Turkish," although formally it was not.

Because the Balkans have always been a sort of frontier peasant society, the rural population, both Muslim and Christian, retained much of its pagan heritage in the form of religious and folk culture as well as its language and customs. When the Balkans urbanized during Ottoman times, the *çarsi*s (markets), *hamam*s (baths), *han*s (inns), *medrese*s, and mosques that sprang up gave the towns a distinctly Islamic-Ottoman character, while villages retained a predominantly ethnic character and continued to practice ancient rituals under Islamic garb. Moreover, because the majority of the Muslim population in the Balkans belonged to a variety of Sufi brotherhoods, practiced a form of folk Islam that was oriented toward worldly matters, and remained relatively aloof from doctrinal strife, major centers of orthodox religious learning did not emerge there as they did in Anatolia. Instead, the Balkan Muslims developed a pluralist cultural and religious outlook that they have preserved to this day. (Religious conservatives have often branded the Rumili as deprived of a true sense of Islamic belief and teetering on the border of heresy. The fact that Mustafa Kemal and many of his associates were born in Macedonia is often cited as a cause of the secularist measures undertaken during the early days of the Republic.) The combination of a strong desire for modernization, the impact of Europe, the awareness of ethnicity, and the pluralist, worldly Islam prevailing in the Balkans were factors that helped make Salonica and Manastir (Bitola) the first center of Turkish nationalism. Many of the Turkish nationalists involved in the Young Turks revolution of 1908 were not ethnic Turks, but they considered themselves as such. Ziya Gökalp recalled that it was an old habit to call people from the Black Sea "Lazes," those from Rumili "Albanians," and those from eastern Anatolia "Kurds," though Turkish was the preferred language of all of their elites and, in effect, they were Turks.[25] Yet they were proud of their ethnic origins as well as being "Turks." The fact was that at this stage being a "Turk" meant to belong to the educated elite associated with the state, progress, civilization, and so on. The main drawback was Abdulhamid's absolutism, opposition to which united them by obscuring their ethnic differences.[26] Migration produced an ethnic mix and a drastic change of identity, both among the incoming "Turks" of all ethnic backgrounds and the receiving society. The ethnolinguistic nucleus for the fusion of the Balkan and Caucasian immigrants was provided by Anatolian society, which was predominantly Turkish both in language and ethnic culture but much more orthodox in religious outlook. After the migrations, a large part of the Ottoman Muslims of Anatolia, Rumili, and the Caucasus were fused into a new sociocultural synthesis that combined a variety of ethnic Muslim groups into a new one that was called Turkish: an ethnic name with a new multiethnic, multilinguistic content.

The Ottoman Empire historically saw continual migration and settlement, but the nineteenth-century migrations dwarfed all previous ones. The main migrations started from Crimea in 1856 and were followed by those from the Caucasus and the Balkans in 1862 to 1878 and 1912 to 1916. These have continued to our day. The quantitative indicators cited in various sources show that during this period a total of about 7 million migrants from Crimea, the Caucasus, the Balkans, and the Mediterranean islands settled in Anatolia. These immigrants were overwhelmingly Muslim, except for a number of Jews who left their homes in the Balkans and Russia in order to live in the Ottoman lands. By the end of the century the immigrants and their descendants constituted some 30 to 40 percent of the total population of Anatolia, and in some western areas their percentage was even higher.[27] Great numbers of immigrants were incorporated relatively easily into the Anatolian environment. The koranic commandments ordering the believers to accord all necessary assistance to the *muhacir* and treat them as brothers were bolstered by the caliph's own instructions and the government's settlement measures. Consequently, the local Muslim communities in Anatolia—sometimes with donations from the Christian inhabitants—built dwellings and agreed to provide food and agricultural equipment for the immigrants. The incorporation of the immigrants also was facilitated by the fact that in the countryside the newcomers' elites were easily accepted by the native Anatolian elites, who had the economic, social, and cultural upper hand there.

The immigrants called themselves Muslims rather than Turks, although most of those from Bulgaria, Macedonia, and eastern Serbia descended from the Turkish Anatolian stock who settled in the Balkans in the fifteenth and sixteenth centuries. They, therefore, were returning "home," although they brought a cultural and religious outlook considerably different from the conservative and formalistic Islam of Anatolia. However, unifying forces such as Islam and Ottoman culture and the desire for modernity, coupled with the Ottomanist and Islamist policies of the government, prevented the population from splitting into native and immigrant political categories, although the terms *yerli* (natives) and *muhacir* (immigrants) may be heard even today describing origin and status in the local society. Some of the immigrants had difficulty adjusting to the Anatolian environment, especially some unruly Circassian tribes; but since the immigrants were not asked to forsake their native tongues and dialects or customs and dress, their integration took place at the local level, dialectically and peacefully. At the upper level, their elites became part of the emerging modern, Turkish-speaking Ottoman elite. For its part, the government helped by preventing tribes or confederations of tribes from settling anywhere in concentration; however, regions in western Anatolia—Biga, Gönen, Hendek, Düzce, and others—became populated by large numbers of Caucasians.[28]

It would be accurate to use the term "restructuring" rather than "integration" to describe the settlement of the immigrants in Anatolia. This restructuring was facilitated by the same economic and social forces of capitalism that had begun the transformation of Ottoman society early in the century. The immigrants were given land—on average from six to twenty acres, depending on the productivity of the soil—as private property and became small landowners, thus speeding up the privatization of state lands and the creation of a landed peasantry. The restructuring would have not been possible or successful without the economic input. The ethnonational identity of the modern Turks developed as the product of the experience of migration and restructuring at the same time the concept of modernity, the new knowledge, and the rationalistic spirit of the modern education were taking hold in the society and creating a new rational understanding of the place of Islam and Ottoman past in their culture. Thus the idea that Turkish nationalism was an "awakening of a dormant national consciousness" and rapid galvanization of ethnic identity, as claimed by most students of Turkish nationalism, including Ziya Gökalp, needs to be restudied. This view assumes that "national" identities were determined historically many centuries or millennia ago but were submerged into supranational organizations until given the opportunity to reappear in the modern form. Since many leading nationalist Ottoman (Turkish) intellectuals, such as Mehmet Murat Mizanci, Ibrahim Temo, Yusuf Akçura, Şemseddin Sami, and Ömer Seyfeddin, were immigrants or descendants of immigrants, and ethnically related to or of non-Anatolian Turkish stock, this view must be reconsidered. The intelligentsia, as mentioned, identified with the state and its "Turkishness" because of the language, but that Turkishness carried little political significance, and Turkishness was anyway not something separate but actually part of a multiple identity. Already by the mid-1880s "Ottoman," "Turk," and "Muslim" had become synonymous, and the identity created by restructuring—that is, the new society—actually was a composite of the three. Being a Tatar, Bosnian, or Kurd was not in conflict with being a Turk in the new sense. "Turkishness" denoted the identity of the emerging society and superseded all the old ethnic identities, including that of the original Turks. This voluntary adoption of Turkishness by non-Turks was facilitated by common faith and history and, perhaps, by some intuitive knowledge that they were helping to build a new society. It is no wonder that some Turkish leaders and intellectuals have compared Turkey's "national" formation to that of the United States. The idea has some validity and calls for a serious study.

In sum, immigration produced in Anatolia a structurally and culturally new society that developed around the state and colloquial Turkish language. Under the impact of new economic conditions and political circumstances, the society emerging in Anatolia after the 1870s, while largely made up of Ottoman-Islamic elements, was actually a new entity composed of the native Turks of Anatolia and Rumili and Balkan and Caucasian immigrants. The cultural effects of the intermixing of ethnic linguistic groups in Anatolia were many and widespread. For example, literally thousands of writers, musicians, politicians, and religious men in Republican Turkey are of immigrant stock. A recent publication gives the name of 282 writers and poets of Caucasian origin who produced many literary works, mainly in Turkish, and are known chiefly as Turks;[29] it does not list some of the best known Turkish writers, such as the novelist Orhan Pamuk, who is of Circassian origin.

The identification of immigrant elites with the newly emerging sociopolitical entity in Anatolia and Rumili, of which they were both the constituents and subjects, was basic. They ceased to be immigrants, although remembering their origin, and became participating citizens of their new homeland, eventually to be named Turkey. The War of Liberation in the years 1919–22, in which a substantial number of immigrants fought, helped convert the historical and cultural bonds politicized and internalized through Ottomanism and Islamism into Turkish national ties. The biographies of 504 army officers who died in the War of Liberation indicates that 64, or 12 percent, were born in Macedonia and Iraq. The list does not indicate how many of the officers' parents or grandparents were born outside the borders of today's Turkey.[30] The percentage of non-Anatolians, thus, would be even higher. It is interesting to note also that a fairly large number of Circassians fought against the nationalist forces in 1919–20, following the caliph's call, but their motives might not be what the official history of Turkey has described them to be. There are some demands today that Ethem, the Circassian rebel leader, should be judged not only by his defection to the invading Greeks but also by his early seminal contribution to the nationalist cause during the early days of the Liberation War.

A territorial fatherland, was precisely defined, eventually, by the National Pact of 1919 and Lausanne Treaty of 1923. To this territory, the heterogenous constituents of the new Turkish sociocultural entity soon became attached. The new nation was not, however, composed of a group that was burning with the desire to avenge historical humiliations, as were the Serbs, Bulgarians, Greeks, and, later, the Arabs. On the contrary, growing out of an old mixture of ethnosocial groups relatively free of historical inhibitions and of nostalgia for the past, the new entity expressed no irredentist desire to revive the Ottoman Empire. In fact, the elites had, in order to legitimize their rebellion against the monarchy, found it expedient to ignore history. And a preoccupation with the future rather than dreams of past glories remains today Turkey's basic philosophical and political orientation.

Ottomanism, Islamism, and Arabism

The late Albert Hourani, in his classic study of Arab thought, begins the chapter on Arab nationalism by emphasizing the historical and cultural factors that expressed the sense of Arabness. Among them were the Wahhabi Revolt and the much quoted statement of Ibrahim paşa, Mehmet Ali's son, about giving back to the Arabs their nationality and political freedom (although the latter probably was more truly French wishful expectation than Ibrahim's real thought).[31] In any event, Hourani divides the Arabs into a pro-Turk group, who thought that a strong monarchy and a united empire would preserve the independence of Islam, and an anti-Turkish, non-Muslim contingent, who believed that the Empire's integrity would be assured by a constitutional monarchy, equality of rights for Muslims and non-Muslims, separation of religion and politics, equal justice, and compulsory education. The main reason for the Arab-Turkish rift, Hourani seems to believe, was that the caliphate, an Arab "national" institution, had been usurped by the Turks. Hourani backs his views with quotations from Wilfrid Scawen Blunt's *The Future of Islam* (1882) and James Finn's *Stirring Times* (1880), whose authors were engaged in the British covert policy to establish an Arab caliphate and turn the Arabs against the Turks. On the rise of Arab nationalism, he mainly relies on the writings of Arab Christians but admits that Muslims did not respond to the Christians' calls—implying that the much touted Arab nationalist literature of the nineteenth century was the product of and appealed to only a small minority. The truth is that the Arab elites, unlike the Turks, had a very well-rooted, strong sense of historical continuity and ethnic identity. They were fully aware that the language of the Koran was Arabic, that the Prophet himself was an Arab, and that the Arabs had played a major role in the rise and spread of Islam. Other Muslims readily recognized the Arabs' special place in Islam; the Turks even accorded them the title of *kavm-i necip* (noble nation). Modernity, Ottomanism, and Islamism did not revive the Arabs' historical identity which always remained strong, but forced them to redefine their old identity in the light of new circumstances, which had deepened the Arabs' self-consciousness and sensitized them to their own changed religious, ethnocultural identity and gave them a new perception of their history. Unlike the Arabs, the Turks identified with Islam on the basis of faith, not language or the Prophet's tribal affiliation, although their Mevlud, Sufism, cultural pluralism, and special *tarikat*s had "Turkified" the outward manifestation of their faith. Still, the Arabs showed little predisposition toward installing or following an Arab caliph, as indicated by Şerif Hüseyin's short-lived tenure and other failed attempts to revive the caliphate after it was abolished in Turkey in 1924. Clearly, then, the Turkish caliphate was not the cause of the Arab-Turkish discord (see chapter 11).

Ernest Dawn and other students of Arab nationalism attributed its rise to the failure of Ottoman civilization to keep pace with Europe, intraelite rivalry, and different concepts of modernism. At the same time, Zeine N. Zeine saw it as a reaction to the imposition of secularism and of the Turkish language in schools; and Bassam Tibi pointed to globalization of the European ideas of nationalism, nation-state, and decolonization.[32] A more recent, collective attempt has tried to break new ground by adopting an eclectic approach.[33] Instead, all those works on Arab nationalism more or less agree that the Arabs as a whole wanted to remain part of the Ottoman Empire at least until 1912–13, if not later. While the growing importance of local culture, regionalism, and individualism strengthened the Arabs' sense of ethnic identity in the latter part of the nineteenth century, many Arabs learned and spoke Turkish with little resentment, as the Ottomanist and Islamist policies of the Ottoman governments from 1856 and 1878 onward were increasingly beneficial to them and did not threaten their culture and identity. Islamism, in openly acknowledging the supremacy of Islam, implicitly recognized the Arabs' special role in creating its institutions and in disseminating it, thus obliquely complimenting Arabs' ethnic pride. Abdulhamid's pro-Arab policy has already been noted.

The benefits of Ottomanism to the Arabs were obvious. It not only allowed the entry of thousands of Arabs into higher government positions, notably at the local level, but it also secured their acceptance into professional schools, granted them some freedom in the conduct of local affairs, and afforded them protection against the French and English intentions to occupy their lands. Practically every educated Turk recognized the existence of an Arab nation with a special place in the Ottoman Empire. Even Ziya Gökalp repeatedly asserted that Arabs and Turks constituted different (ethnic) nations and were together the component parts of the Ottoman Empire. That a "modern Arab nation," like the Turkish nation, was rising as response to changed circumstances was put forth by Arab intellectuals, such as Abdal Rahman Kawakibi (1849–1902), a Syrian of Kurdish origin, who was a fierce critic of Abdulhamid's despotism and an advocate of an Arab caliphate. He fled to Egypt in 1899 and there published sections of his famous book, *Taba-i al-Istibdad* (Nature of Tyranny). Earlier (1882) he had published *Umm al-Qura* (Mother of villages) in which he eulogized Mecca and the unique virtues of the peninsula Arabs.[34] He was not the first, or the last, to point out the existence of a new type of Arab political entity. Already the "Arabists" of all varieties who emerged in Syria after 1890 were openly discussing the separate existence of an Arab *ümmet* (*ummah*) or *qawm* (*millet*, or ethnic nation), as did Arab students in Istanbul and other Turkish cities. The obvious discrepancy between a rising Arab ethnic consciousness among the elites and the desire of the most to remain part of the Ottoman state, at least until 1913 shall be explained later.

It is not correct, therefore, to claim that Arab nationalism was a political reaction to the increased use of the Turkish language in courts and government offices. Nor is it true that the replacement of Arab officials in provincial and local administrative offices by ethnic Turks caused political reaction, although it did stir some protests. This Turkification aimed chiefly at upgrading administrative efficiency and facilitating communication, and the Arabs registered no strong objections.[35]

Even the so-called Arab nationalists, such as Salahaddin al-Kasimi, the organizations, such as al-Ahd of Aziz al-Misiri and the Syrian Arab Congress, and the critics of Abdulhamid, such as Raşid Rida (1865–1935), initially did not ask for separation from the Ottoman state, only for a larger degree of autonomy. Rida opposed Abdulhamid's absolutism but defended Ottoman unity. After the Young Turks' takeover in 1908, he went on to establish a school of Muslim missionaries in Istanbul and to mediate between the Arabs and Turks. Finally, he became anti-Turkish; but his Arab Association was established only in 1911, and his campaign to have the Arabs secede from the Ottoman Empire and establish their own pan-Arab empire began still later.[36] Although the continuing Arab attachment to Ottomanism might have derived more from practical considerations than from genuine belief in the system, Arabs, not Turks, remained supporters of Ottomanism and of Abdulhamid's Islamism to the end of the Empire. In a recent study of Turko-Arab relations, Hasan Kayali argued that Arabs remained firmly committed to Ottomanism, despite some contrarian views, and that even Şerif Hüseyin's so-called Arab Revolt had limited impact, though it was a watershed.[37] The Arab-Turkish rift, which put an end to Ottomanism, probably cannot be attributed to one or two causes but to the cumulative effect of various grievances and the ethnic, cultural, and political developments that differentiated the relatively well-established Arab ethnohistorical society from the emerging Turkish protonation. As long as the Ottoman state and its various institutions served Arab interests and respected Arab culture, language, and history while ignoring its own ethnic Turks, the Arabs had no reason to complain. In fact the state's modernization policies were facilitating the rise of a modern Arab nation.

The truth is that the Arab "nation" to which the intellectuals referred was a new entity, different in identity and mentality from traditional Arab society. This modern Arab nation was the consequence of the same forces that transformed the Turkish segment of the Empire. Youssef M. Choueiri, after critically analyzing and dismissing disjointed statements about modern Arab history and the national question, arrives at the conclusion that Arab historiography needs to give the Ottoman option a central position. He attributes the rise of a concept of a fatherland with definite boundaries and distinct identity not to Tahtawi's *Takhlis al-Ibiz* but to the Ottoman endeavor for reforms. In Choueiri's view, "Ottomanism slowly disintegrated into localized patriotic movements," as local patriotism and later Arab nationalism took the place of receding Ottoman influence; however, in sum, Arab "regions or systems beyond the reach of Ottoman power failed to embrace a modern concept of nation state."[38]

We have mentioned the fact that Turkish became the language of education, the superior courts, and the central press, and that this stemmed from the need for wider communication, administrative efficiency, and the newspapers' search for a wider readership. However, the increased use of colloquial Turkish—or linguistic populism—was accompanied by identification with the local culture, which was ethnic. The interest in folklore and in the *hece*, the syllabic meter preferred by lower-class Turkish poets, led to the decline of the *aruz*, the Arabic poetic meter. Indeed, the *hece* eventually would be defined as the Turkish "national" meter. Behind this seemingly natural linguistic and literary development was a social factor with explosive political potential. The promoters of colloquial Turkish soon discovered—maybe because the use of colloquial Turkish sensitized them to the fact—that the "Turks" in villages and towns, who were their own cultural kinsmen, were also the least-developed segment of the population. In any event, as discontent with the government coincided with mounting criticism of Abdulhamid's despotism, the growing interest in a Turkish language and literature appeared as a form of literary populism that was at the same time an implicit criticism of the upper political order and the absolutism for which Ottomanism and Islamism provided a convenient legitimacy. Thus the political alienation of the Turks from the Arabs was preceded by the growing tension between the emerging Turkish ethnic folk culture and the cosmopolitan, Islamo-Ottoman (Turkish) culture of the establishment that had appealed to the Arabs. The defense of the colloquial Turkish and of the modern literature, which took the living society as subject, was a convenient means to criticize the ruling establishment and, ultimately, promoted the cause of ethnic Turkish nationalism. Only the state could resolve this complex and ambiguous clash between folk and elite cultures, as it did by siding ultimately with the Turks. It was the state that forced Arab nationalism to come into the open by deciding to create a Turkish nation by bringing together various ethnic, cultural, historical factors necessary to build a modern nation.

The Young Turks Revolution

The Young Turks came to power in 1908 with the purpose of re-establishing a constitutional order and of implementing it in "ideal" fashion by giving freedom of expression to all the ethnic groups in the Empire. The Arabs, Christians, and Jews envisaged Ottomanism as freedom to develop themselves as they wished and eventually to gain autonomy. The Young Turks soon realized that this "Ottomanism" would lead to the liquidation of the Ottoman Empire, with little if any land left to "Turks." That, in turn, would have left the Young Turks with no country to rule and no profession to practice. (The Sèvres Treaty of 1920, signed by the sultan and the allies, did exactly that, giving the Turks only the northwest corner of Anatolia.) The Young Turks developed their own version of Ottomanism, proposing to merge the Albanians, Greeks, and other smaller groups into one homogenous Ottoman nation, which was being Turkified. Because the Young Turks initially ruled in association with old-time bureaucrats known for their administrative ability and anti-Hamidian attitude, such as Sait and Kiamil paşas, who were made premiers, the Ottoman old guard was able to maintain some of its influence until the Young Turks were ousted from power in the elections of 1912. In January 1913, the Young Turks returned to government through a coup after the country's defeat in the Balkan War. Their new government decided that the survival of the state and the Ottoman Empire and the fate of the ethnic Turks called for the creation of a Turkish core, that is, a group identified with Turkishness, regardless of ethnic origin, to make up the backbone of the state. As there was not yet a fully formed Turkish nation capable of undertaking that task, the leadership of the Young Turks hastened to produce one, using all the means of state at their disposal. The state was no longer to serve Islam or Ottoman ideals but the Turkish nation (still under the guise of Ottomanism and Islamism) which would consist of the amalgam of the groups living in Anatolia who shared a common Islamo-Ottoman experience. Centuries-old traditions of power and authority were pushed aside overnight as the state took the charge to create a Turkish nation out of the Ottoman Islamic mold. A Muslim critic of nationalism expresses best the changed role of the Islamic state: "Nationalism has been injected . . . through one and only one source: the control and manipulation of political power. The point that has to be understood is that the State is the ultimate source of good and evil in any society. . . . The Islamic State is an essential and integral part of Islam. Indeed, Islam is incomplete without an Islamic state."[39] Ismail Kemal bey, the Albanian nationalist, summarized best the nationalist aspects of Ottomanism. "By [Ottoman] Union," wrote Ismail Kemal, "the Albanians understood a grouping of different races under the flag of the Ottoman Constitution," which would strengthen the Empire guaranteeing its national existence. "The Committee [CUP] on the other hand only thought of uniting all the different races by forcing them to deny their origin."[40]

The state and its vast military-bureaucratic structure were placed in the service of the nation, which decided for the first time in the entire history of the Turks to "establish a state bearing its own ethnic name"—to paraphrase Atatürk's famous speech announcing the establishment of the Turkish Republic in 1923. The Arabs had not minded remaining loyal to the Ottoman Empire, despite the Turkishness of its administrative language, as long as the state had or appeared to serve the faith and, thus, the Muslims, regardless of their different ethnic origins and languages. Now that the state had become the exclusive instrument of a Turkish nation, however, the Ottoman partnership became meaningless for the Arabs.

It was at this point that the discussion on Arab nationalism took a new track, seeking to reconcile political power (the state) with Islam and Arab ethnicity. For instance, Abd al-Rahman Bazzaz, after questioning whether it was possible for an Arab to be a "loyal nationalist and a sincere Muslim" answered that "Islam is a political religion" and stated that Arab nationalism is based on linguistic, historical, cultural, and spiritual ties and vital interests. He asserted that Islam conformed to and expressed the spirit and culture of the Arabs, who were its propagators. In his view, pan-Islamism aimed at forming a comprehensive political organization, which all Muslims would be obliged to obey, but that such an organization could not be established for social and geographical reasons, whereas an Arab union was possible, even though in some countries the most violent opponents of pan-Arabism were the pan-Islamists. Al-Bazzaz believed that *true* nationalism can, on no account, contradict true religion because it is in essence "a spiritual movement . . . to resurrect the internal forces of the nation." Obviously, this was an Arab effort to nationalize Islam and place it in the service of an *ethnic nation* that sought to define its identity within the framework of its own historical and cultural experience and language, using Islam as its basic cement.[41]

The reconciliation of national identity (which is essentially a secular concept) with religious identity was then, and remains today, one of the basic dilemmas of nationalism among Muslims. The leaders of Republican Turkey have tried to circumvent the issue by ignoring the Islamic dimension of their nationalism. Being unable to offer any acceptable explanation for the survival of Islam, except for platitudes, they have labeled discussions on how to reconcile faith and nationality as "subversive" and jailed the discussants as criminals. Obviously, the "three ideas of state, religious community, and linguistic nation" cannot be easily dissociated from one another.[42] Turkish governments have used the state power to perpetuate the view that the meaning of state, nation, faith, and identity is decided and maintained by the state—often in the name of "secularism" and democracy, although such a view and policy is the antithesis of both.

Conclusion

The central theme of this chapter is that structural change undermined the traditional society of the Ottoman Empire. Ottomanism itself was a primary factor in weakening the traditional community and paving the way for the new one, while seeking to provide it with a political identity. Islamism gave a psychological content to Ottomanism and expedited its transforming effects. The Turkish segments of the Empire, namely Rumili and Anatolia, transformed themselves in a manner substantially different from the Arab segments, due to the historical and ethnic peculiarities of the area. The lack of a well-established ethnic identity among the Ottoman elites and their openness to contemporary civilization—that is, to the European type of modernization—facilitated the emergence of a composite identity that was called Turkish. The fact that the language of the state was Turkish and the modern culture was expressed in that tongue promoted the formation of a new "ethnic" Turkish identity (to be examined in the next chapter). The Young Turks took over power swiftly, without at first realizing that the entity they were governing was no longer an empire of diverse ethnoreligious groups but a conglomeration of emerging ethnonational groups. They knew that they had, sooner or later, to take charge of one of these, the Turks—who, by virtue of their geography, history, and association with the early Ottoman state, could claim its legacy and so claim to be both the "oldest" and "newest" nation to emerge from its matrix. Propaganda glorified the revolution of 1908 as the heroic achievement of "patriots" dedicated to the cause of freedom and the "salvation of the nation"; for example, *Hatirat-i Niyazi*, the self-glorifying memoirs of Ahmed Niyazi bey, a Macedonian Albanian known as the *kahraman-i hürriyet* or "hero of freedom," became for a short time for the revolutionaries a sort of Bible.[43] A closer scrutiny of the events preceding the "revolution" and the actual event itself, however, shows that it succeeded by virtue of the sultan's confusion, hesitation, and realization that he could do little in the face of the fait accompli that was the new society, the proto–Turkish nation, which he had helped create but could not control or understand.[44]

Abdulhamid's wide network of spies penetrated the Union and Progress Society and kept him informed of all the activities in Paris of and its supporters. The sultan knew the names of all the leaders of the crucial Salonica branch, which was established in 1906 and was dominated partly by army officers and Freemasons and which subsequently directed the revolution of 1908. Although Abdulhamid possessed sufficient political, military, and financial means to liquidate all the secret organizations in Macedonia, he did not do so. Why? This question has become controversial.

Cemal Kutay, a prolific but controversial writer and publisher of numerous memoirs by Turkish statesmen, in publishing the memoirs of Talat paşa (1874–1921), head of the Union and Progress branch in Salonica, member of parliament, interior minister, and prime minister between 1909 and 1918, has once more raised the issue of the rapidity with which the sultan decided to restore the constitution.[45] In his effort to draw attention to the special nature of the Young Turks revolution, Kutay refers to Şemseddin Günaltay (1883–1961), a professor and Islamist reformer, member of the Ottoman parliament in 1915–20, and prime minister in 1949–50, and to Celal Bayar, the third president of Turkey, both of whom suggested that the Young Turks should be seen and studied in different frame of reference than the long-accepted one.[46] According to Talat paşa, who met and talked to Abdulhamid and allegedly asked his advice on some state questions, the sultan said that he considered the "revolution" the consequence of uncontrollable historical circumstances and that he bore no grudge against the Young Turks.[47] M. Şükrü Hanioğlu states that "except for small donations . . . it is ironic that the Young Turk movement was subsidized by the palace with money extorted by the sale of 'journals' [secret denunciations] and by the blackmail with which some members obtained state positions."[48] Others have attributed the restoration of the constitution to Abdulhamid's desire to avoid bloodshed and thus spare the lives of the professionals he had educated in his schools. The German kaiser also boasted of telling Abdulhamid that absolutism had no future and that he should reinstate the constitution. Others claimed that the restoration of the constitution was an acknowledgment by the sultan that his subjects had become capable of charting their own political destiny and that he therefore could no longer cite their ignorance to justify the suspension of the constitution. The truth is that the sultan saw both freedom and Turkification as inevitable and he complied with their force. Toward the end of his reign, Abdulhamid identified with the fate of the ethnic Turks. Fethi Okyar claims that the sultan showed a deep concern that the number of Turkish army officers was diminishing (Von der Goltz told him the same) and that he felt "honored to be a member of the Turkish nation" and that the "Turks are the basic [*asli*] group of the state."[49] The last Ottoman sultans, Reşat (1909–1918) and Vahideddin (1918–22), and Caliph Abdulmecid (1922–24) similarly identified themselves as Turks, as do their descendants today, many of whom live in Turkey. According to a study authored by a member of the Ottoman dynasty, in 1999, 82 descendents of Osman were living, including 24 imperial princes and 20 imperial princesses. Of these, 23 lived in Turkey, 28 in Europe, 10 in the United States, and 21 in Arab lands.[50]

The imperial family's ethnic identification with the Turks, the rapidity with which Abdulhamid capitulated to CUP demands and restored the constitution, the extraordinary initial public support and the outburst of intellectual energy in the form of the great variety of journals and books and so on issued after the revolution indicates that, indeed, the Ottoman society had undergone massive fundamental quantitative and qualitative change, including a startling change of identity, during Abdulhamid's reign. The revolution of 1908 itself, if its background is properly studied, proves this.

We have examined the elements that combined to bring the remarkable transformation of the society. Suffice it here to say that, by the turn of the century, the society was no longer passive but was ready to turn revolutionary if need be. The Young Turks revolution was, in fact, preceded by series of popular uprisings in 1905–1907 protesting new taxes, such as Hayvanat-i Ehliye Rüsumu, which broadened the scope of the old *agnam* (sheep) tax to cover other farm stock, and a new head tax. Practically every major province in the east, notably Erzurum, Bitlis, and Van, witnessed violent popular demonstrations against the government that resulted in the death of government officials.[51] These demonstrations were usually led by local notables who asked specifically how the new revenue would be spent and wanted a voice in local administration. The Union and Progress party tried to involve itself in these protest movements, while the sultan tried to quell the demonstrations, first, by persuasion, using his best administrators, and then by force, but without success. This unprecedented and prolonged disobedience was the work of a new social group, the new middle class, which could defy, for the sake of their own interest and political vision, all previous traditions and norms of government. The unrest opened the era of modern politics and ethnic nationhood. Turks found out that if they were to become part of the European civilization they had to accept its principle of political organization, namely, national statehood. They did so in 1923, incurring the wrath of the Muslim world, which nonetheless followed Turkey's footsteps and organized itself into some fifty national territorial states between 1925 and 2000.

16

Turkishness of the Community
From Religious to Ethnic-National Identity

Turkish nationalism remains a little understood political phenomenon because it has been studied out of its historical, social, and cultural context as just another imitation of its Western or Balkan counterparts. A particular difficulty in properly understanding Turkish nationalism derives also from the way its birth and evolution was perceived and presented by the two ideologues of Turkish nationalism. Indeed, the last version of Ziya Gökalp's ideas on the origin of Turkish nationalism, which appeared in *Türkçülüğün Esaslari* in 1923, and Yusuf Akçura's interpretation, published in *Türk Yili* in 1928, were framed to serve the policies of the government in power. There are of course fundamental differences between the two, as shall be discussed in more detail in the next chapter. Briefly, Gökalp envisioned a national Turkish elite that would turn the disparate ethnic categories of Turks into a homogeneous ethnic community—or nation—based on culture and language, while Akçura regarded the Ottoman Turks as already part of a political Turkish nation embracing all Turks in the world. The "them" for Turkish nationalists was not a foreign oppressor but the dynasty—and the dark forces of ignorance—that is, the religious establishment, and even the faith itself—that prevented the Turks from marching in tandem with contemporary civilization. Antihistoricism eventually became one of the key features of Turkish nationalism. The ideologues of Turkish nationalism, including Gökalp, as well as the early Turkish republican government, purposely denied the Selçuki and Ottoman historical roots of the emerging Turkish nation, to avoid the stigma Europeans put on everything "Ottoman," "Turkish," or "Muslim" and keep the nation from being identified with the dynasty-monarchy, and to eradicate the roots of irredentism and orient the nation toward the future. The state thus deprived the nation of its history or, in George Orwell's terms, erased history in order to control the present.

Turkish official nationalism in the Republic rejected Ottomanism and Islamism but, when necessary, made extensive references to the Turks' Islamic and pre-Islamic past—seen now in ethnic terms—to lend that vital historical support to its claims. Specifically, the nationalists held that, while the ancient Turks possessed inherently modernistic and democratic tendencies and a pure ethnic culture, they were prevented from keeping up with the world (Western) civilization and from founding their national state by imperial dynastic regimes and Islam. Worse, the Republic contended that the Ottoman dynasty used its ethnic affiliation with the Turks to press them into the continuous service of meaningless, imperial, Islamist goals and prevented them from absorbing science and achieve progress.

Today those views are being challenged by a growing number of Turkish intellectuals, precisely because a correct grasp of Europe and its true intellectual legacy has enabled them to review freely and objectively their own immediate history and to conclude that there would not have been a Turkish nation as we know it today without its Ottoman and Islamic past. These new approaches bear the imprint of Europe, not the colonialist one but the universalist, objective, and humanist West. Turkey is much more modern and European today than during the period of the imposed historical amnesia that lasted until the 1960s, after democracy began to lift the barriers to free inquiry and encouraged the Turks to search for their historical Ottoman and Islamic roots. The search was neither the result of nostalgia for the past nor of rejection of modernity or Atatürk; it was a healthy inquiry into the sources of the Turks' identity. One of the key questions asked today in Turkey is "Who are we?" or "What kind of nation are we?" The question became acute after generations of Turks had embraced Europe and its civilization and believed themselves to have become part of it, only to be denied membership at first in the European Union (possibly because they are Muslims). (Turkey was admitted only in 1999, following great pressure and promises of compliance with the EU's strict entry requirements.) The late President Turgut Özal, in a book that is little read, tried to make a strong case to prove that Turks were Europeans. He had the right intuition but lacked the necessary intellectual background to prove his case. Indeed, Turkish history was determined by continuous interaction with Europe, which helped produce a "new Turk" who remained Muslim. Others have theorized that the Ottomans did not acknowledge their Turkish ethnic origin because they had a very low opinion of the nomadism and tribalism of the early Turks, and also because there was continuous warfare between Türkmen-Oğuz (considered authentic ethnic Turkish tribes) and the Ottoman administration.[1]

The Young Turks and Ottomanism

The downfall of Sultan Abdulhamid's absolutism and the rise of Turkish nationalism are attributed to the 1908 revolution of the Young Turks.[2] Credited with organizing from their centers in Europe, mainly Paris and Geneva, a steady opposition to Abdulhamid, the Young Turks are viewed as having absorbed Western ideas of democracy and nationalism in order to apply them to the Ottoman Empire; but this image is an erroneous one. The Young Turks' secret organization was established as the Ittihad-i Osmani Cemiyeti (Society of Ottoman Unity) at the Royal Medical School in 1889 in Istanbul by four or five students led by Ibrahim Temo, an Albanian, and Abdullah Cevdet, a Kurd. It became the nucleus and the catalyst of opposition to Abdulhamid's reign. It soon combined with a similar organization established at the Royal War College. Discovered by the sultan's agents, many members fled to join other exiles in Europe. By 1895, under the direction of Dr. Ahmet Riza, a positivist and implacable enemy of Abdulhamid, and some others, the society changed its name to Ittihad ve Terakki Cemiyeti, the Committee of Union and Progress (CUP; formerly Progress and Union) and engaged in systematic political activity, including the publication of reviews and newspapers. From this date onward, the CUP tried to contact every anti-Hamidian opposition group in the Ottoman lands. Many of its would-be allies, however, although opposed to absolutism, rejected CUP's positivist and materialist "scientific" philosophy. CUP's key purpose was to keep the Empire united and to modernize Ottoman society by, first of all, restoring the constitution and reconvening the parliament of 1876. It attracted some leading members of the ulema, of the Cemiyet-i Islamiye (Islamic society) of Şeyh Muhiddin, and of the religious orders, including such Nakşbandi *şeyh*s as Erbilli Mehmed Esad and others from the Mevlevi, Malamati, and Bektaşi orders. (Şeyh Muhiddin wrote the sultan that the six-hundred-year-old Ottoman nation had awakened and nobody could stop it; the best service the sultan could render to the nation was to restore its constitution. Muhiddin claimed that the freedom and the parliament demanded by the Young Turks conformed to Islamic principles and that absolutism undermined the existence of the Ottoman state.)[3] CUP also attracted various Arab opposition groups, both intellectuals and notables, as well as a variety of individuals studying or working in Europe who did not formally join the organization. In addition, CUP sought to establish relations with the Ottoman bureaucrats, Premier Kiamil Paşa and Governor Ismail Kemal among them. CUP used every means available to persuade the British and French governments to pressure Abdulhamid, or directly intervene, to implement reforms and, eventually, to oust him.

The true architect and agent of the 1908 revolution was the Osmanli Hürriyet Cemiyeti (Ottoman Freedom Society), established in 1906 in Salonica by a number of Balkan officers, intellectuals, and notables. Using the military forces under the command of its members, this society compelled Abdulhamid on 23 July 1908, to reinstate the constitution and reconvene the parliament but kept the sultan formally in power. Ten months later, in 1909, taking a religious uprising as their pretext, they replaced Abdulhamid with Reşad efendi (Mehmet V), who became their docile tool.[4] The Ottoman Freedom Society had formally merged with CUP in Paris but in fact became the dominant segment of the CUP and decided the Empire's destiny according to its own philosophy and objectives. Except for Ahmet Riza and a few other individuals, many of the original CUP members stayed in Europe. The founders and members of the Ottoman Freedom Society were born, grew up, and were educated within the Empire and were subject to the cultural, political, and ideological forces present in Ottoman society, especially the revolutionary nationalist and liberal Islam of the Balkans.[5] They did not constitute a debating society like CUP, for which European philosophies had become an intellectual pastime rather a plan of social action. The Young Turks of the CUP, as shall be indicated, had ignored nationalism while in Europe, and even their domestic friends regarded them as somewhat alienated from their own society, culture, and traditions. However, the members of the Ottoman Freedom Society who carried out the revolution of 1908 and took control of the government were both Ottoman nationalists and "Turks," a name that initially denoted association with the state and modernism, rather than ethnicity.

It is of seminal importance to understand how so many Young Turks became "Turkified" without any evident plan or program to accomplish this. The level of "Turkification" among educated Muslim elites in the Balkans was widespread, and one is led to ask how a "Turkish nationalism" could have developed in a region where a substantial number of Muslims were not of Turkish ethnic origin. The first answer is that they shared an all-embracing faith that is Islam (like Jews speaking so many different tongues) and that conditions in the Balkans favored the convergence and merger of Ottomanism and Islamism into Turkishness. This happened not because of a prearranged plan but because the spread of education and literacy and the infusion of new ideas, especially through modern literature and the socialization in schools—all of which was more intensive in the Balkans than in Anatolia—generalized the use of the Turkish language as a medium of expression for intellectual elites that had developed with similar modes of thought. The emerging "modern" or "national" identity superseded but did not obliterate the identity derived from kinship, class, region, social position, and so on. Non-Muslims could not become "Turks" but could easily choose their ethnic identity as the occasion warranted it. Cases of optional identity among the Balkan Christians were frequent: it was not unusual, for example, to find three brothers declaring such different identities as Serb, Greek, and Bulgarian respectively. Muslims might claim to be simultaneously Turk and Albanian, and so on, since for Muslims ethnicity and faith were not exclusive. Macartney wrote in 1934 that although certain areas could be defined as predominantly Greek, Albanian, or Serbian, "there was left a great intermediary zone in which the population was not merely mixed, but to a large degree of uncertain nationality."[6]

The situation of the ethnic Turks was different from that of the Albanians, Greeks, and other fairly compact ethnic groups inhabiting well-defined territories and sharing some folk institutions. In fact, it can be argued that in the Rumilian Turkish community tribal identities had long been superseded and the population culturally homogenized and closely identified with the Ottoman state so as to make it more receptive to new policies of Ottomanism and Islamism, which, in turn, became the ideological instruments of unification and indoctrination. The Balkan Turks were the immediate beneficiaries of the combination of Ottomanism, Islamism, and modernism that turned their old ethnic identity into a new one that was the product of enlightenment and modernity.

The burgeoning of Turkishness was a natural growth, the consequence of a series of nonpolitical, modernist endeavors that helped raise also the ethnic consciousness of other groups besides the Turks; and Turkishness subsequently developed into "Turkism." These two similar terms need to be differentiated. "Turkishness" is used as the equivalent of *Türklük*, or ethnic identity, while "Turkism" is equal to *Türkçülük*, the expression of Turkish political nationalism. Eventually the terms *Türklük* and *Türkçülük* were superseded by *milliyetçilik*, a term developed chiefly in the Republic and equivalent to "nationalism." The evolution of ethnic consciousness and the crystallization of the Turkish identity was divided into three phases: (1) the historical cultural process of identity formation or Turkishness from 1839 to 1908; (2) the articulation and expression of statist ethnic nationalism or Turkism in the periods 1908–1913 and 1913–18; and (3) Republican nationalism, 1920–50. The last phase is not treated in this book.

The Emergence of Turkishness

The "core" of the Ottoman state until the nineteenth century, consisted of the imperial elite or status group that ruled the Empire and spoke mainly Turkish but did not assert any ethnic affiliation. The lack of an ethnic "core" distinguished it from its Hapsburg and Romanov contemporaries, which, with their multiple ethnic, religious, and linguistic groups, at first glance seemed to resemble the Ottoman Empire; but each of these had an ethnic and cultural core, German or Russian respectively, and a bureaucracy that identified itself with that core. Even czarist Russia, which never created a truly ethnic Russian nation, had a czar and an Orthodox imperial Russian culture with which the "Russians," including a variety of assimilated groups, could identify themselves. The Ottoman bureaucracy, on the other hand, regarded itself as an elite without formal ties to any ethnic or linguistic group that was administering a dynastic state belonging to the house of Osman and serving the faith.

After the reforms of 1839 and 1856 undermined the social, legal, and political bases of the old order and the values that tied the subject to the state, the state sought to base itself on a broader social foundation, and Ottomanism was developed as the result of this effort. It viewed Ottoman citizenship as conferring on the citizens of the "nation" a common identity, which initially was a legal one. Yet many people, including Europeans, viewed the Ottoman state as "Turkish" because the Turks constituted the most numerous ethnic group. Hungarian and Polish revolutionaries who had taken refuge in the Ottoman lands between 1849 and 1851, some of whom converted and went into government service, routinely referred to the Ottoman state as "Turkistan."[7] Ali and Fuat paşas, who seemed to have liked the name, certainly did not think to turn the Ottoman Empire into a Turkish nation-state, although they might have perceived the rise of ethnicity as a major factor of political life.

The Islamic character of the emerging nation would not be contested but its identity became subject to dispute among intellectuals, who could be divided into "populist" and "statists." Ahmet Mithat efendi considered the Ottoman state as inhabited by a variety of *kavm*s (ethnic groups), all of which owed primary loyalty to the sultan, the personification of the state and the dynasty. He regarded the Turks within the Empire as the least-developed and the least-educated ethnic group but believed that, being the most numerous group, they had a right to gain a place for their culture similar to that enjoyed by the largest ethnic groups in the European nation-state system. Placing the utmost importance on education, Mithat, therefore, felt a sincere individual responsibility (nationalists attributed it later to his sense of national solidarity) for bringing the Turks up to the level of the relatively better-developed ethnic groups, chiefly the Balkan Christians, possibly as preparation for an ethnic federation in the Balkans. To facilitate the education of the lower classes, he used simplified language in his writings, being one of the first to do so.

Contrasted with Ahmet Mithat's populist philosophy was the statism of Namik Kemal, who regarded the individual as the mere tool of the ideal corporate entity, the activist state. Religion, according to Ahmet Mithat, was the source of individual ethics, identity, and spiritual nourishment; for Namik Kemal, Islam was the source of collective identity and state vitality and justified the state's claim to loyalty, service, and sacrifice from the individual. Thus, Namik Kemal used patriotism to reaffirm the state's traditional supremacy over the individual, unlike the modernist, who mobilized it on behalf of modernity. He criticized Sultan Abdulaziz's personal absolutism and condemned the sultan's relatively liberal economic policies as deviations from state traditions and as likely to corrupt society's ethics for the benefit of selfish individuals and foreigners, and he called upon the individual to save the state by defending it against its enemies, including rulers unworthy of their political and historical mission. Aware of the role played by Turks in the establishment and maintenance of the Ottoman Empire (he romanticized it by claiming that four hundred mounted Kayi tribesmen had established it), Namik Kemal attributed its existence to selfless devotion to Islam rather than to ethnic pride. Likewise aware that ethnic and state loyalties might clash, he advocated the Turkification of all Ottoman Muslims in order to enhance the unity of the Ottoman Empire. He too advocated use of a simplified Turkish, championed the cause of the commoner (not for his or her sake but for the good of the state), praised the virtue of realism in literature, and spoke for liberal constitutionalism—all in order to strengthen the state. His version of modernity was romantic, corporate, and elitist, even though it was forward-looking. The influence of Namik Kemal's statism appeared in Ziya Gökalp's thinking and in the Young Turks' policies and, later, in modernist Kemalist endeavors.

Ahmet Mithat was a sort of Turkish Edmund Burke, believing in evolution and social harmony but also in the individualistic and traditionalist, populist and pragmatic version of modernity. Ahmet Mithat might be called a traditionalist-modernist. Although respectful of the supremacy of the old, benevolent state, he believed that the situation of the Christians and Muslims alike would improve through education, material progress (which he called civilization), and interaction with the outside world. He defended women's right to emancipation and modern education in his *Hanimlara Mahsus* (Special for women) and was entrusted by his friend Cevdet paşa with the education of his daughter, Fatma Aliye, who became a leader of the cause for Muslim women's emancipation (although the immediate group for which she spoke were the Turkish women).[8] Fatma Aliye (1862–1924) is one of the figures of the period who deserves study. She is considered to be one of the first, if not the first, Ottoman woman writer. She was the wife of Faik paşa, one of Sultan Abdulhamid's aides. She wrote the novels *Muhadarat* (The veiled) (1892), *Nisvan-i Islam* (Muslim women) (1892), *Refet* (1898), *Taaddud-u Zevcat* (Polygamy) (1899), a biography of philosophers, and one historical piece. Her books were displayed at the Chicago World Fair. Fatma Aliye wrote also a short biography of her distinguished father and analyzed the events of his time. *Ahmet Cevdet Paşa ve Zamani* (Ahmet Cevdet paşa and his time) was first published in Istanbul (Kanaat) in A.H. 1332 (1916) and reissued in Istanbul in 1994. The introduction is a defense of modern objective historiography as well as an implicit criticism of those who held children responsible for their parents' faults. Her teacher, Ahmet Mithat efendi, wrote in 1894 a short biography of his pupil in which he described her as "an unimaginable event and a defiance to those who censure the [women] who aspire to be [a writer like her]."

Namik Kemal's stand in defense of freedom and his play, *Vatan*, glorifying Ottoman patriotism, earned him the permanent title of "national poet," but after 1908 Ahmet Mithat was consigned to oblivion as a single-minded pragmatist and opportunist serving an absolutist sultan. Until the Committee of Union and Progress came to power, however, the modernist traditionalism of Ahmet Mithat was the dominant current in society. Ahmet Mithat's once numerous followers came mainly from the provincial upper and urban lower strata of the new middle classes, while Namik Kemal, whose origins were in the pre-Tanzimat imperial bureaucracy, appealed to upper- and mid-level imperial bureaucrats and urban *umera* (plural of *amir*)—that is, the old, ruling upper class. Ahmet Mithat's followers were pragmatists, whose writings and ideas reflected the changing lives and mores of the society amidst which they lived. They neither manipulated symbols, myths, and expectations as did Namik Kemal nor considered themselves reformers or revolutionaries, although they were committed proponents of *medeniyet* (civilization), which they defined as a new world order that also preserved the virtues and accomplishments of the old. They were never credited with establishing a formal school of thought, as were Namik Kemal's statists, the moving force behind the Constitution of 1876. Nonetheless, Ahmet Mithat claimed as early as 1878, in his anti-Tanzimat publication, *Uss-i Inkilap*, that a new Ottoman nation with its own specific identity and culture was emerging around the caliph-sultan, thus demonstrating his own sensitivity to the ethnic mixing and cultural transformation taking place in Anatolia.[9] After 1890, however, even Ahmet Mithat mentioned the term *Ottoman nation* less and less and referred more frequently to Turks as being a sort of nation in their own right. Similarly *millet*, after 1895, seemed to mean for him an ethnic group, rather than a religious community, and he called the non-Muslims *ansir-i muhtelife*, literally "various elements." Yusuf Akçura, who stood ideologically on the opposite side, praised Ahmet Mithat as *hacce-i evvel* (first teacher) and expressed satisfaction that someone "different from [Namik] Kemal and his friends grasped correctly the idea of nationality and of the European civilization in which it [nationalism] occupies such an important place. This understanding brought Mithat efendi close to the people . . . actually to Turkism. The spirit, science, and know-how of the contemporary European civilization is democratic [populist]. Ahmet Mithat discovered this spirit and spent his entire life propagating this 'principle.'"[10]

Ahmet Mithat and, to a lesser extent, Namik Kemal both engaged in the discussion about adopting a simple written Turkish, and this brought out the inadequacy of the Arabic alphabet for Turkish phonetics. The early Turks had devised and abandoned many alphabets: nine early Turkic alphabets, such as Göktürk and Uygur, were abandoned, either for political reasons or because of their inability to render generally acceptable sounds. Finally, all Muslim Turks accepted the Arabic alphabet for religious reasons, although the script had several consonants ill suited to Turkish and lacked the short vowels that are basic to Turkish. Thus the word "pen," which was expressed in three letters (*klm*) in Arabic, had to be expressed as a five-letter word (*kalem*) in Turkish, while *MHMD* became variously *Muhammet* or *Mehmet* or *Mahmud*. The Tanzimat intellectuals, such as Namik Kemal, Ibrahim Şinasi, and others, were newspapermen interested in devising a language and even an alphabet suitable to the colloquial Turkish used by the urban, lower-class readers of their newspapers. The search for an alphabet suitable to Turkish in fact led to the advocacy of the Latin alphabet long before the Turkish government formally adopted it in 1928. As mentioned, the first concrete proposal to adopt the Latin alphabet was made in the 1863 by Ahunzade Mirza Fethali (1812–78) and he was later seconded by two army officers, Major Ömer and Menemenlizade Tahir.[11] The idea of a new alphabet and the use of a simplified language, therefore, were an integral part of a type of populism that took ethnic form, since the language to be simplified was Turkish, and simplification brought it closer to the language spoken by the lower-class ethnic Turks. In 1914 Enverpaşa, one of the three Young Turks, leaders while minister of war, introduced his own alphabet, which spelled words according to the Turkish phonetics, that is, each vowel and consonant was represented by a separate letter. The alphabet was abandoned, however, because of the confusion it created.

The press had become the channel for the linguistic populism and Turkishness. Newspapers such as *Ikdam*—along with Ahmet Mithat's *Tercüman-i Hakikat*—became the main voice of the complex modernist, Islamist, Ottomanist, individualistic form of Turkishness. *Ikdam*'s publisher, Ahmet Cevdet (1862–1935), who had been a staff writer for Ahmet Mithat's *Tercüman-i Hakikat*, adopted as the motto for his own publication "This is a Turkish newspaper." *Ikdam* attracted several leading intellectuals, among them Necip Asim (Yaziksiz, 1861–1935). Born in Kilis, north of Aleppo, to an old family of Turkish *sipahi*s (cavalrymen administering *timar*s or state land fiefs), Asim became a linguist and orientalist well respected in Europe. He was educated in Damascus, where the discrimination against Turks gave him a strong anti-Arab bias. The newspaper attracted also Veled Çelebi (Izbudak, 1868–1950), who was born in Konya to a family descended from Mevlana Rumi, the great mystic poet and founder of the Mevlevi religious order. More important, *Ikdam* provided an outlet for expression to the first popular social realists of Turkish literature: Ahmet Refik; Halid Ziya (Uşakligil), some of whose books were banned until 1908; Ahmet Rasim; and Ali Kemal, who published the *Turk* in Cairo and for a while also acted as chief writer and correspondent for *Ikdam*.

Ikdam was established in 1903 and survived until 31 December 1928, publishing a total of 11,384 issues. Some of its writers seemed to lean definitely toward ethnic Turkishness, but it remained respectful of Ottomanism and Islamism. *Ikdam* was criticized, but not prosecuted or closed, by Abdulhamid. Its populist philosophy led it to promote simplified Turkish and moderate ethnic Turkishness, but apparently it was not political enough to please Akçura, who in his highly selective history of Turkish nationalism, written in 1928, dismissed the *Ikdam* group as insufficiently aware of Turkism. Akçura acknowledged indirectly, however, that the Turkishness promoted by *Ikdam* had been popularized to some extent. He reported that publisher Ahmed Cevdet had informed him that around 1893 the public began to display Turkish ethnic sentiments, that unknown common people came to his office suggesting he publish books about their own—that is, the Turks' old literary and scientific achievements—and that, consequently, *Ikdam* published the *Kamus-i Alem*, and other basic encyclopedic and linguistic works dealing with Turks' history and language.[12] Cevdet said his effort was cut short by the government's censorship of Turkish publications. Gökalp, whose basic work *Türkçülüğün Esaslari* begins with a survey of the history of Turkism, acknowledged the Turkist role played by *Ikdam* but claimed that it lost popularity after one of its contributors, Fuad Raif, proposed to eliminate all the Arab and Persian words from Turkish. In sum, both Gökalp and Akçura, the theorists of Turkism, acknowledged *Ikdam*'s pivotal role in raising Turks' ethnic awareness, but they criticized its lack of nationalist political-ideological commitment.

The cultural and literary Turkishness of *Ikdam* was carried further and given a much more definitive linguistic and semipolitical cast by the poet Mehmet Emin (Yurdakul). The first populist advocate of Turkishness, he belongs in a special category of his own.[13] Mehmet Emin was born in 1869 to Turkish parents of village origin; his father was a fisherman and his mother a peasant girl from a village in the vicinity of Istanbul. He studied in a military school and then in the law school in Istanbul, which he did not finish. Şemseddin Sami (Fraseri) urged him to write in simple colloquial Turkish as did Cemaleddin Afghani, who had a profound political and nationalistic influence on him. Mehmet Emin was interested in the language, life, and aspirations of the lower classes, whom he viewed as Turks and Muslims. His first known poem, published in 1897 under the title "Kuran'i Kerim" (The Great Koran), was followed by a sixty-six-page book of pictures and only nine poems, bearing the revolutionary title *Türkçe Şiirler* (Turkish poems) in 1899. The most quoted line in those poems encapsulating Mehmet Emin's philosophy was: "Ben bir Türküm, dinim, cinsim uludur" (I am a Turk, my faith and my stock [or breed-race], are great). It was a clear statement of identity and pride in the culture and origin of the Turks at a time when "Turk" was used to describe the uncouth, the villagers, and the undesirables. Emin's other poems include "A Voice from Anatolia," in which he declares "This is my ancestral hearth [*ocak*], my house, my village are its parts." He expresses his determination to defend it in "Cenge Giderken" (Going to war). Clearly Mehmet Emin's patriotism and natural love of people and of the land had an authentic Turkish quality, rather than being a parody of the French or Persian feelings. Modernists such as the romantic Abdulhak Hamit; the realist novelist Recaizade Ekrem; Tevfik Fikret, the humanist, secularist poet, and teacher at the American Roberts College; and Riza Tevfik, the philosopher, all praised Emin's poems. They found them natural and realistic, using the *hece* or the syllabic meter deemed to be specially Turkish; only Ömer (Muallim) Naci, a defender of the old Ottoman literary styles, objected to Emin. The leading European orientalists and students of Ottoman literature—E. J. Gibb, Vladimir Minorski, P. Horn, and Arminius Vambery—wrote personal letters to Mehmet Emin, praising him for expressing and describing in simple language the real life, beliefs, and aspirations of the common Turks.[14] "Turks" no longer appeared solely as martyrs, sacrificing themselves for the glory of their faith and sultan, as idealized by the statist and Islamist writers, or as cruel savages living beyond the pale of "civilization," as they were represented in European writings, but as simple human beings aspiring to a secure and dignified life in their own country, speaking their own language, and practicing their own culture—not that of the Arabs, Persians, French, or other symbols of "high" civilization.

The expression of humanist Turkishness in simple language and realistic fashion flourished during Abdulhamid's reign and represented a milestone in the development of a national Turkish literature, political thought, and identity—all revolving around the country's people, land, and aspirations. The writers described ordinary Turks first as human beings, having their own patriotic feelings, specific esthetic tastes, ethical principles, and a language in which to express pride in being Turkish. The powerful political message of their works found a warm reception among thousands of students enrolled in the Empire's schools. Mehmet Emin's poetry represented a turning point—it was, in fact, a synthesis of all the various themes that contributed to a thirty-year process of identity formation. Akçura, while acknowledging Emin's basic contribution to the rise of Turkishness, viewed it as just an evolutionary step toward his own political version of ethnic nationalism or Turkism. Also, Akçura ignored completely Ömer Seyfettin (1884–1920), probably the greatest narrator and social satirist of his time and definitely a leading advocate of popular Turkishness. Ömer Seyfettin, the son of an officer of Circassian origin in the Ottoman army, born in Gönen, a small town near the eastern shores of the Sea of Marmara, studied in a military school. He became one of the major writers for the *Genç Kalemler*, to be discussed later. In one of his stories—actually a novel consisting of six short stories satirizing the ideologies of his time—he mercilessly attacked Yusuf Akçura as a racist and false noble.[15] (Seyfettin wrote a political tract in 1914 at the time the Ottoman Empire entered World War I. It is basically anti-Russian but also expresses sympathy for pan-Turkism. He was, however, opposed to political Ottomanism and the revival of the empire.)[16]

These developments leading toward Turkishness were by no means limited to Ahmet Mithat's group. Literature, "the soul of society," more than any other branch of the humanities reflecting the actual feelings and thoughts of society helped define the inner and true identity of the emerging nation. The rise of a modern Turkish literature, in which Mithat efendi played a leading role, was affected profoundly by Western, especially French, writing. Established by Şinasi (1826–71), the Tanzimat modern literary school produced a variety of works, some in simplified Turkish dealing with modern themes and the individual. Namik Kemal, who was also a staunch defender of modern literature, which, his statism notwithstanding, he viewed as a means of self-expression and a mirror of life. As an early disciple of literary realism, and believing that traditionalist themes could use modern (Western) forms of expression, he was a pathbreaker for future generations. Indeed, Namik Kemal took the first step toward bringing into the stream of Turkish thought, paradoxically, a broader sense of empathy with the human social and ethnic dimensions in the traditionalist Ottoman-Muslim frame of reference. The intelligentsia's growing interest in the appalling social and economic situation of Turkish peasants was the consequence of this enhanced sense of empathy as much as of the rising consciousness of their social own position midway between the peasantry and the upper imperial order.

It was Ahmet Mithat efendi, who began to write his novels and stories in the 1870s, who laid his distinctive individualistic, realistic, and "national" imprint on the emerging Turkish literature and soul. He dealt with native topics, searching for styles of expression suited to society's taste and reflecting its feelings. By reflecting the cultural and esthetic predispositions of the "Turks," this modern literature distinguished itself from the old Ottoman court and Arab and Persian literatures and was the "birth certificate" of the new Turks.[17] Its spirit was best captured by the Edebiyat-i Cedide movement (1896–1901) and its review *Servet-i Fünun* (Treasure of science-knowledge), published under the direction of Recaizade Mahmut Ekrem. The review was begun in reaction to the conservatism of the journal *Malumat* (Knowledge), with its inability to address the problems and aspirations of the new generations. Although Muallim Naci, the son-in-law of Ahmet Mithat and the private historian of Sultan Abdulhamid, as well as the literary editor of *Tercüman-i Hakikat*, eloquently defended the virtues of the old literature, the exponents of the new literature managed to hold to their own.

So the "old" and "new" literatures coexisted for a while, until the "new" prevailed. The writers for Edebiyat-i Cedide were the sons of middle-class merchants and government officials, had studied the European languages and literatures, and were committed modernists, expressing views opposed to the prevailing concepts. Among them were the poet Tevfik Fikret (1864–1915), who dealt with ethical-social themes and advocated the adoption of rational faith, for he no longer believed in the traditional Islam. (His son Haluk, the subject of one of his poems, converted to Protestantism and became a church minister; he died in the United States.) In 1905 Fikret wrote the poem "Tarih-i Kadim" (Ancient history) describing the misery and suffering caused by war and glorification of the past; and in another poem, he lamented the failure of an attempt to assassinate Abdulhamid. He was fiercely criticized by Mehmet Akif (Ersoy), a Turk of Albanian origin. Halit Ziya (Uşakligil), the creator of the modern Turkish social novel; the critic Ahmet Şuaip; Faik Ahmet (Ozansoy); Süleyman Nazif, the nationalist Turkish poet of Arab origin; Mehmet Rauf; Ahmet Mithat (Müftüoğlu) and many others expressed a new concept of the human being of the "national" society. All these poets and novelists of Edebiyat-i Cedide, along with Muallim Naci, are studied today in the Turkish schools, not as Ottomans but as founders of modern Turkish national literature. Although they adhered to the view that art was for art's sake and indulged in romanticism, elitism, and subjectivism, they sought to devise also new forms of expression and sometimes created new words, often out of Arabic and Persian, to express the individual's new problems and sentiments. Some of these Cedidist writers openly followed the French naturalists and realists, such as Émile Zola, in portraying the force of human nature, worldly desires, and aspirations challenging the austere restriction of the old order that stifled the natural tendencies of human beings.

The subjects of modern Turkish literature, written in relatively simple Turkish, were the individual members of everyday society, increasingly viewed as members of a distinct cultural group of individuals with special personalities and perceptions—that is, as "Turks." The writers for Edebiyat-i Cedide could be considered the representatives of the first national Turkish literary current that found its expression within the political frame of Ottomanism and Islamism. The themes, values, and aspirations reflected in their literature would become an intrinsic part of Turkish modernism and, to some extent, part of the Turks' ethnic-national ethos. Sometimes, though, themes of apparently limited scope were used to veil the larger and more difficult issues tackled by the modern writers. The criticism of household slavery was really a defense of women's individual rights and their freedom to choose their husbands according to their own natural wishes. Many of the first modern novels in Turkish are, in fact, attacks on female slavery and on men who used women as objects of pleasure. Ahmet Mithat's lengthy novels, *Hasan Mellah* and *Hüseyin Fellah*, several pieces in his well-known series *Letafet-i Rivayet* (Pleasant rumors), and an early (1870) long story, *Esaret* (Slavery), condemned slavery.[18] Other enemies of slavery included the famous poet Abdulhak Hamit, who wrote the heartbreaking poem *Validem* (My mother) in memory of his slave mother. Recaizade Mahmut Ekrem wrote a play, *Vuslat* (literally, "The lovers' reunion"), in 1874 in order to dramatize the female slave's plight. Namik Kemal and many others also condemned slavery (*Uncle Tom's Cabin* was well known by these early Turkish writers).

The most influential antislavery book—often described as the first Turkish defense of women's rights and an important milestone in the development of modern literature—was Samipaşazade Sezai's classic *Sergüzeşt* (Adventure). Sezai, who was born to a slave mother and raised in his father's palace, a place full of female Circassian slaves, used the heroine, Mihriban, a beautiful slave woman who is left pregnant by the master's son and then is sold to cover the "adultery" and resold again, to dramatize the plight of the women slaves and society's indifference to their fate. Actually, slavery was officially abolished by the Ottoman government in 1854–67 but continued to be practiced both in the capital and, especially, in the Arabian peninsula.[19] The starting point of all the antislavery literature was the idea, taken from the American and French Revolutions, that human beings are born free and equal; this idea was personalized in accordance with the readers' traditional sense of mercy, ethics, and respect for family. The unlimited sexual freedom permitted males, and the resulting abuses, were implicitly portrayed as a violation of Muslim family values and an exploitation of the poor by the rich and powerful; a new class dimension thus was added to the antiestablishment sentiment by these populist writers, many of whom originated in the middle and lower classes.

By the late nineteenth century, literature became the subject of books about the literature, first viewed as "Ottoman" then "Turkish." The first of these books, published by Abdulhalim Memduh in 1889, was titled *Tarih-i Edebiyat-i Osmani* (History of Ottoman literature), as were works by Şehabeddin Süleyman and by Ali Ekrem Bolayir (Namik Kemal's son), published in 1912. Although virtually no literary work identified as "Ottoman" appeared before 1860, Şehabeddin's history of "Ottoman" literature traced it back to Aşikpaşa (1272–1333) and his famous historian son, Aşikpaşazade (d. 1400), both of whom had lived supposedly in the "pure" Turkish era of the Ottoman Empire. Finally, in 1914, M. Fuat Köprülü brought out his textbook on the subject, *Türk Tarihi Edebiyati Dersleri* (Lectures on historical Turkish literature); later editions, in 1921 and 1926, were retitled *Türk Edebiyati Tarihi* (History of Turkish literature). In 1928 he published a relatively little-known nationalist piece, *Milli Edebiyat Cereyaninin Ilk Mubeşirleri ve Divan-i Türk-i Basit* (The first precursors of the national literature and the *divan* [collection of poems] of simple Turkish). In it he claimed that poets had advocated the use of colloquial Turkish as early as the sixteenth and seventeenth centuries but found no support in government circles; he cited Ahmet Nedim (1680–1730), the foremost court poet of the eighteenth century, who occasionally wrote in colloquial Turkish as one who was fully aware of his ethnic identity. Toward the end of the century, Ottoman history began to be treated as "Turkish" history in scores of textbooks. Abdurrahman Şeref in 1895 wrote *Tarih-i Devleti Osmani* (History of the Ottoman state), a textbook that conceived the state as being something apart from the House of Osman. The public identification of some Ottoman statesmen with Turkishness also became frequent. Sait paşa, premier many times during and after Abdulhamid's reign, and the main force behind many educational reforms, boasted that he could trace the Turkishness of his family back two hundred years. My contention is that the linguistic, literary, and intellectual bases of modern Turkish intellectual life and ethnic identity were laid during the last two decades of the nineteenth century at the same time that a reevaluation of the Ottoman past was taking place. This reevaluation actually helped lay some historical-classical foundations for the emerging national culture.

There was an outburst of book publication of both older classical works from the Ottoman past and newer volumes looking toward the Turkish future. For instance, the *Seyyahatname*, the widely known seventeenth-century travel book of Evliya Çelebi, previously banned from circulation, was printed by *Ikdam* along with other "classical" works, such as *Sicil-i Osmani, Lugat-i Tarihiyye ve Cografiyye, Mesahir-i Islam*, the dictionary *Kamus-u Alem*, and so on. The monumental biographical study, *Osmanli Müelli-fleri, 1299–1915* (Ottoman authors), by Bursali Mehmet Tahir (1861–1925) and his *Encyclopedia of Turkish Sciences and Learning* stand as major classical foundations in the development of Turkish national culture. Published in three volumes over the period 1915–24, the encyclopedia contains the biographies of more than sixteen hundred "Ottoman" mystics, religious scholars, poets, writers, historians, physicians, mathematicians, and geographers, whom the author selected after consulting some eight thousand to ten thousand books and manuscripts. Mehmet Tahir graduated from the Harbiye in 1883 and became a teacher in the Monastir and Salonica military schools and a founding member of the Ottoman Freedom Society. An amateur biographer, he followed the well-established Islamic biographical tradition of collecting material about the order of the Melami (Melamatiyya) to which he belonged. In 1896, Tahir published in *Ikdam* 163 biographies of Ottoman intellectuals, and by popular demand, he issued them in 1897 as a book, *Türklerin Ulum ve Fününa Hizmetleri* (The Turks' contribution [service] to the sciences and art). The book's excellent reception and the urgings of his good friends at *Ikdam*, including Veled Çelebi and Necip Asim, persuaded Tahir efendi to compile the *Osmanli Müellifleri*.[20] An original work still used as a basic biographical source, the *Osmanli Müellifleri* should be judged not by its uneven quality but by the message it conveyed. In the introduction, Tahir repeated the claim he had made in *The Turks' Contribution* that the scientists and scholars "who rose from among the Ottoman Turks of whom I am honored to be a part" prove the Turks' creativity and their love of learning and the sciences. Tahir, however, contrasted the recognition Westerners accorded to even the smallest contribution of their scholars with the Turks' disdain for their own kin who served the faith, the state, and learning. He also published several other biographies of illustrious Turks, such as the seventeenth-century philosopher Katip Çelebi, who regarded the Ottomans and Turks as being identical. Indeed, Tahir efendi insisted that at least one-third of the great Muslim thinkers, including Farabi and Ibn Sina, and as many as half the ulema who studied the *Hadis*, were Turks, not Arabs or Persians, although they wrote in those languages.[21]

Ahmed Refik (Altinay) (1880–1937), a distinguished and prolific historian, wrote *Alimler ve San'atkarlar* (Scholars and artists) in 1924; it deals with fifteen Ottoman historians and writers. This book, along with ninety other important studies by Ahmed Refik on various aspects of Ottoman history and that of the early Republic, never received the recognition it deserved, for his defense of the Ottoman past as an inextricable part of the Turks' culture was met by official displeasure. Ahmed Refik, a truly great scholar, was a graduate of the War College who had occupied important positions in the government of the Ottoman Young Turks. He lost his job in the Republic, disgraced by official order, and spent his last years in poverty, selling his books and furniture to survive.[22] His reputation still awaits full rehabilitation.

There is ongoing discussion about Abdulhamid's attitude toward the Turkish ethnic awakening and his identification with Turkishness after 1890 and, especially,

after his dethronement in 1909. True, the sultan banned the open promotion of Turkism, but he did not prevent activities promoting Turkishness. Several examples have
been cited already to indicate the sultan's interest in Turkishness, such as his introduction of Turkish into modern schools and Nizamiye courts, the substitution of
Turkish for Arabic in the *huzur dersleri* (the religious debates during the Ramadan),
his alleged advice to schoolteachers in Manastir to use Turkish, the repair of Gazi
tombs in Söşüt, his well-known admonition of the Albanian officer who had insulted
a Turkish gardener, and so on. To all of this one may add the testimony of Ali Said,
an amateur historian and Abdulhamid's personal secretary from 1885 to 1908. Said,
who handled some of the sultan's most delicate affairs, noted in his memoirs that after
he wrote in his history of the Selçuki Turks that the Ottoman and Iranian dynasties
were related, the angered sultan send a special investigator to him. Said exonerated
himself by telling the investigator that the Selçukis ruled Iran but were of pure Turkish stock "and that the Kayi tribe to which the sultan's [ancestors] belonged was
Turkish."[23] The very fact that the sultan identified with the Kayi, an ethnic tribe to
which Osman, the founder of the state, supposedly belonged is indeed significant.[24]
    It was during the latter years of Abdulhamid's reign that Turkishness finally en-
tered the stream of historical thinking—that is, the interpretation of the past—and
expressed itself in an institution. The Ottoman Historical Society (Tarih-i Osmani
Encumeni) was established in 1909 by the order of the new sultan Mehmet V (Reşat,
r. 1909–1918). Headed by Abdurrahman Şeref, the official court chronicler, the society promoted a version of Ottoman history that emphasized the dynasty's relation
to its subjects, perhaps in order to legitimize its own existence. Because the founding
act of the society did not mention the Turks by name as the founders of the state, it
drew irate criticism from Akçura. Articles published in its journal and the first volume of an Ottoman history it published in 1917, however, reflect rather comprehensive and relatively objective Turkist views. Members included some of the most
distinguished historians and Turko-Ottomanist writers of the period: Necip Asim,
Mehmed Arif, Ahmet Mithat, Ibnul Emin Mahmud Kemal, Ahmet Refik (Altinay),
and Avram Galante, the historian of the Ottoman Jews. Their published works, some
of which have permanent value, portrayed Ottoman history essentially as that of a
Turkish-Ottoman people (nation) rather than as a chronicle of the sultan's deeds and
sayings as in the past. (The depersonalization of history was symbolized by the replacement by a palace secretary of the old *sir katibi*, the scribe who accompanied the
sultan and recorded his every move, decision, and activity.) Although the "nation"
envisioned by the members of the historical society was called "Ottoman," in reality
they viewed Ottoman and Turkish as synonymous, and eventually the society saw
Ottoman history as part of overall Turkish history and published some important
manuscripts. Its journal, *Tarih-i Osmani Encümeni Mecmuasi*, published forty-nine
issues from 1910 to 1918 and then two more issues in 1919–23, with a total of 249
articles. The society also began the classification and cataloguing of archival documents, which marks the establishment of what is today the Başbakanlik Arşivi,
Turkey's chief historical archive. The newspaper *Ikdam* was a supporter of the society.[25] A more detailed analysis of the society and its role in the transition from an
imperial to a national Turkish historiography, although outside the immediate scope
of this study, could clarify the developmental phases of Turkish nationalism. Surviv-

ing in the Republic, it changed its name first to Türk Tarih Encümeni (in 1923–24), then to *Türk* Tarihi Tetkik Cemiyeti, and, ultimately, to Türk Tarih Kurumu (in 1931–32). In its last form it was led by nationalists, chiefly Yusuf Akçura and his students.[26]

The First Turkish Historical Congress, held 2–10 July 1932 under Atatürk's patronage and dominated by Yusuf Akçura, sought to define what came to be known as the "Turkish thesis of history." To that end, the participants, teachers from the mid- and upper-level schools and a handful of chosen historians, emphasized the Turks' pre-Islamic Central Asian history. They also sealed the periodization of Turkish history into the pre-Tanzimat (up to 1839), Tanzimat (including the time of the Young Turks to 1918), and Turkish national phases that Atatürk had outlined in his *nutuk* (speech) of 1927. The Tanzimat phase was roundly criticized by all sides, conservatives and modernists alike. (The period lasted from 1839 to 1876.) Akçura's long and rather banal piece read at the concluding session made extensive reference to European historians and historiographers and recommended that historians should henceforth write, and teachers teach, "Turkish history."[27] In addition, the congress gave the Kazan-born refugee historians such as Yusuf Akçura (who acted through a proxy, Reşit Galip, the secretary of the society), Sadri Maksudi (Arsal), and Şemseddin (Günaltay) an excellent chance to settle their long-standing score with Zeki Velidi (Togan) over the failed unity of Russia's Turks. Zeki Velidi Togan (1890–1970) was mercilessly criticized, first, for his "unscientific" views on the impact of drought on Central Asian urban and cultural life, but particularly for allegedly having opposed the Russian Turks' unity, and, finally, for holding a university position without having the necessary qualifications. It should be noted that it was the foremost Turkish historian, Mehmet Fuat Köprülü who, after hailing Togan's advanced and mature approach to the study of history, had hired him as a teacher at the University of Istanbul in 1926. Togan's real "fault" was his criticism of the questionnaire submitted to the would-be participants in the conference. He had objected to its shaky historical methodology and had portrayed in a relatively favorable manner the Nakşbandis, who had been outlawed by the new regime. Subsequently, Togan resigned his position and went to Germany, where he completed his doctorate and became a honorary professor. He returned to Turkey in 1939 to become an outstanding historian. Togan, a Başkir by origin, was for a while a sympathizer with the progressive aspects of the Bolshevik Revolution and as president of Başkordstan refused to accept at the Muslim Congress of 1917 a unified Turco-Islamic entity under the leadership of Kazan. He was in favor of regional autonomy, which would have recognized the independence of Başkordstan and other Turkic regions. It is ironic that in 1944 Togan was arrested and condemned to ten years in prison for being a "pan-Turkist" and "racist."[28]

Meanwhile interest in political history and national historical methodology grew as the works of Charles Seignobos (1854–1942) on political history—he de-emphasized social and economic history in his lucid textbooks written for French schools—were translated and became popular among intellectuals. The state finally stepped in to tell the Turks who they were and that their "national" roots were in Central Asia. The clash, long in the making, between a historically conditioned and popularly accepted Turkishness with a powerful ethos of its own and the state's artificially construed ethnic identity finally had come into the open. The clash still continues under the rubric of secularism versus religious reaction.

The Young Turks and Turkishness

The "Turkist" policy of the Young Turks must be judged first in the light of the intellectual and linguistic developments associated with "Turkishness" during Abdulhamid's reign. The removal of Abdulhamid and the ascent to power of the Young Turks did not put an immediate end to the development of ethnic Turkishness. Although the Committee of Unity and Progress, the true power behind the government, encouraged the Turkists to assert their views, it did not yet openly espouse, or even support, Turkism as an ideology. After all, the Young Turks "revolution" did not begin as a "national" one. As mentioned, the Young Turks in exile in Europe had been interested primarily in consolidating Ottoman unity through the restoration of the constitution and the reconvening of parliament. The very name of their party, Union (of Ottomans) and Progress (of the country), expressed their Ottomanist political and philosophical positivist views. They did not discard Ottomanism or Islamism, although the latter was somewhat soft-pedaled. The more basic factor that affected the Young Turks policies and, ultimately, their politicizing of Turkishness was the clash between statism and individualism, or centralization-decentralization, that had appeared earlier in the modernist writings of Namik Kemal and Ahmed Mithat efendi. Prince Sabahaddin, the son of Damat Celaleddin paşa and Seniha sultan, Sultan Abdulhamid's sister (the family had fled to Europe in 1899 and rejuvenated the moribund CUP), was the leader of the group arguing for decentralization and private enterprise, while the group represented chiefly by Ahmet Riza bey, the publisher of the *Meşveret*, favored statism and positivism. Although Ahmet Riza displayed considerable ethnic awareness—some call him, mistakenly, a "Turkish nationalist"—his Turkishness remained a latent part of his Ottomanism-statism. The Young Turks abroad, initially showed little interest in nationalism. They wrote extensively on every major European intellectual current yet avoided discussing their own ethnic "Turkishness."[29] The Young Turks in Paris were interested mainly in the positivist ideas of Auguste Comte, the elitist Pierre Lafitte, and a variety of other thinkers and writers whose ideas and views were shaped by the industrializing society of the West and had little relevance to the Ottoman Empire. However, a few of the Young Turks in Europe, usually the lesser-known individuals, expressed also an interest in the fate of the ethnic Turks, as indicated by the titles of their books.[30] Nevertheless, although a few of the Young Turks had began to look upon the Ottoman Empire as a Turkish state and showed real interest in the ethnic Turks, most were interested primarily in perpetuating the Empire's multiethnic Ottoman existence, not in creating a Turkish nation.

The short period of political and social peace and harmony that followed the Young Turks ascendancy to power ended not because of disagreement over Turkishness, or even "secularism," but over the new government's centralization policy designed to strengthen Ottoman unity. Before the year 1908 was out, the agrarian groups, provincial notables, and most of the religious establishment, as well as the Greeks, Armenians, and Macedonians began to attack CUP's centralist policies. In time, the opposition to CUP coalesced around, first, the Ahrar (People) and then the Itilaf (Liberal) Parties, which outwardly adopted an Ottomanist-Islamic ideology and Prince Sabahaddin's liberal economic views. The statists, gathered around the leading cadres of CUP, regarded the views of their opponents as ideas that would hasten the disintegration of the Empire. Throughout the era of the Young Turks these issues—statism and centralization versus expanded local autonomy and some recognition for local culture—were the key issues separating the party in power from the opposition. The question of who was a "Turk," although discussed privately, had not affected, and would not affect, the policies of CUP yet, although ethnic Turks were increasingly regarded as having been exploited economically by their own upper classes in association with the Greek and Armenian minorities and European interests and having faced total disappearance. From this economic perspective, Ottomanism appeared now to be the ideology of the upper classes, while nationalism acquired a populist dimension by appearing to defend the economic interests of the lower classes, which were seen as consisting predominantly of ethnic Turks.[31] Those who called themselves "Turks" were immediately accepted as such by CUP, provided they were Muslim, not closely identified with the Hamidian regime, and acted properly. At the same time, ethnic ties, rather than the old historical-cultural relationship between the Ottoman Turks and the Turks of Russia, acquired increased political importance, and a series of publications emphasized ethnicity as the basis of nationhood.[32]

The Young Turks' view of Turkishness and of Ottomanism was affected but not changed by the Bulgarian declaration of independence and Hapsburg occupation of Bosnia-Herzogovina, both in 1908. However, the Italian occupation of Libya, the Albanian revolts and independence in 1910–1912, and, especially, the two Balkan wars of 1912–13, which led to the partitioning of Macedonia and Thrace among Greece, Serbia, and Bulgaria and put an end to the Ottoman presence in the Balkans, brought to the fore the question of an ethnic "core" sincerely dedicated to holding together the remainder of the Empire in Asia. The leaders of the Young Turks began to look to the "Turks" as the most trustworthy ethnic group to be such a "core," especially as most of Anatolia was inhabited by people who now mostly called themselves Turks. The urge to turn to history to emphasize the role of the Turks in the founding of the Ottoman Empire was opposed by futurists, for whom Ottoman history was a reminder of regression and decadence. An exchange of views, in verse, between Yahya Kemal Beyatli and Ziya Gökalp, provides excellent insight into the clashing views about modernity and history among the Young Turks' intelligentsia. At one of their drinking parties, Gökalp chided Beyatli for his infatuation with the Ottoman past, describing him as looking like a destitute vagabond in tatters, for he had his eyes fixed on history. Beyatli, born in Üsküp (Skopje) in Macedonia, educated in Paris, and romantically interested in Ottoman glories, replied, "I am neither in tatters nor a vagabond [bohemian]; I am the future rooted in the past."[33]

The Albanians, unwittingly, acted as a catalyst in the decision of the Young Turks to turn Turkishness into Turkism, but without formally abandoning Ottomanism and Islamism. The Albanians had played a vital role throughout the Ottoman history as reliable soldiers and statesmen; and, in the nineteenth century, they had emerged as intellectuals, journalists, and political activists in the Union and Progress societies. Historically speaking, the Albanians had entered the fold of Islam during the time of Ottoman rule in the Balkans as well-formed ethnic communities; consequently, they retained a strong sense of ethnic identity and attachment to their language, and as early as 1878 they established the League of Prizerin in order to proclaim Albanian independence if the Ottoman state disintegrated. Although Sultan Abdulhamid accorded the Albanians privileged treatment, including tax exemptions, they expressed their nationalist-separatist sentiments after the Serbians and the Greeks, anticipating the disintegration of the Ottoman Empire, and appeared determined to divide and annex Albania. It was at this point that many Albanians, including high officials in the service of the Porte, such as Ismail Kemal and Naim Fraşeri, some of whom had established their political organizations as branches of the Union and Progress Party, began openly to promote Albanian separatism in a manner no different from that of the Christian separatists.[34] When the Albanians did declare independence in 1912, largely to forestall the annexation of their lands by Serbia and Greece, the Young Turks felt betrayed by their most loyal Ottoman brothers and became fearful the Arabs would do the same, although the latter had not expressed such intentions yet.

Nonetheless, the Young Turks continued formally to defend Ottomanism, although their Ottomanism was no longer the supraethnic, supranational identity envisaged by the Tanzimatists; it was only a formula that would allow the CUP to transform the Ottoman Empire into a Turkish entity, "imperial in form and national in content."

Conclusion

The CUP gave "Turkishness" some protection and encouragement from 1908 to 1912, but not open support. In 1913 the CUP ceased to act as a secret ruling society and took over the government itself. The idea that the Ottoman state could be saved by a leadership group dedicated to rationalism, modernism, and positivism and resting upon an ethnic group dedicated both to "its own land" and to modernity was taking root. However, confronted with the staying power of Ottomanism and Islamism, the Young Turks sought somehow to reconcile the three ideologies. They more or less abandoned Islamism in the interior because it appeared to legitimize Sultan Abdulhamid's old policies, and they emphasized Ottomanism as a principle of unity there. Otherwise, they valued the power of Islam as still the most meaningful bond of social cohesion and as an instrument of foreign policy. At the insistence of the Germans, who like the English overestimated the influence of the caliphate among the overseas Muslims, the Young Turks turned Islamism into pan-Islamism and used it to nurture pan-Turkism. A handful of the leaders of the Young Turks, headed by Enver paşa, despite the opposition of the cabinet and the population at large, dragged the Ottoman Empire into the First World War on the side of the Central Powers. On 11 November 1914 the şeyhülislam issued the call to *cihad* in the form of five *fetvas* calling on the Muslim peoples, and especially on the Muslims of Turkish stock in Kazan, Central Asia, Crimea, India, Afghanistan, and Africa, to rise against their Russian and European masters.[35] Abdulhamid had never issued the call to *cihad* (except pro forma in the Greek war of 1897); the Young Turks, who denounced Islamism while out of power, resorted to it at the discretion of the Germans. Their *cihad* had a very limited impact on the war, but it helped discredit the caliphate. It made the caliphate appear to be the tool of any opportunistic ruler rather than the central symbol and representative of unity and defender of the faith as Abdulhamid strove to make it (see also chapter 11).

After 1913, and including the war years, the CUP undertook a series of basic measures that marked the beginning of a new reformist era, which continued, with some changes, into the Republic. "Turkishness" was gradually turned into "Turkism," not as a state ideology or even as specific policy (except for the disastrous effort to introduce Turkish in minority schools) but encouraged discreetly as a distinct ideological school of thought dedicated to progress and, ultimately, the political supremacy of the ethnic Turk. While the development of Turkishness during Abdulhamid's reign had caused little reaction among conservative Islamists, the rise of Turkism during the CUP's rule, as a distinct ideological category different from and opposed to Ottomanism and Islamism, prompted the Islamists, Westernists, and other groups to claim an autonomous sphere for their own ideas. True, Islamism, Turkism, positivism, Westernism, and so on, existed in embryonic forms before the CUP came to power, but none had established organizations and developed their own program of action.[36] After the Turkists began to establish their ethnically oriented organizations, however, the proponents of other ideologies sought to formalize their views, establish organizations and even political parties, and publish their own newspapers and reviews in order to define and promote whatever ideology they espoused. The idea of a national economy free of the control of the non-Muslim Ottomans and of its dependency on the West, which emerged during CUP rule, aimed ultimately to benefit the ethnic Turks. The free enterprise, largely financed by foreign capital, that had started during Abdulaziz's reign and gained momentum during Abdulhamid's tenure, benefited a small urban group but not many Turkish Muslim villagers. In the *vilayets* of Istanbul, Izmir (Aydin), and Bursa (Hüdavendigar), impoverished peasant women resorted to widespread abortion, which, combined with spread of diseases such as syphilis, brought in with the "civilization of Europe," produced a substantial decrease in the Muslim population. The problem, hardly noted by scholars, had far-reaching efforts in dramatizing the plight of ethnic Turks and in increasing the economic appeal of Turkism. British consular reports mentioned massive infant mortality among rural Turks in the Aegean areas, while in the Marmara Sea littoral, abortion and venereal diseases, fostered by poverty, had reached such a level as to force Abdulhamid to undertake an antiabortion campaign.[37]

Probably the greatest conflict was generated by the differing meanings attributed to science, positivism, modernity, and faith. Indeed, modernism and positivism were seen as closely related, if not synonymous, thanks to the Young Turks' leader, Ahmet Riza bey, and his newspaper *Meşveret*. It is highly debatable whether Westernism had developed as a full-fledged school of thought before 1908, despite Niyazi Berkes's claim that the Westernists advocated the radical moral and material transformation of their society by emulating Europe before the Young Turks came to power.[38] It is true that Abdullah Cevdet (1869–1932), the leading Westernist, in his journals *Osmanli* (1897) and *İçtihat* (1897–99, 1904), advocated positivism as the avenue to progress; but he also defended Islam and, like some other writers, asserted that faith and religion were not one and the same. Cevdet was a Kurd by origin and an early opponent of Abdulhamid's absolutism; he was banished to Tripoli and then fled to Europe but remained aloof from the Young Turks' leaders. Berkes described him as being an enemy "neither of Islam nor of religion in general," while Tarik Zafer Tunaya regards him as a bitter critic of Islamic practices and Şükrü Hanioğlu defines him as a materialist and atheist. The *Ictihat* was read by many modernist Westernists who occupied leading positions in the Republic.[39]

The distinction many drew between faith and religion defined faith as representing the inner commitment to God, the Prophet, and their teachings, while religion provided the man-made organization—the religious bureaucracy—and identities through which the faith was filtered to the masses and could be manipulated. Many positivists believed that the manipulation of religion by ignorant clergymen and oppressive governments had caused the stagnation of Muslim societies. Because the sultan-caliph controlled the *şeyhulislam* and his office, the anticlerics, influenced partly by French radicalism, accused him of having created a state-controlled clergy in violation of Islam's long-standing traditions. The modernists tended to regard *iman* (faith) as a natural, God-given spiritual capacity. It was to be preserved through a reform of the institutional, legal, and educational accoutrements of religion that would make the relations between faith and religion correspond to the norms of modern civilization—whatever that meant. This idea seemed to be that religion could be manipulated according to social and political needs, but that the faith would still remain intact and pure. Born out of social and political rather than theological considerations, the discussion actually was an indirect effort to portray the sultanate and caliphate as political institutions created by humans. Mustafa Kemal Atatürk's "secularism" may be described as an effort to do away with the institutions harmful to the nation created in the name of religion, while respecting the faith alone and allowing for freedom of worship, observance of Ramadan, and the like, these being deemed related to the faith and not to the worldly ambitions of the religious establishment. (Later developments in Turkey have demonstrated that the distinctioin *iman ve din*, of faith and religion, the essence and the form, cannot be kept separate forever.) Concomitant with this view, there arose for the first time also a new "national," Turkish view of Islam.

All the discussions involving religion, faith, ethnic identity, and so on, were of only incipient issues. Most of the Young Turks were modernist, Ottomanist, and Islamist and, to some degree, positivist, Turkist, and nationalist. Ziya Gökalp, an early victim of this confused ideological situation and the alienation it engendered, found his salvation in making Turkism-cum-civilization the repository of the faith, while converting Turkishness into Turkism. Indeed, Gökalp can be viewed both as a thinker and as a missionary and preacher of the new faith of Turkism in its modern "national" garb. In Gökalp's view, Turkish nationalism and civilization went hand in hand because "civilization is exactly like religion. It is necessary to believe in it and bond oneself from the heart to it."[40] This is an exact conversion. For him, civilization and national identity were inseparable and became the Turks' new faith. In his *Dini Türkçülük* (Turkism in religion), Gökalp again discussed the use of Turkish in prayers as the best way to enhance and express one's faith. Turkism, to Gökalp, was the vehicle both for adopting the civilization of Europe and thus establishing a bond of unity with the West and for preserving the Turks' new-found national identity. By substituting *national modernistic faith* for *religious faith* Gökalp made himself the enemy of the Islamists, who censured him for having materialized, politicized, and nationalized the faith. At the same time, the positivists and atheists (Marxists) opposed him for granting the faith a sphere of existence above materialism, which he abhorred. In any case, the Turks' identity developed within the frame of the multiple identities of modernity, Ottomanism, Islamism, and Turkishness. Each one was based on concrete historical, religious, and linguistic foundation and, despite the state's manipulation of all these identities for its own interest, they left a lasting imprint on contemporary Turks' identity and personality. That civilization-modernity could become a new faith was and is a matter of seminal importance for the Turks, for it pits a faith created by humans against the revealed one.

17

The Turkist Thinkers

Ziya Gökalp, Yusuf Akçura, Fuat Köprülü

In the preceding chapter I established the ideological and historical context for the views of Ziya Gökalp, Yusuf Akçura, and Mehmet Fuat Köprülü, the fathers of Turkish nationalism.[1] All three attempted to define for the Turks a new national identity within the frame of Ottomanism and Islamism, and all three were modernist, democratically minded constitutionalists, who had opposed Abdulhamid's absolutism on principle as much as for personal reasons. Gökalp and Akçura suffered imprisonment and exile for having done so. Moreover, the three were closely acquainted with Western ideas, knew one or more European languages, and possessed knowledge and intellectual capacity well above that of many of their contemporaries. They also were well versed in Islamic culture; with the exception of Köprülü, however, they had only a superficial knowledge of Ottoman history. Having participated to various degrees in the War of Independence of 1919–22, Gökalp, Akçura, and Köprülü all supported the Kemalist national movement and accepted the place of Islam in Turkish life, although they wanted to curtail the influence of the religious institutions on society and government. Ethnically, they reflected to some extent the contemporary ethnic composition of Turkey in that none of them had a "pure" Turkish ancestral origin. Even more significant, the issue never became the subject of debate, indicating that the intelligentsia viewed Turkishness not as a revived historical ethnic identity but mainly as a new one. In the next sections I shall assess Akçura and Gökalp's contribution to the discourse on Turkish nationalism, by analyzing both their frequently studied main works and their various minor writings along with Köprülü's seminal historical contribution. This will not be an exhaustive study of their ideas but will focus only on those aspects that related to Abdulhamid's reign: Ottomanism, Islamism, and nationalism. The chief goal of all three of them was to reconcile Ottomanism, and/or Islamism with nationalism, or Turkishness-Turkism—or if necessary, to eliminate them. The most basic pieces on Turkish nationalism written by Ziya Gökalp and Yusuf Akçura, "Üç Cereyan" (Three currents) and *Üç Tarz-i Siyaset* (Three political ways) respectively, were efforts to find some sort of accommodation, within the framework of modernism and the changing needs of the state, between the ideologies. Köprülü wrote a less important article on the subject.

Ziya Gökalp (1878–1924)

Ziya Gökalp was born in Diyarbakir in southeast Anatolia to a family of lower-class civil servants. He always claimed that he was a Turk, although one of his ancestors might have been of Kurdish origin. In any case, Gökalp's father believed firmly in the Western type of education, at the same time holding Islam and oriental culture in high esteem. Consequently, as a youth Gökalp read the works of Gazali, Farabi, and the other Muslim thinkers, studied mysticism, and became a committed Sufi. At the same time, he learned to read French in the Idadi school and acquainted himself with the ideas of Gabriel Tarde, Emile Durkheim, Albert Sorel, and other French luminaries. Because his town was used as a place of exile, young Gökalp also came to know the anti-Hamidian intellectuals banished there, including Abdullah Cevdet, whose materialism challenged Gökalp's mysticism and idealism and drove him to an almost fatal suicide attempt. After the traumatic encounter with Cevdet's beliefs, Gökalp turned to nationalism as an antidote to positivism. In particular, he embraced the views of Durkheim, who represented the European reaction to positivism. Gökalp enrolled in the veterinary school in Istanbul, but by 1896 he had been sentenced to ten months in prison for "subversive" (anti-Hamidian) activities and then exiled back to his native town. There he eventually joined the local secret branch of the Union and Progress Society. During this period in Diyarbakir, from 1902 to 1908, Gökalp read the works of European thinkers and was employed by the local chamber of trade and the provincial council. He thus became aware of, in Taha Parla's words, the "close relationship between the Committee of Union and Progress (CUP) and the local notables—*eşraf*—of Anatolia."[2] The exiled Gökalp also studied the land situation of the local peasantry, collected folklore, wrote poems, and became acquainted with the ethnic culture of the Turkish villagers.[3] After Union and Progress took power in 1908, Gökalp first became party inspector in his province; as early as 1909, however, he was invited to Salonica. One year after that he joined the powerful Central Committee of the Union and Progress, along with Russia's famous Azeri Turkists, Hüseyinzade Ali and Ahmet Ağaoğlu, who had a profound ideological impact on him.

Hüseyinzade Ali (1864–1942), born in Baku and educated in St. Petersburg as a physician, came to Istanbul in 1889 to join the staff of the military medical school.[4] There he disseminated the ideas on ethnic nationalism and populism that he had learned from the Russian intellectuals and from Ahunzade Mirza Feth Ali, the first nationalist-modernist Azerbaycani. Thus he helped turn the school into a major Turkist center. Although modest, retiring, and disliking publicity, Hüseyinzade was very influential and persuasive in private, as was Gökalp himself. Gökalp accepted fully Hüseyinzade's idea that the Turks had triple identity (Turkish-Islamic-modern) and made it the subject of his famous article and, later, a book. Actually, Hüseyinzade had formulated the Turks' threefold identity as *Türkleştirmek, Islamlaştirmak, Avrupalilaştirmak*, but Gökalp changed *Avrupalilaşmak* (Europeanization) to *Muasirlaşmak* (contemporaneity). Hüseyinzade believed the linguistic and cultural unity of all the Turks could be achieved under the leadership of the Ottoman government. The idea of territorial unity embodied in the concept of *Turan* (lands inhabited by Turks), however, remained for both Hüseyinzade and Gökalp a myth employed to mobilize and unite youth, rather than a practical program for action.

Gökalp's other friend, though less influential than Hüseyinzade, was Ahmet Ağaoğlu (1869–1939), a native of Susha in the Karabağ province of Azerbaycan. After studying in Russian schools and then in Paris in 1888, Ağaoğlu settled in Baku, where he taught French and participated in the political and intellectual movements of his country, until Russian pressure forced him to take refuge in Turkey in 1908. The Ağaoğlu family has played an important part in Turkish political and intellectual life ever since. Ahmet Ağaoğlu himself became a member of the opposition party, Serbest Firka, in 1930. His son, Samet, was a nationalist writer and a leading member of the Democratic Party from 1947 to 1960; Ahmet's grandson, a poet and writer, was a militant Marxist, while his granddaughter excelled as a lawyer.

The date at which the leading Turkists from Russia became advisors to CUP's Central Committee corresponds more or less with the Young Turks' efforts to help Turks develop a degree of ethnic consciousness within the framework of Ottomanism. Specifically, it was about 1908 when these Turkists, Ziya Gökalp and their followers, including students in the professional schools, established the associations and began to publish reviews dedicated to the discussion and dissemination of Turkist ideas. The first major nationalist organization, Türk Derneği, was established in 1908, on Yusuf Akçura's initiative, by Necip Asim and other staff members of the newspaper *Ikdam*, along with some immigrants from Russia.[5] Its goal was to study the history of all the Turkic groups in the world, although it devoted special attention to the Turks of Russia. The association advocated language reform—that is, the adoption of the colloquial as the means of written communication—and promoted the study of folklore and Ottoman patriotism, disseminating its views and findings in the publication bearing its name.

The *Genç Kalemler*, published originally as a literary review under the name of *Hüsnü Şirin* in Manastir (Bitola), was in a way the counterpart of the *Türk Derneği* and initially advanced a cultural form of Turkism. It was first published, with financial help from CUP, in 1910 by Ali Canip (Yöntem) at the suggestion of Ziya Gökalp. The publication, through the pen of Kazim Nami (Duru), echoed the nationalist themes that the Ottoman state was established by Turks, that Ottomanism was internalized only by Muslims as a religious-political identity, and that Turks, despite their long existence in the nonethnic Ottoman state, had retained their language, and the "Ottoman" language was Turkish. Gökalp published in the *Genç Kalemler* his famous poem "Turan," the last lines of which stated that the fatherland of the Turks was not Turkey or Turkistan but a vast and eternal land called "Turan." Gökalp's pan-Turanism, however, was not consistent and much of what he wrote and published later was contradictory, especially after he stopped using the term in 1916. One may assume it reflected in the early influence of Hüseyinzade Ali. By 1912 Gökalp apparently had abandoned Ottomanism and favored ethnicity as the source of political identity. In Diyarbakir, before 1908, in articles he wrote for the *Peyman*, Gökalp had compared the multiethnic and multireligious composition of the Ottoman population to that of the United States of America, in effect claiming that the Ottoman Empire could likewise become one nation with one single political identity.[6] (The idea that the Ottoman and American identities resemble each other merits some elaboration.)

By 1915 Gökalp had distanced himself not only from Hüseyinzade but also from Akçura, who regarded *soy* (race or lineage) as the basis of national identity, while

Gökalp now viewed ethnic culture as its foundation. Akçura viewed the nation as a well-formed political body, while Gökalp saw it as an ethnic-cultural community to be politically indoctrinated and turned into a nation. Already in 1913, after the *Genç Kalemler* and its staff had moved to Istanbul, the rising nationalist historian Fuat Köprülü had criticized the review for confusing "nation" with "race," for adopting a narrow, sectarian view of ethnicity and nationality, and for ignoring international political trends and developments. The *Genç Kalemler* replied that the term *race* (*irk*) was synonymous with "ethnic nation," for many Albanians, Kurds, and so on, were part of the Türklük (Turkishness), and *Türklük* could be used interchangeably with *Osmanlilik* (Ottomanism).[7] The debate marked Gökalp's search for a concrete basis of identity that was specifically Turkish but not such as to alienate non-Turkish Muslims. Consequently he spoke of an "Islamo-Ottoman culture" of which the Turks and Arabs were part, each with their own language and identity. In turn, the review *Türk Yurdu* (discussed shortly) argued that the *Genç Kalemler* was confusing the purely ethnic content of Turkism with the "cosmopolitan" Ottoman Islamo-Turkic culture espoused by Ottomanist Turkists. Obviously Gökalp found it difficult to make clear that the Turkish identity he sought to define resulted not from a pure racial stock but from the amalgam of numerous Muslim ethnic groups that had cohabited the Ottoman Empire and produced an Ottoman-Islamic Turkish culture.

The important Turkist association Türk Yurdu emerged as the forum of the debate. Founded in 1911 by Mehmed Emin, Ahmet Hikmet, Akil Muhtar, Ahmet Ağaoğlu, Ali Hüseyinzade, and Yusuf Akçura—the last three being close friends and collaborators from Russia—it started publishing the review bearing its name in 1912, apparently with money provided by the rich Huseyinof family of Orenburg; but probably the money was supplied to *Turk Yurdu* by the CUP, and the Huseyinof name was used as a cover. The *Türk Yurdu* soon replaced the *Türk Derneği* as the most important political nationalist journal of the period, attracting many of the writers from the *Genç Kalemler*, including Ziya Gökalp. It criticized the Tanzimat reformers for having undermined the Turkishness of the Ottoman state, and it censured their superficial understanding of modernization-Westernization and their hesitant reformism. The Russian and Ottoman groups in the Türk Yurdu association both rejected Ottomanism, but for different reasons; Gökalp believed that it ignored Turkish ethnic identity and culture, while Akçura criticized the very imperial concept itself for denying national-ethnic identity as basis of political nationhood and hindering the development of panturkic sentiment. In other words, Gökalp favored strengthening the Ottoman Turks' sense of ethnic-cultural identity, but Akçura thought all the Turks in the world shared a common identity and could collaborate politically. Akçura claimed that any Anatolian Turk, if asked what his *soy* was, would respond "I am a Türk." The *Türk Yurdu*, however, did not openly advocate political panturkism but, rather, a loose cultural relationship between the Ottoman Turks and their kin abroad.

The Türk Ocağı, the other influential nationalist organization, was established formally in 1912 by some 190 students enrolled at the military medical school; they were later joined by students at the administrative school, or Mülkiye. Their stated purpose was to achieve through education the social, economic, and national development of the ethnic Turks. Ahmet Ağaoğlu and Yusuf Akçura were associated with the Ocak from the start, more by coincidence than design, when the students sought their advice on organizing the association. Although Akçura actually tried to take control of the Türk Ocağı, he finally accepted Hamdullah Suphi (Tanriöver) as chairman, and Akçura and his friend Ahmed Ferit remained as directors. The Türk Ocağı deserves an in-depth study because it applied Gökalp's ideas on nationalism and strove to maintain a degree of cultural continuity with the Turkishness of Ahmet Mithat as it developed prior to 1908. The leader of the Ocaks, Hamdullah Suphi Tanriöver (1886–1966) was a modernist Turkist and, like Gökalp, believed that *hars* (culture) was a key link among all Turks. His concept of culture was ethnic and secular. As ambassador to Bucharest, Romania, in the 1930s, he was instrumental in opening schools among the Turkish-speaking Orthodox Christian Gagauzes, and he tried unsuccessfully to arrange for their migration to Turkey. His father, Abdurrahman Suphi paşa, was descended from a well-known family and had played an important role in generalizing education in the Ottoman Empire, while his uncle, Samipaşa-Sezai, was a critic of slavery and of the restrictions imposed on women. In the 1950s Tanriöver re-established the Ocaks, which are still active as a conservative nationalist organization.[8] The panturkism of the Ocaks was cultural, rather than political, as Landau implies.[9] The association's purpose, according to its bylaws, was to provide "national education to the Turks, who form the most important Muslim nation [in the Ottoman Empire], in order to raise their scientific, social and economic standards and to perfect the Turkish race (nation) and language."[10]

Ziya Gökalp (and most of the publishers of the *Genç Kalemler* as well) eventually joined the Türk Ocağı and made it "his" association, while the *Türk Yurdu* followed Akçura's ideas. Gökalp used his increasing influence to raise the ethnic consciousness of the Ottoman Turks, while Akçura was more interested in Russia's Muslims, especially the Tatars. Akçura even devised the idea of a Turco-Tatar nation, which found little following. Gökalp was also instrumental in establishing four populist weeklies, *Halka Doğru* (1913), *Türk Sözü* (1914), *Islam Mecmuasi* (1914), and *Yeni Mecmua* (1917), the latter two with direct CUP financial support. The Türk Ocağı, though relatively active during the war years, did not become involved in politics. Only later, in the Republic, did it emerge as the chief nationalist organization, until it was replaced by the People's Houses in 1931–32.[11]

Gökalp's relations with Akçura deteriorated. In 1913 he, with Talat paşa, invited Akçura to become a member of CUP, but the latter refused on the rather flimsy pretext that he could not take the oath on the Koran without *abdest* (ritual ablution). Akçura remained aloof from the CUP, criticizing it for involving the army in politics, for usurping all of the sultan-caliph's powers, and, especially, for retaining Ottomanism as a principle of state, thus jeopardizing the rise of the Turks' ethnic-national consciousness. Because Gökalp did not want to divide the Turkists, he strove to remain on friendly terms with Akçura, despite the tensions between them. At the same time, Gökalp also was facing criticism on another front. His religious nationalist reformism, promoted in the *Islam Mecmuasi*, created a reaction among conservative Islamists. They viewed ethnic nationalism and racism as identical; so they accused Gökalp of promoting racism. This criticism of Gökalp is still heard in Turkey today. An Islamist writer has claimed that God created all individuals in the same way and that any claim to superiority based on race or *soy* was anti-Islamic, that Gökalp was the "merciless enemy of religion" and an imitative philosopher and that Turkism was alienation in the form of Westernization;[12] and one critic claims that Gökalp took his secularist views from an "evil genius," Tekinalp (Moise Cohen).[13] In 1919, after the Ottoman defeat in the war, the British interned Gökalp and other leading nationalists and CUP members on the island of Malta. Staying there until 1921, Gökalp had time to review, revise, and assemble his main writings in his *Türkçülüğün Esaslari*, the handbook of Turkish nationalism. He died in 1924, in relative obscurity but highly respected by his followers.

In his writings Gökalp seemed to have started from the premise that the key unit of human organization was the community. It, in turn, consisted of equal individuals bound to each other by a sense of solidarity grounded in a common language and in the culture that embodied their values and faith. Gökalp viewed political and social associations as variations on the community, but with more complex structures and additional forms of solidarity. The nation, as Gökalp defined it in 1917, well after his views had undergone considerable evolution, was a cultural community. It was not a racial, ethnic, geographical, political, or voluntary association. Instead, it consisted of men and women who shared the same education and language and, as the result of having the same culture, the same religious and aesthetic values and tastes. The definition acquired its final form in 1923 in Gökalp's classic *Türkçülüğün Esaslari* under the title *Türkçülük Nedir*? (What is Turkism?).[14] True and durable political associations, such as the nation, were based on commonality of language, culture, and faith, which produced shared sentiments. Gökalp rejected the materialism of Karl Marx and the pragmatism and economic liberalism of Adam Smith, making duty toward the collectivity an absolute norm. The community, meaning the nation, had priority over the individual and the individual's rights, as expressed in the slogan "Ferd yok millet var, hak yok vazife var" (There is no individual but nation; there are no rights but duties). Identity therefore derived from the culture of the community. Anyone who shared the culture of the community was a Turk, regardless of ethnicity or country of origin; and the community had to be made conscious of its Turkish ethnic culture, which was unique, as were its patterns of settlement, social organization, and temperament. According to Gökalp, after becoming settled entities, the Turkish villages with their mosques, schools, common pastures, common woods, and self-reliant, self-governing folk organizations, became democratic minirepublics; Arab villages, on the other hand, were always ruled by a chief or a landlord and looked to a master for guidance. However, Gökalp refused to accept the separatist implications of the organizational and behavioral differences he posited. When his close friend, Sati al-Husri, decided that he was an Arab, Gökalp denounced him as a traitor, and al-Husri became a leading Arab nationalist ideologue.

Although ethnic culture was thus the source of norms, principles, and even political action, it could become a source of political identity only in a true nation, which Gökalp defined as a democratic society based on centralization, homogeneity, and division of labor. By contrast, nations composed of tribes and city states were segmentary societies. A *kavm* (ethnic group) became a nation in Gökalp's eyes once it acquired a national conscience (*milli vicdan*), politics, religion, morality, science, law, and aesthetics. According to Gökalp, because ethnic groups that had developed their national conscience could not be subdued or made colonies, the Turks remained free, while Iraq and Syria, without a national conscience, were turned into colonies after World War I.[15] In fact, Gökalp had a rather tenuous understanding of history, which led him to contradictory views about the emergence of nations. On the one hand, he said nationality resulted from evolution and willpower, when he wrote that Turks, after having lived in tribal organizations and the Muslim *ümmet*, decided to become a nation. On the other hand, he maintained that the Turks as an ethnic group had existed since time immemorial and the love of fatherland and moral and patriotic ideals that were the characteristics of modern nationhood had always been present in the Turkish culture. "The Turkish *kavm*," stated Gökalp, "existed before the Islamic *ümmet* and the Selçuk and Ottoman empires. It had its own ethnic civilization before it entered into common Iranian civilization [which along] with the [Islamic] *ümmet* and [Ottoman] imperial organization [all three supranational entities,] destroyed many of the [Turks'] ethnic institutions." Then he added an exceptionally insightful remark to the effect that "this participation in [supranational organizations] prepared the way for the Turks to develop into a nation."[16]

Gökalp did not elaborate how the Ottoman Turks' identity was shaped by membership in the Islamic community and the Ottoman Empire. Instead he jumped back into the convenient view that the Turks' identity was formed millennia ago, claiming that Turks had preserved their "national" identity within the Ottoman Empire and reasserted it at the proper historical moment: "Nation-states arise when these [multi-ethnic] empires disintegrate. In Europe the nation state rose only after the Roman and German Empires disintegrated. . . . [T]he nation is that ethnic group which, as it emerges after a long period of fusion within an empire, strives to regain and prove its identity." He elaborated further on the same idea. "The nation," he wrote, "is that ethnic group which, as it emerges after a long period of fusion within an empire, strives to regain and revive its identity . . . [T]he future of all states will be in the direction of nation states. . . . [A] *kavm* [nation] seeks to achieve perfection by creating *an ethnic religion, an ethnic state, and an ethnic civilization*" provided that it can achieve political and civic unity.[17] Obviously, Gökalp viewed the nation and national identity as permanent, while the imperial or religious format in which the "nation" was preserved was evolutionary and subject to change. He did not care to deal with, or was not aware of, the seminal fact that the Turks had an ethnic identity but not a national political one, and that the political identity was formed in the second half of the nineteenth century within the framework of Ottomanism and Islamism, the first he rejected. Gökalp perceived political nationalism as different from national-ethnic identity and patriotism. Relying on Gabriel Tarde, the French sociologist, he portrayed nationalism as the consequence of the manipulation of national identity and ego. Newspapers, Gökalp claimed rather simplistically, were its instigators, for to boost circulation, they glorified their readers' national achievements in art and science and battlefield bravery, thus giving readers a sense of power and superiority.

According to the late Tarik Zafer Tunaya, the rise of national consciousness among all the other ethnic groups in the Ottoman Empire made it imperative for the state to "nationalize" the Turks by freeing them from their atomic existence and making them aware of higher collective goals: the *ben* (I, or me) was to be changed to *biz* (us). Tunaya claimed that Gökalp's real aim in imbuing the individual with the idea of belonging to the nation was to free him from total subservience to the state. An exclusive attachment to statehood bred servility and selfishness and was depersonalizing, while belonging to the nation was elevating, humanizing, liberating, and altruistic.[18]

The question of "civilization" occupied a central place in Ziya Gökalp's thinking and is given considerable space in most of the studies about him.[19] He saw it as the sum of the science, material achievement, and commonly shared international values that supported relationships with other nations but did not supplant its own unique culture. In other words, civilization was international and could be appropriated by any nation without risk of losing its own culture and identity. As a result, the Turks were simultaneously acquiring the contemporary civilization of Europe and developing their own national identity and culture. According to Gökalp, the unique source of the emerging national Turkish culture was the folk culture, which was to be assimilated, refined, and expressed by the "national" elites or the "güzideler," as he called them. These elites were predominantly political and were distinguished by high intellect, artistic ability, and motivation for achievement; they were the carriers of civilization to the masses, whose culture they had to absorb if their patriotic, civilizing mission were to succeed.

Gökalp's idealization of the elites as the instrument of civilization and modernism, along with his usual neglect of the economic and social forces behind the elites' rise to power, provided the best justification for the elitist political rule of the Young Turks and the Republic. He elaborated upon these themes mainly in various reviews such as *Halka Doğru* (Towards people) and *Ictimayat Mecmuasi* (Sociological review), whose populism was cultural not social. Gökalp became increasingly aware of the growing sociocultural and political dichotomy between the elites and masses and tried to remedy it, not by advocating equality of power and income, which the elites monopolized, but by appeal to ethnic-national solidarity. Ultimately, the preservation of national unity became the convenient argument with which the ruling elites silenced all demands for social justice and economic opportunity.

The leader, or *kahraman* (hero), occupied a central place in Gökalp's thinking. He described the "great men" as charismatic leaders who appeared to fight for social and religious causes but, in reality, were the epitome of national genius and rose in times of crisis. Because they expressed basic national sentiments, they could rapidly awaken their people's national consciousness and rally them into action.[20]

Gökalp's original and constructive views on Islam satisfied neither the "secularists," who were mostly positivists, nor the conservative "Islamists." For the positivists, progress and science were irreconcilable with religion, while to the Islamists, ethnic nationalism was racism and any lay culture would infringe upon the integrity of the faith. Gökalp considered Islam, as a faith, to have an autonomous sphere as the religious component of culture and identity. He did his best to reconcile religion with modernity by persuading the religious establishment to accept some legal reforms and implement changes in its organization. He also rejected panislamism, the political unity of all Muslims based solely on the faith, as being contrary to Turkism, although he did not reject alliances among Muslim nations. Gökalp was not an agnostic or an atheist but a modernist. He helped to start *Islam Mecmuasi* (Review of Islam) in order to reconcile modernity with Islam. The weekly adopted as its motto "Dinli bir hayat, hayatli bir din" (A life with religion and a religion with life), which was in line with the revivalists' concept of *ihya* (revival) and sought to define the place of Islam in an emerging modern Turkish national state.[21] *Islam Mecmuasi* has been described by Berkes as "secularist," by T. Z. Tunaya as "Islamist," and by A. Bennigsen-Quelquejay as reflecting the reformist views of the Russian Muslims. Actually, Gökalp wanted to reassess Islam's place and function not within the frame of the universal religious *ümmet* but within the confines of a national-political *ümmet*—the nation—whose members were tied together by bonds of national and patriotic solidarity and their mutual dedication to civilization or progress. National Islam was bound to remain cultural as long as it remained domestic and became political once it was internationalized.

Gökalp believed that there was perfect harmony between Islam and science and that both could be placed in the service of the nation. The contributors to *Islam Mecmuasi* consisted not only of Gökalp's own disciples but also of recognized authorities on Islam, such as Şerafettin Yaltkaya (1887–1949), who played an important role in the Republic as the head of Diyanet (Religious Affairs); Kazim Musa, who was *şeyhulislam* from 1910 to 1918 and worked on a Turkish Koran together with Ahmet Mithat; Mansurzade Sait; and many other modernist Islamists. Yusuf Akçura, however, unlike many other Muslims from Russia, Ağaoğlu included, did not contribute to the review because it was not secular enough to suit his political ethnic panturkism. The review regarded Islam in Turkey proper as being still mired in superstition and as less reformed and modernized than its counterparts in Russia, Egypt, and even India.[22] Gökalp considered religion as a source of ethical norms and solidarity and a means of personal transcendence and identification with some superior entity. In the same way, the nation offered a higher level of collective identification than the tribe or the ethnic group, but its unique nature necessitated special laws to regulate its daily life; hence Gökalp placed the utmost importance on *örf* (customary lay law) without denying the importance of the Şeriat.

The state, according to Gökalp, had the duty to serve the nation by protecting and preserving its morality and by promoting solidarity and culture within society. He thus placed the state in the service of the nation rather than the faith as in the past, and this alienated the Islamists further. Despite his opposition to state totalitarianism, Gökalp was a statist. He used Durkheim's corporatist ideas to advocate a modern statism, which in reality amounted to retaining the old Ottoman concept of state supremacy. It might have escaped him that the state's new self-defined mission to serve the nation could legitimize its authoritarianism and eventually lead it to use the nation for its own political ends, in the same way the Ottomans had used Islam for state purposes. Gökalp saw the modern nation-state as a democratic institution, but he failed to devise the means for popular participation. Nevertheless, his seminal point that the state was no longer a divine entity but a worldly institution serving the nation remained.

The bitterest and most tenacious opponents of Turkish nationalism, as mentioned, were the conservative Islamists. In an article entitled "Ills Befallen Turkishness," Gökalp responded to their criticisms:

> Turkism has been accused of being the opposite of Islamism. In reality the Turkists' purpose is [to create] a Muslim modern [contemporary] Turkishness. The ideal of Turkists is Turkishness as much as their communal [ümmet] ideal is Islamization. I believe that the Turkists should have also a *ümmet* [religious communal] program whose main principles should appeal to all Muslims [for which it is necessary] to preserve the Arabic alphabet.[23]

Gökalp proposed that Muslims hold conferences to discuss common projects, such as the development of an Islamic scientific language and educational system, establishing permanent communications among muftis, and the adoption of the crescent as the symbol of the Islamic *ümmet*. Concluding that "Turkism is also Islamism," he advocated the unity of Muslim nations but not their national fusion into a single supranational religious community: "The Turkists can distinguish themselves from Muslim nationalists [fundamentalists] only by becoming Muslim communalists [*ummetci*; united as nations]. The Muslim who does not accept the national identity-ideal of the specific ethnic nations [*kavim*s, from Arabic *kavin*] such as the Turks, Arabs, Indians, Afghanis . . . cannot be expected to unite [with them as nation]."[24] Gökalp decried the fact that Arab and Albanian nationalists such as Abdullah Nadim and Naim Fraşeri, "who did not understand the real meaning of Muslim communalism, that is, alliance of Muslim nations, preached hate of Turks." In the process of describing a school curriculum for a modern, national Islamic education, Gökalp condemned the religious men who, rejecting modern science simply because it had emerged after the Prophet's death, advocated the separation of religious education from the scientific and national Turkish education. Arch-Islamists responded by calling Gökalp an anti-Muslim renegade and racist—as they still do.

Gökalp's inclusion of a scientific and progressive Islam among his modernist national goals became much more categorical after 1914–15, as did his unequivocal rejection of Ottomanism. He had taken a milder stand in his seminal article, "Üç Cereyan," published in somewhat rough form in 1913.[25] Then he had stated that the Turks had proclaimed Ottomanism in order to maintain understanding among nationalities, even though, in the age of nationalism, rulers should share the same national identity and sentiments as the ruled. "Turkism," in his view, was "not in competition with Ottomanism. Actually it is its most powerful supporter . . . although there are young extremist Turkists who create the wrong impression. Turkism is the real foundation of Islam and Ottomanism against cosmopolitanism."[26] The Turkish national identity, still in the making, rested on the three foundations—ethnicity (Turkishness), Islam, and modernity, which did not contradict but complemented each other. In short, the Turkish nation belonged simultaneously to the Uralic-Altaic group of peoples, to the Islamic community, and contemporary Western civilization.[27] Gökalp was criticized for ignoring modernism-Westernism as a separate current of thought. Peyami Safa, one of the most prominent advocates of Turkish nationalism in the 1930s and 1940s, claimed that Gökalp failed to mention Westernism because of his dispute with Abdullah Cevdet, the publisher of *Osmanli* and later *Ictihat*.

Gökalp claimed that the three identities derived from very specific needs and experiences. Turkism represented the *hars*, or the ethnic culture, which was unique and national; Islam was the spiritual and ethical foundation of that culture; and modernism represented civilization—that is, science, technology, and internationality. The Turks thus were free to adopt the theoretical and practical sciences of Europe but not its faith. It should be noted that most of these views did not appear, or appeared in much different form, in his last work, *Türkçülüğün Esaslari*, published in 1923. By that time Gökalp had a new *kahraman* (hero), Mustafa Kemal (Atatürk), whom he praised more than he had praised Talat paşa, the chief leader of the Young Turks; Atatürk, in his mind, epitomized the special sort of leader that a true nation could produce in times of crisis: a leader with foresight and courage who embodied the national genius and willpower.

Ziya Gökalp's work is open to wide criticism. Its major shortcoming was rejection of economic factors and the formative processes rooted in history. Indeed, he deemed history a superfluous, dysfunctional, and artificial branch of learning that would eventually melt and disappear into sociology, the queen of social sciences. In addition, Gökalp's deductionism, his instrumentalist view of the social sciences, his dogmatic view of certain concepts, and his idealization of myths all narrowed his understanding of the transformation of Ottoman society and led him to partisan judgments about Ottomanism. Despite his defense of rigorous methodology and logical constructions, he relied on intuition more than facts, and his Sufi mystical leanings colored his understanding of social problems and his proposals for solutions. However, it was precisely the traits of dogmatism, idealism, and Turkishness that made Gökalp exceptionally effective in stirring young people and the educated waiting for a national messiah. To this day, Gökalp remains the idol of the ultranationalists, although few understand the scope and implications of his ideas, which they often use selectively. At the same time, Marxists and other leftists dismiss him comtempteously as an "idealist" thinker, without bothering to read his works. Gökalp saw an irreconcilable difference between everything Ottoman and everything Turkish. For him the language, music, and art of the Ottomans were cosmopolitan and derivative, and those of the Turks were authentic, national, unique.

The implication was that everything Ottoman was artificial and imposed from above and should be eliminated; but actually the "Ottoman" language used by newspapers and reviews had become "simplified"—that is, "Turkified"—and well understood by rank-and-file Turks. In fact, even the language spoken at the court of Abdulhamid, aside from a number of expressions necessitated by court etiquette, was Turkish rather than "Osmanli." Anyway, the "Osmanli" language was basically Turkish and not an *aşure* (a dish of mixed dried fruits)—that is, a string of Persian and Arabic words haphazardly put together, as charged by its critics. Gökalp urged creation of a "national" Turkish music, which in his views would consist of folk music; he termed Ottoman music, resting on Farabi's version adopted from the Byzantine, an alien import.[28] This idea was sharply criticized by Rauf Yekta, one of the leading authorities on Turkish music.[29] Yekta found little difference between Western and eastern music and claimed that there was a classical Turkish music, derived from Persian, Western and Indian music, as much as a Turkish folk music spread in all the areas inhabited by the Turkic peoples. Yekta rejected Gökalp's view that prior to the introduction of Western music, first in the form of military marches (substituting for the *mehter* of the Janissaries abolished in 1826), the only classical music the Turks (Ottomans) possessed was Farabi's music copied from the Byzantine. Yekta stated, "I could not believe my eyes: the master [Gökalp] advanced views totally opposed to the realities of the history of music and drew unexpected and strange conclusions . . . which I do not believe are the fruit of his own research and analysis . . . [views] which neither an oriental nor occidental musical authority would endorse." Yekta also stated that he could no longer remain silent in the face of such unfounded attacks upon "our national music" and answered and corrected, paragraph by paragraph, Gökalp's views.[30] Today, Ottoman music has a large following and has become the "classical" Turkish music, as the key Ottoman poets have become "classical" Turkish poets.[31]

Gökalp's view of Ottomanism remained one-sided. Had he possessed a true understanding of the concrete economic and social forces that shaped the destiny of societies in general, and of Ottoman society in particular, his judgment of Ottomanism probably would have been different. As mentioned, he realized intuitively that Turkishness was a by-product of Ottomanism, but he regarded the two as politically and ideologically irreconcilable as long as Turkishness was not strong enough to stand on its own. Gökalp pictured Ottoman society as divided into two groups, the elite (Ottomanists) and the masses (ethnic Turks), but he attributed the division to cultural factors and not to its real cause, which was class differences. Furthermore, the court and folk cultures were never divided as absolutely as envisaged by Gökalp. Topics and literary styles percolated from the upper culture to the lower and vice versa during the eighteenth and, especially, the nineteenth century, as social mobility increased and many lower-class individuals joined the ranks of the ruling elites and brought their folk culture with them. The political elite knew and, when necessary, spoke the colloquial Turkish throughout Ottoman history. Furthermore, the first advocates of "Turkishness" were not lower-class nationalists but "cosmopolitan" Ottoman ministers and premiers (Mustafa Reşit and Fuat paşas), who claimed that the Ottoman *hükümet* (government) was always "Turkish." Other high Ottoman officials, such as Ahmet Vefik (1823–91) and Münif and Süleyman paşas, pleaded the cause of linguistic Turkism. Thus it may be seen, Turkishness began to surface within an Ottoman-Turkish modernist context much before Gökalp's arrival on the scene, although it was expressed without a clear political goal.

Gökalp considered the nationalist elites, the *güzideler*, of which he was one, the carriers of civilization and "teachers" of the masses; but these very elites in the Republic not only distanced themselves from the *cahil halk* (ignorant people) and made a shambles of their authentic Turkish language in order to make it "pure" Turkish, but also adopted agnosticism as proof of their own modernity. A claim to be a Turk, a diploma, and official anointment was enough to turn a pedestrian opportunist into a missionary of civilization and Turkism. Monopolizing political and economic power in order to "civilize" the very folk regarded as "authentic Turks," this modernizing elite destroyed folk culture under the pretext of making it national. When they acted in the name of modernity, they meant the civilization of Europe, but they deprived it of its democratic, natural, humanistic, and progressive dimensions. The perennial identity crisis in Turkey—which has recently reached a crucial point—has been the result of their ill-understood modernism and Turkism, which became the religion of the bureaucracy and the intelligentsia and the unofficial religion of the state as well. Gökalp would have never approved of the attacks on the spoken Turkish, traditions, and religion, had he lived long enough to see them, although he bears his share of responsibility for having given to these attacks a degree of legitimacy in his *Türkçülüğün Programi*, the second half of his *Türkçülüğün Esaslari*.

Because Gökalp attached supreme value to all collective and statist entities as the best defense against anomie caused by individualism, he was labeled with the misleading epithet of *socialist*. In fact, he had nothing to do with socialism as generally understood, rejecting the existence of class divisions and the class struggle and accepting only the division of the labor force into occupational categories. To the end of his life he remained a true modern Sufi, both in feeling and action. In his recollections, Yusuf Akçura wrote sarcastically that Gökalp was a man of action but acted more like a "*şeyh*, a spiritual guide . . . who helped persuade today's Turkish youth to enter the most perfect brotherhood that ever existed, the brotherhood of Turkish nationalism."[32] Akçura also stated that Turkism and Turkists were in existence before Gökalp's time but that he evaluated them according to his own biases. (Ironically, Akçura did the same to promote *his* version of Turkism.) Gökalp was in his heart a humanist and a democratically minded, well-meaning intellectual. He truly wanted to raise the Turks' national consciousness and bring them into the modern age, but he thought doing so required detaching the Turks from their own Ottoman past. He viewed everything Ottoman as inseparable from Ottomanism and so an impediment to national consciousness. During the Republic, therefore, he provided the most authoritative argument for rejecting the study and understanding of Ottoman history, which really amounted to a denial of national history. Taha Parla claims that Gökalp tried sincerely to reconcile the dichotomies of "tradition-modernity, continuity-change, nationalism-internationalism, and Islamism-secularism."[33] There is no question that Gökalp hoped to find a way out of those apparent conflicts, but by rejecting the historical Ottomanist-Islamist framework in which these seemingly contradictory identities developed and coexisted, he actually made the dichotomy permanent and exclusive. He was, after all, in the service of a political party, CUP. His reliance on state power to reshape the society and its identity both affected his views and hindered an open and free dialogue about Turkish identity.

Ziya Gökalp's work is replete with contradictions, dogmatic judgments uttered without supporting evidence, selective use of data, and ideas borrowed randomly from European sources. Of course, his main writings came out from 1908 to 1924, amidst constantly changing political circumstances. Gökalp had to adapt his thinking to the collapse of the Hamidian regime, the Young Turks' rise to power, the disintegration of the Ottoman Empire, the Turkish War of Liberation, the abolition of the monarchy, and the establishment of the Republic. In addition, as a loyal member of CUP's leadership, he was bound to defend his party's policies. However, despite his shortcomings, Ziya Gökalp must be considered the most important Turkish thinker of the twentieth century. He was the first to discuss the basic questions of the sociology of organizations and to use analytical concepts, methods, and approaches suitable to the study of social phenomena. Gökalp sought to place the last phase of the Ottoman Empire in a theoretical framework and tried to conceptualize the identity changes taking place within his own society. Because he had no native sociological model to guide him, he was forced to borrow many concepts and methods, which expressed the problems of an industrial society, from Europe, even though they were unsuitable to the study of Ottoman society. Nonetheless, he laid the foundations of what could have become a Turkish school of sociological thought if his followers had only properly understood and developed and corrected his ideas. Still, by looking at the Turkish transformation from inside, Gökalp provided, as Parla put it, the "only plausible, comprehensive, cognitive map for Turkey's passage from a six-hundred-year empire to a new nation-state."[34] To be sure, the map was incomplete and faulty, like all maps of new-found lands, but it still was a guide to new discoveries. Gökalp's writings were didactic and committed, for he acted both as the analyst of events and as the teacher-promoter of his own ideas and subjective judgments. As a teacher, he showed great zeal along with intellectual curiosity, vigor, and courage. Above all, however, he demonstrated personal modesty. To the end he maintained these qualities, amidst the shifting loyalties, the personal ambitions, corruption, and materialism of his contemporaries; his sole worldly possession at the time of his death was a small, modest house. It is fitting to end this section with some key quotations from Ziya Gökalp's writings on modernization, secularism, and civilization. These quotations are freely translated from *Türkçülüğün Esaslari*, the M. Kaplan edition (1990), with page numbers given in parentheses.

> There is no relation between civilization and religion. There is no Christian civilization, just as there is no Islamic civilization. (57)

> Russians began to advance after Peter the Great introduced innovation [*yenilik*] by force. This historical fact is the cause of the rise of the Western civilization; the lack of it [innovation] accounts for the absence of progress in the oriental civilization. (63)

> Civilization consists of the totality of given [scientific-technological] institutions [that all nations can share]; institutions that belong specifically to a single nation constitute the national culture, like the institutions that belong solely to a [religious] faith. (53)

> There is one single means for progressing and reaching the Europeans, namely, "entering fully into the civilization of Europe." The Tanzimatist reformers understood this truth but adopted European civilization only halfway, hoping to create a Western and Eastern synthesis; instead they created a dichotomy in every field. Only the Harbiye and Tibbiye [War College and Medical School] adopted a pure European type of education and trained the great [*kumandan*] military leaders and doctors who saved our national existence. (64)

> The Japanese entered Western civilization preserving their religion and nationality and thus reached the European [level of development]. Can't we enter Western civilization preserving our Turkishness and Islamic faith? (66)

> Obviously we [Muslims] had adopted our old sciences from the Byzantine. Now if we [Muslims] should replace the Greeks' sciences with European sciences, we shall lose nothing from our faith and culture. If these issues were clearly spelled out, nobody could sincerely object to our leaving the oriental civilization in order to enter into the occidental one. (67)

Gökalp also claimed that the Oğuz Turks, who lived in Turkey, Azerbaycan, Iran, and Horezm (Turkmenistan), were closely related to one another and could be culturally united, but as far as political unity was concerned the answer was that it was "şimdilik hayir" (not for the time being).

> The long-range goal of Turkism is Turan, which may involve the non-Oğuz, that is the Kipçak Turks, who may evolve and become nations. The term Turan is a common ethnonational denominator and expresses the possibility of unity embodied in the communality of language, literature, and culture. (25)

Turan was used as a utopian ideal to develop Turkism. Turkism, therefore, has three levels: Turkishness (the identity of Turkey's Turks), Oğuzism, and Turan.

Gökalp also disseminated his political views in the form of poems, to "use verse to educate the people." The titles of these didactic poems, all written in very simple Turkish, indicate their content: "Fatherland," "Nation," "Duty," "Loyalty," "Language," and so on. Two poems, both titled "Istida" (Petition), are addressed to Mustafa Kemal and call him a genius and ask him to deliver the nation from ignorance and poverty and free the nation from the "black sultan" through science and nationalism.[35]

Yusuf Akçura (1876–1935)

After Ziya Gökalp died in 1924, Yusuf Akçura rapidly rose to an important and unique place as an intellectual leader. Akçura not only had established and guided the organizations and publications that provided a forum for Turkish ethnic nationalist ideas, including his own, but from 1929 through 1932 he also helped Mustafa Kemal give direction to the development of Turkish cultural and political life. Yet he remains a controversial and neglected figure because history has proved that his teachings were off the mark and showed his opportunism. A book of reminiscences by leading Turkish intellectuals, planned to be published in Akçura's honor in 1936, was never written, and biographies in Turkish and in foreign languages remain unusually brief and incomplete. Furthermore, his 150-odd published articles are virtually ignored. There are few monuments or streets in Turkey bearing Akçura's name while Gökalp's is seen everywhere. The main information we have about Akçura derives from an autobiography that appeared in the 1928 *Türk Yili* and from one book-length analytical study of Akçura's life and some of his ideas published in Europe.[36] The importance of his legacy is, in fact, debatable.

Akçura (Akçurin) was born in the village of Süyebaşi in the district of Simbirsk (Simbirs) in Kazan in 1876 to a family of rich Tatar merchants; he was related on his father's side to the *hans* of Crimea. He was also related to Gaspirali's wife, who helped him financially to publish the *Tercüman* in Crimea. He came to Istanbul in 1883 with his mother, Bibi Kamer Banu, a descendent of the well-known Yunusoğullari family, in part to avoid the harassment of creditors following his father's death in 1878. In Istanbul Akçura attended the *rüşdiye* school, then enrolled in the Harbiye in 1896. After spending some six or seven years in Istanbul, Akçura took a trip to his native Kazan, and this profoundly affected his views about the power of ethnicity and cultural continuity. In the Ottoman capital Akçura lived in a modest house in Aksaray, the dilapidated quarter inhabited mostly by Muslim Turks. In contrast, he saw the cultivated, rich Christian bourgeoisie, protected by the European powers, living in the prosperous Pera section of Istanbul (today's Beyoğlu). Then, during his visit to his native Kazan, Akçura met his wealthy, well-educated relatives, who were part of the local Tatar bourgeoisie and also enjoyed the respect of the Russian bureaucracy. They had fought for four hundred years to maintain their ethnic identity and Islamic faith under czarist rule and had managed to reform and modernize their society by remaining Tatar and Muslim. Akçura seems to have concluded that ethnic-racial purity, freedom from economic bondage, and a new, dynamic bourgeoisie were the ingredients necessary for a national revival and that the monarchy and Ottomanism were the main obstacles to it.

Akçura's anti-Hamidian feelings developed mainly after his visit to Kazan. He was arrested, but forgiven, because of his open defense of freedom, for he was not a member of the secret Union and Progress Society. In 1897, however, he was not forgiven but exiled to Fezzan in Libya, along with his friend and nationalist colleague, Ahmet Ferit (Tek). Instead of staying in the south Saharan city of Fezzan, they actually stayed in Tripoli until 1899, when they escaped to Paris. From 1889 to 1903 Akçura studied at the École Libre des Sciences Politiques, receiving an excellent education in philosophy, sociology, history, and linguistics from Albert Sorel, Anatole Leroy-Beaulieu, Levy-Bruhl, Tarde, and Durkheim. In short, he was one of the few Turkish intellectuals to receive a sound and complete Western education, which he understood and internalized, while maintaining his own identity as a Tatar-Türk and Muslim. In Paris, Akçura established close relations with the Union and Progress Society and published several articles in its journal, *Meşveret,* though he did not join the group. Rather, he became increasingly disenchanted with the low intellectual caliber of the Young Turks and their dedication to Ottomanism. His graduation thesis on Ottoman institutions lacks originality. In 1904 he returned to Russia and there wrote his famous pamphlet, *Üç Tarz-i Siyaset* (Three political ways). This was reprinted by the Cairo newspaper *Türk,* a little-known paper published by Ali Kemal and a strong defender of Ottomanism, in its issues of 14–28 April and 5 May 1904. Akçura's pamphlet recently has been hailed as the "manifesto" of Turkish nationalism by one of his Kazan compatriots, a distinguished scholar.[37]

While in Russia between 1904 and 1908, Akçura published extensively and became closely involved in the political nationalist movements of the Muslims. When the well-known Russian orientalist V. D. Smirnov denounced one of his articles to the authorities as being seditious, however, Akçura left the country. Back in Istanbul, Akçura soon became involved in the establishment of all the major nationalist organizations and contributed articles to their publications. Yet, his continuing refusal to join the Union and Progress Party resulted in a rift with Gökalp and loss of his teaching job at the University of Istanbul. His two brief forays into nationalist party politics, including the establishment of Milli Meşrutiyet Firkasi (National Constitutional Party) in 1912, were unsuccessful; he failed to be elected a deputy. Regardless, the CUP government sent Akçura to Switzerland to negotiate the release of the Ottoman prisoners of war in Russia.[38] He then became involved in a variety of conferences and meetings and returned once more to Kazan to seek, among other goals, freedom for the Muslims of Kazan and Başkordstan. Akçura defended the Ottoman entry into the First World War on the side of Germany in the belief that a German victory would lead to the liberation of Russia's Muslims and thwart British and French designs on the Ottoman lands. Upon his return to Istanbul from Russia in 1919, after the Ottomans lost the war, Akçura was arrested by the British, but he was released because he had not joined CUP and its party. Akçura's distance from CUP actually helped drew him closer to Atatürk; in 1920, leaving his young bride behind, he joined the nationalist group of Mustafa Kemal in Ankara and remained his staunch supporter throughout his life. In 1924 Akçura was made a deputy in the National Assembly and taught in the Law School of Ankara. Having published in the *Türk Yili* of 1928 his history of

Turkish nationalism as a unilinear evolutionary process, he played, on Atatürk's instructions, a major role in 1931 as the "founder" and then the president of the Türk Tarihi Tetkik Cemiyeti (TTTC), the parent of the Türk Tarih Kurumu (Turkish Historical Society). In the following year Akçura organized the first convention of the TTTC, aimed at giving a new direction to the study of Turkish history. However, he suffered from multiple sclerosis and subsequently was compelled to leave Ankara and return to Istanbul, where he taught at the university until his death on 11 March 1935.

Akçura had a brilliant mind and considerable artistic ability (he was a good portraitist), to which systematic and serious training in the social sciences added a well-rounded, realistic understanding of human affairs. He accepted as a fundamental political truth Sorel's view that the rise of nations was the greatest event of the twentieth century. Akçura also developed a dialectical understanding of social and political phenomena, along with a great appreciation of the role of the social classes and the state in shaping the destiny of human societies and nations. For Akçura, the nation was a recent phenomenon that resulted from economic changes and social evolution as well as from will, preconceived ideas, and, especially, state action. Akçura pointed out that the introduction of capitalism in Russia ruined the old Muslim aristocracy and produced a Muslim bourgeoisie who fostered the national revival of their people, just as the Christian merchants did in the Ottoman Empire. Akçura thus advocated the development of an Ottoman national economy and bourgeoisie; and he charged Parvus (Alexander Helphand, 1867–1924), who was a socialist, to write articles on economic issues for the *Türk Yurdu*. Akçura himself urged the government to undertake all necessary measures, including the use of European capital, to promote the rapid rise of a national Turkish bourgeoisie; this idea had been previously expressed by some Tanzimat reformers, especially Ali paşa.[39]

The Turkish bourgeoisie envisaged by Akçura was to be subservient to the national goals of the state, not a free agent acting for its own interest. He dismissed the Young Turks in Europe as the sons or grandsons of the "rich beys and *paşa*s of Istanbul" who defended the status quo and remained oblivious to the nationalist and populist currents and the democracy of Europe. Toward the end of Abdulhamid's reign, according to Akçura, Ottoman society consisted of the following groups: (1) the military and civil bureaucrats who had amassed great fortunes; (2) Muslim and non-Muslim merchants who controlled internal and external trade; (3) the lower classes of Istanbul, who were protected and cared for by the government; (4) province notables eager to defend their interest and communal influence. He believed that the latter three groups, which coincide with what we called the new middle class, became the backbone of the opposition parties. Eventually the CUP, in order to win over these groups, ceased to be the party of the discontented and became the spokesman of the rich. Still unable to draw popular support, it had changed by 1918 into a defender of the economic interests of the petty Turkish-Muslim proprietors and merchants.[40] The true Turkish nation in Akçura's view consisted of small landowners, artisans, merchants, and wage earners, that is the lower classes, whom the nationalists wanted to "protect" against the rich, the notables, businessmen, and their patron, the sultan.

Akçura believed that nations differed from one another in their racial characteristics, attributing the victory of the Germans over the French in 1870 to their racial superiority. History for Akçura was not only a means of understanding international

economic forces but also a record of an ethnic group's past, genealogy, and achievements that nourished modern nationalism. Akçura was also known as the leading
exponent of panturkism, even though he did not openly advocate a political union
of all the Turks and was, in fact, rather selective. Half of his long piece in *Türk Yili* in
1928 was dedicated to the history and geography of Russia's Muslims—that is, the
Tatars and Azeris—but not the Turks of Central Asia. Similarly, he maintained close
relations with and published numerous articles on the Muslim Tatar emigrés of Kazan
and Crimea but wrote relatively little about the Turks of Turkey. As a result, he was
accused of trying to use the Ottoman state to liberate his Kazan fellows. In any event,
his devotion to the cause of Russia's Turks earned him the title of panturkist.[41]

Akçura's idea that a nation was based on kinship or race was derived from the
particular situation of his native Kazan society. Having maintained, against incred-
ible odds, a high degree of linguistic, religious, cultural, and ethnic continuity since
the Russian conquest in 1552, the Kazan Tatars in the nineteenth century became a
relatively cohesive ethnonational group and even transformed a variety of related
groups into "Tatars." Indeed, the Kazan Tatars were so sure of their own ethnic identity and origin that they often looked down condescendingly upon the Ottoman Turks
for mixing with Arabs, Persians, Circassians, converted Slavs, Greeks, and Jews. It was
in this context, then, that Akçura saw Ottomanism and Islamism as cosmopolitan
obstacles to the development (or discovery) of the Ottoman Turks' ethnic-national
identity. Akçura considered both Ottomanism and Islamism (not Islam) as artificial
devices that had failed to hold the Ottoman Empire together, and he advocated replacing them with ethnic nationalism in order to save and preserve the Ottoman Turks
as an ethnic group. This view is best expressed in *Üç Tarz-i Siyaset*, still known as his
major work, and deserves a critical analysis.[42]

Akçura debated Ottomanism, Islamism, and nationalism in terms of their practical potential and concluded that the political goals of Ottomanism and the religious
goals of Islamism conflict with the ethnic purposes of nationalism. Ottomanism,
according to Akçura, was an artificial state creation designed to be a new supranational identity, riding over the existing ethnoreligious ones, by granting equal rights
and freedoms to non-Muslims for the purpose of preserving the integrity of the Ottoman Empire. Inspired by the French Revolution and promoted by Napoleon III in
the Ottoman Empire, it had been discredited after Germany defeated France in 1870,
though Akçura claimed that he could still accept Ottomanism if it were used solely
in the service of the Muslim Turks. Meanwhile, the failure of Ottomanism to hold
the Empire together had led the Ottoman government to adopt Islamism, with the
purpose of establishing the same French-inspired type of homogeneous nation toward which Ottomanism had been directed. The Islamists overlooked, however, both
the multireligious structure of the Ottoman Empire and the idea of ethnic nationality emerging even among Muslims. Furthermore, according to Akçura, not only was
the panIslamist policy of Abdulhamid a natural corollary of Ottomanism, but it also
was continued under the Young Turks, despite the emergence of a nationalist school
of thought. Akçura found the nationalism—previously promoted as Turkishness by
the newspaper *Ikdam*—that emerged in the Ottoman Empire prior to 1908 to be
deficient, for it was apolitical and not based on race (lineage, ethnicity): "The idea of
a Turkish political nationality based on race is very new and was not present in the

Ottoman state and in the past Turkish states. . . . [T]he desire of a circle in Istanbul to [create] a Turkish nationality had a scientific [academic] rather political character."[43]

Akçura made a crucial distinction between Islam and Islamism. Islam, in his view, was an "important element in the formation of a great Turkish nation" and had helped the state assimilate the non-Turkish Muslims; but Islamism unnecessarily alarmed Ottoman non-Muslims and Europeans, and it ultimately divided even the Muslims, for it ignored their ethnicity. Akçura noted that worldwide Muslim unity was unachievable, for many of the Islamic lands were under European occupation, and "the influences of race [ethnicity] and other events have undermined the political unity based on faith . . . despite Islam's desire to destroy the ethnic and national sentiments [*kavim ve milliyet taassubu*] which Western ideas have, in a limited way, helped resurrect."[44] Akçura used the term *taassub*, which, it should be noted, in his day had the meaning of "passion" and "zeal" rather than "fanaticism," as it was translated by European and Russian writers. Nevertheless, the common use of Arabic alphabet and the implementation of Islamic laws made a degree of Muslim unity possible, Akçura said, advancing the unusual idea that should the Muslims' laws depart from the Şeriat, they would still remain "Islamic" if the law were implemented in a Muslim society ruled by a "Muslim" government. Akçura believed that religion could become an ingredient of nationality and could contribute to the Turks' unity, provided that "Islam changed itself as did Christianity in such a way as to allow for the emergence of nationalities [recognition of ethnicity]." Akçura accepted the fact that some nationalists regarded religion as an indispensable component of nationality, but he believed that if "Islam were to have a [real] function in the unification of the Turks, it is necessary for it to undergo change [from inside] in such a manner as to accommodate the birth of nations, as Christianity has done recently. This change is virtually imperative."[45] (Note that Abdulhamid suggested that Islam rid itself of dogmatism, as Christianity did, to become progressive.) Like Gökalp, Akçura believed that modernization and national religious awakening would go together; a modernized society needed a modernized faith.

Akçura freely argued that, although Turkism lacked the appeal of Islam, its strength lay in the Turks' common language, race, customs, and religion and that the Turks' unity posed no immediate threat to any other state or nation. He criticized *Türk*, the newspaper that had printed his famous article, for the limited scope of its Turkishness, which comprised only the Ottoman Turks. He had sent his article to the newspaper because its name appealed to him, but then he realized that *Türk* "ignored these Turks living in an area extending from Peking to Montenegro" and regarded as Turks only "the western Turks who are Ottoman citizens . . . and [who trace their beginning] only to the fourteenth century [when the Ottoman Empire was established,] something they learned from French sources . . . and want to protect only their [the Ottoman Turks'] rights. [For these Ottomanist Turks] the military, political, and civilizational past of the Turks includes only [the Ottoman sultans] Hüdavendigar [Murat I, d. 1389], Fatih [Mehmet II, d. 1481], Selim [the First, d. 1520], [only Ottoman intellectuals] Ibni Kemal [historian], Nefi [poet], Baki [poet], Evliya Çelebi [seventeenth-century traveler], [Namik] Kemal, rather than [Central Asian figures such as] Oğuz [the ancestral father of Turks], Cengiz, and Timur [*han*s] Ulug bey [astronomer and ruler of Samarkand], Farabi [philosopher], Ibn Sina [Avicenna],

Taftazani [scholar], Neva'i [poet and statesman]."[46] The passage is exceptionally il-luminating for it describes Akçura's preference for the Turks' transnational identity stemming from remote, reconstructed ethnic memories, rather than the Ottoman past.

Akçura's article produced an immediate answer from Ali Kemal, who argued that the Ottoman government did not pursue any specific Ottomanist or Islamist policy and that, anyway, the Turks were too weak to undertake grandiose political schemes and should devote themselves to raising the intellectual, educational, and economic standards of their conationals. Ali Kemal (1869–1922), the son of a self-made candle merchant originally from a village in Anatolia, was an Ottomanist and opposed CUP's nationalist policy. He believed in the internal peaceful strengthening of society and in individual progress within the existing political and social system and in accord with the reformist principles of the Tanzimat. He went to Paris in the 1890s and then went to Egypt to administer the estates of the ruling dynasty. In Cairo he published *Mecmua-i Kemal* and, finally, in 1902, the *Türk*. He returned to Istanbul about 1908, and, besides teaching at Mülkiye, he involved himself in politics. As the chief writer of *Ikdam*—he had been its correspondent in Paris—he used the paper to attack CUP's policies and joined the opposition Ahrar and then the Hürriyet ve Itilaf (the Free-dom and Unity Party, also known as the Liberal Party). He opposed the Kemalists for ignoring the country's traditions and the spirit of the Tanzimat and for adopting unrealistic reform schemes. The circumstances that led to his violent death in 1922, in Izmit, on his way to Ankara, are still unclarified.[47]

In a truly significant rejoinder, Ahmet Ferit (Tek), Akçura's school friend, sup-porter, and confident, told Ali Kemal that the Ottoman governments had indeed implemented a policy of Ottomanism and Islamism, and he cited examples. Ahmet Ferit, in fact, believed that the Ottomanist policy of the government was a direct con-sequence of modernization and the Tanzimat, "[which] meant the abandonment of medieval traditions . . . the reformist politicians of the [Tanzimat] era accepted as they should have the [idea of people's representation] brought about by the great [French] revolution and strived to achieve the administrative unity of the Ottoman subjects."[48] In Ahmet Ferit's view, Ottomanism allowed the state to use Islam and the idea of Islamic unity to strengthen itself and thus enhance, when conditions per-mitted, the success of Turkism. He called Ottomanism "the most powerful shield, the greatest defense policy and the most suitable goal" of the Ottoman government. Asserting that there currently existed an Ottoman nation and that "we should strive to preserve as much of it as possible," he cited the maintenance and enforcement of the Tanzimat policy as the first goal of the government. He thought of the caliphate as "a vehicle to make Islam a foundation of our society" but seemed to anticipate that the policy of Islamic union would fail eventually. He stated that there was no existing Turkist policy but that the Ottomanist policy would be useful "in preserving our national existence" when the Islamic policy lost effectiveness.[49]

Akçura and Ahmet Ferit had come to the same conclusion: the purpose of the state was first to prepare for the rise of and then to assure the survival of the Turkish na-tion. Akçura, however, saw Ottomanism as an obstacle, while Ferit regarded it as an asset and opportunity. The truth is that, in 1904, when this discussion took place, the term *Türk* was synonymous with the terms *Ottoman* and *Muslim*. As Masami Arai

puts it, "'Türklük' and 'Osmanlilik' were interchangeable in the thought of nationalist Ottomans. Even the non-nationalist Ali Kemal . . . used the term 'Turkish state'
[*Türk Devleti*]."[50] Indeed, the cultural-linguistic Turkification of the Ottoman state
had advanced to such a degree that after the turn of the century, Ottoman sultans
and caliphs claimed to be "Turks." Abdulhamid's identification with Turkishness has
been noted. The sad case of the last Ottoman caliph is another example. Abdulmecid II
(1868–1944) died in Paris in poverty after the Turkish government refused the transfer
his assets to France. He asked to be buried in Turkey, "my own country," as he described it in his testament. His daughter Dürrüşehvar, who was married to the nizam
of Hyderabad at the time, asked the Turkish government for permission to bury the
caliph in Turkey. Her petition was refused, as were all the requests of Salih K. Nigar,
the caliph's secretary. New requests addressed to the government of Adnan Menderes,
who took power in 1950 and who reportedly was sympathetic to the Ottoman dynasty, had no effect, despite a law passed in 1952 permitting the return of some 144
of the members of the dynasty exiled in 1924. Finally, after a wait of ten years in cold
storage in Paris, the lifeless body of the last Ottoman caliph, thanks to the efforts of
the nizam of Hyderabad, was buried on 3 March 1954 in the cemetery Cennet-ul
Bakiiye in Medina. S. K. Nigar, the secretary, described the burial: "The coffin was carried to Cennet-ul Bakiiye at dusk. The soil in the place chosen for the grave was
stony. The Sudanese grave diggers worked it with difficulty. The coffin finally was
lowered into the grave amidst chanted prayers. Then the grave was filled with dirt
and stones, and following the Wahhabi custom no sign was put on the grave. . . . [At
long last] Abdulmecid II received an honor that no other Ottoman sultan had: he
was entombed close to the Prophet." It is ironic that the Turkish National Assembly
answered the final request for permission to bury Abdulmecid in Turkey years after
it was submitted and after he had been already buried. The Assembly asked the peti-
tioner "whether you still insist on your earlier demands [to bury the caliph in Tur-
key] now that the corpse is buried in Medina." In answer, Nigar replied, "I leave it to
the conscience of the nation to judge the mentality of those people who defied all
notions of humanity and did not allow the lifeless body of an innocent man to be
buried in the soil of his fatherland. . . . He died with a profound love for his *vatan*
Turkey."[51]

Some other members of the Ottoman dynasty, although permitted to, did not
choose to return to Turkey. For instance, Prince Lütfullah (1880–1973), the son of
Damad Celaleddin paşa and of Seniha sultan, the daughter of Abdulmecid and sister
of Abdulhamid, stated that although he was attached to Turkey, he preferred to live
in France "which gave him hospitality." Lütfullah had fled with his father to Europe
in 1899 and returned in 1908 with his famous brother Sabahaddin (1877–1948), who
became involved in politics as a defender of decentralization and private enterprise
and as an opponent of CUP. Sabahaddin fled to France in 1914 after being suspected
of organizing the plot to kill Mahmut Şevket paşa, a pillar of the CUP government.
Lütfullah was not involved in politics but was exiled in 1924, along with other members of the caliph's family. Incidentally, Lütfullah gave one of the best descriptions of
Atatürk to his interviewers and a proof of impartiality and objectivity.[52]

The official attitude toward the members of the Ottoman dynasty reflects the changing nature of Turkey's politics and interpretation of history. Following my program

to check contemporary developments against their historical background, I visited, in October 1996, the *mezar* (grave) of Mahmud II, Abdulaziz, and Abdulhamid II, all buried under the roof of the same *türbe* (mausoleum) on Divan Yolu in Istanbul. The repairs and upkeep of the building were undertaken by the Türbeleri Koruma ve Yaşatma Derneği (Society for the Protection and Perpetuation of Mausoleums), which repaired the tombs of many sultans. The mausoleum of the three sultans is located in a cemetery in which the members of the Ottoman dynasty are buried, including those who died in Egypt and elsewhere. The new epitaph on Abdulaziz's grave accuses Mithat paşa of having been involved in the sultan's murder, thus absolving him of the sin of suicide—the only sultan reportedly to have killed himself out of a total of thirty-six rulers since 1299. The cemetery is declared a museum and open to the public but under the supervision of a pretentious and arrogant religious man who claimed to know all about Islam and the Ottomans but did not know where Sultan Abdulmecid was buried. (His tomb is in the courtyard of Istanbul's Selimiye mosque.)

The loss of the remainder of Balkans in 1912–13 had a crucial impact, strengthening the position of Akçura and bolstering his plea for ethnic nationalism. The Turkist associations and reviews proliferated, but their aggressive defense of ethnic Turkism continued to provoke sharp rebuttal from conservative nationalists and Islamists for whom "national" and "religious" identity were identical. After being sharply criticized by Ali Kemal and Ahmed Ferid in 1904, Akçura seemed to have abandoned for a while his version of panturkism and came closer to Ottomanism. In fact, he confessed that he had erred in confusing *tevhid-i Etrak* (unity of Turks) with *tevhid-i Islam* (Muslim unity) and agreed that the Ottoman government could have pursued Turkist and Islamist policies in the interior without a corresponding policy abroad. He reverted to pan-Turkism in 1911—that is, in the year he republished the *Üç Tarz-i Siyaset* and CUP began to support Turkism. That date also coincides with the establishment of the review *Türk Yurdu* and the organization of the same name that defended ethnic Turkism based on language and kinship. However, Akçura attacked Ottomanism openly in the *Türk Yurdu* only after the Balkan War and, as usual, provoked sharp reaction: Ebuzziya Tevfik, the famous literary critic and an Ottomanist, not only criticized Akçura but also denigrated the term *Tatar* by equating it with *hunhar* ("bloodthirsty") and went on to advocate the fusing of Greeks, Kurds, and Arabs into an Ottoman-Turkish nation.

Ahmet Naim, writing in the Islamist *Sebil-ul Reşat* (the former *Sirat-i Müstakim*), divided the Turkists into "pure Turkists," who rejected religion, and "Islamist Turkists," who accepted Islam but also kinship and language as the bases of Turkish identity. Ahmed Naim stated that nationalism—or *asabiyet-i kavmiye*—would destroy the unity and brotherhood of the Muslims. In reply, Ahmet Ağaoğlu (Agaev), who had a very sound background in Islam, wrote that Islam rejected tribalism, not ethnicity; he saw no conflict between Islam and nationality and went on to eulogize the Turks' contribution to Islam. Discussions of this sort continued well into Republic, but the analysis of them would exceed the scope of this work.[53] The fact that the Republic prohibited such debates did nothing to alleviate many Turks' uneasiness about the state-defined identity forced upon them.

The discussions on ethnicity, religion, and Ottomanism revealed the essentially different meanings the Ottoman intellectuals attached to these terms. Some sought to define the Turks' emerging ethnic identity, or Turkishness, in historical-cultural terms by accommodating it with Ottomanism, Islamism, and modernism, all of which stemmed from the Ottoman Turks' immediate past. Others, including the two ideologues, Ziya Gökalp and Yusuf Akçura, viewed the Turks' identity from the vantage point of sociological theories positing a futuristic utopia. Masami Arai was probably correct in stating that there were differences in the understanding of nationalism between the Ottoman Turks and the immigrants from Russia, although both groups cooperated in overcoming these.[54]

Judging ideology strictly on its practical utility for the formation of a nation, Akçura regarded ethnic nationalism as offering the best means for assuring not the Empire's survival, but that of the Turks as an ethnic group.[55] Although he condemned European imperialism and the formulation of the Eastern Question as aimed at the destruction of the Ottoman state and as part of the ongoing struggle between Christianity and Islam, Akçura still advocated the adoption of Western civilization and culture. Unlike Ziya Gökalp, who claimed that culture was national and unique and so could not be borrowed without endangering national cultural existence, Akçura made little distinction between culture and civilization. Rather, he believed that a nation's racial and ethnic peculiarities sufficed to preserve its separate existence and, as mentioned, that Islam would survive and thrive by becoming the cultural and historical components of ethnic nationalism. Akçura also was a populist, advocating measures to help the peasantry, the bulk of which was Turkish, to achieve a higher standard of education and life. The populism of Ziya Gökalp, by contrast, was cultural; *halkçilik* (populism), for him, called for the elites to take civilization to the masses while absorbing, in return, the folk culture and spirit. After testing the two theories against the development of nationalism, Islam and modernity (Westernization) in Turkey, one could say that Akçura was correct, in that his theory prevailed at state level, while Gökalp's found acceptance among the society of intellectuals and modernist-nationalists.

Mehmet Fuat Köprülü (1890–1966)

Köprülü is seldom viewed as a nationalist ideologue because his international reputation and stature as a historian have obscured his nationalist side, but he is considered the father of Turkish national historiography.[56] While Ziya Gökalp was born to a humble family in a provincial town and Yusuf Akçura, was a refugee from Russia, Fuat Köprülü was born in Istanbul to illustrious parents. His great-grandfather, Mehmet Köprülü, grand vizier from 1655 to 1661, was of Albanian origin but was fully Turkified; he married the daughter of a noble Turkish family living in the town of Köprü in the region of Amasya. Fuat Köprülü's own parents, owners of one of the richest libraries in Istanbul, belonged to the Ottoman establishment: his father served in the judiciary, and his mother was the daughter of Arif Hikmet, an Islamic scholar.

Köprülü's intelligence showed itself early. After attending the elementary and *rüşdiye* schools, he enrolled in the Istanbul Law School, but he found the academic level to be so pedestrian that he decided to study on his own in his family's library. Having learned Persian and Arabic, as well as French, in 1905 he began, at age fifteen, his distinguished writing and publishing career. He joined the newspaper *Türk Derneği* in 1908 and also was active on the *Türk Yurdu* and *Türk Ocağı*, where he fell under the influence of Gökalp. From the beginning, they seemed to agree on a basic issue. Köprülü's main historical thesis was that the early Ottoman state was established by ethnic Turks whose folk culture blended heterodox Islam with ancient Turkic traditions and beliefs; this paralleled Gökalp's staunch belief in a grassroots, purely Turkish ethnic culture that had survived centuries of Ottoman cosmopolitanism. Obviously the two influenced each other. Both had considerable interest in French culture and philosophy; for example, Köprülü translated several of Gustave le Bon's books along with literary pieces by other French writers. In 1919 Köprülü published his monumental work on the place of the religious mystics in Turkish literature and society.[57] This brought him rapid international recognition, including several honorary doctoral degrees.[58] (In 1948 Stalin rescinded the degree awarded to Köprülü by the Moscow Academy after Köprülü criticized Stalin's territorial demands on Turkey. Once Köprülü became foreign minister, in 1950, the Soviets offered to reinstate his degree; Köprülü rejected the offer.) In 1923 he became professor of Turkish literature at the University (Darulfünun) of Istanbul.

Eventually Gökalp introduced and recommended Köprülü to Mustafa Kemal (Atatürk), who admired the young historian and in 1924 made him a counselor of the Ministry of Education. Köprülü's association with the Republican rulers was tenuous from the beginning, as he discreetly opposed the regime's assault on Ottoman history and culture. In 1927, however, he became the head of the Ottoman Historical Society and was one of the few to criticize the wholesale rejection of Ottoman past. He took part in the first Turkish History Congress, held in 1932 and dedicated to devising a national approach to the study of Turkish history; yet Köprülü, though recognized as Turkey's foremost historian, remained a rather passive and unwilling participant. His communication read at the congress was a perfunctory summary of his published views on the history of Turkish literature, and he intervened only once to answer a criticism.[59] Meanwhile, the congress itself represented a turning point in Turkish intellectual history. Headed by Yusuf Akçura (the minister of education was formally the chair), it hardly dealt with Ottoman history but concentrated instead on the Turks' pre-Islamic Asian history, and gave the emigrés from Russia a chance to settle their scores.

Köprülü directed, or was instrumental in, the publishing of the *Türkiyat Mecmuasi*, *Milli Tetebbular Mecmuasi* (1915), and the Turkish version of the Encyclopedia of Islam. He also was the chief editor of the *Ülkü* (1936–41), the main publication of the People's Houses. After Atatürk's death, Köprülü was given a seat in the parliament in 1943, probably as a reward for his grudging reconciliation with the ruling Republican People's Party (RPP). Nevertheless, along with Celal Bayar, Adnan Menderes, and Refik Koraltan, he resigned from the RPP and established in 1946 the opposition Democratic Party (DP). When his party won the elections and came to power in 1950, Köprülü became foreign minister in the new government; but he left the post in 1956 and one year later resigned from the DP altogether as a protest against the leaders' authoritarianism. He had been part of the Democratic government that from 1950 to 1954 passed a series of laws to correct some of the reformist excesses and dilute some of the anti-Ottoman and anti-Islamic measures taken by the RPP between 1923 and 1945. Arrested along with all the leaders and deputies of DP by military junta that took over the government in 1960, Köprülü was acquitted in the Yassiada mass trials. The doyen of Turkish national history did not write much of significance after 1950, and he died in 1966 as a result of injuries received in a traffic accident. The miscarved inscription on Köprülü's tombstone, because the masons did not know the meaning of the "old" words, is a pathetic and symbolic example of the rupture between the old and new culture of Turkey.

Köprülü's nationalist-modernist philosophy is epitomized in his speech welcoming the decision of the North Atlantic Council in September 1951 to accept Turkey as a member. "We are entering the Atlantic Alliance, which is not only a military and political community," declared Köprülü, "but a community of culture and civilization, and of democratic nations. . . . [T]he Alliance consists of democratic nations which have attained a high level of [development in the] contemporary civilization."[60] Turkey's final acceptance into the North Atlantic Treaty Organization on 18 February 1952 signaled formal admission into what Gökalp would have called the international civilization, or the West.

Köprülü factually and comprehensively analyzed a mass of historical, sociocultural, and political writings hardly known or used previously by European and Turkish scholars. He held that the Turks had their own venerable and distinguished ethnic culture, which was expressed in religious terms—often in an unorthodox fashion; that the founders of the early Ottoman state were Turks rooted in a literary-religious, ethnic Turkish cultural tradition; and that the core of the Ottoman Empire remained Turkish despite its "internationalization" after the mid-fifteenth century. Köprülü did not formulate a nationalist ideology of his own but instead, he used an immense body of cultural and historical data to establish an ethnic-cultural basis for the Turks' national identity. Köprülü believed, as did his mentor Gökalp, that the folk culture and language formed the basis of the Turkish national identity. But whereas Gökalp ignored the force of history, Köprülü regarded the folk culture as the product of historical evolution and subject to a variety of influences, including court styles and literature. According to Köprülü, the Turks' specific ethnic culture and identity, although rooted in their Central Asian past, had evolved independently throughout the Selçuki era and took new form in the life, institutions, and, especially, the literature of the early Ottoman state. Köprülü paid utmost attention to the methodology needed to study ancient Turkish folk literature and its close association with the folk religion. He stressed, in particular, the literary origins, evolution, and role of the folk minstrels (*aşiks*) of the sixteenth and seventeenth centuries in creating the Turkish literary styles. Because he believed that literature expressed the ethnocultural characteristics of a nation, he claimed that Turks, through their folk literature, had maintained their "national" attributes under the Ottoman system. Köprülü's populist-ethnic approach to folklore marked a sharp departure from the old Ottoman school of literary thought, which had regarded the Ottoman literature as derived basically from Persian and Arabic.

Köprülü's *Türk Edebiyatinda Ilk Mutasavviflar* has survived the test of time. It is a literary historical study of the popular Turkish poets who were also founders and/or members of the mystic *tarikat*s (mostly Sufi religious orders). Köprülü was the first to call attention to the ideas, forms of expression, and literary styles of the Central

Asian mystic Ahmet Yesevi (d. ca. 1166) and to Yunus Emre, Haci Bektaş, and the other successors who continued the Yesevi tradition in the Turks' new homeland in Anatolia. Köprülü believed that the origins of Turkish folk literature predated Islam and evolved, preserving its own heterodox character, even after the Turks converted to Islam and adopted specific Islamo-Turkish forms during the Selçuki and early Ottoman Empires. He developed this basic theme in a seminal, but little used, article, on the role of Islam in the formation of Turkish identity and culture in Anatolia, published in 1922 and, significantly enough, not reissued in Turkey since.[61] In the article Köprülü pointed out that, prior to coming to Anatolia, both nomadic and settled Oğuz Türkmen had practiced shamanism and had adopted at various times Mandaeanism, Buddhism, Manichaeism, and Christianity. Moreover, strong traces of these early religions and practices remained as part of the Turks' ethnic culture after their conversion to Islam. The Sufi *baba* or *dede* gave this heterogenous folk religion-culture a Turkish-Islamic character during the Selçuki and Ottoman Empires. The *baba*s (father, an honorific title given to popular Sufi "saints") and dervishes, according to Köprülü, were the "Islamized version of the Turkish *kam* or *ozan* [shaman/wandering minstrel]," who continued the old Turkish cults in Anatolia.

Köprülü argued that many Türkmen *baba*s, who belonged to the Yeseviyya brotherhood or were Melamatiyya *şeyh*s or "Sufis of Khorasan," as well as numerous "other people of all creeds from Iran, Iraq, and Syria went to Anatolia, to *dar al-cihad*." The *baba*s, however, played the main role in inspiring the Oğuz—that is, the ethnic Turkish tribes and the forefathers of the Anatolian and Azeri Turks—to action "in a language they could understand [by endowing] it with mystical but simple and popular images of Islam that conformed to their old ethnic traditions."[62] The same free-thinking *baba*s later were instrumental in inciting the Türkmen tribes to rise against the religious-political order of their own sultans—in other words, against the promoters of orthodoxy and the oppressive political order of the Selçuki and the early Ottoman sultanate.

Köprülü's ideas have been revived, but in a changed form. One of the current revisionists, seeking an accommodation between Ottoman history, Islam, and modern Turkey, claims that in the early Ottoman state the rulers and the ruled shared the same folk Islam of the nomadic tribes as represented by the *abdallar*, the mystics of Anatolia and Rumili. Sunni Islam was politicized and became dogmatic because of the political reaction against the Safavids and was used to legitimize the sultan's absolute authority. After the Tanzimat of 1839, this dogmatic Islam was blamed for the Empire's regression. The first constitutional movement of 1876, as the writer imagines it, was the intelligentsia's reaction to this politicized, absolutist Islam as well as an attempt to return to the early folk Islam of the Turks, while Sultan Abdulhamid's Islamism was a part of the reaction to the distortion of the early Islam of the Turks.[63]

In Köprülü's view the extremist Alawi (Shiite) tendencies of the Qalandariyya, a Sufi brotherhood, influenced the Türkmen tribes, especially in Syria, where the *batini* beliefs of the Ismailis had been dominant. In short, the *baba*s were instrumental in spreading Shiite doctrines and *batini* beliefs among the Türkmen. For example, Köprülü believed that Baba Ishak, instigator of the ferocious revolt of 1240 against the Selçuk sultan Kaikusrev, was a Qalandari and an extremist Alawi.[64] Köprülü further held that Baba Ishak was the doctrinal precursor of Haci Bektaş Veli, Sari Saltuk, and Bedreddin Simavnali; once praised by socialists for pursuing equality and social justice, all three men today are regarded as representing the ethnic Turkic element. Although Köprülü saw Turkish ethnic culture as rooted in the Central Asian folk religion, he made it abundantly clear that this culture assumed a truly Turkish (national) character in Anatolia; it developed from the eleventh through thirteenth centuries, and continued to evolve under the early Ottomans. In Köprülü's opinion the Sufi representatives of this Turkish ethnic culture were different from the Arab and Persian Sufis, who spent quiet and contemplative lives secluded in *tekkes* (lodges), while the *babas* and *abdals* (the Sufis of Rum) were active cihadists, and Islamic-Turkish missionaries. Köprülü concluded that Anatolia was Turkified ethnically and Islamized religiously from the eleventh to the fourteenth centuries by various Oğuz Turkish tribes led by the *babas*. Thanks to them, the nomadic Türkmen tribes and the rural classes maintained their Turco-Islamic folk culture, even when the cities formally adopted Sunnism; but the rural areas, folk Islamic Turkish culture and urban Sunnism reached an accord to respect each other's specific spheres of influence and religious beliefs. Actually, the nomadic Turkish states established in east Anatolia and Azerbaycan in the fourteenth and fifteenth centuries played a key role in the Turkification of Anatolia and the creation of a new ethno-Islamic culture.[65] Nonetheless, the Türkmen often succumbed to the call of their unorthodox beliefs and clashed with the Selçuki and Ottoman authorities and the religious establishment and incited their Türkmen brothers to join the Muslim adversaries of the Ottomans, such as the Akkoyunlu and the Safavids.

Köprülü elaborated further on the Turkish background of the Ottoman state in a series of talks given at the Sorbonne in Paris in 1934.[66] He claimed, in effect, probably in error, that the Ottoman founders, Ertuğrul and his son Osman, belonged to the Kayi tribe, although he acknowledged that the Kayi was not numerically large enough to dominate the rest of the Türkmen tribes and establish a state by itself. Paul Wittek, based on a mass of philological sources, claimed that the Kayi tribe could not be the Ottomans' ancestors and that probably Ertuğrul and Osman belonged to another small Turkish tribe.[67] After claiming that the Rumili (Balkan) Turkish culture was an extension of the Anatolian Turkish culture, Köprülü concluded that the Ottoman state was neither an imitation of the Byzantine Empire nor the result of a spontaneous outburst of religious zealotry and mass conversion to Islam, as claimed by a few Western historians but had followed a logical sequence in the Turko-Selçuki history of Anatolia.[68] The Turkish *beyliks* (principalities) that arose with their own specific cultures in Anatolia in the eleventh through thirteenth centuries eventually became part of the Selçuki state, which, in turn, was dispersed by the Mongols and split into some twenty petty fiefdoms. The subsequent effort to reunify these fiefdoms-principalities and further Turkify Anatolia was undertaken by one of them, the Germianoğullari, and then by the Ottomans who completed the process. The early Ottoman state, therefore, Köprülü pointed out, "was not a new ethnic and political body unrelated to the defunct Selçuki Sultanate and its successor *beyliks*. . . . [I]t was in fact a new synthesis, a new historical composition [*terkip*] emerging from the political and social evolution of the Anatolian Turkishness of the thirteenth to fourteenth centuries, which had been at the basis of the Selçuki state, the Danişmends and Anatolian *beyliks*.[69]

The founders of the early Ottoman state, in Köprülü's view, chose their elites and bureaucrats from among the Turkish aristocracy, except for the Mihaloğullari and a few other converts, and placed the Turks in all the high positions. After the middle of the fifteenth century, as the Ottoman state began to acquire the features of an empire, however, a variety of other *Ottomanized* elements, that is, converts to Islam, joined the administration and "internationalized" the state.[70] Still, this Ottoman state structure remained anchored in the old Turkish-Islamic ground. According to Köprülü, the Ottoman Empire did not succeed in creating a Turkish nation because it ignored the history and the core composition of the state. Similarly, although the Tanzimatists and the Young Turks did want to create such a people, or nation, they did not succeed because they clung to the idea of empire. In an article written in 1918, Köprülü defined Ottomanism as trying to establish a comity of ethnic groups, such as the Arabs, Greeks, and Armenians, that was impossible to achieve. Köprülü rejected race as the basis of nationalism and defined Turkish nationalism as antiracist and humanist and as recognizing the equality of nations.[71] Then, latter-day efforts to create a nation overlooked the fact that the classical Ottoman state rested on the dynasty and Islam. Without elaborating further upon this key point, Köprülü stated that some six years earlier he had submitted recommendations for restructuring the Ottoman state based on a Turkish Muslim sultanate and on Turkism.[72]

As summarized above, Köprülü's views on Turkish nationalism indicate that he, like Gökalp, believed the lower classes had maintained their Turkish national ethnic culture and identity during the "international" periods of the Ottoman Empire and could somehow rediscover it by removing the nonnational accretions. Köprülü ignored the fact that Ottomanism in the nineteenth century was a wholly new type of nation-building process and that the socioeconomic forces restructuring Ottoman multiethnic society had a power of their own to give a new shape to the traditional elements and a new identity to the emerging nation. There is no evidence to suggest that the folk culture would have produced a modern nation on its own without the sophisticated administrative, social, and legal suprastructure developed in the nineteenth century, largely as the result of Ottomanism. It was Ottomanism, implemented by a central government in a new social, economic, and structural framework, that brought together the disparate ethnic Turkish urban and tribal nuclei and fused them into the new, broad ethnic unit that eventually became political and national. The traditional Ottoman elite, who controlled the state for centuries, could not have steered society toward a new form of organization as long as they lacked the ideology, social structure, and motivation necessary for creating a nation.

Köprülü's contribution to the rise of Turkish nationalism is vitally important. He provided a theory to support the view that Turks had possessed, since ancient times, their own ethnic culture and their own language, and he backed this cultural theory with extensive historical data from the Turks' own immediate past.[73] His theory failed to gain official support only because of the Republican regime's decision to ignore the Turks' Islamic and Ottoman past. However, Köprülü's breadth of knowledge, objectivity, and power of analysis, as well as his predominant interest in methodology and the correct use of sources, gives his interpretations credibility. Indeed, Köprülü provided Gökalp with the historical underpinning for his view that lower-class Turks possessed their own unique ethnic culture. Gökalp took that culture out of its historical context, however, and made it appear to be a purely secular ethno-national culture, deprived of a true historical basis.

Conclusion

Turkish nationalism evolved through three distinct stages of identity change. The first long, historical stage (1865–1908) was not a deliberately planned process but the by-product of increased communication, literacy, and the rise of new elites. The process of identity change began among these elites, whose initial identity, regardless of eth-nic origin, was determined chiefly by their association with the state and their self-proclaimed Ottomanism, supplemented ideologically by their acceptance of progress, or *medeniyet* (contemporary civilization) as a common goal. They developed a pro-prietary attitude toward the state, seeking to replace the sultan-dynasty as its titular owner. Benedict Anderson has suggested that a sense of community that involves a shared identity is essential for the rise of political nationalism.[74] Within such a com-munity, individuals acknowledge that a political compact links them to others with whom they share a recognized affinity wider than lineage alone. True, in the Turkish case, the new community emerged within the frame of Ottomanism and Islamism, which provided the political link; but the elites, instead of seeking a corresponding identity reflecting the multiple identities of the community (despite some debate on this point) leaned toward ethnicity as the sole, exclusive identity of the emerging new Turkish nation.

The second stage of identity change began after the Young Turks came to power in 1908 and Abdulhamid, the symbol of the old Ottoman-Muslim order, was deposed in 1909. It was characterized by government support given to groups that espoused or promoted Turkishness, although the government had no clear-cut ethnic Turkist policy of its own. The Young Turks government formally defended Ottomanism and, in order to eliminate Abdulhamid's political appeal, de-emphasized Islamic ritualis-tic ceremonies and curtailed some of the "political" power of clerics and traditional leaders; for example, the *şeyhulislam* was excluded from the ministerial cabinet. The "secularism" of the Young Turks, after an initial phase of positivist rhetoric, remained confined mainly to measures inspired by the desire to achieve bureaucratic efficiency rather than to promote the secularist ideology. Yet many intellectuals increasingly viewed positivism as equal to adopting science as the only sure road to progress and modernism, and this view remained the hidden ideology of many leading Young Turks. In the meantime, the idea of the "nation" underwent a basic change. The origi-nal idea of nation embodied in Ottomanism and Islamism was a political commu-nity above ethnicity. Indeed, Ottomanism established the rudimentary legal and political foundations of modern nationhood but was unable to generate the ideo-logical ingredients of true solidarity and unity. It was not able to supersede the origi-nal image of the nation as political religious community; the resulting Ottoman *mil-let* (nation) was comprised mostly of Muslims, regardless of the concept of common citizenship and the idea of political participation embodied in the constitution and parliaments of 1876 and 1878. As the nation emerged as basically an Ottoman Mus-lim political community, it alienated the non-Muslims, who became minorities in a

unitary state dominated by a Muslim majority. In a strange and ironic way, the old
Ottoman system, which had treated all religious communities as self-governing, culturally and linguistically autonomous units, was being replaced by the European
model of the centralized nation-state in which the culture and language of the dominant majority prevailed. From roughly 1912–13 to 1918, efforts were made to transform the Ottoman-Muslim nation—which was not cohesive but divided into a variety of ethnolinguistic groups—into an ethnic Turkish nation. Ottomanism and
Islamism were abandoned in practice, although they were maintained as state principles. The Young Turks and the two principal exponents of Turkism, Yusuf Akçura
and Ziya Gökalp, tried to convert the Ottoman *millet* to Turkism during this time.
They denounced everything associated with Abdulhamid and his reign, against which
their revolution had taken place; they sought to attain sufficient economic, scientific,
and military strength to assure the survival of the state and prove the superiority of
the new regime over the Hamidian one; and, finally, at the same time, they needed to
base the state on a new political community anchored in a core ethnic group—that
is, in a nation identified with and entirely loyal to the state.

Class considerations also played a crucial role during the Young Turks' search for the
proper ethnic identity. The commoner Turks were the poorest and least-developed
ethnic group in their "own" state, while "their" imperial leaders, regardless whether
they called themselves Muslims, Ottomans, or Turks, lived in opulence. As the leaders
of the Young Turks came from the lower middle classes, they easily came to regard
the rich, upper imperial stratum as indifferent to the plight of ethnic Turks, who were
regarded as the very foundation of the state. In his play *Memiş Çavuş*, Tunali Hilmi
(1891–1928) (*Memiş*, a corruption of *Mehmet* is a half-pejorative diminutive name
given to peasant Turkish boys) dramatized the lamentable poverty of a peasant boy
who is, nevertheless, staunchly attached to his country and serves loyally in the army.
The Young Turks therefore made veiled appeals to egalitarianism to justify their control of state on behalf of the common Turks, though they themselves were not truly
egalitarian, socialist, or even populist.

The Young Turks decided to place the state in the service of the nation rather
than serve a cosmopolitan body of Ottoman Muslims, and the ethnic Turk was to
be the foundation of nation. A rising journalist and apologist for CUP, Hüseyin
Cahit (Yalçin), stated forcefully in the party paper, *Tanin*, that the state's sole preoccupation was the Turks. Both Yusuf Akçura and Ziya Gökalp believed that ethnic Turkishness should define the identity of the nation and that Turkism was the
ideology necessary to create and disseminate this identity. It was Akçura's view that
one's identity was determined historically by the ethnic lineage (race) of the group in
which one was born and that it was buttressed by common religion and language.
He attributed the Ottoman Turks' lack of national political consciousness not to the
absence of ethnic awareness but to the lack of a modern national bourgeoisie and an
economic system identified with the ethnic Turks, as well as to the failure of the state
to develop a program of ethnic-national indoctrination. He regarded the Ottoman
rulers as a status group that had gained economic power, refinement, and erudition
through reforms and association with Europe but that had failed to absorb the European concept of nationality and a sense of social and national responsibility. Akçura
therefore advocated that the government use its power to create a Turkish bourgeoi-

sie with a national identity to become the sustaining foundation of the state. Gökalp, on the other hand, believed that the essence of nationhood was its culture, which was formed by the blending of language, faith, customs, and a special ethnocultural ethos. Such a "nation" could survive for centuries under a variety of political systems but would regain its basic identity when the political system that prevented its self-assertion disintegrated. In short, Gökalp believed that the disintegration of the Ottoman Empire would allow the Turks simply to reassert their ethnic identity and culture in the new political framework of national statehood.

Akçura and Gökalp both considered the twentieth century the age of nations and nationalism. While Akçura held that the state had an almost limitless ability to create and reshape a nation's identity and culture by selecting and emphasizing the elements most suitable to its purposes, Gökalp seemed to place less importance on direct government intervention, except in education. According to Gökalp, creating a nation out of an ethnic community (which in the Turkish case was barely developing) was a process of grassroots voluntarism, and government's role was to help define, channel, and popularize its identity thorough education. Gökalp envisaged the ideal Turkish nation as a classless, monolithic society, which, freed of social and ethnic conflicts, would allow the ethnic Turkish folk culture to percolate upward and become, with due refinement and adaptation, the culture of the entire nation, built around one language. Gökalp and Akçura considered the *milli kahraman*, the national leader possessing charisma and extraordinary insight, to be uniquely qualified to express the national will and identity. Both eulogized Atatürk as such a leader, although Gökalp had praised Talat paşa, the Young Turks' leader, in similar terms. Both Akçura and Gökalp implied that an authentic Turkish ethnic culture had existed before the advent of Islam and the Ottomans and that nationalism would somehow link the Turks to that historical culture.

Meanwhile, Mehmet Fuat Köprülü noted key cultural and historical continuities in the history of the modern Turks, although he failed to make the connection between the Ottomans and present-day Turks more definitive through a judicious evaluation of economic and social forces. The Turks did have influential Central Asian roots, and Russia's Muslims had a special political-cultural impact in the nineteenth century, but the basic course of Ottoman history was determined by forces germane to the Ottomans. Akçura and Gökalp used history arbitrarily only to link the Turks to their pre-Islamic origins rather than to understand how Turkish-speaking Ottomans evolved to call themselves Turks. Because their major intent was to distance the Turks as much as possible from their Ottoman political past and the sense of inferiority that was associated with it and, instead, to orient them toward the future through acceptance of European modernity and civilization in toto, they ignored Köprülü's emphasis on the Turks' early Ottoman past in Rumili and Anatolia and selectively accepted his other view: namely, that Central Asian literature and folk Islam were the sources of Turkish national culture and identity. Köprülü accepted the Central Asian origins of folk Islam but also emphasized its transformation in Anatolia and acquisition of unique "Turkish" features.

Akçura, Gökalp, and Köprülü all rejected Islamism as a state ideology and pan-islamism as its extension in foreign affairs. All three regarded Islam as a necessary cultural and spiritual ingredient of the national culture but viewed religion as a mat-

ter of individual choice and disposition. They appeared to give the state some responsibilities toward religion, and the state-faith conflict that became one of the distinguishing features of the Republic apparently was absent from the thinking of these
three early nationalist writers. Nonetheless, ultraconservative Islamists, who rejected
ethnicity as part of political identity and the state's efforts to manipulate it for its own
ends, attacked both Gökalp and Akçura as racists and heretics. Actually, all these
debates revolved around the problem of the reconciliation of the universalist identities engendered by Ottomanism and Islamism with the more specific ethnonational
identity of the emerging Turkish state-nation. The key issue was whether the identities and values engendered and internalized by Ottomanism and Islamism could be
incorporated and retained in a homogenous nation-state's culture. The precise identity and name of the emerging nation was another thorny issue.

The satisfactory assessment of the place of Ottomanism and Islamism in the making of Turkish identity to this day remains the key issue of Turkish identity and nationalism. The transformation of the Turks from being just one of the ethnic groups
in the Empire, although the most numerous and intimately associated with Ottoman
history, into the masters of the state was complicated by at least two crucial issues.
First, the state that had created these multiple identities in order to preserve itself could
no longer remain impartial but had to take a position in favor of one of the ethnic
groups, namely the Turks. Second, having decided to embrace and promote the language, culture, and customs of the Turks, it needed to culturally homogenize and
secularize the nation accordingly.[75]

Akçura, Gökalp, and, to a lesser extent, Köprülü sought initially to reconcile, or at
least relate to one another, Ottomanism, Islamism, and Turkishness, as the three ideologies were so closely and organically related. Gökalp, in line with the thinking of
his Azeri mentor, Hüseyinzade Ali, recognized unequivocally that Turkishness, Islam,
and modernity (the civilization of Europe) were inseparable parts of the modern
Turks' identity, but he dismissed the Ottomans altogether while remaining an advocate of worldly (secularized) Islam as part of the national culture. Akçura used utility
as criteria for accepting or rejecting Ottomanism and Islamism, and a closer scrutiny
of his seminal writing on these issues shows that while he placed priority on Turkism
he did not reject the first two universal identities until 1912–13, when the last of the
Empire's Balkan territories was wrested from it.

The third stage in the development of Turkish nationalism took place during two
phases of the Republic, 1923–30 and 1930–46. The Republic now inherited the question of the Turks' triple identity and resolved the issue by fiat. It ignored entirely the
Ottoman-Islamic past and decided that lineage was the basis of the Turks' political
identity. However, even state power cannot change everything. There remained fundamental social, ideological, cultural, and historical continuities between the Ottoman past and the contemporary Republic. Consequently, an endless identity crisis
was engendered in Turkey because some groups chose to stress only Islam; others,
the imperial Ottoman past; and most, the Republic's teachings. The state obviously
took an ambiguous position but ultimately sided with the "reform," and made "secularism" its creed. The state created the People's Houses in 1932 specifically with the
purpose of replacing the *hars*—that is, Islamo-historical concept of Turkish culture
of the Türk Ocaklari, with a purely secular, materialistic folk culture. The People's

Houses were all dismantled by 1953, however, and all efforts to revive them have been fruitless. I visited the headquarters of the People's Houses in Ankara in 1995. It was headed by one of the members of the military group that overthrew the popularly elected Democratic Party government in 1960 and sought to revive the Houses as part of Atatürk's legacy. The organization was dispirited and disoriented; it had become a relic, like the Ottoman past it had sought unsuccessfully to obliterate.

The society-community as living organism evolved on its own, often in conflict with and in contradiction to the state's policies, making Ottoman history and Islam part of its "national" ethos and identity, the essence of which is different from the official identity defined by the state and maintained and promoted by the military. The gradual introduction of democracy after 1946 challenged the official dogma of lineage-based Turkish identity. Since then, constant change in the form of massive urbanization and the resulting interaction of urban and rural folk cultures, the spread of literacy, industrialization, intensive communication, and generational changes (40 percent of the population is now below the age of twenty-five) has molded a fairly cohesive nation, which is an amalgam of the old Ottoman ethnic groups. The name *Turks* which is rejected by some groups, including nationalist Kurds, defines not so much a lineage group but a nation that bears the cultural characteristics of its immediate Ottoman-Islamic past and uses its language—that is, Turkish—as did the Ottoman government throughout its existence. The recent history of the Ottoman state, from the perspective of the Turks, shows a high degree of continuity meshed with change. Despite political rejections, denunciations, and condemnation of one another, the societies of the Hamidian and Young Turks eras and of the Republic exhibit a structural cultural and social continuity, all built around the common goal of modernization. State power was used to build a cohesive unitary nation, in good measure by relying upon the solidarity and common identity engendered by Ottomanism and Islamism, which had blended into each other and became part of everyday culture. These ideologies shaped cultural symbols, identities, and patterns of thought and behavior that ultimately entered into the stream of Turkish nationalism—not a nationalism charted by the Republican government but one that followed its own dialectical course and remained faithful to its past. Thus there are today in Turkey two nationalisms: one official nation-nationalism charted and defined by government according to its own blueprint and a "nation of the people" that has evolved naturally, drawing its essence from the structural transformation, identity change, faith, and history.

The overwhelming majority of Turks belong to the "people's nation," which is in effect the continuation of the multiethnic multilinguistic, tolerant, and pluralist Ottoman society-community where one can speak one's own language and practice one's own customs. There is continuous interaction and growing overlapping between the two "nations," except for a self-secluded small elite claiming to be the state, and the gap between them is narrowing.

The rise of Turkish nationalism studied here in the context of Ottomanism and Islamism should help illuminate the source of the endless crises in Turkey that have given the outside world a false perception of what really happened and is happening in Turkey. The major shortcoming of this modern Turkish nation lies in the matter of self-definition and self-perception. The elites, in control of the real government, which is above the parliament, continue to see Turkey through the narrow ethno-ideological glasses of the generation of the 1930s and 1940s and, in the name of "national unity," prevent others from expressing any different views. Recently, however, the discourse on the relationship between state and nation and on the virtues of the nation-state in Turkey has taken a new form, because elites rising from the grassroots have developed a new perception of what the state and the nation are and what their relationship with the citizens ought to be. Specifically, the prevailing demand is that the state apparatus not be used by any group to impose its ideology and prescribed culture on society or on any ethnic group and that the government refrain from social engineering while maintaining security, law, and order, in a democratic fashion.

The measure of a nation's maturity lies in the ability of its citizens to see their entire past with all its good and bad sides and judge it according to their own individual sense of identity, rather than by norms imposed by the state. It is in this context that the ideas of both Gökalp and Akçura should be recognized as part of the formative phases of modern Turkish nationhood that must be supplemented and even replaced by ideas that reflect more accurately the historical evolution, structural transformation, and identity formation of the contemporary Turkish nation.

Conclusion

The Muslim world in general and the Ottoman state in particular experienced two unprecedented movements of change in the nineteenth century, one welling up from below and embodied in grassroots revivalist movements and another that stemmed from above and was led by the state, supported by the middle classes, intellectuals, notables, and many religious men. Both movements were responses to the new European socioeconomic order created by the industrial revolution and the ensuing capitalist system, and both were searching for ways to adapt a society to the new conditions. Capitalism steadily took over the Ottoman state, aided by the existing Islamic concepts of *mülk*, or private property, and freedom of trade, which were used by the new middle classes to challenge state control of the economy in general and, particularly, its control of land. The segment of the Ottoman population that was engaged in the production and marketing of agricultural commodities welcomed the freedom brought by capitalism to adapt production and prices to the interplay of market forces rather than abiding by strict state regulations governing the economy—even though such regulations were based on legitimate social and political considerations. The painfully slow but steady penetration of capitalism, both culturally and socially, decided the outcome of the struggle between commercial interests and the state for control of the economy and community. The struggle had been going on for over a century. It had started with the reforms introduced by the Köprülü viziers in the second half of the seventeenth century and by Nevşehirli Ibrahim paşa early in the eighteenth. Intended to adapt Ottoman trade and finances to the changes in Europe, these reforms failed because the groups holding state power were too strong and those clamoring for some change, usually the producers, were too disorganized and weak to transform the system.

As the central government lost its power in a series of wars with Russia and the Hapsburgs in the period 1768–1830 and its revenues (mostly tithes) dwindled, the state sought to increase agricultural production and achieve social peace by gradually offering a variety of incentives to villagers, first to the Christian peasants in the Balkans and ultimately to the Muslims, including the right to own land and freely sell their crops. The weakness of the central government facilitated the rise of the notables, who served as tax collectors and administrators of state lands, as the forerunners of a new middle class and of the community as new sources of power. In opposing the center, the notables relied on economic power, the community on faith. The Ottoman state, finally, in order to assure its own survival, was forced to initiate changes, and these in effect laid the administrative, legal, and institutional bases for the development of a primitive, dependent form of capitalism and also of modern education, communications, the press, and so on. These reforms enabled the bureaucracy, which had been an appendix to the dynasty (the sultan), gradually to become de facto masters of the state and to formally seek legitimacy for their authority in the will of the community—the "people," or the "nation."

Thus the old fiction that the state was an indivisible part of the faith (*din-u devlet*) and served it under the divine guidance of the sultan was shattered, and it became evident that the status group controlling power acted primarily according to its own needs, and interests. Sultan Abdulhamid had sought to use the *şeyhulislam*'s religious authority to give a stamp of approval to his actions, which were designed to use the caliphate as the basis of his temporal power as sultan—as in the Umayyad and Abbasid eras—and to delegitimize the bureaucracy in favor of the "community" as the source of his authority. But this old arrangement, whereby the *şeyhulislam* issued his *fetva* (religious opinion) attesting to the government's compliance with Şeriat (religious law), although formally maintained, lost its raison d'être in the nineteenth century. The *şeyhulislam* still retained his formal authority to sanction the enthronement and dethronement of the sultan, but in a much attenuated form: the divestitures and investitures of sultans Abdulaziz, Murat, Abdulhamid, and Reşat in the period 1876–1909 were not decided upon independently on their merit by the ulema or the *şeyhulislam* but by the modernist bureaucracy bent on using constitutionalism to limit the sultan's authority. The *şeyhulislamate*, which had been more or less subservient to the state/sultan since the sixteenth century, was now transformed, totally and finally, from a supposedly detached umpire between the state and the faith into an office for legitimizing actions of the bureaucracy. (In this context it is essential to note that despite the formal demise of the *şeyhulislamate*, the Republican government transferred many of its functions to the Directorate of Religious Affairs and thus preserved it, although few Turks would admit to any continuity between the new office and the old.)

The emergence of the community, referred to as the "people" or *millet* (nation), as an inchoate source of power and legitimacy coincided with the rise of the middle class, notably in the countryside, as the new sociopolitical force created by capitalism. The change in the land tenure system—that is, the transfer of state lands (some 50–70 percent of the arable land) to individuals as private property—and the commercialization of agriculture promoted the ascendancy of this class, made up of Muslims (who overwhelmingly controlled rural property), as a powerful social, cultural, and ultimately, political force. Contributing vitally to its rise was this state's own view that the cultivation of all arable lands and the expected growth of agricultural production would increase state revenue and help the government meet the vast expanses caused by the modernization of the army, expansion of bureaucracy, education, and so on. This apparent alliance between the government and the rising middle classes was greatly aided by the outward continuity of state, dynasty, culture, and faith and some sort of tacit agreement that the acquisition of *medeniyet* (civilization) could save the state and strengthen the community (society).

By the time the nature, scope, and origin of civilization—whether it was materialistic, Western, and/or Christian, created or borrowed—became subject to debate, the idea itself had been largely accepted and incorporated into the elites' culture. The concept of civilization embodied ideas of change and progress rooted in rationalism and enlightenment that were ultimately used to scrutinize Islam itself, the society, the world, and the state. Although the participants in the debate could be classified as Islamist, conservatives, modernists, Westernists, and the like, they shared a rational, dynamic, and worldly approach and outlook. The modern educational system and the professional schools introduced mainly during Abdulhamid's time helped generalize the new modes of thought and also provided a channel for upward mobility of the middle class, especially for the sons of the country notables, to government positions. Islam increasingly was regarded as *medeniyet*, as having worldly, material aspects and as open to enlightenment, progress, and achievement—a development that was anathema to those defending the unadulterated spirituality of Islam, including the Wahhabis. Since the state promoted this very idea of change—with the sultan-caliph's blessing—and of civilization in order to save and strengthen itself, and since the state still possessed its Islamic credentials, the idea of civilization as something desirable percolated from the top to the lower layers of society, which viewed it more in material terms.

The new middle class and especially the agrarian sector that rose and gained power after 1856 apparently believed that civilization and Islam were perfectly compatible and that change could assure the material and moral welfare of society. The fact that the Ottoman state was independent and Islamic and had preserved its historical and cultural continuity made change appear the result of its own decision and therefore somehow in harmony with Islamic values. As Yusuf Akçura noted, a society ruled formally by an Islamic government would remain "Islamic" regardless of the intensity of change—and, I may add, could reassert its Islamic identity without rejecting change, progress, and so on, as happened in Turkey after the 1950s. In contrast to the Ottoman State, most of the other Muslim states were occupied by various European Christian states and Russia. These occupying powers imposed change, often by destroying the traditional Islamic governments and institutions and undermining the continuity of local culture by depriving it of its Islamic socioeconomic foundations. At the same time, European occupation inadvertently freed the local community from the tutelage (often bondage) of state elites and compelled it to seek its own salvation and to preserve its faith and identity by utilizing its own resources, often under the leadership of grassroots, self-taught Islamist leaders. Revivalist movements in Asia and Africa were communal reactions to this destruction of the traditional system and were intended to preserve Islamic order and identity and to protest foreign occupation and local collaborators. The revivalist movements also facilitated the upward movement of local and regional vernaculars, customs, and ways of life that became ultimately the cultural marks of the Muslim national states that emerged in the twentieth century. In the Ottoman state, thanks to its formal independent statehood and political, social, and cultural continuity, the struggle for modernization and change could be aimed at liberating the community not from foreign occupation but from the oppression of the bureaucracy, a part of which used the very concept of modernity to establish and legitimize its own political supremacy. Thus the Ottoman Muslim community was freed from bondage to the state not by the sudden and painful collapse of the traditional system but by a process of alternating conflict and cooperation between the bureaucracy and the new middle class, which gradually transformed both the state and society and produced new elites that were both modern and Islamic. Unprovoked by the trauma of foreign occupation, not a single popular revivalist movement arose in the Ottoman lands; even the Sanusiyya sided with Istanbul after 1881 in order to thwart French and Italian occupation, while Şeyh Şamil's movement arose outside Ottoman boundaries.

The conflict-cooperation between the bureaucracy and the middle class had confusing peculiarities. There was disagreement about the categories of land. The landowning middle class defended the sanctity of property rights based on Islamic laws, while considering the status of *miri*, or state lands, which were subject entirely to the *kanunname*, or secular state laws, as lacking strong religious credentials, having been created not by the Prophet but by Caliph Umar (d. 644). (Shiites were particularly skeptical about the validity of their status.) Another disagreement concerned the control of the community. The centralization measures of the 1820s had put an end to the de facto autonomy of local and regional notables, who had helped the center control the communities and the land prior to the nineteenth century. Later, unable to control the provinces with its still miniscule central bureaucracy, the government tried to enlist the support of the lower middle class, whose children were usually educated in the modern schools. This lower class, in turn, sought to maintain good relations with the state by supporting its reformist and centralizing endeavors and defending its interests but, at the same time, strongly supporting Islamic culture and ways of life. Thus the lower strata of the middle class were allied with the central government against the old, semifeudal landlords and notables and supported change in the judiciary and administrative systems in order to legalize and consolidate their own wealth and position while expanding their control of the community by identifying closely with its faith, culture, and local interests.

The state had prevented real challenge to its power in the past by using a variety of subtle (and not-so-subtle) means to prevent the accumulation of wealth in private hands, including those of its own dignitaries. Now, seeking to increase revenues, it permitted the countryside groups to become owners of the country's most valuable asset—the land—and gain and expand their control of the community, that is, the *millet* that the "reformed" state wanted to make the new foundation of its power. This bizarre switch of positions made the new middle class the defender of the community's Islamic culture against the very state that for five hundred years had claimed to embody the faith, to be *din-u devlet*. Yet the new middle class had to rely on the state for defense, order, security, legalization, and legitimacy, vis-à-vis the community it claimed to represent and defend. It should be noted that this middle class, which would develop an individualistic, rational, interest-oriented, pragmatic, and worldly mode of thought and behavior, remained deeply attached to its Islamic identity and developed an increasingly political view of the world and its own government. This class became increasingly Muslim, both culturally and politically, while developing a close interest in Western science and material achievement and oddly, in its own society and culture. Ahmet Mithat efendi was the best intellectual representative and spokesman of this class, while the Nakşbandia, itself a very old Sufi order, re-emerged in a modern Islamic form and sought to adapt somehow the new social and cultural order to the basic tenets of orthodox Islam.

It should also be noted that although the first movement toward change in the Ottoman State was initiated, with the sultan's approval, by a small bureaucratic group descending from old bureaucrats, ulema, and so on within a span of some sixty-five years between 1839 and 1908, the bulk of the bureaucracy came to consist mainly of new recruits from the lower ranks of the urban population and countryside notables. Eventually the foreign ministry, the army, and a few technical services came to represent the statist, modernist viewpoint, while the rest of the bureaucracy, deprived of real levers of power, tended to side with the community. However, few escaped the strong, binding power of the statist culture—that is, the material and psychological gratification of being part of the ruling elite.

Already, by the end of Abdulmecid's reign in 1861, the reformist (Western) wing of the bureaucracy, rooted in the foreign ministry, came to dominate the government and the sultan himself; and, when faced with Abdulaziz's efforts to reinstate absolutism, the bureaucracy and its allies in the intelligentsia turned modernity into an ideology and promoted it as the means most capable of assuring the state's survival. However, without the sultan's support, the power of the bureaucracy lacked legitimacy, so it sought to make the "people," through the constitution and parliament of 1876, the source of both legitimacy and power. Consequently, Mithat paşa, prime mover behind these seminal changes, enlisted the support of the notables, both Muslims and non-Muslims, to make the sultan a constitutional monarch, promising the community or *millet* (nation) civilization, modernity, and a share of power—more illusion than real. In answer the sultan, notably Abdulhamid, sought the support of the same community by upholding the virtues of Islam and tradition and by granting its middle-class representatives economic, administrative, and educational incentives and distinctions (medals and pensions). In sum, by the time Abdulhamid came to the throne, the classical Ottoman state, established Islam, and, especially, the social structure of Anatolia had undergone fundamental changes. The political and social effects of this transformation, fueled by increased literacy, social mobility, and opening to the outside world, were magnified and popularized by the press, which institutionalized the imperceptible, but ever present, changes. Old names were appropriated by Muslims and given new meanings: *millet*, traditionally applied to non-Muslim religious communities, became the term for the Muslim community-nation; the Osmanli identity, initially bestowed on all the Ottoman subjects, regardless of faith or ethnic origin, came to be viewed as a Muslim identity; and the epithet *Turk* came to apply to all Muslims designated the holders of state and political power rather than to members of a particular ethnic group.

The reign of Abdulhamid (1876–1909) witnessed the explosive growth of the middle class (split along ethnic-religious lines as Muslim and non-Muslim), of free enterprise, foreign investment, the further privatization of state lands, the professionalization and growth of the bureaucracy, the rise of a new corps of army officers, and unprecedented development in transportation and communication. At no time in its history had the Ottoman society undergone such a profound transformation.

The emerging Ottoman society, with its new identities and political culture, was profoundly and uniquely affected by the migration of several million Muslims from the Crimea, Caucasus, the Balkans, and the Mediterranean islands. In fact, the consolidation of the capitalist system, the emergence of the community, the reshaping of its Islamic identity and culture into a national one, and the state's changing relations with other countries owe much to migration.

After the 1860s the transformation was speeded up and conditioned, both positively and negatively, by Ottoman relations with England, France, and Russia. Having defeated Russia in the Crimean War of 1853–55 and given the Ottomans a much needed respite, Europe, especially England, was not content merely to see all Ottoman doors wide open to its cultural and economic influences but actually wanted to become a de facto partner in the administration of the Empire. Europe had promoted the introductory "reforms" in order to consolidate their influence over the Ottoman Empire—under the pretext of promoting the "equality" and welfare of the Christian subjects of the Ottoman government.

The turning point, in fact, the event that defined the last decades of Ottoman history, was the resurgence of Islam as a political ideology. This was triggered by the change of British policy toward the Ottoman State in 1875–76, when London turned from an ally and protector into a devious, whimsical critic and, ultimately, an enemy. This British change of attitude was in fact caused by a shift in the European balance of power and was subtly exploited by Russia, which used the events in the Balkans in 1875–76 to turn the British public against the Ottoman state and thus isolate it. Russia then launched, without any provocation, the war of 1877–78 that put a virtual end to the Ottoman presence in the Balkans. (The final blow to the Ottoman Empire was inflicted by the British themselves in 1918 on the Palestinian and Iraqi fronts.) The defeat of France in 1870 established Germany as the newest imperial power of Europe and produced a rapprochement between London and St. Petersburg, easing their fears of France, the other contender for Ottoman lands. Public opinion in England was at this time a rising political force; with its growing sense of Christian consciousness and its association with liberalism, so well expressed by Gladstone, it turned against the Ottoman state and Islam and their brand of "nationalism." Mithat paşa, the leading Ottoman modernist bureaucrat, was a friend of the British and French but became suspect as an Ottoman nationalist who viewed the modern reforms as necessary measures to strengthen the state—paradoxically, against the political ambitions of the British and French and, especially, Russia, which distrusted him fiercely. As the Ottomans became more attached to their Islamic identity and culture even as they modernized, the British, French, and Russians concluded that Muslims were motivated by religious fanaticism and opposition to "civilization" and Europe—that is, to their colonial rule. Consequently, Europeans viewed the proclamation of the constitution—the most Westernist Ottoman endeavor—as a meaningless "oriental trick" designed to preempt the Constantinople conference that sought to bring to the Balkans reforms that amounted to a partial dismemberment of the Ottoman state in the name of freedom, modernity, and progress.

The war of 1877–78 was an immense tragedy for the Ottoman state and Muslims and general: over 300 thousand Muslims were massacred and one million uprooted in the Balkans and Caucasus, and the Balkan provinces of Serbia, Romania, Montenegro (which became independent), and Bulgaria (which became autonomous) were lost. The Berlin Treaty of 1878 sealed the Ottoman defeat and, contrary to its claim that it would settle the national question in the Balkans, generated a series of new ethnic-national-religious conflicts, which had been markedly absent during four centuries of Ottoman rule, and which culminated in the creation of a group of ethnic national states, including Turkey.

A cynical view, supported by a great deal of circumstantial evidence, is that England, in order to chastise the Ottoman government for its independent stand, subtly prepared the ground for the Russian attack from which it would then "save" and "protect" it, acquiring in exchange control of its administration and resources and some of its lands. Abdulhamid faced the dilemma of defending his country against Britain while yearning for its help and seeking for ways to force London to return to Palmerstonian policy of 1844–75 of friendship and protection against Russia.

The disastrous defeat in the war and the Berlin Treaty of 1878 produced a revolution in the thinking of the Ottoman public, turning it against its own government and crystallizing demands for efficient administration, economic development, education, and material progress as well as for a consensus between the ruler and the ruled—in a word, for authentic modernization and popular participation in government rather than haphazard institutional tinkering. Various field reports by British consuls in Anatolia quoted at length in this book indicate that the war compelled rank-and-file Muslims to search rationally for the worldly causes of their state's defeat and the economic stagnation of their society and to arrive at the point of holding their leaders responsible for all that failure. While practically no Muslim regarded Islam as the cause of their plight, an increasing number blamed the religious leaders for misinterpreting the faith, failing to relate it to living society, the human being, and the land they inhabited. This was in effect the beginning of an inward-looking Islamic nationalism, triggered by foreign wars and territorial losses, which produced, as many scholars have noted, an identity change.

This was the background against which Sultan Abdulhamid developed his modernist Islamist policy after 1878. His first goal was to strengthen society by modernizing it materially and his second to keep the Muslims living in the Ottoman state united against European-backed separatism. His widespread improvements in education, transportation (railroads), urbanization, economic investments, sanitation, and so on aimed at strengthening society. The sultan emphasized Islam as an ideology and backed it with the state power and incentives in order to integrate the Arabs, the Shiites, and the millions of migrants into a cohesive Muslim-Ottoman community. Actual organic integration occurred mainly among the core people of the Ottoman state in Rumili and Anatolia. The sultan also used an Islamist ideology to mobilize and manipulate the citizens in order to gain power for himself, ignoring the essential fact that power is a worldly, material tool that, in the hands of the state, can turn a religious community into a political body and faith into a *dünyevi*, or worldly creed (if a worldly faith can be called a faith at all).

The caliphate became central to Abdulhamid's internal policy of reform and unity and to his relations with Europe and Russia. Paradoxically, it was the British who, in their naïve belief that the caliph was a kind of Muslim pope and that whoever controlled the Muslim religious leaders could control the Muslim masses, enhanced the caliphate's international visibility. In the 1790s they asked the Ottoman caliph, as the head of the Muslim community, to advise the rebellious Sultan Tipu of Mysore to accept British rule; in 1857, he was asked to tame the Sepoy rebels; and, in 1878, he was pressured to persuade the emir of Afghanistan to stop his opposition to the British and to mobilize the Muslims of Central Asia against the Russians. Meanwhile, appeals by many Muslim rulers and notables in Asia and Africa to the Ottoman caliph for help against foreign occupation in exchange for political allegiance and submission not only enhanced the caliphate's international prestige and appeal among Muslims but also turned it into a central Muslim institution.

Abdulhamid used the caliphate to support his absolutism and establish control over the bureaucracy but also to silence his critics, especially after he suspended the constitution and disbanded parliament in 1878: the restoration of these institutions became the chief ideology of the anti-Hamidian opposition, both liberal Islamic and Westernist. There is no question that Abdulhamid's use of the caliphate to consolidate the authority of the sultanate caused irreparable damage both to his own historical legacy and to the image of Islam, making it appear a faith that could be used for political purposes by whoever had the credentials to do so. On the other hand, the sultan's religious policy, despite its Islamist label, prepared the ground for the separation of faith and state. Abdulhamid preached the superiority of the faith, claiming that the caliphate had priority over the sultanate, although his real power derived from the sultanate, which he used to change society and speed up secularization. If one analyzes correctly the changes in the judiciary system, the secular training of judges, the educational reforms, the neutralization of the şeyhulislamate as a purely religious body, and so on, one comes to the surprising conclusion that these were, in fact, secularizing measures that created autonomous spheres of activity for the faith and state under the supervision of the state for lack of other bodies to fulfill the task. It is understandable, therefore that Abdulhamid showed a great interest in the separation of church and state in the United States, which he believed conformed to the Islamic standards that had prevailed in the pre-modern Ottoman state. In effect, Abdulhamid tried to revive the classic de facto separation of state and faith while seeking again, as in the old days, to maintain the fiction that the state and faith were united—this time entirely in his person. He was bitterly criticized by leading Muslim scholars—for example, Haci Muhiddin efendi, the deputy head of the Cemiyet-i Islamiye (Islamic Society) and Musa Kazim (1858–1920), three times *şeyhulislam* in 1910–18—and many others, who claimed that constitutionalism was not a "European" import but an Islamic requirement. Abdulhamid, in fact, very effectively used his credentials as caliph to institute far-reaching change that modernized and brought the Ottoman state into the present age while maintaining and strengthening the community's Islamic culture and identity. Unfortunately, his absolutism, his mistrustful and suspicious nature and hesitant character, and the personal nature of his authority obscured much of his achievement. In the end he was judged not on the basis of his remarkable accomplishments but solely on his political record as an absolutist.

The second basic goal of Abdulhamid was to maintain the territorial integrity of the Ottoman state by avoiding war and the interference of the European powers. After William Gladstone became prime minister of Britain in 1880, Abdulhamid became fully convinced that the British (and French) would use every opportunity to divide the Ottoman lands among themselves (as they actually did after World War I) and to subdue every Muslim land in the world. In order to prevent such interfer-

ence, Abdulhamid dangled before British eyes the threat of *cihad* while cultivating
the friendship of overseas Muslims through respect for their faith, culture, and values. The British and the French, at the height of their imperialism, attempted through
tortuous means to undermine Abdulhamid's caliphal authority by seeking, among
other things, to replace him with an Arab caliph; this effort did not succeed. After
Turkey abolished the caliphate in 1924, Şerif Hussein of Mecca proclaimed himself
caliph, but he was defeated by the Saudis in 1925, and the institution has been dormant ever since.

A substantial part of this work is dedicated to the study of the transformation of
the Ottoman Muslim communities under Abdulhamid into semimodern societies and
nations as the consequence of emerging regional, ethnic, and, ultimately, national
identities. Paradoxically, this transformation came about both because of and in open
contradiction to the supposedly unifying ideologies of Ottomanism and Islamism. I
have explained how universalist attachment to Islamic tradition and faith can develop
simultaneously and coexist peacefully with a commitment to a particular region, language, and community; and I have indicated how the adoption of small local and
regional administrative units, the creation of the modern educational system, the rise
of local elites, the development of regional historiography, and so on stimulated the
rise of regional and local identity and a sense of local cultural and ethnic awareness
that both reinforced the emerging "national" identity and opposed it if the "national"
failed adequately to recognize the local. Finally, I have attempted to explain how new
identities emerge and how the old ones acquire modern forms under the protective
shield of old historical and religious labels, maintaining thus a degree of continuity.
In this context I have indicated that the rise of modern Turkey was conditioned by
the introduction of capitalism, the development of a new middle class, the migration
and settlement of the Crimean, Caucasian, and Balkan Muslims and nomadic tribes,
by urbanization, professionalization, and the like. In the ultimate analysis, the new
way people saw themselves and the social position and the physical and cultural environment with which they associated themselves—that is, the fatherland or fatherlands—were ideas entertained mainly by the new middle class. These new modes of
thought, and a wide spectrum of nontraditional feelings, were part of the new identity of traditional Muslims, as they were transformed politically first into Ottoman-
Islamists and then into Turks (or Arabs, Albanians, and so on).

The new society emerging in Anatolia used the new literature, defined eventually
as Turkish, in which prose (the short story, the novel) acquired priority over poetry
to develop its readers' perception of the nation in which they lived, of themselves as
individuals, and, ultimately, of the world at large. Thus the personality and psychology of modern Turks was created. The emerging historiography, the publication of
encyclopedias, dictionaries, and biographies of Turks who contributed to science and
learning established the intellectual foundation of the modern Turkish nation. It is
essential to emphasize that *Türklük* (that is, the identity of modern Turks) was shaped
initially not by ethnicity but by Ottomanism and Islamism. Ottomanism created the
seminal notion of territorial nationhood, which in turn engendered a new sense of
solidarity, allegiance, and loyalty revolving around the *vatan*/fatherland—which did
not exist in this concrete form in the traditional Ottoman state. The territory linked
the community and the faith in a new entity, the nation. Islam, and later Islamism

under Abdulhamid, provided the psychological and ideological force that amalgamated believers into a new, politicized group and turned the religious community into a protonation by shifting to the *millet* many of the ties that had bound individuals to their faith. Ottomanism eventually helped develop a historical context in which the Turks appeared as the founders and the mainstay of the state, and their language and "ethnic" culture were seen as the distinct features of Anatolia and the Balkans, where the core of the state was located.

There is no question that Anatolia was settled from the eighth century onward by a variety of Turkic groups. They preserved their language, customs, and folk culture, but, until about the end of the nineteenth century, these "authentic" Turkish communities called themselves Muslims, not Turks or Ottomans, and had little, if any, organic association with the actual state except as its obedient servants. The new upper-class "Turkish" society that emerged toward the end of the nineteenth century included many traditional groups—bureaucrats, intelligentsia, and upper-middle-class people, who were located mainly in cities and small agrarian towns. It was conscious of its superior position vis-à-vis the rural-tribal segment of the population and identified with the state as much as with faith and tradition and modernism—the nature and degree of this identification depending upon the quality and degree of their affiliation with the state and/or community and economic interests. Ethnic nationalists eventually viewed the villagers and tribesmen who comprised a substantial part of the "authentic" ethnic Turks as an underprivileged group that was misguided culturally and exploited by the upper cosmopolitan group associated with the Empire and sultan. The option to identify ethnically with this lower class on the basis of ethnic lineage was thus created. Social mobility, modernism, economic differentiation, education, and so on, revealed the social and economic dichotomy between the upper Ottoman and lower "Turkish" societies and provided fuel for populism and ethnic nationalism, the two key ideologies that ultimately determined the fate of Ottomanism, Islamism, and Turkism.

The key to understanding the rise of Turkish nationalism lies in this complex situation, created by both concrete historical and social factors and ideologies. On the one hand, there was an upper layer of urbanites who were modernized, Islamized, and Ottomanized politically but also "Turkified" culturally and linguistically. Many of them favored the monarchy and the status quo. On the other hand, there were the destitute lower classes made up of ethnic Turks, migrants, and various marginal elements who were seeking a better life, and who had, in fact, amalgamated with one another on the basis of common faith. The modernist strata of intellectuals, consisting of Turks, Arabs, Albanians, Caucasians, Kurds, and so on, came mostly from the middle and lower middle classes. They were the backbone of the Young Turks movement and ultimately identified themselves with the lower classes against the monarchy and the notables of their own class, most of whom sided with the monarchy. Most of the middle-class modernists and traditionalists favored constitutionalism and change, although they differed about the method for achieving these ideals.

The Young Turks Revolution of 1908, although carried out formally by the officers of the Macedonian army, was actually prepared for and brought to fruition by a series of local uprisings between 1905 and 1908. These uprisings were engineered by the local landowners, merchants, and craftsmen, that is, the provincial middle class in the towns of Anatolia and Rumili. Ultimately, the control of the parliament and government was assumed by the statist-military group, which acquired control of the state apparatus. Once more, questions about the source of authority and, especially, the legitimization of that authority surfaced as key issues: that is, the debate was over control of the state by popular consensus versus imposition of power from above in the name of an ideology. Sultan Abdulhamid had claimed control of the state apparatus based on divine right. The Young Turks (members of the Committee of Union and Progress or CUP) took over the power on behalf of the "people" and the freedoms enshrined in the constitution and used free elections in the hope of gaining the community's support and legitimization. They did not, however, win a majority; indeed, the elections, held over several months beginning in the fall of 1908, produced a total of about 280 deputies, of whom only 53, mostly ethnic Turks, identified themselves openly as supporters of the CUP. The rest of the deputies, including most of the notables, landlords, merchants, and minority groups (Armenians initially supported CUP), soon united behind the opposition Ahrar (People's) and Itilaf (Alliance) Parties. These parties bore the liberal mark of Prince Sabahaddin's Decentralization and Private Enterprise Society, and they favored the cultural and social status quo but demanded a degree of autonomy for local and provincial governments, freedom of enterprise, reforms of the administrative and tax systems, and material progress. The small Union and Progress group in control of power were dedicated modernists—many were openly Westernists and some positivists—but also anticolonialist nationalists. They believed that the Ottoman Empire could be saved by unity and rapid progress to be undertaken by a government—that is, their government—dedicated to progress; they pledged support for Ottomanism and Islamism, mainly in order to preserve the state's territorial integrity. The Young Turks leadership, associated as they were with the upper middle class and with opposition to the sultan and the monarchy and branded by their selfishness and conservatism, increasingly found themselves accused of lacking true dedication to the "nation," the state, and the fatherland. It was at this point, around 1910, that the Young Turks began to take note of "Turks" in the countryside as the depressed, exploited, and underdeveloped element of the population and gradually decided to make them the "core" of the state and nation.

The discovery of Turks, whether real or imagined, at the lower end of the social ladder provided the Young Turks with an ideal but rather mythical constituency with which to identify and a way to condemn the old order that kept the Turks, the nominal masters of the state, so backward. The nationalist discourses of Ziya Gökalp, Yusuf Akçura, and Mehmet Köprülü revolved basically around two major themes: the discrediting of the old Ottoman imperial order and the finding of a new national constituency to support the rule of the Young Turks and modernism. The genesis of Turkish nationalism lay in this sociopolitical situation, which eventually resulted in making ethnicity the source of political identity. Gökalp dismissed the Ottoman order (the monarchy and imperial bureaucracy) as a social class that had oppressed and prevented the national development of the "real Turks," who somehow had managed to preserve their ethnic and cultural purity in their pristine villages. Gökalp viewed Ottomanism and Islamism (not Islam) as the instruments used by the ruling order to stifle the culture of the ethnic Turks—although much of what Gökalp considered to be "Turkish" culture was, like his own identity, of recent origin and represented essentially the culture of the new upper-class society created in the nineteenth century. Gökalp tried to distance Turks from this cosmopolitan Ottoman society by imagining the Turks of Anatolia and Rumili as constituting an ethnic community, homogenized by a common culture, language, and outlook for the future; but fully aware that his own group, in control of the power, was different in culture, behavior, and orientation from his idealized Turkish ethnic community, he urged the elites to take the civilization of the century to the "pure" villages and in turn to absorb from them their pure ethnic Turkish culture. Akçura, on the other hand, believed that nationality and nationalism was the universal ideology of the twentieth century and was rooted in the middle class, which was to be created if necessary by the state and taught to work for the nation's good. The "nation" for Akçura was a political entity rooted in *soy* or ethnic (racial) origin that had existed for centuries, even though its many subgroups remained unaware of their common identity. The duty of the state was to make all the members of the Turkish nation living in both the Ottoman Empire and abroad aware of this identity. Akçura dismissed Ottomanism and Islamism, primarily because, contrary to the opinion of some of his best friends, because Ottomanism-Islamism served no longer the interests of the state and nation. Ignoring the specific historical and social events that conditioned the rise of modern Turkey, he portrayed the Turkish nation as having existed from time immemorial and chided Turks who were preoccupied only with the Ottoman Turks and ignored those of Russia. Köprülü in turn recognized the Turkishness of Anatolian society and the early Ottoman state but condemned the latter's cosmopolitanism, although he acknowledged that practically everything Ottoman, except the political regime of the last century, was actually Turkish, as was the Islam of Rumili and Anatolia. He was not much interested in the non-Ottoman Turks.

These three ideologues were aware of the enduring influence of Ottomanism and Islamism and sought to relate them to the emerging ethnic nationalist Turkist ideology of the state or simply to discard them. Like many other nationalist ideologies of the twentieth century, they did not seek the identity of the new Turk in the complex historical and social factors that had transformed the Ottoman state but in the ethnic purity of the villages and tribes.

The discussions revolving around Ottomanism-Islamism and Turkish nationalism were analyzed in the last chapter and need not be repeated. Suffice it to say that the Republican regime conducted a Turkification and nationalization policy based partly on blueprints produced by Gökalp and Akçura but also on the crucial experience of the War of Liberation in 1919–22, which led to the establishment of the national territorial Turkish state and added a true national dimension to the Turks' identity. The democratization process, which began in 1945–46, challenged the statist, semiracist ideology of Turkism and opened the way for recognition of the obvious truth that the identity and culture of today's Turks is the product of their own historical experience as Ottomans, Muslims, and modernists. In this context, Turkish modernism appeared not as a copy of the West, despite numerous examples that would seem to support this view, but as the product of the Turks' own history and culture and concept of civilization.

This empirical analysis of the Ottoman transformation supports the idea that nation states are born as the result of a combination of economic factors (capitalism, expansion of trade and wealth), intellectual forces (enlightenment, modern education), intensive communications (press, speed of transportation), and so on, which produce new patterns of social stratification, new identities, and a culture that reflects the historical experience and identity of a given group of people as well as the "national" concepts of a willful, calculating people in control of the state. In the emerging identity there are as many older historical, social, and cultural ingredients as there are contemporary visionary, mythical, and haphazardly chosen new inputs. In the Turks' case, the society that emerged was one whose elites had developed a rational outlook, individualism, and an awareness of their nation's social, political, and historical background and, ultimately, its ethnic and linguistic affiliation. Essential to note is the fact that the new nation was taught to downgrade its own Ottoman past and nostalgia for past grandeur. Until about the nineteenth century its rational, utilitarian, and pragmatic character seemed to inhere only in the imperial bureaucracy, which used it to rule and dominate the rest of society. The bureaucracy maintained its dominant political and intellectual position by preventing the access of the rest of the population to economic power and enlightenment. The Palace School, a secular institution, was open only to bureaucrats, while the *medreses* (religious schools) taught mainly religious subjects without criticism, analysis, or self evaluation. The middle class, thanks to the modern education rapidly acquired rational modes of thought, and through capitalism it gained economic power; it used these new acquisitions not only to defy the bureaucracy but also to cement its relationship with the community, both by embracing and defending its values and cultures and by endowing it with its own rational, worldly, and pragmatic modes of thought. The new middle class became at the same time more Islamic and more worldly while developing its own literary, cultural, and communication styles, which became part of the new Turkish-Islamic modern culture. There was of course borrowing from the West (and sometimes the East) at times on an indiscriminate basis by those who failed to understand their own culture and faith. As mentioned, the new identities often emerged under old names and labels and provided the community with a sense of continuity and psychological security derived from the belief that its transformation was in harmony with its own past and identity. Its reliance on faith and the caliph increased, not only because of the psychological reassurance these afforded but also because they legitimized change and facilitated the acceptance of the new identity by reconciling the community with the culture of the living society.

In this context, Islam must be seen not as an obstacle but as the multisided, cultural-religious mechanism that combined tradition with continuity and the Islamic ethos and facilitated the adaptation to change and modernity. The revivalist movements, notwithstanding their orthodoxy, were vehicles of change and adaptation to the new order at the grassroots level that, among other things, gave respectability to and assured the wide use of the vernacular of local culture. Islam never forbade the use of the vernacular or of ethnic identity, but it did not authorize their employment as a means to dominate and destroy other ethnic groups. Furthermore, aside from a small group of dogmatists, few Muslims seem to have opposed progress—that is a better material existence and a higher form of moral life, both of which classical Islam had promoted and defended.

Through numerous citations and examples I have shown that, in the name of Islam, Abdulhamid was the architect of profound change in every aspect of Ottoman life—even of the move toward political liberalism, which he inadvertently triggered with his absolutism. In fact, he maintained and broadened the reforms of Tanzimat to such an extent as to create the basic sociocultural and educational foundations supporting the emergence of the intelligentsia that put an end to his absolutism and his reign. The sultan was an admirer of the European civilization and of Christianity's ability to rid itself of dogmatism, even as he believed in Islam's basic superiority and openness to science.

In sum, Ottoman society underwent a profound secularization that redefined the place of Islam as a source both of faith for the individual and of the nation's culture. Indeed, secularization made Islam part of what can be called the "national culture" of the new collectivity, namely, the nation. At the same time, Islam modernized it-self, not by changing the Koran or the Sunna but by redefining its relationship first to the political community (nation) and second to the individual in that commu-nity. Abdulhamid had inadvertently brought this change to maturity through his use of Islamism as an ideology both to secularize Islam and to make the society face the new world with its modern Islamic identity. Behind this process of secularization, which took place rather peacefully in the period 1876–1908, lurked grave dangers. First, there was the slow pace of development, which showed how much more was left to be done. The small group of positivists and the Young Turks' leaders in Paris (Ahmet Riza was its chief representative) claimed in private that religion in general and Islam in particular were the main obstacles to the adoption of science and, ulti-mately, to progress and a better, more harmonious world. It was therefore clear that any ruler, including Abdulhamid, using religion to justify his authority could easily be seen as an opponent of science and progress. This was an obvious ideological stand in response to Abdulhamid's own ideological use of Islam to legitimize absolutism. The positivists used the promise of freedom (constitutionalism) to gain the support of the middle class, and then used the government power thus obtained to oust the sultan and place themselves in power, castigating anyone opposed to their power as reactionary and Islamist. In the end, the modernist positivists turned secularization into secularism. This happened gradually, as nationalism, Turkification, and the de-mand for rapid progress, which were originally the natural outcome of the vast pro-cess of socioeconomic change and secularization, came increasingly to be viewed from the narrow, ideological secularist perspective. By the end of the Young Turks era in 1918, the secularization-versus-secularism clash was evident, although the first still had the upper hand. The mixture of class, faith, and ideology followed its course in the Republic. The new regime first denied the fact that the War of Independence of 1919–22 had been won by a coalition of countryside notables (some nationalists, some Islamists, some monarchists), army officers, and intellectuals, giving the credit for victory only to a handful of leaders. The Republican People's Party viewed the oppo-sition to one-party rule, which came from the community at large, as being stoked by religious reactionaries and their allies, the countryside notables.

Secularism was placed first as a principle of the RPP program 1931; it was incor-porated into the constitution as late as 1938, and has remained since then a principle—in fact the basic ideology—of the state, thus assuring the supremacy of self-proclaimed secularists. Religious "revivals" in Turkey, the proliferation of the popular brother-hoods, the battle over the wearing of the headscarf, and a myriad of other "Islamic"

actions have been reactions to this politically motivated secularism—not to secularization. The fact is that secularism provided constitutional cover and legitimacy for
the one-party rule of the RPP (Republican People's Party) until 1950 (it abandoned
it formally after 1965) and for the first two military interventions and, in part, also
the third. It has, in fact, become a major impediment to democracy, giving a small
number of people the right to take any action in the name of secularism and thus
encouraging extremist Islamists to respond in kind in the name of Islam by condemning modernism and democracy as means to promote strong rule by self-appointed
guardians of modernism.

The overwhelming majority of Turks are in the middle—they are modernist,
Kemalist, progressivist, and democratic-minded as much as they are Muslim, be they
observant or only nominally faithful. Today in Turkey, modernity, democracy, and
Islam tend to supplement and complement each other rather than stand in isolation.
A large majority of Turks view Islam the way the people of the United States view it,
as allowing full freedom for individuals to chose and believe (or not believe) in a given
faith but without involving the government in the service of one creed. This was the
original intent of the Turkish republican leaders, Mustafa Kemal Ataturk's secularism ultimately wanted to achieve this goal, which in fact has materialized. However,
self-proclaimed "secularists-Ataturkists" stubbornly refuse to acknowledge this accomplished fact both for reasons of ideology and group interest. The modernist-
Islamist conflict carries a dangerous potential and needs to be defused by defining,
in a correct fashion, the real relation of modernism and Islam. Modernism, Kemalism,
secularization, and republicanism have been accepted in their basic form by the overwhelming majority of Turkish Muslims, whatever they may chose to call themselves.
But the overwhelming majority of Turks also consider themselves *Muslims* and abide
in various ways and degrees by Islamic customs and values. The only thing still to do
is to have reliable, respected figures from both sides step forward and acknowledge
each other's position. The first move must come from the representatives of the state,
especially the army and upper echelons of the bureaucracy, the press, and academia—
the bastions of ideological secularism and the self-styled progressivists who claim to
guide and represent modernism. Some of these figures, unfortunately, are vocifer-
ous, aggressive, opportunistic, and intellectually shallow imitators, often distant from
their own culture and society. There is no doubt that a high degree of old-style
positivism, irreligiosity, political elitism, and authoritarianism prevails among them,
just as fanaticism, narrow dogmatism, bigotry, and denial of democracy prevail among
some Islamists. The secularists must acknowledge that the country is Muslim, that
all Turkish citizens are free to practice their faith (as the constitution states) in full
freedom and have no inhibition or fear about calling themselves Muslim. The Islamists in turn must openly declare that they accept modernism, Kemalism, republicanism, and the freedom to practice one's faith as one deems fit, not as a tactic to win
power but as an essential part of their Islamic faith and identity. That is this book's
basic message.

Notes

INTRODUCTION

1. Ernest Gellner, *Encounters with Nationalism* (Oxford, 1994), p. 83.
2. Ibid., p. 89.
3. Antonio Gramsci, *Selections from the Prison Notebooks of Antonio Gramsci*, ed. and trans. Q. Hoare and Geoffrey Nowell Smith (New York, 1971). These views of the uses of ideology are also expressed in George Rude, *Ideology and Popular Protest* (New York, 1980), pp. 21–22, and E. P. Thompson, "Eighteenth-Century English Society: Class Struggle without Class," *Social History* 3 (May 1978): 133–65.
4. Ernest Gellner, *Nations and Nationalism*, 3rd ed. (Ithaca, 1991), pp. 4–5.
5. Change and modernity in the Muslim world produced in the end nation-states that were neither "Eastern" nor "Western," but a new, sui generis type of Islamic state that embodied many elements of traditional society but also the material and cultural features of European culture. Social groups in the modern Muslim states, which played a supporting role in this process, sometimes grew out of existing groups; in other cases they evolved independently but then developed linkages with the old ones. For example, the new entrepreneurial middle classes resulted primarily from market relations, but the merchants, craftsmen, and religious scholars of the old order frequently changed their professions or adapted themselves to market conditions to join the entrepreneurs within the new social strata. The significance of the rise of nation-states in the Muslim world is discussed by James P. Piscatori, *Islam in a World of Nation-States* (New York, 1986). For the nature of change see the suggestive article Bernard Lewis, "The Middle East, Westernized Despite Itself," *Middle East Quarterly* 3(1996): pp. 53–61, and the references cited in this book.
6. Tuncer Baykara, *Osmanli Medeniyet Kavrami ve Ondokuzuncu Yuzyila Dair Araştirmalar* (Izmir, 1992), pp. 11–22.
7. Anthony D. Smith, *National Identity* (London, 1993), pp. 20, 21.
8. Dwight E. Lee, "The Origins of Pan-Islamism," *American Historical Review* 47 (January 1942): 279.
9. C. H. Becker, "Panislamismus," in *Islamstudien* II (Leipzig, 1932), p. 242 (reprinting an article that appeared originally in 1904).
10. See E. G. Browne, "Pan-Islamism," in *Lectures on the History of the Nineteenth Century*, ed. F. A. Kirkpatrick (Cambridge, 1902), pp. 306ff; D. S. Margoliouth, "Pan-Islamism," in *Proceedings of The Central Asian Society* (1912), pp. 3–17; Ikbal Ali Shah [Sirdar], "Ferments in the World of Islam," *Journal of the Central Asian Society* 14 (1927): 130–34; and, more recently, Wilford Cantwell Smith, *Islam in Modern History* (Oxford, 1986).

11. "Abdul Hamid, Sultan and Khalif, and the Pan-Islamic Movement," *Blackwood's Magazine* (September 1906): 291, 292. For a detailed and extensive study of Abdulhamid II's foreign policy, see F. A. K. Yasamee, *Ottoman Diplomacy: Abdulhamid II and the Great Powers, 1878–1888* (Istanbul, 1996).

12. Arminius Vambery, "Pan-Islamism," *The Nineteenth Century* 60 (July–December 1906): 548.

13. Lee, "Origins of Pan-Islamism," pp. 278–87.

14. Anthony Reid, "Nineteenth-Century Pan-Islam in Indonesia and Malaysia," *Journal of Asian Studies* 26 (February 1967): 267.

15. Benhjet Wahby bey, "Pan-Islamism," *The Nineteenth Century* 60, no. 363 (January–June 1907): 862.

16. Ibid., pp. 862–63. Emphasis in original.

17. See Browne, "Pan-Islamism"; Margoliouth, "Pan-Islamism"; Ali Shah, "Ferments."

18. See, e.g., Gabriel Charmes, *L'Avenir de la Turquie: Le panislamisme* (Paris, 1883).

19. Smith, *Islam in Modern History*, p. 82. Smith believes that the attempts to activate the Muslims' sentiment of cohesion "into concrete form, to express the unity on political or other levels, have in modern as in earlier history broken on the rocks of restive actuality" and that the "political expression that it found, in Ottoman plans of Abdul Hamid, was, to say the least, unfortunate" (p. 83). Yet Smith is exceptionally perceptive when he relates panislamism to nationalism: he finds the two ideologies to be different but *not in conflict* (p. 84). We shall explore the issue in the next chapters.

20. Nikki R. Keddie rightly claims that "Pan-Islam . . . was an important step in the transition from Islamic to national loyalties" and that "on closer examination, Pan-Islam seems to have more resemblance to modern nationalist movements than to older Islamic feelings." "Pan-Islam as Proto-Nationalism," *Journal of Modern History* 41 (March 1969): 18.

21. Lee, "Origins of Pan-Islamism," pp. 286–87.

22. Hans Kohn, *The Idea of Nationalism* (New York, 1945); Karl W. Deutsch, *Nationalism and Social Communication* (Cambridge, Mass., 1953); Benedict Anderson, *Imagined Communities: Reflections on the Origin and Spread of Nationalism*, 6th ed. (London, 1990); E. J. Hobsbawm, *Nations and Nationalism since 1780: Programme, Myth, Reality* (Cambridge, 1990); Ernest Gellner, *Nations and Nationalism* (Oxford, 1983), pp. 4–5; Anthony D. Smith, *Theories of Nationalism*, 2nd ed. (London, 1983), *National Identity* (New York, 1991), and *The Ethnic Origins of Nations* (Oxford, 1986); John Alexander Armstrong, *Nations before Nationalism* (Chapel Hill, N.C., 1982); Niyazi Berkes, *The Development of Secularism in Turkey* (Montreal, 1964); Bernard Lewis, *The Emergence of Modern Turkey* (London, 1961).

CHAPTER 1

1. See John L. Esposito, *Islamic Revivalism* (American Institute for Islamic Affairs), The Muslim World Today Occasional Paper, no. 3 (Washington, D.C., 1985).

2. See Patrick Bannerman, *Islam in Perspective: A Guide to Islamic Society, Politics, and Law* (London, 1988), pp. 157ff, and Emmanuel Sivan, *Radical Islam: Medieval Theology and Modern Politics* (New Haven, 1985), p. x.

3. See Youssef M. Choueiri, *Islamic Fundamentalism* (Boston, 1990). There is, in fact, a very rich literature on contemporary Islamic fundamentalism, which is outside of the scope of this study: see Sami Zubaida, *Islam, the People and the State: Essays on Political Ideas and Movements in the Middle East* (London, 1989); Bruce B. Lawrence, *Defenders of God: The Fundamentalist Revolt against the Modern Age* (New York, 1991); Daniel W. Brown, *Rethinking Tradition in Modern Islamic Thought* (New York, 1996); Martin E. Marty and R. Scott Appleby, eds., *Fundamentalism Observed* (Chicago, 1991); and Gilles Kepel, *The Revenge of God: The Resurgence of Islam, Christianity, and Judaism in the Modern World* (University Park, Pa., 1994).

4. John O. Voll, "Renewal and Reform in Islamic History, Tajdid and Islah," in *Voices of Resurgent Islam*, ed. John L. Esposito (New York, 1983), pp. 32, 33.

5. Ibid., p. 35.

6. See Abul 'Ala Mawdudi, *The Process of Islamic Revolution* (Lahore, 1977) and *Islamda Ihya Hareketleri* [Revival movements in Islam] (Istanbul, 1986).

7. Bradford G. Martin, *Sömürgeciliğe Karşi Afrika'da Sufi Direniş* [Sufi resistance to colonialism in Africa], trans. F. Tatlicioğlu (Istanbul, 1988); the original was titled *Muslim Brotherhoods in Nineteenth-Century Africa* (New York, 1976). According to one source, the work of J. Spencer Trimingham is also being translated into Turkish.

8. Seyyed Vali Reza Nasr, *Mawdudi and the Making of Islamic Revivalism* (New York, 1995); Charles J. Adams, "Mawdudi and the Islamic State," in *Voices of Resurgent Islam*, ed. Esposito, pp. 99–133.

9. For the history of the major popular Sufi orders, see Alexandre Popovic and Gilles Veinstein, eds., *Les Voies d'Allah* (Paris, 1996).

10. See, e.g., John L. Esposito, *Islam: The Straight Path* (New York, 1988), pp. 120–21; Wilfred Cantwell Smith, *Islam in Modern History* (New York, 1963), p. 49; Lansine Kaba, *The Wahhabiyya: Islamic Reform and Politics in French West Africa* (Evanston, Ill., 1974). For an opposite view, see, M. S. Zaharaddin, "Wahhabism and Its Influence outside Arabia," *Islamic Quarterly* 33 (1979): 146–57.

11. On these issues, see Ayman Al-Yassini, *Religion and State in the Kingdom of Saudi Arabia* (Boulder, Colo., 1985); David Holden and Richard Johns, *The House of Saud: The Rise and Rule of the Most Powerful Dynasty in the Arab World* (New York, 1981); Nadav Safran, *Saudi Arabia: The Ceaseless Quest for Security* (Cambridge, Mass., 1985); John O. Voll, *Islam, Continuity and Change in the Modern World* (Boulder, Colo., 1982); and Mohammed Almana, *Arabia Unified: A Portrait of Ibn Saud* (London, 1980). For additional background information on the Saudis, see Gary Troeller, *The Birth of Saudi Arabia: Britain and the Rise of the House of Sa'ud* (London, 1976); James P. Piscatori, ed., *Islam in the Political Process* (Cambridge, Mass., 1983); Michael C. Hudson, *Arab Politics: The Search for Legitimacy* (New Haven, 1977); and John Lewis Burckhardt, *Notes on the Bedouins and Wahabys* (London, 1831). For a friendly history of the Wahhabis, see Harry St. John Bridger Philby, *Arabia* (London, 1930), and *Arabia of the Wahhabis* (New York, 1973). The idea that the Saudis created their own version of modernity is hardly tenable. See E. Long, *The Kingdom of Saudi Arabia* (Gainesville, Fla., 1997).

12. Ahmet Cevdet, *Tarih-i Cevdet*, vol 6. (Istanbul, 1994 ed.), pp. 2647–48.

13. See Semiramis Çavuşoğlu, "The Kadizade Movement: An Attempt of Şeriat-Minded Reform in the Ottoman Empire," Ph.D. diss., Princeton University, 1990. See also Madeline C. Zilfi, "The Kadizadelis: Discordant Revivalism in Seventeenth-Century Istanbul," *Journal of Near Eastern Studies* 45 (1986): 251–69. See also chapter 10.

14. William Hunter, *The Indian Musulmans* (Calcutta, 1945; 1st. ed. 1871).

15. Even today, in modern Turkey, the historical importance of the *vakif* to society is recognized, as the government strives to maintain the "Islamic" appearance of the old *vakif* lands while using their revenues for financial operations that have nothing to do with Islam. The successor to the Ottoman Ministry of Vakifs is the General Directorate of the Vakifs, which administers about five thousand such institutions of one sort or another. Fadil Ünver, director in 1995, told a reporter from the newspaper *Cumhuriyet* on 7 May 1995, that the total annual budget of his agency amounted to about 5 trillion liras, or roughly 115 million dollars. Part of that income was derived from *vakif* lands that the Ottoman government had "left" or rented to some individuals and institutions; but other lands were appropriated. For instance, the exceptionally valuable *vakif* lands at Okmeydani in Istanbul were occupied by squatters (*gecekondu*), who were to acquire them as private property, build houses on them, and join the rank of the rich. The interesting part of Ünver's story, however, was that much of the *vakif* income was used as capital by the Vakiflar Bankasi, a regular state-owned lending and credit institution that, for mercantile reasons, refuses to sell its shares to the public. There are also in Turkey today several hundred other new types of *vakif*s established by private individuals, dedi-

cated to education, the arts, and other purposes and subject to a law modeled after the one regulating U.S. foundations. Their total worth is several billion dollars.

16. Hunter, *Indian Musulmans*, p. 176.

17. Ibid., pp. 177–78.

18. Qeyamuddin Ahmad, *The Wahhabi Movement in India* (Calcutta 1966), p. xi. See also Fazlur Rahman, *Islam* (New York, 1968), pp. 240–45; Fasihuddin Balkhi, *The Wahabi Movement* (New Delhi, 1983); three anonymous articles, "The Wahabis of India," *Calcutta Review* 50 (1870): 73–104 and 51 (1870): 177–92, 381–99; Narahari Kaviraj, *Wahabi and Farazi Rebels of Bengal* (New Delhi, 1982); Akbar S. Ahmed, *Discovering Islam: Making Sense of Muslim History and Society* (London, 1987); Gail Minault, *The Khilafat Movement: Religious Symbolism and Political Mobilization in India* (New York, 1982).

19. On Shah Waliullah, see Smith, *Islam*, pp. 51ff. See also Fazlur Rahman, s.v. "Islam" *The Encyclopedia of Islam* (E1), new ed., (Leiden 1960), pp. 240–49, and Sirdar Ikbal Ali Shah, *Islamic Sufism* (Lahore, n.d., ca. 1933).

20. Ahmad, *Wahhabi Movement*, p. 14.

21. Ibid., p. 102.

22. On the Faraizi, see Sashi Bhusan Chaudhuri, *Civil Disturbances During the British Rule in India, 1765–1857* (Calcutta, 1955).

23. Quoted by Hunter, *Indian Musulmans*, p. 209.

24. *Wahhabi Movement*, pp. 336–38.

25. See Sayyid Ahmad Khan, review of Hunter's book in *Calcutta Review* (1870): 382 (oddly, he claimed that the Indian Muslims were not anti-British but anti-Sikh); and see also K. H. Ansari, "Pan-Islam and the Making of the Early Indian Muslim Socialists," *Modern Asian Studies* 20 (1986): 509–37; Hafeez Malik, *Sir Sayyid Ahmad Khan and Muslim Modernization in India and Pakistan* (New York, 1980); and Barbara Daly Metcalf, *Islamic Revival in British India: Deoband, 1860–1900* (Princeton, 1982).

26. Ahmad, *Wahhabi Movement*, p. 337.

27. The main sources on muridism are N. A. Smirnov, *Miuridizm na Kavkaze* (Moscow, 1963); and also the recent revisionist work of Shah Ahmadov, *Imam Mansur: The National Liberation Movement in Chechnya and the Northern Caucasus at the End of the Eighteenth Century* (Grozny, 1991), in Russian.

28. See Moshe Gammer, "Shamil and the Muslim Resistance to the Russian Conquest of the North-Eastern Caucasus," Ph.D. diss., University of London, 1989. This dissertation was published in a substantially revised and enlarged form as *Muslim Resistance to the Tsar: Shamil and the Conquest of Chechnia and Daghestan* (London, 1994). See also M. Izzat Quandour, "Muridism: A Study of the Caucasian Wars of Independence, 1819–1859," Ph.D. diss., Graduate University, 1964, published (without change) first in the Republic of Kabardina Balkaria in 1995, and then in the United Kingdom, Jersey, Channel Islands in 1996, under the title *Muridism: A Study of the Caucasian Wars, 1819–1859*. The Turkish sources contain a great deal of historical information but provide only limited treatment of the intellectual aspects of the movement: see Aytek Kunduk, *Kafkasya Muridizmi, Gazavat Tarihi* (Istanbul, 1987); the review *Sebilurreşad*, nos. 510–17 (1922); and Ahmet Hazer, *Kuzey Kafkasya Hürriyet ve Istiklal Davasi* (Ankara, 1961). The standard sources in English on the Russian advance in the Caucasus and on Şamil are W. E. D. Allen and Paul Muratoff, *Caucasian Battlefields: A History of the Wars on the Turco-Caucasian Border, 1828–1921* (Cambridge, 1953), and John F. Baddeley, *The Russian Conquest of the Caucasus* (London, 1908). For a recent reappraisal of Caucasian history, see the proceedings of a conference, Marie Bennigsen Broxup et al., eds. *The North Caucasus Barrier: The Russian Advance towards the Muslim World* (London, 1992); see also Ismail Barkök, *Tarihte Kafkasya* (Istanbul, 1958), and *Islam Ansiklopedisi* (1A), new ed. (Istanbul, 1990), s.vv. "Çerkesler," "Kafkasya," "Şeyh Şamil," as well as "bulletins" published by various Caucasian organizations in Turkey, Jordan, and Russia, and the communications of the World Caucasian Conference held in Russia in 1998.

29. See the account in Franco Venturi, "La riforma dell'Alcorano, ossia il mito italiano dello sceicco Mansur," *Rivista Storica Italiana* 98 (1986): 47–77.

30. Gammer, *Shamil and the Muslim Resistance*, pp. 45–50.

31. See Cemal Gökçe, *Kafkasya ve Osmanli Imparatorluğu'nun Kafkasya Siyaseti* (Istanbul, 1979), pp. 156–82 (much of the material on the Caucasian campaign of Battal paşa in this work is based on Ottoman archival material).

32. Mansur's teachings are to be found in *Adab-ul Merziye* (Istanbul, 1869) and A. Bennigsen, "Un mouvement populaire au Caucase de XVIIIe siècle: La guerre sainte du Sheikh Mansur (1785–1794)," *Cahiers du Monde Russe et Soviétique* 5 (April–June 1964): 159–205. See also A. V. Fadeev, "The Intrinsic Social Bases of Murid Movement," *Voprosy Istorii* 16 (1955); Apollon Runovski, *Miuridizm i Gazavat po Obiasneniiu Shamilia* (Tiflis, 1863); Irene Melikoff, "L'Idéologie religieuse du muridisme caucasien," *Revue de Kartvelologie* 25 (1968): 27–45; and, for a local source, Burhaneddin al-Dagistani, *Arrisalan*, no. 720 (Cairo, 16 June 1947).

33. The literature on Şeyh Şamil is very rich. The basic source is the Arabic chronicle of Muhammad Tahir al-Qarakhi, who was Şamil's secretary; it was published in Arabic with a Russian heading, I. Iu. Krachkovskii, *Trudy Instituta Vostokovedeniia* 35 (Moscow, 1941); see also Moshe Gammer, "Shamil and the Murid Movement, 1830–1859; An Attempt at a Comprehensive Bibliography," *Central Asian Survey* 10 (1991): 189–247. In addition to the works cited above, see J. Milton Mackie, *Life of Schamyl; and Narrative of the Circassian War of Independence against Russia* (Boston, 1856); Kenneth Mackenzie, *Shamil and Circassia* (London, 1854); Vladimir Minorsky, *Studies in Caucasian History* (London, 1953); Edmund Spencer, *Turkey, Russia, the Black Sea, and Circassia* (London, 1854); M. Canard, "Chamil et Abdelkader," *Annales de l'Institut d'Études Orientales* 44 (Algiers, 1956): 231–56 (summarizing French literature on the subject); V. A. Sollogub, *La Caucase . . . reponse aux biographes parisiens de Chamil* (St. Petersburg, 1855); Mehmet Fetkerey, *Çerkeslerin Asli* (Istanbul, 1922); Mustafa Z. Hizaloğlu, *Şeyh Şamil (Şimali Kafkasya Istiklal Mücadeleleri)* (Ankara, 1958); and Tarik M. Göztepe, *Imam Şamil, Kafkasyanin Büyük Harp ve Ihtilal Kahramaninin Esareti ve Ölümü* (Istanbul, 1950). Göztepe's book went through several editions; the seventh edition was issued under the title *Dağistan Aslani Imam Şamil* (Istanbul, 1991).

34. Quandour, "Muridism," p. 101.

35. Allen and Muratoff, *Caucasian Battlefields*, p. 48.

36. Ibid., pp. 107ff.

37. Quandour, "Muridism," p. 148.

38. See Kemal H. Karpat, *Ottoman Population, 1830–1914: Demographic and Social Characteristics* (Madison, Wis., 1985); Justin McCarthy, *Death and Exile: The Ethnic Cleansing of Ottoman Muslims, 1821–1922* (Princeton, 1995).

39. The letter, written in May 1828, was apparently given by some of the Caucasian chiefs to the Ottoman authorities. This and other letters are in the Başbakanlik Arşivi and have been published in a collection of documents: *Kafkas Araştirmalari* 1 (Istanbul, 1988), docs. 34, 35, and 38, pp. 120–22.

40. Ibid., doc. 41, pp. 126–27.

41. Ibid., doc. 43, p. 131.

42. Ibid., doc. 45, pp. 132–33; see also Mustafa Budak, "1853–1856 Kirim Harbi Başlarinda Doğu-Anadolu Kafkas ve Şeyh Şamil," ibid., pp. 52–57.

43. Ibid., doc. 46, p. 134. The document in the archives is not Şamil's original communication but a summary transcribed by a clerk.

44. Ibid., docs. 46, pp. 134–35, and 45, p. 13 (24 May 1854). Other correspondence between Şamil and the Ottoman sultan appears in Sh. V. Tsagareishvili, ed., *Shamilstavlennik Sultanskoi Turtsii i Angliiskikh Kolonizatorov* (Tiblisi, 1953) (a publication of the Directorate of Archives of the Georgian SSR).

45. Mahmud Celaleddin paşa, *Mirat-i Hakikat*, 3 vols., ed. Ismet Mirağlu (Istanbul, 1983), p. 312 (his memoir deals basically with events in 1875–76).

46. For the controversy on Şamil, see Lowell Tillett, *The Great Friendship: Soviet Historians on the Non-Russian Nationalities* (Chapel Hill, N.C., 1969), pp. 130–60, 194–220. See also Moshe Gammer, "Shamil and the Ottomans: A Preliminary View,"

V. Milletlerarasi Türkiye Sosyal ve Iktisat Tarihi Kongresi: Tebliğler (Ankara, 1990), pp. 387–93, and "The Siege of Akhulogoh: A Reconstruction and Reinterpretation," *Asian and African Studies* 25 (July 1991): 103–118.

47. Mirza Kazem-Bek, "Miuridizm i Shamil," *Russkoe Slovo* (St. Petersburg, 1859).

48. For the continuing praise of Şamil, see, e.g., a pamphlet by Maryam Jameelah, *Two Great Mujahadin of the Recent Past and Their Struggle for Freedom against Foreign Rule: Sayyid Ahmad Shahid; Imam Shamil: A Great Mujahid of Russia* (Lahore, 1976). For Şamil's influence in Turkey, see Hasan Ali Aydemir, "Şeyh Şamil ve Günümüze Olan Etkileri," B.A. thesis, University of Istanbul, 1976. For Şamil's correspondence with Mehmet Ali of Egypt, after the Egyptian army defeated the Ottomans in 1839 and Ibrahim paşa promised to conquer the eastern Caucasus, see Moshe Gammer, "The Imam and the Pasha: A Note on Şamil and Muhammad Ali," *Middle Eastern Studies* 32, no. 4 (1966): 336–42.

49. Başbakanlik Arşivi (hereafter BA), Yildiz Collection (hereafter Yildiz), Sadaret Hususi Maruzat (hereafter SHM), doc. no. 172/142, March 1883.

50. On how Islam used democracy to regain spiritual strength, see the view of one leading Turkish islamist, Fehmi Koru, "Democracy and Islam: The Turkish Experiment," *Muslim Political Report*, no. 9, (September–October 1996): 1, 4–6.

51. For a general background see A. Bennigsen, "The Qadiriyah (Kunta Hajji) Tariqah in North-East Caucasus: 1850–1987," *Islamic Culture* 62 (1988): 63–78.

52. For a typical Soviet view, see O. A. Sukhareva, *Islam v Uzbekstane* (Tashkent, 1960). For bibliography, see Ann Sheehy, "The Andizhan Uprising of 1898 and Soviet Historiography," *Central Asian Survey* 14 (1966): 139–50, and Edward Dennis Sokol, *The Revolt of 1916 in Russian Central Asia* (Baltimore, 1954), pp. 56–60.

53. A. Temimi, "La Politique ottomane face à l'insurrection du constantinois en 1871," *Revue d'Histoire Maghrebine* (1980): 17.

54. For the details of this Algerian migration, see Pierre Bardin, *Algeriens et tunisiens dans l'empire ottoman de 1848 à 1914* (Paris, 1979). The involvement of the Algerians in Ottoman and Syrian politics is dealt with by Eliezer Tauber, "The Political Role of the Algerian Element in Late Ottoman Syria," *International Journal of Turkish Studies* 5 (winter 1990–91): 27–47; on the involvement of Abdelkader and successors in the Syrian reformist and nationalist movements, see S. Tufan Buzpinar, "Opposition to the Ottoman Caliphate in the Early Years of Abdulhamid II, 1877–1882," *Die Welt des Islams*, 36, no. 1 (1996): 59–89.

55. Some of the main works on the Sanusiyya are E. E. Evans-Pritchard, *The Sanusi of Cyrenaica* (Oxford, 1949); Nicola A. Ziadeh, *Sanusiyah: A Study of a Revivalist Movement in Islam* (Leiden, 1958); Bradford G. Martin, *Muslim Brotherhoods in Nineteenth-Century Africa* (Cambridge, 1976); Gabriel Charmes, *La Tunisie et la Tripolitaine* (Paris, 1883); Louis Rinn, *Marabouts et Khouan: Étude sur l'Islam en Algérie* (Alger, 1884); and Ahmad Sidqi, *Al-Harakat al-Sanusiya, Nashatiha wa Namuwwuha fi'l-Qarn al-Tasi Ashar* (Cairo, 1967).

56. See Ziadeh, *Sanusiyah*; Martin, *Muslim Brotherhoods*, ch. 4.

57. See Raphael Danziger, *Abd al-Qadir and the Algerians: Resistance to the French and Internal Consolidation, 1832–1839* (New York, 1977), and Jamil M. Abun-Nasr, *A History of the Maghrib* (Cambridge, 1971).

58. Abun-Nasr, *Maghrib*, p. 306.

59. Hayrettin Yücesoy, *Senusilik: Sufi bir Ihya Hareketi* (Istanbul, 1985), pp. 197–78.

60. Sehbenderzâde Filibeli Hilmi, *Senusiler ve Sultan Abdulhamid: Asr-i Hamidi'de Alem-i Islam ve Senusiler* (Istanbul, 1992), esp. p. 66 (for the author's view of Abdulhamid), and pp. 19–26 (for an excellent description of Sanusi lodges as centers for education, social assistance, etc.). The first edition of this work was published in Istanbul in 1909, its long title expressing Hilmi's admiration for the Sanusi: *On Üçüncü Asrin En Büyük Mütefekkir-i Islamisi Seyyid Muhammed es-Senusi: Abdulhamid Seyyid Muhammed al-Mehdi Asr-i Hamidi'de Alem-i Islam ve Senusiler*. The work deserves more elaboration than this brief citation.

61. Yücesoy, *Sanusilik*, p. 146.
62. Uwe Halbach, "'Holy War' against Czarism: The Links between Sufism and Jihad in the Nineteenth-Century Anticolonial Resistance against Russia," in *Muslim Communities Reemerge: Historical Perspective on Nationality, Politics, and Opposition in the Former Soviet Union and Yugoslavia*, ed. Edward Allworth (Durham, N.C., 1994), pp. 251–75.
63. John O. Voll, *Islam: Continuity and Change in the Modern World* (Boulder, Colo., 1982), p. 280.

CHAPTER 2

1. See Mahibbul Hasan, *History of Tipu Sultan* (Calcutta, 1971).
2. Most of the correspondence between Tipu and the Ottoman sultans is available. See Yusuf Bayur, "Maysor Sultan Tipu ile Osmanli Padişahlarindan Abdulhamid, III Selim Arasindaki Mektuplaşma," *Belleten* 12 (1948): 617–54, including the text of the original letters in Farsi and the Osmanli translations. Additional information on Tipu's embassy is found in *Cevdet Tarihi*, vol. 3 (Istanbul, 1893), pp. 270–90, passim.
3. See, for the history of the trip, Hasan, *Tipu Sultan*, pp. 128–38.
4. I. H. Qureshi, "The Purpose of Tipu Sultan's Embassy to Constantinople," *Journal of Indian History* 24 (1945): 77–84. Qureshi claimed that Haidar Ali Khan had become the most formidable power of south India, and the British saw him as the chief obstacle to their own ambitions.
5. Ibid., p. 83.
6. The Porte asked for information about Mysore and Tipu from the British ambassador in Istanbul. The British ambassador's letter is in BA, Cevdet Tasnifi collection, doc. 6455; and Bayur, "Maysor Sultan," pp. 636–37. Note that the caliph at that time was not Selim III (r. 1789–1807), as some sources identify him, but Abdulhamid I (r. 1774–89).
7. Bayur, "Maysor Sultan," p. 639.
8. The copies of these letters were found by the British in Tipu's palace. They were purchased before the Bolshevik Revolution by a Russian citizen in Paris and were catalogued in the Institute of History in Leningrad. The correspondence was published first in *Narody Azii i Afriki* AN/SSSR, no. 4 (1962), and republished in English in *Central Asian Review* 11 (1963): 72–88.
9. The original of the first letter, written on 20 September 1798 with notations in the margin, along with a Turkish translation from the Farsi, can be found in the BA, Name Defteri, doc. 9; it is reproduced in Bayur, "Maysor Sultan," p. 643, and appears in an English translation as a footnote to the earl of Mornington's letter to Tipu in *The Despatches, Minutes and Correspondence of the Marquess Wellesley During His Administration in India*, 5 vols., ed. Robert Montgomery Martin (New Delhi, 1984), vol. 1, pp. 414–17. The copy of Selim III's second letter, brought by an Ottoman emissary to Tipu, is dated 7 June 1799, that is, several weeks after Tipu's death on 4 May 1799.
10. Bayur, "Maysor Sultan," pp. 645ff.
11. Martin, *Despatches*, vol. 1, p. 417.
12. Ibid., p. 414.
13. Ibid., p. 418.
14. See Kabir Kausar, *Secret Correspondence of Tipu Sultan* (New Delhi, 1980), p. 301.
15. Ibid., p. 307.
16. Ismail Hakki Uzunçarşili, *Osmanli Tarihi*, vol. 2 (Ankara, 1949), pp. 388–89; vol. 3 (1951), pp. 31–33.
17. Some of the standard works on Atjeh are C. Snouck Hurgronje, *The Achehnese*, trans. A. W. S. O'Sullivan (Leiden, 1906); J. Kreemer, *Atjeh*, 2 vols. (Leiden, 1922–23); also *Islam Ansiklopedisi*, s.v. "Atjeh." See also James T. Siegel, *The Rope of God* (Berkeley, 1969); and Clifford Geertz, *Peddlers and Princes: Social Change and Economic Modernization in Two Indonesian Towns* (Chicago, 1963). For a detailed historical treatment, see

Anthony Reid, *The Contest for North Sumatra: Atjeh, the Netherlands, and Britain, 1858–1898* (New York, 1969).

18. Anthony Reid, "Nineteenth-Century Pan-Islam in Indonesia and Malaysia," *Journal of Asian Studies* 31 (1967): 267–83. Reid defines a movement to be panislamic "if it provides an ideological basis for cooperation between or beyond individual political units in a political struggle under the banner of Islam." Though he agrees that the caliph was a central figure, Reid rightly states that "it does not follow that every outburst of pan-islamic enthusiasm formed part of a centrally directed international movement" (p. 267).

19. Quotations are from Bertram J. O. Schrieke, as reported by Reid, "Pan-Islam," p. 273.

20. Ibid., p. 269.

21. The first document dealing with Shah Mansur's request is a memorandum sent by the grand vizier's office to the Imperial Palace reporting on a communication received from the governor in Jedda. The memorandum, signed "M" for Mehmet Emin Fuat paşa, is dated 28 Ramazan 1266 (7 August 1850). In view of the time necessary for the communication to reach Istanbul, the first contact probably took place at the beginning of 1850 or late in 1849. See BA, Irade division, Hariciye section, (hereafter Irade, Hariciye), doc. 3270. (After the Tanzimat in 1839 the "Irade" title was given to the most important government, that is, sultan's decisions. Prior to this date these orders were classified under the title "Muhimme.") For the relations between Atjeh and Istanbul, see also Reid, *Contest for North Sumatra*, pp. 69ff.

22. BA, Irade, Hariciye, doc. 3270.

23. Ibid.

24. The correspondence is in BA, Irade, Meclis-i Vala, doc. 7706, 11 December 1851. (Several documents pertaining to the same issue are listed under a single reference.)

25. Ibid. See also Mehmet Kurtulmuş, *Ace-Sumatra Dosyasi* (Istanbul, 1986).

26. BA, Irade, Meclis-i Vala, doc. 7707, 11 December 1851.

27. Ibid., doc. 7935, 11 February 1852. (The letter is signed "M," again for Mehmet Emin Fuat paşa, the reformist minister accused nowadays of being one of the chief "culprits" of European-type modernization.)

28. BA, Irade, Meclis-i Mahsus (Mahsusa), doc. 1524, 29 April 1869.

29. Ibid. See the memorandum of the Porte addressed to the sultan in this file, which contains several documents on this subject.

30. Ibid.

31. BA, Irade, Hariciye, doc. 15586, 2 September 1873.

32. The newspapers *Basiret* and *La Turquie* of May and June 1873 contain detailed accounts about these events. There is also a rather comprehensive account in Reid, *Contest for North Sumatra*, pp. 119–29.

33. BA, Idare, Hariciye, doc. 15586, draft of the memo addressed to the Dutch. Further investigation in Dutch archives may determine whether the memorandum was actually delivered.

34. BA, Yildiz, sec. 14, folder 8, doc. 253, 24 June 1886. See report of Ali Galip, the Ottoman consul general in Bombay.

35. Siegel, *Rope of God*, pp. 11ff.

36. Ibid.

37. Anthony Reid has pointed out that Marie W. F. Treub, a political adviser to the Dutch economic interests in east India, defined the native resistance movement as consisting of nationalism, communism, and Islam. (This view was also Soekarno's basic ideology. He "rejected the intellectual's mutual distrust of the common man as an opponent of modernist enlightenment and instead argued that the folk possessed a progressive general will"; see Soekarno, *Nationalism, Islam and Marxism*, trans. Karel H. Warouw and Peter D. Weldon [Ithaca, 1970]). For the relationship among Islam, social change, and nationality, see Anthony Reid, *The Indonesian National Revolution, 1945–1950* (Hawthorn, Vic., 1974); and *The Blood of the People: Revolution and the End of Traditional Rule in Northern Sumatra* (Kuala Lumpur, 1979).

38. For the history of Comoro, see Malyn D. D. Newitt, *The Comoro Islands: Struggle against Dependency in the Indian Ocean* (Boulder, Colo., 1984).

39. The letter is in the BA, Irade, Meclis-i Mahsus, Heyet-i Vekile, 11 January 1865. (The documents are not numbered.)

40. For a rather extensive roster of names and a history of Comoro, see Jean Martin, *Comores: Quatre îles entre pirates et planteurs*, 2 vols. (Paris, 1983).

41. BA, Idare, Meclis-i Mahsus, Heyet-i Vekile, letter of the council, 12 October 1862.

42. Ibid.

43. Ibid., memorandum of 12 January 1865.

44. The classic work on Yakub bey is Demetrius Charles Boulger, *The Life of Yakoob Beg; Athalik Ghazi, and Badaulet; Ameer of Kashgar* (London, 1878); see also Boulger, *Central Asian Portraits: The Celebrities of the Khanates and the Neighboring States* (London, 1880). For more recent and objective appraisals see Ho-dong Kim, "The Muslim Rebellion and the Kashgar Emirate in Chinese Central Asia, 1864–1877," Ph.D. diss., Harvard University, 1986, and G. J. Alder, *British India's Northern Frontier, 1865–1895* (London, 1963). For additional literature, see Wen-Djang Chu, *The Moslem Rebellion in Northwest China, 1862–1878* (The Hague, 1966); Henry Trotter, "The Amir Yakub Khan and Eastern Turkistan in Mid-Nineteenth Century," *Journal of the Royal Central Asian Society* 4, part 4 (1917): 95–112; Tsing Yuan, "Yakub Beg (1820–1877) and the Moslem Rebellion in Chinese Turkistan," *Central Asiatic Journal* 6 (1961): 134–67; G. Macartney, "Eastern Turkistan: The Chinese Rulers over an Alien Race," *Proceedings of the Central Asian Society* (March 10, 1909); Robert B. Shaw, "Central Asia in 1872," *Proceedings of the Royal Geographical Society of London* 16 (Session of 1871–72) (London, 1872): 395–409; Ch'enching Lung, "Çin ve Bati Kaynaklarina Göre 1828 Isyanlarindan Yakub Bey'e Kadar Doğu Türkistan Tarihi," Ph.D. diss., Ankara University, 1967; Akdes Nimet Kurat, "Atalik Gazi Yakub Bek" (manuscript, 1930, Istanbul Türkiyat Enstitüsü Kütüphanesi Library); and Ram Lakhan Shukla, *Britain, India and the Turkish Empire, 1853–1882* (New Delhi, 1973).

45. Boulger, *Yakoob Beg*, p. 57.

46. On these missions and foreign relations of Yakub bey, see Paul Henze, "The Great Game in Kashgaria: British and Russian Missions to Yakub Bey," *Central Asian Survey* 8 (1989): 61–95.

47. For the Russian conquest of Central Asia, see Seymour Becker, *Russia's Protectorates in Central Asia: Bukhara and Khiva, 1865–1924* (Cambridge, 1968). The diplomatic aspect is best described in Walter Millar Thorburn, *The Great Game: A plea for a British Imperial Policy* (Toronto, 1875); see also Peter Hopkirk, *The Great Game: The Struggle for Empire in Central Asia* (London, 1990).

48. The *Lutfi Vekainamesi*, as it was called, was published for the first time as *Vak'a-nuvis Ahmed Lutfi Efendi Tarihi*, ed. M. Münir Aktepe (Ankara, 1988–90). Lutfi's description of the government's supposed indifference to Yakub bey's envoy is rather subjective. Chroniclers generally submitted their "history," usually in successive volumes, to the ruler of the time, most likely the successors to the rulers under whom the events recorded took place. Lutfi recorded the events taking place after 1825. He replaced the famous Cevdet paşa (discussed in this study in another context) about 1878–79 and presented the fourteenth volume to Sultan Abdulhamid II probably around 1890. One may assume that he wanted to praise Abdulhamid's interest in overseas Muslims by stressing his predecessor's lack of concern for them.

49. BA, Irade, Dahiliye, doc. 15524.

50. Ibid., doc. 46454 of 27 *Rebiyülevvel* 1290 (25 May 1873). Information on the visit, based on British diplomatic correspondence, is provided also by Shukla, *Britain, India*, p. 125.

51. BA, Irade, Dahiliye, letter of 28 *Rebiyülevvel* 1290 (26 May 1873).

52. Ibid., doc. 46753 of 13 August 1873.

53. Shukla, *Britain, India*, pp. 126–27.

54. BA, Yildiz, sec. 33, folder 91, doc. 1481. The report does not have a date, but its content indicates that it was written in late 1878 or early 1879; it provides one of the best descriptions available of events in Kaşgaria in 1876 and 1877.

55. Ibid.

56. BA, Irade, Dahiliye, doc. 49343, 12 August 1875.

57. Ibid., doc. 49059.

58. Eugene Schuyler, *Turkistan: Notes of a Journey in Russian Turkistan, Khokand, Bukhara and Kuldja*, 2 vols. (New York, 1876), pp. 315–60 passim.

59. BA, Irade, Dahiliye, doc. 49343, 12 August 1875.

60. Ibid., doc. 60716, 8 April 1877 (24 *Rebiyülevvel* 1294). The best day-to-day information on these visits, including occasional information on what was discussed, as well as on developments in Central Asia could be found in the newspaper *Basiret*, the nationalist Islamist publication. Issue numbers 1913 (20 September 1876) to 2400 (at the end of 1877) contain some key news.

61. BA, Irade, Dahiliye, doc. 60710, 10 April 1877.

62. Henze, "Great Game," pp. 86–88.

63. BA, Yildiz, sec. 33, folder 91/33, doc. 1638 of 25 *December* 1879. (The *rumi* and *hicri* dates are 13 Kanun-i evvel 1295 and 10 Muharrem 1297). The registrar of the document uses the term *elçi* (ambassador) in referring to Eddai Yakub efendi.

64. Ibid., file 36, doc. 1211 (n.d.).

65. Ibid., sec. 14, file 9, doc. 382 of 20 Zilhicce 1298 (13 November 1881), "Memorandum on the later situation of Kashgar submitted as requested by Bey Kuli Bey the son of the late Yakub Khan, the amir of Kashgar." (A version of this report in modern Turkish by Abdullah Yaman appeared in *Doğu Türkistanin Sesi* 1 [December 1984]: 50–52.)

66. The newspaper *Russian World* of 17 July 1877 accused England of conspiring against Russia in Kaşgar and of inciting more Muslim rulers to follow the example of Yakub bey by accepting the supremacy of the caliph; see Shukla, *Britain, India*, p. 131. See also Hopkirk, *The Great Game*.

67. See, on the general topic of the Gulf, Gary Troeller, *The Birth of Saudi Arabia: Britain and the Rise of the House of Sa'ud* (London, 1976); Sheikh Mohammad Iqbal, *Emergence of Saudi Arabia: A Political Study of King Abd al-Aziz ibn Saud, 1901–1953* (Srinagar, 1977); Robert Lacey, *The Kingdom* (London, 1981); Harry St. John Bridger Philby, *Sa'udi Arabia* (New York, 1955), and *Arabia of the Wahhabis* (New York, 1973); and R. Bayly Winder, *Saudi Arabia in the Nineteenth Century* (New York, 1965); the politics of the area and the history of the ruling families in the Gulf are treated at length in J. B. Kelly, *Arabia, the Gulf and the West* (London, 1980). See also chapter 1.

68. BA, Irade, Dahiliye, doc. 33349, 9 July 1862.

69. Ibid., the letter of Mehmet Namik paşa, "Muşir-i Ordu-yu Irak ve Vali-i Bagdat," 21 May 1862 (as usual, he spelled the Arabic names according to Turkish phonetics).

70. See Ahmet Nuri Sinapli, *Şeyhül Vüzera, Serasker Mehmed Namik Paşa* (Istanbul, 1987).

71. The correspondence concerning Emirs Faisal and Abdullah is in BA, Irade, Meclis-i Mahsus, folder 1381, communications from 23 November 1866 to 4 January 1867. According to letters written by the governors of the Hicaz and Baghdad, Nejd was a *kaymakamlik* in the 1860s and was attached to the governorate of Baghdad. The information presented here is only a synopsis of about three hundred pages of documentary information. For greater detail see Frederick F. Anscombe, *The Ottoman Gulf: The Creation of Kuwait, Saudi Arabia, and Qatar* (New York, 1997).

72. BA, Irade Meclis-i Mahsus, doc. 1381.

73. Ibid., letter of Mehmed Namik paşa, 3 October 1866.

74. Ibid., letter of 23 November 1866.

75. BA, Irade, Dahiliye, doc. 33349, 8 July 1862.

CHAPTER 3

1. For a survey of the Russian historiography on relations with their Muslim subjects, see Seymour Becker, "The Muslim East in Nineteenth Century Russian Popular Historiography," *Central Asian Survey* 5 (1986): 25–48. For a comprehensive account of the

Russian efforts to convert Muslims see Chantal Lemercier-Quelquejay, "Les Missions orthodoxes en pays musulmans de Moyenne- et Basse-Volga: 1552–1865," *Cahiers du Monde Russe et Soviétique* 8 1967: 369–403. On the Golden Horde, see Bertold Spuler, *Die goldene Horde: Die Mongolen in Russland, 1223–1502* (Wiesbaden, 1965), and Charles J. Halperin, *Russia and the Golden Horde* (Bloomington, Ind., 1987). See also Donald Ostrowski, "The Mongol Origin of Muscovite Political Institutions," *Slavic Review* 49 (winter 1991): 525–43.

2. Quoted by Jaroslaw Pelenski, *Russia and Kazan: Conquest and Imperial Ideology (1438–1560s)* (The Hague, 1974), p. 191. This is one of the most detailed studies in English based on Russian primary sources that deals with the genesis of Russian anti-Islamic messianism.

3. Ibid., chap. 9, "The Religious Struggle against the Kazanian Tatars: Comments, Projects and Exhortations," pp. 177–209.

4. Ibid., p. 208. Russian historiography attempted to describe Kazan and other conquered Muslim lands as having been inhabited by Russians who were forced out by bellicose "pagans" (e.g., *Kazanskaia Istoriia*, written by Ioann Glazatyi in 1564 and based on unreliable sources). Later books such as *Kniga Stepennaia tsarskago rodosloviia*, by an unnamed author (2 vols.) (Moscow, 1617), defended the idea of expansion to the east, pp. 122ff. See also A. Bennigsen and Chantal Lemercier Quelquejay, *La Presse et le Mouvement national chez les mussulmans de Russie avant 1920* (Paris, 1964).

5. The question of Russia's Muslims and the *hac* is treated in D. Lombard, "L'Empire ottoman vu d'Insulinde," in *Passé Turco-Tatar, Présent Soviétique* (Louvain, 1986), pp. 158ff. See Azade-Ayse Rorlich, *The Volga Tatars: A Profile in National Resilience* (Stanford, 1986).

6. For a comprehensive treatment of this issue, see *Islam Ansiklopedisi* (IA, new ed.), s.vv. "Kirim" and "Kazan," and Özalp Gökbilgin, *1532–1577 Yillari Arasinda Kirim Hanliği'nin Siyasi Durumu* (Ankara, 1973).

7. See Becker, "Muslim East," pp. 29–45.

8. On Crimea, see Alan W. Fisher, The Russian Annexation of the Crimea, 1772–1783 (Cambridge, 1970), pp. 57ff., and Müstecib Ülküsal, Dobruca ve Türkler (Ankara, 1966).

9. For the Crimean migration and community, see Kemal H. Karpat, "Ottoman Urbanism: The Crimean Migration to Dobruca and the Establishment of Mecidiye," *International Journal of Turkish Studies* 3 (winter 1984–85): 1–26, and relevant bibliography therein. For the current situation, see Gyorgy Lederer, "Islam in Romania," *Central Asian Survey* 15 (1996): 349–68. The second international congress of Tatars, mostly Crimeans, was held in Constanta-Dobruca (Romania) on 6–10 October 1998.

10. Mahmut Celaleddin paşa, *Mirat-i Hakikat*, 3 vols., ed. Ismet Miroğlu (Istanbul, 1983), pp. 27–28. Note that there were two other prominent Mahmut Celaleddin paşas in the nineteenth century: (1) Damat Mahmud Celaleddin paşa (1838–1884), husband of Cemile sultan, took an active role in the deposition of Abdulaziz and was killed in prison in Taif in 1884; (2) Mahmud Celaleddin paşa (1853–1903), the husband of Seniha sultan and father of Prince Sabaheddin and Lutfullah, who was of Caucasian origin, went into exile in 1899 and died in Brussels. The family played a seminal role in the Young Turks movement in 1902–1908.

11. Gilles Veinstein, ed., *La Question du califat*, (Paris, 1994), pp. 25–36; this is a publication of the Institute of Oriental Languages and Civilizations.

12. Ram Lakhan Shukla, *Britain, India and the Turkish Empire, 1853–1882* (New Delhi, 1973), p. 25.

13. See Kemal H. Karpat, "The Impact of Hungarian Refugees in the Ottoman Empire, 1849–1851," *Hungarian Heritage Review* (March 1990): 131–53.

14. Mustafa Reşit paşa, *Hristiyan Tebaya Dair Layiha* (Istanbul University Library), I. M. Kemal Inal manuscripts, nos. 2612, 2975.

15. See Roderic Davison, *Reform in the Ottoman Empire, 1856–1876* (Princeton, 1963). Ilan Karmi, "The Tanzimat and the Non-Muslims, 1839–1878: The Implications of the Reforms in Nineteenth-Century Ottoman Empire on the Legal, Political, Economic and Social Status of Non-Muslims" Ph.D. diss., University of Wisconsin–Madison, 1986.

16. BA, Yildiz, sec. 18, folder 39, doc. 1858, 17 November 1879.

17. Ibid., carton 39, doc. 1863, 15 February 1849.

18. BA, Irade, Dahiliye, doc. 12447, session of 27 November 1849.

19. See ibid., 24 April 1850.

20. The negative reaction is portrayed vividly in Cevdet Ahmet paşa, *Tezakir*, ed. Cavid Baysun (Ankara, 1953–67), pp. 61–70; see also Davison, *Reform*, chap. 2.

21. Cevdet paşa, *Tezakir*, pp. 64–89 (see especially *tezkire* (memorandum) 9 and 10). It should be noted that most publications on the Ottoman bureaucracy deal almost exclusively with the Foreign Ministry and ignore the position and views of other ministries; see Carter Findley, *Ottoman Officialdom: A Social History* (Princeton, 1989).

22. See Davison, *Reform*, chap. 2.

23. On Russia's expansion into Central Asia, see Michael Rywkin, ed., *Russian Colonial Expansion to 1917* (London, 1988); Richard A. Pierce, *Russian Central Asia, 1867–1917: A Study in Colonial Rule* (Berkeley, 1960); George Nathaniel Curzon, *Russia in Central Asia in 1889 and the Anglo-Russian Question* (London, 1889); H. Sutherland Edwards, *Russian Projects against India from the Czar Peter to General Skobeleff* (London, 1885); H. Blerzy, "Les Révolutions de l'Asie centrale," *Revue Deux Mondes* 5 (1874): 138, 141–44; G. Lejean, "La Russie et l'Angleterre," *Revue Deux Mondes* 69 (1867): 702ff.; Gabriel Charmes, "La Situation de la Turquie," *Revue Deux Mondes* 47 (1881): 741; Friedrick von Hellwald, *The Russians in Central Asia* (London, 1874); Eugene Schuyler, *Turkistan: Notes of a Journey in Russian Turkistan, Kokand, Bukhara, and Kulja* (New York, 1876); R. Bosworth Smith, *Muhammad and Muhammadanism* (Lahore, [1974]), pp. 246–47; M. A. Tretev, *Russia and England in Central Asia* (Calcutta, 1876); Arminius Vambery, *Sketches of Central Asia* (London, 1868) and *Central Asia and the Anglo-Russian Frontier Question: A Survey of Political Papers* (London, 1874).

24. Shukla, *Britain, India*, p. 28.

25. See Beatrice F. Manz, *The Rise and Rule of Tamerlane* (New York, 1989). For a broad background, see Zeki Velidi Togan, *Bugünkü Turkili Turkistan ve Yakin Tarihi* (Istanbul, 1981), and V. V. Bartold, *Histoire des turcs d'Asie centrale* (Paris, 1945). For Turkish translation, see V. V. Bartold, *Moğol Istilasina Kadar Turkistan*, trans. Hakki D. Yildiz (Ankara, 1990).

26. H. Baki Kunter, "Tarsus'taki Türkistan Zaviyelerin Vakfiyeleri," *Vakiflar Dergisi* 6 (Istanbul 1965): 31–64. See also the classic source, Shams al-Din Ahmad Aflaki, *Manaqib al-'Arifin*, ed. Tahsin Yazici, 2 vols. (Ankara, 1976–80).

27. Kunter, "Tarsus'taki."

28. Ali Arslan, "Türkistan ile Osmanli Türkiyesi Arasindaki Ilmi Münasebetler (XV–XIX. yüzyillarda)," Ph.D. diss., University of Istanbul, 1988, pp. 48–87. One of the most comprehensive studies in English is Dina Le Gall, "The Ottoman Naqshbandiyya in the Pre-Mujaddidi Phase: A Study in Islamic Religious Culture and Its Transmission," Ph.D. diss., Princeton University, 1992. For a recent conference on Ahmet Yesevi held in Turkistan in October 1990, see my account in the newsletter of the Association for Central Asian Studies (ACASIA), (1991).

29. Adnan Adivar, *Osmanli Türklerinde Ilim* (Istanbul, 1982), pp. 36ff. See also Mehmet Arif, "Devlet-i Osmaniye'nin Teessüs ve Takarruri Devrinde Ilim ve Ulema," *Darülfünun Edebiyat Fakültesi Mecmuasi* 1 (1914): 137–44.

30. For the list of şeyhs see Arslan, "Türkistan," pp. 127–37.

31. The Ottoman classical sources such as *Tarihi Peçevi, Tarihi Selaniki, Netayic-ul Vukuat*, etc., contain useful information on Uzbek-Ottoman relations. A detailed chronological survey is in J. Audrey Burton, "Relations between the Khanate of Bukhara and Ottoman Turkey, 1558–1702," *International Journal of Turkish Studies* 5 (winter 1990–91): 83–104. Two dissertations that contain good information on Ottoman sources dealing with Central Asia are Ayten Sariyar, "XV ve XVI. Yüzyillarda Osmanli-Özbek Münasebetleri," Ph.D. diss., University of Istanbul, 1965, and Mustafa Budak, "Osmanli-Özbek Siyasi Münasebetleri (1510–1740)," (Ph.D. diss., University of Istanbul, 1987. For a comprehensive treatment, see Mehmet Saray, *Rus Işgali Devrinde Osmanli Devleti ile*

Türkistan Hanliklari Arasindaki Siyasi Münasebetler (1775–1875) (İstanbul, 1984). A very useful collection of documents on these relations was published by the General Directorate of Turkish Archives, *Osmanli Devleti ile Kafkasya, Türkistan ve Kirim Hanliklari Arasindaki Münasebetlere Dair Arşiv Belgeleri*: vol. 1, *1687–1908 yillari arasi* (İstanbul, 1992), referred to hereafter as *Osmanli Devleti—Orta Asya Münasebetleri*.

32. *Osmanli Devleti—Orta Asya Münasebetleri*, doc. 41, pp. 98–100 (original in BA, Hatt-i Humayun, doc. 36547).

33. Ibid., doc. 46, p. 103 (original in BA, Hatt-i Humayun (imperial decrees), doc. 76/6). There are several other communications dealing with Shah Haydar's embassy.

34. BA, Yildiz, sec. 14, carton 38, doc. 553/618, ca. 13 February 1894.

35. Ibid. Cevdet uses the term *temeddün*, which can be translated as "in need of settlement and civilization."

36. See *Osmanli Devleti—Orta Asya Münasebetleri*, doc. 73 (original in BA, Irade, Hariciye, doc. 13785).

37. BA, Yildiz, sec. 18, carton 39, doc. 1863, 15 February 1894.

38. BA, Irade, Meclis-i Mahsus, doc. 1627 of 7 October 1870. The language of the handwritten letter is an interesting mixture of Arabic words, Ottoman political expressions, and native terms.

39. For other examples, see the communications between Istanbul and Central Asia in *Osmanli Devleti—Orta Asya Münasebetleri* and sources cited in note 31.

40. *Basiret*, 31 January 1877.

41. Ibid., 13 December 1876.

42. Ibid., 20 September 1876; 10 December 1876; 8 February 1877.

43. Ibid., 8 February 1877.

44. See chapter 2, and Arminius Vambery, "Pan-Islamism," in *The Nineteenth Century* 60 (July–December 1906), 547–58; 61 (January–June 1907), 860–72.

45. *Russian World*, 17 July 1877, cited by Shukla, *Britain, India*, p. 131.

46. *Lytton Papers*, MSS. Eat. E. 218 (India Office Library), cited by Shukla, *Britain, India*, pp. 131–32.

47. *Basiret*, 8, 10 February 1877.

48. Dwight E. Lee, "A Turkish Mission to Afghanistan, 1877," *Journal of Modern History* 13 (1941): 337. The wide-ranging implications of this mission are discussed in several different contexts in this article.

49. Saray, *Rus Işgali Devrinde*, pp. 26–45.

50. Mahmud Celaleddin paşa, *Mirat-i Hakikat*, pp. 316–19. On Layard's embassy, see Yuluğ Tekin Kurat, *Henri Layard'in Istanbul Elçiliği: 1877–1880* (Ankara, 1968).

51. Celaleddin, *Mirat-i Hakikat*, p. 517; also BA, Yildiz, sec. 31, file 86, doc. 156 (n.d., ca. 1877).

52. Celaleddin, *Mirat-i Hakikat*, p. 517.

53. Azmi Ozcan, "Indian Muslims and the Ottomans: A Study of Hindu-Muslim Attitudes to Pan-Islamism and Turkey," Ph.D. diss., University of London, 1990.

54. BA, Yildiz, sec. 36, file 18, doc. 139/9, 16 March 1877.

55. Shukla, *British, India*. pp. 120–55 passim.

56. The mission's report is in BA, Irade, Hariciye, 1, doc. 16873. See also M. Cavid Baysun, "Şirvanizade Ahmet Hulusi Efendinin Efganistan Elçiliğine Aid Vesikalar," *Tarih Dergisi* (September 1948): 151–56; Lee, "Turkish Mission," p. 851; Özcan, "Indian Muslims"; Mehmet Saray, *Rus Işgali Devrinde Osmanli Devleti ile Turkistan Hanliklari Arasindaki Siyasi Münasebetter (1775–1875)* (İstanbul, 1984), pp. 15ff., reproducing Hulusi efendi's memoirs; and Shukla, *British, India* , pp. 135ff. Shukla's account is based mainly on British diplomatic dispatches and a few published articles.

57. Letter reproduced in Lee, "Turkish Mission," p. 841.

58. Celaleddin, *Mirat-i Hakikat*, p. 311.

59. Ibid., pp. 311–12.

60. For the correspondence and other relevant material on these events, see BA, Irade, Dahiliye, nos. 61009–61133/January–April 1878.

61. See the excellent publication about the Caucasian front by an insider who was an aide to Ahmed Muhtar paşa, the commander of the Anatolian armies in 1877, Mehmet Arif, *Başimiza Gelenler* (Istanbul, 1973). Unfortunately, General Kondukov, in his interesting memoirs, does not discuss the war of 1877–78; see *General Musa Kondukov'un Anilari*, prepared by Murat Yağan (Istanbul, 1978), a publication of the Kafkas Cultural Society.

62. Celaleddin, *Mirat-i Hakikat*, pp. 312–14.

63. I. V. Evdokimov, "Panislamizm i Panturkizm," *Voennyi Sbornik* 12 (1911): 85–112.

CHAPTER 4

1. For background, see Kemal H. Karpat, *An Inquiry into the Social Foundations of Nationalism in the Ottoman State: From Social Estates to Classes, from Millets to Nations,* Woodrow Wilson School of International Relations (Princeton, 1973).

2. Hanna Batatu, *The Old Social Classes and the Revolutionary Movements of Iraq* (Princeton, 1978), introduction, esp. pp. 11, 14ff.

3. See Haim Gerber, *The Social Origins of the Modern Middle East* (Boulder, 1987). Gerber relies conceptually on Barrington Moore's *Social Origins of Dictatorship and Democracy* (Boston, 1967) to analyze the Ottoman Land Code of 1858. See also Ann Elizabeth Mayer, ed., *Property, Social Structure and Law in the Modern Middle East* (Albany, 1985); A. M. Shah et al., eds., *Social Structure and Change,* 4 vols. (The Hague, 1996–97) (this book dealing with India offers many concepts valid for the Middle East); Keiko Kiyotaki, "Ottoman Land Policies in the Province of Baghdad, 1831–1881," Ph.D. diss., University of Wisconsin–Madison, 1997; Tsugitaka Sato, *State and Rural Society in Medieval Islam: Sultans, Muqtas and Fallahun* (London, 1997); Albert Hourani, "Ottoman Reform and the Politics of Notables," in *Beginnings of Modernization in the Middle East,* ed. William R. Polk and Richard L. Chambers (Chicago, 1968), pp. 41–68; and Kemal H. Karpat, "The Land Regime, Social Structure, and Modernization in the Ottoman Empire," in ibid., pp. 69–92. For additional information on the political role of the new middle classes, see Philip S. Khoury, *Urban Notables and Arab Nationalism: The Politics of Damascus, 1860–1920* (New York, 1983); and C. A. O. van Nieuwenhuijze, ed., *Commoners, Climbers and Notables* (Leiden, 1977), esp. Kemal H. Karpat, "Some Historical and Methodological Considerations Concerning Social Stratification in the Middle East: Property Rights and Social Structure," pp. 83–101 and chapters 15, 16.

4. For the early pressure to commercialize agriculture, see Suraiya Faroqhi, *Towns and Townsmen of Ottoman Anatolia* (Cambridge, 1984); Çağlar Keyder and Faruk Tabak, eds., *Landholding and Commercial Agriculture in the Middle East* (Albany, 1991); and Şevket Pamuk, *The Ottoman Empire and European Capitalism, 1820–1913* (New York, 1987). For the size of land properties in the Ottoman Empire, see Bruce McGowan, *Economic Life in Ottoman Europe: Taxation, Trade and the Struggle for Land, 1600–1800* (Cambridge, 1981), and David Dean Commins, *Islamic Reform: Politics and Social Change in Late Ottoman Syria* (New York, 1990). For general history, see Ahmet Tabakoğlu, *Türk Iktisat Tarihi* (Istanbul, 1986).

5. For background, see Tevfik Yazgan, "1840–1910 Osmanli Tarim Ekonomisine Giriş: Yapisal Sorunlar, Tarimsal Kredi ve Tarim Politikasi," Ph.D. diss., University of Istanbul, 1980.

6. Kiyotaki, "Ottoman Land Policies," pp. 144–45.

7. For further information and bibliographical data, see Karpat, *Inquiry.*

8. For some background information, see Halil Inalcik, *Tanzimat ve Bulgar Meselesi* (Ankara, 1943; repr. 1992); Traian Stoianovich, "The Conquering Balkan Orthodox Merchant," *Journal of Economic History* 22, no. 2 (June 1960): 234–313; and Kemal H. Karpat, "Millets and Nationality: The Roots of the Incongruity of Nation and State in the Post-Ottoman Era," in *Christians and Jews in the Ottoman Empire: The Functioning*

of a Plural Society, ed. Benjamin Braude and Bernard Lewis, 2 vols. (New York, 1980), vol. 1, pp. 141–70. For a special concept of bourgeoisie, see Fatma M. Göcek, *Rise of the Bourgeoisie, Demise of Empire: Ottoman Westernization and Social Change* (New York, 1996).

9. Keyder and Tabak, *Landholding*, passim.

10. For the history of the Ottoman Jews and the relevant bibliography, see Stanford J. Shaw, *The Jews of the Ottoman Empire and the Turkish Republic* (New York, 1991), and Aron Rodrigue, *French Jews, Turkish Jews* (Bloomington, 1990), a book dealing with the Ottoman Jews' modernization.

11. For the relations between the Muslims and Christians, see Jeremy Salt, *Imperialism, Evangelism, and the Ottoman Armenians, 1878–1896* (Newbury Park, U.K., 1993). See also Orhan Koloğlu, *Abdulhamid Gerçeği*, 2nd ed. (Istanbul, 1987), pp. 181ff., and Roderic H. Davison, "Turkish Attitudes Concerning Christian-Muslim Equality in the Nineteenth Century," *American Historical Review* 59 (April 1954): 853ff. The impact of European occupation on elite formation in North Africa is admirably analyzed by Roger Le Tourneau, "Position sociale et culturelle de l'élite dirigeante d'Afrique du Nord," *Cahiers de Linguistique d'Orientalisme et de Slavistique*, nos. 1–2 (1973): 7–27.

12. See Kemal H. Karpat, "Gli stati balcanici e il nazionalismo: L'immagine e la realtà," *Quaderni Storici* 28 (1993): 679–718. The very social change that occurred as the consequence of the Christians rapid opening to the West exposed them to and made them the early beneficiaries of the new modes of communication which initially had economic motives. For instance, the first private newspaper in the Ottoman state was (note the title) *Le Mercure Oriental*, published in 1796 by a French merchant, Marti-Joseph Arnould. The paper proposed to provide information to Europeans to sell their industrial products and find source of raw material in the Ottoman Empire. The paper also conveyed a strong message that a determined elite can change the course of history, that politics and economics were inseparable and had superseded religious motives. See Gerard Groc, "*Le Mercure Oriental*: Une tentative de presse commerciale ou le premier journal privé" *Toplum ve Ekonomi*, 7, 1994: 27–48.

13. Kemal H. Karpat, *Ottoman Population, 1830–1914* (Madison, Wis., 1985), chap. 4. Two important works on migration, based largely on the same archival sources used by this writer for a forthcoming publication, have been published in Turkey: Nedim Ipek, *Rumeli'den Anadolu'ya Türk Göçleri, 1877–1890* (Ankara, 1994); and Ahmet Halaçoğlu, *Balkan Harbi Sirasinda Rumeli'den Türk Göçleri, 1912–1913* (Ankara, 1994). The earlier work of Bilal Şimşir, *Rumeli'den Türk Göçleri*, 3 vols. (Ankara, 1989), consists mainly of British documents concerning the Muslim migration in 1876–78. See also chapters 1 and 17.

14. See Karpat, *Ottoman Population*, chap. 5. See also Zeynep Çelik, *The Remaking of Istanbul* (Seattle, 1986); and Daniel Panzac, ed., *Les Villes dans l'empire ottoman: Activités et societés*, vol. 2 (Paris, 1994). On the various categories of merchants, see Ali Ihsan Bağiş, *Osmanli Ticaretinde Gayri Müslimler* (Ankara, 1983); Bruce Masters, "The Sultan's Entrepreneurs: The Avrupa Tuccaris and the Hayrie Tüccars in Syria," *International Journal of Middle East Studies* 24 (1992): 549–79.

15. See Martin Strohmeier, "Muslim Education in the Vilayet of Beirut, 1800–1918," in *Decision Making and Change in the Ottoman Empire*, ed. Caesar E. Farah (Kirksville, Mo., 1991), pp. 215–41, quotation p. 215. See also Commins, *Islamic Reform*.

16. See H. Hüsrev Hatemi, *Türk Aydini: Dünü Bügünü* (Istanbul, 1991), p. 7; this work, written by a conservative revisionist Turkish scholar, offers a new perspective on the Turkish intelligentsia.

17. There is a lack of reliable studies on education. The enrollment figures, some of which are tentative, are based on Bayram Kodaman, *Abdulhamid Devri Eğitim Sistemi* (Istanbul, 1980), which uses a variety of primary sources; Mahmud Cevad, *Maarif-i Umumiye Nezareti, Tarihçe-i Teşkilat ve Icraati* (Istanbul, 1922); Reşat Özalp, *Milli Eğitimle Ilgili Mevzuat (1857–1923)* (Istanbul, 1982); and Hasan Ali Koçer, *Türkiye'de Modern Eğitimin Doğuşu ve Geliğimi (1773–1923)* (Istanbul, 1974). There also are several useful

articles in the collection Tanzimat I (Ankara, 1940). See also Osman Ergin, *Türkiye Maarif Tarihi*, 5 vols. (Istanbul, 1940–41; repr. 1977), B. C. Fortuna, "Education for the Empire: Ottoman State Secondary Schools During the Reign of Sultan Abdulhamid II (1876–1909)" Ph.D. diss., University of Chicago, 1997, and Mehmet Alkan, "Ölüçülebilen Verilerle Tanzimat Sonrasi Ösmanli Modernleşmesi," Ph.D. diss., University of Istanbul, 1996.

18. Bedii Şehsuvaroğlu, "Ali Suavi ve Galatasaray Lisesi," *Belgelerle Türk Tarihi Dergisi* 2 (1968).

19. Ibrahim Temo, *Ittihad ve Terakki Cemiyetinin Teşekkülü ve Hidemat-i Vataniye ve Inkilab-i Milliye Hatiralarim* (Mecidiye, Romania, 1939).

20. See Bayram Kodaman, *Abdulhamid Devri Eğitim Sistemi*, pp. 197–98.

21. All figures are taken from Mehmet Ö. Alkan, "Ölçülebilen Verilerle Tanzimat Sonrasi Osmanli Modernleşmesi," Ph.D. diss., University of Istanbul, 1996, pp. 45–51, 466; this exceptionally valuable work provides quantitative date to support the idea that considerable growth occurred in the 1876–1914 period. For an analysis of the content of the textbooks, see his article in *Ottoman Past and Today's Turkey*, ed. K. H. Karpat, forthcoming.

22. Some information on this matter may be found in Donald Quataert, *Social Disintegration and Popular Resistance in the Ottoman Empire, 1881–1908* (New York, 1983).

23. See Maria Todorova, "Mithat Paşa's Governorship of the Danube Province," in *Decision Making and Change in the Ottoman Empire*, ed. Caesar E. Farah (Kirksville, Mo., 1993), pp. 115–28.

24. On the parliament of 1877–78, see Robert Devereux, *First Ottoman Constitutional Period* (Baltimore, Md., 1963). See also Kemal H. Karpat, "The Ottoman Parliament of 1877 and Its Social Significance," *Notes du Premier Congrès International de l'Association Internationale d'Études du Sud-est Europe* 1969: 247–57. The late Hakki Tarik Us, a journalist who gathered and published the records of the first Ottoman parliament, mentioned that he was preparing a biographical study of the deputies of the parliament of 1877, but despite intensive efforts, including a search of the library named after him in Bayezit, Istanbul, no such manuscript could be located.

25. This issue is discussed at length by Kemal H. Karpat in "Abdulhamid'in Panislam Politikasi, Yanliş bir Görüşün Düzeltilmesi," *Türk Dünyasi Araştirmalari* (November 1987).

26. This information is culled from a collection of documents in BA, Yildiz Collection, sec. 18, carton 39, December 1868. On Cevdet's philosophy, see Ümid Meriç Yazgan, *Cevdet Paşa'nin Toplum ve Devlet Görüşü*, 3rd ed. (Istanbul, 1992), p. 52, and Ercüment Kuran, "Türk Tefekkür Tarihinde Ahmet Cevdet Paşa'nin Yeri," in *Türkiye'nin Batilaşmasi ve Milli Meseleler*, ed. Ercüment Kuran (Ankara, 1994), pp. 141–47.

27. Commins, *Islamic Reform*, p. 13.

28. A comprehensive treatment of the Nakşbandi is in Marc Gaborieau et al., eds., *Nakşbandis* (Istanbul, 1990). See also Hamid Algar, "The Naqshibandi Order: A Preliminary Survey of Its History and Significance," *Studia Islamica* 44 (1976): 129, and Hamid Algar, "A Brief History of the Naqshbandi Order," in *Nakşbandis*, ed. Marc Gaborieau et al. (Istanbul, 1990), pp. 3–44. (Algar should be given the credit for first pointing out the sociopolitical dimension of the order.) For additional background information, see Bandirmalizade Ahmed Munib, *Mecmua-i Tekâyâ* (Istanbul, 1980), and Thierry Zarcone, "Histoire et croyances des derviches turkestanais et indiens à Istanbul," *Anatolia Moderna* 2 (1990): 160–64.

29. This view was first expressed by Martin Van Bruinessen, *Agha, Shaikh, and State: The Social and Political Structures of Kurdistan* (Ryswick, The Netherlands, 1978). For support of the nationalist thesis see David McDowall, *The Kurds* (London, 1997).

30. Dzemal Cehajic, "Socio-Political Aspects of the Naqshbandi Dervish Order in Bosnia and Herzegovina and Yugoslavia Generally," in Gaborieau, *Nakşbandis*, p. 667.

31. The relationship between Bosnian Islam and the Turks is studied extensively in Tone Bringa, *Being Muslim the Bosnian Way: Identity and Community in a Central Bosnian Village* (Princeton, 1995). See also my review in *American Historical Review*, no. 102 (1997): 1189–90.

32. Arminius Vambery, *Travels in Central Asia* (London, 1864), p. 232.

33. See M. Fuat Köprülü's monumental work, *Türk Edebiyatinda Ilk Mutasavviflar* (The first mystics in Turkish literature), originally published in 1919 and last reprinted in Istanbul in 1976.

34. Ibid., pp. 108–11.

35. See *Islam Ansiklopedisi*, s.v. "Ahmet Yesevi" and "Nakşbendi."

36. Devin Deweese, "The Masha'ikh-i Turk and the Khojagan: Rethinking the Links between the Yasavi and Naqshbandi Sufi Traditions," *Journal of Islamic Studies* 7 (1996): 180–207.

37. This story was related to this writer in 1989 by one of the Bukhara *alims*; it derives from the *Silsilaname-i Khwajagan-i Naqshiband*, cited by Algar, "The Naqshibandi Order," p. 139. The migration of the ulema and scientists from Bukhara to the Ottoman state is recounted in Shams al-Din Ahmad Aflaki, *Manaqib al-'Arifin*, ed. Tahsin Yazici, 2 vols. (Ankara, 1976–80). See also Mehmet Arif, "Devlet-i Osmaniye'nin Teessüs ve Tekarrürü Devrinde Ilim ve Ulema," *Darülfünun Edebiyat Fakültesi Mecmuasi* 1 (1914): 137–44. For the rich bibliography on Hoca Ahrar, see Jo-Ann Gross, "Khoja Ahrar," Ph.D. diss., New York University, 1982.

38. See Yohanan Friedmann, *Shaykh Ahmad Sirhindi* (Montreal, 1971); Fazlur Rahman, *Selected Letters of Sirhindi* (translation of Ahmad Sirhindi's *Intikhabat-i Maktubat* [Karachi, 1968]); and Richard Foltz, "The Central Asian Naqshbandi Connections of the Mughal Emperors," *Journal of Islamic Studies* 7 (1996): 229–39.

39. Algar, "The Naqshibandi Order," pp. 142ff.

40. Butrus Abu-Manneh, "The Naqshbandiyya-Mujaddidiyya in the Ottoman Lands in the Early 19th century," *Die Welt des Islams*, vol. 22 (Leiden, 1982), p. 3.

41. Ibid., p. 13.

42. Uriel Heyd, "The Ottoman Ulema and Westernization in the Time of Selim III and Mahmud II," *Studies in Islamic History and Civilization* (Jerusalem, 1961), pp. 63–96.

43. See Albert Hourani, "Shaik Khalid and the Naqshbandi Order," in *Islamic Philosophy and the Classical Tradition*, ed. S. M. Stern et al. (Columbia, S.C., 1972).

44. See Mehmed Esad efendi, *Uss-i Zafer* (Istanbul, A.H. 1293 [1876]), pp. 97–126.

45. See Jemaleddin of Kazikumukh, *Al-Adab ul-Marziyya—Naqshbandi Treaty* [sic], Society for Central Asian Studies, Reprint no. 10 (Oxford, 1986); and Muhammad Tahir al-Qarakhi, *Bariqat al-Suyuf al-Daghestaniyya fi Ba'd al-Ghazawat al-Shamiliyya* (Moscow, 1946). For fuller bibliographical and factual information, see Moshe Gammer, *Muslim Resistance to the Tsar: Shamil and the Conquest of Chechnia and Daghestan* (London, 1994), pp. 39–80 and passim.

46. The literature on Şeyh Ahmed is collected in one file in BA, Yildiz, SRM, file 35/38; the quotation is from a communication of 5 December 1886. I have presented only an outline of Şeyh Ahmet's case, which certainly deserves extended study because of its ethno-regional significance.

47. The only major biographical study of Gümüşhanevi is Irfan Gündüz, *Gümüşhanevi Ahmed Ziyaüddin (KS) Hayati, Eserleri, Tarikat Anlayişi ve Halidiyye Tarikati* (Istanbul, 1984).

48. Frederick de Jong, "The Naqshbandiyya in Egypt and Syria," in Gaborieau, *Nakşbandis*, pp. 589–91.

49. Butrus Abu-Manneh, "Shayk Ahmed Ziya'üddin El-Gümüşhanevi and the Ziya-i-Khalidi Suborder" in *Shi'a Islam, Sects and Sufism*, ed. Frederick de Jong (Utrecht, 1992), pp. 105–17. I used also a Turkish translation. See also de Jong's article on Nakşbandia in Egypt and Syria in Gaborieau, *Nakşbandis*, pp. 589–601.

50. See Gümüşhanevi's reissued works, *Ehl-i Sünnet I'tikadi* (Istanbul, 1988; orig. ca. 1860).

51. Gündüz, *Gümüşhanevi Ahmed Ziyaüddin*, pp. 149ff.

52. Cemal Kutay, *Kurtuluşun ve Cumhuriyetin Manevi Mimarlari* (Ankara, 1973), pp. 76ff.; Mustafa Kara, *Tekkeler ve Zaviyeler*, 2nd ed. (Istanbul, 1980); and Mustafa Kara, *Bursa'da Tarikatlar ve Tekkeler*, 2 vols. (Istanbul, 1980).

53. Thierry Zarcone, "Remarques sur le rôle socio-politique et la filiation historique des şeyh Nakşbendi dans la Turquie contemporaine," in Gaborieau, *Nakşbandis*, pp. 407–20.

54. For Coşan's speeches see *II. Abdulhamid ve Dönemi Sempozyum Bildirileri 2 Mayis 1992*, ed. Coşkun Yilmaz (Istanbul, 1992), pp. 17–18, 227–28.

55. Coşan expressed all of these ideas in *Gayemiz* [Our purpose] (Istanbul, n.d.), apparently written (with Halil Necatioğlu) as a preface to a review. In my interview with him (October 1996) in his *dergah*, the Iskender paşa mosque in Fatih-Istanbul, he repeated his views convincingly.

56. See the collection of Coşan's essays, *Islam Çağrisi* [Call of Islam] (Istanbul, 1989; 2nd pr. 1990). The above views were confirmed in my interview with Coşan at the Iskender paşa mosque, October 1996.

CHAPTER 5

1. On the impact of the printed word, See Walter J. Ong, *The Presence of the Word: Some Prolegomena for Cultural and Religious History* (New Haven, 1967), and *Orality and Literacy: The Technologizing of the Word* (London, 1982); William A. Graham, *Beyond the Written Word: Oral Aspects of Scripture in the History of Religion* (Cambridge, 1987). See also chap. 8, sec. 4, which supplements this chapter.

2. Francis Robinson, "Technology and Religious Change: Islam and the Impact of Print," *Modern Asian Studies* 27 (1993): 239.

3. Ali Çelebi Kinalizade, *Ahlak-i Alai* (Istanbul, 1980; 1st ed. Cairo, 1830).

4. Niyazi Berkes, *The Development of Secularism in Turkey* (Montreal, 1964), pp. 42–49. The literature on the history of the Ottoman printing is repetitive.

5. The most complete treatment of the constitution in English is still Robert Devereux, *The First Ottoman Constitutional Period: A Study of the Midhat Constitution and Parliament* (Baltimore, Md., 1963). See also Doğu Ergil, ed., *Türk Parlamentoculuğunun Ilk Yüzyili: 1876–1976* (Ankara, 1976).

6. Scholars who have worked on this issue prefer to use the term "Islamism" instead of "panislamism": see Selim Deringil, "II. Abdulhamid'in Diş Politikasi," *Tanzimattan Cumhuriyete Türkiye Ansiklopedisi*, vol. 3, pp. 304ff.

7. Hilmi Ziya Ülken, *Türkiye'de Çağdaş Düşünce Tarihi* (Konya, 1966), p. 39; also see Kemal H. Karpat, "The Mass Media: Turkey," in *Political Modernization in Japan and Turkey*, ed. R. E. Ward and Dankwart A. Rustow (Princeton, 1964), pp. 255–82; Selim Nüzhet Gerçek, *Türk Gazeteciliği: Yüzüncüyil Dönümü Vesilesile* (Istanbul, 1931); and Fahriye Gündoğdu, "II. Abdulhamit Dönemi Türk Basin Teknolojisi ve Modern Türk Basimciliğina Giriş," *Edebiyat Fakültesi Dergisi* (special issue) (Ankara, 1983), pp. 101–109.

8. See the memoirs of Ali efendi, *Istanbul'da Elli Yillik Önemli Olaylar* (Istanbul, 1976). This is the new, "Turkified" version of the original *Istanbul'da Yarim Asirlik Vakayi Muhimme* (Istanbul, 1909). The memoirs were written after the author had spent more than thirty years in exile and contain little new information, critical analysis, or interpretation of events but are frank enough to provide a glance at the forces behind the newspaper.

9. Further information on *Basiret* and other newspapers may be found in A. D. Jeltyakov, *Türkiye'nin Sosyo-Politik ve Kültürel Hayatinda Basin: 1729–1908 Yillari* (Ankara, 1979); this is a translation of the Russian original published in Moscow in 1972.

10. See Mahmud Celaleddin paşa, *Mirat-i Hakikat* (Istanbul, 1983), pp. 171–201; also Ahmet Cevdet paşa, *Tezakir*, vols. 1, 2 (Ankara, 1953), p. 90 (see chaps. 2 and 3).

11. There is a definite need for a detailed study of *Basiret*; some articles are reproduced in Gökhan Çetinsaya, "II. Abdulhamid Döneminin Ilk Yillarinda Islam Birliği Hareketi (1876–1878)," B.A. thesis, Ankara University, 1988.

12. See *Basiret*, no. 2325, 8 January 1878.

13. Ibid., no. 2326, 9 January 1878.

14. Ibid., no. 2365, 17 February 1878.
15. See ibid. nos. 2075–2082, 26 April–4 May 1877. Some *nasihat* letters are reproduced as appendices by Çetinsaya, "II. Abdulhamid," pp. 170–87; also see Ram Lakhan Shukla, *Britain, India and the Turkish Empire, 1853–1882* (New Delhi, 1973), p. 177.
16. *Ittihad*, 5 September 1876.
17. For additional information, see M. Nuri Inugur, *Basin ve Yayin Tarihi* (Istanbul, 1982); Hasan Refik Ertuğ, *Basin ve Yayin Hareketleri Tarihi* (Istanbul, 1970); and Orhan Koloğlu's numerous articles and books.
18. Albert Habib Hourani, *Arabic Thought in the Liberal Age, 1798–1939* (Oxford, 1962), p. 99. A fuller account of *Al-Javaib* is by A. Çetin, "El-Cevaib Gazetesi ve Yayini," *Tarih Dergisi* 34 (1984): 475–81. The newspaper was more Islamic-Ottomanist than ethnically Arab-oriented as Hourani depicted it.
19. Hourani, *Arabic Thought*, p. 99.
20. See *Basiret*, no. 1946, 27 November 1876, and no. 2082, 4 May 1877.
21. See ibid., no. 1915, 25 September 1876.
22. The correspondence and other relevant material on the call to rebellion addressed to Russia's Muslims is found in the Ottoman archives, BA, Irade, Dahiliye, docs. 61009–61133 (1877–78).
23. Şerif Mardin, *The Genesis of Young Ottoman Thought* (Princeton, 1962), pp. 360–84, quotation on p. 360; see also Roderic H. Davison, *Reform Movement in the Ottoman Empire, 1856–1876* (Princeton, 1963), pp. 216ff. In Turkish, probably the best sources that reproduce extensive excerpts from Suavi's writings are Neşet Halil Atay, "Kendi Ifadesine Göre Ali Suavi," *Istanbul Dergisi*, December 1944–April 1945; Hilmi Ziya Ülken, *Türkiye'de Çağdaş Düşünce Tarihi*, vol. 1, pp. 74–76; and Cemal Kuntay, *Sarikli Ihtilalci Ali Suavi* (Istanbul, 1946); see also Enver B. Şapolyo, *Türk Gazeteciliği Tarihi* (Ankara, 1942), which was published by the General Secretariat of the Republican People's Party; and Celaleddin, *Mirat-i Hakikat*, pp. 320, 690–12. A recent publication that brings a new perspective is Ismail Doğan, *Tanzimatin Iki Ucu: Münif Paşa ve Ali Suavi* (Istanbul, 1991); see also Hüseyin Çelik, "Ali Suavi, Hayati ve Eserleri," Ph.D. diss., University of Istanbul, 1990.
24. See Mardin, *Young Ottoman Thought*, p. 364.
25. FO (Foreign Office, London) 424, vol. 70, enclosure 711, 21 May 1878, p. 435.
26. Celaleddin, *Mirat-i Hakikat*, pp. 618–20.
27. Hüseyin Kocabaş, "Ali Suavi Vakasi Üzerine Verilmiş Olan Fetva." This short manuscript is in the Library of the Turkish Historical Society (Ankara), AII/1516.
28. Extract in FO 424, vol. 70, enclosure 2, p. 437.
29. FO 424, vol. 70, enclosure 711/1, p. 437.
30. There is no major study of the Rhodope Muslim resistance, but I have collected considerable information on the subject, which will be treated in another study. Meanwhile some information is available in Tevfik Biyiklioğlu, *Trakya'da Milli Mücadele* (Ankara, 1955); Nevzat Gündağ, *1913 Garbi Trakya Hükümet-i Müstakilesi* (Ankara, 1987); Bilal Şimşir, *Rumeli'den Türk Göçleri*, 3 vols. (Ankara, 1968–70); and Bernard Lory, "Ahmed Aga Tamraslijata: The Last Derebey of the Rhodopes," *International Journal of Turkish Studies* 4 (1989): 179–201.
31. Ismail Hami Danişmend, *Izahli Osmanli Tarihi Kronolijisi*, vol. 4 (Istanbul, 1961), p. 313.
32. See Doğan, *Tanzimat'in Iki Ucu*, pp. 14–65.
33. Namik Kemal, *Celaleddin Harzemşah* (Istanbul, 1975), pp. 1–28; quotes on p. 9; this work was first published in Cairo in about 1880 and then reissued in 1899.
34. A recent publication by a former General Press director portrays Abdulhamid as the virtual prisoner of the Western press. See Orhan Koloğlu, *Avrupa Kiskaçinda Abdulhamid* (Istanbul, 1998). On Novikov's salon see J. Baylen, "Madame Olga Novikov, Propagandist," *American Slavic and East European Review* 10 (1951): 255–71.
35. See the documents in BA, Yildiz, SHM, folders 218/18 and 203/36, 5 June 1882 and 11 October 1888; BA, Kamil paşa Collection, add. folder 86/22, doc. 2182; and folder 86/23, doc. 2229, 28 September 1904.

36. See BA, Yildiz, SHM, folders 218/26 and 164/92, 12 October 1888 and 5 February 1905; and Yildiz, Kamil paşa Collection, folder 86/21, doc. 2281; folder 86/25, doc. 2450; and folder 86/23, doc. 2280; all of 3 and 5 February and 11 April 1905. Also Koloğlu, *Avrupa Kiskaçinda Abdulhamid*, 54–64, 406.

37. Gündoğdu "Ikinci Abdulhamit Dönemi," p. 109.

38. The correspondence on Vambery is in BA, Yildiz, SHM, folder 220/32, doc. 2232/226/42, 16 December 1888, 4 March 1889, and 17 June 1889. For the *Correspondance de l'Est* and *Correspondance de Wien* see BA, Yildiz, SHM, folders 219/43 and 219/60, 25 November 1888 and 2 December 1888, and 225/24, 9 May 1889.

39. For the government's view of education, see an interesting exchange of letters between Sait paşa and Abdulhamid, BA, Irade, Meclis-i Mahsus, doc. 5448, 23 December 1891; and BA, Yildiz, sec. 31/82, doc. 1927, 25 July 1893; BA, Irade, Dahiliye, docs. 40 and 53, 9 December 1893 and 24 April 1895. See also an order by the sultan asking that courses on Ottoman history be given special attention. BA, Yildiz, sec. 11, doc. 1763/5, 10 January 1900.

CHAPTER 6

1. See Louis Lataillade, *Abd el-Kader, adversaire et ami de la France* (Paris 1984); Paul Azan and Jean Louis, *L'Emir Abd el Kader, 1808–1883, du fanatisme musulman au patriotisme français* (Paris, 1925); also chapter 1, section on the Sanusiya, and chapter 4.

2. Ali Pacha, "Testament Politique," *Revue de Paris* 17 (1910). See the Turkish translation, along with the relevant bibliography, in Engin D. Akarli, *Belgelerle Tanzimat, Osmanli Sadrazamlarindan Ali ve Fuad Paşalarin Siyasi Vasiyyetnameleri* (Istanbul, 1978). For biographical information, see the standard basic biographical references, Ibnulemin Mahmud Kemal Inal, *Osmanli Devrinde Son Sadrazamlar*, 6 vols. (Istanbul, 1958–64); Mehmed Zeki Pakalin, *Son Sadrazamlar ve Başvekiller*, 5 vols. (Istanbul, 1940–48); Engin D. Akarli, *The Long Peace: Ottoman Lebanon, 1861–1920* (Berkeley, 1993).

3. One of the most comprehensive accounts of the Algerian revolt of 1871 is Louis Rinn, *Histoire de l'insurrection de 1871 en Algérie* (Algiers, 1891).

4. These two letters are in the Başvekalet Arşivi in Istanbul. They have been translated into French and published by A. Temimi, "La Politique ottomane face à l'insurrection du constantinois en 1871," *Revue d'histoire Maghrebine* 3 (1980): 11–20, 64–68, quotations, pp. 67–68. The first letter is dated 25 September 1871—that is, eighteen days after Ali paşa's death; the second is dated 28 March 1872. (Copies of the letters exist also in the archives of the French foreign ministry.)

5. Ibid., pp. 67–68.

6. Letters in BA, Yildiz, Perakende (Miscellaneous), vol. 23, secs. 303 and 607, 27 May 1866.

7. Archives of the French Foreign Ministry (hereafter cited as AFFM), Correspondence politique des consuls (CPC), Turkey, vol. 440, pp. 231–32, Tissot to Freycinet, 12 August 1880; see also A. Temimi, "La Politique ottomane," pp. 11–20, 64–68.

8. Temimi, "Politique."

9. AFFM, CPC, Turkey, vol. 447, pp. 284ff., Moutholon to Sainte Hilaire, 21 July 1881. (Copies of the letters addressed by the Algerians to Mahmud Nedim paşa are in this file.)

10. For the standard treatment of the Eastern Question, see Gerald David Clayton, *Britain and the Eastern Question: Missolonghi to Gallipoli* (London, 1971), also M. S. Anderson, *The Eastern Question, 1774–1923: A Study in International Relations* (London, 1966).

11. Richard Millman, *Britain and the Eastern Question, 1875–1878* (Oxford, 1979), p. 15. Note that Richard Millman's description of the events of 1875–76 also fits the situation in Bosnia-Herzogovina in 1992–95.

12. Ibid., p. 25.

13. The following literature provides a rather good view of this event: Richard Shannon, *Gladstone and the Bulgarian Agitation 1876* (London, 1963); David Harris, *Britain and the Bulgarian Horrors of 1876* (Chicago, 1939); W. E. Gladstone, *Bulgarian Horrors and the Question of the East* (London, 1876); Ronald J. Jensen, "Eugene Schuyler and the Balkan Crisis," *Diplomatic History* 5 (Winter 1981): 23–37. The literature on Gladstone is voluminous, one of the latest and most comprehensive works, which includes also an excellent selected bibliography, is Sir Roy Jenkins, *Gladstone* (New York, 1977). The work, although sympathetic to Gladstone, is detached and multisided; Jenkins sees Gladstone as a mixture of Little Englander caution and concert of Europe idealism and as having a sense of "British dignity, perhaps even a subconscious one of the superiority of white Anglo Saxon men" (p. 500).

14. See John Morley, *The Life of William Ewart Gladstone*, 3 vols. (New York, 1903), vol. 2, pp. 549, 551.

15. Jenkins, *Gladstone*, pp. 500–502 passim.

16. On the pro- and anti-Turkish attitudes of the British, including the Israeli-Gladstone rivalry, see Bernard Lewis, "The Pro-Islamic Jews," *Judaism*, 17 (1968): 391–404.

17. Stanford J. Shaw and Ezel Shaw, *History of the Ottoman Empire and Modern Turkey*, 2 vols. (New York, 1977), vol. 2, pp. 155–56.

18. BA, Yildiz, sec. 18, file 38, doc. 553/594 n.d., probably ca. 1890.

19. In his article, "The Sultan and the Bureaucracy: The Anti-Tanzimat Concepts of Grand Vizier Mahmud Nedim Paşa," *International Journal of Middle East Studies* 22 (1990): 257–74, Butrus Abu-Manneh has attached much importance to Nedim's little sixty-one-page booklet defending absolutism, *Ayniye-i Devlet* (Mirror of State), addressed to Sultan Abdulaziz; the booklet remained in manuscript form until 1909.

20. The declaration, which was translated into Urdu, appeared in the *Englishman* of 18 November 1876. For quotations see BA, Yildiz, sec. 18, folder 28, carton 128, no. 525/414. A full account of these events is also in Ram Lakhan Shukla, *Britain, India, and the Turkish Empire, 1853–1882* (New Delhi, 1973), pp. 94–154; Azmi Özcan, "Indian Muslims and the Ottomans, 1877–1914: A Study of Indian Muslim Attitudes to Pan-Islamism and Turkey," Ph.D. diss., University of London, 1990. It was translated into Turkish and published in 1992 under title *Pan-Islamizm: Osmanli Devleti, Hindistan Müslümanlari ve İngiltere, 1877–1914* (Istanbul, 1992) and has been published in English: *Pan-Islamism: Indian Muslims, the Ottomans and Britain, 1877–1924* (New York, 1997).

21. The letter is in BA, Yildiz, SHM, doc. 195/14, 11 August 1877.

22. Millman, *Britain and the Eastern Question*, p. 217.

23. On these events, in addition to the literature cited elsewhere, see Barbara Jelavich, *The Ottoman Empire, the Great Powers, and the Straits Question, 1870–1877* (Bloomington, 1973); G. D. Clayton, *Britain and the Eastern Question: Missolonghi to Gallipoli* (London, 1971); and for a different view on the British foreign policy during the reign of Abdulhamid, see Cedric James Lowe, *The Reluctant Imperialists: British Foreign Policy, 1878–1902* (London, 1967).

24. *Basiret*, 13 December 1876.

25. Quoted by Millman, *Britain and the Eastern Question*, p. 240.

26. See Mustafa Müftüoğlu, *Her Yönü ile Sultan İkinci Abdulhamid* (Istanbul, 1985), pp. 78–79, 82.

27. These reports are in the British Record Office under FO 78 and FO 242. Most of the British and French dispatches have been assembled. See Bilal Şimşir, *Rumeli'den Türk Göçleri*, vol. 3 (Ankara, 1989); and also Kemal H. Karpat, *Ottoman Population, 1830–1919* (Madison, Wis., 1985), chap. 4. A lengthy treatment of these atrocities against Muslims is Justin McCarthy, *Death and Exile: The Ethnic Cleansing of Ottoman Muslims, 1821–1922* (Princeton, 1995); and my review in *International Migration Review*, 31 (1997): 420–24.

28. Millman, *Britain and the Eastern Question*, pp. 314–16.

29. For the texts of the San Stefano and Berlin treaties, see *Der Berliner Kongress 1878, Protokolle und Materialien* (Boppard am Rhein, 1978).

30. See Bernard Lory, *Le Sort de l'heritage ottoman en Bulgarie: L'example des villes bulgares: 1878–1900* (Istanbul, 1985). For the campaign of 1985–89 to "Bulgarize" the Turks of Bulgaria see Kemal H. Karpat, ed., *The Turks of Bulgaria: The Fate of a Minority* (Istanbul, 1990), and *Ottoman Population*, chap. 4.

31. The impact of the Berlin Treaty on the nationality issue is treated at length in Kemal H. Karpat, "The Ottoman Attitude towards the Resistance of Bosnia and Hercegovina to the Austrian Occupation in 1878," *Naucni Skup Otpor Austrougarskoj Okupaciji 1878 Godine u Bosni i Hercegovini* (Sarajevo, 1979), pp. 147–72 (the entire book deals with this issue), and Benjamin Braude and Bernard Lewis, *Christians and Jews in the Ottoman Empire.*

32. See Karpat, *Ottoman Population*, pp. 51–55.

33. Arminius Vambery reported that Ahmed al-Barzinji al-Hussaini, a theologian from Mecca, as early as the 1850s wrote a pamphlet, entitled *General Advice to the Kings and Peoples of Islam*, in which he described the increasing power of the Christian world and advised the kings that the successful emulation of European scientific and economic efforts was the only way to escape total destruction. The truth of what he said had now been proven.

34. From an Italian report obtained by the French consulate in Izmir, AFFM, CPC, Smyrna, vol. 8, p. 34, Rome, 19 January 1881.

35. Emphasis added. FO 78, vol. 2622, Bilotti to Derby, 22 January 1877.

36. AFFM, CPC, Turkey, Trebizond, vol. 5, 21 September 1878.

37. Emphasis added. FO 424, vol. 71, pp. 85–86, Chermside to Hornby, 22 May 1878.

38. Ibid., p. 86.

39. AFFM, CPC, Salonica, vol. 6, p. 135, report of Consul Dozon, 12 October 1881.

40. FO 78, vol. 2787, confidential report of Layard of 2 May 1878.

41. FO 424, vol. 126, p. 18.

CHAPTER 7

1. On the export of wine, see BA, Yildiz, SHM, doc. 215/17, 19 July 1888; and BA, Yildiz, Sadaret Resmi Maruzat (Kiamil paşa's letter), doc. 43/25, 24 June 1888. The export of alcoholic beverages had been regulated by some bylaws, the Muskirat Resm-i Murisi Nizamnamesi.

2. Ahmet Nuri Sinapli, *Seyhül Vüzera: Serasker Mehmed Namik Paşa* (Istanbul, 1987), pp. 250–51.

3. See BA, Yildiz, SHM, doc. 165/87, 15 August 1880.

4. The voluminous correspondence on Daghestani Şeyh Ahmet is in BA, Yildiz, Sadaret Resmi Maruzat (Prime Ministry's official), doc. 35/38, 5 December 1886; see chapter 1 for a full discussion of Şeyh Ahmet.

5. The long controversy about the origins of the Ottoman state is summarized in Cemal Kafadar, *Between Two Worlds: The Construction of the Ottoman State* (Berkeley, 1995); unfortunately, Kafadar, following a well-established tradition among modernist Turkish intellectuals, ignores the basic role of popular Islam in the formation of the Ottoman state.

6. Earlier and rather subjective popular Western works on Abdulhamid II include Georges Dorys (Anastase Adossidis—son of Adossidis paşa, ex-governor of Crete), *The Private Life of the Sultan of Turkey*, trans. A. Hornblow (New York, 1901); Barry Unsworth, *The Rage of the Vulture* (London, 1982); Abdul Hamid Hidayette, *Revolutionnaire, ou, ce qu'on peut pas dire en Turquie* (Zurich, 1896); Alma S. Wittlin, *Abdulhamid: The Shadow of God* (London, 1940), which strives to be factual; Philip Paneth, *Turkey: Decadence and Rebirth* (London, 1943). For somewhat more detailed but still biased accounts, see Edwin Pears, *Life of Abdulhamid* (New York, 1917); Paul Andre Desjardin, "Au Pays de l'espionnage: Les sultans Mourad V et Abd-ul-Hamid," *Les Bas-fonds de Constantinople* (Paris, 1892). A better work, though incomplete, is by Sir Henry George Elliot (edited by his daughter), *Some Revolutions and Other Diplomatic Experiences* (London, 1922); W. S.

Monroe, *Turkey and the Turks* (London, 1895). See also several novels dedicated to Abdulhamid, Michel de Grèce, *Le Dernier Sultan*, and Nahid Sirri Orik, *Sultan Hamid Düşerken*, 3rd ed. (Istanbul, 1944), originally published in 1937, dealing with the last year of Abdulhamid's reign, which he spent under the watchful eyes of the Young Turks. Orik (1894–1960) wrote novels and short stories in both Turkish and French and represents rather well the views of the anti-Hamidian generation of 1908–60. A play by Orhan Asena, *Yildiz Yargilanmasi* (Istanbl, 1990), staged first in Izmir in 1995, featured Mithat paşa's trial in 1881. A book that stands above the rest is Joan Haslip, *The Sultan: The Life of Abdul Hamid II* (London, 1958).

In Turkish the basic sources are the classic work of Osman Nuri, *Abdulhamit-i Sani ve Devr-i Saltanati, Hayat-i Hussusiye ve Siyasiyesi*, 3 vols. (Istanbul, 1327 [1907]), and Sait paşa, *Sait Paşanin Hatirati*, 3 vols. (Istanbul, 1928). The article in the old edition of *Islam Ansiklopedisi* (IA), written ca. 1940 by A. H. Öngünsu, is superficial and reflects the official negative viewpoint of the Republican leaders. A new Turkish version of *Islam Ansiklopedisi*, which is being prepared by the Diyanet Vakfi, has given Abdulhamid a more balanced treatment. Cevdet Küçük, *IA*, pp. 216–24. The "official" view on Abdulhamid of the Republican period also is reflected in the main general source of the period: Enver Ziya Karal, *Osmanli Tarihi, Birinci Meşrutiyet ve Istibdat Devirleri, 1876–1907*, vol. 8 (Ankara, 1962). Efforts to rehabilitate Abdulhamid occurred sporadically after the political liberalization of 1945–46. See Necip F. Kisakurek, *Ulu Hakan II. Abdulhamid Han* (Istanbul, 1965); Nizamettin Nazif Tepedelenlioğlu, *Sultan Ikinci Abdulhamid ve Osmanli Imparatorluğunda Komitacilar*, 2nd ed. (Istanbul, 1972; first published in 1964); and Stanford J. Shaw and Ezel Shaw, *History of the Ottoman Empire and Modern Turkey*, 2 vols. (New York, 1977), vol. 2, which places Abdulhamid in a more balanced frame of reference as does Orhan Koloğlu, *Abdulhamit Gerçeği* (Istanbul, 1987). One of the most detailed and balanced accounts is by Abdulhamid's secretary Tahsin paşa, *Sultan Abdulhamid: Tahsin Paşa'nin Yildiz Hatiralari* (1931; reprint, Istanbul, 1990). See also Aydin Talay, *Eserleri ve Hizmetleriyle Sultan Abdulhamid* (Istanbul, 1991). For sympathetic approaches, see Y. K. Necefzade, *1908–1918 Sultan Ikinci Abdulhamid ve Ittihad-ü Terakki* (Istanbul, 1967), and Mustafa Müftüoğlu, *Tarihin Hükmü: Her Yönü ile Sultan Ikinci Abdulhamid* (Istanbul, 1985). There is also a variety of lesser writings on Abdulhamid, mostly in Turkish. Ahmet Refik (Altinay), *Abdulhamid-i Sani ve Devri Saltanati* (Istanbul, 1031). For the anti-Hamidian campaign, see Suleyman Kani Irtem *Abdulhamid Devrin' de Hafiyelik ve Sansür* (Istanbul, 1999). This is a collection of articles written 1933–45 by Irtem (1871–1945), a unionist who occupied high positions in the Young Turks era but lost popularity in the Republic. He published articles in the newspaper *Akşam* to supplement his income.

Probably among the best sources of trustworthy insights into Abdulhamid's personality and political views are his own memoirs; he was the first Ottoman sultan to have engaged in personally written political reminiscences. Several versions are available:

(1) The memoirs dictated to his secretary Ali Muhsin bey in Salonica, where he was exiled after his dethronement in 1909. The fate of the memoirs dictated in Salonica is not known. The officers guarding him confiscated the memoirs and arrested the secretary after Ali Muhsin rejected "some proposals."

(2) In Abdulhamid's lifetime, Allinger Frères of Paris and Neuchatel published *Avant la débâcle de la Turquie: Pensées et souvenirs de l'ex-sultan Abdul-Hamid* (Paris, 1914). The title page indicates that these memoirs were collected by Ali Vehbi bey, who translated them into French. It is known that during his tenure Sultan Abdulhamid occasionally dictated to his secretaries his views and reactions concerning current political events and personalities. Most of these piecemeal memoirs, bearing specific dates, go back to 1891 and 1892. They have been translated into Turkish as Sultan Abdulhamit, *Siyasi Hatiratim*, ed. Ismet Bozdağ (Istanbul, 1974); additional editions published in 1975, 1984, and 1987 are identical to the original 1974 edition. These appear to be the most reliable and have been used extensively in this work.

(3) A series of memoirs-notes by Abdulhamid, published first by Ibnulemin Mahmut Kemal (Inal) in *Turk Tarih Encumeni Mecmuasi* (1926), were found among documents stored in the Yildiz Palace. A version of these memoirs was published in *Utarit* (a review with limited circulation issued in 1918–20, which I was not able to find). These memoirs were dictated by the sultan himself to his secretary in 1333 (1917), while he was living at Beylerbeyi Sarayi in Istanbul. According to later accounts, the sultan sent these memoirs to a publishing house in Leipzig with the instruction that they be issued five years after his death. Abdulhamid died in 1918, but the Leipzig house never published the memoirs. Ismet Bozdağ, a publisher and writer, claimed that he purchased some old books in Bursa in 1941 and found among them a manuscript with a note that described the manuscript as "a copy of the original sent to Leipzig except for some important topics which were omitted." It was this truncated version that was first published by Selek Publishers as *Ikinci Abdulhamid'in Hatira Defteri* (Istanbul, 1960). Bozdağ claims that in 1961 he engaged in a search for the full text of the memoirs sent to Leipzig. Eventually staff from the newspaper *Tercüman*, which published an edition for Turks working in the then Federal Republic, discovered in Leipzig the elderly son of the owner of the publishing house (whose real name is not given) to which Abdulhamid's memoirs had been entrusted and which was closed in 1923. The publisher had not been able to publish Abdulhamid's manuscript but had given it to his son for safekeeping. In 1973 the son presented the manuscript to Bozdağ, who finally published it in 1974 as *Sultan Abdulhamid'in Hatira Defteri*. (I have used the eighth edition, which came out in 1988 from Pinar publishers of Istanbul.) Bozdağ's "Leipzig story" has been challenged but not the veracity of the memoirs. See Alaeddin Yalçinkaya, *Sultan II Abdulhamid Han'in Notl'ari* (Istanbul, 1996).

The memoirs Abdulhamid dictated in 1917 and sent to Leipzig represent his efforts to rehabilitate himself politically. Following his loss of power in 1908–1909, the sultan had witnessed the annexation of Bosnia by Austria, the disastrous Balkan war of 1912–13, and the Ottoman entry into World War I on the side of Germany, which brought the Empire to its end. He accused his enemies, mainly the Young Turks and the constitutionalists of 1876, for all the losses, but also devoted considerable space to defending himself against the accusation of having ordered the killing of Mithat paşa, whom he describes as being in the service of England. (He claims that Hüseyin Avni paşa received money and support from England and engineered along with Mithat paşa in 1876 the ousting of Sultan Abdulaziz.) The memoirs of 1917 are subjective and self-righteous—and in places full of inaccuracies—despite the existence of some very useful factual information. Consequently, the memoirs translated into French seem to be the most reliable and illuminative. Some of Abdulhamid's personal views and utterances are in Atilla Çetin and Ramazan Yildiz, *Sultan Ikinci Abdulhamid Han: Devlet ve Memleket Görüşlerim* (Istanbul, 1976).

Another set of memoirs on Abdulhamid's personal life and palace affairs are the reminiscences published by his daughters. Ayşe Osmanoğlu, the tenth child (sixth daughter) of the sultan, spent most of her adult life in exile (1924–52) in Europe and published the first book. See *Babam Sultan Abdulhamid (Hatiralarim)*, 3rd ed. (Ankara: Selçuk, 1986; 1st ed. 1960). The second book was published by Sadiye Osmanoğlu, *Hayatimin Aci ve Tatli Günleri* (Istanbul, 1966). On the artistic aspects of Abdulhamid, see Nihat Ergin, *Yildiz Sarayinda Müzik: Abdülhamid II Dönemi* (Ankara, 1999).

The Turkish archives contain other piecemeal memoirs attributed to Abdulhamid. These consist of eleven handwritten papers that end abruptly in the middle of a sentence. A part of these memoirs has been reproduced in the *Ikinci Abdulhamid'in Hatira Defteri* (Istanbul, 1960). See BA, Yildiz, sec. 8 (Hatirat-i Seniye), folio 77/3, doc. 2009.

There are a series of memoirs, in addition to those mentioned elsewhere in this study, by prominent officials who worked for Abdulhamid. Most of these writers worked as palace secretaries. Known as *mabeyin kâtipleri*, they were usually graduates of the Mulkiye. Among these memoirs, the following are worthy: Fahri bey (secretary to Abdulaziz), *Ibretnuma: Mabeyinci Fahri Bey'in Hatiralari ve Ilgili Bazi Belgeler*, ed. Behir S. Baykal (Ankara, 1968); Ali Cevat, *Ikinci Meşrutiyet'in Ilani ve Otuzbir Mart Hadisesi: II. Abdulhamid'in Son Mabeyn Başkatibi Ali Cevat Beyin Fezlekesi* (Ankara, 1960); Halid Ziya (Uşakligil), *Saray ve Ötesi: Son Hatiralar*, ed. Faik R. Unat (Istanbul, 1965); Mehmet Tevfik (Biren), *II. Abdulhamid Meşrutiyet ve Mütareke Devri Hatiralari*, 2 vols. (Istanbul, 1993) (Biren, the son of Ahmed Hamdi efendi, was from a prominent ulema family); and Ali Fuad Türkgeldi, *Görüp Işittiklerim* (Ankara, 1957). Ruth Haerkötter has studied the publications on Abdulhamid (mainly those compiled after 1980) and the controversy in Turkey about his policies: *Sultan Abdulhamid II in der türkischen Publizistik seit Gründung der Republik* (Frankfurt, 1996). For a fierce attack on the defenders of Abdulhamid see the Marxist *Aydinlik*, no. 454 (1996).

7. Sultan Abdulhamid, *Sultan Abdulhamid'in Hatira Defteri*, 8th ed. (Istanbul, 1988), p. 104.

8. Public Records Office, FO 800/32 (Vambery papers); see also Vambery's own writings, including his autobiography, *His Life and Adventures* (London, 1883) (there are several editions of this work, each including information not found in the other editions); and "Personal Recollections of Abdulhamid and His Court," *Nineteenth Century and After* 65 (June 1909): 69–88, and 66 (July–December 1909): 980–94, which are expanded versions of sections of his memoirs. Vambery's letters regarding his conversations with Abdulhamid have been translated and published in Turkish with a rather misleading, sensational title: see Mim Kemal Öke, *Vambery, Belgelerle Bir Devletlerarasi Casusun Yaşam Öyküsü* (Istanbul, 1985).

9. Öke, *Vambery*, p. 4.

10. Fethi Okyar, *Üç Devirde Bir Adam* (Istanbul, 1980); this memoir was given a title and published by Cemanl Kutay.

11. See Tahsin paşa, *Sultan Abdulhamid: Tahsin Paşa'nin Yildiz Hatiralari* (Istanbul, 1990), p. 227.

12. For details, including copies of articles appearing in the European press, see BA, Yildiz, SHM, doc. 221/40, 221/54, 20–29 January 1889; also *Le Temps*, 20 January 1889.

13. His development plan is in FO 78/2951, doc. 442, 28 May 1879; published by Stanford Shaw in *International Journal of Middle East Studies* 4 (1973): 359–68.

14. For the dependency views, see Şevket Pamuk, *The Ottoman Empire and European Capitalism, 1820–1913* (New York, 1987); and my review in the *Middle East Journal* 22 (October 1987): 103–8; also Reşat Kasaba, *The Ottoman Empire and the World Economy: The Nineteenth Century* (Albany, 1988). History does not appear to support Wallerstein's dependency theory; see Steve J. Stern, "Freedom, Capitalism and the World System in the Perspective of Latin America and the Caribbean," *American Historical Review* 93 (October 1988): 829–72, and replies pp. 873–97. On finances, see Engin D. Akarli, "Economic Policy and Budgets in the Ottoman Turkey, 1876–1909," *Middle Eastern Studies* 28 (1992): 443–76. On capitalism, see Nicolai Todorov, "The Genesis of Capitalism in the Balkan Provinces of the Ottoman Empire," *Exploration in Economic History* 7 (1970): 313–24; and Edhem Eldem, *Banque Imperiale Ottomane: Inventaire commenté des archives* (Istanbul, 1994) (records of bank transactions showing that these consisted mainly of loans to Ottoman high officials, the royal family, upper-class bureaucrats, and non-Muslim merchants); Edhem Eldem, "The Late Hamidian Regime through the Imperial Ottoman Bank Archives," paper presented to the Symposium on the Hamidian Era, Bad Hamburg, July 1993; A. Biliotti, *La Banque Imperiale Ottomane* (Paris, 1909); J. Thobie, *Intérêts et imperialisme français dans l'empire ottomane, 1895–1914* (Paris, 1977). For a broad survey of the introduction of technology in the Ottoman Empire, see Ekmeleddin Ihsanoğlu and Mustafa Kaçar, eds., *Çağini Yakalayan Osmanli* (Istanbul, 1995). The title (The Ottoman catching up with the contemporary age) is tantalizing.

15. Sultan Abdulhamid, *Siyasi Hatiratim*, ed. Ismet Bozdağ (Istanbul, 1974), p. 157.
16. See BA, Yildiz collection, sec. 8, folio 77/3, doc. 2009. The brief biography of Hayrullah efendi is in I. H. Uzunçarşili, *Midhat Paşa ve Taif Mahkumlari* (Ankara, 1985), p. 131.
17. See Sultan Abdulhamid's memoirs, *Siyasi Hatiratim* (Istanbul, 1990).
18. Tahsin paşa, *Tahsin Paşa'nin Yildiz Hatiralari*, p. 53.
19. See Ayşe Osmanoğlu, *Babam Sultan Abdulhamid (Hatiralarim)*, 3rd ed. (Ankara, 1986), p. 259; for the life histories of Ottoman imperial family members, see Murat Bardakçi, *Son Osmanlilar: Osmanli Hanedaninin Sürgün ve Miras Öyküsü* (Istanbul, 1992). Kenize Mourad, *De la part de la princesse morte* (Paris, 1987). The author describes the life of Selma, her mother, one of the exiled abroad.
20. Ayşe Osmanoğlu, *Babam Sultan*, pp. 35–36.
21. M. Sait Halim paşa, *Toplumsal Çözülme (Buhranlarimiz)* (repr. Istanbul, 1983), p. 9. On Sait Halim, see M. Hanefi Bostan, *Bir Islamci Düşünür: Said Halim Paşa* (Istanbul, 1992). Halim was Young Turks Premier when the decision to enter WWI on the German side was taken.
22. Sultan Abdulhamit, *Siyasi Hatiratim*, pp. 15, 19 (introduction by an anonymous writer).
23. Mabeyinci Fahri bey, *Ibretnuma: Mabeyinci Fahri Bey'in Hatiralari ve ilgili Bazi Belgeler*, ed. Bekir S. Baykal (Ankara, 1968). The author, a Palace official of Abdulaziz claimed that Abdulhamid forced him to testify that his uncle was murdered.
24. One of the most authoritative Ottoman sources on these events, although very supportive of Abdulhamid, is Mahmut Celaleddin paşa, *Mirat-i Hakikat*, 3 vols., ed. Ismet Miroğlu (Istanbul, 1983), pp. 117–27. See also Ahmet Cevdet paşa, *Maruzat*, ed. Yusuf Halacoğlu (Istanbul, 1980), pp. 207ff.
25. See Uzunçarşili, *Midhat Paşa*, and Bilal Şimşir, *Fransiz Belgelerine Göre Midhat Paşa'nin Sonu: 1878–1884* (Ankara, 1970); the trial of Midhat is detailed in the French diplomatic dispatches.
26. For an analysis of the debates in the parliament, based on the available minutes, see Kemal H. Karpat, "The Social Significance of the Ottoman Parliament of 1876," in *Proceedings of the First International Conference of South East European Studies* (Sofia, 1969). The constitution and the structure of the parliament is analyzed in Robert Devereux, *The First Ottoman Constitutional Period* (Baltimore, Md., 1963).
27. See, e.g., Niyazi Berkes, *The Development of Secularism in Turkey* (Montreal, 1964).
28. Quoted by Ali Haydar Mithat, *The Life of Midhat Pasha* (London, 1903: repr. New York, 1973), p. 80. Ali Haydar was the son of Midhat paşa.
29. Sultan Abdulhamid, *Hatira Defteri*, p. 119.
30. Ibid., p. 118, 119–20.
31. *Siyasi Hatiratim*, pp. 80–81, contains a series of pejorative allusions to Mithat paşa.
32. Ismail H. Danişmend, *Izahli Osmanli Tarihi Kronolojisi*, 1st ed., vol. 4 (Istanbul, 1955), p. 289.
33. Shaw and Shaw, *History*, vol. 2, pp. 184. For rather unpersuasive reasons for the sultan's seclusion see F. Georgeon, "Le Sultan caché: Reclusion du souverain et mise en scene du pouvoir a l'époque de Abdulhamid II (1876–1909)" *Turcica* 23 (1997): 93–124. Orhan Gologlu has pointed out that the "seclusion" of the sultan, in addition to ensuring his security, was a precaution against providing information to the foreign press always avid to magnify and distort any news and the utterances of the sultan: *Avrupa Kiskaçinda Abdulhamid* (Istanbul, 1998).
34. "Imperial Self-Portrait: The Ottoman Empire as Revealed in Sultan Abdulhamid II's Photographic Albums," *Journal of Turkish Studies* 12 (1988); the entire issue consists of photographs and explanations. There are other published versions of the same photographs. Another view of traditional Ottoman life comes from drawings, mostly by Europeans: see Turkish Republic Ministry of Culture and Tourism, *Ottoman Empire in Drawings* (Istanbul, 1987); Engin Çizgen, *Photography in the Ottoman Empire: 1839–1919* (Istanbul, 1987).

35. Tahsin, *Sultan Abdulhamid,* pp. 25–28; see also Engin Akarli, "Friction and Discord within the Ottoman Government under Abdulhamid II (1876–1909)," *Boğaziçi Üniversitesi Dergisi 7* (1979): 3–26; and F. A. K. Yasamee, *Ottoman Diplomacy: Abdulhamid II and the Great Powers 1878–1888,* (Istanbul, 1996), pp. 36–39.

36. The story of how and why Abdulhamid wanted a modern population survey is in S. S. Cox, *Diversions of a Diplomat in Turkey* (New York, 1887), pp. 37–38.

37. Ömer Faruk Akgün, "II. Abdulhamid'in Kültür Faaliyetleri Üzerine Bazi Dikkatler," *II. Abdulhamid ve Dönemi Sempozyum Bildirileri* (Istanbul, 1992), pp. 75–84, 139–140.

38. Emphasis added. BA, Yildiz collection, doc. 2022; reproduced by R. Yücel Özkaya, "II. Abdulhamid'e Sunulan Güzel Sanatlar Hakkinda Bir Layiha," *Osmanli Tarihi Araştirma ve Uygulama Merkezi Dergisi,* 4 (Ankara, 1993), pp. 645–85, quotation on p. 663.

39. On the establishment of these museums, see Zeynep Rona, ed., *Osman Hamdi Bey ve Dönemi Sempozyum, 17–18 Aralik 1992* (Istanbul, 1993).

40. See Şevket Toker, *Hüseyin Rahmi Gürpinar'in Romanlarinda Alafranga Tipler* (Izmir-Bornova, 1990). (See chapters 15, 16.)

41. Evangolos Misailidis, *Temaşa-i Dünya ve Cefakar-ü Cefakeş,* prepared by R. Anhegger and Vedat Günyol (Istanbul, 1986), quotations on pp. xxi, xxvii. For the literature on the long-forgotten Karamanlis (a small Turkish-speaking Orthodox congregation with a church of its own survives in Istanbul), who settled in Greece after 1926, see Ramire Vadala, *Essais sur l'histoire des Karamanlis* (Paris, 1900), and Evangelia Balta, *Karamanlikida: XXe siècle bibliographie anatolique* (Athens, 1987).

42. The original of the eight-volume *Seyahatname* is in the library of the Topkapi Palace; the *Ikdam* version was incomplete, altered, and occasionally mistranslated (as were the subsequent 1969–71 and 1975–85 popularized versions, which used *Ikdam*'s text and are still read in Turkey today).

43. On the Ottoman army see M. A. Griffiths, "The Reorganization of the Ottoman Army under Abdulhamid II, 1890–1897," Ph.D. diss., University of California, 1965; J. Parry and Malcolm Yapp, eds., *War, Technology and Society in the Middle East* (London, 1975); and Colmar Freiherr von der Goltz, *Nation in Arms: A Treatise on Modern Military Systems and Conduct of War* (London, 1906). See also the Turkish translation, *Millet-i Muselleha* [Armed nation] (Istanbul, 1884), and Gül Tokay, *Makedonya Sorunu: Jön Türk Ihtilalinin Kökenleri 1903–1908* (Istanbul, 1996). One of the best accounts of the army during Abdulhamid's reign is in Rifat Uçarol, *Gazi Muhtar Paşa (1839–1919): Askeri ve Siyasi Hayati,* 2nd ed. (Istanbul, 1989). The best factual account of the uprising of 1909 is provided by the court chronicler Abdurrahman Şeref, *Son Vak'anüvis Abdurrahman Şeref Efendi Tarihi: II. Meşrutiyet Olaylari (1908–1909),* ed. Bayram Kodaman and M. A. Ünal (Ankara, 1996).

44. Sultan Abdulhamid, *Siyasi Hatiratim,* p. 161. The word "thinking" was used by Abdulhamid in the sense of intellectual effort.

45. Ibid., p. 170.

46. Ibid., p. 171. On Ottoman slavery, see Y. Hakan Erdem, *Slavery in the Ottoman Empire and Its Demise, 1800–1909* (London, 1996).

47. Ahmet Uçar, "II. Abdulhamid'in Milletlerarasi Sergilere Müdaheleleri," *Ilim Dünyasi* (spring 1996): 3–10.

48. Ayşe Osmanoğlu, *Babam Sultan,* pp. 24–25.

49. Sultan Abdulhamid, *Siyasi Hatiratim,* p. 162.

50. Fethi Okyar, *Üç Devirde Bir Adam* (Istanbul, 1980), published by C. Kutay, who claimed to have used the hand-written manuscript kept by Okyar's family. The title of the book is chosen by Kutay. (The actual memoirs were published by Iş Bankasi [Labor bank], the first major bank in the republic established by Celal Bayar.) In view of Kutay's controversial use of sources, I investigated his sources. My investigation showed that Kutay did have a series of long interviews with Okyar while working as correspondent for the newspaper *Ulus,* the government's journal in Ankara in the 1930s. Osman Okyar believes that Kutay's view of his father's opinion about Abdulhamid is correct. Ayşe

Osmanoğlu, Abdulhamid's daughter, in her memoirs also stated that her father held Fethi Okyar in high esteem.

51. Fethi Okyar, *Üc Devirde Bir Adam*, p. 100.

52. Ibid., pp. 104, 105.

53. Ibid., pp. 210–15. A rather lengthy summary of these debates is in Berkes, *The Development of Secularism in Turkey*, pp. 359–66.

54. The notes are in the Library of the Turkish Historical Society. No. Y-255.

55. Sultan Abdulhamid, *Siyasi Hatiratim*, pp. 164–65.

56. Ibid., p. 166.

57. Ibid., p. 166–67.

58. Shaw and Shaw, *History*, pp. 220–46, and n. 13.

59. A succinct summary of these events is in Celaleddin, *Mirat-i Hakikat*, vol. 3, pp. 145–48; see also Karpat, *Ottoman Population*, chap. 4; Bilal Şimşir, *Rumeli'den Türk Göçleri*, vol. 3 (Ankara, 1968–70); Justin McCarthy, *Death and Exile: The Ethnic Cleansing of Ottoman Muslims, 1821–1922* (Princeton, 1995).

60. Prince Petar II, *The Mountain Wreath of P. P. Nyegosh, Prince-Bishop of Montenegro, 1830–1851*, trans. James W. Wiles (London, 1930); quoted in Asim Zubcevic, "Pathology of a Literature: Some Roots of Islamophobia," *Journal of Muslim Minority Affairs* 16 (1996): pp. 309–15, passim (Zubcevic places the Bosnian Catholic Ivo Andric's [1892–1975] works, including his Nobel prize–winning novel *Bridge on the Drina*, in the anti-Muslim category). For an overall view of Bosnia and its religious conflicts, see Noel Malcom, *Bosnia: A Short History* (London, 1994).

61. For Rosebery and his policies, see R. R. James, *Rosebery: A Biography of Archibald Philip, Fifth Earl of Rosebery* (London, 1963).

62. BA, Yildiz, sec. 9, file 72/4, doc. 2622 (no date given, probably written in 1878/79).

63. See, e.g., a report on measures that follow closely the sultan's directives that was sent to the palace by the Porte: BA, Yildiz, SHM 164/20, 16 June 1880. The British ambassador was aware of these reforms and reported them to London; see report in *International Journal of Middle East Studies* 4 (1973): 359–68, prepared for publication by Stanford J. Shaw. See ftn. 58 and 13.

64. Haslip, *The Sultan*, pp. 123, 124.

CHAPTER 8

1. See Kemal H. Karpat, *Ottoman Population, 1830–1914* (Madison, Wis., 1985), chap. 4.

2. Sultan Abdulhamid II, *Siyasi Hatiratim*, prep. Ismet Bozdağ (Istanbul, 1974), p. 57.

3. BA, Yildiz, Perakende (Miscellaneous), envelope 13/311, no. 1421, 19 May 1894.

4. Ibid., envelope 105/313, doc. 1400, 14 December 1899; it is interesting that this report was sent directly to the sultan by Colonel Yusuf Kenan, a staff officer in the imperial army.

5. Ibid., envelope 103/317, doc. 1144, 14 November 1899.

6. Stephen Duguid, "The Politics of Unity: Hamidian Policy in Eastern Anatolia," *Middle Eastern Studies* 9 (1973): 139–56; the article provides extensive information on the panislamic and administrative policy of Abdulhamid toward the Kurdish tribes.

7. Ayşe Osmanoğlu, *Babam Sultan Abdulhamid (Hatiralarim)*, 3rd ed. (Ankara, 1986), pp. 25–26.

8. Duguid, "Politics of Unity," p. 144.

9. See Kemal H. Karpat, "Ottoman Urbanism: The Crimean Migration to Dobruca and the Establishment of Mecidiye," *International Journal of Turkish Studies* 3 (winter 1984–85): 1–26.

10. G. P. Gooch and Harold Temperley, eds., *British Documents on the Origins of the War, 1898–1914* (11 vols.) (London, 1926–1938); ibid., vol. 5 (London, 1938), p. 27, quoted in Duguid, "Politics of Unity," p. 140.

11. For specific works on the Islamist activities discussed in this chapter, see Cezmi Eraslan, *II. Abdulhamid Devrinde Osmanli Devleti Dahilinde ve Afrika Kitasinda Islam Birliği [Panislamism] Faaliyetleri* (Istanbul University, Institute of Social Sciences, 1989); I. Süreyya Sirma, *II. Abdulhamid'in Islam Birliği Siyaseti* (Istanbul, 1985), and "Ondokuzuncu Yüzyil Osmanli Siyasetinde Büyük Rol Oynayan Tarikatlere Dair Bir Vesika," *Tarih Dergisi* 31 (Istanbul, 1978), pp. 163–83; *Sultan Abdulhamid II, Devlet ve Memleket Görüşlerim*, ed. Atilla Çetin and Ramazan Yildiz (Istanbul, 1976); Mehmet Hocaoğlu, *Abdulhamid Han'in Muhtiralari* (Istanbul, 1976); F. A. K. Yasamee, "The Ottoman Empire and the European Great Powers, 1882–1887," Ph.D. diss., University of London, 1984.

12. On *Maruzat*, see Ahmet Cevdet paşa, *Maruzat* (Istanbul, 1980), ed. Yusuf Halacoğlu; for Cevdet's philosophy, see Ümid Meriç Yazgan, *Cevdet Paşa'nin Toplum ve Devlet Görüşü*, 3rd ed. (Istanbul, 1992), pp. 80–95, and *Ahmet Cevdet Paşa Semineri* (Istanbul, 1986), a series of papers submitted to a seminar held 27–28 May 1985, and Ebul-ula Mardin, *Medeni Hukuk Cephesinden Ahmet Cevdet Paşa* (Istanbul, 1948). For a recent in-depth analysis of Cevdet as a historian, see Christoph K. Neumann, "Das indirekte Argument, Ahmed Cevdet paşa: Tarih als Plädoyer für die Tanzimat," Ph.D. diss., University of Hamburg, 1992 (a Turkish translation was published).

13. BA, Yildiz, sec. 18, file 38, doc. 553/588; also BA, Idare, file 3, doc. 156/125.

14. E. Kuran, "Küçük Said Paşa as a Turkish Modernist," *International Journal of Middle Eastern Studies* 1 (1970): 124–32.

15. (Küçük) Sait paşa, *Sait Paşa'nin Hatirati*, 3 vols. (Istanbul, 1928). For an appraisal of Sait paşa, see also Tahsin paşa's memoirs, *Sultan Abdulhamid: Tahsin Paşa'nin Yildiz Hatiralari* (1931; reprint, Istanbul, 1990), pp. 41–43.

16. Kiamil's views concerning some of the main events during his vizierate as well as polemics exchanged with Sait paşa concerning foreign policy decisions have been published: *Kiamil Paşa'nin Anilari*, ed. Güldağli-Güven (Istanbul, 1991); the papers of Kiamil paşa are classified and catalogued in the archive under his own name.

17. Von Goltz's stay in and influence on the Ottoman military deserves a far more extensive and detailed study than accorded here. See his article, C. F. von der Goltz, "Stärke und Schwäche des Turkischen Reiches," *Deutsche Rundschau* 93 (1897). Von Goltz's own work, *Nation in Arms* (1883), was translated into Turkish as *Millet-i Muessela* [Armed nation]. See also Wilhelm van Kampen, *Studien zur Deutschen Türkeipolitik in der Zeit Wilhelm II* (Kiel, 1968). F. A. K. Yasamee, "Colmar Freiherr von der Goltz and the Rebirth of the Ottoman Empire," *Diplomacy and Statecraft* 9 (2 July 1998): 91–128, has a rich bibliography. See also Pertev Demirhan, *Generalfeld marschall Colmar Freiherr von der Goltz: Das Lebensbild eines grossen Soldaten* (Göttingen, 1960).

18. On these two officials see Ali Karaca, *Anadolu Islahati ve Ahmet Şakir Paşa, 1838–1899* (Istanbul, 1993), and Ahmet Nuri Sinapli, *Şeyhul Vüzera, Serasker Mehmet Namik Paşa* (Istanbul, 1987); a list of Abdulhamid's palace "cabinet" is in F. A. K. Yasamee, *Ottoman Diplomacy: Abdulhamid II and the Great Powers, 1878–1888* (Istanbul, 1996), pp. 36–39.

19. See Butrus Abu-Manneh, "Sultan Abdulhamid II and Shaikh Abulhuda al-Sayyadi," *Middle Eastern Studies* 15 (1979): 131–53; this author somewhat exaggerates Abdulhuda's importance. See also B. Gürfirat, "Ebul Huda'nin II. Abdulhamid'e Sunduğu Arizalar," *Belgelerle Türk Tarihi* 18 (1969): 27–28; Engin D. Akarli, "Abdulhamid II's Attempts to Integrate Arabs into the Ottoman System," in *Palestine in the Late Ottoman Period*, ed. David Kushner (Leiden, 1986), pp. 74–89. For Abdulhamid's "Arab Secretary," his contact man with Syrian notables, see E. Caesar Farah, "Arab Supporters of Sultan Abdulhamid II: Izzet al-Abid," *Archivum Ottomanicum* 15 (1997): 189–220.

20. Zafir wrote several books, e.g., *Akrab-ul Vesail* and *Al-Rihla-ul Zafiriyye*. For some general information on Zafir, see C. E. Caffarel's report of 1888, excerpted in Jacob Landau, *The Politics of Pan-Islam: Ideology and Organization* (Oxford, 1990), pp. 322–23; Caffarel was the French military attaché in Istanbul. See also discussion on Sanusiya, chaps. 1 and 12.

21. Emphasis added. See Mustafa Kara, "Şazeliye Tarikati ve Üç Büyük Şeyhi," *Haraket*, September 1981, pp. 23–35, quotation on p. 32.

22. See S. Tufan Buzpinar, "Abdulhamid II and Sayyid Fadl Pasha of Hadramut," *Journal of Ottoman Studies* 13 (1993): 227–39. For Abid, see ftn. 19.

23. See Irfan Gündüz, *Gümüşhanevi Ahmed Ziyauddin (KS) Hayati, Eserleri, Tarikat Anlayişi ve Halidiyye Tarikati* (Istanbul, 1984).

24. This view was put forth by Gabriel Charmes, "La Situation de la Turquie: La politique du caliphat et ses consequences," *Revue Deux Mondes* 47 (1881): 740–45. A second article, with the same title, ibid., 49 (1882): 833–69, deals more with Abdulhamid's life and personality. These articles with some additions were reissued by the author in book form, *L'Avenir de la Turquie: Le panislamisme,* (Paris, 1883).

25. Ahmet Mithat's articles on autocracy appeared in the *Tercüman-i Hakikat,* issues of 3–18 July 1878. Some Europeans also espoused these views; see Sidney Whitman, "Abdul Hamid an Autocrat Not a Despot," *New York Herald,* 17 August 1896. Also Sidney Whitman, *Turkish Memoirs* (London, 1914), pp. 24–28, 216–24. (Whitman was asked but refused to enter the sultan's service.)

26. Ahmet Mithat efendi, *Uss-i Inkilab* (Istanbul, 1294 [1878]), pp. 10–13.

27. BA, Yildiz, Dahiliye, sec. 9, doc. 2638/72. This memorandum, along with a few similar communications issued by Abdulhamid, is included in Mehmet Kocaoğlu, ed., *Abdulhamit Han'in Muhtiralari* (Istanbul, 1989), pp. 125–28.

28. See Ahmet Mithat efendi, "Islamiyet ve Medeniyet ve Yahut Hala Ingiltere Münasebeti," *Tercüman-i Hakikat,* 9 January 1880.

29. Ibid.

30. Ibid., 23 August 1880.

31. Ahmet Mithat's reformist views are treated at length in N. M. Orhan Okay, *Bati Medeniyeti Karşisinda Ahmet Midhat Efendi* (Istanbul, 1989).

32. Ahmet Hamdi Tanpinar, *Ondokuzuncu Asir Türk Edebiyati Tarihi* (Istanbul, 1976), pp. 458, 459–60.

33. BA, Yildiz, sec. 18, file 38, doc. 553/610 (n.d.).

34. BA, Yildiz, Idare, Dahiliye, doc. 96880, 21 July 1891. A lengthy analysis of the Shiite problem in Iraq appears in Gökhan Çetinsaya, "Ottoman Administration in Iraq, 1890–1908," Ph.D. diss., University of Manchester, 1994, pp. 221–86; also Selim Deringil, "The Struggle against Shiism in Hamidian Iraq: A Study in Ottoman Counter-Propaganda," *Die Welt des Islams,* 30 (1990): 45–62. An important discussion about Iranian panislamism is in Mehrdad Kia, "Pan-Islamism in Late Nineteenth-Century Iran, *Middle Eastern Studies* 32 (1996): 30–52.

35. BA, Yildiz, sec. 14, file 10, doc. 1623, memorandum of Ali Galip, 13 August 1894. This long memorandum is presented here only in summary. The archives contain many other memoranda dealing with the ethnic and religious situation in Iraq; see Süleyman paşa's letter of 7 April 1892, BA, Yildiz, sec. 14, doc. 1188; and the report of Hoca Ishak efendi, BA, Irade, Dahiliye, doc. 75963. On the question of Iranian citizens, see Bruce Masters, "The Treaties of Erzurum (1823 and 1848) and the Changing Status of Iranians in the Ottoman Empire," *Iranian Studies* 24 (1991): 3–17.

36. For a picture of the economic situation of the Sunni officialdom see Eraslan, "II. Abdulhamid," pp. 50–52; for the number of *mujtahids,* see Çetinsaya, "Ottoman Administration," p. 224.

37. The orders issued by the government concerning these activities, covering roughly the years from 1882 to 1895, are in BA, Yildiz, Idare, Dahiliye; they are presented here in summary form.

38. Ibid., doc. 96880, 21 July 1891.

39. Niyazi Berkes, *The Development of Secularism in Turkey* (Montreal, 1964), p. 267; Nikki R. Keddie, "The Pan-Islamic Appeal: Afgani and Abdulhamid II," *Middle Eastern Studies* 3 (1966): 46–67, and *Sayyid Jamal ad-Din "al-Afghani"* (Berkeley, 1972), pp. 373ff.

40. The publisher was Ismet Bozdağ, cited previously. For Afghani's influence in Turkey, see Alaeddin Yalçinkaya, *Cemaleddin Efgani ve Türk Siyasi Hayati Üzerindeki Etkileri* (Istanbul, 1991).

41. See letters in Keddie, "The Pan-Islamic Appeal," pp. 54ff.

42. BA, Irade, Dahiliye, doc. 98319, letter of the Palace Secretariat to the Porte, 1 December 1891. The correspondence between Cevdet paşa and Abdulhamid indicates that the sultan's main interest in Afghani was his possible role as an intermediary between the Shiites and Sunnis of Iraq.

43. BA, Yildiz, sec. 14, file 38, doc. 553/586 (n.d.).

44. Ibid., sec. 1, Muhtira-i Humayun, file 3, doc. 156/XXV.

45. Nikki R. Keddie, "Religion and Irreligion in Early Iranian Nationalism," *Comparative Studies in Society and History* 4 (1962): 265ff.; also Kia, "The Struggle against Shiism." A good part of Abdulhamid's correspondence on Islamism is found in the Yildiz Collection; but some letters, though deposited in the archives, have reportedly not been made available to the public yet. Moreover, maps, letters, articles, etc., alluded to in various communications often fail to accompany the files.

46. A. Osmanoğlu, *Babam Sultan*, pp. 57–58.

47. See letter of Afghani in BA, Yildiz Collection, sec. 14, file of doc. 1103 (n.d.).

48. BA, Yildiz, sec. 14, file 7, doc. 211, 8 May 1893. The report includes extensive information on the tribes of the Gulf.

49. Ibid., file 8, doc. 257; there is no date, but the content indicates that it was issued as an answer to a telegram from Baghdad dated 26 August 1907.

50. Ibid., file 7, doc. 212 (n.d.); see also Çetinsaya, "Ottoman Administration."

51. Sultan Abdulhamid, *Siyasi Hatiratim*, pp. 166–67.

52. For a description of the situation in Yemen, see BA, Yildiz, Idare, Dahiliye, sec. 14, file 8, doc. 293/126, letter of Hüseyin Hilmi paşa, 24 February 1907; also Eraslan, *II. Abdulhamid*, pp. 86–98.

53. A. Osmanoğlu, *Babam Sultan*, p. 25; and Eraslan, *II. Abdulhamid*, p. 95.

54. BA, Idare, Dahiliye, doc. 97741, 22 September 1891, report of Abdulkadir, governor of Mosul, and Ömer Vefik paşa, commander of the reform units.

55. Ibid., doc. 56/2, 24 September 1892, memoranda of governor of Mosul and Ömer Vefik paşa.

56. BA, Irade, Meclis-i Mahsus, doc. 4867, 7 July 1890.

57. See entries in the Irade (Evkaf) catalogue in the BA.

CHAPTER 9

1. For the Ottoman concerns about the British attitude, see BA, Yildiz, SHM, docs. 163/106 and 164/40, 16 February and 13 April 1880. Much of the Ottoman correspondence is supported and duplicated by the British communications in FO 78 (Turkey); many (if not most) of Henry Layard's papers in the British Museum consist of copies of this diplomatic correspondence. For the spirit of the time, see Owen Chadwick, *The Secularization of the European Mind in the Nineteenth Century* (Cambridge, 1975), and also Norman Daniel, *Islam, Europe and Empire* (Edinburgh, 1966).

2. Kemal H. Karpat, *Ottoman Population, 1830–1914* (Madison, Wis., 1985), pp. 53–55.

3. House of Commons, Accounts and Papers, 100/44 (1881) p. 61, Goschen to Granville, 3 September 1880.

4. FO 424/86, p. 109.

5. The Armenian patriarch's figures are reproduced without any critical analysis by Marcel Leart, *La Question arménienne à la lumière des documents* (Paris, 1913), pp. 50–59. (Leart's real name was Krikor (Grigor) Zohrab; he was an Armenian from Istanbul, and his "documents" are figures collected from propaganda pamphlets and the like.)

6. This British diplomatic correspondence is in HCAP (House of Commons, Accounts and Papers) 100/44 (1881) and comprises Ambassador Goschen's exchange of communications with Patriarch Nerces and Consuls Trotter, Wilson, and Chermside. See also Karpat, *Ottoman Population*, pp. 51–55.

7. The confidential population reports prepared at the sultan's request are reproduced in Karpat, *Ottoman Population*, pp. 194–97.

8. Ram Lakhan Shukla, *Britain, India and the Turkish Empire, 1853–1882* (New Delhi, 1973), pp. 158–59.

9. The British correspondence concerning the *Peyk-i Islam* is found in FO 78, and 424 (passim) 1877–81.

10. The initial information about the paper supplied by the vizier's office to the sultan is in BA, Yildiz, SHM, doc. 164/92, 20 March 1880; see also Orhan Koloğlu, *Abdulhamid Gerçeği*, 2nd ed. (Istanbul, 1987), pp. 185–90.

11. Most of the Ottoman correspondence concerning the *Peyk-i Islam* and related issues is in BA, Yildiz, sec. 18, file 38, docs. 553 to 594, as is Cevdet paşa's memorandum; he regarded the *Peyk-i Islam* affair as one of the chief reasons for the English-Ottoman discord and alienation from each other. See also Yuluğ Kurat Tekin, *Henri Layard'in Istanbul Elçiligi, 1877–1880* (Ankara, 1968).

12. Ram Lakhan Shukla, "Indo-Turkish Activities," chap. 8 of *Britain, India*, pp. 155ff.

13. For a documented study of this case see Azmi Özcan, "Özbekler Tekkesi Postnişini Buharali Şeyh Süleyman Efendi Bir Double Agent mi idi?" *Tarih ve Toplum*, 17 (1992): 204–8.

14. AFFM, Correspondence Politique (CP), Turkey, vol. 444, p. 124, Tissot to Saint Hilaire, 23 January 1881.

15. Ibid., vol. 441, pp. 263–65, Tissot to Saint Hilaire, 29 September 1880.

16. Ibid.

17. Ibid., vol. 447, pp. 18ff., Tissot to Saint Hilaire, 1 June 1881.

18. *Osmanli*, 29 May 1881.

19. AFFM, CP, Turkey, vol. 447, pp. 81 and 294. Saint Hilaire to Montholon, 23 July 1881, and Ministry to Tissot, 13 June 1881.

20. Ibid., vol. 449, p. 157, Saint Hilaire to Tissot, 14 November 1881.

21. Ibid., vol. 455, p. 30, letter dated 22 December 1882, enclosure.

22. Ibid., vol. 444, pp. 286ff., Grevy, governor general of Algeria, to Saint Hilaire, 9 February 1881.

23. Ibid., vol. 451, pp. 152ff., consul of Hodeida to Noailles, 25 October 1882.

24. Ibid., pp. 102–12 (copies of reports sent to the French Embassy in Istanbul), 21 November 1881.

25. AFFM, (Correspondence Politique, Syrie) CPS, Turkey, Salonica, vol. 6, 22 July 1882.

26. These issues are discussed in a plethora of publications; for the relevant bibliography, see Michael Van Vleck, "British Educational Policy in Egypt Relative to British Imperialism in Egypt, 1882–1922," Ph.D. diss., University of Wisconsin–Madison, 1990.

27. Most of the local employees of the French and British embassies in Istanbul were Christian; see AFFM, CPS, Turkey, Izmir, vol. 8, 23 July 1882.

28. See FO 424, vol. 126, Wilson to Dufferin, report of 25 August 1882.

29. Ibid., p. 59.

30. Ibid., p. 61.

31. FO 424, vol. 126, Blunt to Dufferin, 8 August 1882, pp. 18, 25.

32. The entire correspondence concerning Gladstone's new anti-Turkish speeches of 1889 is in BA, Yildiz, SHM, docs. 233/78, 79; 230/51; 231/43; 12–19 February 1889.

33. The report from the Ottoman embassy in St. Petersburg and a copy of the article are in ibid., doc. 232/9, 28 December 1889.

34. FO 424, vol. 186, p. 167, Fitzmaurice to Carrie (report from Aleppo), 30 September 1896; see also the similar report, FO 424, vol. 183, p. 13, Longworth to Currie (report from Trebizond), 17 June 1895. The views expressed in these reports were accepted as true and appeared as such in many books. Niyazi Berkes reproduced almost verbatim the passage of the report accusing the sultan of surrounding himself with "Khojas, Sheikhs," et al.; see *The Development of Secularism in Turkey* (Montreal, 1964), passim.

35. AFFM, CPC (Correspondence Politique des Consuls), Aleppo, 1878–1881, report of 3 December 1880, pp. 230–33, quotation on p. 252.

36. Ibid.

37. Ibid., reports of 9 October 1881 (Aleppo file), pp. 340ff. On French-Ottoman relations, see Jacques Thobie, *La France impériale, 1880–1914* (Paris, 1982).
38. BA, Yildiz, SHM, 232/68, 21 January 1890.
39. See Robert Herly, "L'Influence allemande dans le panislamisme contemporain," *Nouvelle Revue Française d'Outre-Mer* 47, no. 12; 48, nos. 1–3 (Paris, Dec. 1955–March 1956).
40. Oppenheim's views are summarized in Jacob M. Landau, *The Politics of Pan-Islam: Ideology and Organization* (Oxford, 1990), pp. 96–98.
41. Selim Deringil, "Abdulhamid'in Diş Politikasi," *Tanzimattan Cumhuriyete Türkiye Ansiklopedisi*, vol. 3.

CHAPTER 10

1. Probably the most complete list of Abdulhamid's Islamic activities is in Cezmi Eraslan, *II. Abdulhamid ve Islam Birliği* (Istanbul, 1992), which idealizes the sultan as a ruler dedicated solely to the cause of Islam, Jacob M. Landau, in *The Politics of Pan-Islam* (Oxford, 1990), adheres to the old view that pan-Islamism was anti-Western and stemmed from a well-defined caliphal political plan of action.
2. See Douglas S. Brookes, "Of Swords and Tombs: Symbolism in the Ottoman Accession Ritual," *Turkish Studies Association Bulletin* 17 (fall 1993): 1–22; Selim Deringil, *The Well-Protected Domain: Ideology and Legitimation of Power in the Ottoman Empire: 1876–1909* (London, 1997), and *Islam Ansiklopedisi* under respective titles.
3. See "arma," "nişan," etc., in Mehmet Zeki Pakalin, *Osmanli Tarih Deyimleri ve Terimleri Sözlüğü* (Istanbul, 1993). For an extensive treatment of the subject, see Zdzislaw Zygulski, *Ottoman Art in the Service of the Empire* (New York, 1992).
4. See M. Sertoğlu, *Osmanli Türklerinde Tuğra* (Istanbul, 1975); Ernst Kühnel, "Die Osmanische Tughra," *Kunst des Orients* 2 (1955): 69–82; Esin Atil, *The Age of Sultan Suleyman the Magnificent* (New York, 1987), pp. 32–38.
5. Selim Deringil, "Symbolism of Power in the Hamidian Regime," paper presented to a colloquium on the Hamidian era, Bad Hamburg, Germany, 12–14 July 1993, and "The Invention of Tradition as Public Image in the Late Ottoman Empire," *Contemporary Study of Society and History* 35 (1993): 3–29.
6. For the history of the modern Ottoman or Turkish marches, see Mahmut R. Gazimihal, *Türk Askeri Muzikalari Tarihi* (Istanbul, 1955); and Etem R. Üngör, *Türk Marşlari* (Ankara, 1965).
7. Carter V. Findley, *Ottoman Civil Officialdom: A Social History,* (Princeton, 1988), pp. 24–25.
8. For the tribal schools, see Bayram Kodaman, "II Abdulhamid ve Aşiret Mektebi," *Türk Kültürü Araştirmalari* 15 (1976): 253–68; also Eugene L. Rogan, "Aşiret Mektebi: Abdulhamid II's School for Tribes: 1892–1907," *International Journal of Middle Eastern Studies* 28 (February 1996): 83–107; and Alişan Akpinar, *Osmanli Devletinde Aşiret Mektebi,* (Istanbul, 1997).
9. The Mülkiye is examined in Ali Çankaya, *Yeni Mülkiye Tarihi ve Mülkiyeliler,* 4 vols. (Ankara, 1968–69).
10. See BA, Evkaf, Irade, docs. 1310–1334 (1894–1918). The history of the Ministry of Vakifs is authoritatively studied by Ibnulemin (Inal) Mahmud Kemal, *Evkaf-i Humayun Nezaretinin Tarihçe-i Teşkilati ve Nüzzarin Teracim-i Ahvali* (Istanbul, 1335 [1919]).
11. BA, Yildiz, SHM, doc. 235/69, 16 February 1890.
12. Ibid., Sadaret Resmi Maruzat 8/27, 3 October 1881.
13. Ibid., doc. 16/46, 2 August 1882.
14. For the organization of and expenditure for the pilgrim caravan, see Münir Atalar, "Hac Yolu Güzergahi ve Masrafi-Kara Yolu, 1253/1837," *Osmanli Tarihi Araştirma ve Uygulama Merkezi Dergisi*, vol. 4 (Ankara, 1993), pp. 43–90. For a more general view, see Suraiya Faroqhi, *Pilgrims and Sultans: The Hajj under the Ottomans, 1517–1683* (London, 1994).

15. On the missionaries' activities, see correspondence in BA, Yildiz, Sadaret Resmi Maruzat, doc. 21/53, 10 October 1883; for the debate on countermeasures against missionaries, see BA, Irade, Şura-i Devlet, doc. 6666, 25 November 1891. See also Jeremy Salt, "A Precarious Symbiosis: Ottoman Christians and the Foreign Missionaries in the Nineteenth Century," *International Journal of Turkish Studies* 3 (1985): 55ff. On the Yezidis, see John S. Guest, *The Yezidis: A Study in Survival* (New York, 1987).

16. For this basic memorandum dealing with Islamic education, see BA, Yildiz, file 11/5, doc. 1763, 10 January 1900.

17. For the weakening of religious feelings in the nineteenth century, see Benedict Anderson, *Imagined Communities: Reflections on the Origin and Spread of Nationalism*, 6th ed. (New York, 1990), pp. 28–40.

18. Sultan Abdulhamid, *Siyasi Hatiratim*, ed. Ismet Bozdağ (Istanbul, 1974), p. 155. The proclamation of Sultan Abdulmecid asking the Muslims not to participate in the Sepoy Revolt is in BA, Irade, Hariciye, doc. 7894, and is reproduced in Y. Hikmet Bayur, *Hindistan Tarihi*, vol. 3 (Ankara, 1987), pp. 315–16.

19. Tahsin paşa, *Sultan Abdulhamid: Tahsin Paşa'nin Yildiz Hatiralari* (Istanbul, 1990), pp. 48–51.

20. See David Fromkin, *A Peace to End All Peace: The Fall of the Ottoman Empire and the Creation of the Modern Middle East* (New York, 1989), pp. 96–97.

21. Samuel Sullivan Cox, *Diversions of a Diplomat in Turkey* (New York, 1887), p. 37; also Kemal H. Karpat, *Ottoman Population, 1830–1914* (Madison, Wis., 1985), p. 31.

22. Oscar S. Straus, *Under Four Administrations: From Cleveland to Taft* (Boston, 1922), p. 46.

23. Ibid., p. 143, 145, 146.

24. On the exhibits see Zeynep Çelik, *Displaying the Orient* (Berkeley, 1992).

25. The extensive correspondence on unity between the sultan and the shah is in BA, Yildiz, sec. 36/xi, doc. 151, 13 February 1879; also SHM, doc. 165/80, 12 August 1880; Sadaret Resmi Maruzat, doc. 6/32, 25 July 1880; SHM, doc. 167/42, 19 April 1881; see also Merdad Kia, "Pan-Islamism in Late Nineteenth-Century Iran," *Middle Eastern Studies* 32 (1996): 30–52.

26. Eraslan, *II. Abdulhamid*, pp. 347–70.

27. See BA, Yildiz, SHM, doc. 794, 21 September 1893; and on Japan, see Hoe-Soo Lee, *Osmanli-Japon Münasebetleri ve Japonya'da Islamiyet* (Ankara, 1989); and Landau, *Politics of Pan-Islam*, pp. 43–45.

28. Eraslan, *II. Abdulhamid*, p. 199.

29. BA, Yildiz, Sadaret Resmi Maruzat, doc. 3/10, 31 March 1879, and SHM, doc. 161/94, 8 August 1879.

30. David D. Commins, *Islamic Reform: Politics and Social Change in Late Ottoman Syria* (New York, 1990), p. 13.

31. Ibid., pp. 49–52.

CHAPTER 11

1. The standard work in English is Sir Thomas Walker Arnold, *The Caliphate* (London, 1965); see also Emile Tyan, *Sultanat et califat* (Paris, 1956). The literature on the caliphate in Turkish is rich and partisan but deserves careful scrutiny, especially recent works, for understanding the state of mind among its apologists and adversaries. I will cite only a few titles, without describing the contents. Mehmet Emin Bozarslan, *Hilafet ve Ümmetçilik Sorunu* (Istanbul, 1969); Suphi Menteş, *Hilafetin Mahiyet-i Şeriyyesi* (Istanbul, 1969), republished in 1970 as *Şeriyat Açisindan Halifeliğin Içyüzü* (Istanbul, 1970) by H. A. Önelçin (apparently a pseudonym); Mahmut Gologlu, *Halifelik Ne Idi? Nasil Alindi? Ne Için Kaldirildi* (Ankara, 1973).

2. Hamilton A. R. Gibb and Harold Bowen, *Islamic Society and the West* 2 vols., vol. 1 (Oxford, 1950), pp. 26–38; also Gibb, "Some Considerations on the Sunni Theory of the

Caliphate," *Archives d'Histoire du Droit Oriental* 3 (1947): 401–10, repr. in *Studies on the Civilization of Islam*, ed. S. J. Shaw (Boston, 1962), pp. 141–50.

3. Halil Inalcik, "Islamic Caliphate, Turkey and the Muslims in India," in *Shariah, Ummah and Khilafah: Lectures*, ed. Yusuf Abbas Hashimi et al., I. H. Qureshi Memorial Lecture Series no. 1 (Karachi, 1987), p. 18, and "The Caliphate and Atatürk's Inkilab," *Belleten* no. 182 (1982): 353–65.

4. Hamilton A. R. Gibb, "Al-Mawardi's Theory of the Caliphate," *Studies on the Civilization of Islam*, pp. 151–65. For other views on the Ottoman caliphate, see G. P. Badger, "The Precedents and Usages Regulating the Muslim Caliphate," *Nineteenth Century* (1877): 274–82; C. A. Nallino, *Notes on the Nature of the "Caliphate" in General and on the Alleged "Ottoman Caliphate"* (Rome, 1919).

5. Lutfi paşa's treatises were analyzed and translated by Hamilton A. R. Gibb, "Lutfi Paşa on the Ottoman Caliphate," *Oriens*, vol. 15 (Leiden, 1962), pp. 288ff., esp. 290.

6. Kazim Musa, *Külliyat* (Istanbul, 1920), p. 36; this book contains the author's writings published over a long period. Kazim Musa, three times *şeyhulislam*, was born in Erzurum in 1858. He received his *icazet* (license to teach) in Istanbul and in 1900 taught the Mecelle (the modernized religious code) in the law school in Istanbul. He also taught Ahmet Mithat efendi the *tefsir* (interpretation of *fikh*, religious law). He became *şeyhulislam* in 1910 in the cabinet of Ismail Hakki paşa, was fired, then reinstated; he entered the cabinet for the third and last time in 1918. Accused of being, among other things, a freemason, he rejected the charge and claimed he was a Nakşbandi. He was tried with the Unionists in 1918 and exiled to Malta, but died in Edirne in 1920, before the sentence was carried out.

7. The issue is debated at length by Gilles Veinstein, ed., *La Question du califat* (Paris, 1994), pp. 25–37.

8. This excerpt is reproduced in John. J. Donohue and John L. Esposito, eds., *Islam in Transition* (New York, 1982), p. 36.

9. See Şemseddin Sami, *Kamus-i Türki* (repr. Istanbul, 1978), 2 vols., p. 586 (originally published in 1899–1900).

10. BA, Irade, Hariciye, doc. 7894. The pamphlets and books written on the caliphate upheld the same view: see Nazif Sururi, *Hilafet-i Muazzama-i Islamiye* [The great Islamic caliphate] (Istanbul, 1898); and S. Tufan Buzpinar, "Abdulhamid II, Islam and the Arabs: The Cases of Syria and the Hijaz (1878–1882)," Ph.D. diss., University of Manchester, 1991, pp. 21–26.

11. William Ochsenwald, *Religion, Society, and the State in Arabia: The Hijaz under Ottoman Control, 1840–1908* (Columbus, Ohio, 1984), pp. 4–7.

12. See Ismail H. Uzunçarşili, *Mekke-i Mükerreme Emirleri* (Ankara, 1972), pp. 4ff.

13. See Butrus Abu-Manneh, "Sultan Abdulhamid II and the Sharifs of Mecca (1880–1900)," *Asian and African Studies* 9 (1973): 2–3; also Saleh Muhammad al-Amr, "The Hijaz under Ottoman Rule, 1869–1914: The Ottoman Vali, the Sharif of Mecca, and the Growth of British Influence," Ph.D. diss., University of Leeds, 1974, published in Riyadh in 1978 as a book. S. Tufan Buzpinar, "Opposition to the Ottoman Caliphate in the Early Days of Abdulhamid II: 1877–1882," *Die Welt des Islams* 36 (1996): 59–89.

14. Ochsenwald, *Religion, Society*, pp. 14–18.

15. Wilfrid S. Blunt, *The Future of Islam* (London, 1882). Niyazi Berkes in *The Development of Secularism in Turkey* (Montreal, 1963), pp. 268–70, gives Blunt exaggerated credit for launching the idea of an Arab caliphate; David D. Commins, *Islamic Reform: Politics and Social Change in Late Ottoman Syria* (New York, 1990), pp. 108–9, repeats this view. For a detailed account of British views of the caliphate, see also Buzpinar, "Abdulhamid II," pp. 46–65.

16. See BA, Yildiz, SHM, docs. 164/147, 28 June 1880; 165/55, 2 August 1880; 164/144, 27 June 1880.

17. Charmes's comprehensive articles were translated in summary and submitted to the sultan, who kept them in his files; see the undated translation in BA, Yildiz, sec. 33, file 91, doc. 1626. The translator mentioned specifically that Charmes had lived in Istanbul

for a while and had visited Syria, implying that he obtained his information from authentic Arab and Turkish sources.

18. See Ismail Hakki Uzunçarşili, *Mithat ve Rüştü Paşalarin Tevkiflerine Dair Vesikalar* (Ankara, 1946); Abdurrahman Çayci, "Mithat Paşa'nin Taif Kalesinden Kaçma Tasavvuruna Dair Yabanci Belgeler," *Belgelerle Türk Tarihi Dergisi* (8 May 1968): 36–42.

19. See the Ottoman correspondence in BA, Yildiz, Sadaret, doc. 165/154, 3 October 1880.

20. This information derives from dispatches to London from Zohrab and the government of India; see the chapter entitled "Anti-Turk Activities of the British among the Arab Chiefs," in Ram Lakhan Shukla, *Britain, India and the Turkish Empire, 1853–1882* (New Delhi, 1973), pp. 86–212, esp. 191; Tufan Buzpinar, "The Hijaz Abdulhamid II and Amir Hussein's Secret Dealing with the British, 1877–80," *Middle Eastern Studies* 33 (1955): 99–123.

21. Foreign Department, Political (Government of India) dispatch 135 (12 January 1880), Zohrab to Alston, cited by Shukla, *Britain, India*, p. 192. The Ottoman knowledge of British intentions was expressed in the *Tercuman-i Hakikat* January 30, 1881, and other publications.

22. Muttalib's letters to the sultan are in BA, Yildiz, SHM, docs. 164/144 and 147, 27 and 28 June 1880. Muttalib's revolt in the 1850s is given extensive treatment by Ahmet Cevdet paşa, *Tezakir*, 3 vols., prep. Cavid Baysun (Ankara, 1953), vol. 1, pp. 101–52.

23. BA, Irade, Dahiliye, doc. 69860; see also Cevdet paşa, *Tezakir*, pp. 110–20; Uzunçarşili, *Mekke-i* pp. 70ff.; Abu Manneh, "Sultan Abdulhamid II," p. 12; Shukla, *Britain, India*, pp. 206ff.

24. On cholera cases, see BA, Yildiz, SHM, docs. 168/65, 28 September 1881; 168/106, 26 September 1881; 165/106, 28 August 1880; and 169/18, 1 December 1881. For an extensive treatment of cholera in the Ottoman Empire and early measures to combat it, see Daniel Panzac, *La Peste dans l'empire ottoman: 1700–1850* (Paris, 1985); and Gülden Sariyildiz, *Hicaz Karantina Teşkilati, 1865–1914* (Ankara, 1996); this book brings the survey to World War I.

25. See Pierre Boyer, "L'Administration française et la réglementation du pèlerinage à la Mècque (1830–1894)," *Revue d'Histoire Maghrebine* (July 1977): 276–93.

26. BA, Yildiz, SHM, doc. 172/85.

27. Quoted in Shukla, *Britain, India*, p. 202.

28. Butrus Abu-Menneh, "Sultan Abdulhamid II," p. 20.

29. Fazil's letters are in BA, Yildiz, sec. 14, file 12, doc. 88/26 (n.d.); see chapter 8.

30. The correspondence between the palace and the Porte on the *Punjab Times* article is in BA, Yildiz, SHM, docs. 211/65 and 214/63, 5 March 1888 and 7 June 1888. On all this correspondence see also Orhan Kologlu, *Avrupa Kiskaçinda Abdulhamid* (Istanbul, 1998), passim.

31. BA, Yildiz, SHM, 214/63.

32. Extracts in ibid., 208/90, 15 December 1887. See also correspondence on other newspapers, BA Yildiz Defteri, doc. 372, sec. 36, Letter 144/XIII of 27 April and 2 May 1891.

33. BA, Yildiz, SHM, 212/60, 5 April 1888.

34. Report to the palace by the prime minister's office. Ibid., doc. 224/3, 2 April 1889.

35. A detailed account of the anticaliph campaign is in Caesar Farah, "The Islamic Caliphate and the Great Powers, 1904–1914," *Studies on Turkish-Arab Relations* 2 (Istanbul, 1987), pp. 37–48, and Tufan Buzpinar, "Abdulhamd II and Sayyid Fadl Pasha of Hadramut," *Journal of Ottoman Studies* 13 (1993): 227–39.

36. The report was sent directly to the palace; see BA, Yildiz, Kiamil paşa collection, doc. 86/9, 880, ca. September 1899.

37. BA, Yildiz, SHM, 215/40, 30 July 1888.

38. Ibid., 180/22, 10 November 1884.

39. See M. Şükrü Hanioğlu, *Osmanli Ittihad ve Terakki Cemiyeti ve Jön Türkler 1889–1902* (Istanbul, 1986), p. 114.

40. BA, Yildiz, sec. 36, file 15, doc. 2467/1, 4 March 1884.

41. See dispatches in BA, Yildiz collection, SHM, doc. 175/47, 28 November 1889.

42. Halil Halit's letter is in BA, Yildiz, Special Section (no numbers), 5 March 1898; the sultan placed only important and sensitive correspondence in the Special Section.

43. Sultan Abdulhamid, *Siyasi Hatiratim*, p. 127.

44. Ibid., p. 144, 145.

45. BA, Yildiz, SHM, doc. 233/48, 12 February 1890.

46. This interesting report is in BA, Irade, Dahiliye, doc. 88495, 11 April 1889, and should be compared with other statistics on the number of *hacis*.

47. Ibid.; also BA, Yildiz, SHM, docs. 175/36–40 and 175/117, 20 and 24 November and 25 and 27 December 1883.

48. BA, Yildiz, SHM, doc. 216/47, 19 August 1888.

49. On the obsession of the British and Kitchener with panislamism, and the image of the influence of Muslim religious leaders, see David Fromkin, *A Peace to End All Peace* (New York, 1989), pp. 96–105; see also chapter 10.

50. The full history of this railway remains to be written, for a huge amount of relevant Ottoman material has become available only recently. To date, the most detailed study in English is by William Ochsenwald, *The Hijaz Railroad* (Charlottesville, Va., 1980). The author used a substantial number of original sources, including figures on the expenses and revenues of the railroad. See also Eleuthere Elefteriades, *Les Chemins de fer en Syrie et au Liban* (Beirut, 1944); H. Slemman (Henri Lammens), "Le Chemin de fer de Damas-La Mecque," *Revue de l'Orient Chrétien* 5 (1900): 507–34; *Hicaz Demiryolunun Varidat ve Masarifi ve Terakk-i İnşaati* [Income and expenses and construction progress of the Hicaz railway] (Istanbul, 1908); Naci Kiciman, *Medine Müdafaasi* (Istanbul, 1971); Jacob M. Landau, *The Hejaz Railway and the Muslim Pilgrimage: A Case of Ottoman Political Propaganda* (Detroit, 1971); Herbert Ponicke, "Heinrich August Meissner Pascha und der Bau der Hedschas und Bagdadbahn," *Die Welt als Geschichte* 16 (1956): 196–210; David Kushner, "The Haifa-Damascus Railway: The British Phase, 1890–1902," in *Decision Making and Change in the Ottoman Empire*, ed. Caesar E. Farah (Kirksville, Mo., 1993), pp. 193–213.

51. Sultan Abdulhamid, *Siyasi Hatiratim*, pp. 144–45, 151.

52. Ibid., 5th ed. (1987), pp. 123, 124.

53. See W. Reuven Hazan, "Peaceful Conflict Resolution in the Middle East: The Taba Negotiations," *Journal of the Middle East Studies Society at Columbia University* 2 (1988): 39–65.

54. Ochsenwald, *Hijaz Railroad*, pp. 98–110.

55. Ibid., pp. 53, 111.

56. For an extensive treatment of the *hac* caravans see Karl K. Barbir, *Ottoman Rule in Damascus, 1708–1758* (Princeton, 1980), and other references to hac.

57. The study of the caliphate after 1918 falls outside the scope of this study, but see especially Veinstein, *La Question du califat.*

CHAPTER 12

1. See correspondence BA, Yildiz, SHM, doc. 172/69, 14 January 1883; Sait paşa, the Ottoman premier, forwarded the ambassador's cable directly to the sultan.

2. See Michel Le Gall, "Ottoman Reaction to the European 'Scramble for Africa': The Defense of the Hinterland of Tripolitania and Cyrenaica," *Asian and African Studies* 24 (1990): 109–35. Comprehensive information is in F. A. K. Yasamee, *Ottoman Diplomacy: Abdulhamid II and the Great Powers, 1878–1888* (Istanbul, 1996).

3. See L. Carl Brown, *The Tunisia of Ahmad Bey, 1837–1855* (Princeton, 1974), pp. 27–35, 63–64.

4. For an extensive treatment of Ottoman-French relations in North Africa, see A. Çayci, *Büyük Sahra'da Türk-Fransiz Rekabeti 1858–1911* (Erzurum, 1970); also Ercü-

ment Kuran, *La Politique ottomane face à l'occupation d'Alger par les français (1827–1847)* (Tunis, 1970), text in Arabic; Celal Tevfik Karasapan, *Libya, Trablusgarp, Bingazi ve Fizan* (Ankara, 1960); and Julia A. Clancy-Smith, *Rebel and Saint: Muslim Notables, Populist Protest, Colonial Encounters (Algeria and Tunisia, 1800–1904)* (Berkeley, 1994).

5. Jacques Thobie et al., eds., *La France imperiale, 1880–1914* (Paris, 1982), p. 122. For Salisbury's attitude on Africa, see Thomas Pakenham, *The Scramble for Africa, 1876–1912* (New York, 1991), pp. 276ff.

6. Harold D. Nelson, ed., *Tunisia: A Country Study* (Washington, D.C., 1979), p. 32.

7. For the Ottoman reaction to the attacks in the French press—notably *La Republique*, published by Gambetta—accusing the caliph of inciting uprisings in Tunisia and Algeria, see communications of the Ottoman Embassy in Paris, BA, Yildiz, SHM, doc. 168/14, 10 July 1881; and ibid., doc. 168/41, 19 August 1882.

8. Dwight L. Ling, *Tunisia, from Protectorate to Republic* (Bloomington, Ind., 1967), pp. 33–34.

9. Several dispatches of the governor of Tripoli are collected in BA, Yildiz, doc. 170/60, 7 June 1882.

10. Ibid., letter of 15 May 1882, doc. 13. Ahmet Rasim paşa, a well-educated administrator who spoke French well, deserves a full biography; the succinct account of his life in Mehmet Süreyya bey, *Sicill-i Osmani* (repr. Istanbul, 1996), vol. 4, pp. 856–57, is insufficient.

11. BA, Yildiz, doc. 170/60, letter of 22 May 1882. On the size of the Ottoman armed forces see *Sultan Abdulhamid ve Devri Semineri 27–29 May 1992* (Istanbul, 1994), pp. 78–79.

12. BA, Yildiz, SHM, doc. 172/5, 27 November 1882; in Zafir, see chapter 8.

13. The rather lengthy correspondence between the *vali*, the military commander, and Istanbul on the question of occupying the salt mines is found in BA, Yildiz, SHM, doc. 172/57, covering the period between August 1882 and January 1883.

14. Ali Abdullatif Ahmida, *The Making of Modern Libya: State Formation, Colonization, and Resistance, 1830–1932* (Albany, N.Y., 1994), pp. 85–88; also Michel Le Gall, "Forging the Nation-State: Some Issues in the Historiography of Modern Libya," in *The Maghrib in Question: Essays in History and Historiography*, ed. Michel Le Gall and Kenneth J. Perkins (Austin, Tex., 1997), pp. 95–108.

15. BA, Irade, Dahiliye, doc. 74139, 27 December 1884. Also Le Gall, "Ottoman Reaction," pp. 119–20.

16. Michel Le Gall, "The Ottoman Government and the Sanusiya: A Reappraisal," *International Journal of Middle Eastern Studies* 21 (February 1989): 90–106, claims that Sanusi-Ottoman relations were determined by practical considerations rather than pan-islamic ideology. See also Şehbenderzade Filibeli Ahmed Hilmi, *Senusiler ve Sultan Abdulhamid* (Istanbul, 1992); Anthony Cachia, *Libya under the Second Ottoman Occupation, 1835–1911* (Tripoli, 1945). For a more detailed account of taxes in Libya, see Nesimi Yazici, "Layihalar Işiğinda II Abdulhamid Döneminde Libya Üzerine Gözlemler," *Sultan II. Abdulhamid Devri Semineri: Bildiriler, 27–29 Mayis 1992* (Istanbul, 1994), pp. 47–84, especially pp. 71–72. Also Rachel Simon, *Libya between Ottomanism and Nationalism (1911–1919)* (Berlin, 1987). (Ahmida overemphasizes the self-propelled action by Sanusiya and gives an exaggerated picture of the social-national factor.)

17. Le Gall, "Ottoman Government," p. 94; see also Jacob M. Landau, *The Politics of Pan-Islam* (Oxford, 1990), pp. 321–24.

18. Çayci, *Büyük Sahra'da*, pp. 22ff.; see also Sehbenderzâde Filibeli Ahmed Hilmi, ftn. 16. His book, published originally in 1909 under a long title, is critical of Abdulhamid. The writer, who spent many years in Fezzan as an exile, gives excellent information on the Sanusi.

19. Bradford Martin, *Muslim Brotherhoods in Nineteenth-Century Africa* (Cambridge, 1976), pp. 95ff.

20. BA, Yildiz, docs. 169/57, 4 February 1882, and 169/149, 30 March 1882; also BA, Hariciye, 12 September 1892, and Cezmi Eraslan, *II. Abdulhamid ve Islam Birliği* (Istanbul, 1992), p. 135.

21. Le Gall, "Ottoman Government," p. 99.

22. See a series of documents in I. Süreyya Sirma, "Fransa'nin Kuzey Afrika'daki Sömürgeciliğine Karşi Sultan II Abdulhamid'in Panislamist Faaliyetlerine Ait Bir Kaç Vesika," *Tarih Enstitüsü Dergisi*, 7–8 (Istanbul, 1977), pp. 157–85, and "Ondokuzuncu Yüzyil Osmanli Siyasetinde Büyük Rol Oynayan Tarikatlara Dair Bir Vesika," *Tarih Dergisi* 31 (Istanbul, 1978), pp. 163–83; these articles are mainly reproductions of Ottoman documents.

23. See reports in BA, Meclisi Vukela, Mazbata, pp. 30–33, in particular, the minutes of 17 May 1888.

24. French Foreign Ministry (new series), Turkey, ser. B, carton 80.38 (1902) (Pan-Islamic propaganda); also Çayci, *Büyük Sahra'da*, pp. 194–95; Bradford G. Martin, *Muslim Brotherhoods in Nineteenth-Century Africa* (Cambridge, 1976), p. 122, and Le Gall, "Ottoman Reaction," pp. 125ff.

25. See report in French Foreign Ministry (new series), Report of 12 February 1902 (reproduced in I. Süreyya Sirma, *Ikinci Abdulhamid'in Islam Birliği Siyaseti* (Istanbul, 1985), pp. 52–62).

26. Jean Louis Triaud, *Tchad, 1900–1902: Une guerre franco-libyenne oubliée? Une confrérie musulmane—la Sanusiyya face à la France* (Paris, 1987), p. 13.

27. See J. Spaulding and L. Kapteijns, eds., *An Islamic Alliance: Ali Dinar and the Sanusiyya, 1906–1916* (Evanston, Ill., 1994).

28. Triaud, *Tchad, 1900–1902*, pp. 51–90 passim.

29. Sultan Abdulhamid, *Siyasi Hatiratim* (1987), pp. 148–49.

30. Ibid., p. 137. The sultan described the Turks as slow and capable of enduring endless difficulties, but their ultimate reaction was overwhelming and determined.

31. For these issues, see Lisa Anderson, *State and Social Transformation in Tunisia and Libya, 1830–1980* (Princeton, N.J., 1986), pp. 110ff. For subsequent relations with Italy, see Timothy W. Childs, *Italo-Turkish Diplomacy and the War over Libya, 1911–1912* (Leiden, 1990).

32. Sultan Abdulhamid, *Siyasi Hatiratim* (1987), pp. 155, 156.

33. See Jamil M. Abun-Nasr, *A History of the Maghrib* (Cambridge, 1971), pp. 306–12; for details, see Muhammad Fuad Şukri, *Al-Sanusiyya Din wa Dawla* (Cairo, 1948); see also chapter 2.

34. Mahmut Faiz's two reports are in BA, Idare, Dahiliye, doc. 15284, 29 November 1852 (the second letter is undated). For the earlier diplomatic missions in the eighteenth century, see M'Hammad Benaboud-M. Menouni, "A Moroccan Account of Constantinople," *Actes du VII'ème Congrès du CIEPO*, ed. A. Temimi (Zaghouan, 1987), pp. 68–75. For a comprehensive account of Ottoman-Moroccan relations see Abderrahman El-Moudden, ed., *Le Maghreb a l'épogue ottomane* (Rabat, 1995).

35. BA, Idare, Dahiliye, doc. 15284, report of 29 November 1852 comprises rich information about the Moroccan economy, army, faith, etc.

36. *Basiret*, 24 September 1876 and 27 November 1876. A special call in the form of "Nasihat" (Advice) to Morocco was issued by the paper on 3 May 1877.

37. *Basiret*, 10 February 1877.

38. BA, Yildiz, SHM, doc. 159/1, letter of 1 February 1877 (written in Arabic).

39. BA, Yildiz, sec. 36, file 18, doc. 139/9, contains a letter stemming directly from the Palace, dated 1 Rebiyyulevvel 1294 (16 March 1877), and the letter from the şeyhulislam of the same date.

40. "I occupy with God's will the caliphate and the imamate as the legacy of my ancestors, the glorious caliphs and conquerors. I am endowed with the heart-felt allegiance [*biat*] of the entire ulema, state dignitaries, military leaders and all the poor and rich people. The almighty God has made my ancestors succeed in their holy wars carried out in honor of all the Prophets and of those who have arrived at the divine truth [the sultan uses the colloquial term "ermişler" rather than the more formal "erenler"], and for the sake of the faith. I beg God to empower me to enhance further the illustrious şeriat of the Prophet Muhammed and to serve the Harameyen with the utmost

veneration. I hope to receive your prayers to God to help me in following this unique and rightful path.

"Although we could not correspond until now, we [know that] we have inherited the duty to revive the friendship that had prevailed among our beloved ancestors. The shared community of faith and doctrine [*mezhep*] compels us to unite and weld together [our people] and unsheathe our swords in order to defeat our enemies. The shame and shortcoming befallen on one community which believes in one God would put to shame other communities of the same kind. [Communities believing in one God would be hurt by the shame and defect afflicting any one of them.]

"It is not a secret to people with foresight to realize that although Muslims are settled far away from each other in the East and West [*masriq-magrib*] they will endeavor to strengthen the person [that is, Abdulhamid] who is endeavoring to keep up the lofty prestige of the caliphate amidst the faithless: all this will no doubt enhance the believers' [Muslims'] stature. Islam possesses many verses [in the Koran], *hadis*es, and proofs in support of unity and wholesomeness. God ordered in the Koran that all believers are brothers in order to . . . reject the proud and conceited. Our Prophet has shown the believers both with words and wise deeds the value of unity and togetherness. . . . Blasphemy [*kufr*] is openly in evidence everywhere and the [growing] power of the infidel is before our eyes. It is our inevitable duty as Muslims to unite and weld to each other to destroy the enemies of our faith and thus uphold eternally the sublime teachings of Islam among all people. Otherwise the ultimate results of all this will cause harm to all the Muslims. One cannot escape the enemy's power by living in faraway lands. I do not want to discuss this situation in detail. I was informed that the learned and virtuous Seyyid Sanusi who was in Istanbul is known to you. I trust him and prefer to communicate to you through him important and secret matters. Consequently I have kept the letter short and leave him to communicate orally the details." (Ibid.)

41. See also Edmund Burke, "Pan-Islam and Moroccan Resistance to French Colonial Penetration, 1900–1912," *Journal of African History* 12 (1972): 97–118.

42. See BA, Yildiz, SHM, doc. 170/95 of 19 June 1882.

43. Ibid., doc. 207/42 and 207/69, 8 and 18 October 1887.

44. BA, Irade, Dahiliye, doc. 90886, letter of 3 December 1889 from the Palace Secretariat addressed to the Porte. On the religious situation in Morocco, see Edmund Burke, "The Moroccan Ulema, 1860–1912," and Kenneth Brown, "Profile of a Nineteenth-Century Moroccan Scholar," in *Scholars, Saints and Sufis: Muslim Religious Institutions since 1500*, ed. Nikki R. Keddie (Berkeley, 1972), pp. 93–126 and 127–48, respectively.

45. BA, Irade, Dahiliye, doc. 90886, 3 December 1889. For historical background, see Jean Brignon et al., *Histoire du Maroc* (Paris, 1967); Thomas Pakenham, *The Scramble for Africa, 1876–1912* (New York, 1991), pp. 631–43 passim; also Henri Terasse, *Histoire du Maroc* (Casablanca, 1950). For the relations of local events to broader national politics, see Clancy-Smith, *Rebel and Saint*.

46. Mustafa Bilge, "II Abdulhamid'in Islam Birliği Çağrisi ve Fas," in *II Abdulhamid ve Dönemi, Sempozyum Bildirileri* (Istanbul, 1992), pp. 45–55; also Jean Deny, "Instructeurs militaires turcs au Maroc sous Moulay Hafidth," in *Memorial to Henry Basset* (Paris, 1928), pp. 1–22.

47. BA, Yildiz, doc. 168/44, 19 August 1882.

48. See the detailed discussion by F. A. K. Yasamee, "The Ottoman Empire, the Sudan and the Red Sea Coast," in *Studies on Ottoman Diplomatic History V: The Ottomans in Africa*, ed. Selim Deringil (Istanbul, 1992) (I am indebted to Prof. Yasamee for providing me an early draft of this article.)

49. On the Mahdi, see Pakenham, *Scramble for Africa*, pp. 217–29, 230–75; Bernard M. Allen, *Gordon and the Sudan* (London, 1931); Bradford Martin, *Muslim Brotherhoods*, pp. 5–8, 171–79; and Albert Hourani, *Arabic Thought in the Liberal Age, 1798–1939* (Oxford, 1967), passim.

50. Yasamee, "Ottoman Empire, Sudan," p. 6.

51. The communications about the occupation of Massawa are in BA, Yildiz, Sadaret Resmi Maruzat, doc. 31/49, 6 December 1885.

52. BA, Irade, Dahiliye, doc. 14794, 27 October 1851. See also Jean-Pierre Greenlaw, *The Coral Buildings of Suakin* (New York, 1995), which contains useful historical information on the Sudanese mahdi revolt and a local religious leader Osman Dinga.

53. See BA, Yildiz, SHM, 224/83, 25 April 1889, report dealing with an alleged Sanusi attack on the mahdi as reported in *Pall Mall*, 26 March 1889.

54. See Yasamee, "Ottoman Empire, Sudan."

55. FO 78/4059, Drummond Wolfe to Salisbury.

56. For further information, see Gabriel Warburg, "Mahdism and Islamism in Sudan" *International Journal of Middle Eastern Studies* 27 (1995): 219–236.

57. Martin, *Muslim Brotherhoods*, pp. 167ff. See also chap. 2, section on Comoro.

58. For the relations of Zanzibar with England, see Pakenham, *Scramble for Africa*, chap. 16.

59. See BA, Yildiz, SHM, doc. 160/30, 20 December 1878 and 13 February 1879, and doc. 163/85, 5 February 1880.

60. For these embassies, see ibid., docs. 220/38, 20 December 1888; 47/22, 28 April 1889 (Abdulkadir's mission); BA, Irade, Dahiliye, docs. 61867, 87811, and 88540, 7 April 1889; also Çayci, *Büyük Sahra'da*, pp. 44–60.

61. BA, Irade, Dahiliye, doc. 36772; also Eraslan, *II. Abdulhamid*, p. 130.

62. See BA, Yildiz, Sadaret, doc. M. 221/30, 14 January 1889, and other communications.

63. BA, Irade, Dahiliye, doc. 88553, 23 April 1889.

64. BA, Yildiz, SHM, doc. 222/27, 7 February 1889.

65. Roland A. Oliver, *The Missionary Factor in East Africa* (London, 1952), pp. 102–108; also Martin, *Muslim Brotherhoods*, pp. 166–67; and Francis Barrow Pearce, *Zanzibar: The Island Metropolis of Eastern Africa* (London, 1920).

66. Martin, *Muslim Brotherhoods*, pp. 174, 175.

67. The correspondence about the slaves is in BA, Irade, Dahiliye, 9553, 31 July 1848.

68. The communications are in BA, Yildiz, Idare, Dahiliye, docs. 36772 (1885), 87811, 61861, 88540. See also Eraslan, *II. Abdulhamid*, pp. 136–45. For an exchange of letters from 1850 to 1898 concerning Borno and Kano see B. G. Martin, "Five Letters from the Tripoli Archives," *Journal of the Historical Society of Nigeria* 2, 1962: 350–71, and especially, Al-Hajj Hassan Gwarzo, "Seven Letters from the Tripoli Archives," *Kano Studies* 4, 1968: 50–60.

69. For details see Le Gall, "Ottoman Reaction," pp. 128–31.

CHAPTER 13

1. Charles J. Halperin, *Russia and the Golden Horde: The Mongol Impact on Medieval Russian History* (Bloomington, Ind., 1985). For Cengiz han, see Paul Ratchnevsky, *Genghis Khan: His Life and Legacy*, trans. and ed. Thomas Nivison Haining (Oxford, 1991); David Morgan, *The Mongols* (Cambridge, Mass., 1992); Leo de Hartog, *Genghis Khan, Conqueror of the World* (New York, 1989).

2. Devin DeWeese, *Islamization and Native Religion in the Golden Horde: Baba Tükleş and Conversion to Islam in Historical and Epic Tradition* (University Park, Pa., 1994), p. 6. See also Allen J. Frank, *Islamic Historiography and "Bulghar" Identity among Tatars and Bashkirs of Russia* (Leiden, 1998).

3. On the Mongols, and their relations with the Turkic peoples, see V. V. Bartold, *Moğol Istilasina Kadar Türkistan*, trans. and prepared with notes by Hakki Dursun Yildiz (Ankara, 1990).

4. On Timur, see Beatrice Manz, *The Rise and Rule of Tamerlane* (New York, 1989).

5. Charles Warren Hostler, *The Turks of Central Asia* (Wesport, Conn., 1993), pp. 75, 76. This book is an updated version of *Turkism and the Soviets* (London, 1957). For a

basic source, see Gerhard von Mende, *Der nationale Kampf der Russlandtürken* (Berlin, 1936). These studies need to be placed within the larger framework of nationalism for all of Russia. See Robert John Kaiser, *The Geography of Nationalism in Russia and the USSR* (Princeton, N.J., 1994).

6. The view that Muslim modernists saw Islam as an obstacle to their assimilation and peaceful relations with Russians is one-sided. See Pinar Batur-Vanderlippe and John Vanderlippe, "Young Ottomans and Jadidists: Past Discourse and the Continuity of Debates in Turkey, Caucasus and Central Asia," *Turkish Studies Association Bulletin* 18 (1994): 59–82.

7. On Cengiz han's revival as a "national hero," see Ötemiş Haci (Utemish-Khadzhi, Ibn Maulan Muhammed Dost), *Cenghiz-name* (Alma Ata, 1992); the author served the Shaybanids, and the original was written at the beginning of the sixteenth century. The surviving republished section of the manuscript deals with the history of the tribes in the Desht-i Kipcak in the fourteenth century.

8. See Josef Glazik, *Die Islammission der russischen-orthodoxen Kirche* (Munster, 1959); Mark Batunsky, "Russian Missionary Literature on Islam," *Zeitschrift für Religions und Geistesgeschichte* 39, no. 3 (1987), and "Russian Clerical Islamic Studies in the Late Nineteenth and Early Twentieth Centuries," *Central Asian Survey* 13, no. 2 (1994): 213–35; Robert Geraci, "Russian Orientalism at an Impasse: Tsarist Education Policy and the 1910 Conference on Islam," in *Russia's Orient: Imperial Borderlands and Peoples, 1700–1917*, ed. Daniel R. Brower and Edward J. Lazzerini (Bloomington, Ind., 1997), pp. 138–62. For additional information, see S. Bagin, *Ob otpadenii v magometanstvo krashchennykh inorodtsev Kazanskoi Eparkhii i o prichinakh etogo pechalnogo iavleniia* (Kazan, 1910), and *Propaganda Islama putem pechati* (Kazan, 1909); L. I. Klimovich, *Islam v Tsarskoi Rossii: Ocherki* (Moscow, 1936).

9. See Tadeusz Swietochowski, *Russia and Azerbaijan: A Borderland in Transition* (New York, 1995), p. 12. For a comprehensive discussion of Russia's Muslims, notably in the nineteenth and twentieth centuries, see A. Zeki Velidi Togan, *Bugünkü Türk Ili Türkistan ve Yakin Tarihi*, 2nd ed. (Istanbul, 1981); the original was completed in 1929 and was published first in Egypt but was not widely distributed.

10. See, e.g., reports in BA, Yildiz, SHM, doc. 178/56, 3 June 1884, and doc. 177/50, 20 March 1884, about the Russian occupation of Merv in Central Asia.

11. Ibid., doc. 214/13, 17 May 1888; and see also chapter 2.

12. Ibid., doc. 203/20, 29 May 1887. The letter of the Ottoman consul in Tiflis, Hasan Hasif, was dated 18 March 1887; the prime minister, Kiamil paşa, received it on 29 May 1887 and forwarded it immediately to the sultan. The file contains newspaper articles and several other letters, referred to below.

13. Ibid.

14. Ibid.

15. Ibid.; and see also Selim Deringil, "L'Empire ottoman et le pan-islamisme dans la Russie turcophone," *Cahiers d'Études sur la Mediterranée Orientale et le Monde Turco-Iranien* 16 (1993): 207–17.

16. See Hostler, *Turks of Central Asia*, p. 95: Kh. Gabidullin and A. M. Arsharuni, *Ocherki panislamizma i panturkizma v Rossii* (Moscow, 1931); J. Stalin, *Marxism and the National and Colonial Question* (London, 1942).

17. Some of the methods used to enlist the native elites into the Russian army are described by former Russian Muslim generals who later joined the Ottoman army. See, e.g., General Musa Kondukov's memoirs, *General Kondukov'un Anilari* (Istanbul, 1978); and Chantal Lemercier-Quelquejay, "Cooperation of the Elites of Kabarda and Daghestan in the Sixteenth Century," *The North Caucasus Barrier: the Russian Advance towards the Muslim World*, ed. Abdurakhman Avtorkhanov, et al. (London, 1992), pp. 18–44.

18. Togan in *Bugünkü Türk Ili* provides extensive biographical on these Muslim leaders, pp. 205–510 passim.

19. BA, Yildiz, SHM, doc. 4/67, 12 November 1879; doc. 4/74, 1 December 1879. On the many other Muslims of Russia seeking Ottoman service, see ibid., doc. 180/58, 14 December 1884.

20. Ibid., doc. 4/67, 12 November 1879; doc. 4/74, 1 December 1879.

21. The best description of these Muslim middle classes is in the writings of Yusuf Akçura, which appeared in the review *Türk Yurdu* after 1911, and in the form of a yearbook (Istanbul, 1928).

22. For the history of Azeri oil, see Robert W. Tolf, *The Russian Rockefellers: The Saga of the Nobel Family and the Russian Oil Industry* (Stanford, Calif., 1976); also Daniel Yergin, *The Prize: The Epic Quest for Oil, Money and Power* (New York, 1993).

23. For a detailed study of the emergence of national identity in Azerbaycan, see Tadeusz Swietochowski, *Russian Azerbaijan, 1905–1920: The Shaping of National Identity in a Muslim Community* (New York, 1985). For alphabet reform in Azerbaijan, see Bilal N. Şimşir, *Azerbaycan'da Türk Alfabesi Tarihçe* (Ankara, 1991). The intellectual developments in Azerbaijan are studied in Ibrahim Yüksel, *Azerbaycan'da Fikir Hayati ve Basin* (Istanbul, 1994).

24. For a positive view of Russian treatment of Muslims, see Andreas Kappeler, "Czarist Policy toward the Muslims of the Russian Empire," *Muslim Communities Reemerge: Historical Perspectives on Nationality, Politics, and Opposition in the Former Soviet Union and Yugoslavia*, trans. from the German and French by Caroline Sawyer, ed. Edward Allworth (Durham, N.C., 1994), pp. 141–56; also Chantal Lemercier-Quelquejay, "Les Missions orthodoxes en pays mussulmans de Moyenne et Basse-Volga, 1552–1865," *Cahiers du Monde Russe et Soviétique* 8 (1967).

25. The information on education among Russia's Muslims derives from well-known sources. Alexander Bennigsen and Chantal Lemercier-Quelquejay, *Islam in the Soviet Union* (New York, 1967); Hélène Carrère d'Encasse, *Islam and the Russian Empire: Reform and Revolution in Central Asia* (Berkeley, 1988); Serge A. Zenkovsky, *Panturkism and Islam in Russia* (Cambridge, 1960); Edward Allworth, *The National Question in Soviet Central Asia* (New York, 1973); Tadeusz Swietochowski, *Russian Azerbaijan*. On Ilminski, see A. Rozhdestvensky, *Nikolai Ivanovich Il'minsky i yego sistema inorodcheskogo obrazovaniya v Kazanskom Kraie* (Kazan, 1900); and M. A. Miropiev, *O polozhenii Ruskikh inorodtsev* (St. Petersburg, 1901).

26. See an early report by missionary Sophy Bobrovnikoff, "Moslems in Russia," *The Muslim World*, 1 (1911): pp. 5–31.

27. Bennigsen and Lemercier-Quelquejay, *Islam in the Soviet Union*, pp. 33ff.

28. For the two historians, see *Vak'a-Nüvis Ahmed Lutfi Efendi Tarihi*, vols. 9–16, prepared by M. Münir Aktepe (Ankara, 1989–93). See also Abdurrahman Eşref, *Tarih Müsahabeleri* (Istanbul, 1923), reprinted as *Tarih Konuşmalari* by Eşref Eşrefoğlu (Istanbul, 1978). Mustafa Nuri, *Netayic-ul Vukuat*, was published by Mehmet Galip, the author's son, in 1911. Two volumes were published by the Turkish Historical Society in 1976, edited by Neşet Çağatay.

29. See *Namik Kemal'in Tarihi Biyografileri*, prepared by Iskender Pala (Ankara, 1989).

30. For a discussion of the impact of the modern school system in Central Asia, see Adeeb Khalid, "The Politics of Muslim Cultural Reform: Jadidism in Tsarist Central Asia," Ph.D. diss., University of Wisconsin, 1993.

31. Arminius Vambery, "Pan-Islamism," *The Nineteenth Century* (1906): 5ff.

32. Bobrovnikoff, "Moslems in Russia," p. 29.

33. Bennigsen and Lemercier-Quelquejay, *Islam in the Soviet Union*, p. 32. See also other works cited in n. 25, and relevant entries in the *Encyclopaedia of Islam*, old and new editions, and new Turkish versions; and Nadir Devlet, *Rusya Türklerinin Milli Mücadele Tarihi: 1905–1917)* (Ankara, 1985). Devlet's bibliography includes references to the main works, some rare, by and about the leading Muslim intellectuals of Russia.

34. Alexander Bennigsen and Chantal Lemercier-Quelquejay, *La Presse et le mouvement national chez les mussulmans de Russie avant 1920* (Paris 1964), pp. 20ff; also

Jo-Ann Gross, ed., *Muslims in Central Asia: Expressions of Identity and Change* (Durham, N.C., 1992). The linguistic revolution—that is, the adaptation of local idioms as literary tongues among Russia's Muslims—deserves a far lengthier treatment than I am able to accord it here. For additional reading see Hostler, *Turks of Central Asia*, pp. 98–110.

35. To the best of my knowledge, there are very few systematic and comprehensive studies about various ethnic and religious Muslim communities in Istanbul and their journals and activities; one available study that gives insightful information about the Iranians, including the Azerbaycanis, is Thierry Zarcone and F. Zarinebaf, *Les iraniens d'Istanbul* (Paris, 1993).

36. For a recent study of Gaspirali see S. Hakan Kirimli, "National Movements and National Unity among the Crimean Tatars, 1905–1916," Ph.D. diss., Univ. of Wisconsin–Madison, 1990, which contains a wealth of bibliographical information; it was published with some change by E. J. Brill under the same name (Leiden, 1996); see also Alan W. Fisher, *The Crimean Tatars* (Stanford, Calif., 1978); Cafer Seydamet Kirimer, *Gaspirali Ismail Bey* (Istanbul 1934). (I take the liberty of adding a personal note here: this book was given as a present to my father by Cafer bey when he visited our home in Dobruca; it played a role in awakening my interest in the history of the Russian Muslims.) See also Edward J. Lazzerini, "Ismail Bey Gaspirinskii (Gaspirali): The Discourse of Modernism and the Russians," in *Tatars of Crimea: Their Struggle for Survival*, ed. Edward Allworth (Durham, N.C., 1988), pp. 149–169; Lazzerini, "Ismail Bey Gaspirinskii and Muslim Modernism in Russia, 1878–1904," Ph.D. diss., University of Washington, 1973, and "Defining the Orient: A Nineteenth-Century Russo-Tatar Polemic over Identity and Cultural Representation," in Allworth, *Muslim Communities*, pp. 33–45.

37. Similar demands for secularization were made by the merchants and professionals in the Ottoman millets. See Roderic Davison, *Reform in the Ottoman Empire, 1856–1876* (Princeton, N.J., 1963).

38. Kirimli, "National Movements," pp. 50–51.

39. See *Tercüman*, 21 November 1905, quoted in Kirimli, "National Movements," p. 56.

40. See Ismail Türkoğlu, "Rusya Türklerinde Abdürreşid Ibrahim," Ph.D. diss., Marmara University, Istanbul, 1993; Nadir Özbek, "Abdürreşid Ibrahim, 1857–1944," M.A. thesis, Boğaziçi University, Istanbul, 1994. For a partial autobiography, see Abdurreşid Ibrahim, *Tercüme-i Halim, Yani Başima Gelenler* (St. Petersburg, n.d.), and *Alem-i Islam ve Japonya'da Intisar-i Islamiyet* (Istanbul, 1911). For additional bibliography, see *Toplumsal Tarih* 19 (July 1995): 7–28, and 20 (August 1955): 6–23. See also Hoe-Soo Lee, *Islam ve Türk Kültürünün Uzak Doğu'ya Yayilmasi* (Ankara, 1988); this work by a Korean scholar provides extensive information on Abdurreşid (pp. 228–58) and Islamic activities in Japan (pp. 108–28). A brief but illuminating description of Abdurreşid appears in Samet Ağaoğlu's portraits of his father's Muslim friends, many from Russia, *Babamin Arkadaşlari*, 3rd ed. (Istanbul, 1969), pp. 73–97.

41. See the minutes of the congress in Ihsan Ilgar, *Rusya'da Birinci Müslüman Kongresi Tutanaklari* (Istanbul, 1988).

42. Bennigsen and Lemercier-Quelquejay, *Islam in the Soviet Union*, pp. 43–44.

43. FO 371/519, p. 17.

44. T. T. Tazhibaev, *Prosveshenie i shkole Kazakhstana v vtoroi polovine XIX veka* (Alma Ata, 1962), p. 196.

45. Kemal H. Karpat, "The Roots of Kazakh Nationalism: Ethnicity, Islam or Land?" *Annals of the Feltrinelli Foundation* (Milan, 1993), pp. 313–33.

46. See Adeeb Khalid, "Tashkent 1917: Muslim Politics in Revolutionary Turkestan," *Slavic Review* 55 (1996): 270–96; see also Seymour Becker, *Russia's Protectorates in Central Asia: Bukhara and Khiva, 1865–1924* (Cambridge, 1968).

47. Some of these issues are discussed in the following essays: Ian M. Matley, "Ethnic Groups of the Bukharan State ca. 1920 and the Question of Nationality"; William L.

Hannaway Jr., "Farsi, the Vatan and the Millat in Bukhara"; and Timur Kocaoğlu, "The Existence of a Bukharan Nationality in the Recent Past," all three of which are in *The Nationality Question in Soviet Central Asia*, ed. Edward Allworth (New York, 1973).

48. Azade-Ayşe Rorlich, "One or More Tatar Nations?" in *Muslim Communities Reemerge: Historical Perspectives on Nationality, Politics, and Opposition in the Former Soviet Union and Yugoslavia*, trans. from the German and French by Caroline Sawyer, ed. Edward Allworth (Durham, N.C., 1994), pp. 61–79. On the exile in 1944, see Anne Sheehy, *The Crimean Tatars and Volga Germans: Soviet Treatment of Two National Minorities* (London, 1971).

49. An excellent description of the panturkist state of mind prevailing among the Ottoman youth, and of the occupation of Baku (including information about the low opinion held by the Russian Muslim revolutionaries toward the "idealism" of Ottoman intellectuals), are found in the memoirs of Şevket Süreyya Aydemir, *Suyu Arayan Adam* (Istanbul, 1967), pp. 62–65, 152–236. For a historical account, see Tadeusz Swietochowski, *Russia and Azerbaijan* (New York, 1995), pp. 71–126.

50. Alexander Bennigsen, "Panturkism and Panislamism in History and Today," *Central Asian Survey*, 3 (1984): 40.

51. Zenkovski erred in claiming that the Azeris were influenced by Afghani and not Turkic considerations. See *Panturkism and Islam in Russia* (Cambridge, 1960) pp. 271–72; also Baymirza Hayit, *Islam and Turkestan under Russian Rule* (Istanbul, 1987); Gerhard von Mende, *Der nationale Kampf der Russlandtürken* (Berlin, 1936); and on identity change, see Edward J. Lazzerini, "Defining the Orient: A Nineteenth-Century Russo-Tatar Polemic over Identity and Cultural Representation," in Allworth, *Muslim Communities*, pp. 46–61.

52. Swietochowski, *Russia and Azerbaijan*, p. 130. Resulzade, the leader of the Azeri nationalists, was freed from prison by Stalin but in 1922 escaped to Istanbul where he became unpopular for engaging in "minority politics." He is regarded today as the founding father of modern Azerbaycan.

53. Yusuf Akçura, *Üç Tarz-i Siyaset* (Istanbul, 1927). See also Paul Dumont, "La Revue *Türk Yurdu* et les musulmans de l'empire russe: 1911–1914," *Cahiers du Monde Russe et Soviétique* 15 (1974), pp. 315–32. See chap. 17.

54. See translation in Robert Devreux in *The Principles of Turkism* (Leiden, 1968), pp. 1–11.

55. Ibid., pp. 4–5.

56. Ibid., p. 5. On Hüseyinzade, see Ali Haydar Bayat, *Ali Bey Hüseyinzade (Prof. Dr. Hüseyinzade Ali Turan) ve Türkiye'de Yayinladiği Eserleri* (Istanbul, 1992).

57. Sultangaliev has become a national figure in Kazan today. A detailed lengthy biography-novel about him was immediately translated from the Kazan Tatar dialect into Turkish and published in Turkey by a foundation dedicated to nationalist causes. It admonished the Turkish marxists for deliberately covering up events in the USSR in not making Sultangaliev known to the Turkish public. Renad Muhammedi, *Sirat Köprüsü: Sultan Galiev* (trans. Mustafa Öner) (Istanbul, 1993).

58. Some of this historical background is analyzed in a contemporary perspective by Igor P. Lipovsky, "Central Asia: In Search of a New Political Identity," *Middle Eastern Journal* 50 (1996): 211–23.

59. See Kemal H. Karpat, "The Socio-Political Environment Conditioning the Foreign Policy of the Central Asian States," in *The Making of Foreign Policy in Russia and the New States of Eurasia*, ed. Adeed Dawisha and Karen Dawisha (New York, 1995), pp. 177–215, and *Foreign Policy of Turkey: Recent Developments* (Madison, Wis., 1996).

CHAPTER 14

1. Charles F. Keyes, "The Dialectics of Ethnic Change," in *Ethnic Change*, ed. Charles F. Keyes (Seattle, 1981), pp. 3–30, passim.

2. Ibid.

3. On these issues, see Nathan Glazer and Daniel P. Moynihan, *Ethnicity: Theory and Experience* (Cambridge, 1975), passim.

4. N. Poulantzas, *State, Power, and Socialism* (London, 1978).

5. Ibrahim Halil Asçidede, *Hatiralar: Geçen Asri Anlatan Kiymetli Vesikalardan Bir Eser* (Istanbul, 1960). See also Marie L. Bremer, *Die Memoiren des türkischen Derwischs Asçi Dede Ibrahim* (Walldorf-Hessen, 1959) (originally the author's Ph.D. dissertation, written in Bonn). The crucial role played by the notables in the transformation of Ottoman society in the eighteenth and nineteenth centuries has finally become a subject of study. See Dina Rizk Khoury, *State and Provincial Society in the Ottoman Empire: Mosul, 1540–1831* (Cambridge, Mass., 1997), and Richard von Leeuwen, *Notables and Clergy in Mount Lebanon, 1736–1840* (Leiden, 1994). See especially chap. 4 and ftn. 11–14 below.

6. Şeyhulislam Mustafa Sabri, *Hilafet-i Muazzuma-i Islamiye, Hilafet ve Kemalizm*, 2nd ed., ed. Sadik Albayrak—who improvised the second part of the title (Istanbul, 1992), quote on p. 33. Sabri's views have found wide circulation among some contemporary Islamists in Turkey.

7. Sait Halim paşa, *Buhranlarimiz* (Istanbul, 1919), pp. 45–46. An opponent of Abdulhamid and Premier during the Young Turks period, Sait (1863–1921) denounced the latter for using the idea of "people" and "national will" to cement their authoritarianism.

8. See *Basiret*, 12 July 1870; and also the issue of 29 July 1870, advising Egypt, Tunisia, Serbia, Montenegro, Wallachia, and Moldavia to remain part of the Ottoman state, or "Ottoman Union," as it called it.

9. See *Ittihad*, 19 July 1876.

10. For a recent account of Midhat see *Uluslararasi Midhat Paşa Semineri Edirne, 8–10 Mayis 1984* (Ankara, 1986). For the trial and death of Mithat paşa, see Bilal Şimşir, *Fransiz Belgelerine göre Mithat Paşa'nin Sonu, 1878–1886* (Ankara, 1970). Mithat has been the darling of the modernist bureaucrats and bête noire of the conservatives-Islamists.

11. Martin van Bruinessen provided a good analysis of the sociopolitical change occurring in southeastern Anatolia and the rise of ethnic consciousness; see *Agha, Shaikh, and State: The Social and Political Structures of Kurdistan* (London, 1992). Von Bruinessen's articles on east Anatolia and the Kurds have been collected, translated, and published in Turkey in a book titled *Kürdistan Üzerine Yazilar*, prep. by N. Kiraç et al. (Istanbul, 1992). On the composition of a cultural system, see Clifford Geertz, *The Interpretation of Cultures: Selected Essays* (New York, 1973).

12. For Syria, see David Dean Commins, *Islamic Reform: Politics and Social Change in Late Ottoman Syria* (New York, 1990), pp. 90–98.

13. See, e.g., classics by M. Çağatay Uluçay, *Onsekiz ve Ondokuzuncu Yüzyillarda Saruhan'da Eşkiyalik ve Halk Hareketleri* (Istanbul, 1955), and *Manisa Tarihi* (Istanbul, 1939); see also M. Şerif Firat, *Doğu Illeri ve Varto Tarihi* (Ankara, 1948); Osman Bayatli, *Bergama'da Yakin Tarih Olaylari XVII–XIX Yüzyil* (Izmir, 1957); and Mehmet Bilgin, *Sürmene* (Istanbul, 1990). My own research (not published) centered on the provinces of Gaziantep (Aintap) and Balikesir provided the empirical evidence for the ideas expressed in the text. See note 5 above.

14. See, e.g., Sami Önal, *Milli Mücadelede Oltu* (Ankara, 1968).

15. See Necmeddin Şahiner, *Bilinmeyen Taraflariyle Bediuzzaman Said Nursi*, 7th ed. (Istanbul, 1988); Şerif Mardin, *Religion and Social Change in Modern Turkey* (Albany, N.Y., 1989); *EI* (new ed.) s.vv. "Nursi" and "Nurdjuluk."

16. Şahiner, *Bilinmeyen*, pp. 84–85.

17. Ibid., p. 90.

18. Peter Hardy, *The Muslims of British India* (London, 1972), p. 58; see also my chap. 1, section on Indian revivalism.

19. See Kemal H. Karpat, "Gli stati balcanici."

20. Eliezer Tauber, "The Political Role of the Algerian Element in Late Ottoman Syria," *International Journal of Turkish Studies* 5 (winter 1990–91): pp. 28–29.

21. Commins, *Islamic Reform*, pp. 41–42, 89–98.

22. See Reeva S. Simon, "The Education of an Iraqi Ottoman Officer," in *The Origins of Arab Nationalism*, ed. Rashid Khalidi (New York, 1991), pp. 156ff.

23. Liah Greenfeld, *Nationalism: Five Roads to Modernity* (Cambridge, Mass., 1992).

24. See Kemal H. Karpat, *Ottoman Population, 1830–1914* (Madison, Wis., 1985), pp. 118–90.

25. The history of the Armenians as a *millet* in the classical Ottoman Empire and the development of Armenian nationalism have generally been treated with considerable subjectivity; for a more balanced view, see Benjamin Braude and Bernard Lewis, eds., *Christians and Jews in the Ottoman Empire* (New York, 1980).

26. A. Synet, *Les Grecs en l'empire ottoman* (Constantinople, 1878).

27. Fikret Adanir, *Die makedonische Frage: Ihre Entstehung und Entwicklung bis 1908* (Wiesbaden, 1979).

28. On the Bosnian identity, see Tone Bringa, *Being Muslim the Bosnian Way* (Princeton, N.J., 1995), and my review in *American Historical Review* 1997 (102): 1189–90.

29. BA, Bab-i Ali Evrak Odasi, no. 318922, 18 January 1914.

30. See the series of diplomatic dispatches in FO, 424; vol. 192, p. 143; vol. 197, p. 39; vol. 198, p. 93; and vol. 202, p. 78.

31. FO 212, vol. 186, p. 62 (Consul Eyres to P. Curie), 25 December 1895.

32. See FO 424; vol. 184, p. 522, 9 December 1895.

33. These views were put forth by P. Risal in a lengthy article with the suggestive title of "Les Turcs à la recherche d'une âme nationale," *Mercure de France* (August 1912): 673–707. The author was actually Munis Tekinalp (Moise Cohen), a Jew from Salonica, who also was involved with the Turkish nationalist movements. For a book-length study that includes most of Tekinalp's principal political writings, see Jacob M. Landau, *Tekinalp, Turkish Patriot 1883–1961* (Leiden, 1984).

34. Quoted in Risal, "Les Turcs," reproduced in Landau, *Tekinalp*, p. 63.

CHAPTER 15

1. See Arminius Vambery, *La Turquie d'aujourd'hui et d'autant quarante ans* (Paris, 1898).

2. Bernard Lewis, "Watan," *Journal of Contemporary History* 26 (1991): 526, provides a number of historical examples of the usage of *vatan*.

3. These questions are dealt with in the ninth-century work of Muqaddasi, *Hudud al'Alam: The Regions of the World: A Persian Geography*, trans. V. Minorsky (Karachi, 1980); and in Shaybani, *The Islamic Law of Nations: Shaybani's Siyar*, trans. Majid Khadduri (Baltimore, Md., 1966); André Miguel, *La Géographie humaine du monde musulman jusqu'au milieu de 11e siècle* (Paris, 1967); Xavier de Planhol, *Les Fondements géographiques de l'histoire de l'islam* (Paris, 1968); Mohammad Tal'at Ghunaymi, *The Muslim Conception of International Law and the Western Approach* (The Hague, 1968). Lack of space prevents an in-depth analysis of the territory in Islam.

4. BA, Yildiz, SHM, doc. 170/6, 7 June 1882.

5. I have used the text edited and published by one of the main authorities on Namik Kemal, namely Mustafa Nihat Özön, ed., *Vatan Yahut Silistre*, 2nd ed. (Istanbul, 1943). All the quotations in the text, if not otherwise specified, are translated by me directly from this edition.

6. Özön, *Vatan*, pp. 80–94. Various articles are reproduced by Özön as appendices.

7. Bernard Lewis, *The Emergence of Modern Turkey* (London, 1965), p. 332.

8. These meanings of the term are discussed in David Kushner, *The Rise of Turkish Nationalism: 1876–1908* (London, 1977), pp. 24–26.

9. Sultan Abdulhamid, *Siyasi Hatiratim* (Istanbul, 1970), pp. 166–67.

10. Ahmet Cevdet paşa, *Tezakir*, 3 vols., ed. Cavid Baysun (Ankara, 1953), vol. 1, p. 85; see also Cemil Meriç, *Cevdet Paşa'nin Toplum ve Devlet Gürüşü*, 3rd ed. (Istanbul, 1992), p. 80.

11. Albert Hourani, *Arabic Thought in the Liberal Age, 1798–1939* (London, 1962), pp. 78–79.

12. On the bureaucracy, see Carter V. Findley, *Ottoman Civil Officialdom: A Social History* (Princeton, N.J., 1988), pp. 22–24.

13. See BA, Yildiz, sec. 11, file 5, 1763, 10 January 1900 (memorandum from sultan's palace to premier's office).

14. Ibid., sec. 18, file 39, 1858.

15. Ibid., sec. 18, file 39 (n.d., ca. 1890).

16. Ibid.

17. I have used the original, which is catalogued in the archives as "Hatirat-i Seniye" (Imperial Memoirs), BA, Yildiz, sec. 8, file 77/3, 2009. These have been printed, with some updating in language, in various editions of Abdulhamid's memoirs.

18. See Ebul'ula Mardin, *Huzur Dersleri*, ed. Ismet Sungurbey, vol. 1 (Istanbul, 1951), vols. 2, 3 (Istanbul, 1966), quotation from vol. 1, p. 7. The late Ebul-ula Mardin, who repeatedly stressed the importance of the "huzur" debates, was a professor of civil law at the University of Istanbul. A truly great mind and a good Muslim, at home with the sciences of both the West and East and the Ottoman Muslim legacy, he had been secretary in the Ottoman Parliament for the Young Turks and a professor of Mecelle (the modernized religious code) in the Darulfünun, the Ottoman University. As a former student of his, I gratefully acknowledge his patience and subtlety in making me appreciate the continuity of history and culture as well as the necessity of change and adaptation.

19. See the Türk Yili of 1928, republished in 1990 as *Türkçülük*.

20. See Kushner, *The Rise of Turkish Nationalism.*

21. Nihad Sami Banarli, "Sultan Abdulhamid'in Türkçeciliği," *Hayat Tarih Mecmuasi* (December 1967).

22. Frances Trix, "The Stamboul Latin Alphabet of S. Sami," paper presented at the Middle Eastern Studies Association conference, Phoenix, Ariz., November 1994. See also bibliography. For a balanced, objective view of S. Sami by an Albanian scholar, see Hasan Kaleshi, *Le Rôle de Chemseddin Sami Frachery dans la formation de deux langues littéraires: Turque et albanaise*, Institut des Etudes Balcaniques, Serbian Academy of Sciences and Arts (Belgrade, 1970), pp. 197–216.

23. William L. Cleveland, *The Making of an Arab Nationalist: Ottomanism and Arabism in the Life and Thought of Sati' al-Husri* (Princeton, N.J., 1971).

24. This is Paul Wittek's basic thesis, that as the conquest of the Balkans laid the Empire's foundations, its loss led to the Empire's doom. See *The Rise of the Ottoman Empire* (New York, 1971).

25. Cited by Niyazi Berkes, *Ziya Gökalp and Turkish Nationalism* (New York, 1959), pp. 43–45.

26. See details in Kemal H. Karpat, "Gli stati balcanici e il nazionalismo: L'immagine e la realtà," *Quaderni Storici* (84) 1993: 679–718.

27. In order to understand better the impact of migration on the formation of modern Turkey treated in this work, I undertook sociological fieldwork on contemporary internal migration in Turkey and published the results in *The Gecekondu: Rural Migration and Urbanization in Turkey* (New York, 1976). The field study permitted me to witness and understand in a concrete, tangible manner the impact of migration on the identity and cultural outlook of the migrants. The insights gained from my work on the Gecekondu led me to research the demographic history of the Ottoman Empire in the nineteenth century, and the quantitative data were published as *Ottoman Population, 1830–1914: Demographic and Social Characteristics* (Madison, Wis., 1985).

28. I am currently preparing a detailed study of the settlement of immigrants in Anatolia, 1850–1914; for general information, however, see my *Ottoman Population*, chap. 4, and "Ottoman Urbanism: The Crimean Migration to Dobruca and the Establishment of Mecidiye," *International Journal of Turkish Studies* 3 (winter 1984–85): 1–26.

29. Sefer E. Berzeg, *Kafkas Diasporasinda Edebiyatçilar ve Yazarlar Sözlüğü* (Samsun,

1995); the author bears the name of one of the smaller but aristocratic tribes of Caucasia that emigrated into the Ottoman Empire in the nineteenth century.

30. Nusret Baycan, *Türk Istiklal Harbinde Şehit Düşen Subaylar* (Ankara, 1988), pp. 677–740.

31. See Hourani, *Arabic Thought*, pp. 260–323; it is possible to argue, based on his latter writings on Ottomans, that Hourani drastically changed his earlier views that had reflected his sympathies for the nationalistic writings of the Arab Christians.

32. For the main works on Arab nationalism see Ernest C. Dawn, *From Ottomanism to Arabism: Essays on the Origins of Arab Nationalism* (Urbana, Ill., 1973); N. Zeine, *The Emergence of Arab Nationalism with a Background Study of Arab-Turkish Relations in the Near East* (Beirut, 1966); Bassam Tibi, *Arab Nationalism: A Critical Enquiry*, 2nd Eng. ed. (New York, 1990) (the original 1971 version is in German); and Rashid Khalidi et al., eds., *The Origins of Arab Nationalism* (New York, 1991). For a bibliography on Arab nationalism see Kemal H. Karpat, *Political and Social Thought in the Contemporary Middle East* (New York, 1968).

33. William W. Haddad and William Ochsenwald, eds., *Nationalism in a Non-National State: The Dissolution of the Ottoman Empire* (Columbus, Ohio, 1977).

34. See Sylvia Haim, *Arab Nationalism: An Anthology* (Berkeley, 1962), pp. 78–81; Hourani, *Arabic Thought*, pp. 271–73.

35. Eliezer Tauber divides the "Arab national societies" formed after 1908 into four categories. One category, made up of al-Ahd, al-Fatat, etc., were a response to the Young Turks' nationalist policies, while the rest followed regional goals. However, there were earlier societies, such as al-Nahda al-Arabiyya, which originated in an educational society established by Tahir al-Cezairi with the purpose of spreading Arabism (*'uruba*) among the youth of Damascus. This Arab society was not revolutionary, separatist, or nationalist; it was, in fact, an Arabic version of the Türk Yurdu. It did not want to separate the Arabs from the Ottoman Empire, but merely to gain recognition for Arabic as an official school language and to increase Arabs' participation in local government. One member, Muhibb al-Din, was caught with the forbidden books of Namik Kemal and had to flee to Istanbul, where he "noticed that the Arab students were ignorant of their language and preferred to speak Turkish." Consequently, by 1907 Muhibb al-Din had begun to teach Arabic to students in Istanbul with the purpose of making "the intellectual Arab youth aware of their Arabism and to encourage them to cooperate in improving Ottoman society." See Tauber, *The Emergence of the Arab Movements* (London, 1993), pp. 45, 47.

36. Eliezer Tauber, "Rashid Rida as a Pan-Arabist before World War I," *The Muslim World* 79, no. 2 (1989): 102–12; also Tauber, *Emergence*. See also Malcolm H. Kerr, *Arab Cold War, 1958–1964; A Study of Ideology in Politics* (London, 1965).

37. Hasan Kayali, *Arabs and Young Turks* (Berkeley, 1997), pp. 1–25.

38. Youssef M. Choueiri, *Arab History and the Nation State* (London, 1989), pp. 198, 201. Khaled Fahmy, *All the Pasha's Men: Mehmed Ali, His Army and the Making of Modern Egypt* (Cambridge, 1999).

39. Salim Siddiqui, "Nation-States as Obstacles to the Total Transformation of the Ummah," in *The Impact of Nationalism on the Muslim World*, ed. M. Ghayasuddin (London, 1986), p. 2.

40. *The Memoirs of Ismail Kemal Bey* (London, 1920), p. 366.

41. Sylvia Haim, ed., *Arab Nationalism: An Anthology* (Berkeley, 1962), pp. 172–88, from which the quotations are taken; the original *Al-Islam wa'l-qawmiyya al-Arabiyya* (Baghdad, 1952) appeared in translation in *Die Welt des Islams* 3 nos. 3–4 (1954).

42. Hourani, *Arabic Thought*, p. 281.

43. Ahmet Niyazi, *Hatirat-i Niyazi yahut, Tarihçe-yi inkilab-i kebir-i Osmanlidan bir sahife* (Istanbul, 1910). These memoirs were serialized in 1908 following the decision of the CUP Congress.

44. The literature in English on the Young Turks is still limited and general. Hanioğlu's published work covers the period up to 1902: see M. Şükrü Hanioğlu, *The*

Young Turks in Opposition (New York, 1995). See also Feroz Ahmad, *The Young Turks: The Committee of Union and Progress in Turkish Politics, 1908–1914* (Oxford, 1969); Hasan Kayali, *Arabs and Young Turks*; and Erik Jan Zurcher, *The Unionist Factor: The Role of the Committee of Union and Progress in the Turkish National Movement, 1905–1926* (Leiden, 1984).

45. See Cemal Kutay, *Şehit Sadrazam Talat Paşa'nin Gurbet Hatiralari*, 2nd ed., 3 vols. (Istanbul, 1983) (henceforth *Talat Paşa Hatiralari*); only 1,500 copies of this work were printed. Talat's memoirs dictated in Berlin were in the possession of Ahmet Hamid Ortaç who delivered them to Kutay. See also Tevfik Çavdar, *Talat Paşa: Bir Örgüt Ustasinin Yaşam Öyküsü* (Ankara, 1984), which provides excellent account of the social and political environment of the Balkans, where Talat grew up. For the respect shown to Talat in Turkey, see Robert W. Olson, "The Remains of Talat: A Dialectic between Republic and Empire," *Die Welt des Islams* 26 (1986): 46–56.

46. Kutay, *Talat Paşa Hatiralari* I, pp. 51–57.

47. Ibid., pp. 16–17. These views about Talat paşa asking Abdulhamid's advice on state affairs are supported also by the memoirs of Fethi Okyar, *Üç Devirde Bir Adam* (Istanbul, 1980).

48. Hanioğlu, *The Young Turks* p. 214.

49. Okyar, *Üç Devirde Bir Adam*, pp. 104–5.

50. Osman S. Osmanoğlu (this is their surname), *The Ottoman Family. On the 700th Anniversary of the Foundation of the Ottoman State* (Istanbul, 1999). The author wrote: "For more than 600 years we served our country faithfully. . . . Our successors . . . made it possible for our nation to remain free and headed for greatness again," Ibid, p. 5.

51. The study of local and regional histories, as mentioned in a different context, could and should shed significant light on national events, especially in Turkey where local history has been almost entirely ignored. For the events of 1906 in Erzurum, see Muammer Demirel, *Ikinci Meşrutiyet Öncesi Erzurum'da Halk Hareketleri 1906–1907* (Ankara, 1990); Mehmet Nusret, *Tarihçe-i Erzurum Yahut Hemşehrilere Armağan* (Istanbul, 1922); and Aykut Kansu, *1908 Devrimi* (Istanbul, 1995), published in English as *The Revolution of 1908 in Turkey* (New York, 1997).

CHAPTER 16

1. Turgut Özal, *Turkey in Europe and Europe in Turkey* (Nicosia, Cyprus, 1991). For a Turkish self-appraisal see Demirtaş Ceyhun, *Ah Şu Biz "Karabiyikli" Türkler* [We the black-mustached Turks] (Istanbul, 1992). Ozal's book was actually written by officials of the Foreign Ministry although he reviewed it closely.

2. For the latest detailed study of the genesis of the CUP and the philosophy of the leaders, see M. Şükrü Hanioğlu, *The Young Turks in Opposition* (New York, 1995). See also Ernest E. Ramsaur, *The Young Turks: Prelude to the Revolution of 1908* (Princeton, N.J., 1957); Feroz Ahmad, *The Young Turks: The Committee of Union and Progress in Turkish Politics, 1908–1914* (Oxford, 1969); and Hasan Kayali, *Arabs and Young Turks* (Berkeley, 1997).

3. R. Yücel Özkaya, "Tanzimatin Siyasi Yönden Meşrutiyete Etkileri ve Cemiyet-i Islamiye ve Başkanvekili Mühaddin Effendi'nin Mesrutiyet Hakkindaki Düşünceleri," *Tanzimat'in 150 Yildönumü Uluslararasi Sempozyumsu* (Ankara, 1944), pp. 301–321. See also Hanioğlu, *Young Turks*, pp. 33–70.

4. The relations between Reşad Efendi and CUP are objectively and excellently described by his secretary and a trusted CUP appointee, see Halit Ziya (Uşakligil), *Saray ve Ötesi: Son Hatiralar*, 3 vols. (Istanbul, 1940–41). A later edition published in Istanbul in 1965 was edited by Faik R. Unat.

5. Ottoman Islam in the Balkans deserves a lengthy, unbiased, and detached study; for some lucid and comprehensive accounts, see Dennison Rusinow, "The Ottoman Legacy in Yugoslavia's Disintegration and Civil War," in *Imperial Legacy: The Ottoman*

Imprint on the Balkans and the Middle East, ed. L. Carl Brown (New York, 1996), pp. 78–99; also H. T. Norris, *Islam in the Balkans: Religion and Society between Europe and the Arab World* (Columbia, S.C., 1993). See also various sections in this study.

6. C. A. Macartney, *National States and National Minorities* (London, 1934), p. 136.

7. Louis Kossuth, the well-known leader of the Hungarian revolution, wrote a Turkish grammar, and David Urquhart, the Russophobe who, as a British member of parliament, became a defender of the Hungarian cause, wrote extensively about the Hungarian Turkish ethnic kinship; see Kemal H. Karpat, "The Impact of Hungarian Refugees in the Ottoman Empire, 1849–1851," *Hungarian Heritage Review* (March 1990): 131–53. For the use of the term *Turkistan*, supposedly inspired by the French, see Masami Arai, "An Imagined Nation: The Idea of the Ottoman Nation as a Key to Modern Ottoman History," *Oriens* 27 (1991): 1–11.

8. See Mübecel Kiziltan, prep., *Fatma Aliye Hanim: Yaşami, Sanati, Yapitlari ve Nisvan-i Islam* (Istanbul, 1993); Carter V. Findley, "La Soumise, la subversive: Fatma Aliye, romancière et féministe," *Turcica* 27 (1995): 153–75.

9. Ahmet Mithat, *Uss-i Inkilap* (Istanbul, 1294 [1878]), pp. 7–13; see also chapter 15.

10. Yusuf Akçura, *Türk Yurdu* (Istanbul, 1914), p. 167.

11. See Ibrahim Yüksel, *Azerbaycan'da Fikir Hayati ve Basin* (Istanbul, 1991); also chapter 13. For an extensive treatment of the history of the Turks' alphabets, see Bilal N. Şimşir, *Türk Yazi Devrimi* (Ankara, 1992).

12. Akçura(oğlu), *Türkçülük: Türklügün Tarihi Gelişimi* (Istanbul, 1978), pp.94–95.

13. For the biographies of these early "Turkists," see Ahmet Hamdi Tanpinar, *19. Asir Türk Edebiyati Tarihi*, 4th ed. (Istanbul, 1976), and Akçura, *Türkçülük*. Tanpinar's elitist history gives only one line to Yurdakul, but Akçura praised him highly (pp. 116ff.). On Yurdakul, see also John Wilkinson Gibb, *A History of Ottoman Poetry*, 6 vols. (London, 1900–10).

14. These were partly reproduced in Akçura, *Türkçülük*, 118n; and, Gibb, *History*, 6, 134–35.

15. See Kemal H. Karpat, "Social Environment and Literature: The Young Turks Era in the Literary Works of Ömer Seyfeddin," *Islamic World from Classical to the Modern Age: Essays in Honor of Bernard Lewis* (Princeton, N.J., 1989), pp. 69–94; also "Ömer Seyfeddin and the Transformation of the Turkish Thought," *Revue des études sud-est européennes* 10 (1972), with bibliography. See also Tahir Alangu's extensive study *Ömer Seyfettin: Ülkücü Bir Yazarin Romani* (Istanbul, 1968).

16. See Ömer Seyfettin, *Yarinki Turan Devleti*, 3rd ed. (Istanbul, 1980), repr. of the original, pub. 1914.

17. The information on modern Turkish literature upon which the following discussion is based is gleaned from numerous works on the history of Turkish literature, including most prominently Ahmet Hamdi Tanpinar, *19. Asir Turk Edebiyati Tarihi*; Ahmet O. Evin, *Origins and Development of the Turkish Novel* (Minneapolis, Minn., 1983); especially Cevdet Kudret, *Türk Edebiyatinda Hikaye ve Roman, 1859–1959*, 3 vols. (Istanbul, 1970–90); and Niyazi Aki, *Ondokuzuncu Yüzyil Türk Tiyatrosu Tarihi* (Erzurum, 1963), and other works. An excellent article by Inci Enginun is in Kemal H. Karpat, *The Ottoman Past and Today's Turkey* (Brill, forthcoming).

18. Ahmet Mithat paşa, *Ahmet Mithat Efendinin Tiyatrolari*, ed. Inci Enginün (Istanbul, 1990).

19. For the antislavery literature, see Ismail Parlatir, *Tanzimat Edebiyatinda Kölelik* (Ankara, 1987), and Y. Hakan Erdem, *Slavery in the Ottoman Empire and Its Demise, 1800–1909* (New York, 1996).

20. For the most up-to-date biographical and bibliographical information on Bursali Ahmed Tahir, see *Türklerin Ulum ve Fününa Hizmetleri* (Ankara, 1996); also the *Islam Ansiklopedisi* (new Turkish ed.) and the introduction to the reprint of Mehmet Tahir, *Osmanli Müellifleri* (Istanbul, 1972).

21. Tahir, *Türklerin Ulum*, pp. 25–26.

22. See the introduction by Vahid Çabuk to the reprint of Ahmet Refik's *Alimler ve San'atkarlar*, publication of the Ministry of Culture, no. 376 (Ankara, 1980). (After 1965

the government began to publish discreetly a series of books on Ottoman history that were taboo before 1950.)

23. Ali Said, *Saray Hatiralari: Sultan Abdulhamid'in Hayati* (Istanbul, 1994), p. 125; the author's name is a pseudonym. The memoirs lauding Abdulhamid were published in Istanbul newspapers only in 1920–23, when the city was under British occupation.

24. For negative portrayal, see *Ibretnuma,* ed. Bekir Sitki Baykal and published by the Turkish Historical Society) (Ankara, 1968).

25. The purposes of the association are stated in "Ifade-i Meram," *Tarih-i Osman-i Encümeni Mecmuasi* 1 (April 1910): 1–3. On the society in general, see Hasan Albayrak, "The Ottoman Historical Society," *Journal of the Middle East Studies Society at Columbia University* (1988): 87–109; Busra Ersanli-Behar, *Iktidar ve Tarih: Türkiye'de "Resmi Tarih" Tezinin Oluşumu, 1929–1937* (Istanbul, 1992); see also the section on Köprülü in chapter 17.

26. Taner Timur, *Osmanli Kimliği* (Istanbul, 1994). It blames Western racial theories of undue influence on the Turkish nationalism of the Republic.

27. For Akçura's communication, see *Birinci Türk Tarihi Kongresi, Konferanslar, Munakaşalar* (Ankara, [n.d., ca. 1932]), pp. 577–607.

28. See Tuncer Baykara, *Zeki Velidi Togan* (Ankara, 1989); Zeki Velidi Togan, *Tarihde Usul,* 2nd ed. (Istanbul, 1969); Togan, *Türklüğün Mukadderati Üzerine* (Istanbul, 1977); and Togan, *Hatiralar* (Istanbul, 1969). Togan's bibliography includes 337 titles. For the post-1908 period, see [S. H. Takizade], "Les Courants politiques dans la Turquie," *Revue du Monde Musulman* 21 (1912): 158–221; and "Le Panislamisme et le panturquisme," *Revue du Monde Musulman* 22 (1913): 179–222.

29. See M. Şükrü Hanioğlu, *Bir Siyasal Örgüt Olarak "Osmanli Ittihad ve Terakki Cemiyeti" ve "Jön Türkler,"* vol. 1 (1889–1902) (1986; 2nd ed., Istanbul, 1989), pp. 627–40, 645–50 passim. The idea that the Young Turks did not develop a theory of nationalism is expressed even more forcefully by Hanioğlu in his *Young Turks in Opposition,* p. 202.

30. Abdulhalim Memduh, *Mazlum Türkler: Meiyze* (Paris, 1902); Tunali Hilmi, *Onbirinci Hutbe: Türkiyalilik, Osmanliliktir, Osmanlilik Türkiyaliliktir* (Geneva, 1902). (Note that Tunali prefers to use the term *Turkiyalilik* (of Turkey, or Turkishness.) Tunali acquired fame after 1908 and especially in the Republic. In his early works he regarded Ottomanism and Turkishness as one and the same. Whether a Turkish nation existed prior to 1908–1918 has recently become subject of debate. Feroz Ahmad, while praising highly M. Şükrü Hanioğlu's *The Young Turks in Opposition* in *American Historical Review* (AHR) (December 1996), criticized his use of the term *millet* as the equivalent of the "nation" instead of a religious community. Hanioğlu answered that the meaning of the term derived from its content and that at the turn of the century for elites the term *millet* defined a nation. Ahmad demurred: in his view, the term *millet* defined basically a religious community, and the Ottoman leaders feared nationalism as a threat to their multiethnic empire. For an exchange of letters between Ahmad and Hanioğlu, see AHR (October 1997). The issue may be answered by a correct understanding of this chapter that there can exist a nation or *millet* even without a well-defined ethnic core.

31. The economic policy of the Young Turks is analyzed extensively in Zafer Toprak, *Türkiye'de "Milli Iktisat" 1908–1918* (Ankara, 1982).

32. See Paul Dumont, "La Revue *Turk Yurdu* et les musulmans de l'empire russe, 1911–1914," *Cahiers du Monde Russe et Soviétique* 15 (1974): 315–32; Yusuf Akçura, *Türk Yili* (Istanbul, 1928). See chap. 13.

33. The quote is from Beyatli's piece on Gökalp in Beysanoğlu, *Ziya Gökalp Için Yazilanlar,* p. 244.

34. The psychological and personal aspects of Albanian nationalism are evident in some memoirs: see, for instance, Kazim Nami (Duru), *"Ittihat ve Terakki" Hatiralarim* (Istanbul, 1957), and *Arnavutluk ve Makedonia Hatiralarim* (Istanbul, 1959); Resneli Niyazi bey, *Hatirat-i Niyazi* (Istanbul, 1826 [1910]); and Ismail Kemal, *The Memoirs of Ismail Kemal Bey* (London, 1920). See also the memoirs of one of the leading Balkan Turkish nationalists and publisher of the *Rumili,* Ethem Ruhi (Balkan), *Balkan Hatiralari, Canli Tarihler* (Istanbul, 1947).

35. On *cihad*, see Jacob M. Landau, *The Politics of Pan-Islam* (Oxford, 1990), pp. 98–142; for the texts of the *cihad fetva*s, see J. L. Lewis, "The Ottoman Proclamation of Jihad in 1914," *Islamic Quarterly* 19 (January–June 1975): 157–63. See chap. 11, where the same information is provided in different context.

36. The ideological situation prior to 1908 is analyzed in some detail in Hanioğlu, *The Young Turks in Opposition*, pp. 7–32, and in Niyazi Berkes, *The Development of Secularism in Turkey* (Montreal, 1964), pp. 337–46.

37. Kemal H. Karpat, "The Alliance of Modern Medicine and Islam: The Anti-Abortion Campaign During the Reign of Abdulhamid II," paper presented to the 7th International Congress of Ottoman Economic and Social History, Heidelberg, 25–29 July 1995.

38. Berkes, *Secularism*, pp. 367–84.

39. See Berkes, *Secularism*, p. 340; Tarik Zafer Tunaya, *Islamcilik Cereyani* Istanbul, 1962), pp. 73–76; M. Şükrü Hanioğlu, *Doktor Abdullah Cevdet ve Dönemi* (Istanbul, 1981).

40. Ziya Gökalp, *Türkçülüğün Esaslari*, ed. Mehmet Kaplan (Ankara, 1990), p. 55.

CHAPTER 17

1. For the most part, Turkish nationalism has been studied as consisting of Ziya Gökalp's ideas and thus deprived of the broad historical-ideological-social context in which it developed. Uriel Heyd, *Foundations of Turkish Nationalism: The Life and Teachings of Ziya Gökalp*, (London, 1950), is a useful but dated book. In Niyazi Berkes, *Ziya Gökalp, Turkish Nationalism and Western Civilization* (New York, 1959), an analysis of Gökalp's ideas is restricted to the introduction to the book, a mere 18 pages out of 327 pages of text and footnotes. It appeared originally in the *Middle East Journal* 4, no. 4 (autumn 1954), but in the book Berkes has provided translations of Gökalp's main writings, some of which are difficult to find, and useful bibliographic footnotes. It is the most useful anthology available to the English reader. In this chapter I have made extensive use of Berkes's translations along with the originals. Taha Parla, *The Social and Political Thought of Ziya Gökalp, 1876–1924* (Leiden, 1985), is a concise, precise, and indispensable piece of scholarship with a very valuable bibliography that helps the reader follow changes in Gökalp's ideas. See also *The Principles of Turkism*, trans. Robert Devereux (Leiden, 1968), which is a translation of Gökalp's main book. See also François Georgeon, *Aux Origines du nationalisme turc, Yusuf Akçura (1870–1935)* (Paris, 1980), and Ahmet Temir, *Yusuf Akçura* (Ankara, 1987). A broad historical survey is provided by David Kushner, *The Rise of Turkish Nationalism, 1876–1908* (London, 1977).

A relatively new, meticulous piece of scholarship on Turkish nationalism is by Masami Arai, *Turkish Nationalism in the Young Turk Era* (Leiden, 1992). Other works on Gökalp and nationalism include Cavit O. Tütengil, *Ziya Gökalp Üzerine Notlar* (Istanbul, 1964); *Ziya Gökalp Hakkinda bir Bibliografya Denemesi* (Istanbul, 1949); M. Emin Erişirgil, *Bir Fikir Adaminin Romani: Ziya Gökalp* (Istanbul, 1951); Kazim Nami Duru, *Ziya Gökalp* (Istanbul, 1975); Hilmi Z. Ülken, *Türkiye'de Çağdaş Düşünce Tarihi*, 2 vols. (Istanbul, 1979); and Orhan Türkdoğan, *Ziya Gökalp Sosyolojisinde Bazi Kavramlar Değerlendirilimesi* (Istanbul, 1978). A very useful compilation of articles written by Gökalp's friends and contemporaries is Şevket Beysanoğlu, ed., *Ziya Gökalp Için Yazilanlar-Söylenenler*, vol. 2 (Ankara, 1975). Gökalp's main writings are mentioned throughout this chapter except for his posthumous *Türk Medeniyet Tarihi* [History of Turkish civilization] (Istanbul, 1926), which has limited value.

Ziya Gökalp's main work is *Türkçülüğün Esaslari* (TE) (Ankara, 1923). It consists of some of his revised and edited articles which appeared in his *Türkleşmek, Islamlaşmak, Muasirlaşmak* in 1918. The name of this last book derives from his article "Üç Cereyan" (Three currents); the book includes articles that do not appear in the TE. The TE includes new pieces as part of the nationalist plan of action implemented as Turkism. The basic and most influential account of the history of Turkism in addition to Gökalp's article on the subject, is Yusuf Akçura's piece in the *Türk Yili* (1928), which was published later separately as *Türkçülük: Türklüğün Tarihi Gelişimi* [Turkism: The historical development of Turkism] (Istanbul, 1978). In this work I relied mainly on the latest edition of *Türkçülüğün Esaslari*, which came out in 1990 as part of the series on Turkish classics and was edited by the late Mehmet Kaplan, a distinguished literary critic and historian, with the assistance of Kenan Akyüz, a literary historian.

2. Parla, *Social and Political Thought*, p. 13.

3. See Gökalp's autobiography, which appeared first in the *Küçük Mecmua*, no. 17 (1923), and is translated in Berkes, *Ziya Gökalp, Turkish Nationalism*, pp. 35ff, and summarized in Parla, *Social and Political Thought*, pp. 10–32. For a critical view of incomplete use of Gökalp's writings see Andrew Davison, *Secularism and Revivalism in Turkey* (New Haven, 1998), pp. 97–100. Uriel Heyd is criticized.

4. Ali Haydar Bayat, *Ali Bey Hüseyinzade ve Türkiye'de Yayinladiği Eserleri* (Istanbul, 1992); see also Akçura, *Türkçülük*, passim.

5. The exact founding dates and the names of the founders of these associations are in Arai, *Turkish Nationalism*, pp. 28–31.

6. For Gökalp's pre-1908 views, see Şevket Beysanoğlu, *Ziya Gökalp'in Ilk Yazi Hayati (1894–1909)* (Istanbul, 1956), pp. 30–105, passim.

7. This interesting and illuminating discussion is summarized in Arai, *Turkish Nationalism*, pp. 42–45.

8. For Tanriover's views, see his writings assembled in *Dağ Yolu* (Ankara, 1928). See also Füsun Üstel, "Türk Ocaklari (1912–1931)," Ph.D. diss., Ankara University, 1986.

9. Jacob M. Landau, *Pan-Turkism from Irredentism to Cooperation* (Bloomington, Ind., 1995), pp. 40–42, 76–77; see also M. Uzun and Y. Hacaloğlu, eds., *Türk Ocaklari Belgeseli: Belgeler, Resimler, 1912–1994* (Ankara, 1994). For a claim that the Ocaks were established in order to endow the Turks with national consciousness and make them a true nation, see Yusuf Sarinay, *Türk Milliyetçiliğinin Tarihi Gelişimi ve Türk Ocaklari: 1912–1931* (Istanbul, 1994).

10. Reproduced in Temir, *Yusuf Akçura*, p. 44. "Race" has the meaning of lineage.

11. See Kemal H. Karpat, "The People's Houses in Turkey," *Middle East Journal* (winter–spring 1963).

12. Kemal Solak, *Islama Göre Millet, Milliyetçilik ve Irkçilik* (Istanbul, 1979), pp. 105–10. See also Şevket Beysanoğlu, ed., *Ziya Gökalp Için Yazilanlar, Söylenenler*, vol. 2 (Ankara, 1975).

13. H. Mustafa Genç, *Islami Açidan Ziya Gökalp ve Türkçüler* (Istanbul, 1978). Marxists rejected Gökalp too because of his antimaterialsim and lack of scholarship. Mustafa Turkeş, "The Ideology of the Kadro (Cadre) Movement: A Patriotic Leftist Movement in Turkey," in *Turkey before and after Atatürk*, ed. Sylvia [Haim] Kedouri (London, 1999), pp. 92–119. See also Şevket Sureyya (Aydemir), "Ziya Gökalp," *Kadro* 1, no. 2 (1932): 29–40. Aydemir was one of the four leaders of the Kadro, an elitist leftist movement. He regarded Gökalp as dated and unscientific.

14. Gökalp, *Türkçülüğün* (Kaplan ed.), pp. 16–23. He had expressed his thought on this issue in other articles titled more accurately "Millet Nedir?" [What is a nation?] *Ictimayat Mecmuasi* 1, no. 3 (1917), *Küçük Mecmua*, no. 281 (1923), and *Yeni Mecmua* 4, no. 70 (1923).

15. Gökalp, "Milli Vicdani Kuvvetlendirmek," *Türkçülüğün* (Kaplan ed.), pp. 81–88. Also Parla, *Social and Political Thought*, p. 75.

16. Berkes, *Ziya Gökalp, Turkish Nationalism*, p. 133.

17. Ibid., p. 128; emphasis added.

18. Tunaya's views appear in Beysanoğlu, *Ziya Gökalp*, pp. 332–33, and were originally published in the *Milliyet*, 27 October–3 November 1974. The discussions were part of the reaction to the marxist drive—led in part by Kurdish nationalists—to downgrade Turkish nationalism in all its aspects.

19. See Heyd, *Foundations of Turkish Nationalism*; Berkes, *Ziya Gökalp*; and Parla, *Social and Political Thought*.

20. See Ziya Gökalp, "Ictimayat ve Fikriyat: Cemiyette Büyük Adamlarin Tesiri," *Ictimayat Mecmuasi* 4, nos. 1 and 2 (1917): 156–70.

21. Arai translated the motto as "Life with religion, religion with life"; see *Turkish Nationalism*, p. 83 and nn. 1, 2.

22. Ibid, pp. 85ff.

23. Gökalp, "Türklüğün Başina Gelenler," *Türkleşmek, Islamlaşmak, Muasirlaşmak,* ed. Ferhat Tamir (Istanbul, 1974), p. 40. Published originally in *Turk Yurdu* (1912).

24. Ibid., p. 41.

25. Ziya Gökalp, *Türk Yurdu* 3 (1913). The three currents of the article, as mentioned, became the title of his book *Türkleşmek, Islamlaşmak, Muasirlaşmak (1918)*, which was published in 1923 as *Türkçülüğün Esaslari*; however, this seminal article does not appear in the *Türkçülüğün Esaslari*, in either the old or new edition. It is reproduced in Berkes, *Ziya Gökalp, Turkish Nationalism*, pp. 71–78.

26. Gökalp, *Türkleşmek*, p. 9.

27. Berkes, *Ziya Gökalp, Turkish Nationalism*, p. 78.

28. Ziya Gökalp, *Yeni Mecmua*, no. 83 (30 August 1923), repr. with some change in *Türkçülüğün Esaslari* (1990), pp. 31–45.

29. See Rauf Yekta's article on Turkish music in *Encyclopedia of Music and Musicians* (New York, 1937), pp. 2945–3065.

30. Rauf Yekta, "Ziya Gökalp Bey ve Milli Musikimiz Hakkindaki Fikirleri," *Servet-i Fünun*, no. 1480 (1925): 89–91; Yekta's article has been reprinted by Ismail Akçay in *Musiki Mecmuasi*, no. 448, (1995): 16–17. Köprülü, who at this time defended the Ottoman heritage, supported Yekta; see *Tevhid-i Efkar*, 28 January 1924.

31. See Kemal Silay, *Nedim and the Poetics of Ottoman Courts* (Bloomington, Ind., 1994). Nedim also wrote in the colloquial Turkish.

32. Yusuf Akçura, "Gökalp Ziya bey hakkinda hatira ve mulahazalar," *Türk Yurdu* 2, ser. 1 (4 December 1924): 156–62, quotation on p. 162.

33. Parla, *Social and Political Thought*, p. 22.

34. Ibid.

35. See Ziya Gökalp, *Yeni Hayat* (Istanbul, 1971). The publisher, Ali Nüzhet Gökçek, in the introduction to the collection of poems, wrote that Gökalp's works had not been printed since his death in 1924 and that one would get the wrong view of what Gökalp thought if one were to rely solely on Yusuf Akçura's views as published in the *Türk Yurdu*.

36. Georgeon, *Aux Origines*. Some of Akçura's works and his short biography are in Temir, *Yusuf Akçura*, pp. 81–93. See also H. Z. Ülken, *Türkiye'de Çağdaş Düşünce Tarihi*, vol. 1 (Istanbul, 1966), pp. 637–49; Abdullah Yusupov, *Gospoda Akcurin* (Kazan, 1974); David Thomas, "Yusuf Akçura and the Intellectual Origins of Üç Tarz-i Siyaset," Ph.D. diss., McGill University, 1976, which has a comprehensive bibliography, pp. 207–14, and Akçura in *Türk Yili* (1928). *Kazan*, a review published by "Kazan Turks" in Ankara, dedicated an issue to Akçura, vol. 18 (1976). See also Muharrem Feyzi Togay, *Yusuf Akçura'nin Hayati* (Istanbul, 1944). A recent work originally submitted as a dissertation in Russian to the Academy of Science of Tataristan (Russia) includes Russian sources on Akçura. I used the Turkish translation, Rafael Muhammetdin, *Türkçülügün Doğuşu ve Gelişimi* (Istanbul, 1998) (It compares Akçura and Gökalp. Translator not indicated.) For a recent book based on the memoirs of Şefika Gaspirali, the wife of Ismail Gaspirali and sister of Yusuf Akçura, see *Şefika Gaspirali ve Rusya'da Türk Kadin Hareketi, 1893–1920*, ed. Şengül Hablemitoğlu and Necip Hablemitoğlu (Ankara, 1998) (a publication of the Menger Foundation, publisher of works on the Tatar Muslims of Russia).

37. Temir, *Yusuf Akçura*, p. 33.

38. See the report, *Rusya Esir Murahassi Yusuf Akçura Bey'in Raporu* (Istanbul, 1335 [1919]).

39. *Türk Yurdu*, no. 12 (August 1917): 3521–22.

40. See Yusuf Akçura's article, written in 1920 and published as "Ittifak'a Dair" [About alliance], in *Siyaset ve Iktisat* (Istanbul, 1924), pp. 24–27. The book consists of a collec-

tion of sixteen articles. See also "Türk Milliyetçiliğinin Iktisadi Meselelerine Dair" [Economic problems of Turkish nationalism], ibid., pp. 140–68.

41. Georgeon, *Aux origines*, pp. 45–59, passim: also, Serge A. Zenkovsky, *Pan Turkism and Islam in Russia* (Cambridge, 1960).

42. The original thirty-two-page article was published in Egypt, in ten installments, in the April–May 1904 issues of the newspaper *Türk* and then as a pamphlet. It was reprinted in Istanbul in 1327 (1911) and several times thereafter. One of the latest editions (1987) has a long introduction that contains little new information by the late E. Ziya Karal, Akçura's student and head of the Turkish Historical Society. The text of the *Üç Tarz-i Siyaset* in Western languages appeared in Georgeon, *Aux origins*, and in an English translation by Ismail Fehmi in *Oriento moderno* 61, nos. 1–2 (1981): 1–20 and a few other places.

43. Akçura, *Üç Tarz-i Siyaset* (Ankara, 1987), p. 23.

44. Ibid, p. 32.

45. Ibid., trans. Ismail Fehmi in *Oriento Moderno*, p. 18.

46. Akçura, *Üç Tarz*, pp. 35, 62.

47. See Ali Kemal, *Ömürüm* (Istanbul, 1985). The memoirs were published by Zeki Kuneralp, Ali Kemal's son, who was a high-ranking member of the Turkish diplomatic corps. His son, Siman, is the head of ISIS, a publisher of scholarly books in Istanbul.

48. Ahmet Ferit, appendix to Akçura, *Üç Tarz*, p. 49.

49. Ibid., pp. 52–55 passim. It is surprising that scholars did not or chose not to notice the Akçura's real views on Islamism and Ottomanism or the realistic opportunism in Tek's views.

50. Arai, *Turkish Nationalism*, p. 65.

51. Salih K. Nigar, *Halife Ikinci Abdulmecid* (Istanbul, 1964), pp. 76–77. (This book consists almost entirely of official correspondence concerning the burial.) On the fate of the dynasty, see also Murat Bardakçi, *Son Osmanlilar. Osmanli Hanedaninin Sürgün ve Miras Öyküsü* (Istanbul, 1992). See chap. 11 on the caliphate. For the fate of the Ottoman dynasty, see chap. 16 and ftn. 50.

52. Cavit O. Tütengil and Vedat Günyol, *Prens Lütfullah Dosyasi* (Istanbul, 1977).

53. The text of the debates between Ahmet Naim and Ahmet Ağaoğlu is reproduced in Ismail Kara, *Türkiye'de Islamcilik Düşüncesi-Metinler, Kişiler*, vol. 1, 2nd ed. (1986). Some information on Ağaoğlu may be found in Tadeusz Swietochowski, *Russian Azerbaijan, 1905–1920: The Shaping of National Identity in a Muslim Community* (New York, 1985).

54. Arai, *Turkish Nationalism*, pp. 4ff. See also his "An Imagined Nation: The Idea of the Ottoman Nation as a Key to Modern Ottoman History," *Oriens* 27 (1991): 1–10.

55. Akçuraoğlu Yusuf, "Nutuk," *Tarihi Osmani Encümeni Mecmuasi* 97 (1929): pp. 1–25, quotations pp. 2, 25. The article eulogized Atatürk's famous speech: the "great man who created one of the greatest events of the twentieth century wrote also the history of that event" and "the establishment of the new Turkish state is the beginning of the great revolution of the Islamic world."

56. There is no comprehensive biography of Köprülü. One of the more detailed works is by George T. Park, "The Life and Writings of Mehmet Fuad Köprülü: The Intellectual and Turkish Cultural Modernization," Ph.D. diss., Johns Hopkins University, 1975. Halil Berktay's *Cumhuriyet Ideolojisi ve Fuat Köprülü* (Istanbul, 1983) is a useful and insightful ideological Marxist analysis of Köprülü's historical philosophy. Orhan F. Köprülü, *Fuad Köprülü* (Ankara, 1987), written by the historian's son, is the best succinct biography, citing also the senior Köprülü's works.

57. M. Fuat Köprülü, *Türk Edebiyatinda Ilk Mutasavviflar* (Istanbul, 1919).

58. For bibliographical studies on Köprülü, see Fevziye A. Tansel, "Prof. Dr. Fuad Köprülü'nun Yazilari için Basilmiş bibliografyalar ve bunlara bazi ilaveler," *Türk Kültürü*, no. 68 (June 1968): 543–56, and nos. 93, 120, 157 (1970–75). Şerif Hulusi, *O. Prof. Dr. Fuad Köprülü'nün Yazilari İçin Bir Bibliografya, 1912–1940* (Istanbul, 1940); Sami N. Özerdim, *Ord. Prof. Dr. Fuad Köprülü bibliografyasi, 1908–1950* (Ankara, 1951).

59. Köprülü's communication appears in the *Birinci Türk Tarihi Kongresi: Konferanslar, Munukasalar* (Ankara, n.d., ca. 1932), pp. 82, 308–20.

60. Mehmet Fuat Köprülü, *Ayin Tarihi* (October 1951): 60.

61. Köprülü's article, "Islam in Anatolia: A Review of the Religious History of Anatolia after the Turkish Invasion and the Sources for this History," was published in the *Darulfunun Edebiyat Fakültesi Mecmuasi* 2 (1922): 281–486, as an answer to Franz Babinger, who in a well-known article, "Der Islam in Kleinasien: Neue Wege der Islamforschung," claimed that Islam in Turkey was of Iranian origin. Gary Leiser has updated with new bibliographical information and has annotated and masterfully translated Köprülü's article as *Islam in Anatolia after the Turkish Invasion* (Salt Lake City, Utah, 1993). This is to my best of knowledge the second publication of Köprülü's article. Reportedly the Turkish version was republished in 1998.

62. Köprülü, "Islam in Anatolia," trans. Leiser, p. 5.

63. Ahmet Yaşar Ocak, "II. Abdülhamid Dönemi Islamciliğinin Tarihi Arka Plani: Klasik Dönem Osmanli Islamina Genel bir Bakiş Denemesi," *Sultan II. Abdulhamid ve Devri Semineri, 27–29 Mayis 1992: Bildiriler* (Istanbul, 1994), pp. 107–25.

64. Köprülü, "Islam in Anatolia," trans. Leiser, pp. 15–18.

65. These are the Akkoyunlu and Karakoyunlu states. See John Woods, *The Aqquyunlu: Clan, Confederation, and Empire* (Princeton, N.J., 1974), and Faruk Sümer, *Kara Koyunlular* (Ankara, 1967).

66. See Mehmet Fuat Köprülü, *Les origines de l'empire ottoman* (Paris, 1935), pp. 5–19. I have used the 1959 edition, which reproduces the introductions to the French and Serbo-Croatian translations. See also M. Fuat Köprülü, *Osmanli Devletinin Kuruluşu* (Ankara, 1959), and M. Fuat Köprülü, *The Origins of the Ottoman Empire*, trans. and ed. Gary Leiser (Albany, N.Y., 1992).

67. See Rudi Paul Lindner, *Nomads and Ottomans in Medieval Anatolia* (Bloomington, Ind., 1983).

68. See Mehmet Fuat Köprülü, *Bizans Müesseselerinin Osmanli Müesseselerine Tesiri Hakkinda bazi Mulahazalar* (Istanbul, 1931); reissued 1981 with a shortened title as *Bizans Müesseselerinin Osmanli Müesseselerine Tesiri*.

69. Köprülü, *Osmanli Devletinin Kuruluşu*, p. 110.

70. Ibid., p. 83.

71. Mehmet Fuat Köprülü, "Milliyetçilik ve Irkçilik," *Ülkü*, no. 80, April 1940.

72. See Mehmet Fuat Köprülü, "Osmanlilik Telakkisi," *Akşam*, 28 October 1918. (Despite a careful search, this "project" could not be located.)

73. For a more comprehensive view of Köprülü's ideas see Mehmet Fuat Köprülü[zade], *Türk Edebiyatinda Ilk Mutasavviflar* [First mystics in Turkish literature] (Istanbul, 1919), and a number of basic articles including "Türk Edebiyatinin Menşe-i" (The origin of Turkish literature), *Milli Tetebbular Mecmuasi* 2, no. 4 (1913): 1–78.

74. Benedict Anderson, *Imagined Communities* (London, 1983).

75. On the Young Turks' true attitude on religion, see Hanioğlu, *The Young Turks*, pp. 201–2.

Select Bibliography

I. PRIMARY SOURCES

1. Turkish Sources

Başbakanlik Arşivi (Prime Ministry Archives—Istanbul)
Yildiz Archive (collection; comprises Sultan Abdulhamid's correspondence from the
    Yildiz Palace)
Yildiz Esas Evraki (principal documents)
Sadaret Resmi Maruzat (correspondence with chief ministries)
Sadaret Hususi Maruzat (correspondence with lesser ministries, which the sultan was
    not expected to answer)
Irade (orders of the sultan)
Dahiliye (interior)
Hariciye (foreign affairs)
Meclis-i Mahsus(a) (special, ad hoc councils)
Meclis-i Vala (supreme council)
Devlet Şurasi (state council)
Muhacirin Komisyonu (migration commission)
Perakende (miscellaneous papers including newspapers)
Kamil paşa Evraki (papers of Premier Kamil paşa—not to be confused with Kamil Kapeci
    Tasnifi. The word *tasnif* [classification] has been translated as "collection.")

2. British Documents in the Public Records Office, London

Foreign Office (FO) 78 (general correspondence)
FO 424 (correspondence between London and British Embassy in Istanbul)
FO 371
FO 212
House of Commons accounts and papers

3. Archives of the French Foreign Ministry (AFFM), Paris

AFFM CP (Correspondence Politique)
AFFM CPC (Correspondence Politique des Consuls)
AFFM (Nouvelle Série)

4. Reviews and Newspapers

Arisalan
Basiret
Belleten
Belgelerle Türk Tarihi
Darülfünun Edebiyat Fakültesi Mecmuasi
Edebiyat Fakültesi Mecmuasi
Hareket
Hayat Tarih Mecmuasi
Ikdam
Ilim Dünyasi
Istanbul Dergisi
Osmanli Tarihi Araştirma ve Uygulama Merkezi Dergisi
Tarih Dergisi
Tarih ve Toplum
Tarih-i Osmani Encumeni Mecmuasi
Tercuman-i Hakikat
Turk Kültürü Araştirmalari
Turk Yurdu
Vakiflar Dergisi

5. Theses and Dissertations

I have used a number of B.A. graduation theses and Ph.D. dissertations in history at Istanbul University. These are listed fully in the footnotes but not in this bibliography. Many of the Ph.D. dissertations have been revised and published as books. These dissertations were prepared in Turkey and, although of mixed quality, nevertheless often contain references to original archival documents and information. In 1982, the requirement of writing a graduation thesis was lifted. A total of 3,433 B.A. theses were prepared. See list in Abdulkadir Özcan, *Istanbul Universitesi, Edebiyat Fakültesi Tarih Bölümü Tezleri*. Istanbul, 1984.

SECONDARY SOURCES

Abdulhamid (Abdulhamit) Sultan. *Abdulhamid'in Hatira Defteri*. Selek publication. Istanbul, 1960.
———. *Siyasi Hatiratim*. Ed. Ismet Bozdağ. Istanbul, 1974. Reprint, 1975 (twice), 1984, 1987.
———. *Sultan Abdulhamid'in Hatira Defteri*. 8th ed. Ed. Ismet Bozdağ. Istanbul, 1988.
II. *Abdulhamid ve Dönemi Sempozyum Bildirileri*. Istanbul, 1992.
Abdulhamid Han ve Muhtiralari (Mehmet Hocaoglu, ed.) Istanbul, 1989.
Abu-Manneh, Butrus. "The Naqshbandiyya-Mujaddidiyya in the Ottoman Lands in the Early Nineteenth Century." *Die Welt des Islams* 22, (1982): 1–36.
———. "Shaykh Ahmed Ziya'üddin El-Gümüşhanevi and the Ziya'i-Khalidi Suborder." In *Shi'a 'Islam, Sects and Sufism*, ed. Frederick de Jong. 104–17. Utrecht, 1992.
———. "Sultan Abdulhamid II and Shaikh Abulhuda al-Sayyadi." *Middle Eastern Studies* 15 (1979): 131–53.
———. "Sultan Abdulhamid II and the Sharifs of Mecca (1880–1900)." *Asian and African Studies* 9 (1973): 2–23.
———. "The Sultan and the Bureaucracy: The Anti-Tanzimat Concepts of Grand Vizier Mahmud Nedim Paşa." *International Journal of Middle East Studies* 22 (1990): 257–74.
Abun-Nasr, Jamil M. *A History of the Maghrib*. 1971. Cambridge, 1973.

Adams, Charles J. "Mawdudi and the Islamic State." In *Voices of Resurgent Islam*. Ed. John L. Esposito. New York, 1983.

Adanir, Fikret. *Die makedonische Frage: Ihre Entstehung und Entwicklung bis 1908*. Wiesbaden, 1979.

Adivar, Adnan. *Osmanli Türklerinde Ilim*. Istanbul, 1982.

Aflaki, Shams al-Din Ahmad. *Manaqib al-Arifin*. 2 vols. Ed. Tahsin Yazici. Ankara, 1976–80.

Ağaoğlu, Samet. *Babamin Arkadaşlari*. 3rd ed. Istanbul, 1969.

Ahmad, Feroz. *The Young Turks: The Committee of Union and Progress in Turkish Politics, 1908–1914*. Oxford, 1969.

Ahmad, Qeyamuddin. *The Wahhabi Movement in India*. Calcutta, 1966.

Ahmadov, Shah. *Imam Mansur: The National Liberation Movement in Chechenia and Northern Caucasus at the End of the Eighteenth Century*. Grozny, 1991.

Ahmet, Refik [Altinay]. *Abdulhamid-i Sani ve Devri Saltanati*. Istanbul, 1931.

Ahmed, Akbar S. *Discovering Islam: Making Sense of Muslim History and Society*. London, 1987.

Ahmida, Ali Abdullatif. *The Making of Modern Libya: State Formation, Colonization, and Resistance, 1830–1932*. Albany, N.Y., 1994.

Akarli, Engin D. "Abdulhamid II's Attempts to Integrate Arabs into the Ottoman System." In *Palestine in the Late Ottoman Period*, ed. David Kushner. 74–89. Leiden, 1986.

———. *Belgelerle Tanzimat: Osmanli Sadrazamlarindan Ali ve Fuad Paşalarin Siyasi Vasiyyetnameleri*. Istanbul, 1978.

———. "Economic Policy and Budgets in the Ottoman Turkey, 1876–1909." *Middle Eastern Studies* 28 (1992): 443–76.

———. "Friction and Discord within the Ottoman Government under Abdulhamid II (1876–1909)." *Boğaziçi Üniversitesi Dergisi* 7 (1979): 3–26.

———. *The Long Peace: Ottoman Lebanon, 1861–1920*. Berkeley, Calif., 1993.

Akçura(oğlu), Yusuf. "Ittifak'a Dair." In *Siyaset ve Iktisat*. Istanbul, 1924.

———. "Nutuk." *Tarih-i Osmani Encümeni Mecmuasi* 97 (1929): 1–25.

———. *Rusya Esir Murahassi Yusuf Akçura Bey'in Raporu*. Istanbul, 1919.

———. *Türkçülük: Türklüğün Tarihi Gelişimi*. Istanbul, 1978.

———. *Türk Yili*. Istanbul, 1928.

———. *Üç Tarz-i Siyaset*. ed. Enver Z. Karal. Ankara, 1927.

———. "Yusuf Akçura's Üç Tarz-i siyaset" (Three kinds of policy), [trans. Fehmi Ismail, *Oriente Moderno* (January–December 1981]: 1–20.

Akgün, Ömer Faruk. "II. Abdulhamid'in Kültür Faaliyetleri Üzerine Bazi Dikkatler." *II. Abdulhamid ve Dönemi Sempozyum Bildirileri*. 75–84. Istanbul, 1992.

Aki, Niyazi. *Ondokuzuncu Yüzyil Türk Tiyatrosu Tarihi*. Erzurum, 1963.

Akpinar, Alisan. *Osmanli Devletinde Aşiret Mektebi*. Istanbul, 1997.

Al-Amr, Saleh Muhammad. "The Hijaz under Ottoman Rule, 1869–1914: The Ottoman Vali, the Sharif of Mecca, and the Growth of British Influence." Ph.D. diss., University of Leeds, 1974.

Alangu, Tahir. *Ömer Seyfettin: Ülkücü Bir Yazarin Romani*. Istanbul, 1968.

Albayrak, Hasan. "The Ottoman Historical Society." *Journal of the Middle East Studies Society at Columbia University* (1988): 87–109.

Al-Daghestani, Burhaneddin. *Arrisalan*, no. 720 (Cairo), 16 June 1947.

Alder, G. J. *British India's Northern Frontier, 1865–1895*. London, 1963.

Algar, Hamid. "The Naqshibandi Order: A Preliminary Survey of Its History and Significance." *Studia Islamica* 44 (1976): 123–52.

———. "*The Present State of Naqshbandi Studies*," in *Naqshbandis*, ed. Marc Gaborjeau et al. Istanbul, 1990. 45–61.

Ali Pacha. "Testament politique." *Revue de Paris* 17, nos. 7 and 9 (1910): 105–24, 505–24.

Allen, W. E. D., and Paul Muratoff. *Caucasian Battlefields: A History of the Wars on the Turco-Caucasian Border, 1828–1921*. Cambridge, 1953.

Almana, Mohammed. *Arabia Unified: A Portrait of Ibn Saud*. London, 1980.

Alkan, Mehmet Ö. "Ölçülebilen Verilerle Tanzimat Sonrasi Osmanli Modernleşmesi." Ph.D. diss., University of Istanbul, 1996.

Al-Qarakhi, Muhammad Tahir. *Bariqat al-Suyuf al Daghestaniyya fi Ba'd al-Ghazawat al-Shamiliyya.* Moscow, 1946.

Allworth, Edward. *The National Question in Soviet Central Asia.* New York, 1973.

Al-Yassini, Ayman. *Religion and State in the Kingdom of Saudi Arabia.* Boulder, Colo., 1985.

Anderson, Benedict. *Imagined Communities: Reflections on the Origin and Spread of Nationalism.* New York, 1983.

Anderson, Lisa. *State and Social Transformation in Tunisia and Libya, 1830–1980.* Princeton, N.J., 1986.

Anderson, M. S. *The Eastern Question, 1774–1923: A Study in International Relations.* London, 1966.

Anhegger, R., and Vedat Günyol. *Temaşa-i Dünya ve Cefakar-ü Cefakeş.* Istanbul, 1986.

Ansari, K. H. "Pan-Islam and the Making of the Early Indian Muslim Socialists." *Modern Asian Studies* 20 (1986): 509–537.

Anscombe, Fredrick F. *The Ottoman Gulf: The Creation of Kuwait, Saudi Arabia and Qatar.* New York, 1997.

Arai, Masami. "An Imagined Nation: The Idea of the Ottoman Nation as a Key to Modern Ottoman History." *Oriens* 27 (1991): 1–11.

———. *Turkish Nationalism in the Young Turk Era.* Leiden, 1992.

Arif, Mehmet. *Başimiza Gelenler.* Istanbul, 1973.

———. "Devlet-i Osmaniye'nin Teessüs ve Takarrüri Devrinde Ilim ve Ulema." *Darülfünun Edebiyat Fakültesi Mecmuasi* 1 (1914): 137–44.

Armstrong, John Alexander. *Nations before Nationalism.* Chapel Hill, N.C., 1982.

Arnold, Thomas Walker. *The Caliphate.* London, 1965.

Arslan, Ali. "Türkistan ile Osmanli Türkiyesi Arasindaki Ilmi Münasebetler (XV–XIX. yüzyillarda)." Ph.D. diss., University of Istanbul, 1988.

Asçidede, Ibrahim Halil. *Hatiralar: Geçen Asri Anlatan Kiymetli Vesikalardan Bir Eser.* Istanbul, 1960.

Asena, Orhan. *Yildiz Yargilanmasi.* Istanbul, 1990.

Atalar, Münir. "Haci Yolu Güzergahi ve Masrafi-Kara Yolu, 1253/1837." *Osmanli Tarihi Araştirma ve Uyglulama Merkezi Dergisi.* Vol. 4, 43–90. Ankara, 1993.

Atay, Neşet Halil. "Kendi Ifadesine Göre Ali Suavi." *Istanbul Dergisi,* (December 1944–April 1945).

Atil, Esin. *The Age of Sultan Suleyman the Magnificent.* New York, 1987.

Aydemir, Hasan Ali. "Şeyh Şamil ve Günümüze Olan Etkileri." Ph.D. diss., University of Istanbul, 1976.

Aydemir, Şevket Süreyya. *Suyu Arayan Adam.* Istanbul, 1967.

———. "Ziya Gökalp." *Kadro* 1, no. 2 (1932): 29–40.

Azan, Paul, and Jean Louis. *L'Emir Abd el Kader, 1808–1883, du fanatisme musulman au patriotisme français.* Paris, 1925.

Baddeley, John F. *The Russian Conquest of the Caucasus.* London, 1908.

Badger, G. P. "The Precedents and Usages Regulating the Muslim Caliphate." *Nineteenth Century* (1877): 274–82.

Bagin, S. *Ob otpadenii v magometanstvo krashchennykh inorodtsev Kazanskoi Eparkhii i o prichinakh etogo pechalnogo iavleniia.* Kazan, 1910.

———. *Propaganda Islama putem pechati.* Kazan, 1909.

Bağiş, Ali Ihsan. *Osmanli Ticaretinde Gayri Müslimler.* Ankara, 1983.

Baldick, Julian. *Imaginary Muslims: The Uwaysi Sufis of Central Asia.* New York, 1993.

Balkhi, Fasihuddin. *The Wahabi Movement.* New Delhi, 1983.

Balta, Evangelia. *Karamanlikida: XXe siècle bibliographie anatolique.* Athens, 1987.

Banarli, Nihad Sami. "Sultan Abdulhamid'in Türkçeciliği." *Hayat Tarih Mecmuasi* (December 1967).

Bannerman, Patrick. *Islam in Perspective: A Guide to Islamic Society, Politics, and Law.* London, 1988.

Barbir, Karl K. *Ottoman Rule in Damascus, 1708–1758.* Princeton, N.J., 1980.
Bardakçi, Murat. *Son Osmanlilar: Osmanli Hanedaninin Sürgün ve Miras Öyküsü.* Istanbul, 1992.
Bardin, Pierre. *Algeriens et tunisiens dans l'empire ottoman de 1848 à 1914.* Paris, 1979.
Barkök, Ismail. *Tarihte Kafkasya.* Istanbul, 1958.
Bartold, V. V. *Histoire des turcs d'Asie Centrale.* Paris, 1945.
————. *Moğol Istilasina Kadar Türkistan.* Trans. Hakki D. Yildiz. Ankara, 1990.
Basiretçi, Ali Efendi. *Istanbul'da Elli Yillik Önemli Olaylar.* Istanbul, 1976.
Batatu, Hanna. *The Old Social Classes and the Revolutionary Movements of Iraq.* Princeton, N.J., 1978.
Batunsky, Mark. "Russian Missionary Literature on Islam." *Zeitschrift für Religions und Geistesgeschichte* 39, no. 3 (1987).
————. "Russian Clerical Islamic Studies in the Late Nineteenth and Early Twentieth Centuries." *Central Asian Survey* 13, no. 2 (1994): 213–35.
Batur-Vanderlippe, Pinar, and John Vanderlippe. "Young Ottomans and Jadidists: Past Discourse and the Continuity of Debates in Turkey, Caucasus and Central Asia." *Turkish Studies Association Bulletin* 18 (1994): 59–82.
Bayat, Ali Haydar. *Ali Bey Hüseyinzade (Prof. Dr. Hüseyinzade Ali Turan) ve Türkiye'de Yayinladiği Eserleri.* Istanbul, 1992.
Bayatli, Osman. *Bergama'da Yakin Tarih Olaylari XVII–XIX Yüzyil.* Izmir, 1957.
Baycan, Nusret. *Türk Istiklal Harbinde Şehit Düşen Subaylar.* Ankara, 1988.
Baykara, Tuncer. *Osmanli Medeniyet Kavrami ve Ondokuzuncu Yüzyila Dair Araştirmalar.* Izmir, 1992.
————. *Zeki Velidi Togan.* Ankara, 1989.
Baylen, J. "Madame Olga Novikov, Propagandist." *American Slavic and East European Review* 10 (1951): 255–71.
Baysun, M. Cavid "Şirvanizade Ahmet Hulusi Efendinin Efganistan Elçiliğine Aid Vesikalar." *Tarih Dergisi* (September 1948): 151–56.
Bayur, Hilmi Kamil. *Sadrazam Kâmil paşa: Siyasi Hayati.* Ankara, 1954.
Bayur, Yusuf Hikmet. *Hindistan Tarihi.* Vol. 3. Ankara, 1987.
————. *Turk Inkilap Tarihi.* Vol. 3. Ankara, 1983.
————. "Maysor Sultan Tipu ile Osmanli Padişahlarindan Abdulhamid, III Selim Arasindaki Mektuplaşma." *Belleten* 12 (1948): 617–54.
Becker, C. H. "Panislamismus." *Islamstudien* 2 (Leipzig, 1932): 240–62.
Becker, Seymour. *Russia's Protectorates in Central Asia: Bukhara and Khiva, 1865–1924.* Cambridge, 1968.
————. "The Muslim East in Nineteenth-Century Russian Popular Historiography." *Central Asian Survey* 5 (1986): 25–48.
Bennigsen, Alexandre. "Un Mouvement populaire au Caucase de XVIIIe siècle: La guerre sainte du Sheikh Mansur (1785–1794)." *Cahiers du monde russe et soviétique* 5 (April–June 1964): 159–205.
————. "Panturkism and Panislamism in History and Today." *Central Asian Survey* 3 (1985): 39–68.
————. "The Qadiriyah (Kunta Hajji) Tariqah in North East Caucasus, 1850–1987." *Islamic Culture* 62 (1988): 63–78.
Bennigsen, A., and Chantal Lemercier Quelquejay. *La Presse et le mouvement national chez les mussulmans de Russie avant 1920.* Paris, 1964.
Berkes, Niyazi. *The Development of Secularism in Turkey.* Montreal, 1964.
————, ed. *Ziya Gökalp, Turkish Nationalism and Western Civilization.* New York, 1959.
Berktay, Halil. *Cumhuriyet Ideolojisi ve Fuat Köprülü.* Istanbul, 1983.
Berzeg, Sefer E. *Kafkas Diasporasi'nda Edebiyatçilar ve Yazarlar Sözlüğü.* Samsun, 1995.
Beysanoğlu, Şevket, ed. *Ziya Gökalp, Tamamlanmamiş Eserler.* Vol. 1. Ankara. 1985.
————. *Ziya Gökalp Için Yazilanlar-Söylenenler.* 2 vols. Ankara, 1975.
————. *Ziya Gökalp'in Ilk Yazi Hayati (1894–1909).* Istanbul, 1956.

Bilge, Mustafa. "II Abdulhamid'in Islam Birliği Çağrisi ve Fas." In *II Abdulhamid ve Dönemi. Sempozyum Bildirileri.* 45–55. Istanbul, 1992.

Bilgin, Ibrahim Edhem. *Devrimci Sufi Hareketleri ve Imam-i Rabban.* Istanbul, 1989.

Bilgin, Mehmet. *Sürmene.* Istanbul, 1990.

Biliotti, A. *La Banque Imperiale Ottomane.* Paris, 1909.

Birinci Türk Tarihi Kongresi. Konferanslar. *Munakâşalar, Muzakere Zabitlari.* Ankara, 1932.

Biyikoğlu, Tevfik. *Trakya'da Milli Mücadele.* Ankara, 1955.

Blerzy, H. "Les Révolutions de l'Asie Centrale." *Revue Deux Mondes* 5 (1874): 137–44.

Blunt, Wilfrid S. *The Future of Islam.* London, 1882.

Secret History of the English Occupation of Egypt. New York, 1922.

Bobrovnikoff, Sophy. "Moslems in Russia." *The Muslim World* 1 (1911): 5–31.

Bostan, M. Hanefi. *Bir Islamci Düşünür: Said Halim Paşa.* Istanbul, 1992.

Boulger, Demetrius Charles. *Central Asian Portraits: The Celebrities of the Khanates and the Neighboring States.* London, 1880.

———. *The Life of Yakoob Beq: Athalik Ghazi, and Badaulet: Ameer of Kashgar.* London, 1878.

Boyer, Pierre. "L'Administration française et la réglementation du pèlerinage à la Mècque (1830–1894)." *Revue d'histoire maghrebine* (July 1977): 276–93.

Bozarslan, Mehmet Emin. *Hilafet ve Ümmetçilik Sorunu.* Istanbul, 1969.

Bozdağ, Ismet. *Sultan Abdulhamid'in Hatira Defteri.* Istanbul, 1988.

Braude, Benjamin, and Bernard Lewis, eds. *Christians and Jews in the Ottoman Empire.* 2 vols. New York, 1980.

Bremer, Marie L. *Die Memoiren des türkischen Derwischs Asçi Dede Ibrahim.* Walldorf-Hessen, 1959.

Brignon, Jean, et al. *Histoire du Maroc.* Paris, 1967.

Bringa, Tone. *Being Muslim the Bosnian Way: Identity and Community in a Central Bosnian Village.* Princeton, N.J., 1995.

Brookes, Douglas S. "Of Swords and Tombs: Symbolism in the Ottoman Accession Ritual." *Turkish Studies Association Bulletin* 17 (fall 1993): 1–22.

Brower, Daniel R., and Edward J. Lazzerini, eds. *Russia's Orient: Imperial Borderlands and People, 1700–1917.* Bloomington, Ind., 1997.

Brown, Daniel W. *Rethinking Tradition in Modern Islamic Thought.* New York, 1996.

Brown, Kenneth. "Profile of a Nineteenth-Century Moroccan Scholar." In *Scholars, Saints and Sufis: Muslim Religious Institutions since 1500*, ed. Nikki R. Keddie. 127–48. Berkeley, 1972.

Brown, L. Carl. *Imperial Legacy: The Ottoman Imprint on the Balkans and the Middle East.* New York, 1996.

———. *The Tunisia of Ahmad Bey, 1837–1855.* Princeton, N.J., 1974.

Browne, E. G. "Pan-Islamism." In *Lectures on the History of the Nineteenth Century*, ed. F. A. Kirkpatrick. Cambridge, 1902.

Broxup, Marie Bennigsen et al., eds. *The North Caucasus Barrier: The Russian Advance Towards the Muslim World.* London, 1992.

Bruinessen, Martin van. *Agha, Shaikh, and State: The Social and Political Structures of Kurdistan.* London, 1992.

———. *Kürdistan Üzerine Yazilar.* Ed. N. Kiraç et al. Istanbul, 1992.

Budak, Mustafa. "Osmanli-Özbek Siyasi Münasebetleri (1510– 1740)." Ph.D. diss., University of Istanbul, 1987.

Burckhardt, John Lewis. *Notes on the Bedouins and Wahabys.* London, 1831.

Burke, Edmund. "The Moroccan Ulema, 1860–1912." In *Scholars, Saints and Sufis: Muslim Religious Institutions since 1500*, ed. Nikki R. Keddie. 93–126. Berkeley, 1972.

———. "Pan-Islam and Moroccan Resistance to French Colonial Penetration, 1900–1912." *Journal of African History* 12 (1972): 97–118.

Burton, J. Audrey. "Relations between the Khanate of Bukhara and Ottoman Turkey, 1558–1702." *International Journal of Turkish Studies* 5 (winter 1990–91): 83–104.

Buzpinar, S. Tufan. "Abdulhamid II and Sayyid Fadl Pasha of Hadramut." *Journal of Ottoman Studies* 13 (1993): 227–39.

———. "Abdulhamid II, Islam and the Arabs: The Cases of Syria and the Hijaz (1878–1882)." Ph.D. diss., University of Manchester, 1991.

———. "The Hijaz, Abdulhamid II and Amir Hussein's Secret Dealing with the British, 1877–80." *Middle Eastern Studies* 33 (1955): 99–123.

———. "Opposition to the Ottoman Caliphate in the Early Years of Abdulhamid II, 1877–1882." *Die Welt Des Islams* 36, no. 1 (1996): 59–89.

Cachia, Anthony. *Libya under the Second Ottoman Occupation, 1835–1911.* Tripoli, 1945.

Canard, M. "Chamil et Abdelkader." *Annales de l'Institut d'Études Orientales* 44 (Algiers, 1956): 231–56.

Çavuşoğlu, Semiramis. "The Kadizade Movement: An Attempt of Şeriat-Minded Reform in the Ottoman Empire." Ph.D. diss., Princeton University, 1990.

Celaleddin paşa, Mahmud. *Mirat-i Hakikat.* Ed. Ismet Miroğlu. 3 vols. Istanbul, 1983.

Cevat, Ali. *Ikinci Meşrutiyet'in lani ve Otuzbir Mart Hadisesi: II. Abdulhamid'in Son Mabeyn Başkatibi Ali Cevat Beyin Fezlekesi.* Ankara, 1960.

Cevat, Mahmud. *Maarif-i Umumiye Nezareti: Tarihçe-i Teşkilat ve Icraati.* Istanbul, 1922.

Cevdet, Ahmet. *Ahmet Cevdet Paşa Semineri 27–28 Mayis 1985.* Ed. Yusuf Halacoğlu. Istanbul, 1986.

———. *Maruzat.* Ed. Yusuf Halacoğlu. Istanbul, 1980.

———. *Tarih-i Cevdet.* Vol. 6. Istanbul, 1984.

———. *Tezakir.* 3 vols. Ed. Cavid Baysun. Ankara, 1953.

Ceyhun, Demirtaş. *Ah Şu Biz "Karabiyikli" Türkler.* Istanbul, 1992.

Chadwick, Owen. *The Secularization of the European Mind in the Nineteenth Century.* Cambridge, 1975.

Charmes, Gabriel. *L'Avenir de la Turquie, Le panislamisme.* Paris, 1883.

———. "La Situation de la Turquie: La politique du califat et ses consequences." *Revue Deux Mondes* 49 (1882): 833–69.

———. *La Tunisie et la Tripolitaine.* Paris, 1883.

Chaudhuri, Sashi Bhusan. *Civil Disturbances During the British Rule in India, 1765–1857.* Calcutta, 1955.

Childs, Timothy W. *Italo-Turkish Diplomacy and the War over Libya, 1911–1912.* Leiden, 1990.

Chirol, Valentine. "Pan-Islamism." *Proceedings of the Central Asian Society* (1906): 1–28.

Choueiri, Youssef M. *Arab History and the Nation-State : A Study in Modern Arab Historiography, 1820–1980.* London, 1989.

———. *Islamic Fundamentalism.* Boston, 1990.

Chu, Wen-Djang. *The Moslem Rebellion in Northwest China, 1862–1878.* The Hague, 1966.

Clancy-Smith, Julia A. *Rebel and Saint: Muslim Notables, Populist Protest, Colonial Encounters (Algeria and Tunisia, 1800–1904).* Berkeley, 1994.

Clayton, Gerald David. *Britain and the Eastern Question: Missolonghi to Gallipoli.* London, 1971.

Cleveland, William L. *The Making of an Arab Nationalist: Ottomanism and Arabism in the Life and Thought of Sati' al-Husri.* Princeton, N.J., 1971.

Coşan, Mahmud Es'ad. *Islam Çağrisi.* 2nd ed. Istanbul, 1990.

Commins, David Dean. *Islamic Reform: Politics and Social Change in Late Ottoman Syria.* New York, 1990.

Cox, S. *Diversions of a Diplomat in Turkey.* New York, 1887.

Curzon, George Nathaniel. *Russia in Central Asia in 1889 and the Anglo-Russian Question.* London, 1889.

Çankaya, Ali. *Yeni Mülkiye Tarihi ve Mülkiyeliler.* 4 vols. Ankara, 1968–69.

Çavdar, Tevfik. *Talat Paşa: Bir Örgüt Ustasinin Yaşam Öyküsü.* Ankara, 1984.

Çayci, Abdurrahman. *Büyük Sahra'da Türk-Fransiz Rekabeti 1858–1911.* Erzurum, 1970.

———. *La Question tunisienne et la politique ottomane, 1881–1913.* Istanbul, 1963.

Çelik, Zeynep. *Displaying the Orient.* Berkeley, 1992.

―――. *The Remaking of Istanbul.* Seattle, 1986.

Çetin, A. "El-Cevaib Gazetesi ve Yayini." *Tarih Dergisi* 34 (1984): 475–81.

Çetin, Atilla, and Ramazan Yildiz. *Sultan Ikinci Abdulhamid Han: Devlet ve Memleket Görüşlerim.* Istanbul, 1976.

Çetinsaya, Gökhan. "II. Abdulhamid Döneminin Ilk Yillarinda Islam Birliği Hareketi (1876–1878)." thesis Ankara University, 1988.

―――. "Ottoman Administration in Iraq, 1890–1908." Ph.D. diss., University of Manchester, 1994.

Çizgen, Engin. *Photography in the Ottoman Empire, 1839–1919.* Istanbul, 1987.

Daniel, Norman. *Islam, Europe and Empire.* Edinburgh, 1966.

Danişmend, Ismail Hami. *Izahli Osmanli Tarihi Kronolojisi.* Vol. 4. 1st ed. 1947–55. Istanbul, 1961.

Davison, Andrew. *Secularism and Revivalism in Turkey: A Hermeneutic Reconsideration.* New Haven, 1998.

Davison, Roderic. "The Death of the Ex-Sultan" [Abdulaziz] *The Lancet:* 10 June 1976, pp. 872–73.

―――. *Reform in the Ottoman Empire, 1856–1876.* Princeton, N.J., 1963.

―――. "Turkish Attitudes Concerning Christian-Muslim Equality in the Nineteenth Century." *American Historical Review* 59, no. 4 (July 1954): 844–64.

Dawn, Ernest C. *From Ottomanism to Arabism: Essays on the Origins of Arab Nationalism.* Urbana, Ill., 1973.

Demirel, Muammer. *Ikinci Meşrutiyet Öncesi Erzurum'da Halk Hareketleri, 1906–1907.* Ankara, 1990.

D'Encasse, Hélène Carrère. *Islam and the Russian Empire: Reform and Revolution in Central Asia.* Berkeley, 1988.

Deny, Jean. "Instructeurs militaires turcs au Maroc sous Moulay Hafidth." In *Memorial to Henry Basset.* 1–22. Paris, 1928.

Der Berliner Kongress 1878: Protokolle und Materialien. Boppard am Rhein, 1978.

Deringil, Selim. "II. Abdulhamid'in Diş Politikasi." *Tanzimattan Cumhuriyete Türkiye Ansiklopedisi.* Vol. 3.

―――. "L'Empire ottoman et le pan-islamisme dans la Russie turcophone." *Cahiers d'Études sur la Méditerranée Orientale et le Monde Turco-Iranien* 16 (1993): 207–217.

―――. "The Invention of Tradition as Public Image in the Late Ottoman Empire." *Contemporary Study of Society and History* 35 (1993): 3–29.

―――. "The Struggle against Shiism in Hamidian Iraq: A Study in Ottoman Counter-Propaganda," *Die Welt des Islams* 30 (1990): 45–62.

―――. "Symbolism of Power in Hamidian Regime." Paper presented to a colloquium on the Hamidian era held at Bad Hamburg, Germany, 12–14 July 1993.

―――. *The Well-Protected Domain: Ideology and Legitimation of Power in the Ottoman Empire: 1876–1909.* London, 1997.

Derengil, Selim, and Sinan Kuneralp, eds. *Studies on Ottoman Diplomatic History.* Vol. 5, *The Otomans and Africa.* Istanbul, 1990.

Desjardin, Paul Andre. "Au Pays de l'espionnage: Les sultans Mourad V et Abd-ul-Hamid." In *Les Bas-Fonds de Constantinople.* Paris, 1892.

Devereux, Robert. *First Ottoman Constitutional Period: A Study of the Midhat Constitution and Parliament.* Baltimore, Md., 1963.

Devlet, Nadir. *Rusya Türklerinin Milli Mücadele Tarihi: 1905–1917.* Ankara, 1985.

Deweese, Devin. *Islamization and the Native Religion in the Golden Horde: Baba Tükles and Conversion to Islam in Historical and Epic Tradition.* University Park, Pa., 1994.

―――. "The Masha'ikh-i Turk and the Khojagan: Rethinking the Links between the Yasavi and Naqshbandi Sufi Traditions." *Journal of Islamic Studies* 7 (1996): 180–207.

Doğan, Ismail. *Tanzimatin Iki Ucu: Münif Paşa ve Ali Suavi.* Istanbul, 1991.

Donohue, John. J., and John L. Esposito, eds. *Islam in Transition.* New York, 1982.

Dorys, Georges. *The Private Life of the Sultan of Turkey.* Trans. A. Hornblow. New York, 1901.

Dresch, Paul. *Tribes, Government, and History in Yemen.* 1989. Reprint, New York, 1989.
Duguid, Stephen. "The Politics of Unity: Hamidian Policy in Eastern Anatolia." *Middle Eastern Studies* 9 (1973): 139–56.
Dumont, Paul. "La Revue *Türk Yurdu* et les mussulmans de l'empire russe: 1911–1914." *Cahiers du Monde Russe et Soviétique* 15 (1974): 315–32.
Duru, Nami. *Ziya Gökalp.* Istanbul, 1975.
Edwards, H. Sutherland. *Russian Projects against India from the Czar Peter to General Skobeleff.* London, 1885.
Eldem, Edhem. *Banque Imperiale Ottomane: Inventaire commenté des archives.* Istanbul, 1994.
Elefteriades, Eleuthere. *Les Chemins de fer en Syrie et au Liban.* Beirut, 1944.
Elliot, Sir Henry George. *Some Revolutions and Other Diplomatic Experiences.* London, 1922.
El-Moudden, Abderrahman, ed. *Le Maghreb à l'époque ottomane.* Rabat, 1995.
Enginün, Inci. *Ahmet Mithat Efendinin Tiyatrolari.* Istanbul, 1990.
Eraslan, Cezmi. "II. Abdulhamid Devrinde Osmanli Devleti Dahilinde ve Afrika Kitasinda Islam Birliği (Pan-Islamism) Faaliyetleri." Ph.D. diss., University of Istanbul, 1989.
———. *II. Abdulhamid ve Islam Birliği.* Istanbul, 1992.
Ersanli-Behar, Buşra. *Iktidar ve Tarih: Türkiye'de "Resmi Tarih" Tezinin Oluşumu, 1929–1937.* Istanbul, 1992.
Erdem, Y. Hakan. *Slavery in the Ottoman Empire and Its Demise, 1800–1909.* London, 1996.
Ergil, Doğu, ed. *Türk Parlamentoculuğunun ilk Yüzyili: 1876–1976.* Ankara, 1976.
Ergin, Nihat. *Yildiz Sarayinda Müzik: Abdulhamid Dönemi.* Ankara, 1999.
Ergin, Osman. *Türkiye Maarif Tarihi.* 5 vols. Istanbul, 1940–41; reprint, 1977.
Erişirgil, M, Emin. *Bir Fikir Adaminin Romani: Ziya Gökalp.* Istanbul, 1951.
Ertuğ, Hasan Refik. *Basin ve Yayin Hareketleri Tarihi.* Istanbul, 1970.
Esad, Mehmet efendi. *Uss-i Zafer.* Istanbul, 1293; reprint 1876.
Esposito, John L. *Islam: The Straight Path.* New York, 1988.
———. *Islamic Revivalism.* American Institute for Islamic Affairs, The Muslim World Today Occasional Paper, no. 3. Washington, D.C., 1985.
———. "Renewal and Reform in Islamic History, Tajdid and Islah." In *Voices of Resurgent Islam,* ed. John L. Esposito. New York, 1983.
Evans-Pritchard, E. E. *The Sanusi of Cyrenaica.* Oxford, 1949.
Evdokimov, I. V. "Panislamizm i Panturkizm." *Voennyi Sbornik* 12 (1911): 85–112.
Evin, Ahmet O. *Origins and Development of the Turkish Novel.* Minneapolis, Minn., 1983.
Fadeev, A. V. "The Intrinsic Social Bases of Murid Movement." *Voprosy Istorii* 16 (1955). In Russian.
Fahmy, Khaled. *All the Pasha's Men: Mehmed Ali, His Army and the Making of Modern Egypt.* Cambridge, 1999.
Fahri bey. *Ibretnuma: Mabeyinci Fahri Bey'in Hatiralari ve lgilii Bazi Belgeler.* Ed. Bekir S. Baykal. Ankara, 1968.
Farah, E. Caesar. "Arab Supporters of Sultan Abdulhamid II: Izzet al-Abid." *Archivum Ottomanicum* 15 (1997): 189–220.
———, ed. *Decision Making and Change in the Ottoman Empire.* Kirksville, Mo., 1991.
———. "The Islamic Caliphate and the Great Powers, 1904–1914." *Studies on Turkish-Arab Relations* 2 (Istanbul, 1987): 37–48.
Faroqhi, Suraiya. *Pilgrims and Sultans: The Hajj under the Ottomans, 1517–1683.* London, 1994.
———. *Towns and Townsmen of Ottoman Anatolia.* Cambridge, 1984.
Fetkerey, Mehmet. *Çerkeslerin Asli.* Istanbul, 1922.
Findley, Carter V. "La Soumise, la subversive: Fatma Aliye, romancière et feministe." *Turcica* 27 (1995): 153–75.
———. *Ottoman Civil Officialdom: A Social History.* Princeton, N.J., 1988.
Firat, M. Şerif. *Doğu Illeri ve Varto Tarihi.* Ankara, 1948.
Fisher, Alan W. *The Crimean Tatars.* Stanford, Calif., 1978.
———. *The Russian Annexation of the Crimea, 1772– 1783.* Cambridge, 1970.

Fisher, John, *Cruzon and British Imperialism in the Middle East, 1916–1919.* Newbury Park, 1999.

Foltz, Richard. "The Central Asian Naqshbandi Connections of the Mughal Emperors." *Journal of Islamic Studies* 7 (1996): 229–39.

Fortuna, B. C. "Education for the Empire: Ottoman State Secondary Schools During the Reign of Sultan Abdulhamid II (1876–1909)." Ph.D. diss., University of Chicago, 1997.

Frank, Allen J. *Islamic Historiography and "Bulghar" Identity among Tatars and Bashkirs of Russia.* Leiden, 1998.

Frères, Allinger. *Avant la débâcle de la Turquie: Pensées et souvenirs de l'ex-sultan Abdul-Hamid.* Paris, 1914.

Friedmann, Yohanan. *Shaykh Ahmad Sirhindi.* Montreal, 1971.

Fromkin, David. *A Peace to End All Peace: The Fall of the Ottoman Empire and the Creation of the Modern Middle East.* New York, 1989.

Gabidullin, Kh., and A. M. Arsharuni. *Ocherki panislamizma i panturkizma v Rossii.* Moscow, 1931.

Gaborieau, Marc, et al., eds. *Nakşbandis.* Istanbul, 1990.

Gall, Dina le. "The Ottoman Naqshbandiyya in the Pre-Mujaddidi Phase: A Study in Islamic Religious Culture and Its Transmission." Ph.D. diss., Princeton University, 1992.

Gall, Michel le. "Forging the Nation-State: Some Issues in the Historiography of Modern Libya." In *The Maghrib in Question: Essays in History and Historiography*, ed. Michel Le Gall and Kenneth J. Perkins. 95–108. Austin, Tex., 1997.

———. "The Ottoman Government and the Sanusiya: A Reappraisal." *International Journal of Middle Eastern Studies* 21 (February 1989): 90–106.

———. "Ottoman Reaction to the European 'Scramble for Africa': The Defense of the Hinterland of Tripolitania and Cyrenaica." *Asian and African Studies* 24 (1990): 109–135.

Gammer, Moshe. "The Imam and the Pasha: A Note on Şamil and Muhammad Ali." *Middle Eastern Studies* 32, no. 4 (1966): 336–42.

———. *Muslim Resistance to the Tsar: Shamil and the Conquest of Chechnia and Daghestan.* London, 1994.

———. "Shamil and the Murid Movement, 1830–1859: An Attempt at a Comprehensive Bibliography." *Central Asian Survey* 10 (1991): 189–247.

———. "Shamil and the Muslim Resistance to the Russian Conquest of the North-Eastern Caucasus." Ph.D. diss., University of London, 1989.

[Gaspirinski-Gaspirali] Ismail Elgasferi. *Salname-i Turki. Sene-i Islamiyye-i Hicri 1300.* Bayçesaray, 1882.

Gazimihal, Mahmut R. *Türk Askeri Muzikalari Tarihi.* Istanbul, 1955.

Geertz, Clifford. *The Interpretation of Cultures: Selected Essays.* New York, 1973.

———. *Peddlers and Princes: Social Change and Economic Modernization in Two Indonesian Towns.* Chicago, 1963.

Gellner, Ernest. *Encounters with Nationalism.* Oxford, 1994.

———. *Nations and Nationalism.* 3rd ed. Ithaca, N.Y., 1991.

Genç, H. Mustafa. *Islami Açidan Ziya Gökalp ve Türkçüler.* Istanbul, 1978.

Georgeon, F. *Aux Origines du nationalisme turc, Yusuf Akçura (1870– 1935).* Paris, 1980.

———. "Le Sultan caché: Reclusion du souverain et mise en scène du pouvoir à l'époque de Abdulhamid II (1876–1909)." *Turcica* 23 (1997): 93–124.

Geraci, Robert. "Russian Orientalism at an Impasse: Tsarist Education Policy and the 1910 Conference on Islam." In *Russia's Orient: Imperial Borderlands and Peoples, 1700–1917*, ed. Daniel R. Brover and Edward J. Lazzerini. 138–62. Bloomington, Ind., 1997.

Gerber, Haim. *The Social Origins of the Modern Middle East.* Boulder, 1987.

Gerçek, Selim Nüzhet. *Türk Gazeteciliği: Yüzüncüyil Dönümü Vesilesile.* Istanbul, 1931.

Gershoni, Israel, and James I. Jankowski, *Egypt, Islam and the Arabs: The Search for Egyptian Nationhood, 1900–1930.* Oxford, 1986.

Ghunaymi, Mohammad Tal'at. *The Muslim Conception of International Law and the Western Approach.* The Hague, 1968.

Gibb, Hamilton A. R., and Harold Bowen. *Islamic Society and the West.* 2 vols. Oxford, 1950.

Gibb, Hamilton A. R. "Al-Mawardi's Theory of the Caliphate." *Studies on the Civilization of Islam,* ed. S. J. Shaw. 151–65. Boston, 1962.

————. "Lutfi Paşa on the Ottoman Caliphate." *Oriens* 15 (Leiden, 1962): 287–95.

————. "Some Considerations on the Sunni Theory of the Caliphate." *Archives d'Histoire du Droit Oriental* 3 (1947): 401–410.

————. "Some Considerations on the Sunni Theory of the Caliphate." *Studies on the Civilization of Islam,* ed. S. J. Shaw. 141–50. Boston, 1962.

Gibb, John Wilkinson. *A History of Ottoman Poetry.* 6 vols. London, 1900–10.

Gladstone, W. E. *Bulgarian Horrors and the Question of the East.* London, 1876.

Glazer, Nathan, and Daniel P. Moynihan. *Ethnicity: Theory and Experience.* Cambridge, 1975.

Glazik, Josef. *Die Islammission der russischen-orthodoxen Kirche.* Munster, 1959.

Gologlu, Mahmut. *Halifelik Ne Idi? Nasil Alindi? Ne için Kaldirildi?* Ankara, 1973.

Goltz, Colmar Freiherr von der. *Nation in Arms: A Treatise on Modern Military Systems and Conduct of War.* Originally *Das Volk in Waffen,* 1883; translated into Turkish as *Millet-i Musellah,* 1884. Eng. ed., London, 1906.

————. "Stärke und Schwäche des Turkischen Reiches." *Deutsche Rundschau* 93 (October–December 1897): 95–127.

Gooch, G. P., and Harold Temperley, eds. *British Documents on the Origins of the War, 1898–1914.* 11 vols. London, 1926–38.

Göçek, Fatma M. *Rise of the Bourgeoisie, Demise of Empire: Ottoman Westernization and Social Change.* New York, 1996.

Gökbilgin, Özalp. *1532–1577 Yillari Arasinda Kirim Hanliği'nin Siyasi Durumu.* Ankara, 1973.

Gökalp, Ziya. *Hars ve Medeniyet.* Ankara, 1964; reprint, 1977.

————. *The Principles of Turkism.* Trans. Robert Devereux, Leiden, 1968.

————. *Türkçülügün Esaslari.* New ed. Ed. Mehmet Kaplan. Ankara, 1990.

————. *Turkish Nationalism and Western Civilization.* Ed. Niyak Berkes. New York, 1958.

————. *Türk Medeniyet Tarihi.* Istanbul, 1926.

————. *Türkleşmek, Islamlaşmak, Muasirlaşmak.* Istanbul, 1918; reprint, 1960, 1976.

————. *Yeni Hayat.* Istanbul, 1918; reprint, 1971.

Gökçe, Cemal. *Kafkasya ve Osmanli Imparatorluğu'nun Kafkasya Siyaseti.* Istanbul, 1979.

Gözaydin, Ethem Feyzi. *Kirim Türklerinin Yerlesme ve Göç-meléri.* Istanbul, 1948.

Göztepe, Tarik M. *Dağistan Aslani Imam Şamil.* Istanbul, 1991.

————. *Imam Şamil, Kafkasya'nin Büyük Harp ve Ihtilal Kahramaninin Esareti ve Ölümü.* Istanbul, 1950.

Graham, William A. *Beyond the Written Word: Oral Aspects of Scripture in the History of Religion.* Cambridge, 1987.

Gramsci, Antonio. *Prison Notebooks: Selections from the Prison Notebooks of Antonio Gramsci.* Ed. and trans. Q. Hoare and Geoffrey Nowell Smith. New York, 1971.

Grece, Michel de. *Le Dernier Sultan.* Istanbul, 1944.

Greenfeld, Liah. *Nationalism: Five Roads to Modernity.* Cambridge, Mass., 1992.

Greenlaw, Jean-Pierre. *The Coral Buildings of Suakin.* New York, 1995.

Griffiths, M. A. "The Reorganization of the Ottoman Army Under Abdulhamid II, 1890–1897." Ph.D. diss., University of California, 1965.

Groc, Gerard. "*Le Mercure Oriental:* Une tentative de presse commerciale ou le premier journal privé." *Toplum ve Ekonomi* 7 (1994): 27–48.

Gross, Jo-Ann. "Khoja Ahrar." Ph.D. diss., New York University, 1982.

————, ed. *Muslims in Central Asia: Expressions of Identity and Change.* Durham, N.C., 1992.

Guest, John S. *The Yezidis: A Study in Survival.* New York, 1987.

Gündağ, Nevzat. *1913 Garbi Trakya Hükümet-i Müstakilesi.* Ankara, 1987.

Gündoğdu, Fahriye. "II. Abdulhamit Dönemi Türk Basin Teknolojisi ve Modern Türk Basimciliğina Giriş." *Edebiyat Fakültesi Dergisi* (special issue; Ankara, 1983): 101–109.

Gündüz, Irfan. *Gümüşhanevi Ahmed Ziyaüddin (KS) Hayati, Eserleri, Tarikat Anlayişi ve Halidiyye Tarikati*. Istanbul, 1984.

Gürfirat, B. "Ebul Huda'nin II. Abdulhamid'e Sunduğu Arizalar." *Belgelerle Türk Tarihi* 18 (1969): 27–28.

Gwarzo, Al-Hajj Hassan. "Seven Letters from the Tripoli Archives." *Kano Studies* 4 (1968): 50–60.

Habicoğlu, Bedri. *Kafkasya'dan Anadolu'ya Göçler*. Istanbul, 1993.

Hablemitoğlu, Şengüland Necip. *Şefika Gaspiralive Rusya'da Türk Kadin Hareketi, 1893–1920*. Menger Foundation. Ankara, 1998.

Haci, Ötemiş. *Cenghiz-name*. Alma Ata, 1992.

Haddad, William W., and William Ochsenwald, eds. *Nationalism in a Non-National State: The Dissolution of the Ottoman Empire*. Columbus, Ohio, 1977.

Haerkötter, Ruth. *Sultan Abdulhamid II in der türkischen Publizistik seit Gründung der Republik*. Frankfurt, 1996.

Haim, Sylvia, ed. *Arab Nationalism: An Anthology*. Berkeley, 1962.

Halaçoğlu, Ahmet. *Balkan Harbi Sirasinda Rumeli'den Türk Göçleri, 1912–1913*. Ankara, 1994.

Halbach, Uwe "'Holy War' against Czarism: The Links between Sufism and Jihad in the Nineteenth-Century Anticolonial Resistance against Russia." In *Muslim Communities Reemerge: Historical Perspective on Nationality, Politics, and Opposition in the Former Soviet Union and Yugoslavia*, ed. Edward Allworth. 251–75. Durham, N.C., 1994.

Halim paşa, Sait. *Buhranlarimiz*. Published originally in seven installments under different titles. Istanbul, 1919.

Halim paşa [Prens Sait] *Toplumsal Çözülme Buhranlarimiz*. Ed. N. Ahmet Özalp. Istanbul, 1983.

Halperin, Charles J. *Russia and the Golden Horde*. Bloomington, Ind., 1985.

Hanioğlu, M. Şükrü. *Bir Siyasal Örgüt Olarak "Osmanli Ittihad ve Terakki Cemiyeti" ve "Jön Türkler."* Vol. 1. 1986. 2nd ed., Istanbul, 1989.

———. *The Young Turks in Opposition*. New York, 1995.

Hannaway, Jr., William L. "Farsi, the Vatan and the Millat in Bukhara." In *The Nationality Question in Soviet Central Asia*, ed. Edward Allworth. 143–50. New York, 1973.

Hardy, Peter. *The Muslims of British India*. Cambridge, 1972.

Harris, David. *Britain and the Bulgarian Horrors of 1876*. Chicago, 1939.

Hartog, Leo de. *Genghis Khan, Conqueror of the World*. New York, 1989.

Hasan, Mahibbul. *History of Tipu Sultan*. Calcutta, 1971.

Haslip, Joan. *The Sultan: The Life of Abdul Hamid II*. London, 1958.

Hatemi, H. Hüsrev. *Türk Aydini: Dünü Bügünü*. Istanbul, 1991.

Hayit, Baymirza. *Islam and Turkestan under Russian Rule*. Istanbul, 1987.

Hazan, W. Reuven. "Peaceful Conflict Resolution in the Middle East: The Taba Negotiations." *Journal of the Middle East Studies Society at Columbia University* 2 (1988): 39–65.

Hazer, Ahmet. *Kuzey Kafkasya Hürriyet ve Istiklal Davasi*. Ankara, 1961.

Heller, Joseph. *British Policy Towards the Ottoman Empire, 1908–1914*. Newbury Park, Calif., 1983.

Hellwald, Friedrich von. *The Russians in Central Asia*. London, 1874.

Henze, Paul. "The Great Game in Kashgaria: British and Russian Missions to Yakub Bey." *Central Asian Survey* 8 (1989): 61–95.

Herly, Robert. "L'Influence allemande dans le Panislamisme contemporain." *Nouvelle Revue Française d'Outre-Mer* 47, no. 12; 48, nos. 1–3 (Paris, December 1955–March 1956).

Heyd, Uriel. *Foundations of Turkish Nationalism: The Life and Teachings of Ziya Gökalp*. London, 1950.

————. "The Ottoman Ulema and Westernization in the Time of Selim III and Mahmud II." In *Studies in Islamic History and Civilization*. 63–96. Jerusalem, 1961.

Hidayette, Abdul Hamid, *Révolutionnaire, ou, ce qu'on peut pas dire en Turquie*. Zurich, 1896.

Hilmi, Şehbenderzâde Filibeli Ahmed. *On Üçüncü Asrin En Büyük Mütefekkir-i Islamisi Seyyid Muhammed es-Senusi: Abdulhamid Seyyid Muhammed al-Mehdi Asr-i Hamidi'de Alem-i Islam ve Senusiler*. Istanbul, 1909.

————. *Senusiler ve Sultan Abdulhamid: Asr-i Hamidi'de Alem- i Islam ve Senusiler*. Istanbul, 1992.

Hilmi, Tunali. *Onbirinci Hutbe: Türkiyalilik, Osmanliliktir, Osmanlilik Türkiyaliliktir*. Geneva, 1902.

Hizaloğlu, Mustafa Z. *Şeyh Şamil (Şimali Kafkasya Istiklal Mücadeleleri)*. Ankara, 1958.

Hobsbawm, Eric. *Nations and Nationalism since 1780: Programme, Myth, Reality*. Cambridge, 1990.

Holden, David, and Richard Johns. *The House of Saud: The Rise and Rule of the Most Powerful Dynasty in the Arab World*. New York, 1981.

Hopkirk, Peter. *The Great Game. The Struggle for Empire in Central Asia*. London, 1990.

Hostler, Charles Warren. *Turkism and the Soviets*. London, 1957.

————. *The Turks of Central Asia*. Westport, Conn., 1993.

Hourani, Albert. *Arabic Thought in the Liberal Age, 1798–1939*. Oxford, 1967.

————. "Ottoman Reform and the Politics of Notables" In *Beginnings of Modernization in the Middle East*, ed. William R. Polk and Richard L. Chambers. 41–68. Chicago, 1968.

————. "Shaik Khalid and the Naqshbandi Order." In *Islamic Philosophy and the Classical Tradition*, ed. S. M. Stern et al. 75–89. Columbia, S.C., 1972.

Hudson, Michael C. *Arab Politics: The Search for Legitimacy*. New Haven, Conn., 1977.

Hulusi, Şerif. *O. Prof. Dr. Fuad Köprülü'nün Yazilari Için Bir Bibliografya: 1912–1940*. Istanbul, 1940.

Hunter, Sir William. *The Indian Musulmans*. Calcutta, 1945.

Hurgronje, C. Snouck. *The Achehnese*. Trans. A. W. S. O'Sullivan. Leiden, 1906.

Ibrahim, Abdurreşid. *Alem-i Islam ve Japonya'da intişar-i Islamiyet*. Istanbul, 1911.

————. *Tercüme-i Halim. Yani Başima Gelenler*. St. Petersburg, n.d.

Ihsanoğlu, Ekmeleddin, ed. *Osmanli Devletinde Modern Haberleşme ve Ulaştirma Teknikleri*. Istanbul, 1995.

Ihsanoğlu, Ekmeleddin, and Mustafa Kaçar, eds. *Çağini Yakalayan Osmanli*. Istanbul, 1995.

Ilgar, Ihsan. "Imperial Self-Portrait: The Ottoman Empire as Revealed in Sultan Abdulhamid II's Photographic Albums." *Journal of Turkish Studies* 12 (1988).

————. *Rusya'da Birinci Müslüman Kongresi Tutanaklari*. Istanbul, 1988.

Inal, Ibnulemin Mahmud Kemal. *Evkaf-i Humayun Nezaretinin Tarihçe-i Teşkilati ve Nüzzarin Teracim-i Ahvali*. Istanbul, 1335 [1919].

————. *Osmanli Devrinde Son Sadrazamlar*. 6 vols. Istanbul, 1958–64.

Inalcik, Halil. "The Caliphate and Atatürk's Inkilab." *Belleten*, no. 182 (1982): 353–65.

————. "Islamic Caliphate, Turkey and the Muslims in India." In *Shariah, Ummah and Khilafah: Lectures*, ed. Yusuf Abbas Hashimi et al. I. H. Oureshi Memorial Lecture Series, no. 1. Karachi, 1987.

————. *Tanzimat ve Bulgar Meselesi*. Ankara, 1943; reprint, 1992.

Inan, Ari, ed. *Enver Paşa'nin Ozel Mektuplari*. Ankara, 1997.

Inugur, M. Nuri, *Basin ve Yayin Tarihi*. Istanbul, 1982.

Ipek, Nedim. *Rumeli'den Anadolu'ya Türk Göçleri, 1877–1890*. Ankara, 1994.

Iqbal, Sheikh Mohammad. *Emergence of Saudi Arabia: A Political Study of King Abd al-Aziz ibn Saud, 1901–1953*. Srinagar, 1977.

Irtem, Suleyman Kani. *Abdulhamid Devrinde Hafiyelik ve Sansür. Abdulhamide Verilen Jurnaller*. Ed. O. S. Kocahanoglu. Istanbul, 1999.

Jameelah, Maryam. *Two Great Mujahidin of the Recent Past and Their Struggle for Free-*

dom against Foreign Rule: Sayyid Ahmad Shahid: Imam Shamil: A Great Mujahid of Russia. Lahore, 1976.

James, R. R. *Rosebery: A Biography of Archibald Philip, Fifth Earl of Rosebery.* London, 1963.

Jelavich, Barbara. *The Ottoman Empire, the Great Powers, and the Straits Question, 1870–1877.* Bloomington, Ind., 1973.

Jeltyakov, A. D. *Türkiye'nin Sosyo-Politik ve Kültürel Hayatinda Basin: 1729–1908 Yillari.* Ankara, 1979.

Jensen, Ronald J. "Eugene Schuyler and the Balkan Crisis." *Diplomatic History* 5 (winter, 1981): 23–37.

Jenkins, Roy. *Gladstone.* New York, 1977.

Jong, Frederick de. "The Naqshbandiyya in Egypt and Syria: Aspects of Its History, and Observations Concerning Its Present-Day Condition." In *Nakşbandis,* ed. Marc Gaborieau et al. 589–601. Istanbul, 1990.

Kaba, Lansine. *The Wahhabiyya: Islamic Reform and Politics in French West Africa.* Evanston, Ill., 1974.

Kafadar, Cemal. *Between Two Worlds: The Construction of the Ottoman State.* Berkeley, 1995.

Kaiser, Robert John. *The Geography of Nationalism in Russia and the USSR.* Princeton, N.J., 1994.

Kampen, Wilhelm van. *Studien zur Deutschen Turkeipolitik in der Zeit Wilhelm II.* Kiel, 1968.

Kandemir, Feridun. *Peygamberimizin Gölgesinde Son Türkler.* Istanbul, 1974.

Kandiyoti, Deniz. *Fragments of Culture. The Everyday of Modern Turkey.* London, 1999.

Kansu, Aykut. *1908 Devrimi.* Istanbul, 1995.

———. *The Revolution of 1908 in Turkey.* New York, 1997.

Kappeler, Andreas, et al., eds. *Muslim Communities Reemerge: Historical Perspectives on Nationality, Politics, and Opposition in the Former Soviet Union and Yugoslavia.* Trans. Caroline Savyer, ed. Edward Allworth. Durham, N.C., 1994.

Kara, Ismail. *Türkiye'de Islamcilik Düşüncesi-Metinler. Kişiler.* 2 vols. Istanbul, 1986–87.

Kara, Mustafa. *Bursa'da Tarikatlar ve Tekkeler.* 2 vols. Istanbul, 1980.

———. "Şazeliye Tarikati ve Üç Büyük Şeyhi." *Hareket.* (September 1981): 23–35.

———. *Tekkeler ve Zaviyeler.* 2nd ed. Istanbul, 1980.

Karaca, Ali. *Anadolu Islahati ve Ahmet Şakir Paşa 1838– 1899.* Istanbul, 1993.

Karal, Enver Ziya. *Osmanli Tarihi: Birinci Meşrutiyet ve Istibdat Devirleri, 1876–1907.* Vol. 8. Ankara, 1962.

Karasapan, Celal Tevfik. *Libya, Trablusgarp, Bingazi ve Fizan.* Ankara, 1960.

Karmi, Ilan. "The Tanzimat and the Non-Muslims, 1839–1878: The Implications of the Reforms in Nineteenth-Century Ottoman Empire on the Legal, Political, Economic and Social Status of Non-Muslims." Ph.D. diss., University of Wisconsin–Madison, 1986.

Karpat, Kemal H. "Abdulhamid'in Panislam Politikasi, Yanliş bir Görüşün Düzeltilmesi." *Türk Dünyasi Araştirmalari* 48 (November 1987): 13–37.

———. *Foreign Policy of Turkey: Recent Developments.* Madison, Wis., 1996.

———. *The Gecekondu: Rural Migration and Urbanization in Turkey.* New York, 1976.

———. "Gli stati balcanici e il nazionalismo: L'immagine e la realtà." *Quaderni storici* 84 (December 1993): 679–718.

———. "The Impact of Hungarian Refugees in the Ottoman Empire, 1849–1851." *Hungarian Heritage Review* (March 1990): 131–53.

———. *An Inquiry into the Social Foundations of Nationalism in the Ottoman State: From Social Estates to Classes, from Millets to Nations.* Princeton, N.J., 1973.

———. "The Land Regime, Social Structure, and Modernization in the Ottoman Empire." In *Beginnings of Modernization in the Middle East,* ed. William R. Polk and Richard L. Chambers. 69–92. Chicago, 1968.

———. "Mass Media in Turkey." In *Political Modernization in Japan and Turkey,* ed. R. E. Ward and Dankwart A. Rustow. 255–282. Princeton, N.J., 1964.

———. "Ömer Seyfeddin and the Transformation of the Turkish Thought." *Revue des Études du Sud Est Européen* 10 (1972): 677–92.

———. "The Ottoman Attitude toward the Resistance of Bosnia and Hercegovina to the Austrian Occupation in 1878." *Naucni Skup Otpor Austrougarskoj Okupaciji 1878 Godine u Bosni i Hercegovini.* 147–72. Sarajevo, 1979.

———. *Ottoman Population, 1830–1914: Demographic and Social Characteristics.* Madison, Wis., 1985.

———. "Ottoman Urbanism: The Crimean Migration to Dobruca and the Establishment of Mecidiye." *International Journal of Turkish Studies* 3 (winter 1984–85): 1–26.

———. "The People's Houses in Turkey." *Middle East Journal* (winter–spring 1963): 55–67.

———. *Political and Social Thought in the Contemporary Middle East.* New York, 1968. 1982

———. "The Roots of Kazakh Nationalism: Ethnicity, Islam or Land?" *Annals of the Feltrinelli Foundation* (Milan, 1993): 313–33.

———. "Social Environment and Literature: The Young Turks Era in the Literary Works of Ömer Seyfeddin." *The Islamic World from the Classical to the Modern Age: Essays in Honor of Bernard Lewis.* 69–94. Princeton, N.J., 1989.

———. "The Social Significance of the Ottoman Parliament of 1876." In *Proceedings of the First International Conference of South East European Studies.* Sofia, 1969.

———. "The Socio-Political Environment Conditioning the Foreign Policy of the Central Asian States." In *The Making of Foreign Policy in Russia and the New States of Eurasia*, ed. Adeed Dawisha and Karen Dawisha. 177–215. New York, 1995.

———, ed. *The Turks of Bulgaria: The Fate of a Minority.* Istanbul, 1990.

Kasaba, Reşat. *The Ottoman Empire and the World Economy: The Nineteenth Century.* Albany, N.Y., 1988.

Kasumov, Ali, and Hasan Kasumov. *Çerkes Soykirimi: Çerkeslerin XIX. Yüzyil Kurtuluş Savaşi Tarihi.* Ankara, 1995.

Kausar, Kabir. *Secret Correspondence of Tipu Sultan.* New Delhi, 1980.

Kaviraj, Narahari. *Wahabi and Farazi Rebels of Bengal.* New Delhi, 1982.

Kayali, Hasan. *Arabs and Young Turks: Ottomanism, Arabism and Islamism in the Ottoman Empire, 1908–1918.* Berkeley, 1997.

Kazem-Bek, Mirza. "Miuridizm: I Shamil." In *Russkoe Slovo.* St. Petersburg, 1859.

Kazim, Şeyhulislam) Musa. *Islamda Cihad.* Istanbul, 1918.

———. *Islamda Usul-u Meşveret ve Hürriyet.* Istanbul, 1908.

———. *Külliyat.* Istanbul, 1920.

Keddie, Nikki R. "Pan-Islam as Proto-Nationalism." *Journal of Modern History* 41 (March 1969): 3–26.

———. "The Pan-Islamic Appeal: Afghani and Abdulhamid II." *Middle Eastern Studies* 3 (1966): 46–67.

———. "Religion and Irreligion in Early Iranian Nationalism." *Comparative Studies in Society and History* 4 (1962): 265–83.

———. *Sayyid Jamal ad-Din "al-Afghani.* Berkeley, 1972.

Kedourie, Elie. *England and the Middle East: The Vital Years. The Destruction of the Ottoman Empire, 1914–1921.* London, 1956.

Kedourie, Sylvia (Haim), ed. *Turkey Before and After Atatürk.* London, 1999.

Kelly, J. B. *Arabia, The Gulf and the West.* London, 1980.

Kemal, Ali. *Ömürüm.* Istanbul, 1985.

Kemal, Ismail. *The Memoirs of Ismail Kemal Bey.* London, 1920.

Kepel, Gilles. *The Revenge of God: The Resurgence of Islam, Christianity, and Judaism in the Modern World.* University Park, Pa., 1994.

Keyder, Çağlar, and Faruk Tabak, eds. *Landholding and Commercial Agriculture in the Middle East.* Albany, N.Y., 1991.

Keyes, Charles F. "The Dialectics of Ethnic Change." In *Ethnic Change*, ed. Charles Keyes. Seattle, 1981.

Khalid, Adeeb. "The Politics of Muslim Cultural Reform: Jadidism in Tsarist Central Asia." Ph.D. diss., University of Wisconsin-Madison, 1993.
———. "Tashkent 1917: Muslim Politics in Revolutionary Turkestan." *Slavic Review* 55 (1996): 270–96.
Khalidi, Rashid, et al., eds. *The Origins of Arab Nationalism.* New York, 1991.
Khoury, Dina Rizk. *State and Provincial Society in the Ottoman Empire: Mosoul 1540–1834.* New York, 1997.
Khoury, Philip S. *Urban Notables and Arab Nationalism: The Politics of Damascus, 1860–1920.* New York, 1983.
Kia, Mehrdad. "Pan-Islamism in Late Nineteenth-Century Iran." *Middle Eastern Studies* 32 (1996): 30–52.
Kiciman, Naci. *Medine Müdafaasi.* Istanbul, 1971.
Kim, Ho-dong. "The Muslim Rebellion and the Kashgar Emirate in Chinese Central Asia, 1864–1877." Ph.D. diss., Harvard University, 1986.
Kinalizade, Ali Çelebi. *Ahlak-i Alai.* Istanbul, 1980.
Kirimer, Cafer Seydamet. *Gaspirali Ismail Bey.* Istanbul, 1934.
Kirimli, S. Hakan. "National Movements and National Identity among the Crimean Tatars, 1905–1916." Ph.D. diss., University of Wisconsin–Madison, 1990.
———. *National Movements and National Identity among the Crimean Tatars, 1905–1916.* Leiden, 1996.
Kisakürek, Necip F. *Ulu Hakan II. Abdulhamid Han.* Istanbul, 1965.
Kiyotaki, Keiko. "Ottoman Land Policies in the Province of Baghdad, 1831–1881." Ph.D. diss., University of Wisconsin–Madison, 1997.
Kiziltan, Mübecel. *Fatma Aliye Hanim: Yaşami, Sanati, Yapitlari ve Nisvan-i Islam.* Istanbul, 1993.
Klimovich, L. I. *Islam v Tsarskoi Rossii: Ocherki.* Moscow, 1936.
Koçak, Cemil. *Abdulhamid'in Mirasi.* Istanbul, 1990.
Kocaoğlu, Timur. "The Existence of a Bukharan Nationality in the Recent Past." In *The Nationality Question in Soviet Central Asia,* ed. Edward Allworth 151–58. New York, 1973.
Koçer, Hasan Ali. *Türkiye'de Modern Eğitimin Doğuşu ve Gelişimi (1773–1923).* Istanbul, 1974.
Kodaman, Bayram. *Abdulhamid Devri Eğitim Sistemi.* Istanbul, 1980.
———. "II. Abdulhamid ve Aşiret Mektebi." *Türk Kültürü Araştirmalari* 15 (1976): 253–68.
Koloğlu, Orhan. *Avrupa Kiskaçinda Abdulhamid.* Istanbul, 1998.
———. *Abdulhamid Gerçeği.* 2nd ed. Istanbul, 1987.
———. *Mustafa Kemal'in Yaninda Iki Libyali Lider.* Ankara, 1981.
Kondukov, Musa. *General Kondukov'un Anilari.* Istanbul, 1978.
Köprülü, M. Fuat. *Bizans Müesseselerinin Osmanli Müesseselerine Tesiri Hakkinda bazi Mülahazalar.* Istanbul, 1931.
———. *Islam in Anatolia after the Turkish Invasion.* Trans. Gary Leiser. Salt Lake City, 1993.
———. "Islam in Anatolia: A Review of the Religious History of Anatolia after the Turkish Invasion and the Sources for this History." *Darülfunun Edebiyat Fakültesi Mecumasi* 2 (1922): 281–486. (In Turkish.)
———. *The Origins of the Ottoman Empire.* Trans. and ed. Gary Leiser. Albany, N.Y., 1992.
———. *Osmanli Devletinin Kuruluşu.* Ankara, 1959.
———. "Osmanlilik Telakkisi." *Akşam* 28 (October 1918).
———. *Türk Edebiyatinda Ilk Mutasavviflar.* Istanbul, 1919; reprint, 1976.
Köprülü, Orhan F. *Fuad Köprülü.* Ankara, 1987.
Koru, Fehmi. "Democracy and Islam: The Turkish Experiment." *Muslim Political Report,* no. 9, September–October 1996.
Krachkovskii, I. Iu. *Trudy Instituta Vostokovedeniia:* Vol. 35: Moscow, 1941.
Kreemer, J. *Atjeh.* 2 vols. Leiden, 1922–23.
Kudret, Cevdet. *Türk Edebiyatinda Hikâye ve Roman, 1859– 1959.* 3 vols. Istanbul, 1970–90.
Kühnel, Ernst. "Die Osmanische Tughra." *Kunst des Orients* 2 (1955): 69–82.

Kunduk, Aytek. *Kafkasya Muridizmi, Gazavat Tarihi*. Prep. T. C. Kutlu. Istanbul, 1987.

Kuntay, Cemal. *Sarikli Ihtilalci Ali Suavi*. Istanbul, 1946.

Kunter, H. Baki. "Tarsus'taki Türkistan Zaviyelerin Vakfiyeleri." *Vakiflar Dergisi* 6 (Istanbul, 1965): 31–64.

Kuran, Ercüment. *La Politique ottomane face à l'occupation d'Alger par les français (1827–1847)*. Tunis, 1970.

————. "Küçük Said Paşa as a Turkish Modernist." *International Journal of Middle Eastern Studies* 1 (1970): 124–32.

————. "Türk Tefekkür Tarihinde Ahmet Cevdet Paşa'nin Yeri." In *Türkiye'nin Batilaşmasi ve Milli Meseleler*, ed. Ercüment Kuran. 141–47. Ankara, 1994.

Kurat, Akdes Nimet. "Atalik Gazi Yakub Bek." Manuscript, 1930; Istanbul, Türkiyat Enstitüsü Kütüphanesi.

Kurat, Yuluğ Tekin. *Henri Layard'in Istanbul Elçiliği: 1877–1880*. Ankara, 1968.

Kurtulmuş, Mehmet. *Ace-Sumatra Dosyasi*. Istanbul, 1986.

Kushner, David. "The Haifa-Damascus Railway: The British Phase, 1890–1902." In *Decision Making and Change in the Ottoman Empire*, ed. Caesar E. Farah. 193–213. Kirksville, Mo., 1993.

————. *The Rise of Turkish Nationalism, 1876–1908*. London, 1977.

Kutay, Cemal. *Kurtuluşun ve Cumhuriyetin Manevi Mimarlari*. Ankara, 1973.

————. *Şehit Sadrazam Talat Paşa'nin Gurbet Hatiralari*. 2nd ed. 3 vols. Istanbul, 1983.

————. *Üç Devirde Bir Adam*. Istanbul, 1980.

Lacey, Robert. *The Kingdom*. London, 1981.

Lammens, Henri. "Le Chemin de fer de Damas–La Mecque." *Revue de l'Orient Chrétien* 5 (1900): 507–34.

Landau, Jacob M. *The Hejaz Railway and the Muslim Pilgrimage: A Case of Ottoman Political Propaganda*. Detroit, Mich., 1971.

————. *Pan-Turkism from Irredentism to Cooperation*. Bloomington, Ind., 1995.

————. *The Politics of Pan-Islam: Ideology and Organization*. Oxford, 1990.

————. *Tekinalp, Turkish Patriot 1883–1961*. Leiden, 1984.

Lataillade, Louis. *Abd el-kader, adversaire et ami de la France*. Paris, 1984.

Lawrence, Bruce B. *Defenders of God: The Fundamentalist Revolt against the Modern Age*. New York, 1991.

Lazzerini, Edward J. "Defining the Orient: A Nineteenth-Century Russo-Tatar Polemic over Identity and Cultural Representation." In *Muslim Communities Reemerge*, ed. Edward Allworth. 33–61. Durham, N.C., 1994.

————. "Ismail Bey Gaspirinskii (Gaspirali): The Discourse of Modernism and the Russians." In *Tatars of Crimea: Their Struggle for Survival*, ed. Edward Alhvorth. 149–169. Durham, N.C., 1988.

————. "Ismail Bey Gaspirinskii and Muslim Modernism in Russia, 1878–1904." Ph.D. diss., University of Washington, 1973.

Leart, Marcel (pseudonym). *La Question arménienne à la lumière des documents*. Paris, 1913.

Lederer, Gyorgy. "Islam in Romania." *Central Asian Survey* 15 (1996): 349–68.

Lee, Dwight E. "The Origins of Pan-Islamism." *American Historical Review* 47 (January 1942): 278–87.

————. "A Turkish Mission to Afghanistan, 1877." *Journal of Modern History* 13 (1941): 335–56.

Lee, Hoe-Soo. *Islam ve Türk Kültürünün Uzak Doğu'ya Yayilmasi*. Ankara, 1988.

————. *Osmanli-Japon Münasebetleri ve Japonya'da Islamiyet*. Ankara, 1989.

Leeuwen, Richard van. *Notables and Clergy in Mount Lebanon: The Khazin Sheiks and the Maronite Church, 1736–1840*. Leiden, 1994 .

Lemercier-Quelquejay, Chantal. "Cooperation of the Elites of Kabarda and Daghestan in the Sixteenth Century." In *The North Caucasus Barrier: The Russian Advance towards the Muslim World*, ed. Abdurakhman Avtorkhanov et al. 18–44. London, 1992.

————. "Les Missions orthodoxes en pays mussulmans de Moyenne et Basse-Volga, 1552–1865." *Cahiers du Monde Russe et Soviétique* 8 (1967).

Lewis, Bernard. *The Emergence of Modern Turkey*. London, 1965.
———. "The Middle East, Westernized Despite Itself." *Middle East Quarterly* 3 (1996): 53–61.
———. "The Pro-Islamic Jews." *Judaism* 17 (1968): 391–404.
———. "Watan." *Journal of Contemporary History* 26 (1991):
Lewis, J. L. "The Ottoman Proclamation of Jihad in 1914." *Islamic Quarterly* 19 (January–June 1975): 157–63.
Lifchez, Raymond, ed. *The Dervish Lodge: Architecture, Art, and Sufism in Ottoman Turkey*. Berkeley, 1992.
Lindner, Rudi Paul. *Nomads and Ottomans in Medieval Anatolia*. Bloomington, Ind., 1983.
Ling, Dwight L. *Tunisia, from Protectorate to Republic*. Bloomington, Ind., 1967.
Lipovsky, Igor P. "Central Asia: In Search of a New Political Identity." *Middle Eastern Journal* 50 (1996): 211–23.
Lombard, D. "L'Empire ottoman vu d'Insulinde" In *Passé turco-tatar, présent soviétique*. Louvain, 1986.
Long, D. *The Hajj Today: The Survey of the Contemporary Pilgrimage to Makkah*. Albany, N.Y., 1979.
Long, E. *The Kingdom of Saudi Arabia*. Gainesville, Fla., 1997.
Lory, Bernard. "Ahmed Aga Tamraslijata: The Last Derebey of the Rhodopes." *International Journal of Turkish Studies* 4 (1989): 179–201.
———. *Le Sort de l'heritage ottoman en Bulgarie: L'example des villes bulgares, 1878–1900*. Istanbul, 1985.
Lowe, Cedric James. *The Reluctant Imperialists: British Foreign Policy, 1878–1902*. London, 1967.
Lung, Chienching. "Çin ve Bati Kaynaklarina Göre 1828 Isyanlarindan Yakub Bey'e Kadar Doğu Türkistan Tarihi." Ph.D. diss., Ankara University, 1967.
Lutfi, Ahmed (Vakanuvis). *Vak'a-nuvis Ahmed Lutfi Efendi Tarihi*. 16 vols. Ed. M. Münir Aktepe. Ankara, 1988–93.
Lütfi, bey Başmabeyinci (Simavi). *Osmanli Sarayinin Son 'Günleri*. Ed. Şemsettin Kutlu. Originally published as *Sultan Mehmet Reşat ve Halefinin Sarayinda Gördüklerim*. Istanbul, 1924.
McCarthy, Justin. *Death and Exile: The Ethnic Cleansing of Ottoman Muslims, 1821–1922*. Princeton, N.J., 1995.
Macartney, C. A. *National States and National Minorities*. London, 1934.
Macartney, G. "Eastern Turkestan: The Chinese Rulers over an Alien Race." *Proceedings of the Central Asian Society* (10 March 1909).
McDowall, David. *The Kurds*. London, 1997.
Macfie, A. L. *The End of the Ottoman Empire, 1908–1923*. New York, 1998.
McGowan, Bruce. *Economic Life in Ottoman Europe: Taxation, Trade and the Struggle for Land, 1600–1800*. Cambridge, 1981.
Mackenzie, Kenneth. *Shamil and Circassia*. London, 1854.
Mackie, J. Milton. *Life of Schamyl, and Narrative of the Circassian War of Independence against Russia*. Boston, 1856.
Malcom, Noel. *Bosnia: A Short History*. London, 1994.
Malik, Hafeez. *Sir Sayyid Ahmad Khan and Muslim Modernization in India and Pakistan*. New York, 1980.
Manz, Beatrice F. *The Rise and Rule of Tamerlane*. New York, 1989.
Mardin, Ebul-ula. *Huzur Dersleri*. Ed. Ismet Sungurbey. Vol. 1, Istanbul, 1951; vols. 2 and 3, Istanbul, 1966.
———. *Medeni Hukuk Cephesinden Ahmet Cevdet Paşa*. Istanbul, 1948.
Mardin, Şerif. *The Genesis of Young Ottoman Thought*. Princeton, N.J., 1962.
———. *Religion and Social Change in Modern Turkey*. Albany, N.Y., 1989.
Margoliouth, D. S. "Pan-Islamism." *Proceedings of The Central Asian Society* (1912): 3–17.

Martin, Bradford G. "Five Letters from the Tripoli Archives." *Journal of the Historical Society of Nigeria* 2 (1962): 350–71.
———. *Muslim Brotherhoods in Nineteenth-Century Africa.* New York, 1976.
———. *Sömürgeciliğe Karşi Afrika'da Sufi Direniş* (Sufi resistance to colonialism in Africa). Trans. F. Tatlicioğlu. Istanbul, 1988.
Martin, Jean. *Comores: Quatre îles entre pirates et planteurs.* 2 vols. Paris, 1983.
Martin, Robert Montgomery, ed. *The Despatches, Minutes and Correspondence of the Marquess Wellesley During His Administration in India.* 5 vols. New Delhi, 1984.
Marty, Martin E., and R. Scott Appleby, eds. *Fundamentalism Observed.* Chicago, 1991.
Masters, Bruce. "The Sultan's Entrepreneurs: The Avrupa Tuccaris and the Hayrie Tüccars in Syria." *International Journal of Middle East Studies* 24 (1992): 549–79.
———. "The Treaties of Erzurum (1823 and 1848) and the Changing Status of Iranians in the Ottoman Empire." *Iranian Studies* 24 (1991): 3–17.
Matley, Ian M. "Ethnic Groups of the Bukharan State ca. 1920 and the Question of Nationality." In *The Nationality Question in Soviet Central Asia*, ed. Edward Allworth. 134–42. New York, 1973.
Mawdudi, Abul 'Ala. *Islamda Ihya Haraketleri.* Istanbul, 1986.
———. *The Process of Islamic Revolution.* Lahore, 1977.
Mayer, Ann Elizabeth, ed. *Property, Social Structure and Law in the Modern Middle East.* Albany, N.Y., 1985.
Melikoff, Irene. "L'Idéologie religieuse du muridisme caucasien." *Revue de Kartveloloqie* 25 (1968): 27–45.
Memduh, Abdulhalim. *Mazlum Türkler: Meiyze.* Paris, 1902.
Mende, Gerhard von. *Der nationale Kampf der Russlandtürken.* Berlin, 1936.
Menouni, M'Hammad Benaboud-M. "A Moroccan Account of Constantinople." In *Actes du VII'ème Congres du CIEPO*, ed. A. Temimi. 68–75. Zaghouan, 1987.
Menteş, Suphi. *Hilafetin Mahiyet-i Şeriyyesi.* Istanbul, 1969.
——— (H. A. Önelçin). *Şeriyat Açisindan Halifeliğin Içyüzü.* Istanbul, 1970.
Meriç, Cemil. *Cevdet Paşa'nin Toplum ve Devlet Görüşü.* 3rd ed. Istanbul, 1992.
Metcalf, Barbara Daly. *Islamic Revival in British India: Deoband, 1860–1900.* Princeton, N.J., 1982.
Midhat Paşa Semineri [Uluslararasi]. Bildiriler ve Tartişmalar, Edirne 8–10 Mayis 1984. Ankara, 1986.
Miguel, André. *La Géographie humaine du monde musulman jusqu'au milieu de 11e siècle.* Paris, 1967.
Millman, Richard. *Britain and the Eastern Question, 1875–1878.* Oxford, 1979.
Minault, Gail. *The Khilafat Movement: Religious Symbolism and Political Mobilization in India.* New York, 1982.
Minorsky, Vladimir. *Studies in Caucasian History.* London, 1953.
Miroğlu, Ismet, ed. *Mirat-i Hakikat.* Istanbul, 1983.
Miropiev, M. A. *O polozhenii Russkikh inorodtsev.* St. Petersburg, 1901.
Mithat, Ali Haydar. *The Life of Midhat Pasha.* London, 1903; reprint, New York, 1973.
Mithat efendi, Ahmet. "Islamiyet ve Medeniyet ve Yahut Hala *Ingiltere Münasebeti.*" *Tercüman-i Hakikat* 9 (January 1880).
———. *Uss-i Inkilab.* Istanbul, 1294. Reprint, 1878.
Monroe, W. S. *Turkey and the Turks.* London, 1895.
Moore, Barrington. *Social Origins of Dictatorship and Democracy.* Boston, 1967.
Morgan, David. *The Mongols.* Cambridge, Mass., 1992.
Morley, John. *The Life of William Ewart Gladstone.* 3 vols. New York, 1903.
Mortimer, Edward, and Robert Fine. *People, Nation and State.* London, 1999.
Müftüoğlu, Mustafa. *Abdulhamid Kizil Sultan mi?.* Istanbul, 1989.
———. *Tarihin Hükmü: Her Yönü ile Sultan Ikinci Abdulhamid.* Istanbul, 1985.
Muhammedi, Renad. *Sirat Köprüsü-Sultan Galiev.* Trans. Mustafa Öner. Istanbul, 1993.
Muhammetdin, Rafael. *Türkçülügün Doğuşu ve Gelişimi.* Istanbul, 1998.
Munip, Bandirmalizade Ahmed. *Mecmua-i Tekâyâ.* Istanbul, 1980.

Muqaddasi. *Hudud al'Alam: The Regions of the World: A Persian Geography.* Trans. V. Minorsky. Karachi, 1980.

Mürsel, Safa. *Bediüzzaman Said Nursi ve Devlet Felsefesi.* Istanbul, 1976.

Nallino, C. A. *Notes on the Nature of the "Caliphate" in General and on the Alleged "Ottoman Caliphate."* Rome, 1919.

Nami, Kazim (Duru). *Arnavutluk ve Makedonya Hatiralarim.* Istanbul, 1959.

———. *"Ittihat ve Terakki" Hatiralarim.* Istanbul, 1957.

Naqavi, Ali Muhammad. *Islam and Nationalism.* Teheran, 1988.

Nasr, Seyyed Vali Reza. *Mawdudi and the Making of Islamic Revivalism.* New York, 1995.

Necefzade, Y. K. *1908–1918 Sultan Ikinci Abdulhamid ve Ittihad-ü Terakki.* Istanbul, 1967.

Nelson, Harold D., ed. *Tunisia: A Country Study.* Washington, D.C., 1979.

Neumann, Christoph K. "Das Indirekte Argument, Ahmed Cevdet Paşa: Tarih als Plädoyer für die Tanzimat." Ph.D. diss., University of Hamburg, 1992.

Newitt, Malyn D. D. *The Comoro Islands: Struggle against Dependency in the Indian Ocean.* Boulder, Colo., 1984.

Nieuwenhuijze, C. A. O. Van, ed. *Commoners, Climbers and Notables.* Leiden, 1977.

Nigar, Salih K. *Halife Ikinci Abdulmecid.* Istanbul, 1964.

Niyazi, Ahmet. *Hatirat-i Niyazi yahut, Tarihçe-yi inkilab-i kebir-i Osmanlidan bir sahife.* Istanbul, 1910.

Norris, H. T. *Islam in the Balkans: Religion and Society between Europe and the Arab World.* Columbia. S.C., 1993.

Nuri, Celal (Ileri). *Ittihad-i Islam.* Istanbul, 1918.

Nuri, Osman. *Abdulhamit-i Sani ve Devr-i Saltanati. Hayat-i Hussusiye ve Siyasiyesi.* 3 vols. Istanbul, 1327. Reprint, 1907.

Nusret, Mehmet. *Tarihçe-i Erzurum Yahut Hemşehrilere Armağan.* Istanbul, 1922.

Ocak, Ahmet Yaşar. "II. Abdülhamid Dönemi Islamciliğinin Tarihi Arka Plani: Klasik Dönem Osmanli Islamina Genel bir Bakiş Denemesi." In *Sultan II. Abdulhamid ve Devri Semineri 27–29 Mayis 1992. Bildiriler.* 107–25. Istanbul, 1994.

———. *Turk Sufiligine Bakişlar.* Istanbul, 1996.

Ochsenwald, William. *The Hijaz Railroad.* Charlottesville, Va., 1980.

———. *Religion, Society, and the State in Arabia: The Hijaz under Ottoman Control, 1840–1908.* Columbus, Ohio, 1984.

Okay, Orhan N. M. *Bati Medeniyeti Karşisinda Ahmet Midhat Efendi.* Istanbul, 1989.

Öke, Mim Kemal. *Vambery, Belgelerle Bir Devletlerarasi Casusun Yaşam Öyküsü.* Istanbul, 1985.

Okyar, Osman and M. Seyitdanlioglu. *Fethi Okyar'in Anilari Atatürk, Okyar ve Çok Partili Türkiye.* 2nd ed. Ankara, 1999.

Olivier, Roland A. *The Missionary Factor in East Africa.* London, 1952.

Olson, Robert W. "The Remains of Talat: A Dialectic between Republic and Empire." *Die Welt des Islams* 26 (1986): 46–56.

Önal, Sami. *Milli Mücadelede Oltu.* Ankara, 1968.

Ong, Walter J. *The Presence of the Word: Some Prolegomena for Cultural and Religious History.* New Haven, Conn., 1967.

———. *Orality and Literacy: The Technologizing of the Word.* London, 1982.

Orik, Nahid Sirri. *Sultan Hamid Düşerken.* 3rd ed. Istanbul, 1944.

Osmanoğlu, Ayşe. *Babam Sultan Abdulhamid (Hatiralarim).* 3rd ed. Ankara, 1986.

Osmanoğlu, Osman. *The Ottoman Family. On the 700th Anniversary of the Foundation of the Ottoman State.* Istanbul, 1999.

Osmanoğlu, Sadiye. *Hayatimin Aci ve Tatli Günleri.* Istanbul, 1966.

Ostrowski, Donald. "The Mongol Origin of Muscovite Political Institutions." *Slavic Review* 49 (winter 1991): 525–43.

Özal, Turgut. *Turkey in Europe and Europe in Turkey.* Nicosia, Cyprus, 1991.

Özalp, Reşat. *Milli Eğitimle Ilgili Mevzuat (1857–1923).* Istanbul, 1982.

Özbek, Nadir. "Abdürreşid Ibrahim 1857–1944." M.A. thesis, Boğaziçi University, Istanbul, 1994.

Özcan, Azmi. "Indian Muslims and the Ottomans, 1877–1914: A Study of Indian Muslim Attitudes to Pan-Islamism and Turkey." Ph.D. diss., University of London, 1990.

———. "Özbekler Tekkesi Postnişini Buharali Şeyh Süleyman Efendi Bir Double Agent mi idi?" *Tarih ve Toplum* 17 (1992): 204–208.

———. *Pan-Islamism: Indian Muslims, the Ottomans and Britain, 1877–1924.* New York, 1997.

———. *Pan-Islamizm: Osmanli Devleti, Hindistan Müslümanlari ve Ingiltere, 1877–1914.* Istanbul, 1992.

Özerdim, Sami N. *Ord. Prof. Dr. Fuad Köprülü bibliografyasi 1908–1950.* Ankara, 1951.

Özkaya, R. Yücel. "II. Abdulhamid'e Sunulan Güzel Sanatlar Hakkinda Bir Layiha." *Osmanli Tarihi Araştirma ve Uygulama Merkezi Dergisi* 4 (Ankara, 1993): 645–85.

———. "Tanzimatin Siyasi Yönden Meşrutiyete Etkileri ve Cemiyet-i Islamiye Başkan Vekili Mühiddin Efendi'nin Meşrutiyet Hakkindaki Düşünceleri." In *Tanzimat' in 150 Yildönümü.* Ankara, 1994.

Özön, Mustafa Nihat. *Vatan Yahut Silistre.* 2nd ed. Istanbul, 1943.

Pakalin, Mehmed Zeki. *Osmanli Tarih Deyimleri ve Terimleri Sözlüğü.* Istanbul, 1993.

———. *Son Sadrazamlar ve Başvekiller.* 5 vols. Istanbul, 1940–48.

Pakenham, Thomas. *The Scramble for Africa, 1876–1912.* New York, 1991.

Pala, Iskender. *Namik Kemal'in Tarihi Biyografileri.* Ankara, 1989.

Pamuk, Şevket. *The Ottoman Empire and European Capitalism, 1820–1913.* New York, 1987.

Paneth, Philip. *Turkey: Decadence and Rebirth.* London, 1943.

Panzac, Daniel, ed. *La Peste dans l'empire ottoman: 1700–1850.* Paris, 1985.

———. *Les Villes dans l'empire ottoman: Activités et societés.* Vol. 2, Paris, 1994.

Park, George T. "The Life and Writings of Mehmet Fuad Köprülü: The Intellectual and Turkish Cultural Modernization." Ph.D. diss., Johns Hopkins University, 1975.

Parla, Taha. *The Social and Political Thought of Ziya Gökalp, 1876–1924.* Leiden, 1985.

Parlatir, Ismail. *Tanzimat Edebiyatinda Kölelik.* Ankara, 1987.

Parry, J., and Malcolm Yapp, eds. *War, Technology and Society in the Middle East.* London, 1975.

Pearce, Francis Barrow. *Zanzibar: The Island Metropolis of Eastern Africa.* London, 1920.

Pears, Edwin. *Life of Abdulhamid.* New York, 1917.

Pelenski, Jaroslaw. *Russia and Kazan: Conquest and Imperial Ideology (1438–1560s).* The Hague, 1974.

Petar II, Prince. *The Mountain Wreath of P. P. Nyegosh, Prince-Bishop of Montenegro, 1830–1851.* Trans. James W. Wiles. London, 1930.

Philby, Harry St. John Bridger. *Arabia.* London, 1930.

———. *Arabia of the Wahhabis.* New York, 1973.

———. *Sa'udi Arabia.* New York, 1955.

Pierce, Richard A. *Russian Central Asia, 1867–1917: A Study in Colonial Rule.* Berkeley, 1960.

Piscatori, James P., ed. *Islam in a World of Nation-States.* New York, 1986.

———. *Islam in the Political Process.* Cambridge, Mass., 1983.

Planhol, Xavier de. *Les Fondements géographiques de l'histoire de l'Islam.* Paris, 1968.

Ponicke, Herbert. "Heinrich August Meissner Pascha und der Bau der Hedschas und Bagdadbahn." *Die Welt als Geschichte* 16 (1956): 196–210.

Popovic, Alexandre, and Gilles Veinstein, eds. *Les Voies d'Allah.* Paris, 1996.

Poulantzas, Nicos. *State, Power and Socialism.* London, 1978.

Poulton, Hugh. *Top Hat, Grey Wolf and Crescent: Turkish Nationalism and the Turkish Republic.* New York, 1997.

Quandour, M. Izzat. *Muridism: A Study of the Caucasian Wars, 1819–1859.* Jersey, U.K., 1996.

———. "Muridism: A Study of the Caucasian Wars of Independence, 1819–1859." Ph.D. diss., Claremont Graduate University, 1964.

Quataert, Donald. *Social Disintegration and Popular Resistance in the Ottoman Empire, 1881–1908.* New York, 1983.

Quelquejay, Chantal Lemercier. "Les Missions orthodoxes en pays musulmans de Moyenne-et Basse-Volga: 1552–1865." *Cahiers du Monde Russe et Soviétique* (1967): 369–403.

Rahman, Fazlur. *Islam.* New York, 1968.

———. *Selected Letters of Sirhindi.* Translation of Ahmad Sirhindi's *Intikhabat-i Maktubat.* Karachi, 1968.

Ramsaur, Ernest E. *The Young Turks: Prelude to the Revolution of 1908.* Princeton, N.J., 1957.

Rasheed(al-) Madawi. *Politics in an Arabian Oasis. The Rashidis of Saudi Arabia.* London, 1998.

Ratchnevsky, Paul. *Genghis Khan: His Life and Legacy.* Trans. and ed. Thomas Nivison Haining. Oxford, 1991.

Refik, Ahmet. *Alimler ve San'atkarlar.* Ministry of Culture, no. 376. Ankara, 1980.

Reid, Anthony. *The Blood of the People: Revolution and the End of Traditional Rule in Northern Sumatra.* Kuala Lumpur, 1979.

———. *The Contest for North Sumatra: Atjeh, the Netherlands, and Britain, 1858–1898.* New York, 1969.

———. *The Indonesian National Revolution, 1945–1950.* Hawthorn, Vic., 1974.

———. "Nineteenth-Century Pan-Islam in Indonesia and Malaysia." *Journal of Asian Studies* 26 (1967): 267–83.

The Religion Reformers in Islam: The Bigots of Science and Religion. Published by Waqf Ihlas. Istanbul, 1987.

Rinn, Louis. *Histoire de l'insurrection de 1871 en Algérie.* Algiers, 1891.

———. *Marabouts et Khouan: Étude sur l'Islam en Algérie.* Algiers, 1884.

Risal, P. "Les Turcs à la recherche d'une âme nationale." *Mercure de France* (August 1912): 673–707.

Riza, Ahmed. *Ahmed Riza Beyin Anilari.* Ed. B. Demirbaş. Istanbul, 1988.

Robinson, Francis. "Technology and Religious Change: Islam and the Impact of Print." *Modern Asian Studies* 27 (1993): 229–251.

Rodrigue, Aron. *French Jews, Turkish Jews.* Bloomington, Ind., 1990.

Rogan, Eugene L. "Aşiret Mektebi: Abdulhamid II's School for Tribes, 1892–1907." *International Journal of Middle Eastern Studies* 28 (February 1996): 83–107.

Rona, Zeynep, ed. *Osman Hamdi Bey ve Dönemi Sempozyumu 17–18 Aralik 1992.* Istanbul, 1993.

Rorlich, Azade Ayse. "One or More Tatar Nations?" In *Muslim Communities Reemerge: Historical Perspectives on Nationality, Politics, and Opposition in the Former Soviet Union and Yugoslavia,* trans. Caroline Sawyer, ed. Edward Allworth. 61–79. Durham, N.C., 1994.

———. *The Volga Tatars: A Profile in National Resilience.* Stanford, Calif., 1986.

Rozhdestvensky, A. *Nikolai Ivanovich Il'minsky i yego sistema inorodcheskogo obrazovaniya v Kazanskom Kraie.* Kazan, 1900.

Rude, George. *Ideology and Popular Protest.* New York, 1980.

Ruhi, Ethem. *Balkan Hatiralari, Canli Tarihler.* Istanbul, 1947.

Runovski, Apollon. *Miuridizm i Gazavat po Obiasneniiu Shamilia.* Tiflis, 1863.

Rusinow, Dennison. "The Ottoman Legacy in Yugoslavia's Disintegration and Civil War." In *Imperial Legacy: The Ottoman Imprint on the Balkans and the Middle East.* Ed. L. Carl Brown. 78–99. New York, 1996.

Rywkin, Michael, ed. *Russian Colonial Expansion to 1917.* London, 1988.

Sabri, Şeyhulislam Mustafa. *Hilafet-i Muazzuma-i Islamiye, Hilafet ve Kemalizm.* 2nd ed. Ed. Sadik Albayrak. Istanbul, 1992.

Safran, Nadav. *Saudi Arabia: The Ceaseless Quest for Security.* Cambridge, Mass., 1985.

Şahiner, Necmeddin. *Bilinmeyen Taraflariyle Bediuzzaman Said Nursi.* 7th ed. Istanbul, 1988.

———. *Said Nursi ve Nurculuk Hakkinda Aydinlar Konuşuyor.* Istanbul, 1974.

Said, Ali. *Saray Hatiralari: Sultan Abdulhamid'in Hayati.* Istanbul, 1994.

Sait paşa. *Sait Paşa'nin Hatirati.* 3 vols. Istanbul, 1928.

Salt, Jeremy. *Imperialism, Evangelism, and the Ottoman Armenians, 1878–1896.* Newbury Park, U.K., 1993.

————. "A Precarious Symbiosis: Ottoman Christians and the Foreign Missionaries in the Nineteenth Century." *International Journal of Turkish Studies* 3 (1985): 53–67.

Şapolyo, Enver P. *Türk Gazeteciliği Tarihi.* Ankara, 1942.

Saray, Mehmet. *Rus Işgali Devrinde Osmanli Devleti ile Türkistan Hanliklari Arasindaki Siyasi Münasebetler (1775–1875).* Istanbul, 1984.

Sarinay, Yusuf. *Türk Milliyetçiliğinin Tarihi Gelişimi ve Türk Ocaklari: 1912–1931.* Istanbul, 1994.

Sariyar, Ayten. "XV ve XVI. Yüzyillarda Osmanli-Özbek Münasebetleri." Ph.D. diss., University of Istanbul, 1965.

Sariyildiz, Gülten. *Hicaz Karantina Teşkilati, 1865–1914.* Ankara, 1996.

Sato, Tsugitaka. *State and Rural Society in Medieval Islam: Sultans, Muqatas and Fallahun.* London, 1997.

Schuyler, Eugene. *Turkistan: Notes of a Journey in Russian Turkestan, Khokand, Bukhara and Kuldja.* Vol. 1. New York, 1876.

Şehsuvaroğlu, Bedii. "Ali Suavi ve Galatasaray Lisesi." *Belgelerle Türk Tarihi Dergisi* 2 (1968)

Şeref, Abdurrahman. *Tarih Müsahabeleri.* Istanbul, 1923; published as *Tarih Konuşmalari,* Istanbul, 1978.

————. *Son Vak'anüvis Abdurrahman Şeref Efendi Tarihi. II. Meşrutiyet Olaylari, 1908–1909).* Ed. Bayram Kodaman and M. A. Önal. Ankara, 1996.

Sertoğlu, M. *Osmanli Türklerinde Tuğra.* Istanbul, 1975.

Seufert, Günter. *Politischer Islam in der Turkei.* Istanbul, 1997.

Seyfettin, Ömer. *Yarinki Turan Devleti.* 3rd ed. Istanbul, 1980.

Shah, A. M., et al, eds. *Social Structure and Change.* 4 vols. The Hague, 1996–97.

Shah, (Sirdar) Ikbal Ali. "Ferments in the World of Islam." *Journal of the Central Asian Society* 14 (1927): 130–34.

————. *Islamic Sufism.* Lahore, ca. 1933.

Shannon, Richard. *Gladstone and the Bulgarian Agitation 1876.* London, 1963.

Shaw, Robert B. "Central Asia in 1872." *Proceedinqs of the Royal Geographical Society of London* 16 (Session of 1871–72): 395–409. London, 1872.

Shaw, Stanford J. *The Jews of the Ottoman Empire and the Turkish Republic.* New York, 1991.

Shaw, Stanford J., and Ezel Shaw. *History of the Ottoman Empire and Modern Turkey.* 2 vols. New York, 1977.

Shaybani. *The Islamic Law of Nations: Shaybani's Siyar.* Trans. Majid Khadduri. Baltimore, Md., 1966.

Sheehy, Ann. "The Andizhan Uprising of 1898 and Soviet Historiography." *Central Asian Survey* 14 (1966): 139– 50.

————. *The Crimean Tatars and Volga Germans: Soviet Treatment of Two National Minorities.* London, 1971.

Shukla, Ram Lakhan. *Britain, India and the Turkish Empire, 1853–1882.* New Delhi, 1973.

Siddiqui, Salim. "Nation-States as Obstacles to the Total Transformation of the Ummah." In *The Impact of Nationalism on the Muslim World,* ed. M. Ghayasuddin. London, 1986.

Sidqi, Ahmad. *Al-Harakat al-Sanusiya, Nashatiha wa Namuwwuha fi'l-Qarn al-Tasi Ashar.* Cairo, 1967.

Siegel, James T. *The Rope of God.* Berkeley, 1969.

Silay, Kemal. *Nedim and the Poetics of Ottoman Courts.* Bloomington, Ind., 1994.

Şimşir, Bilal. *Azerbaycan'da Türk Alfabesi Tarihçe.* Ankara, 1991.

————. *Fransiz Belgelerine Göre Mithat Paşa'nin Sonu, 1878– 1884.* Ankara, 1970.

————. *Rumeli'den Türk Göçleri.* 3 vols. Ankara, 1989.

————. *Türk Yazi Devrimi.* Ankara, 1992.

Simon, Rachel. *Libya between Ottomanism and Nationalism (1911–1919).* Berlin, 1987.

Simon, Reeva S. "The Education of an Iraqi Ottoman Officer." In *The Origins of Arab Nationalism,* ed. Rashid Khalidi. 151–66. New York, 1991.

Sinapli, Ahmet Nuri. *Şeyhül Vüzera, Serasker Mehmed Namik Paşa.* Istanbul, 1987.
Sirma, I. Süreyya. *II. Abdulhamid'in Islam Birliği Siyaseti.* Istanbul, 1985.
———. "Ondokuzuncu Yüzyil Osmanli Siyasetinde Büyük Rol Oynayan Tarikatlara Dair Bir Vesika." *Tarih Dergisi* 31 (Istanbul, 1978): 163–83.
———. "Fransa'nin Kuzey Afrika'daki Sömürgeciliğine Karşi Sultan II Abdulhamid'in Panislamist Faaliyetlerine Ait Bir Kaç Vesika." *Tarih Enstitüsü Dergisi* 7–8 (Istanbul, 1977): 157–85.
———. *Ikinci Abdulhamid'in Islam Birliği Siyaseti.* Istanbul, 1985.
Sivan, Emmanuel. *Radical Islam: Medieval Theology and Modern Politics.* New Haven, Conn., 1985.
Smirnov, N. A. *Miuridizm na Kavkaze.* Moscow, 1963.
Smith, Anthony. *The Ethnic Origins of Nations.* Oxford, 1986.
———. *Theories of Nationalism.* 2nd ed. London, 1983.
Smith, R. Bosworth. *Muhammad and Muhammadanism.* Lahore, 1974.
Smith, Wilfred Cantwell. *Islam in Modern History.* New York, 1963.
Soekarno. *Nationalism, Islam and Marxism.* Trans. Karel H. Warouw and Peter D. Weldon. Ithaca, N.Y., 1970.
Sokol, Edward Dennis. *The Revolt of 1916 in Russian Central Asia.* Baltimore, Md., 1954.
Solak, Kemal. *Islama Göre Millet, Milliyetçilik ve Irkçilik.* Istanbul, 1979.
Spaulding, J., and L. Kapteijns, eds. *An Islamic Alliance: Ali Dinar and the Sanusiyya, 1906–1916.* Evanston, Ill., 1994.
Spencer, Edmund. *Turkey, Russia, the Black Sea, and Circassia.* London, 1854.
Spuler, Bertold. *Die goldene Horde: Die Mongolen in Russland, 1223–1502.* Wiesbaden, 1965.
Stalin, J. *Marxism and the National and Colonial Question.* London, 1942.
Stern, Steve J. "Freedom, Capitalism and the World System in the Perspective of Latin America and the Caribbean." *American Historical Review* 93 (October 1988): 829–72.
Stoianovich, Traian. "The Conquering Balkan Orthodox Merchant." *Journal of Economic History,* 22, no 2 (June 1960): 234–313.
Straus, Oscar S. *Under Four Administrations: From Cleveland to Taft.* Boston, 1922.
Sukhareva, O. A. *Islam v Uzbekstane.* Tashkent, 1960.
Sultan Abdulhamid'in Hatira Defteri. 8th ed., ed. Ismet Bozdağ. Istanbul, 1988.
Sümer, Faruk. *Kara Koyunlular.* Ankara, 1967.
Süreyya bey, Mehmet. *Sicil-i Osmani.* Reprint, Istanbul, 1996.
Sururi, Nazif. *Hilafet-i Muazzama-i Islamiye.* Istanbul, 1898.
Swietochovski, Tadeusz. *Russia and Azerbaijan: A Borderland in Transition.* Cambridge, 1985.
———. *Russian Azerbaijan, 1905–1920: The Shaping of National Identity in a Muslim Community.* New York, 1995.
Synet, A. *Les Grecs en l'empire ottoman.* Constantinople, 1878.
Tabakoğlu, Ahmet. *Türk Iktisat Tarihi.* Istanbul, 1986.
Tahir (Bursali), Mehmet. *Osmanli Müellifleri.* Istanbul, 1972.
———. *Türklerin Ulum ve Fününa Hizmetleri.* Ankara, 1996.
Tahsin paşa. *Sultan Abdulhamid: Tahsin Paşa'nin Yildiz Hatiralari.* 1931. Reprint, Istanbul, 1990.
Takizade, S. H. "Les Courants politiques dans la Turquie." *Revue du Monde Musulman* 21 (1912): 158–221.
———. "Le Panislamisme et le panturquisme." *Revue du Monde Musulman* 22 (1913): 179–222.
Talay, Aydin. *Eserleri ve Hizmetleriyle Sultan Abdulhamid.* Istanbul, 1991.
Tanpinar, Ahmet Hamdi. *Ondokuzuncu Asir Türk Edebiyati Tarihi.* 4th ed. Istanbul, 1976.
Tanriöver, Hamdullah. *Dağ Yolu.* Ankara, 1928.
Tansel, Fevziye A. "Prof. Dr. Fuad Köprülü'nun Yazilari için Basilmiş Bibliyografyalar ve Bunlara bazi Ilaveler." *Türk Kültürü* 68 (June 1968): 543–56.
Tauber, Eliezer. *The Emergence of the Arab Movements.* London, 1993.

―――. "The Political Role of the Algerian Element in Late Ottoman Syria." *International Journal of Turkish Studies* 5 (winter 1990–91): 27–47.

―――. "Rashid Rida as a Pan-Arabist before World War I." *The Muslim World* 79, no. 2 (1989): 102–12.

Tazhibaev, T. T. *Prosveshenie i shkole Kazakhstana v vtoroi polovine XIX veka.* Alma Ata, 1962.

Temimi, A. "La Politique ottomane face à l'insurrection du constantinois en 1871." *Revue d'Histoire Maghrebine* 3 (1980): 11–20, 64–68.

Temir, Ahmet. *Yusuf Akçura.* Ankara, 1987.

Temo, Ibrahim. *Ittihad ve Terakki Cemiyetinin Teşekkülü ve Hidemat-i Vataniye ve Inkilab-i Milliye Hatiralari.* Mecidiye, Romania, 1939.

Tepedelenlioğlu, Nizamettin Nazif. *Sultan Ikinci Abdulhamid ve Osmanli Imparatorluğunda Komitacilar.* 2nd ed. Istanbul, 1972.

Terasse, Henri. *Histoire du Maroc.* Casablanca, 1950.

Tevfik, Mehmet (Biren). *II Abdulhamid Meşrutiyet ve Mütareke Devri Hatiralari.* 2 vols. Istanbul, 1993.

Thobie, Jacques et al., eds. *La France impériale, 1880–1914.* Paris, 1982.

―――. *Intérêts et imperialisme français dans l'empire ottomane, 1895–1914.* Paris, 1977.

Thomas, David. "Yusuf Akçura and the Intellectual Origins of Üç Tarz-i Siyaset." Ph.D. diss. McGill University, 1976.

Thompson, E. P. "Eighteenth-Century English Society: Class Struggle without Class." *Social History* 3 (May 1978): 133–65.

Thorburn, Walter Millar. *The Great Game: A plea for a British Imperial Policy.* Toronto, 1875.

Tibi, Bassam. *Arab Nationalism: A Critical Enquiry.* 2nd Eng. ed. New York, 1990.

―――. *The Crisis of Modern Islam: A Preindustrial Culture in the Scientific-Technological Age.* Salt Lake City, Utah, 1988.

Timur, Taner. *Osmanli Kimliği.* Istanbul, 1994.

Todorov, Nicolai. "The Genesis of Capitalism in the Balkan Provinces of the Ottoman Empire." *Exploration in Economic History* 7 (1970): 313–24.

Todorova, Maria. "Mithat Paşa's Governorship of the Danube Province." In *Decision Making and Change in the Ottoman Empire*, ed. Caesar E. Farah. 115–28. Kirksville, Mo., 1993.

Togan, A. Zeki Velidi. *Bugünkü Türkili Türkistan ve Yakin Tarihi.* 2nd ed. Istanbul, 1981.

―――. *Hatiralar.* Istanbul, 1969.

―――. *Tarihde Usul.* 2nd ed. Istanbul, 1969.

―――. *Türklüğün Mukadderati Üzerine.* Istanbul, 1977.

Togay, Muharrem Feyzi. *Yusuf Akçura'nin Hayati.* Istanbul, 1944.

Tokay, Gül. *Makedonya Sorunu: Jön Türk Ihtilalinin Kökenleri 1903–1908.* Istanbul, 1996.

Toker, Şevket. *Hüseyin Rahmi Gürpinar'in Romanlarinda Alafranga Tipler.* Izmir-Bornova, 1990.

Tolf, Robert W. *The Russian Rockefellers: The Saga of the Nobel Family and the Russian Oil Industry.* Stanford, Calif., 1976.

Toprak, Zafer. *Türkiye'de "Milli Iktisat," 1908–1918.* Ankara, 1982.

Topuz, Hiszi. *Pariste Son Osmanlilar. Mediha Sultan ve Danat Ferit.* 12th ed. Istanbul, 2000 (orig. publ. May 1999).

Tourneau, Roger le. "Position sociale et culturelle de l'élite dirigeante d'Afrique du Nord." *Cahiers de Linguistique d'Orientalisme et de Slavistique* 1–2 (1973): 7–27.

Tretev, M. A. *Russia and England in Central Asia.* Calcutta, 1876.

Triaud, Jean Louis. *Tchad, 1900–1902: Une guerre franco-libyenne oubliée? Une confrerie musulmane—la Sanusiyya face à la France.* Paris, 1987.

Trix, Frances. "The Istanboul Alphabet of Shemseddin Sami Bey: Precursor to Turkish Script Reform." *International Journal of Middle Eastern Studies* 31, no. 2 (May 1999): 255–272.

Troeller, Gary. *The Birth of Saudi Arabia: Britain and the Rise of the House of Sa'ud.* London, 1976.

Trotter, Henry. "The Amir Yakub Khan and Eastern Turkestan in Mid-Nineteenth Century." *Journal of the Royal Central Asian Society* 4, no. 4 (1917): 95–112.

Tsagareishvili, Sh. V., ed. *Shamil-stavlennik Sultanskoi Turtsii i Anqliiskikh Kolonizatorov.* Tiblisi, 1953.

Tunaya, Tarik Zafer. *Islamcilik Cereyani.* Istanbul, 1962.

Turfan, M. Naim. *Rise of the Young Turks. Politics, The Military and Ottoman Collapse.* London-New York, 2000.

Türkdoğan, Orhan. *Ziya Gökalp Sosyolojisinde Bazi Kavramlar Değerlendirilimesi.* Istanbul, 1978.

Türkgeldi, Ali Fuad. *Görüp Işittiklerim.* Ankara, 1957.

Turkish Republic Ministry of Culture and Tourism. *Ottoman Empire in Drawings.* Istanbul, 1987.

Türkoğlu, Ismail. "Rusya Türklerinde Abdürreşid Ibrahim." Ph.D. diss., Marmara University, Istanbul, 1993.

Türköne, Mumtaz'er. "Siyasi Ideoloji Olarak Islamciliğin Doğuşu (1867–1873)." Ph.D. diss., Ankara University, 1990.

Tütengil, Cavit O. *Ziya Gökalp Hakkinda bir Bibliografya Denemesi.* Istanbul, 1949.

———. *Ziya Gökalp Üzerine Notlar.* Istanbul, 1964.

Tütengil, Cavit O., and Vedat Günyol. *Prens Lütfullah Dosyasi.* Istanbul, 1977.

Tyan, Emile. *Sultanat et califat.* Paris, 1956.

Uçar, Ahmet. "II. Abdulhamid'in Milletlerarasi Sergilere Müdaheleleri." *Ilim Dünyasi* (Spring 1996): 3–10.

Uçarol, Rifat. *Gazi Muhtar Paşa (1839–1919): Askeri ve Siyasi Hayati.* 2nd ed. Istanbul, 1989.

Ülküsal, Müstecib. *Dobruca ve Türkler.* Ankara, 1966.

Uluçay, M. Çağatay. *Manisa Tarihi.* Istanbul, 1939.

———. *Onsekiz ve Ondokuzuncu Yüzyillarda Saruhan'da Eşkiyalik ve Halk Hareketleri.* Istanbul, 1955.

Üngör, Etem R. *Türk Marşlari.* Ankara, 1965.

Unsworth, Barry. *The Rage of the Vulture.* London, 1982.

Uşakligil, Halid Ziya. *Saray ve Ötesi: Son Hatiralar.* Ed. Faik R. Ünat. Istanbul, 1965.

Üstel, Füsun. "Türk Ocaklari (1912–1931)." Ph.D. diss., Ankara University, 1986.

———. *Imparatorluktan Ulus-Devlete, Türk Milliyetçiliği: Türk Ocaklari, 1912–1931.* Istanbul, 1997.

Uzun, M., and Y. Hacaloğlu, eds. *Türk Ocaklari Belgeseli: Belgeler, Resimler, 1912–1994.* Ankara, 1994.

Uzunçarşili, Ismail Hakki. *Mekke-i Mükerreme Emirleri.* Ankara, 1972.

———. *Midhat Paşa ve Taif Mahkümlari.* Ankara, 1985.

———. *Mithat ve Rüştü Paşalarin Tevkiflerine Dair Vesikalar.* Ankara, 1946.

———. *Mithat Paşa ve Yildiz Muhakemesi.* Ankara, 1967.

———. *Osmanli Tarihi.* Vols. 2 and 3. Ankara, 1949, 1951.

———. "Sultan Abdülaziz Vak'asina dair Vak'anüvis Lütfi Efendinin bir Risalesi." *Belleten.* VII (1943): 349–373.

Vadala, Ramire. *Essais sur l'histoire des Karamanlis.* Paris, 1900.

Vambery, Arminius. *Central Asia and the Anglo-Russian Frontier Question: A Survey of Political Papers.* London, 1874.

———. *His Life and Adventures.* London, 1883.

———. "Pan-Islamism." *The Nineteenth Century* 60 (July–December 1906): 547–58; 61 (January–June 1907): 860–72.

———. "Personal Recollections of Abdulhamid and His Court." *Nineteenth Century and After* 65 (June 1909): 69–88.

———. "Personal Recollections of Abdulhamid and His Court." *Nineteenth Century and After* 66 (July-December 1909): 980–94.

———. *Sketches of Central Asia.* London, 1868.

———. *Travels in Central Asia.* London, 1864.

————. *La Turquie d'aujourd'hui et d'autant quarante ans.* Paris, 1898.

Van Vleck, Michael. "British Educational Policy in Egypt Relative to British Imperialism in Egypt, 1882–1922." Ph.D. diss., University of Wisconsin–Madison, 1990.

Veinstein, Gilles, ed. *La Question du califat.* Paris, 1994.

Venturi, Franco. "La riforma dell'Alcorano, ossia il mito italiano dello sceicco Mansur." *Rivista Storica Italiana* 98 (1986): 47–77.

Voll, John O. *Islam: Continuity and Change in the Modern World.* Boulder, Colo., 1982.

————. "Renewal and Reform in Islamic History, Tajdid and Islah." In *Voices of Resurgent Islam,* ed. John L. Esposito. 32–47. New York, 1983.

Wahby bey, Behdjet. "Pan-Islamism." *The Nineteenth Century* 60, no. 363 (January–June 1907): 860–72.

Whitman, Sidney. "Abdul Hamid an Autocrat Not a Despot." *New York Herald* 17 (August 1896).

Winder, R. Bayly. *Saudi Arabia in the Nineteenth Century.* New York, 1965.

Wittek, Paul. *The Rise of the Ottoman Empire.* New York, 1971.

Wittlin, Alma S. *Abdulhamid: The Shadow of God.* London, 1940.

Woods, John. *The Aqqoyunlu: Clan, Confederation, and Empire.* Princeton, N.J., 1974.

Yalçinkaya, Alâeddin. *Cemaleddin Efgani ve Türk Siyasi Hayati Üzerindeki Etkileri.* Istanbul, 1991.

————. *Sultan II. Abdulhamid Han'in Notlari.* Istanbul, 1996.

Yasamee, F. A. K. *Ottoman Diplomacy: Abdulhamid II and the Great Powers, 1878–1888.* Istanbul, 1996.

————. "The Ottoman Empire and the European Great Powers, 1882–1887." Ph.D. diss., University of London, 1984.

————. "The Ottoman Empire, the Sudan and the Red Sea Coast, 1883–1889." In *Studies on Ottoman Diplomatic History.* Vol. 5; and Sinan Kuneralp. *The Ottomans in Africa.* Ed. Selim Deringil. Istanbul, 1992.

Yazgan, Tevfik. "1840–1910 Osmanli Tarim Ekonomisine Giriş: Yapisal Sorunlar, Tarimsal Kredi ve Tarim Politikasi." Ph.D. diss., University of Istanbul, 1980.

Yazgan, Ümid Meriç. *Cevdet Paşa'nin Toplum ve Devlet Görüşü.* 3rd ed. Istanbul, 1992.

Yazici, Nesimi. "Layihalar Işiğinda II Abdulhamid Döneminde Libya Üzerine Gözlemler." *Sultan II. Abdulhamid Devri Semineri: Bildiriler, 27–29 Mayis 1992.* 47–84. Istanbul, 1994.

Yekta, Rauf. "Ziya Gökalp Bey ve Milli Musikimiz Hakkindaki Fikirleri." *Servet-i Fünun* 1480 (1925): 89–91.

Yergin, Daniel. *The Prize: The Epic Quest for Oil, Money and Power.* New York, 1993.

Yuan, Tsing. "Yakub Beg (1820–1877) and the Moslem Rebellion in Chinese Turkestan." *Central Asiatic Journal* 6 (1961): 134–67.

Yücesoy, Hayrettin. *Senusilik: Sufi bir Ihya Hareketi.* Istanbul, 1985.

Yüksel, *Ibrahim. Azerbaycan'da Fikir Hayati ve Basin.* Istanbul, 1991.

Zaharaddin, M. S. "Wahhabism and Its Influence outside Arabia." *Islamic Quarterly* 33 (1979): 146–57.

Zarcone, Thierry. "Histoire et croyances des derviches turkestanais et indiens à Istanbul." *Anatolia Moderna* 2 (1990): 160–64.

————. *Les iraniens d'Istanbul.* Paris, 1993.

————. "Remarques sur le rôle socio-politique et la filiation historique des şeyh Nakşbendi dans la Turquie contemporaine." In *Nakşbandis,* ed. Marc Gaborieau et al. 407–420. Istanbul, 1990.

Zeine, N. *The Emergence of Arab Nationalism with a Background Study of Arab-Turkish Relations in the Near East.* Beirut, 1966.

Zenkovsky, Serge A. *Pan-Turkism and Islam in Russia.* Cambridge, 1960.

Ziadeh, Nicola A. *Sanusiyah: A Study of a Revivalist Movement in Islam.* Leiden, 1958.

Zilfi, Madeline C. "The Kadizadelis: Discordant Revivalism in Seventeenth-Century Istanbul." *Journal of Near Eastern Studies* 45 (1986): 251–69.

Zubaida, Sami. *Islam, the People and the State: Essays on Political Ideas and Movements in the Middle East.* London, 1989.

Zubcevic, Asim. "Pathology of a Literature: Some Roots of Islamophobia," *Journal of Muslim Minority Affairs* 16 (1996): 309–315.

Zurcher, Erik Jan. *The Unionist Factor: The Role of the Committee of Union and Progress in the Turkish National Movement, 1905–1926.* Leiden, 1984.

Zygulski, Zdzislaw. *Ottoman Art in the Service of the Empire.* New York, 1992.

Index

509

as finance minister of, 11; and *cihad*,
274; and coat of arms, 226; Committee
of Union and Progress (CUP) of, 163;
coup of 1908, 129, 326, 349, 351, 352,
354, 355, 417–18; coup of 1913, 349;
early development of, 354–55;
economic policies of, 162; and
education, 99, 102; and England, 179,
197; and ethnicity, 328–29; in Europe,
354–55, 368, 390; French influences
on, 220, 221; Gregorian calendar
adopted by, 163; and Islamism and
pan-Islamism, 87, 368, 370, 418;
Kiamil as grand vizier under, 191; and
Mahmud Celaleddin paşa's family,
433n.10; and Mehmet Cemalleddin
efendi, 163; military alliance with
Germany, 222, 256; modernism of,
305; and Morocco, 268; and
Nakşbandia, 113; and nationalism,
109, 176, 349; and Ottomanism, 12,
326–27, 349, 354–56, 368, 369, 370,
389, 402, 418; and party politics, 93;
positivism of, 299, 305; and
privatization of state lands, 185; Sait as
grand vizier under, 190; and
seyhulislamate, 163, 224, 314, 402; and
social class, 403; Turkification of, 356;
and Turkish language as state
language, 339; and Turkishness, 349,
368–71; and Turkism, 305, 306, 369,

402–4; and von der Goltz's pupils,
192–93; and World War I, 370; Young
Ottomans as precursor of, 96. *See also*
Committee of Union and Progress
(CUP)
Yugoslav multiculturalism, 109

Zafir al-Madani efendi, Şeyh
Muhammed, 174, 186, 194, 262, 271,
338
Zahir, Ali ibn al-, 215
Zahrawi, Abdulhamid al-, 239
Zaid bin Ali Zeynelabidin, 204
Zaidis, 187, 200, 204
Zaid, Mehmet, 113
Zanzibar, 263, 272–74
Zardabi (Zerdabi), Abbaskulu, 289
Zarifi, G., 155, 325
Zeine, Zeine N., 346
Zeki paşa, 261
Zerdabi, Hasan Melikzade-, 289, 295
Zeynullah bin Habibullah, Şeyh, 112
Ziver efendi, 274
Ziya, Halid, 360, 363
Ziya paşa, 127, 133, 156, 165, 338
Ziyaeddin (Ziyaettin), Ahmet, 195
Ziyauddin, Ömer, 113
Zographos, Christaki efendi, 325
Zohrab, James, 247, 248
Zola, Émile, 363
Zülüm (tyranny), 157, 196